Yugoslav Folk Music

NUMBER II IN THE NEW YORK BARTÓK ARCHIVE
STUDIES IN MUSICOLOGY

THE NEW YORK BARTÓK ARCHIVE

Benjamin Suchoff, *Trustee*

The Béla Bartók Archives:
History and Catalogue

Rumanian Folk Music
I Instrumental Melodies
II Vocal Melodies
III Texts
IV Carols and Christmas Songs (*Colinde*)
V Maramures County

Turkish Folk Music from Asia Minor

Béla Bartók Essays

Yugoslav Folk Music
I Serbo-Croatian Folk Songs (with Albert B. Lord)
II Tabulation of Material
III Source Melodies: Part One
IV Source Melodies: Part Two

Yugoslav Folk Music

VOLUME THREE

Yugoslav
FOLK MUSIC
Volume Three

Source Melodies: Part One

by BÉLA BARTÓK

Edited by BENJAMIN SUCHOFF

State University of New York Press

1978

Published by
State University of New York Press
Albany, New York 12246

Printed in the United States of America

Library of Congress Cataloging in Publication Data

Bartók, Béla, 1881–1945.
Yugoslav folk music.

(New York Bartók Archive studies in musicology; no. 9)
Vol. 1 originally published in 1951 by
Columbia University Press, New York,
which was issued as no. 7 of its
Studies in musicology.
Includes bibliographies and indexes.
CONTENTS: v. 1. Serbo-Croatian folk songs and
instrumental pieces from the Milman Parry collection.
1. Folk-songs, Yugoslav—History and criticism.
2. Folk-songs, Croatian—History and criticism.
I. Lord, Albert Bates, joint author.
II. Suchoff, Benjamin.
III. Herzog, George, 1901–
IV. Series: Béla Bartók Archives.
Studies in musicology; no. 9.
V. Series: Columbia University studies in musicology; no. 7.
VI. Title.
ML3590.B32 784.4′9497 78-8188
ISBN 0-87395-383-5

Contents

Editor's Preface

When Béla Bartók and his wife set out for the United States during October, 1940—travelling by autobus and train from Budapest to Lisbon via Italy, the south of France, and Spain—their week-long journey was made a few short months after Germany had conquered France and was engaged in aerial assault and naval blockade of Britain.

The emigrant Bartóks brought with them six trunks containing their personal belongings and, among other manuscripts and documents, the thousands of slips comprising Bartók's collection of published and unpublished Yugoslav folk song source melodies that form the third and fourth volumes of this publication. En route to the port of embarkation, however, their baggage was left behind "somewhere along the Portuguese Frontier."

The various letters exchanged among Bartók, his publisher, Boosey & Hawkes, and the concerned governmental offices and travel agents, reveal the difficulties that had to be surmounted during that frenzied wartime period in order to locate and retrieve the lost possessions. And, too, there were the anguished days of uncertainty until mid-November, when word came that the six trunks had been found in Portugal.

> But let me tell you: perhaps you have already heard of the temporary loss of our luggage. The strain of those past three months has taken much out of me. And the expense! At least a few 100 dollars. Finally our vagabond chattels arrived at the beginning of February, without any loss. I really cannot tell you how I could have borne the loss. My dictionaries, my collection of folk songs, contracts, manuscripts, all were there.[1]

Agatha Fassett's poignant memoir of this event underscores Bartók's trauma, for the fair copy of all the Rumanian folk music notations was also in one of the missing trunks.[2] But at long last, on February 10, 1941, the precious possessions arrived in New York. With their arrival,

[1] Letter from Béla Bartók to Emma and Zoltán Kodály in Budapest, dated December 8, 1941, New York Bartók Archive [*NYBA*] Correspondence File.

[2] *The Naked Face of Genius* (Boston: Houghton Mifflin, 1958), pp. 18–24, 41.

Bartók's obsessive ambition was refreshed: to complete his Rumanian and Turkish folk music studies, and to embark on the planned Serbo-Croatian folk song project which was now made feasible by the recovery of the Yugoslav music notations and their tabulations.

ORDERING OF THE SOURCES

After the Bartóks had settled in their spacious Riverdale (New York) apartment, in the early Spring of 1941, the opportunity arose to unpack and sort the various folk music manuscripts and other source materials brought from Hungary. The music examples comprising this volume were arranged in numbered envelopes but not in their ultimate chronological sequence. It seems useful to provide the reader here with a listing of the envelopes and their contents but in current enumeration as presented in the Tabulation of Material (Vol. II of the present publication), in lieu of a more formal Table of Contents to this volume, since this procedure permits the addition of Bartók's own descriptions which appear on the respective envelopes.

Current No.	*No. and Type of Sections*	*Other Structural Features*	*No. of Variants*	*Envelope No.*
1–35	One		10	57.
36–110	Two: Isometric	*5, 6, 7,*-syll. lines	56	58.
111–201		*8 (4 + 4),*	141	59.
202–256		*8 (3 + 2 + 3), 9,*	62	40.
257–322		*10,* [VI]–[1] caesuras	121	46.
323–406		*10,* [♭2] on	62	41.
407–460		*11, 12, 13,*	51	38.
461–581	Heterometric	**Zz**	79	39.
582–619		**zZ**	29	36.
620–659	Three: Isometric	with □ [caesurae	14	53.
660–727		] □	45	54.
728–832	Heterometric	□ [; 1) groups	89	35.
833–919		2), 3)	64	37.
920–1023		] □; 1), 2), 3)	113	43.
1024–1053	Four: Special	"Specific" Serbo-Croatian structure	34	51.
1054–1171	Isometric	*5, 6,*-syllable lines	89	52.
1172–1308		*7, 8, 9,*	100	50.
1309–1364		*10, 11, 12, 13, 14,*	57	49.

Current No.	*No. and Type of Sections*	*Other Structural Features*	*No. of Variants*	*Envelope No.*
1365–1485	Heterometric	1.–4. groups and *7,6,7,6,* from 5.	71	47.
1486–1540		*8,5,8,5* from 5.	74	45.
1541–1638		*8,6,8,6,* etc. from 5.	118	48.
1639–1733		6.–16.	54	42.
1734–1830		17.–24.	24	44.
1831–1855	No definite structure	Dance and Play Songs	2	55.
1856–1896	Undeterminable structure		2	55.
Parry 1–54			(21)	109.

Following the Tabulation of Material in Vol. II is a list of the seventy-five Parry melodies published in Vol. I. In like manner, therefore, the second draft of those melodies appears in Vol. IV after source melody No. 1896. Comparison of this draft with the published version—ornamented as well as skeleton forms—should be of particular interest to the reader: the MS facsimile is another indicator of Bartók's concept of what notes constitute the principal tones of the Parry transcriptions. Moreover, Parry Nos. 27e, 29, 34–35, 37–39b, 44b, 48–49, 52, and 54, which do not have the skeleton form in smallhead notation, are thus available for comparative purposes in the author's stripped-down form.

SUPPLEMENTARY MATERIALS

A more or less fair copy of 423 Kuba *B.H.* melodies, including the 160 unpublished ones, intermixed with seventy-five *Iz Levča* melodies, were found in Envelope 60 (see Fig. 1).[3] The notations, for the most part of the first melody stanza and its underlying text, essentially are exact copies of the source melodies published below. One exception: all of the latter which are untransposed have their counterparts in this draft with g^1 as final tone. Because of its incompleteness (742 *B.H.* melodies

[3] The 498 slips, of various sizes, were cut from Circle Blue Print (New York) ten- and twelve-stave, octavo-size transparent master sheets. The notations are in india ink, and there are pencil and red crayon annotations in Hungarian and English. Certain of the additions, including structural ones, and which do not appear in the source melodies (published below), apparently were added to "Tab. of Mat." drafts as final improvements.

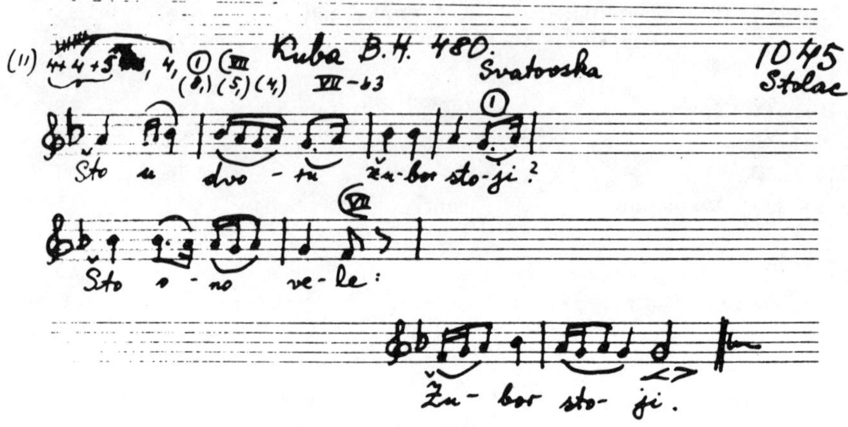

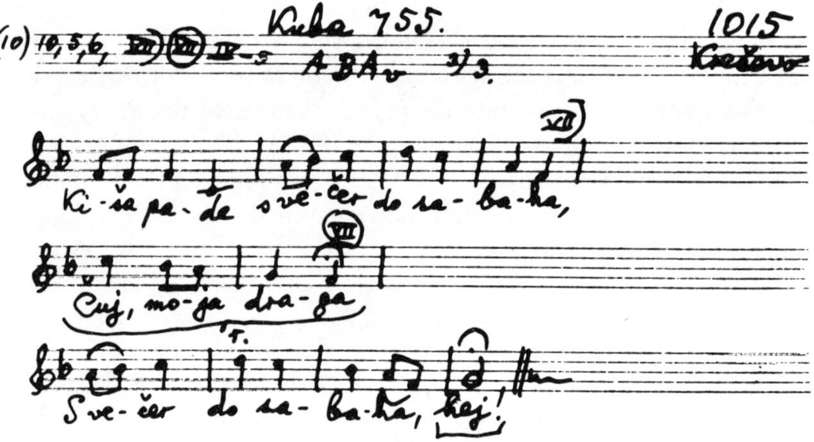

Fig. 1 Bartók's holograph of Kuba transcriptions of folk songs from Bosnia and Hercegovina

were not re-notated) and general appearance, Bartók's reason for preparing this material is unclear: perhaps he may have considered preparing a limited-reference compilation of melodies as a companion to "Tab. of Mat."

Envelope 56 contained fifty-three instrumental tunes: thirteen from

Iz Levča and forty from Đorđević (*Pred. Srb.*).[4] These holdings, together with Bartók's transcription of Parry Collection instrumental pieces (see in Vol. I, Appendix One; see also the Serbian transcriptions in Appendix Two), reinforces the notion that Bartók's original plan may have been to include instrumental as well as vocal music in his study of Serbo-Croatian folk music material.

In the Notes to the Music Examples of Vol. I (pp. 231–44) are Bartók's references to text variants: those to melody Nos. 13, 14, and 51 list specific "Tab. of Mat." sources. It is therefore mentioned here that Bartók made Hungarian translations of 255 Kuhač (206), Kuba (42), *Iz Levča* (3), and Đordević (4) poetic texts, in order to compare their contents with the Parry material and his Rumanian folk song collection.[5]

The various concordances to "Tab. of Mat." in Vol. II show extensors instead of current tabulation numbers. These extensors indicate discarded melodies whose notations were placed by Bartók in Envelope No. 61/A, since the folk songs represent German, Bulgar, Slovak, urban, etc. contaminations. An extensor followed by question mark indicates that the notation, ostensibly a discarded one, is missing from Bartók's collection of materials.[6]

ADDENDA TO THE TABULATION OF MATERIAL

In the editorial preface to Vol. I (pp. xxii f.) a brief account of Bartók's multidimensional activities is narrated, beginning in 1941,

[4] The smaller collection is in Bartók's hand, the larger was copied by someone else. According to information received from the Budapest Bartók Archivum, the various "Tab. of Mat." source melodies were copied by a number of persons, among them Márta Ziegler-Bartók (Bartók's first wife), Edith Pásztory-Bartók (his second wife), and Jenő Deutsch, former Bartók pupil, who autographed most of the fair copy version of the *Rumanian Folk Music* notations. The copying was done as early as 1920 (many were made in the 1930's).

[5] Few of the texts are more than four lines in length. The MS is in india ink on blank master sheet paper, in various sizes, with Rumanian, Hungarian, Serbo-Croatian, and Slovak variant relationships indicated in pencil and red crayon. Some of the remarks are also entered in the "Tab. of Mat." drafts. It remains an open question whether Bartók may have intended this draft to serve as the nucleus for a full-fledged topical classification of his Serbo-Croatian folk song material.

[6] Examination of the Kuhač publications shows that the "missing" notations are either instrumental pieces or folk or urban songs of foreign (i.e., Russian, Bulgar, Slovak) provenance.

during the time he was primarily involved in the transcription and study of Parry Collection materials. These activities, illness, and various personal problems may have impelled him to terminate prematurely his data gathering for entry into the "Tab. of Mat.": there is a substantial number of remarks to be found among the source melodies published below that Bartók did not tabulate, although the remarks are identical in scope with "Tab. of Mat." entries. For the convenience of the reader, therefore, the extracted data are given below. (The first number in the detailed enumeration refers to the "Tab. of Mat." designation which also appears in the upper right-hand corner of each source melody published below.)

18 Similar to *Kádár Kata* [Hungarian] text.
22a. Unintelligible text!
70a. Suspicious text: Slovenian tinge.
73a. Urban song-like text.
74 Cf.: a Rumanian melody? [Compare the given notations with *Rumanian Folk Music* IV, melody No. 12a.]
98b. Cf. with a Rumanian (urban song) melody.
99a. Urban [song-like] text?
124 [With *gusle* part.]
127 Patriotic urban song.
134f. Ballad text.
135a. Urban song-like text.
156 Ugly and artificial laments.
161 Like a [Rumanian] *colindă.*
165b. Arabic.
179 Pentatonic.
180b. [Text is missing.]
185b.c. Pentatonic.
187 Urban-like text.
196e. Ballad-like.
201b. Urban-like text [three-part song? Not listed in Vol. I, p. 71].
226 The lower of the two parts played by a two-stringed *gusle.*
231a. The second melody section has the appearance of a Rumanian *colindă.*
243j. [Two-part song with drone in the lower part. Not listed in Vol. I, p. 71.]

244 Pentatonic.
257 Two-part?! [Not listed in Vol. I, p. 70.]
301a. Pentatonic?
341 Bloodthirsty epic text.
345 Italian?
359b. [Two-part song. Not listed in Vol. I, p. 71.]
380 Pentatonic?
389 Hungarian variant.
433a. Variant of Parry 15.
463 *Tamburica* postlude.
487 [Two-part song. Not listed in Vol. I, p. 71.]
511a. Apparently an urban text.
521 Dance?
569 Mourning (at home) song.
599 *Sibinjanin Janko.*
632 Hungarian variant?
688 Pentatonic.
691b. Variant of *Rumanian Folk Music* II, No. 360.
709b. Apparently a nice urban text.
713c. Pentatonic.
757 The last [melody section] has the appearance of a Rumanian *colindă.*
788f. The second melody section resembles a Hunedoara [Rumanian county] *colindă.*
841a.b. Hungarian, Slovak text variants.
851 Urban song-like.
852a. Sentimental, urban text.
852bis. Reminiscent of a Rumanian song.
874 Beethoven "Pastorale" [Sym. No. 6].
914 Urban Hungarian [refrain].
961a. *Barcsai* [Hungarian text].
971a. Urban text?
986a. Parry variant.
1001a. Unusual form.
1002a. *Colindă*-like text.
1033g. Text is similar to [the Hungarian song] *Elveszettem én ludaim.*
1075 Pentatonic?
1084 Rumanian text similarity?

1093 Urban-like text.
1095a. Urban song?
1096 Like a Rumanian *colindă.*
1105b. Urban song-like.
1107c. Slovak?
1108 Slovak?
1124a.c. Song of Solomon (*Canticum, canticorum*) text.
1133 Pentatonic?
1135a. *Szeretnék szántani* [Hungarian] type.
1142b. Cf. *Rumanian Folk Music* IV, Nos. 14, 28.
1146 Slovak?
1148a. Slovak? Hungarian?
1153 Hungarian?
1155bis b. Slovak variant?
1159 Slovenian text variant.
1172–1173 *Colindă* text variant.
1181a. *Colindă* text variant.
1206b. Soldier text.
1208 Rumanian?
1209b. *Colindă* text variant.
1246g. Urban-like.
1246k. Urban text.
1255d. Urban-like text.
1258 Parry text?
1260 Urban text.
1261 *Colindă*-like text.
1276 Urban text.
1277a. Rhyming text (a a).
1277c. German. Urban text?
1278 Bulgarian?
1288 Rumanian variant?
1303b. *Doica Firă* [Rumanian] text variant.
1310i. *Colindă*-like text.
1335–1336 Urban text.
1344 Urban text.
1347 Urban text.
1354 Urban-song text.
135a. [Conjectural notation given of the missing first two melody sections.]

1359 Rumanian?
1372–1373 Urban-like text.
1379 Urban song?
1380 Slovak-Hungarian?
1409 Slovenian?
1436 Bulgarian variant?
1478 Reminiscent of a Rumanian *colindă.*
1481a. Slovenian influence?
1506a.b. Haydn *Gott erhalte.*
1506c. [See remark to 1532c. below.]
1521a. gigaga.
1532c. Well-known Rumanian melody from the Banat [region].
1540k. Soldier's song.
1546a. Urban-like text.
1546c. Violin postlude after each stanza, played by the singer.
1557b. Urban text.
1584a. Hungarian variant [text].
1584b. Rumanian [text] similarity.
1585g. Sentimental urban text.
1616. Urban-like text.
1617. German.
1619b. Parry variant [No. 51].
1658c. Urban text.
1658f. Old urban-song text?
1664a. Slovenian-influenced text.
1686. [Refrain with Rumanian untranslatable words: see *Rumanian Folk Music* IV, p. 217.]
1737b. *Lelița* refrain [cf. *Rumanian Folk Music* II, No. 403.]
1774. Urban text?
1775. Slovak? Not peasant text.
1794 Slovak similarity.
1805. *Kolomejka* rhythm.
1867. Two-part song!
1873, 1874 [Two-part: *Ojkanje.*]
1886 Turkish text.
1887 Mostly in Turkish language.

Editor's Preface

SUPPLEMENTARY DATA

In his studies on musical folklore Bartók devotes considerable attention to the listing and description of variant melodies and texts. In Vol. I of the present publication, for instance, Hungarian and Turkish (pp. 55–56, 64, 241), Serbo-Croatian, Slovak and Moravian (pp. 64, 231–244), and Rumanian (p. 235) variants are given. The "Tab. of Mat." in Vol. II and the Addenda listed above provide the reader with other variant indications, for the most part with respect to melody.[7] It will be observed, however, that there are a substantial number of annotations in the Source Melodies published below, that make specific or general reference to text variants in the Serbo-Croatian materials collected by Bartók. It is therefore not feasible in this publication to tabulate the data on the more than four-hundred references to "Tab. of Mat." text variants.

Rhythm schemata.—The following source melodies contain rhythm schemata that Bartók did not notate in the sixth column of "Tab. of Mat.": (Current Nos.) 73c.d., 74, 123j.k.t.u.v.z.aa.ff., 258, 261d., 309b., 335b., 418, 423a., 433e., 457, 562, 930a., 983a., 984a.i., 1048, and 1415.

Skeleton melodies.—The attention of the reader is directed to the following source melodies which contain skeleton notations (that is, the form stripped of all ornamental tones), since their comparative study may prove enlightening in the examination of Bartók's procedures for solving the problem of principal tone determination (see Vol. I, pp. 17–18). Current Nos.:

1a.b.	125a.	271e.f.	344f.
11	138	284	365–66c.d.
24a.	160a.	286f.g.	372
62	164b.	290a.	384a.b.d.
64a.	171	301a.	392a.
72b.	183f.	312c.	435d.e.
82a.	208b.	320b.	464
107	210c.	321c.	479a.b.
117a.	243i.	323b.c.	488a.
122b.	265a.d.	328	490

[7] Other Rumanian variants of Serbo-Croatian materials will be found in *Rumanian Folk Music* II (p. 40), III (pp. lxxxi [refrains], xcvii–xcviii), and IV (pp. 35–36).

510b.	714	859	1249
519a.	751	890	1254a.b.
521	752c.	1026f.	1325d.e.
533a.	770a.e.	1039g.	1327a.g.
538a.	771	1054a.	1392a.
543a.	772	1091	1488
562	773c.	1102a.d.	1489
581	775a.	1158a.	1492
583	779b.c.	1203b.	1502c.
592a.	782a.-f.	1210	1512a.
598	787	1215	1514a.b.d.e.
628	804b.	1230b.	1519b.
638a.b.	808	1241a.	1532c.h.i.
658	809	1243e.	1553
690b.	810a.c.	1247a.	

A COMPARATIVE SURVEY OF RELATED SOURCES[8]

Each of Yugoslavia's six republics—Bosnia and Hercegovina, Croatia, Macedonia, Montenegro, Serbia, and Slovenia—has research institutes, university departments or museum sections that collect, study, and publish the results of scholarly investigations of musical folklore.[9] Since World War II, a substantial number of such publications have appeared in Yugoslavia, printed in Latin and Cyrillic alphabets, in book form as collections of transcribed, annotated, and classified folk melodies, and in shorter form as essays on morphological and other aspects of the collected materials or as summary articles of encylopedic nature. Translations and revised versions of a number of these sources,

[8] Published and unpublished materials that are more closely connected with Bartók's own study of Serbo-Croatian folk music, are described in the editorial preface to Vol. I of the present publication.

[9] The republican boundaries are transcended by cultural zones as follows: Alpine—the Slovenian area, which is connected with central European cultural patterns; Pannonian—the northern part of Yugoslavia contiguous with Hungary, that is, Croatia north of the Sava River, and the Vojvodina region (north Serbia); Adriatic—a narrow belt along the Dalmatian coast, including the islands; Dinaric—the remainder of Croatia (including Dalmatia), Bosnia and Hercegovina, and Montenegro; Moravian—southern Serbia, including the Kosmet region; and Vardar—Macedonia. These cultural zones have been determined in part by musical folklore.

as well as some original writings, have been published in foreign journals, in English, German, and French. There are, too, various articles on Yugoslav folk music by foreign ethnomusicologists.

The purpose of this chapter, however, is to provide the reader with an update summary of those available source materials that deal with Serbo-Croatian folk song within the geographic terrain and delimited to the morphological aspects covered by Bartók (Vol. I, pp. 21–87).[10] The results of the editorial comparative survey are described below in the topical order followed by Bartók. Complete publication details concerning the surveyed sources and certain untreated materials (for example, folk song collections and other unavailable writings) will be found in the Selected Bibliography (below, pp. xxxv–xxxix).

PRINTED MATERIAL (Vol. I, pp. 22–25)

The fifth volume of Fr. Š. Kuhač's *Južno-Slovjenske narodne popijevke* bears the publication date of 1941. Bartók, however, was unaware of its existence.[11] Edited by B. Širola and V. Dukat, without the usual piano accompaniments (which Bartók deplored as wasted time and space in folk music collections), the publication contains melody Nos. 1,600 to 2,000. The tunes are published according to their genre, as follows: patriotic, highwayman, travelling, children's (lullabies, naive [snail, bedtime prayers], religious and serious [heroic themes], wishing, play types), New Year's gift, harvesting, miscellaneous foreign Christian ritual, mourning, and mythological types. The children's songs, Nos. 1676–1823, represent the largest category: about one-third of the volume.

Although Bartók lists A. Dobronić's *Ojkanje* publication as unavailable (Vol. I, p. 25), three of its eight music examples are facsimiles of Kuba *N.g.u.D,* Vol. IV which Bartók had on hand.[12]

The format of the Stanković publication (*Srbske narodne pjesme,* Vienna, 1862) would surely have amused Bartók, for each of its twelve melodies (No. 4 is a variant of Tschaikovsky's *Marche Slave,* Op. 31)

[10] See Vol. I, p. 24 for Bartók's explanations with respect to exclusion of Slovenian, Macedonian, and Međimurje folk song materials.

[11] Yugoslavia was occupied by the German army in April, 1941.

[12] Nos. 58[?], 59, and 64. Two melodies are from Vol. III: Nos. 2 and 20; and another was published in Kuba's article "Píseň jihoslavanská a mohamedanism," *Hudební Revue* (God) Vol. VI, p. 495.

are treated in three ways: for voice and piano, for piano solo, and for four-part chorus of male voices!

The reader interested in biographical and other details concerning some of the authors of the collections tabulated by Bartók, should refer to "The Brothers Tihomir and Vladimir Djordjević: Pioneers of Ethnomusicology in Serbia," by Ljubica S. Janković (edited by Barbara Krader) and "Die Volksmusik der Kroaten" by Božidar Širola.[13]

Bartók's assertion that "Serbo-Croatian scholars never used recording instruments, for reasons unknown to me." (Vol. I, p. xii) is in a sense refuted by the field work of Mathias Murko, a Slovenian ethnologist interested in musical folklore, who recorded epic folk songs in Bosnia and Hercegovina, and neighboring regions of Croatia and Dalmatia, during the summers of 1912 and 1913.[14]

In 1975 Walter Graf, the Viennese musicologist, transcribed and annotated the intelligible recordings, including the song texts, performer's data, and other descriptive remarks, which had been copied from the original ones made in 1912. He published the results of his work in the essay "Murko's Phonogramme bosnischer Epenlieder aus dem Jahre 1912" (Graz, 1975), and it should be noted that record No. 1718 is a text variant (*Himzibeg*) of mus. exx. 35 and 36 in Vol. I —there is also a similarity in melodic contour with mus. ex. 35—and record Nos. 1726 and 1727 have text portions in common with mus. ex. 20 (*Dva Morića*).

MELODY-STANZA STRUCTURES (Vol. I, pp. 36–47)

Cvjetko Rihtman calls attention to a Bosnia and Hercegovina tune type, found in villages and towns, and in other Yugoslav regions, which seems to be a vestige of an old Slav tradition. This tune type, designated by Rihtman as "the long tune" (the other type is "the short tune"), is a more complex structure of melody section which, if formed by the repetition of hemistichs of one or, at the most, two lines, is found in

[13] See publication details in the Selected Bibliography. The Širola essay describes the research findings of Kuhač and Kuba.

[14] Since Bartók was thoroughly familiar with the listings in *Folklore Musical* (Paris: Institute International de Coopération Intellectuelle, 1939)—Murko's recordings, among others, are described on p. 219—it would appear that Bartók's use of the term "Serbo-Croatian scholar" was restricted to men such as himself, who collected, transcribed, and published folk song collections over a period of years.

other Slav countries such as Bulgaria, Slovakia, and Russia, but not among other neighboring peoples.[15]

Radmila Petrović points to ancient patterns, designated *kajda* or *glas* by performers, that indicate that the ancient Slavic peoples may have created a basic repertory of melodic types for different occasions and needs. All ritual melodies have their own types of *glas,* classified according to function (wedding, harvest, shepherd, *Lazarička,* etc.), which are used with song texts having the same characteristics of syllabic number, position of accents, and so forth, even though the texts have different subject matter. The *glas* varies with respect to melodic line, interval size, and rhythmic values from area to area and even from village to village, but the text structure and the musical form remain constant. Although the *glas* is not identical or structurally uniform throughout the various regions, the fact that the several types of *glas* are called by the same name in every region suggests their probable antiquity.[16]

PRINCIPLES OF FORM CONSTRUCTION (Vol. I, pp. 47–52)

Bartók's collected materials show an overwhelming preponderance of two- and three-section melodies, a structural feature he points to as evidence of the great difference between Yugoslav folk song melodies and the basically four-section ones of the Slovaks and Hungarians. More recent findings, specifically those contained in Miodrag Vasiljević's 1953 study of five-hundred Sandžak[17] folk songs, provide supportive data:

Two-section melodies. 216 (43.2%), of A B (25.2%) and A A (18%) content-structure;

Three-section melodies. 129 (25.8%), of A B C (11.8%), A B B (11%), A A A (2%), and A B A (0.6%) content-structure;

[15] Cvjetko Rihtman, '2. Bosnia and Hercegovina. (*iii*) *Melopoetic forms.*' in "Yugoslavia: II, Folk Music," *The New Grove Dictionary of Music and Musicians* (1979).

[16] Radmila Petrović, "Some Aspects of Formal Expression in Serbian Folk Songs," (*Yearbook of the International Folk Music Council,* 1971), pp. 74–76. See also her article, "The Place of Ethnomusicology in Yugoslav Music Study," in *Papers of the Yugoslav-American Seminar on Music* (edited by Malcolm H. Brown. Bloomington: Indiana University, 1970), pp. 169–170.

[17] Sandžak is a locality in Bosnia and Hercegovina, about one hundred kilometers northwest of Sarajevo.

Four-section melodies. 146 (29.2%), of A B C D (8.2%), A B A B (7.8%), A A B B (6.2%), and other (7%) content-structure.[18]

Vinko Žganec's later (1957) collection of Međimurje folk songs should be touched on here, even though Bartók excluded material from this Hungarian-influenced region (Vol. I, p. 24), because of the classification procedure followed by the Croatian ethnomusicologist. The 163 melodies are published according to syllabic structure—from seven to fifteen syllable sections—and are listed in a somewhat similar format to Bartók's tabulation, Metric Scheme of the Lines (Vol. I, p. 39). Žganec has added a useful symbolic representation of the heavy and light accents, for each of his metric schemata. In addition the melodies are provided with caesura, content-structure, and syllabic-designation symbols, and metronome marks.[19]

RANGE (Vol. I, pp. 52–59)

Bartók's statement that extra-narrow range melodies which occur in the ceremonial songs of Slovak and Serbo-Croatian materials, and therefore may be the remnants of a common ancient Slavic style, is modified by his question whether there is a connection between such melodies and the narrow range Arabic ones (p. 54). Recent research on the subject of range, while providing additional classification principles in the determination of stylistic age, does not address Bartók's hypothesis.

Valens Vodušek, summarizing Slovenian folk music, describes a recent, surprising discovery made in Rezija (Val di Resia, Italy), an isolated valley in the western Julian Alps. More than half the song repertory has tunes within a trichord; the root tone also serving as the drone. Another 25 per cent shows the fifth above the drone as an addition to the trichord.) The upper tone in some trichordal tunes is

[18] M. A. Vasiljević, *Mélodies populaires du Sandžak* (Belgrade: Institut de Musicologie Monograph No. 5, 1953), pp. LIV–LVI. The author has also determined that more than half the melodies are isometric in rhythmic structure.

[19] V. Žganec, *Međimurje u svojim pjesmama* [Međimurje in its own songs] (Zagreb: Savez muzičkih društava nr Hrvatske, 1957). The analysis of metric schemata appears on pp. 111–113. The author's list of content-structures clearly indicates a dominating Hungarian influence (pp. 117–118). Four melodies are two-section structures, nine are three-section, and the remaining one-hundred sixty are four-section, including a substantial number with descending (that is, A A_5 types) structure and in architectonic form. And the majority of tunes are in some form of the pentatonic scale (pp. 118–119).

unstable: it generally changes from a very low minor third to a very high major one. Almost all these songs—which show very slight differences but are sharply distinguished by the people—have the same metrical verse structure. The average singer has one "personal" tune only (many tunes are called by their authors' names), which is applied to most song texts. And it is perhaps noteworthy that Rezija's dance music has a "characteristic rhythm, predominating in tetratonic and pentatonic wide range tunes, which may have its origins in a pre-Slavic substratum."[20]

SCALES (pp. 59–65)

Bartók has organized his Serbo-Croatian materials into five scale categories: (1) F major or minor tetra-, penta-, and hexachords (the majority of melodies show these structures), with the second degree as final tone; (2) a major scale, with the third degree as final tone; (3) a minor scale with an augmented second between the third and fourth or fourth and fifth degrees, the second degree as final tone; (4) "a very peculiar scale formation"[21] consisting of a minor pentachord with its fifth degree lowered a half step (less frequently the range is extended to include the major or minor sixth degree: in this case the third also may be major or minor)—"intermediate between the diatonic and 'chromatic' scales," (5) "chromatic" melodies of narrow range, that is, with pentachordal segments of a twelve-hemitone scale in which the third and fourth degrees are chromatic and the final tone is fixed.

Jerko Bezić has developed seven categories of tonal relationships, including scale structure, cadence, final tone, tone frequency of occurrence, and part-singing. The abridged descriptions that follow below are limited to range and scale.

1. The Narrow-Intervals Style. Tetrachords and pentachords with successive semitones, a whole tone between two semitones, or combinations of whole and semitones [see Bartók (5) and (4), above]. The single degrees are not as emphasized in their function as they are in scales of more developed modes, and there are some cases in which

[20] V. Vodušek, '5. Slovenia. (*i*) *Partsinging.*' in "Yugoslavia: II, Folk Music," *The New Grove Dictionary of Music and Musicians* (1979).

[21] The so-called Istrian scale.

certain degrees show chromatic fluctuation. Intervals often diverge vigorously from the tempered system. This style is primarily found in mountainous regions, among cattle breeders, and is widespread in the Dinaric zone. It is also found in Istria and parts of Serbia, and, to a lesser extent, in Macedonia and the border area between Slovenia and Croatia.

2. *The Oligotonic Tunes Style.* Bichord and trichord melodies comprising semitones, whole tones, and larger intervals, in which the root tone may be the lowest one, or, more often, the midpoint of the range [see in the preceding section on Range, above, Bartók's statement on extra-narrow range melodies]. This style is common in traditional ritual songs, children's songs, narrative songs, and even dance songs, and it is found in geographically very different regions.

3. *The Diatonic Narrow-Range Style.* Very abundant and varied tetra-, penta-, and hexachord melodies whose roots are the first or the second degree in the tonal series [see Bartók (1), above]. The two larger ranges are expansions of a diatonic tetrachord which may have the semitone at the beginning, midpoint, or end of the tonal series. Temperament and chromatic fluctuation similar to the first style. When the semitone is at the midpoint, the root tone is the final tone, otherwise, the close is on the second degree. This style occurs throughout Yugoslavia except in Slovenia.

4. *The Style of Unison Singing in a Wider Range.* Mostly hexachords are found, commonly structured in the Dorian and Aeolian modes which show obviously elements of anhemitone-pentatonicism (some melodies have the fifth transposition of Hungarian folk music). This style occurs in the Alpine and Pannonian zones, also in the Vardar zone [see Bartók's commentary in Vol. I, pp. 54–59].

5. *The Oriental Elements Style.* There are two elements: (a) the *maqāms*—the Arabic system of melodic construction for performances—and (b) the more widespread, richly-ornamented melodies of wider range, in which the interval of the augmented second (usually appearing in the lower tetrachord) frequently occurs. This style is found primarily in larger settlements along the main traffic routes of the former Ottoman Empire and in the western and southeastern parts of Yugoslavia. The augmented-second element appears occasionally in eastern Croatia and Slovenia. Two *tambura*-type (chordophone) instruments

represent the oriental elements style: the *saz* and the *šargija* [see Bartók (3), above].

6. "In Bass" (na bas) Singing Style. Mostly two-part songs, some multi-part, constructed of diatonic tetra- or pentachords, with possible expansion to a hexachord, ending on the second degree which is accompanied by a perfect fifth below it. Rarely found in Slovenia, unknown in Montenegro and Macedonia, this style is nevertheless the most widespread in Yugoslavia [see Bartók (1), above].

7. The Major Part-Singing Style. One- to four-part singing (five-part in Slovenia) in the major mode whose range is usually smaller than an octave. Parallel thirds are frequent in two-part singing, and the melodic line of the leading part usually ends on the third or first degree. The style is found in Slovenia and Croatia (and in Macedonian urban songs only), and is slowly spreading out of these territories [see Bartók (2), above].[22]

Turning now to Bartók's "unsolved problem"—whether the augmented-second interval is a sign "of oriental (Arabic) influence (perhaps through Turkish intermediation)"—Bezić's Oriental Elements Style (category *5.*, above) evidently provides a clear-cut solution which is further supported by Cvjetko Rihtman's findings with respect to the influence of string instruments on Yugoslav tonal relationships: "Additional important factors were the use . . . of chordophones fretted in the oriental scales in the small-town tradition [where chromaticism is] characterized by an augmented 2nd between two semitones."[23] Rihtman describes these *tambura*-type instruments—the *saz* and the *šargiya*—as probably introduced by Turkish performers who are mentioned in Sarajevo documents dating back to the 15th century.[24]

In the preceding discussion of principles of form construction statistical data are given for frequency of occurrence of content-structure in Vasiljević's collection of Sandžak folk melodies (see note 18, above). Similar treatment is given to scale types, including mode and range; in fact the melodies are classified on the basis of these aspects. The ma-

[22] J. Bezić, "The Tonal Framework of Folk Music In Yugoslavia," in *The Folk Arts of Yugoslavia* (Pittsburgh: Duquesne University Tamburitzans Institute of Folk Arts, 1976), pp. 195–201. See also his article, '3. Croatia. (*i*)–(*vi*)' in "Yugoslavia: II, Folk Music," *The New Grove Dictionary of Music and Musicians* (1979).

[23] Rihtman, *op. cit., (ii) Characteristics of scale, metre and rhythm.*

[24] C. Rihtman, "Yugoslav Folk Music Instruments," in *The Folk Arts of Yugoslavia* (see note 22 for bibliographic details), pp. 218–221.

jority of melodies (292 or 58%) are F major or minor scale fragments, for the most part tetra-, penta-, and hexachords, a frequency of occurrence which agrees with Bartók's data [see Bartók (1), above].[25] In two other collections Vasiljević computes this scale type—which he terms *Le majeure antique* (*de quinte*)—as predominant: Kosmet, with 259 of 522 melodies (49.62%),[26] and Macedonia, 154 of 421 melodies (36.56%).[27]

RHYTHM FORMATION (Vol. I, pp. 65–70)

Because of the unreliability of the published material, Bartók's discussion of rhythm formation is based mainly on the seventy-five melodies in Vol. I. He refers to the scarcity of real *parlando-rubato* rhythm (free rhythm which does not involve the recurrence of equal values or, in other words, the performance is without any systematic succession of note values), assumes the pre-existence of simple original rhythmic patterns for eight-, ten-, and eleven-syllable lines and provides a tabulation of six types of permutation of those patterns, and concludes only that—on the basis of the Parry Collection—the so-called "Bulgarian" [that is, Turkish *aksak*] formations are completely lacking in the Serbo-Croatian material (Vol. I, p. 86). The presently available collections and sources, other than Macedonian publications (see note 27), devote less attention to rhythm structure than to such other morphological aspects as range, scale, part-singing, and genre.

Although Bartók excludes Vinko Žganec's 1924 Međimurje collection, because of its Hungarian or international character (Vol. I, p. 24), the latter's more recent collection of Zagorje[28] folk songs, similarly "contaminated" to a certain extent, is annotated here in view of its

[25] Vasiljević, *op. cit.*, pp. XLI–XLVII. See also his article, "Les bases tonales de la musique populaires serbes," *Journal of the International Folk Music Council,* Vol. IV, 1952, pp. 19–23.

[26] M. A. Vasiljević, *Jugoslovenski muzički folklor. I. Kosmet.* Belgrade: Prosveta izdavačka preduzeće Srbije, 1950, pp. 379–390.

[27] *II. Macedonia.* 1953, pp. LXXV–LXXXI (see note 26 for publication series title and other details).

With regard to oriental scales, the three collections show the augmented second occurring between the third and fourth degrees. The proportion of these scales is as follows: Sandžak (Bosnia and Hercegovina), 60 melodies (12%); Kosmet (autonomous province in southern Serbia), 83 (15.88%); Macedonia, 31 (7.3%).

[28] Zagorje is a Croatian locality north of Zagreb, in the northeastern part of the Pannonian cultural zone.

classification according to rhythmic types. Žganec has ordered the 745 melodies (excluding variants and nine instrumental pieces) according to the syllabic length of the first textline (four to fourteen syllables). Further classification is made according to rhythmic types, that is, note patterns, of which there are 203 (including two types for mourning songs). Bartók's "simple original" patterns *a*) 1.–3.) appear in Žganec as types 69, 139, and 173, respectively; Bartók pattern *b*) 1.) appears as Žganec type 88, and so forth. The Zagorje material is for the most part eight-syllable in first textline length (141 rhythmic types), with six-syllable (36 types) and seven-syllable (19 types) structures in greater abundance than dekasyllabic ones.[29]

Turning next to the matter of *parlando-rubato* and *non-parlando* (that is, *tempo giusto* or fixed) rhythm, this subject is touched by Yugoslav encyclopedists as follows:

Bosnia and Hercegovina. In his review of Vlado Milošević's 1964 pubication of Bosnian folk songs (*Bosanske narodne pjesme IV*. Banja Luka: Muzej Bosanske Krajine. 550 melodies) Cvjetko Rihtman states that "The indisputable value of this collection lies above all in the great number of amusing and attentively transcribed tunes among which there are many of small township centres known as 'uravan'—plain (with changeable unit of duration in the style of tempo rubato), which is very characteristic of older tradition."[30] Elsewhere Rihtman cautions that asymmetrical groupings of simple duple and triple bars (*potkorak*), a frequent phenomenon, are not to be confused with *aksak* rhythm—specifically, the division of nine beats into 2 + 2 + 2 + 3—which is a Turkish element only in the urban repertory.[31]

Croatia. Folk music rhythm is either strict (*giusto*) or free (*rubato*). The latter occurs particularly in solo songs such as laments, narrative songs; the former is found in dance songs and many other forms. In addition to simple, compound, and mixed meters there are also asymmetrical ones with unequal bar units. Syncopation and dotted notes occur more rarely.[32]

[29] V. Žganec, *Narodne popijevke hrvatskog Zagorja* [The Folk Songs of Croatian Zagorje] (Zagreb: Jugoslavenska akademija znanosti i umjetnosti, 1952), pp. 433–440.

[30] *Journal of the International Folk Music Council,* Vol. XVIII, 1964, p. 87.

[31] See note 23 above. See also "Bosansko-Hercegovacka muzika," in *Muzička enciklopedija* (2nd ed.; Zagreb: Yugoslav Lexicographical Society, 1971), Vol. I, p. 227.

[32] Jerko Bezić, "Hrvatska muzika," in *Muzički enciklopedija* (see note 31 for publication details), Vol. I, p. 172; and in *Grove VI* (see note 22): (*vii*) *Rhythm and form.*

Serbia. The "old-time *glas*", a melodic type or model which represents a traditional Serbian musical idiom (see the description on p. xxii, above) offers great variety in stylistic features, and thus can be further typified by such designations as "short *glas*" and "drawn-out *glas*." The latter term ordinarily signifies rhythmic organization, specifically, a prolonged melody in free rhythm.[33] On the surface of the matter, there appears to be at least a semantic relationship between "drawn-out" and the Bartókian appellation "long-drawn" for the Rumanian *Cântec lung* melody type.[34]

PART-SINGING (Vol. I, pp. 70–73)

The polyphonic specimens in Bartók's Yugoslav material, published and unpublished, led him to conclude that part-singing occurs mostly in the northern and western border territories and in Dalmatia. Bezić's study of the various styles of folk music in Yugoslavia (see note 22, above), however, demonstrates that part-singing is widespread throughout Yugoslavia.

So far as place of origin is concerned, Bartók believed that "The geographical extension of polyphony in Yugoslavia points to Western influence, especially when it is remembered that the folk music of the neighbouring Germans of Carinthia and Styria is almost exclusively polyphonic . . . As I feel it, polyphony is, in general, somewhat contrary to the spirit of folk music and must, therefore, be regarded with due suspicion."[35]

Bartók's discussion of part-singing styles is organized in terms of (a) "normal" two-, three-, and four-part songs which use the "simpler harmonies and intervals of Western European art music," including the dominant semicadence ending in melodies whose final tone is the second degree of the scale, and in which two-part songs have a drone, in the lower part, that follows the melodic rhythm; and (b) "peculiar

[33] R. Petrović, *op. cit.*, p. 75.

[34] A *parlando-rubato,* non-ceremonial single melody with variants, improvisatory in character but with a sustained phrase opening, a richly ornamented middle section, and a declamatory cadence on the final tone. See Béla Bartók, *Rumanian Folk Music* (edited by Benjamin Suchoff. The Hague: Martinus Nijhoff, 1967, 1975), Vol. II, pp. 24–25; Vol. V, pp. 9–11. See also Vol. I of the present publication, pp. 59 and 77.

[35] Béla Bartók, "Some Problems of Folk Music Research in East Europe," in *Béla Bartók Essays* (selected and edited by Benjamin Suchoff. London: Faber & Faber [New York: St. Martin's Press], 1976), p. 173.

kind of two-part singing," in major seconds, occurring in Dalmatia in connection with chromatic-style melodies, which may be a transformation of a kind of normal part-singing, an antique style of an extinct art music, or—as a most acceptable explanation—simply "compressed" normal thirds.

Bartók bipartite categorization may have been influenced by Božidar Širola's encyclopedic article in *Zenei Lexicon,* 1931 (see Vol. I of the present publication, p. 37, note 31, for publication details), which postulates that polyphony is a peculiar phenomenon of Yugoslav song: simple homophonic structures based on tonic and dominant chords as the basic harmonies or, in the case of the Croatian coastal regions and islands, a different type—heterophonic diaphony, known in ancient history as *cantus gemelius.* In a later summary of Croatian folk music research Širola asserts that diaphony in remote mountain townships could not have been influenced by Istrian church choirs.[36]

Another classification of polyphonic forms, also in two categories, was described in the early 1950's by Cvjetko Rihtman. Category I consists of forms in which the upper voice takes the lead while the lower, of secondary importance, accompanies in parallel thirds or sixths, or as drones, *ostinati,* or (rarely) canons. Category II comprises forms in which the leading voice occasionally underlaps the accompanying one, that are found only in the central mountainous regions (among herdsmen) where there are eight performance types, including the singing of consecutive seconds.[37] In his most recent encyclopedic essays on the musical folklore of Bosnia and Hercegovina, Rihtman—again in two major categories—has reorganized his concept of polyphonic forms which can be enumerated in outline as follows:

I. Polyphonic forms derived from western European harmonic practice:
   a. with drone;
   b. with parallel motion in 3rds or 6ths;
   c. *na bas* forms (most widespread): the sections end on an open 5th, so that the final note of the melody assumes the function of a dominant;

[36] B. Širola, "Die Volksmusik der Kroaten," in *Studia Memoriae Belae Bartók* (Budapest: Akédemiai kiadó, 1958), p. 99.

[37] C. Rihtman, "Polifoni oblici u narodnoj muzici Bosne i Hercegovine," *Bilten instituta za proučavanje folklora u Sarajevu,* Sarajevo, 1951, pp. 7–30. Abridged forms of this essay appear in *Journal of the International Folk Music Council* ("Les formes polyphoniques dans la musique populaire de Bosnie et d'Herzegovine"), Vol. 4, 1952, pp. 30–35; in *Grove V* ("Folkmusic: Yugoslav."), Vol. III, 1954, p. 416; and in *MGG* ("Jugoslawien. II. Die Volksmusik. 5. Bosnien und Herzegowina."), Vol. VII, 373–74.

d. *ostinato* forms.

These forms are part of the town tradition and represent a later layer in development.

II. Non-European or earlier European polyphonic forms:

a. both voices move in the same direction but with a difference in rhythm and words;
b. in the same direction, using different intervals, so that the first voice is sometimes a 2nd below the second voice and vice versa;
c. in parallel 2nds, so that the second voice stays on a drone, while the first voice plays around it in various ways;
d. the second voice—the drone—in certain places rises or descends in the form of an accent;
e. the first voice occasionally assumes the role of a drone;
f. the motif of the first voice merges with the second voice;
g. various combinations of the above.

A prominent and common feature of Category II polyphonic forms is the occurrence of the interval of the 2nd at the end of sections, that is, its treatment as a consonance. This extremely important characteristic cannot be explained by elements of European peoples or by conditions of their development.[38]

PECULIARITIES OF PERFORMANCE (Vol. I, pp. 73–81)

Bartók's discussion includes ornamental tones, interruptions (line, word, and syllable), swallowing of syllables and their emphatic rendition, clucking sounds, stuttering entrance of words, syllabification of consonants, structurally unessential preparatory upbeats, and hiatus-filling consonants.

In the first section of his *Grove VI* essay (note 15, above) Rihtman offers a brief description of performance peculiarities in Bosnia and Hercegovina.[39] These are listed below, with parenthetical indications of apparent or possible identicalness with Bartók's register.

(1) singing *na glas*—"on top of the voice": an older style of outdoors

[38] C. Rihtman, in *Grove VI* (see note 15); and in *Muzička enciklopedija* (note 31), pp. 228–229. Rihtman lists a third type of "girls' form", which does not belong in either category: the voices intersect but the 2nd appears more rarely and is not always treated as a consonance. Bezić (note 22) includes the various polyphonic forms as part of the tonal framework of Yugoslav folk music.

[39] See also his remarks in *Muzicka enciklopedija* (note 31, above), pp. 225–227; and in *Grove V,* p. 413.

group performance, therefore sung loudly and with an open-throated quality, typical of the country tradition. [Petrović adds that melismatic ornamentation of tones, part of the small-town (Moslem) tradition, represents an Eastern element derived from Turkish influence.[40]]
(2) *potresanje*—"trembling": a sort of rudimentary trill (Bartók: clucking sounds).
(3) *deleganje:* singing while tapping the throat with the fingers. Used by cowherds to produce an intensely vibrating tone and thus encourage two bulls to fight each other.
(4) *od uha*—"from the ear": singing with the palm of the hand turned toward the mouth and with the fingers touching the ear.
(5) *upramase:* the singers face each other at an angle and end on a higher or lower tone of indefinite pitch.
(6) skipping of syllables (Bartók: syllable interruption).
(7) deformation of vowels.
(8) insertion of superfluous syllables such as *j* (pronounced *y*), thus transforming, for example, *od sokola* into *od sojkojlaj.*
(9) prolongation of consonants *n, j,* etc. (Bartók: syllabification of consonants?)
(10) singing to the turning of a *tepsija:* one woman rapidly turns a large shallow metal pan, while another crouches next to her and sings across it.

Another performance peculiarity, observed in all national groups, is the ancient antiphonal style of singing ritual songs. Before the first group of singers has come to the end of the first melody section, the second group enters and sings the same section. Then the first group sings the next section, the second group again entering later on in the same manner. This procedure continues until all melody sections have been sung.[41] This peculiarity is somewhat similar to the change song practice in Rumanian *colinde* (carols) singing, with the exceptions that in Rumania the second group enters with the next melody section,

[40] R. Petrović, "The Concept of Yugoslav Folk Music in the Twentieth Century," *Journal of the International Folk Music Council,* Vol. XX, 1968, p. 23. In her *Grove VI* on the folk music of Serbia, Macedonia, and Montenegro (*"iii Musical Characteristics"*) Petrović also lists *na glas* singing as a performance peculiarity in these territories: "an older music layer—characteristic of cattle breeders and mountain dwellers."

[41] R. Petrović, "Folk Music of Yugoslavia," in *The Folk Arts of Yugoslavia* (see note 22 for publication details), p. 190.

the change occurs from section to section, and the interchange takes place without any pause in the melody.[42]

RELATION BETWEEN TEXT AND MELODY (Vol. I, pp. 81–84)

Bartók's classification of song text genres comprises seven categories of ceremonial and non-ceremonial folk songs. The related literature on this subject is far too extensive to attempt revision or even extension of Bartók's presentation. The current approach in Yugoslav ethnology and ethnomusicology is tripartite: EPIC SONGS, formerly designated as heroic songs, which are of historical nature and for the most part in connection with battles and fighting;[43] FOLK BALLADS or narrative folk songs, which are designated in Yugoslav folk song collections as *lirsko-epske pesme* (lyric-epic songs), *ženske* (women's songs), among other expressions, and which may be sung for listening or for accompanying the dance;[44] and LYRIC SONGS, heterogeneous material of broad thematic spectrum, "interpreted by individuals and groups of singers at various celebrations, gatherings of mourners and other events even without listeners, [these songs] express the spiritual life in all its nuances and the people's daily life in all its details, from birth to death."[45]

[42] Bartók, *Rumanian Folk Music,* Vol. IV, pp. 25, 28–29.

[43] Djenana Buturović, "Oral Epic Poetry of the Peoples of Yugoslavia," in *The Folk Arts of Yugoslavia* (see note 22, above), pp. 137–166. The following points have bearing on Bartók's comments in Vol. I, p. 21: a) the *tambura* and other instruments, in addition to the *gusle,* may provide the accompaniment; b) unaccompanied performances occur; c) women, too, perform epic songs in some parts of Serbia and eastern Hercegovina.

[44] Zmaga Kumer, "The Folk Ballads of Yugoslavia," in *The Folk Arts of Yugoslavia,* pp. 117–134. Kumer states that in Bosnia and Hercegovina the ballad is sung more by women than by men, in some cases into the *tepsija* (metal pan).

[45] Blaže Ristovski, "Oral Lyric Poetry of the Peoples of Yugoslavia," in *The Folk Arts of Yugoslavia,* pp. 167–182. Ristovski's classification is in five major groups, each with subgroups and further divisions: I. Ritual, II. Mythological and Religious, III. Social, IV. Lullabies and Children's songs, V. Patriotic and Revolutionary.

Selected Bibliography

ENCYCLOPEDIAS AND COMPILATIONS

The Folk Arts of Yugoslavia (with an Introduction by W. W. Kolar). Pittsburgh: Duquesne University Tamburitzans Institute of Folk Arts, 1976.

I. "Transition of Folk Culture in Yugoslavia," Dunja Rihtman-Auguštin
II. "Folk Customs—A Survey," Zorica Rajković
III. "Customs and Beliefs," Slobodan Zečević
IX. "The Folk Ballads of Yugoslavia," Zmaga Kumer
X. "Oral Epic Poetry of the Peoples of Yugoslavia," Djenana Buturović
XI. "Oral Lyric Poetry of the Peoples of Yugoslavia," Blaže Ristovski
XII. "Folk Music in Yugoslavia," Radmila Petrović
XIII. "The Tonal Framework of Folk Music in Yugoslavia," Jerko Bezić
XIV. "Yugoslav Folk Instruments," Cvjetko Rihtman
XV. "Folk Dances in Various Regions of Yugoslavia," Ivan Ivančan

Grove's Dictionary of Music and Musicians, 5th edition (edited by Eric Blom). London: Macmillan, 1954. Vol. III, "Folk Music: Yugoslavia," Cvjetko Rihtman.

———, 6th edition (edited by Stanley Sadie). London: Macmillan, 1979. "Yugoslavia: *II. Folk Music.*"

1. "Introduction," Radmila Petrović
2. "Bosnia and Hercegovina," Cvjetko Rihtman
3. "Croatia," Jerko Bezić
4. "Serbia, Macedonia and Montenegro," Radmila Petrović
5. "Slavonia," Valens Vodušek

Muzička enciklopedija, 2nd edition. Zagreb: Jugoslavenski leksikografski zavod. Vol. 1 (1971): "Bosansko-hercegovačko muzika. Narodna," Cvjetko Rihtman; "Crnogorska muzika. Narodna," Jerko Bezić and Miodrag Vasiljević. Vol. 2 (1974): "Hrvatska muzika. Narodna," Jerko Bezić; "Makedonska muzika. Narodna," Aleksandar Linin and Jerkó Bezić. Vol. 3 (1976): "Slovenačka muzika. Narodna," Zmaga Kumer; "Srpska muzika. Narodna," Radmila Petrović.

Selected Bibliography

Die Musik in Geschichte und Gegenwart (edited by Friedrich Blume). Kassel: Bärenreiter, 1958. *Band* 7: "Jugoslawien II. Die Volksmusik."

1. "Slowenien," Zmaga Kumer
2. "Kroatien," Vinko Žganec
3a. "Serbien," Stojan V. Lazarević
3b. "Montenegro," Stana Djurić-Klajn
4. "Mazedonien," Žirko Firfov
5. "Bosnien und Herzegovina," Cvjetko Rihtman

Papers of the Yugoslav-American Seminar on Music (edited by Malcolm H. Brown). Bloomington: The University of Indiana, 1970.

XIII. Problems of Music Bibliography in Yugoslavia," Ivan Klemenčić
XX. "The Place of Ethnomusicology in Yugoslav Music Study," Radmila Petrović

Studia Memoriae Belae Bartók Sacra (edited by B. Rajeczky and L. Vargyas). Budapest: Akadémiai kiadó, 1956. Božidar Širola, "Die Volksmusik der Kroaten"; Vinko Žganec, "Die Elemente der jugoslawischen Folklore-Tonleitern im serbischen liturgischen Gesange."

Zenei Lexicon (edited by Bence Szabolcsi and Aladár Tóth). Budapest: Gyözö Andor, 1931. Vol. II, "Szerb-horvát-szlavon zene," Božidar Širola.

FOLK SONG COLLECTIONS

Bosnia and Hercegovina:

Milošević, Vlado. *Bosanske narodne pjesme*. Banja Luka: Muzej Bosanske Krajine, 1954–1964.

Rihtman, C., Simic, L. and Fulanović-Šošić. *Zbornik napjeva narodnih pjesama Bosne i Hercegovine*. Sarajevo: Muzička akademija, Vol. I (*Dječje pjesme*), 1974.

Croatia:

Bersa, Vladimir. *Zbirka narodnih popievka iz Dalmacije*. Zagreb, 1944.

Kuhač, Fr. Š. *Južno-slovjenske narodne popievke* (edited by B. Širola and V. Dukat). Zagreb, 1941. Vol V: melody Nos. 1,600–2,000.

Žganec, Vinko. *Narodne popijevke hrvatskog Zagorja*. Zagreb: Jugoslavenska akademija znanosti i umjetnosti, Vols. I–III, 1950–1952. Eleven-hundred and fifty melodies.

———. *Medimurje u svojim pjesmama.* Zagreb: Savez muzičih društava nr Hrvatske, 1957. One-hundred and sixty-three melodies.

———. *Hrvatske narodne popijevke iz Koprivnice i okaline.* Zagreb, 1962.

Macedonia:

Firfov, Živko. *Makedonski muzički folklor, Pesni I.* Skopje, 1953. Two-hundred and eight melodies.

——— and M. Simonovski. *Makedonskite melografi od krajot na XIX vek.* Skopje, 1962. Three-hundred and ninety-nine melodies.

———, ———, and R. Prodonov. *Makedonski muzički folklor, Pesni II.* Skopje, 1956. Four-hundred and eighty-one melodies.

Hadžimanov, Vasil. *A bre, Makedonče,* Skopje, 1962. Forty-seven melodies.

———. *Makedonski narodni pesni,* Vols. I–IV. Skopje, 1953–56. Two-hundred melodies.

———. *Momi Tikvešanki.* Skopje, 1968. Two-hundred melodies.

———. *Saborski narodni pesni.* Skopje, 1964. One-hundred and eight melodies.

Traerup, Birthe. *East Macedonian Folk Songs.* Copenhagen: Acta Ethnomusicologica Danica No. 2, 1970. Seventy melodies.

Vasiljević, Miodrag. *Jugoslovenski muzički folklor II, Makedonija.* Belgrade: Prosveta izdavačka preduzeće Srbije, 1953. Four-hundred and twenty-one melodies.

Montenegro:

Lazarević, Stojan. *Muzički folklor Boke Kotorske.* Belgrade: Srpska akademija nauka, Spomenik CIII, 1953. Fourteen melodies.

Vasiljević, Miodrag. *Narodne melodije Crne Gore.* Belgrade: Srpska akademija nauka i umetnosti, 1965. Five-hundred and sixty-eight melodies.

Serbia:

Ilić, Sava. *Antologija srpskih narodnih pesama-Temišvarska oblast.* Bucharest: Folklorni institut, 1958. One-hundred and forty-nine melodies.

Manojlović, Kosta. *Narodne melodije iz istočne Srbije.* Belgrade: Muzikološki institut SANU, 1953. Three-hundred and thirty-seven melodies.

Mokranjac, Stevan. *Zapisi narodnih melodija*. Belgrade: Muzikološki institut SANU, 1966. One-hundred and sixty-three melodies.

Petrović, Radmila. *Narodne melodije Hanske oblasti*. Vranje: Vrankski glasnik No. VII, 1971.

Stanković, Živojin. *Narodne pesme u Krajini*. Belgrade: Muzikološki institut SANU, 1951. One-hundred and twelve melodies.

Vasiljević, Miodrag. *Jugoslovenski muzički folklor I, Kosmet*. Belgrade: Prosveta izdavaćka predužeće Srbije, 1950. Five-hundred and twenty-two melodies.

———. *Narodne melodije iz Sandžaka*. Belgrade: Muzikološki institut SANU, No. 5. Four-hundred melodies.

———. *Narodne melodije leskovačkog kraja*. Belgrade: Muzikološki institut SANU, 1960. Four-hundred and sixteen melodies.

Slovenia:

Dravec, J. *Glasbena Prekmurja: pesmi*. Ljubljana, 1957.

Kumer, Z., Matičetov, B., Merhar, B., and Vodušek, V. *Slovenske ljudske pesmi*. Ljubljana, 1971.

LITERATURE

Bartók, Béla. "Some Problems of Folk Music Research in East Europe," in *Béla Bartók Essays* (selected and edited by Benjamin Suchoff), No. 25. London: Faber & Faber; New York: St. Martin's Press, 1976.

———. "The Parry Collection of Yugoslav Folk Music," *Essays,* No. 21.

———. *Rumanian Folk Music* (edited by Benjamin Suchoff). The Hague, Martinus Nijhoff, Vols. II (1967) and IV (1975).

Janković, Ljubica S. "The Brothers Tihomir and Vladimir Djordjević: Pioneers of Ethnomusicology in Serbia" (edited by Barbara Krader), *Yearbook of the International Folk Music Council,* Vol. 2, 1970.

Kuba, Ludvik. "Pisen jihoslovanská a mohamedanism," *Hudební Revue* (God), Vol. VI, 1912–1913.

Laade, Wolfgang and Dagmar. "The Diaphonic Music of the Island of Krk, Yugoslavia." New York: Folkways Records, Album No. FE 4060, 1975.

Petrović, Radmila. "The Concept of Yugoslav Folk Music in the

Twentieth Century," *Journal of the International Folk Music Council,* Vol. XX, 1968.

———. "Folk Music of Eastern Yugoslavia: a Process of Acculturation," *International Review of the Aesthetics and Sociology* of Music (Symposium of the International Music Society), No. 1, Zagreb, 1974.

———. "Some Aspects of Formal Expression in Serbian Folk Songs," *Yearbook of the International Folk Music Council,* Vol. 2, 1971.

———. "Two Styles of Vocal Music in the Zlatibor Region," *Journal of the International Folk Music Council,* Vol. XV, 1963.

Rihtman, Cvjetko. "Les formes polyphonique dans la musique populaire de Bosnie et d'Herzégovine," *Journal of the International Folk Music Council,* Vol. IV, 1952.

———. "Mehrstimmigkeit in der Volksmusik Jugoslawiens," *Journal of the International Folk Music Council,* Vol. XVIII, 1966.

———. "Le microton dans las aspects les plus anciens de la musique traditionelle en Bosnie et d'Herzégovine." *Izvestija na Instituta za muzika* (Sofia), Vol. XIII, 1969.

———. "Orientalische Elemente in der traditionellen Musik Bosniens und der Herzegowina," *Grazer und Műnchener Balkanologische Studien* (Munich), 1967.

Vasiljević, Miodrag A. "Les bases tonales de la musique populaires Serbes," *Journal of the International Folk Music Council,* Vol. IV, 1952.

Žganec, Vinko. "La gamme istrienne dans la musique populaire yougoslave," *Studia musicologica* (Budapest), Vol. IV, Nos. 1–2, 1963.

———. "The Tonal and Modal Structure of Yugoslav Folk Music," *Journal of the International Folk Music Council,* Vol. X, 1958.

Part One

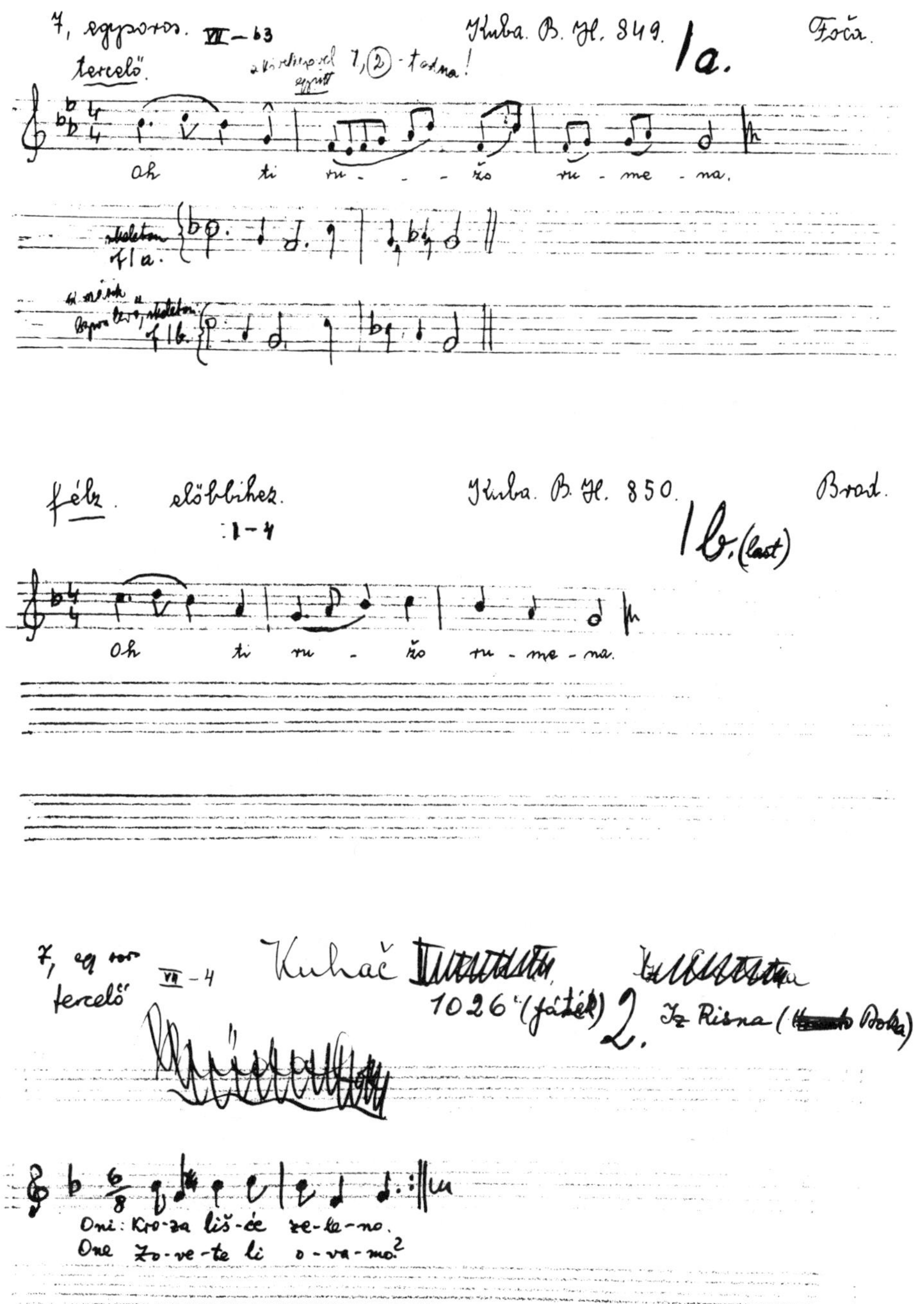
7, egysoros. VII–63
terelő
Kuba. B. H. 849.
1a.
Foča.
Oh ti ru - - - žo ru - me - na.
Kuba. B. H. 850.
1b.
Brod.
Oh ti ru - žo ru - me - na.
7, egy sor
terelő
VII–4
Kuhač
1026.
2.
Iz Risna (Boka)
Oni: Kro-za liš-će ze-le-no.
One Zo-ve-te li o-va-mo?

Dj.: Pred. srb. 583.

3.

Ogladjenovac

1–4

7, egysoros

♩ = 92

Svi dil-be-ri pro-djo-še

Kuhač Oro Iz Srbije

1028.

Kapitan Jovo

4.

7, egysoros
(3+4) fé'Iz.

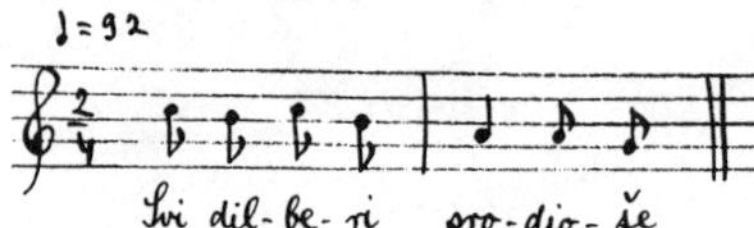

♩ = 69

Ti mo-mo ti de- -voj-ko
ti mo-ga bra-ta ma-miš.

Dj.: Pred. srb. 525.

5.

Adrani

VI–1

8, egysoros

♩ = 92

Oj! Reče či-ča da me že-ni,

8, egysoros, # VII-2 Kuhač III. 1076. 6.

♩= 60. U ženskom kolu. Iz Dubice. (Hrvatska)

Jedni (II. o Drugi)

Za-re-koh se, za-te-koh se.

Var. hogy kicsiben nem megyek.
Kuba Is mégis stb.
stb.

Dj.: Pred. zb. 254. Lázárnapi 7a. Crnoljevica

1–63, 8, egysoros

♪= 152

Car Ko-stadin banju gradu

Dj.: Pred. zb. 255. 7b. Crnoljevica

1–63, 7, előbbihez.

♪=152

Oj! Ovde dvori mete-ni, ov-de dvori me-te-ni

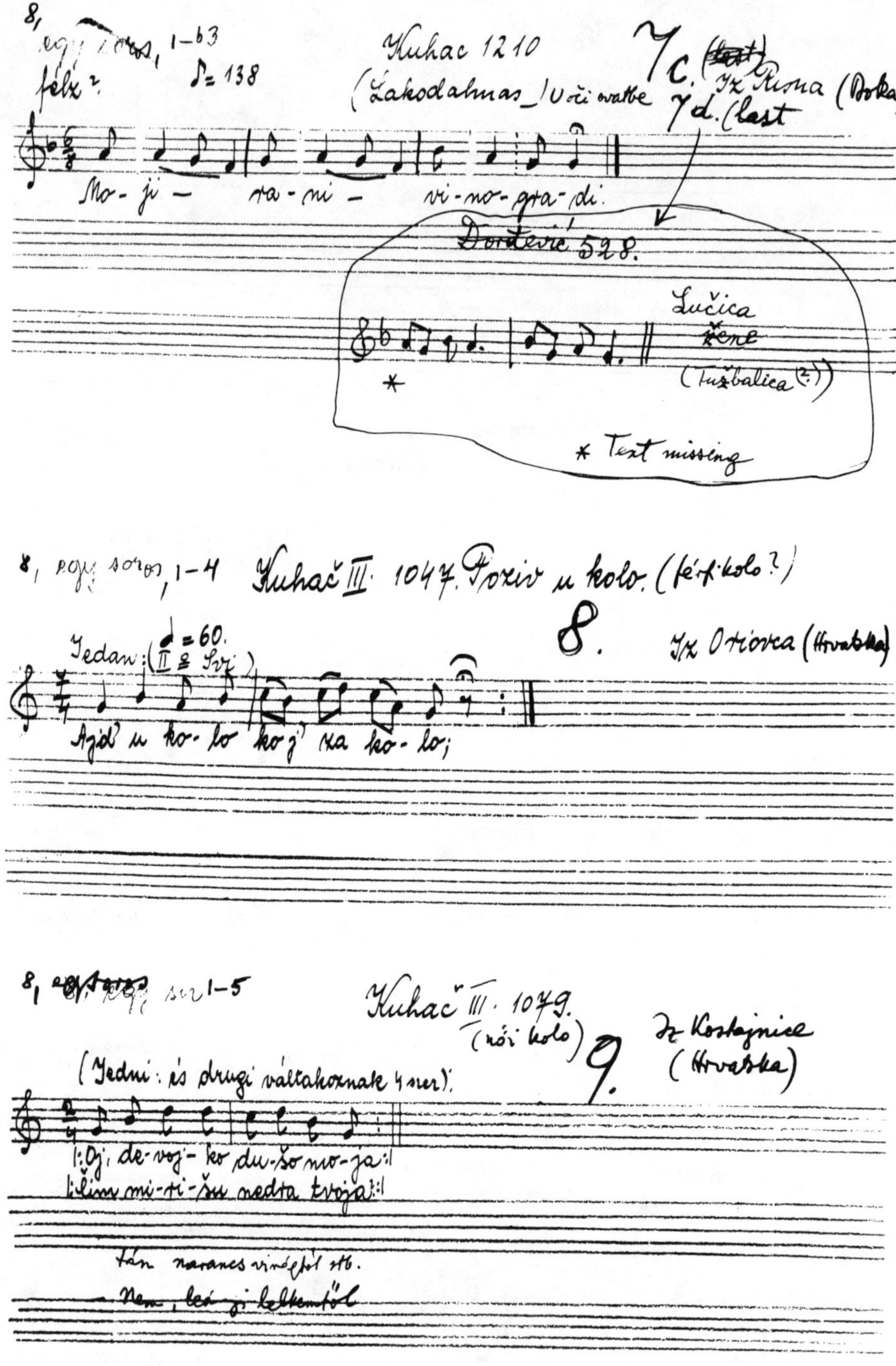

félz. ♪= 138
Kuhac 1210
U oči svatbe
7c. Iz Risna (Boka)
7d.
Mo- ji - ra- ni - vi-no-gra-di.
Đorđević 528.
Lučica
žene
(Tužbalica?)
* Text missing
8, egy soros, 1–4
Kuhač III. 1047. Poziv u kolo.
8.
Jedan: (II & Svi) ♩= 60.
Ajd' u ko- lo ko j' zna ko- lo;
Kuhač III. 1079.
(női kolo)
9.
Iz Kostajnice (Hrvatska)
Oj, de-voj-ko du-šo mo-ja

töredek
♩= 60
Kuhač III. 834.
10. Stara melodija iz Budve. (u austr. Albaniji)
Ko-li-ko noć-ie no-ćas bi.
Kuba B.H. 792.
Moderato.
11. Jajce.
Spletak sple-la dje-te-lina tra-va jadna dajna dao
vidanoj-lo, spletak sple-la
djete-lina tra-va.
Kuba B.H. 486.
Andante
12. Nevesinje.
Ja i-ma-dok dje-voj-ku ja-ra-na,
ja i-ma-dok djevojku ja-ra-na.

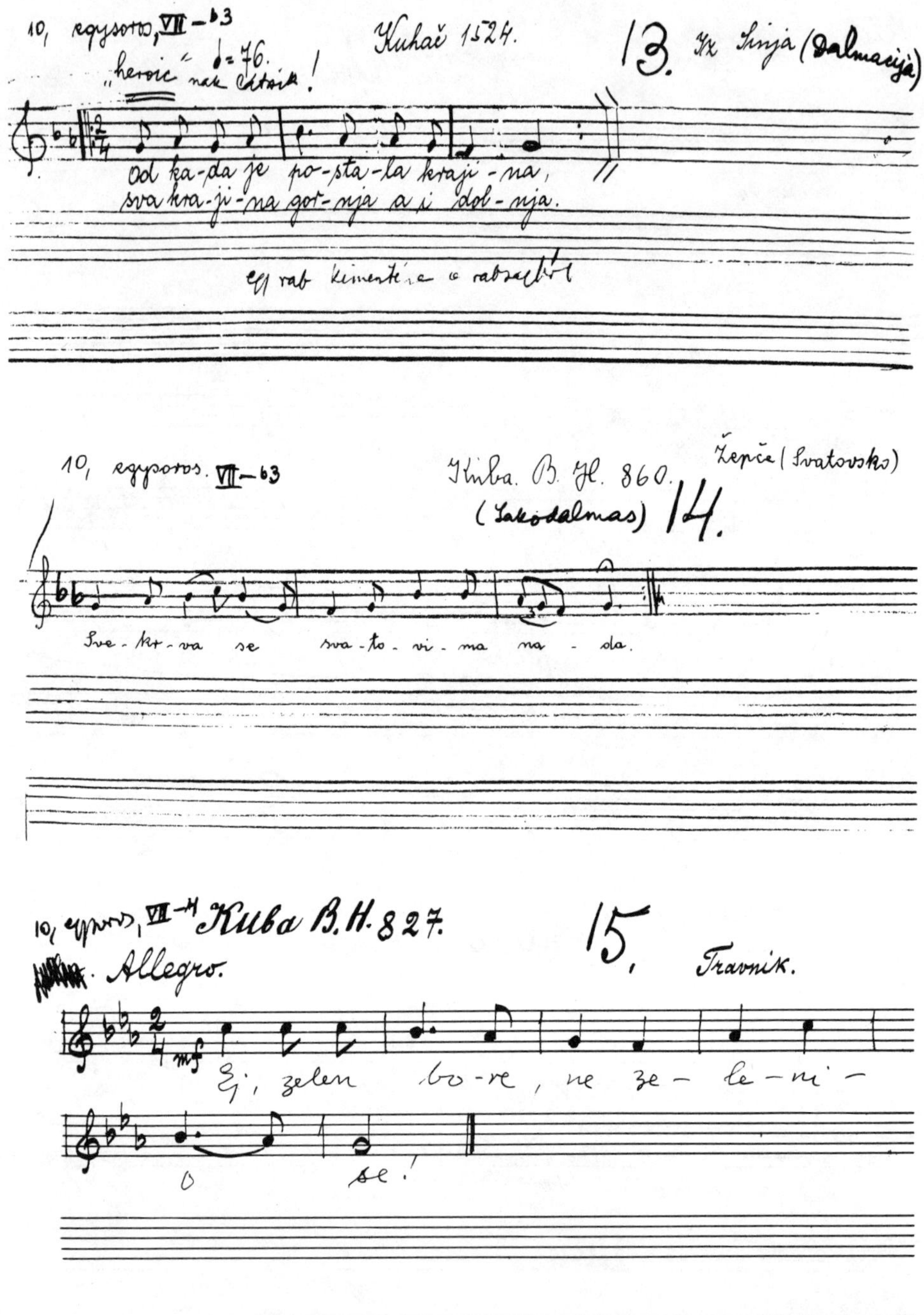

Kuhač 1524.
13.
Sinja (Dalmacija)
♩= 76.
Od ka-da je po-sta-la kraji-na,
sva kra-ji-na gor-nja a i dol-nja.
Kuba. B. H. 860.
Žepče (Svatovsko)
(Lakodalmas) 14.
Sve-kr-va se sva-to-vi-ma na-da.
Kuba B.H. 827.
15.
Travnik.
Allegro.
mf
Ej, zelen bo-re, ne ze-le-ni-
o se!

10, eeftoros, 1–62 Kuba XI. 56. Kolašin

16. Ukolébavka

Dj.: Pred. srb. 325. Davidovci

Lázárnapi

17a.

1–63, 10, eaydoros

= 326.

Dj.: Pred. srb. 326. Davidovci

17b. (last)

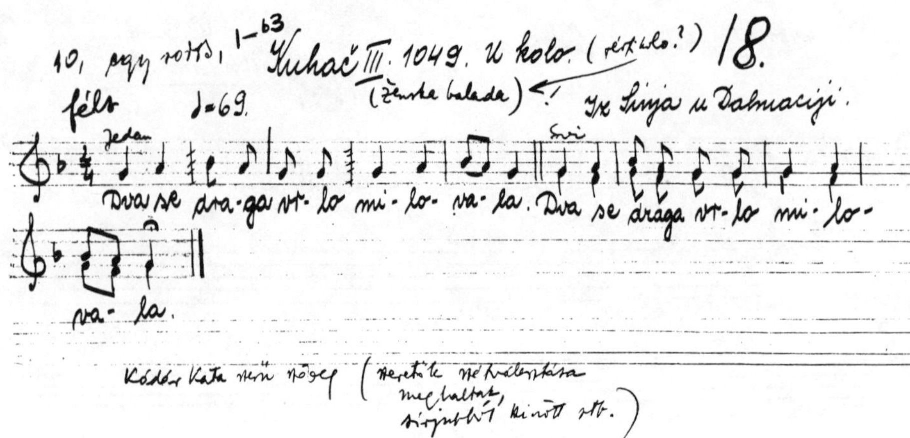

10, egy sor, 1–63
Kuhač III. 1049. U kolo.
18.
(Ženska balada)
Iz Sinja u Dalmaciji.
♩=69.
Dva se dra-ga vr-lo mi-lo-va-la. Dva se draga vr-lo mi-lo-va-la.

10, egyetlen sor. 1–4
lásd 480.?
Kuhač II. 476.
19.
Iz Gline.
♩=60.
A joj me-ni, ko-ja nemam dra - gog!

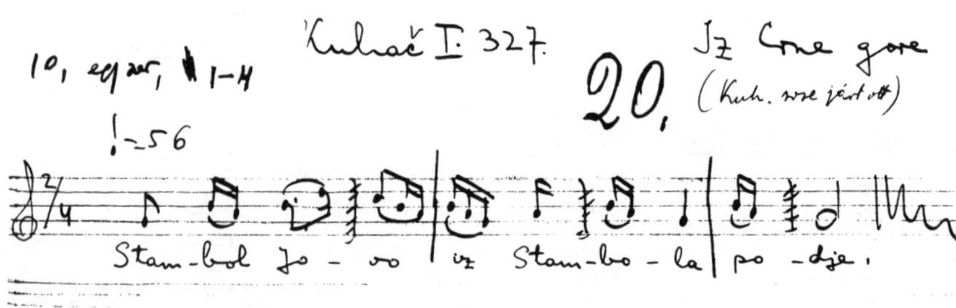

Kuhač I. 327.
10, egy sor, 1–4
20.
Iz Crne gore
!=56
Stam-bol Jo - vo iz Stam-bo-la po - dje.

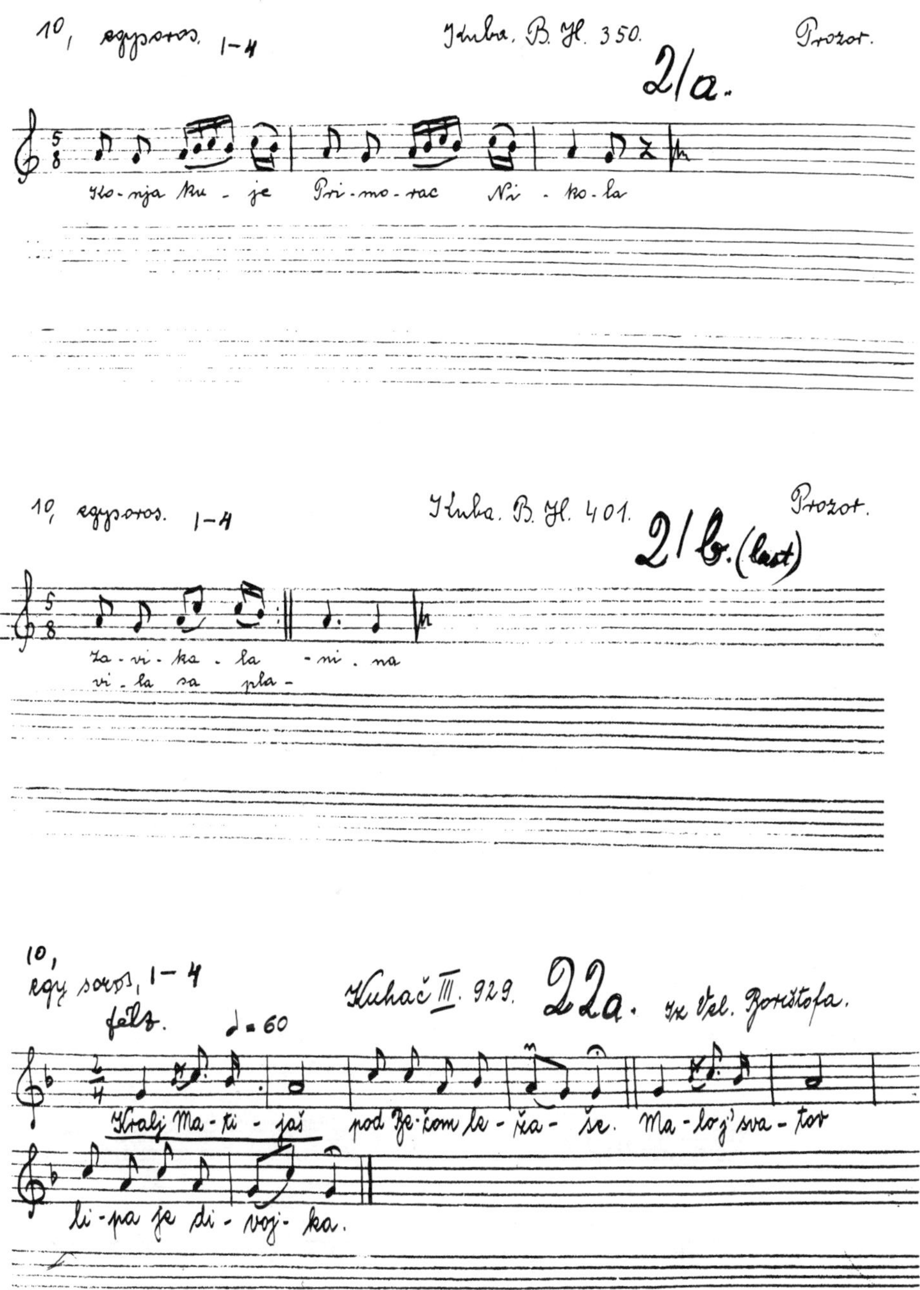

érthetetlen szöveg!

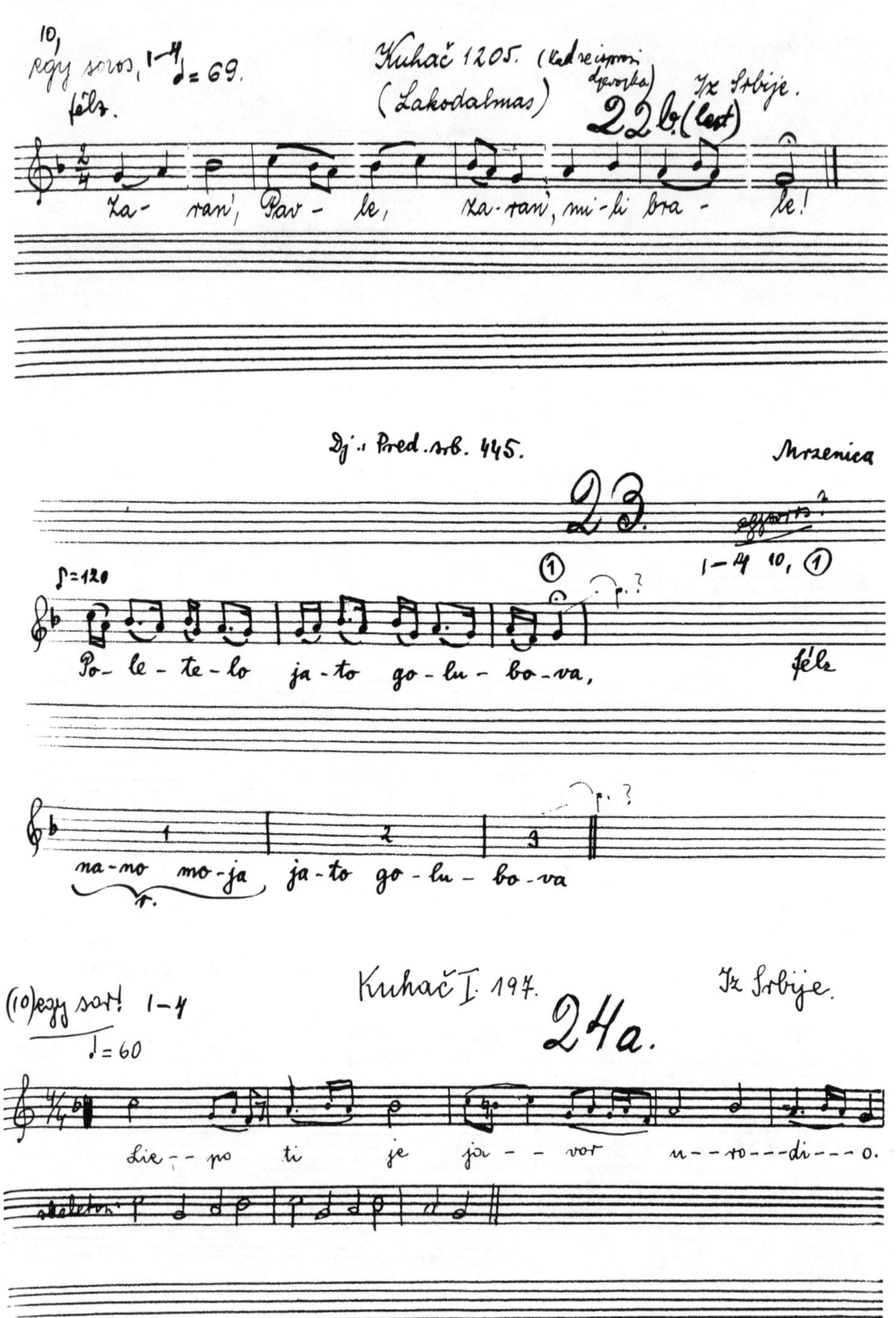
10, egy soros, 1–4, ♩= 69.
félz.
Kuhač 1205.
(Lakodalmas)
Iz Srbije.
22b. (lent)
Za- ran', Pav- le, za-ran', mi-li bra- le!
Dj.: Pred. srb. 445.
Mrzenica
23.
1–4 10, ①
féle
Po- le- te- lo ja- to go- lu- bo- va,
na-no mo-ja ja-to go- lu- bo-va
Kuhač I. 197.
Iz Srbije.
(10) egy sor! 1–4
24a.
Lie- - po ti je ja- - - vor u- - ro- - - di- - - o.

10, egy sor! 6+4
félzárlat. 1–4
Kuhač II 448.
Iz Vukmanića u Hrvatskoj.
24 b.
Da su, da su me-ni, da su me-ni
ze-le-ne ka-či-je, aj, de- - voj-ko!
Dj.: Pred. zb. 247.
24 c.
Toplica
1–4,
10, egysoros
Ma-lo se-lo ra-no ve-če-ralo.
Dj.: Pred. zb. 586.
24 d.
Ogladjenovac.
1–4
10, egysoros
Vi-diš, di-ko, tu ze-le-nu tra-vu,

Dj.: Pred. sb. 588.

Ogladjenovac

~~24 ... (last)~~

№ 586. hoz.

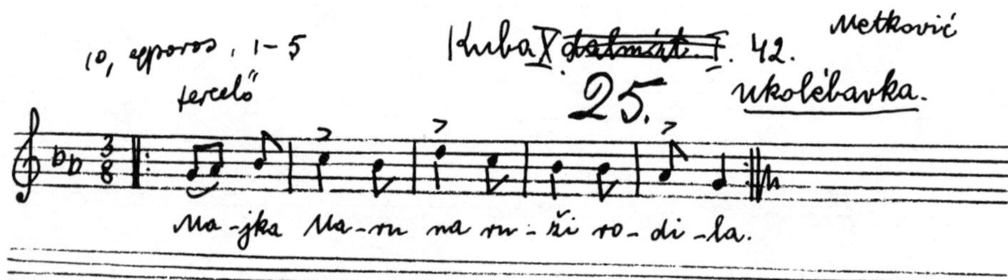

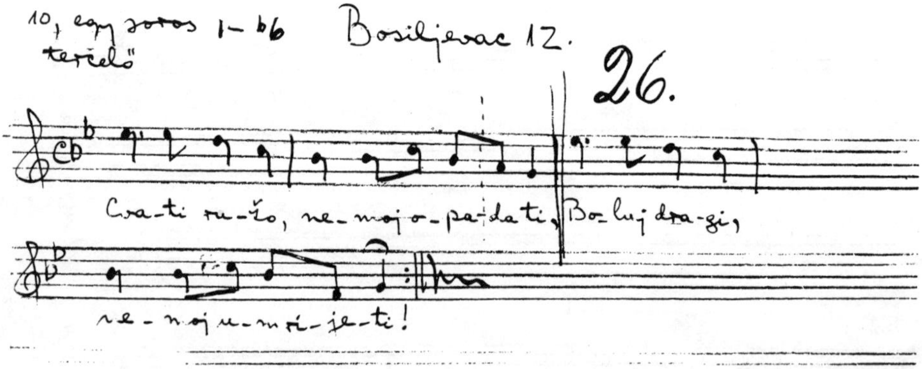

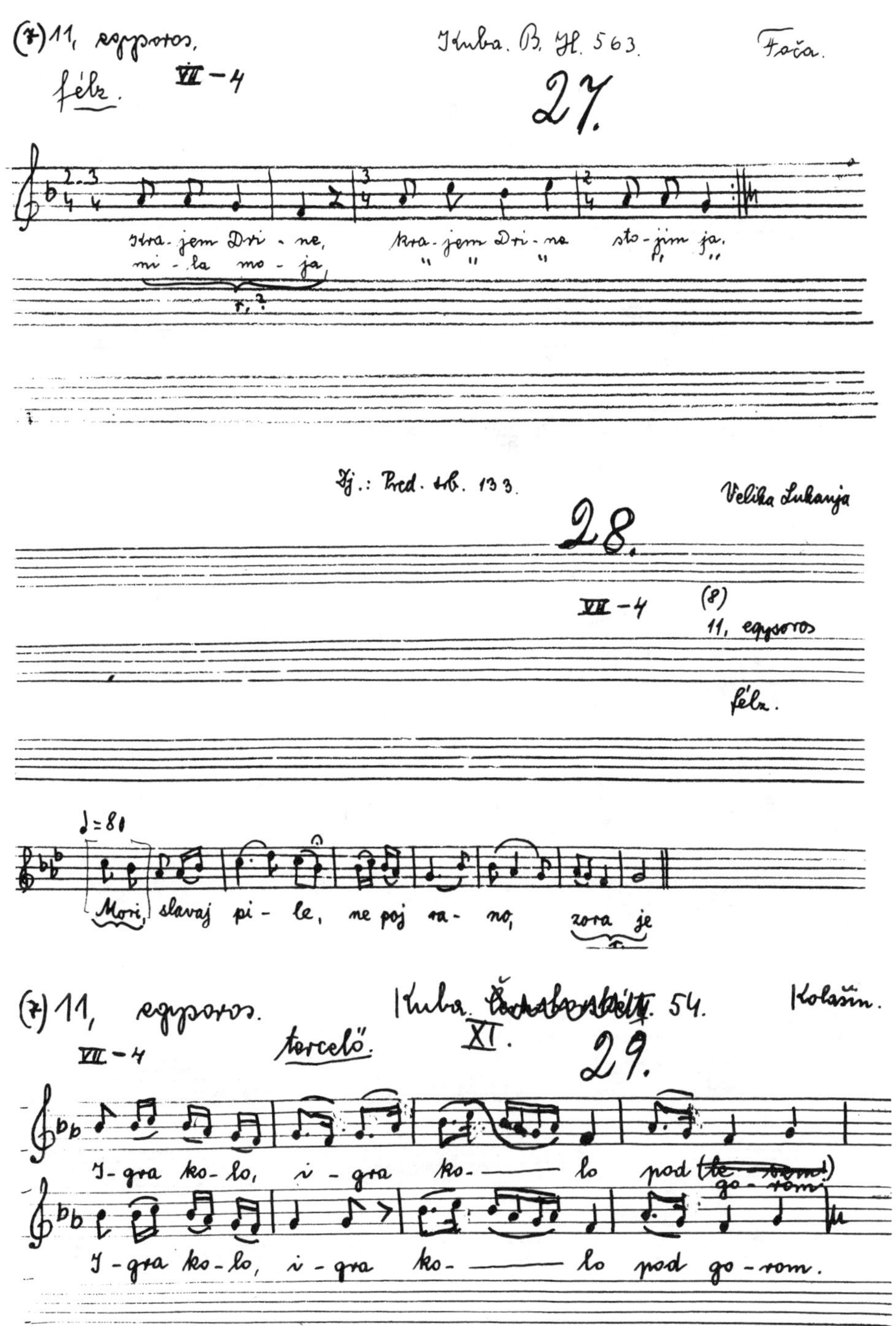

Foča.
27.
Kra-jem Dri-ne, kra-jem Dri-na sto-jim ja.
mi-la mo-ja
Velika Lukanja
28.
♩=81
Mori, slavaj pi-le, ne poj ra-no, zora je
Kolašin.
XI.
29.
I-gra ko-lo, i-gra ko-lo pod go-rom.

Dj.: Pred. zb. 441.

30.

Arzenica

1–4, (8) 11, egysoros

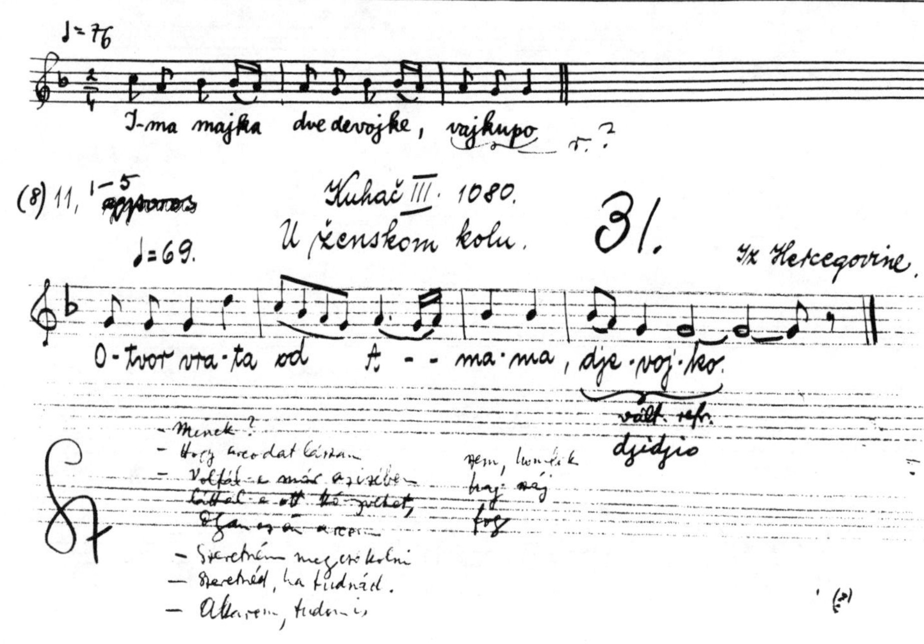

Sedeljka

Pesme iz Levča, 53. (t. 129. 130.)

32.

4+3+4

(7), 11, 1–4 egysoros

Me-se-či-na, Da-vi-na, va-raj ka-do! ih!

r.

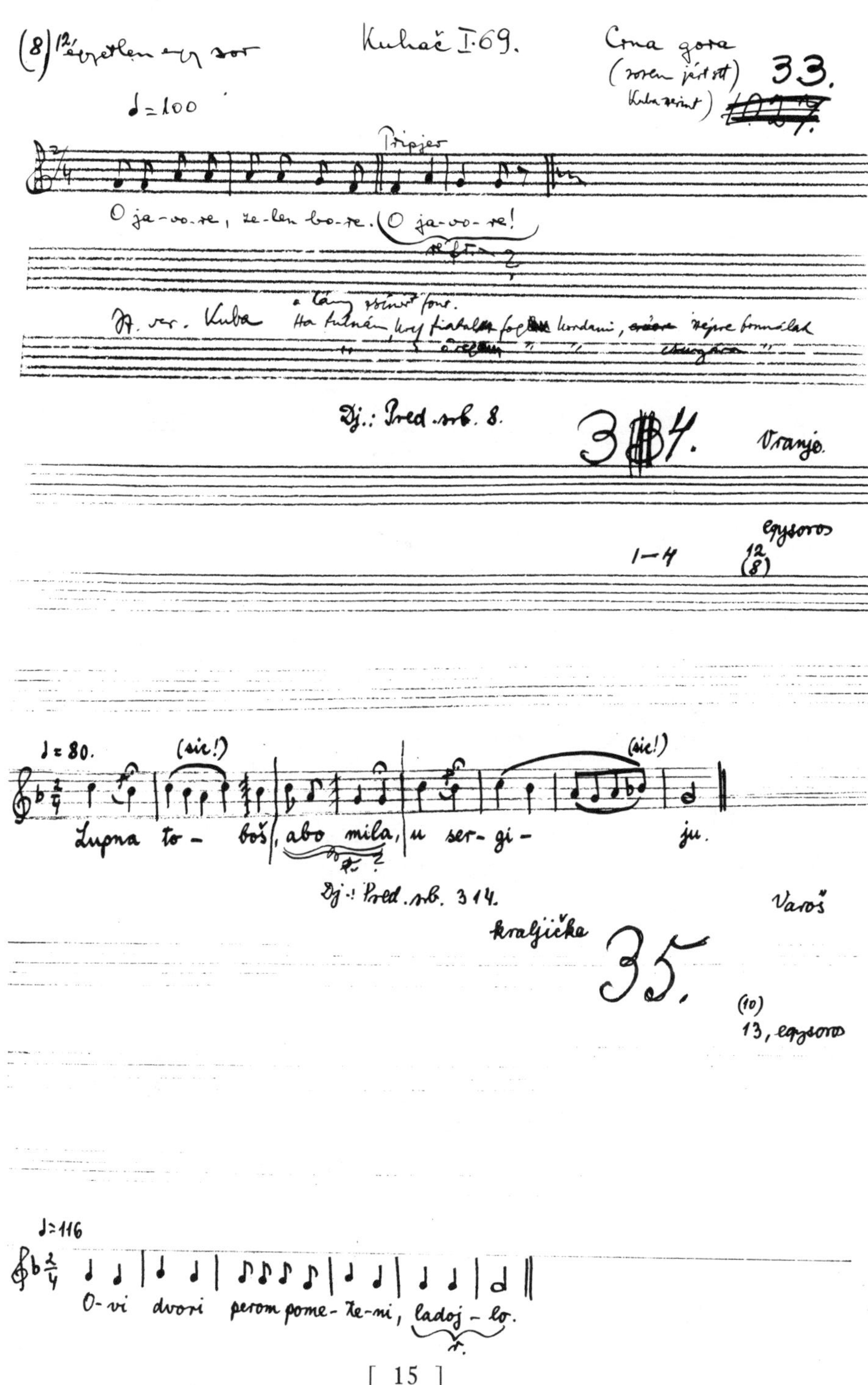
(8) 12, egyetlen egy sor
Kuhač I.69.
Crna gora
33.
♩=100
O ja-vo-re, ze-len bo-re. O ja-vo-re!
Dj.: Pred. srb. 8.
34.
Vranje
egysoros
1—4
12 (8)
♩=80.
(sic!)
(sic!)
Lupna to- boš, abo mila, u ser- gi- ju.
Dj.: Pred. srb. 314.
Varoš
kraljička
35.
(10)
13, egysoros
♩=116
O-vi dvori perom pome-te-ni, ladoj- lo.

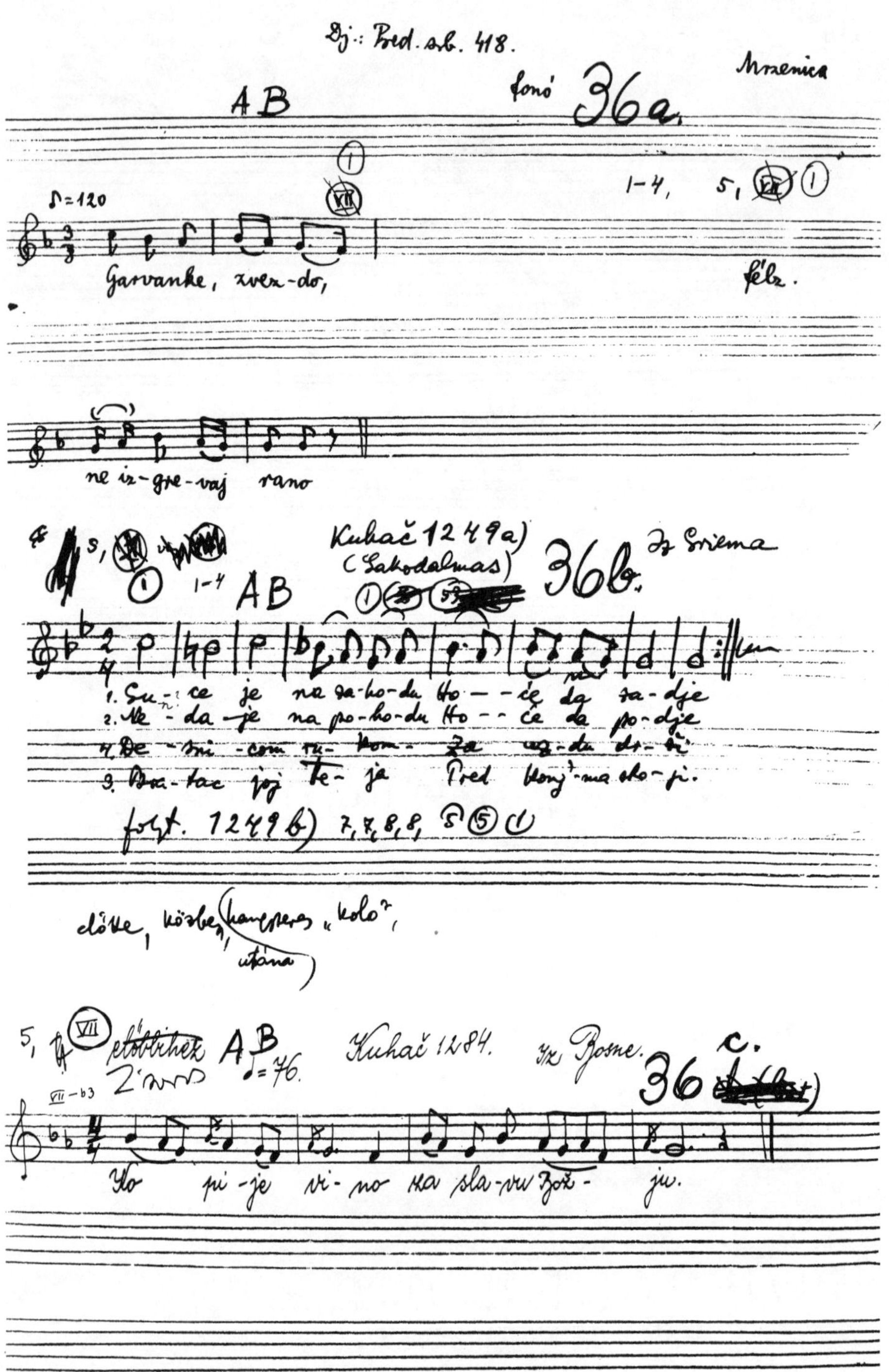

Dj.: Pred. sb. 418.
AB
fonó 36a.
1-4, 5,
♪=120
Garvanke, zvez-do,
félz.
ne iz-gre-vaj rano
Kuhač 1249a)
36b.
Iz Srijema
1-4 AB
1. Sun-ce je na za-ho-du Ho-će da za-dje
2. Ne-da je na po-ho-du Ho-će da po-dje
3. Bra-tac joj te-ja Pred konj-ma sto-ji.
1249b) 7,7,8,8,
AB
♩=76
Kuhač 1284.
Iz Bosne.
36 c.
Ko pi-je vi-no na sla-vu Bož-ju.

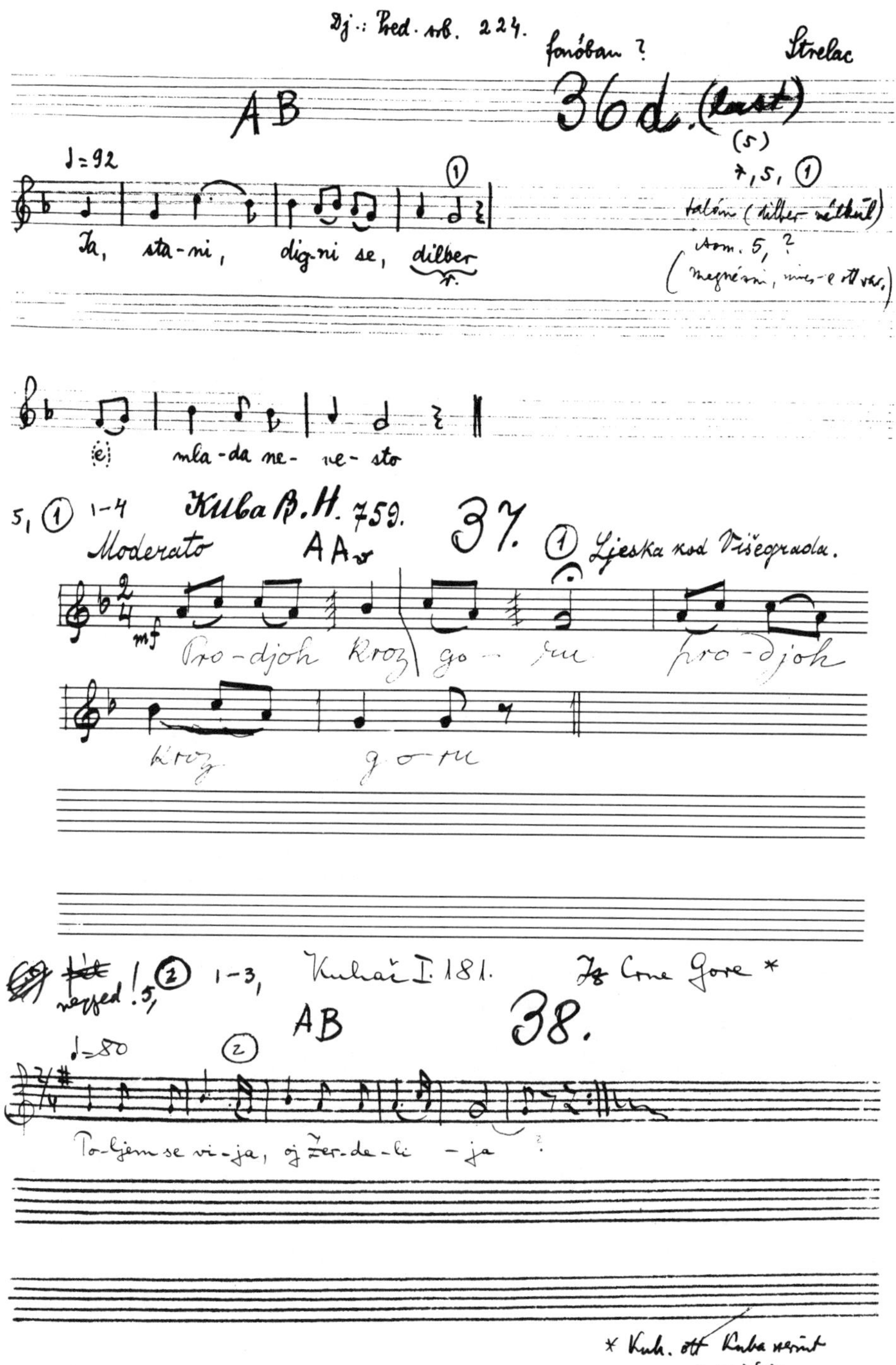

* Kuh. ott Kuba szerint rosse járt.

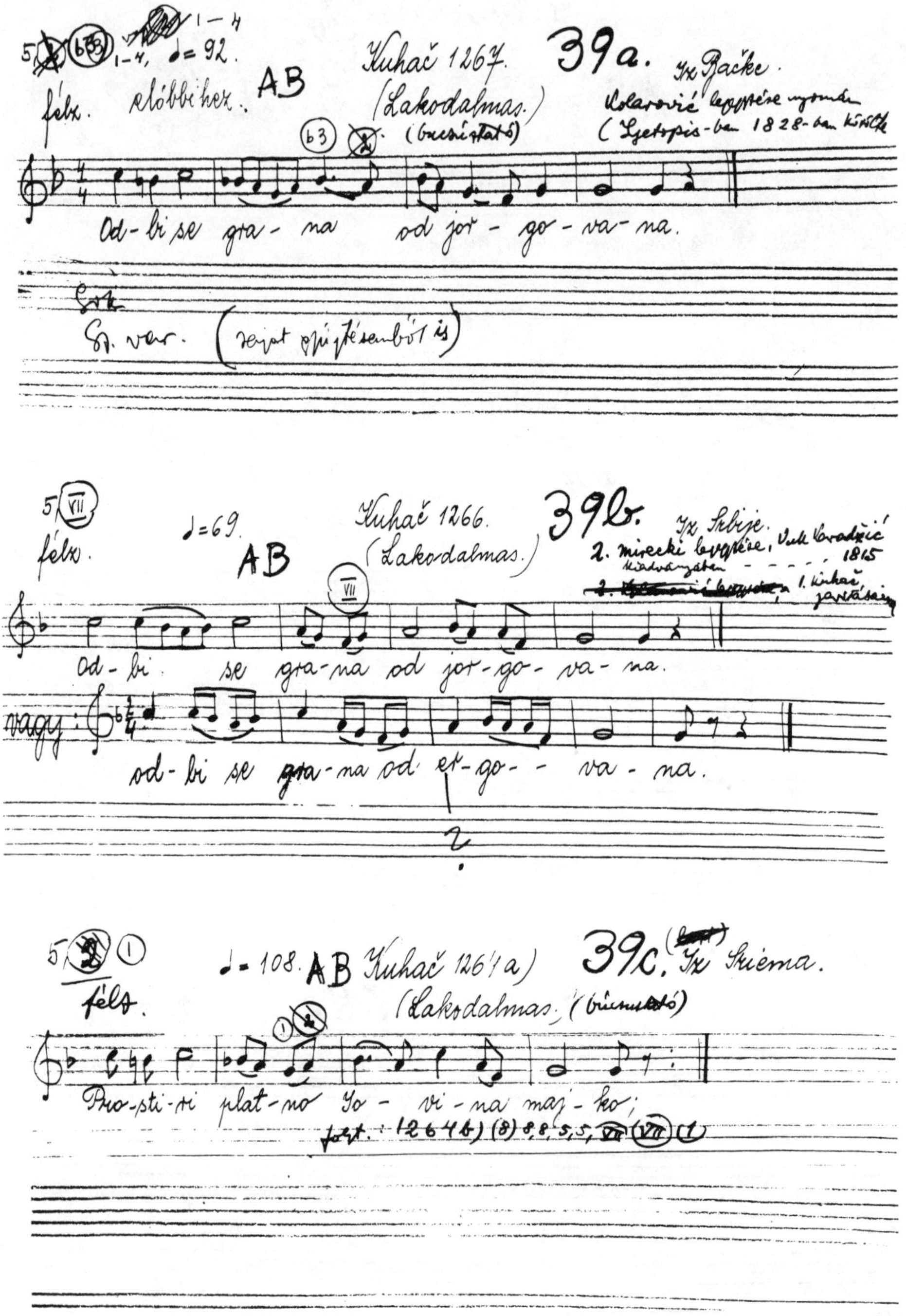
39a. Iz Bačke.
Kuhač 1267.
(Lakodalmas.)
AB
félz. előbbihez.
Od-bi se gra-na od jor-go-va-na.
39b. Iz Srbije.
Kuhač 1266.
(Lakodalmas.)
AB
♩=69.
félz.
Od-bi se gra-na od jor-go-va-na.
vagy:
od-bi se gra-na od er-go-va-na.
39c. Iz Srijema.
♩=108. AB Kuhač 1264 a)
(Lakodalmas.)
Pro-sti-ri plat-no Jo-vi-na maj-ko;

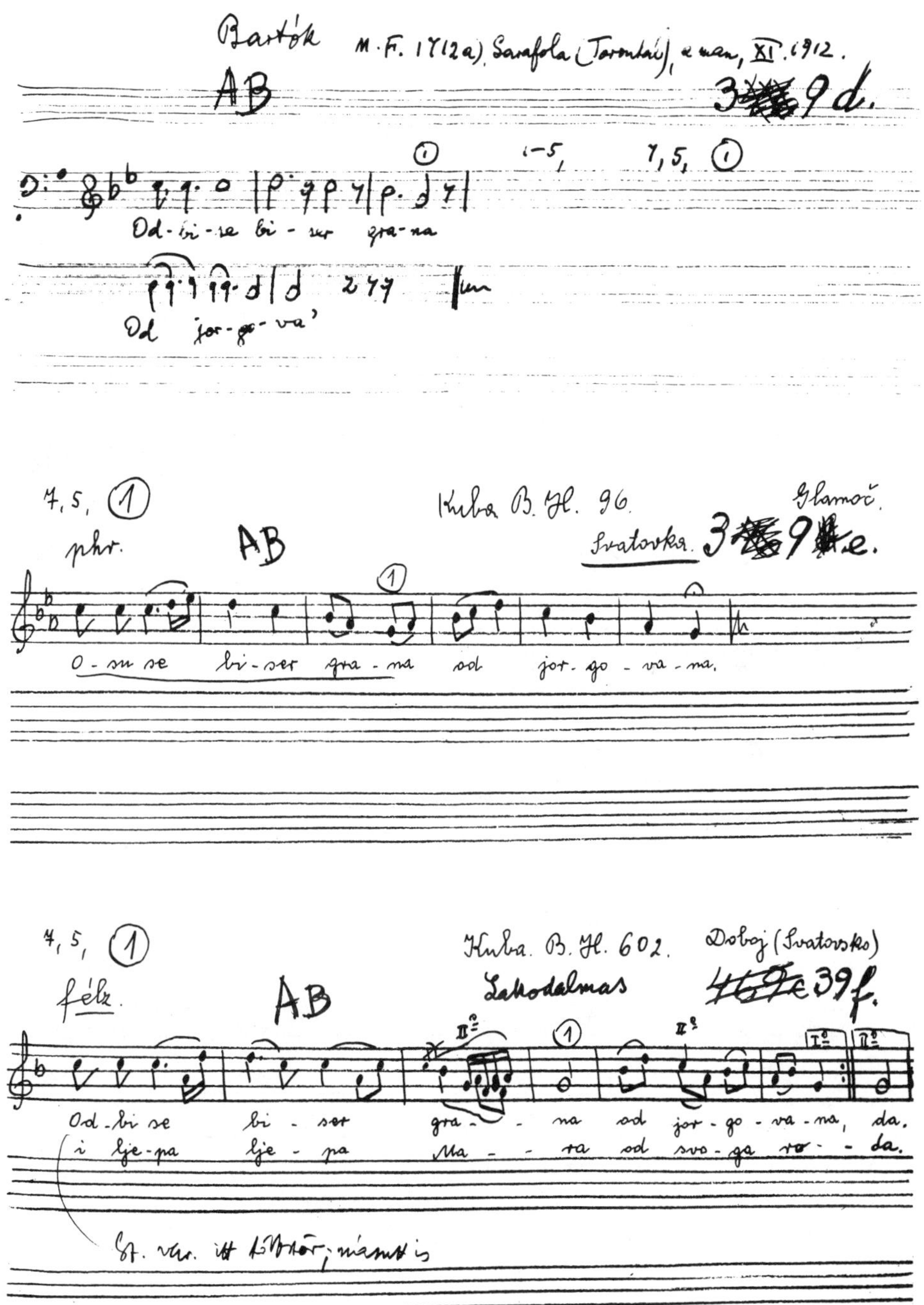

Bartók
AB
Od-bi-se bi-ser gra-na
Od jor-go-va'
7, 5, (1)
Kuba B. H. 96.
Glamoč.
phr.
AB
Svatovka.
O-su se bi-ser gra-na od jor-go-va-na.
4, 5, (1)
Kuba. B. H. 602.
Doboj (Svatovsko)
félz.
AB
Lakodalmas
39f.
Od-bi se bi-ser gra-na od jor-go-va-na, da.
i lje-pa lje-pa Ma-ra od svo-ga ro-da.

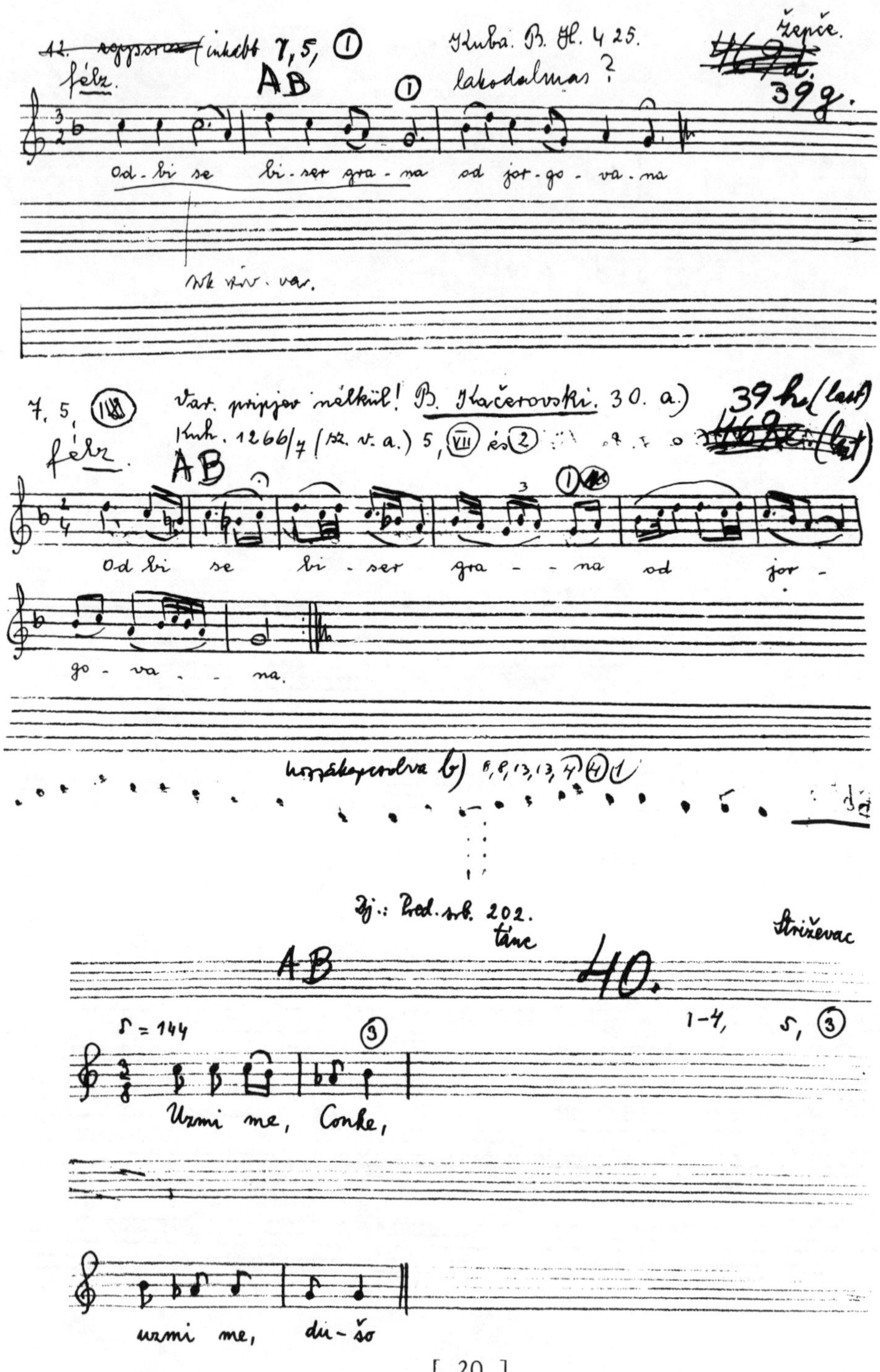

7, 5, (1)
Kuba. B. H. 425.
žepče.
félz.
AB
lakodalmas ?
39 g.
Od-bi se bi-ser gra-na od jor-go-va-na
7, 5,
Var. pripjev nélkül! B. Kačerovski. 30. a.)
39 h. (last)
félz.
AB
Od bi se bi-ser gra--na od jor-go-va--na.
Zj.: Prod. srb. 202.
tánc
Striževac
AB
40.
♪ = 144
1-4, 5, (3)
Uzmi me, Conke,
uzmi me, du-šo

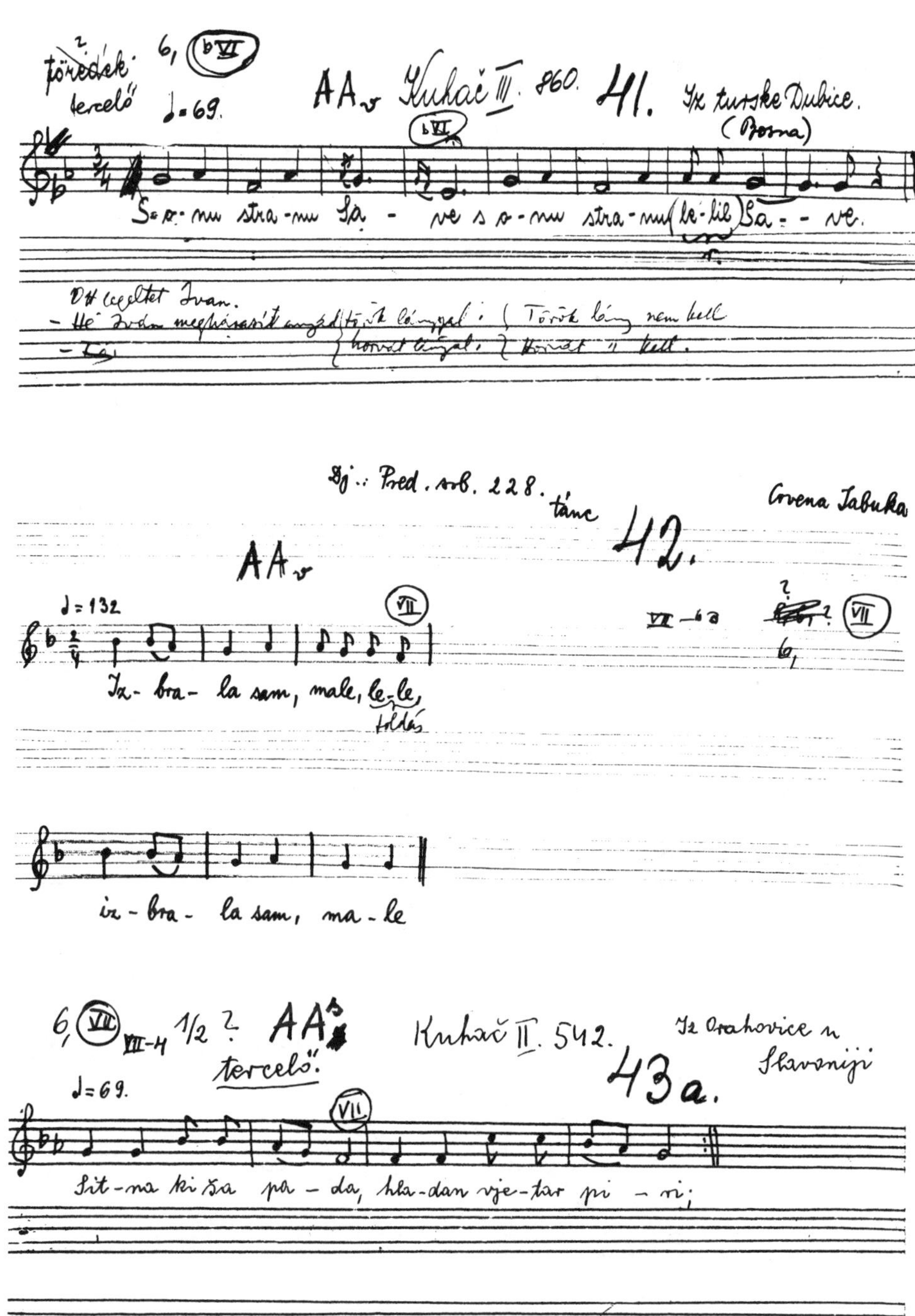

töredék
tercelő
♩=69
AA
Kuhač III. 860.
41.
Iz turske Dubice.
(Bosna)
Sa-mu stra-mu Sa-ve sa-mu stra-mu le-lil Sa-ve.
Dj.: Pred. sb. 228.
tánc
42.
Crvena Jabuka
AA
♩=132
Iz-bra-la sam, male, le-le,
toldás
iz-bra-la sam, ma-le
AA
tercelő
Kuhač II. 542.
Iz Orahovice u Slavoniji
43a.
♩=69
Sit-na ki-ša pa-da, hla-dan vje-tar pi-ri;

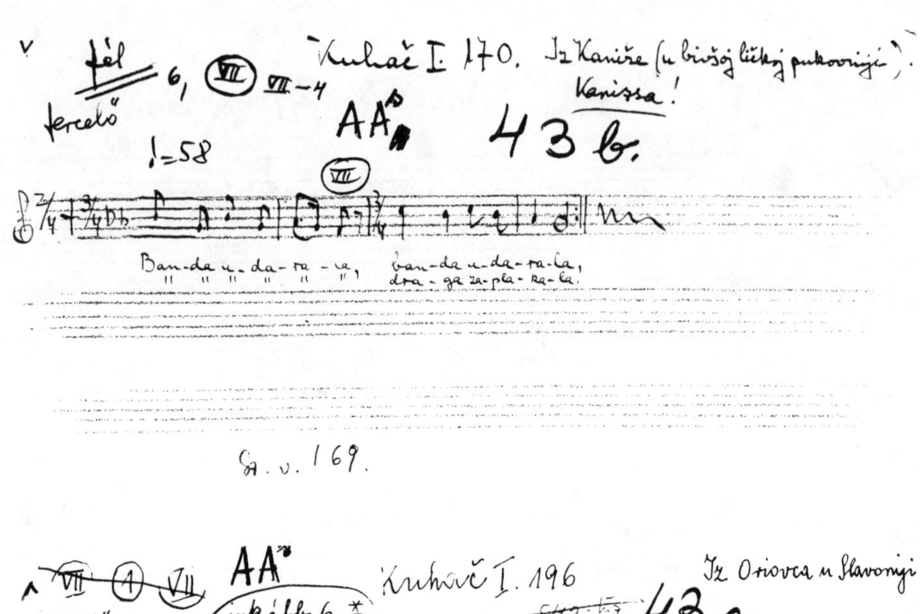
fél 6, VII VII-4
tercelő
Kuhač I. 170. Iz Kaniže (u bivšoj ličkoj pukovniji).
Kanissa!
AA
43 b.
♩=58
Ban-da u-da-ra-la, ban-da u-da-ra-la,
dra-ga za-pla-ka-la.
Sz. v. 169.

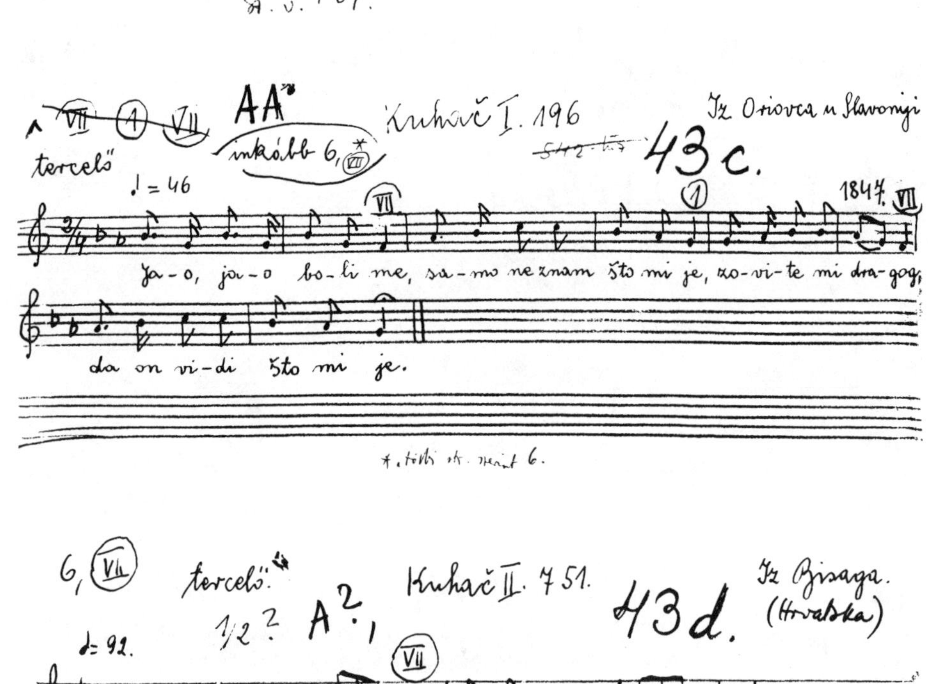
VII 1 VII
AA
inkább 6, VII
Kuhač I. 196
Iz Oriovca u Slavoniji
43 c.
tercelő
♩ = 46
1847.
Ja-o, ja-o bo-li me, sa-mo ne znam što mi je, zo-vi-te mi dra-gog,
da on vi-di što mi je.
*, többi st. szerint 6.

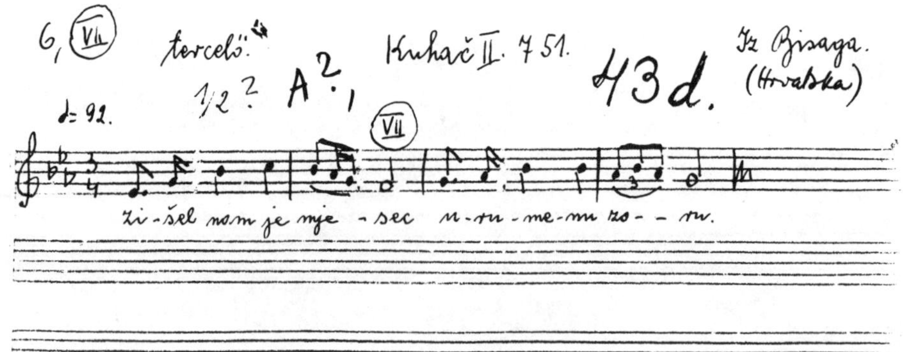
6, VII
tercelő
Kuhač II. 751.
Iz Bisaga. (Hrvatska)
43 d.
♩= 92.
zi-šel nam je mje-sec u-ru-me-nu zo-ru.

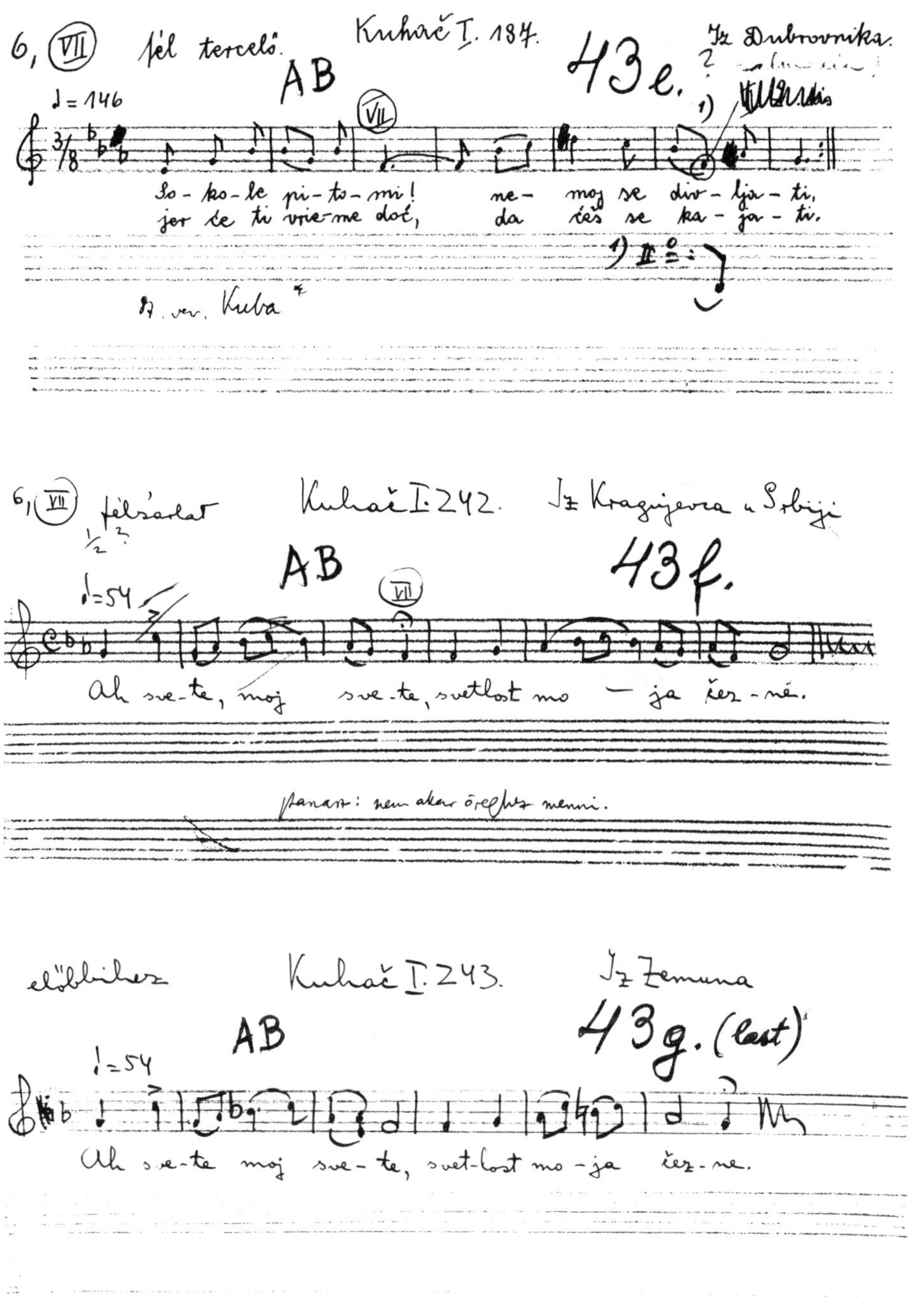
6, VII fél tercelő
Kuhač I. 187.
AB
43e.
Iz Dubrovnika.
♩= 146
So-ko-le pi-to-mi! ne-moj se div-lja-ti,
jer će ti vrie-me doć, da ćeš se ka-ja-ti.
6, VII félszárlat
Kuhač I. 242.
Iz Kragujevca u Srbiji
AB
43f.
♩=54
Ah sve-te, moj sve-te, svetlost mo-ja čez-né.
elöbbihez
Kuhač I. 243.
Iz Zemuna
AB
43g. (last)
♩=54
Ah sve-te moj sve-te, svet-lost mo-ja čez-ne.

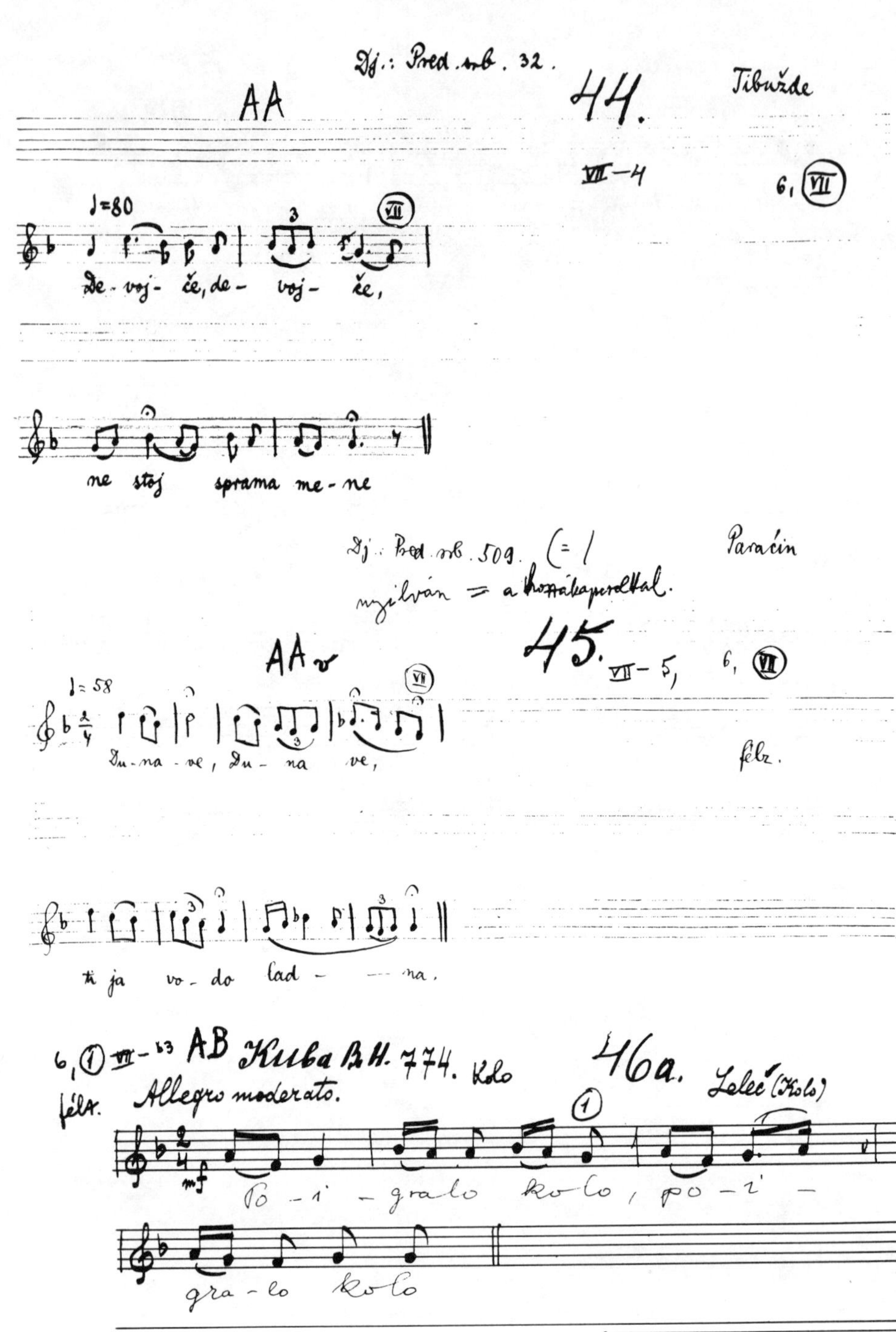

Dj.: Pred. zb. 32.
AA
44.
Tibužde
VII—4
6, (VII)
♩=80
De-voj- če, de- voj- če,
ne stoj sprama me-ne
Dj.: Pred. zb. 509.
Paraćin
nyilván = a kottakapcsolattal.
AA
45.
VII—5,
6, (VII)
♩=58
Du-na-ve, Du- na ve,
félz.
ti ja vo-do lad- — na.
6, (1) VII-b3
AB
Kuba B.H. 774. Kolo
46a.
Leleć (Kolo)
félz.
Allegro moderato.
Po - i - gralo kolo, po-i -
gra-lo kolo

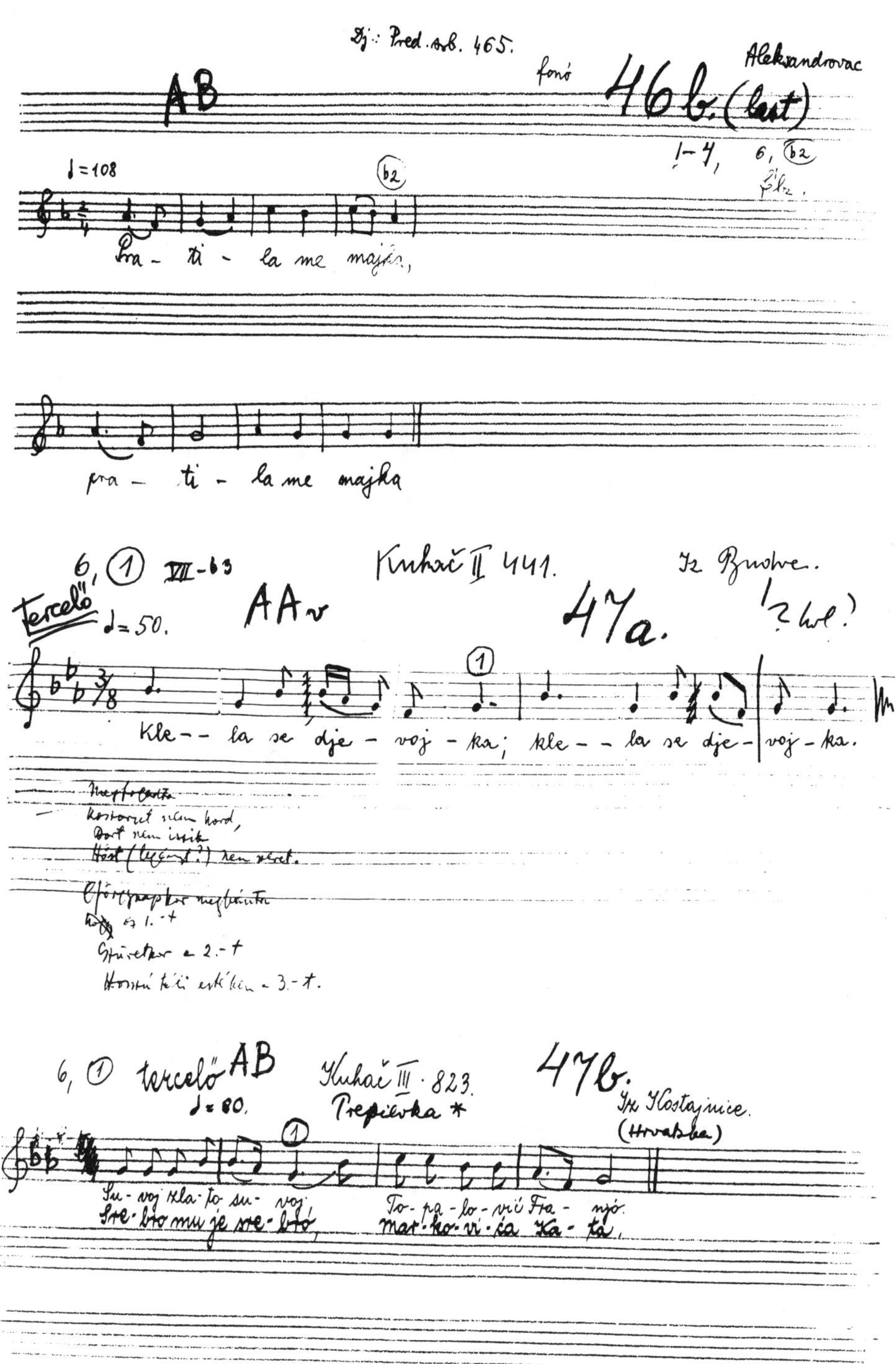
fonó
46b. (lent)
Aleksandrovac
AB
♩=108
Pra - ti - la me majka,
pra - ti - la me majka
Kuhač II 441.
tercelő
AA
♩=50.
47a.
Kle - - la se dje - voj - ka; kle - - la se dje - voj - ka.
tercelő AB
♩=80.
Kuhač III · 823.
47b.
Iz Kostajnice.
(Hrvatska)
Su - voj zla - to su - voj,
Sre - bro mu je sre - bro,
To - pa - lo - vić Fra - njo.
Mar - ko - vi - ća Ka - ta.

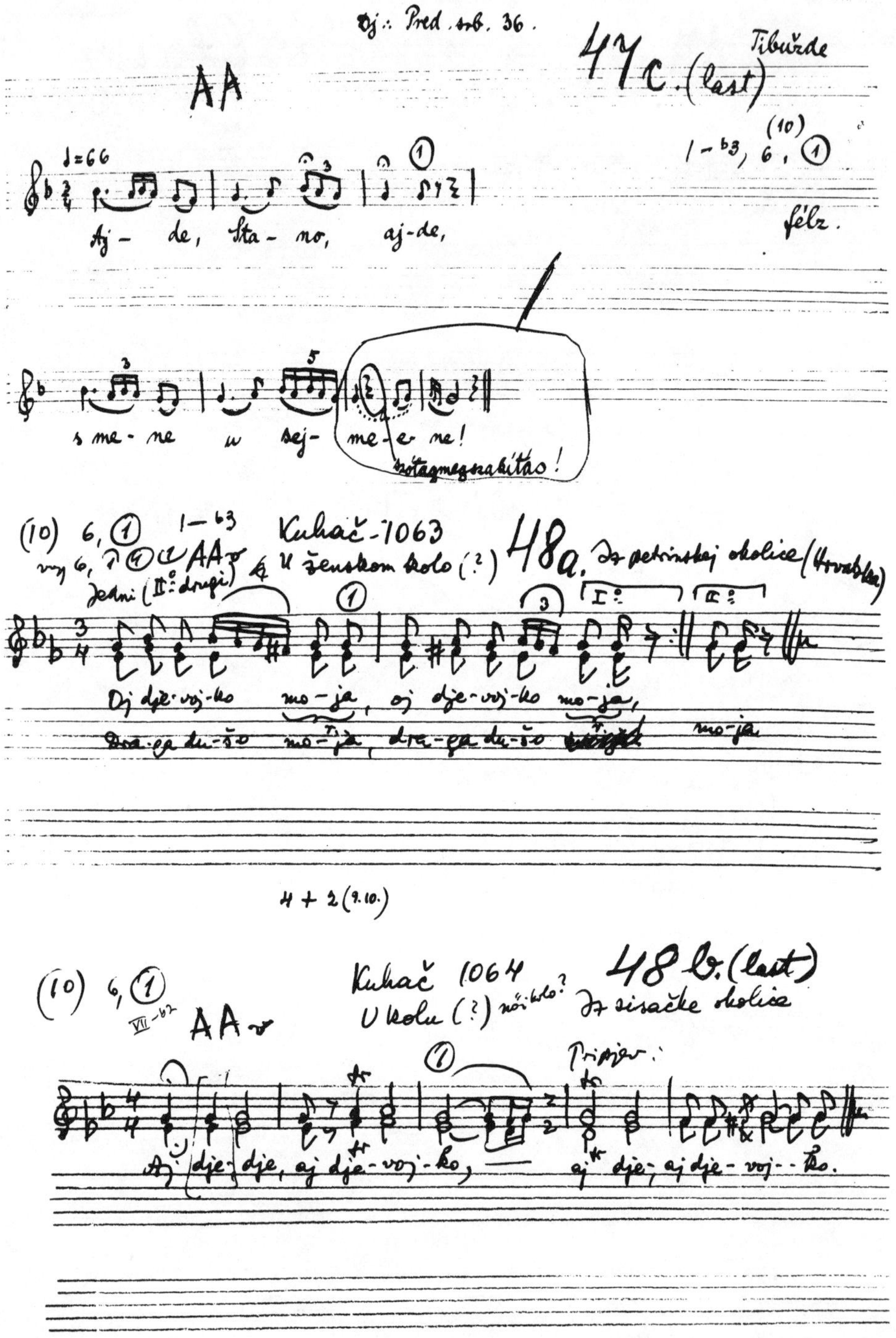
47c. (last)
Tibužde
AA
félz.
Aj - de, Sta - no, aj-de,
s me - ne u sej- me - e ne!
Kuhač-1063
U ženskom kolo (?)
48a.
Oj dje-voj-ko mo-ja, oj dje-voj-ko mo-ja,
4 + 2 (9.10.)
Kuhač 1064
U kolu (?)
48 b. (last)
Aj dje-dje, aj dje-voj-ko, aj dje, aj dje-voj--ko.

6, ① 1–4
Kuba. B. H. 911.
Zenica.
AB
49a.
Mlad nam ko - vač ku - je; a što
ko - vač ku - je?
6, ① 1–63
Kuba B. H. 828. AAv 49b.
Allegro moderato.
Kolo
Doboj (Kolo)
Mlad nam kovač ku - - je,
a što nam ga ko - vač ku - je?
Dj.: Pred. zb. 471.
49c. (last)
Aleksandrovac.
AA
1–4, 6, ①
Što grad Smedere - vo,
što grad Smede - re - vo

Dj.: Pred. sb. 541. 50–51. Pavlica

1–4, 6, ①

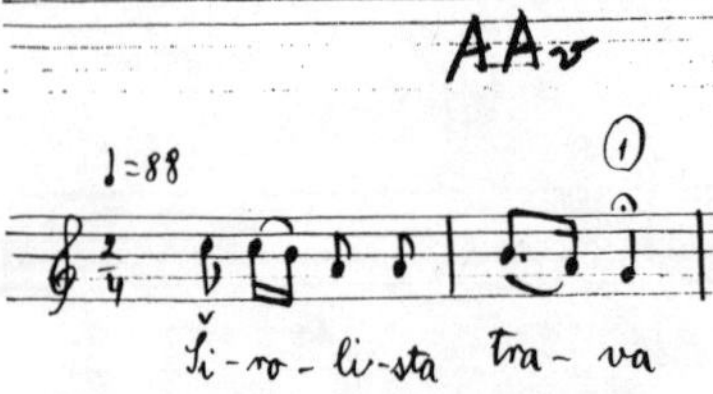

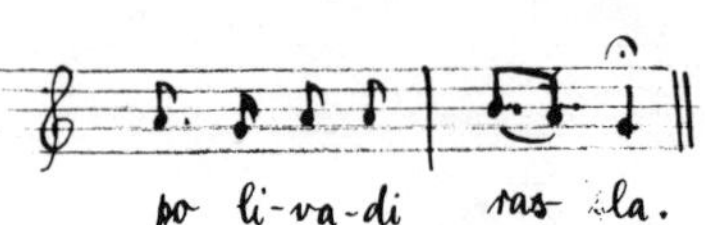

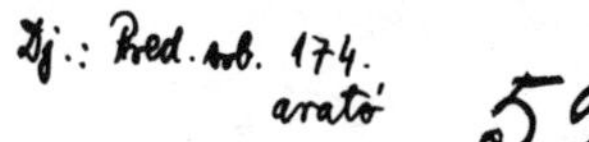

52. Kalna.

1–4 (10)
6, ①

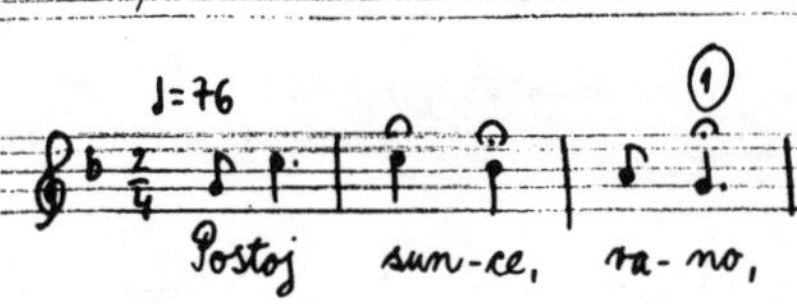

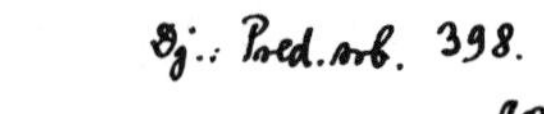

53. Mrzenica

1–5 (10)
6, ①

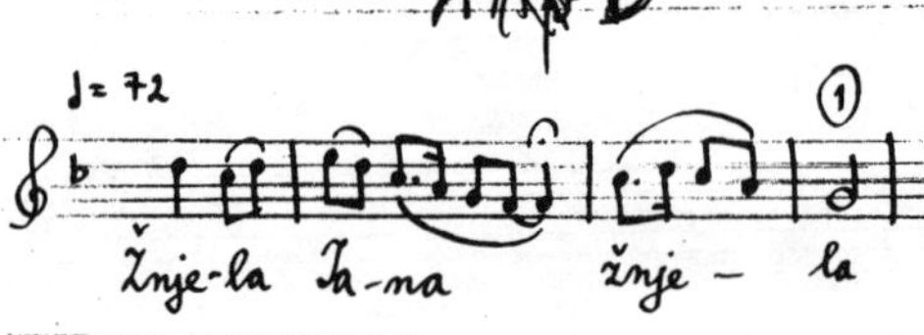

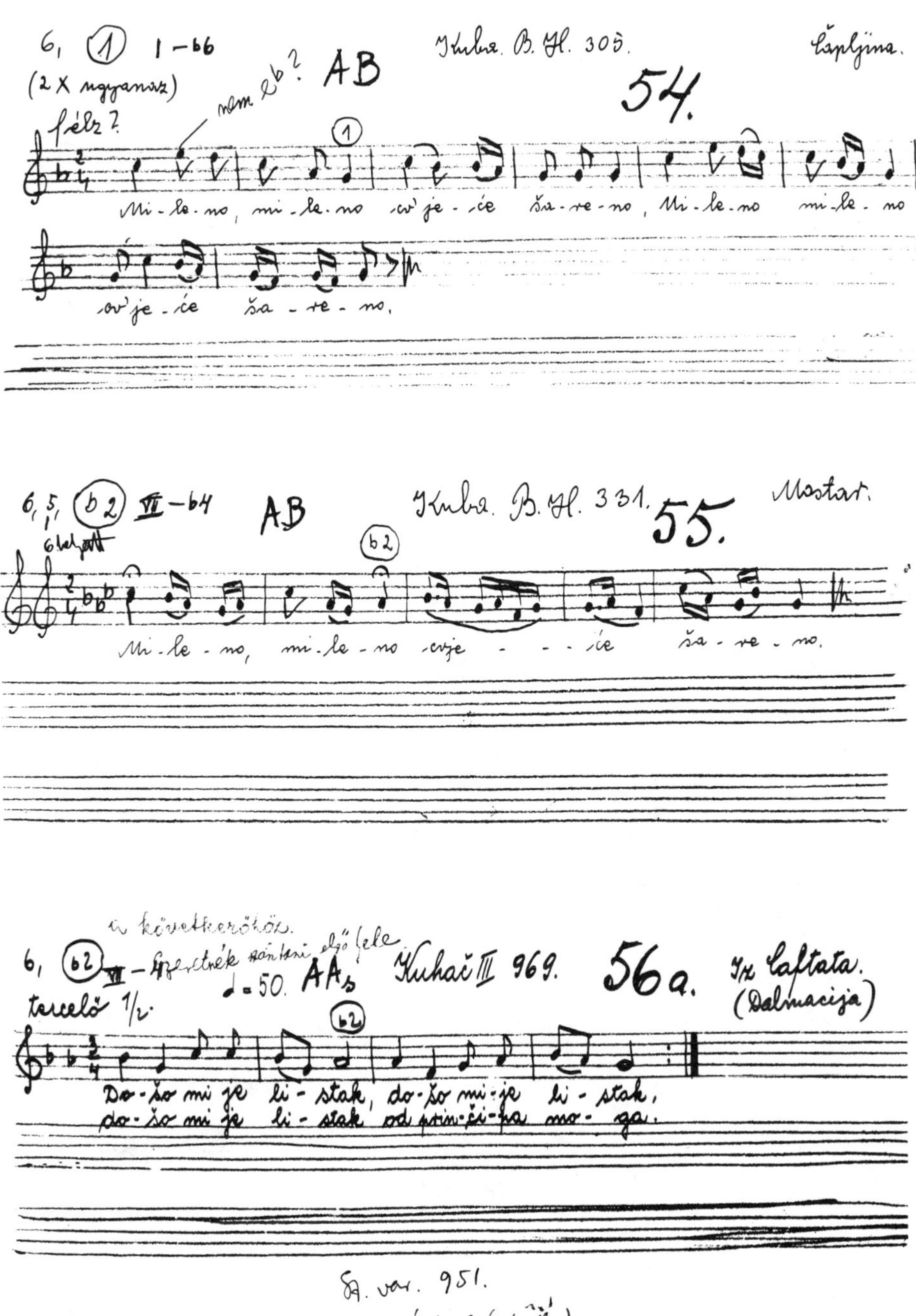
6, (1) I–66
(2 X ugyanaz)
AB
Kuba. B. H. 305.
Čapljina.
54.
Mi-le-no, mi-le-no ov'je-će ša-re-no, Mi-le-no mi-le-no
ov'je-će ša-re-no,
AB
Kuba. B. H. 331.
55.
Mostar.
Mi-le-no, mi-le-no ovje - - - će ša-re-no.
♩=50.
Kuhač III 969.
56a.
Iz Caftata.
(Dalmacija)
Do-šo mi je li-stak, do-šo mi je li-stak,
do-šo mi je li-stak od prin-či-pa mo-ga.
Sz. var. 951.

6, b2 VII -b3
tercelő. AA♭ Kuhač II. 416.
Od stoka Hvara, iz sela Brusja.
56 b.
♩.=56.
b2
Ži-lju moj pri-bi- - li, slav- - - no - - ga si i-
me - - - - na.
6, b2
VII -4
Kuba X II. 24.
Trogir.
AA♭ b2
56 c.
Dívči sbor.
Ve-se-la mla-do-sti
Kru-no-vi-to bla-go
Sve mo-je ža-lo-sti, Mo-je mi-lo dra-go.
6, b2 tercelő.
Kuba X II. 20.
Omiš.
1-4
müdal? tk. csak két sor.
56 d.
Sbor.
AA♭ b2
A-ko si le-gla spat, a-ko si le-gla spat, a-ko si le-gla spat,
bi-la to lah-ka noć.

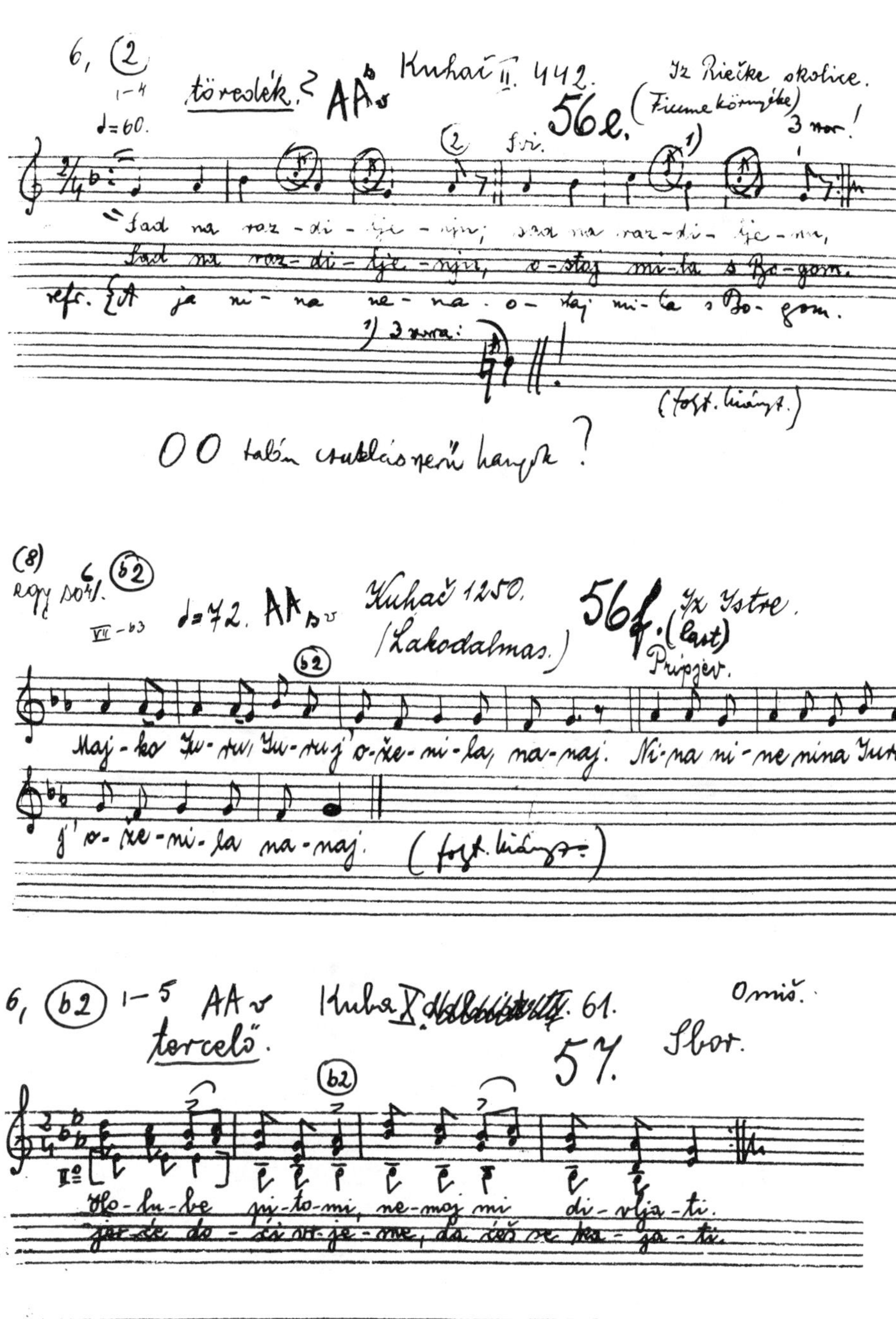
Kuhač II. 442.
Iz Riečke okolice.
56e.
♩=60.
Sad na raz-di-lje-nju, sad na raz-di-lje-nju,
A ja ni-na ne-na o-staj mi-la s Bo-gom.
Kuhač 1250.
(Lakodalmas.)
56f.
Iz Istre.
♩=72.
Pripjev.
Maj-ko Ju-ru, Ju-ru j'o-že-ni-la, na-naj. Ni-na ni-ne nina
j'o-že-ni-la na-naj.
61.
Omiš.
57.
Sbor.
Ho-lu-be pi-to-mi, ne-moj mi di-vlja-ti.

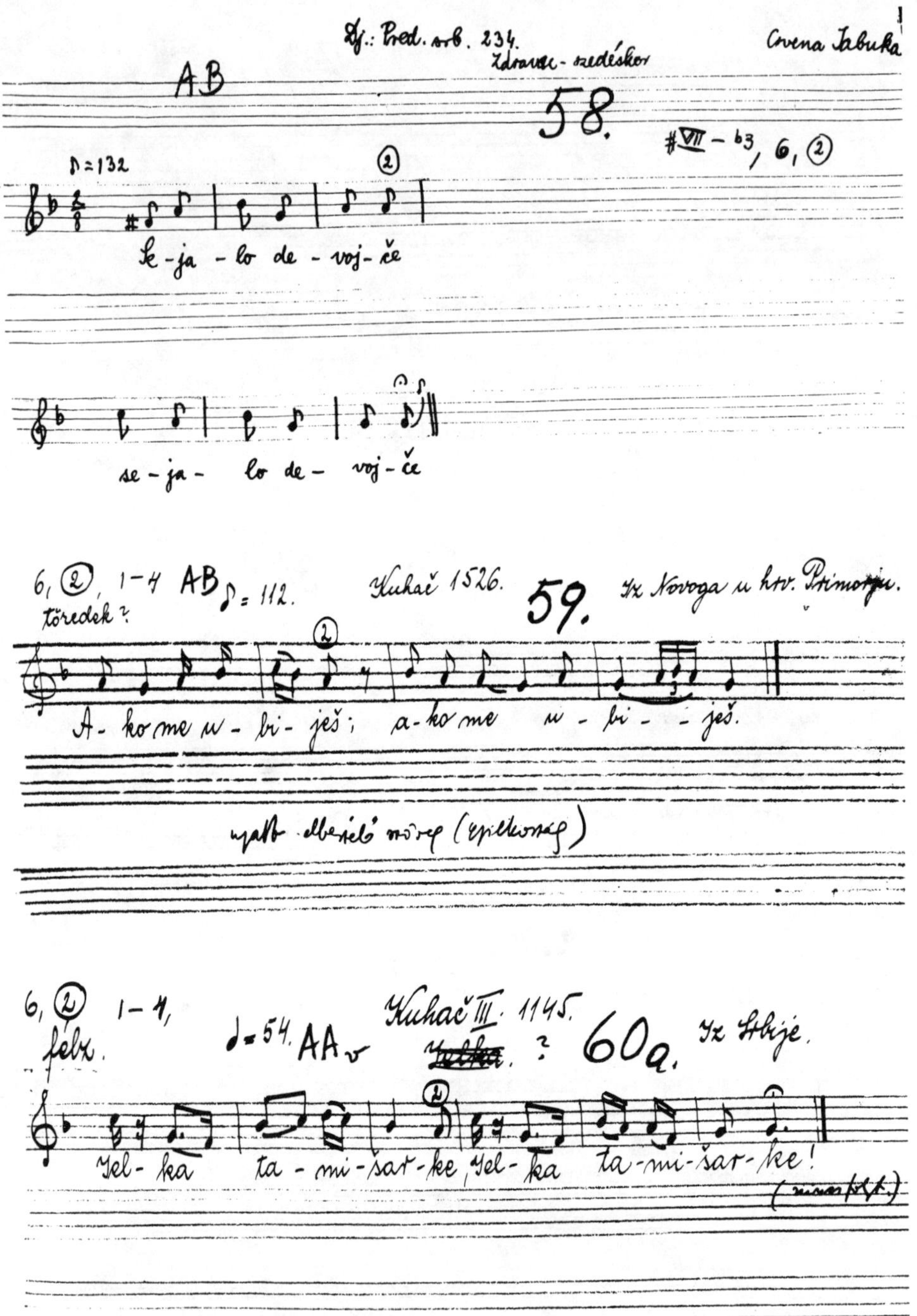
Dj.: Pred. srb. 234.
Zdravac-szedéskor
Crvena Jabuka
AB
58.
#VII – b3, 6, ②
♪=132
Se-ja-lo de-voj-če
se-ja-lo de-voj-če
6, ②, 1–4 AB ♪=112.
töredék?
Kuhač 1526.
59.
Iz Novoga u hrv. Primorju.
A-ko me u-bi-ješ; a-ko me u-bi-ješ.
6, ② 1–4,
félz.
♩=54. AA
Kuhač III. 1145.
60a.
Iz Srbije.
Jel-ka ta-mi-šar-ke, Jel-ka ta-mi-šar-ke!

6, (2) VII–4
Djordjević. Nar. Por. 104/2.
St. St. Mokranjac Peta Rukovet.
félz.
AA
60 b. (last)
|: Po-ve-la je Jel-ka dva ko-nja na vo-du :|
6, (b3) bVII–7
tercelő. AA
Kuba X
29.
Omiš.
61.
mužský sbor.
Gr-li-ce moj' mi-la, slu-šaj glas služ-be-ni!
Dj.: Pred. srb. 34.
62.
Tibužde
AB
VII–b3, 6, (b3)
O-ti-še-ja Dre-lja
skeleton
ta-mo do-le, Dre-lja.

AB
Kuba. B. H. 332.
63.
Mostar
u Tre-bi-nju gra--du vel'-ku ža-last ka-žu, - žu.
AB
Kuba. B. H. 258.
64a.
Stolac.
félz.
skeleton
AB
Kuba. B. H. 868.
64b.
Trebinje.

6, b3
tótos
AB
Kuba. B. H. 870.
64c. (last)
Blagaj.
U Tre-bi-nju gra-du vel' ku ža-lost ka-žu žu.
Dj.: Pred. zb. 235.
Crvena Jabuka
AA
Na premlaz (?)
65.
♪ = 144
1–b3, 6, b3
Dobra sreča, Ne-jo,
dobra sreča, Nejo.
6, b3
1–b3
AB
66.
Iz staroga kaštela u Dalmaciji.

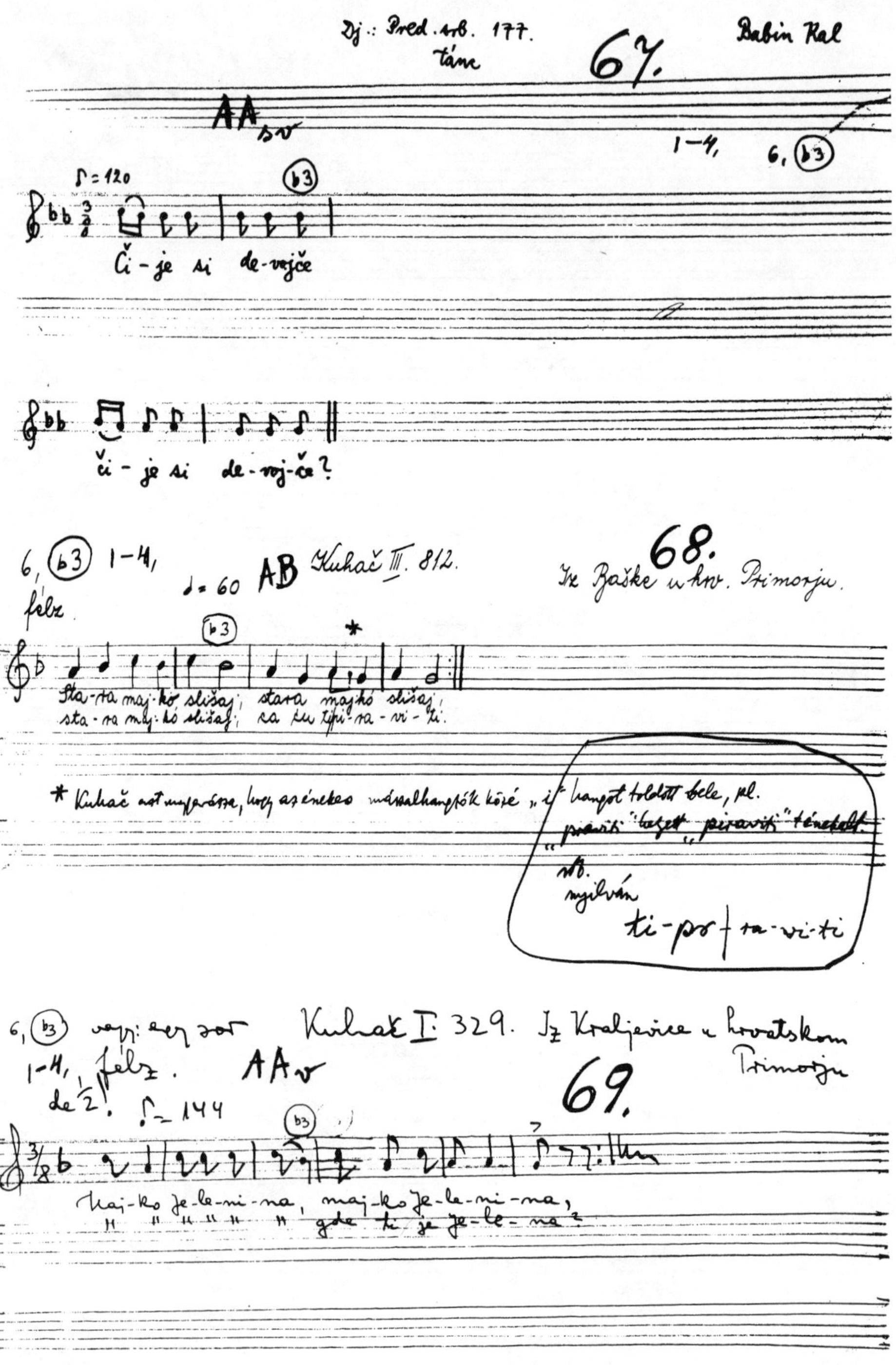

Dj.: Pred. arb. 177.
tánc
67.
Babin Kal
AA sv
1—4, 6, b3
♪ = 120
b3
Či - je si de - vejče
či - je si de - voj - če?
6, b3 1—4,
félz
♩ = 60 AB Kuhač III. 812.
68.
Iz Baške u hrv. Primorju.
b3
Sta - ra maj - ko slišaj; stara majko slišaj;
sta - ra maj - ko slišaj; ka ću tipi - ra - vi - ti.
ti - pr | ra - vi - ti
6, b3
1-4, félz.
de 1/2! ♪ = 144
Kuhač I. 329. Iz Kraljevice u hrvatskom Primorju
AA
69.
b3
Maj - ko Je - le - ni - na, maj - ko Je - le - ni - na,
gde ti je Je - le - na?

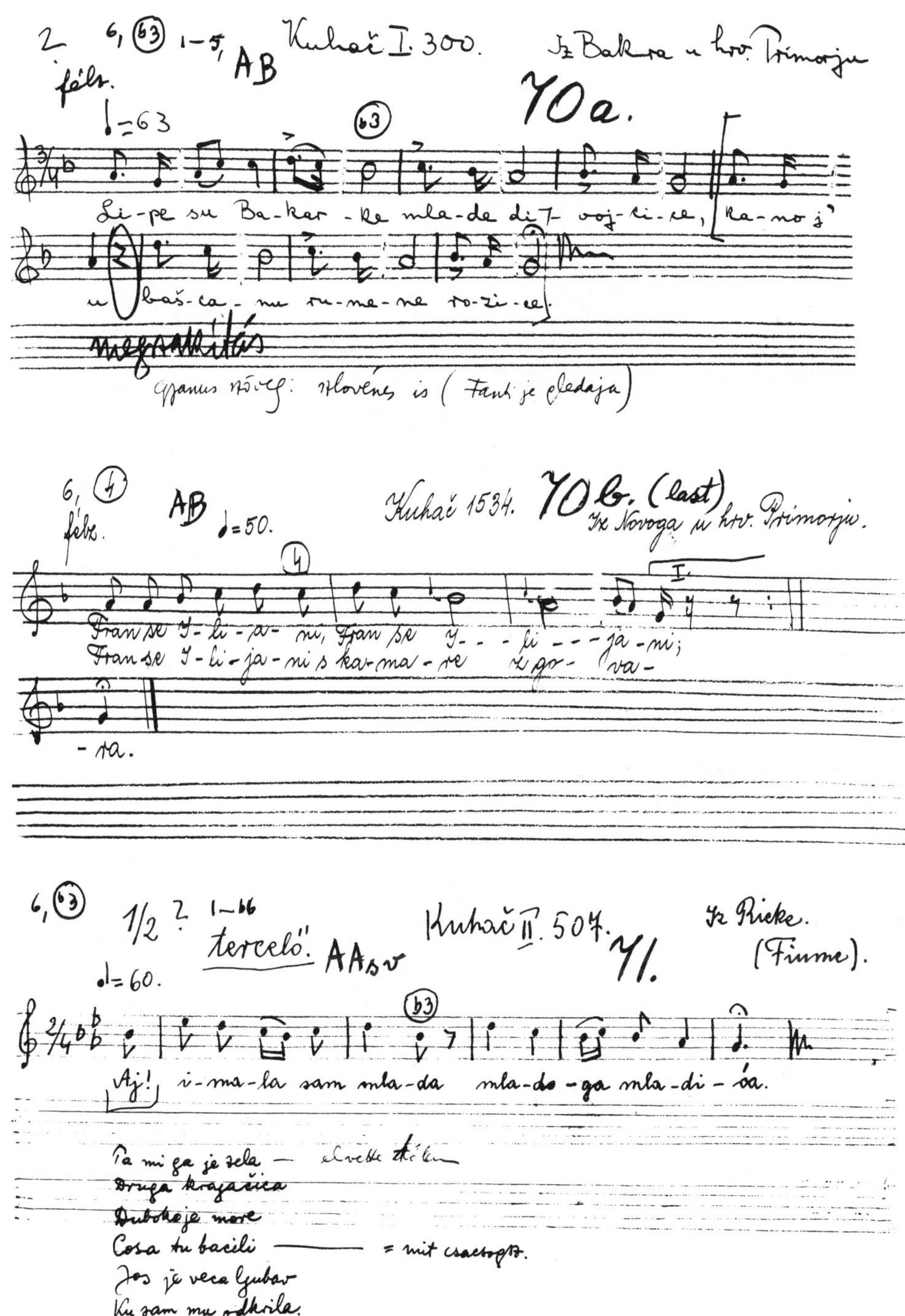

Kuhač I. 300.
Iz Bakra u hrv. Primorju
70a.
Li-pe su Ba-kar-ke mla-de di-voj-či-ce, ka-no j'
u baš-ča-nu ru-me-ne ro-ži-ce.
Kuhač 1534.
70b. (last)
Iz Novoga u hrv. Primorju.
Fran-se I-li-ja-ni, Fran-se I-li-ja-ni;
-va.
Kuhač II. 507.
71.
Iz Rieke.
(Fiume).
tercelő.
Aj! i-ma-la sam mla-da mla-do-ga mla-di-ća.
Ta mi ga je zela
Druga krajačica
Duboko je more
Cosa tu bacili
Jos je veca ljubav
Ku sam mu odkrila.

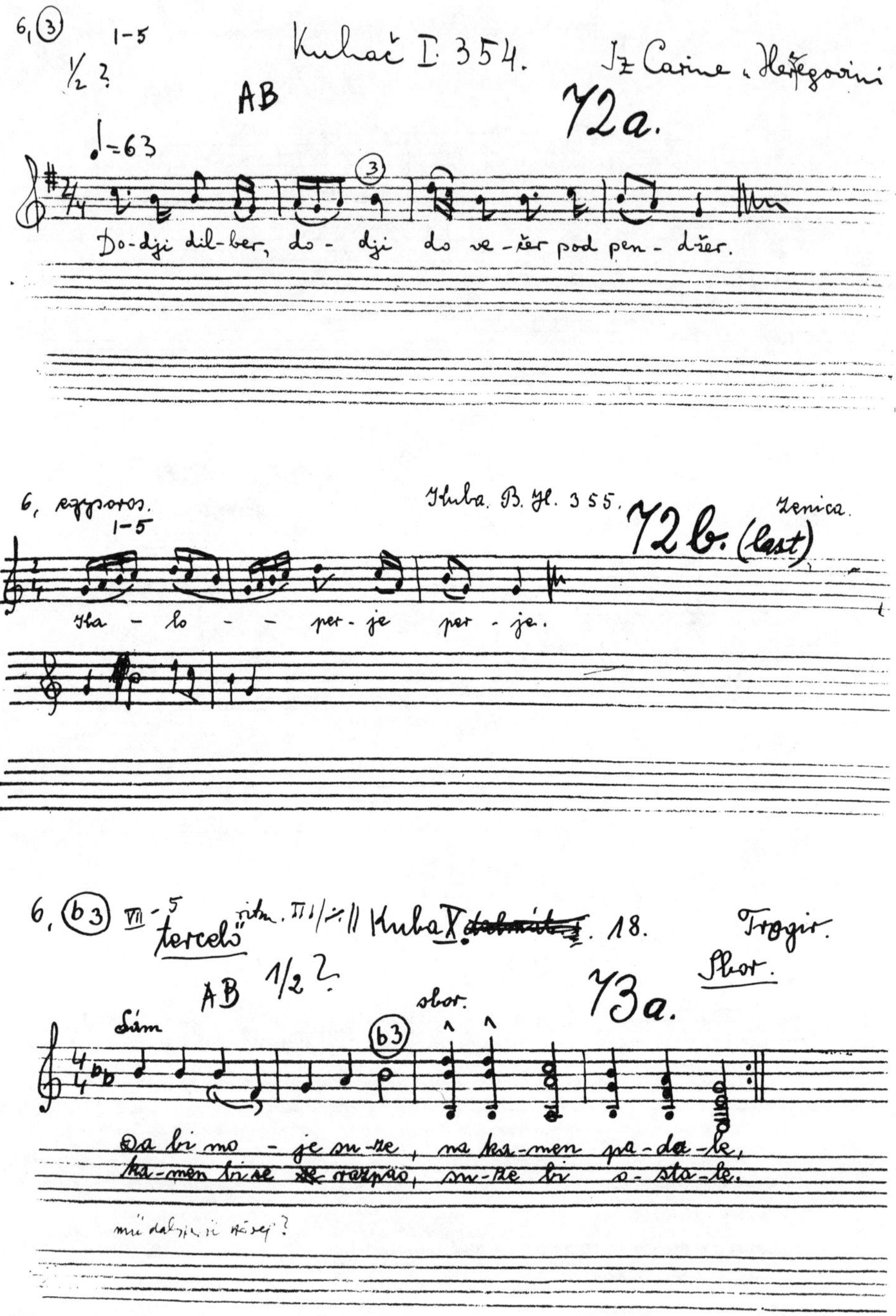

Kuhač I. 354.
Iz Carine u Hercegovini
AB
72a.
Do-dji dil-ber, do-dji do ve-čer pod pen-džer.
355.
72b. (last)
Zenica.
Kuba X. 18.
Trogir.
Sbor.
AB
73a.
sbor.
Da bi mo-je su-ze, na ka-men pa-da-le,
ka-men bi se raspao, su-ze bi o-sta-le.

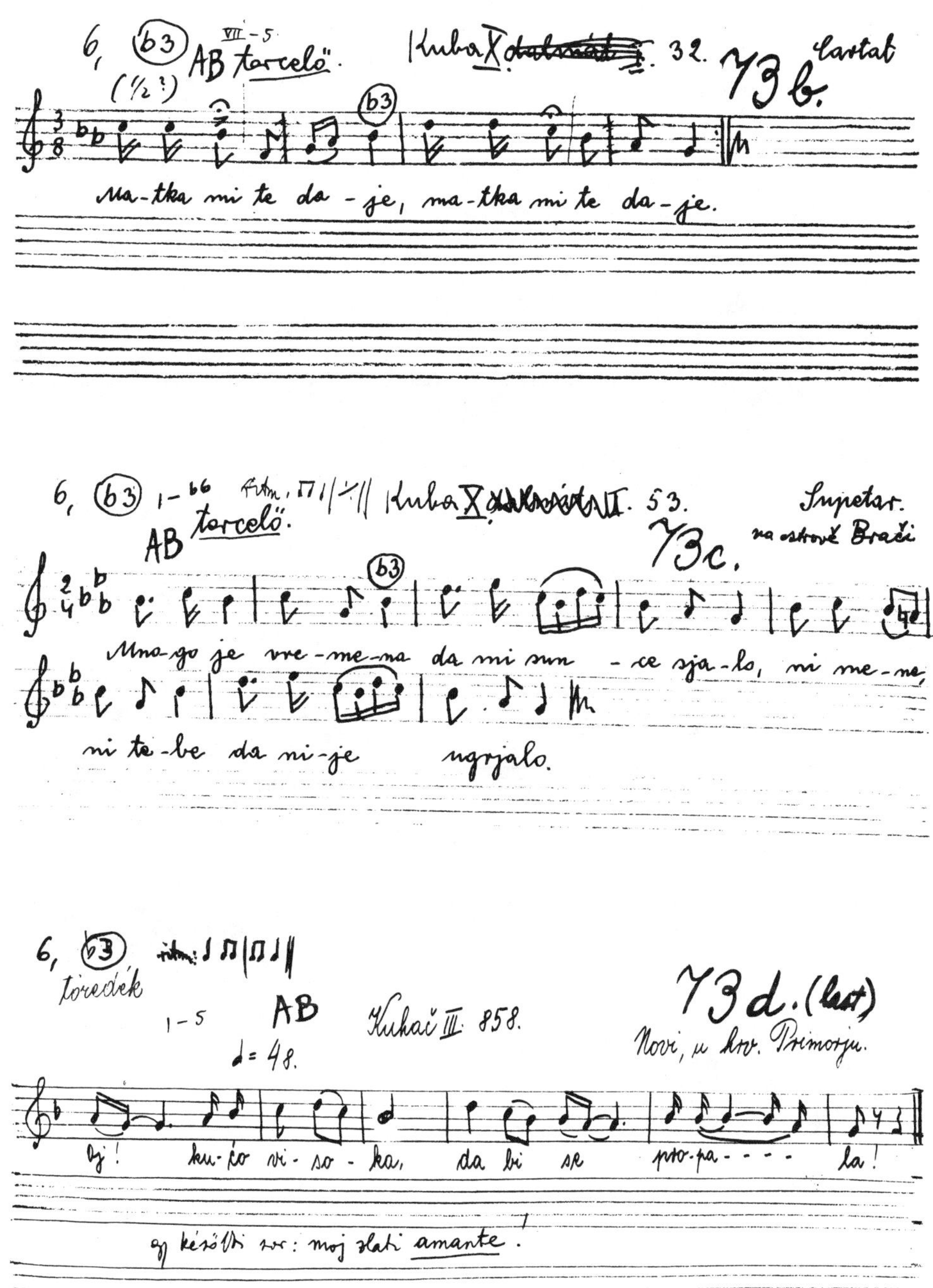

73 b.
ma-tka mi te da - je, ma-tka mi te da-je.
73 c.
Supetar.
Mno-go je vre-me-na da mi sun - ce sja-lo, ni me-ne,
ni te-be da ni-je ugrjalo.
73 d.
AB
Kuhač III. 858.
Oj! ku-ćo vi-so-ka, da bi se pro-pa - - - la!

AB
Kuhač III. 856.
Od otoka Krka.
Ma-ri-ji-ce du-šo, ča mi se j sa-nja-lo; Ma-ri-ji-ce du-šo,
ča mi se j sa-nja-lo.
AA
Kuhač III. 805.
75a.
Iz Dugerese u Hrvatskoj:
Dvi su, dvi su dru-ge, dvi su dvi su dru-ge,
li-po dru-gó-va-le, li-po dru-gó-va-le.
804. 806.
Pred. srb. 412.
AA
75b.
Mrzenica
Oj de-voj-ko, Ja-no
u-bi-la te tu-ga

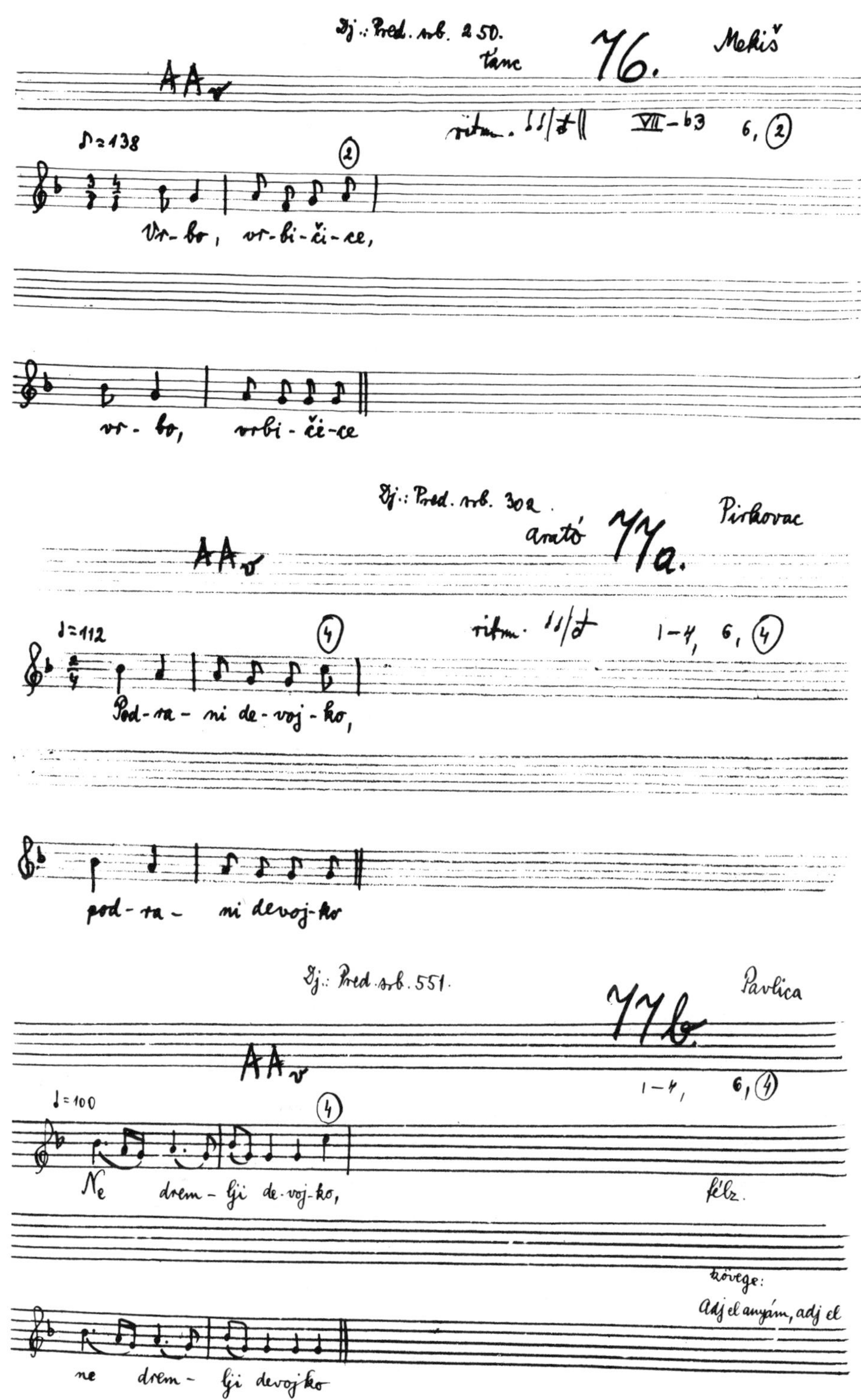
Dj.: Pred. srb. 250.
tanc
76.
Mekiš
AA$_v$
ritm.
VII – b3
6, (2)
♪ = 138
(2)
Vr - bo, vr - bi - či - ce,
vr - bo, vrbi - če - ce
Dj.: Pred. srb. 30a.
arató
77a.
Pirkovac
AA$_v$
♩ = 112
(4)
ritm.
1–4, 6, (4)
Pod - ra - ni de - voj - ko,
pod - ra - ni devoj - ko
Dj.: Pred. srb. 551.
77b.
Pavlica
AA$_v$
1–4, 6, (4)
♩ = 100
(4)
Ne drem - lji de - voj - ko,
félz.
kövege:
Adj el anyám, adj el
ne drem - lji devojko

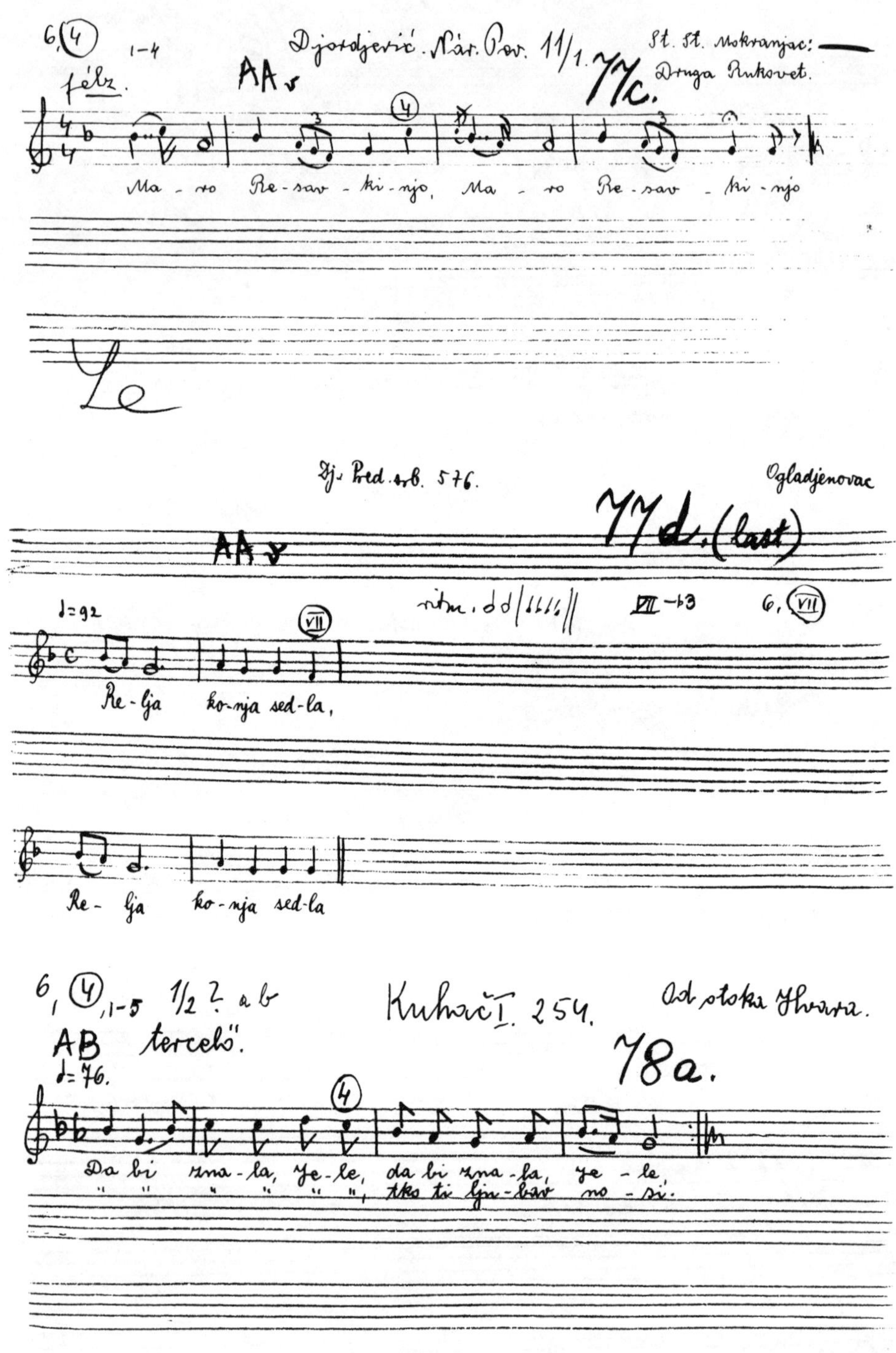

6, (4) 1-4
Djordjević. Nár. Pev. 11/1.
St. St. Mokranjac: Druga Rukovet.
félz.
AA
77c.
Ma - ro Re - sav - ki - njo, Ma - ro Re - sav - ki - njo
Dj. Pred. srb. 576.
Ogladjenovac
77d. (last)
AA
♩=92
VII–b3
6, VII
Re - lja ko - nja sed - la,
Re - lja ko - nja sed - la
6, (4), 1-5 1/2 ? a b
Kuhač I. 254.
Od otoka Hvara.
AB tercelő.
78a.
♩=76.
Da bi zna - la, Je - le, da bi zna - la, je - le,
tko ti lju - bav no - si.

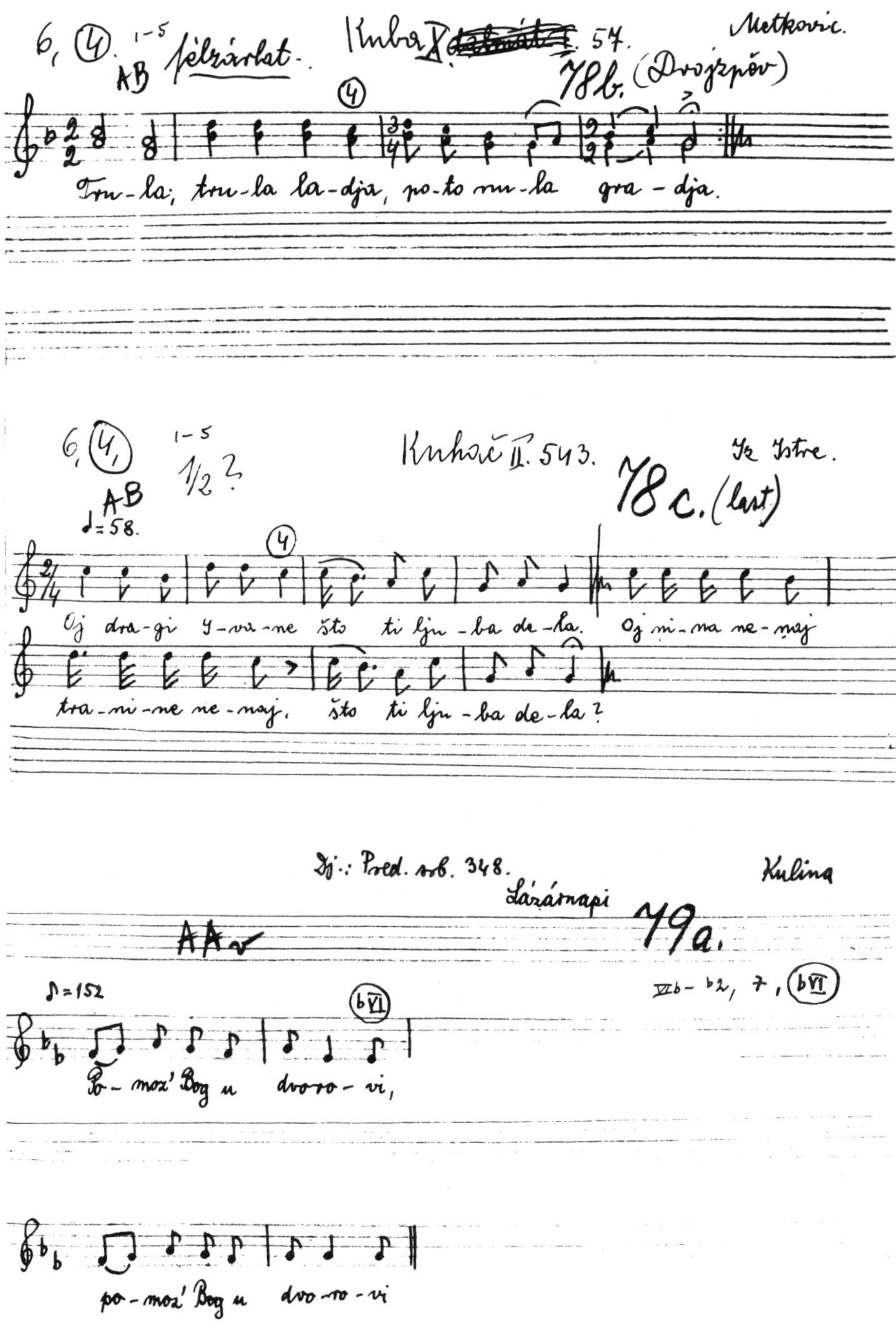
6, (4). 1–5
AB félzárlat.
Kuba X. 57.
Metković.
78b.
Tru-la; tru-la la-dja, po-to-nu-la gra-dja.
6, (4), 1–5
1/2?
AB
Kuhač II. 543.
Iz Istre.
78c. (last)
Oj dra-gi I-va-ne što ti lju-ba de-la. Oj ni-ma ne-maj
tra-ni-ne ne-maj, što ti lju-ba de-la?
Dj.: Pred. sb. 348.
Kulina
Lázárnapi
79a.
AA
Po-moz' Bog u dvoro-vi,
po-moz' Bog u dvo-ro-vi

Dj.: Pred. sb. 312.

Lázárnapi

Varoš

79 b.

VII — 62

7, egysoros

= 313!

♩=80

O- vi dvori dvo-ro-vi

Dj.: Pred. sb. 313.

Lázárnapi

Varoš

79 c.

7, egysoros

♩=80

Ig-raj, igraj lazare, la-zari-ce devojko.

Dj.: Pred. sb. 372.

Lázárnapi

Veliki Šiljegovac

79 d. (last)

VII — 63

7, egysoros féle.

♩=104

Dj.: Pred. srb. 300.
Pirkovac.
Lázárnapi
80a.
AAv
VII-1
7, VII
VII
Oo-de lani mi-nu-mo,
ov-de la-ni mi-nu-mo
Dj.: Pred. srb. 73.
Leskovačka okolina
Lázárnapi
80b. (last)
AAv
VII-b2,
7, VII
♩= 132
VII
Oj, u-ba-va de-voj-ko,
oj, u-bava de-voj-ko!
7, VII
VII-4
1/2?
AB
Kuhač III. 806.
Iz Selnice u hrv. Zagorju.
♩= 69.
81.
VII
Hoj sta-ri-na, sta-ri-na, tri si čer-ke shra-ni-la;
804. 805.

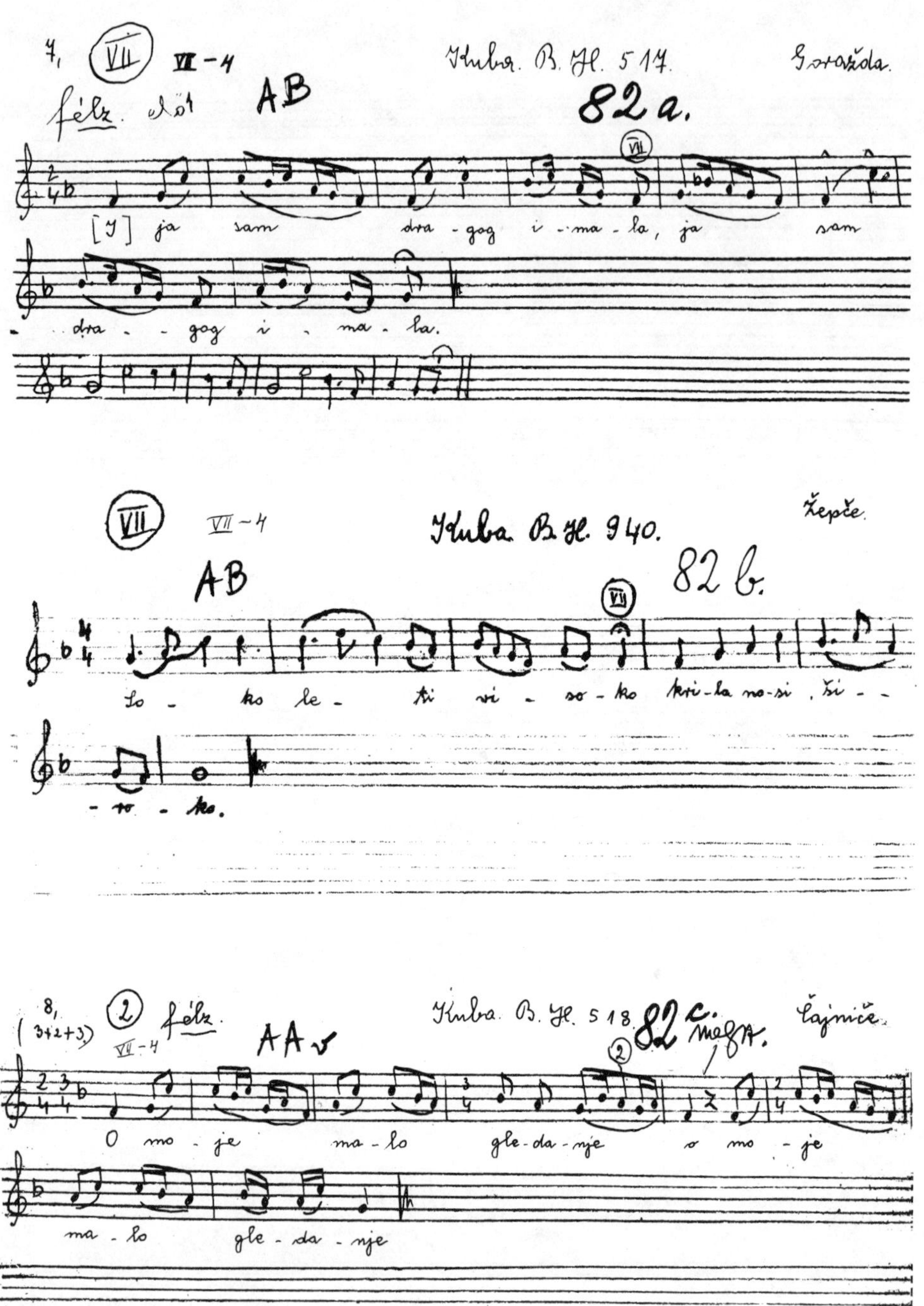
7,
VII
VII – 4
Kuba. B. H. 517.
Goražda.
félz.
AB
82 a.
[J] ja sam dra - gog i - ma - la, ja sam
dra - gog i - ma - la.
VII
VII – 4
Kuba. B. H. 940.
Žepče.
AB
82 b.
So - ko le - ti vi - so - ko kri - la no - si, ši -
- ro - ko.
8,
(3+2+3)
2
félz.
VII – 4
Kuba. B. H. 518.
82 c.
Čajniče.
AA
O mo - je ma - lo gle - da - nje o mo - je
ma - lo gle - da - nje

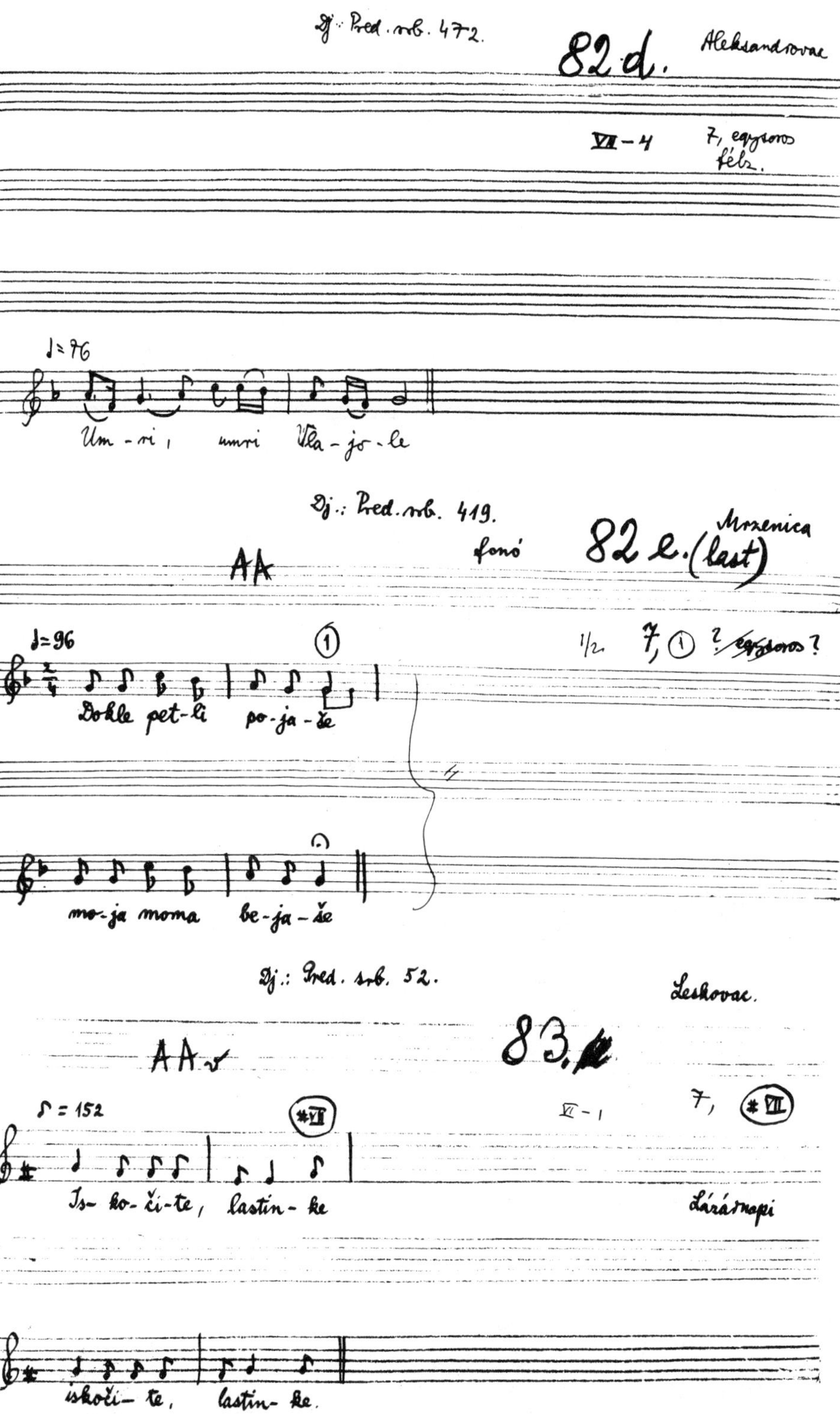

Dj.: Pred. srb. 472.
82 d.
Aleksandrovac
VII – 4
7, egysoros félz.
♩= 76
Um - ri, umri Vla - jo - le
Dj.: Pred. srb. 419.
82 e. (last)
Mrzenica
AA
fonó
♩= 96
1/2 7, ① ? egysoros ?
Dokle pet - li po - ja - še
mo - ja moma be - ja - še
Dj.: Pred. srb. 52.
Leskovac.
83.
AA
♪ = 152
VI – 1
7, (♯VII)
Is - ko - či - te, lastin - ke
Lázárnapi
iskoči - te, lastin - ke.

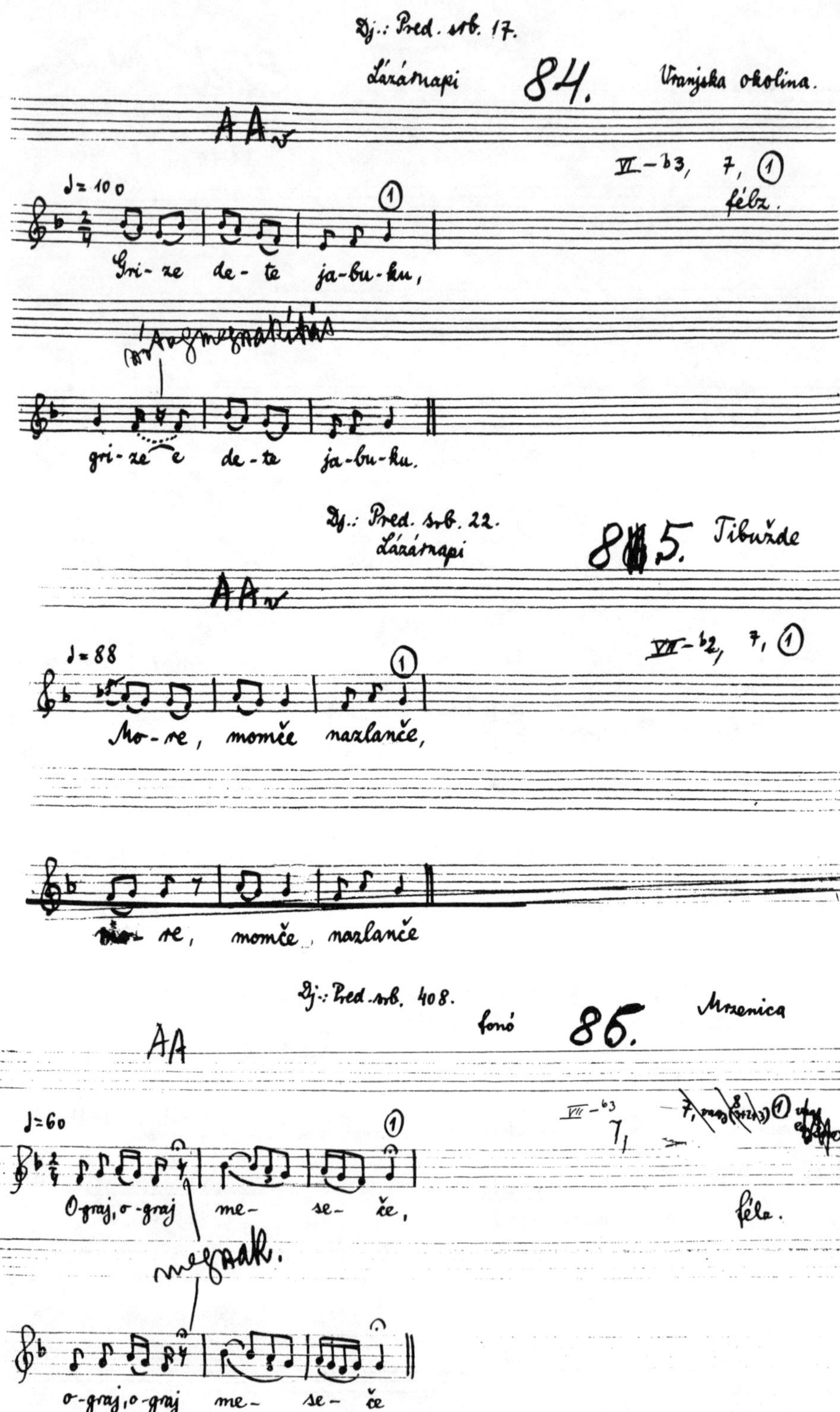

Dj.: Pred. srb. 17.
Lázárnapi
84.
Vranjska okolina.
AA
♩= 100
VI – b3, 7, ①
félz.
Gri- ze de- te ja-bu-ku,
gri- ze e de- te ja-bu-ku.
Dj.: Pred. srb. 22.
Lázárnapi
85.
Tibužde
AA
♩= 88
VII – b2, 7, ①
Mo- re, momče nazlanče,
re, momče nazlanče
Dj.: Pred. srb. 408.
fonó
86.
Mrzenica
AA
♩= 60
VII – b3
7,
Ogmj, o-graj me- se- će,
féle.
megállás.
o-graj, o-graj me- se- će

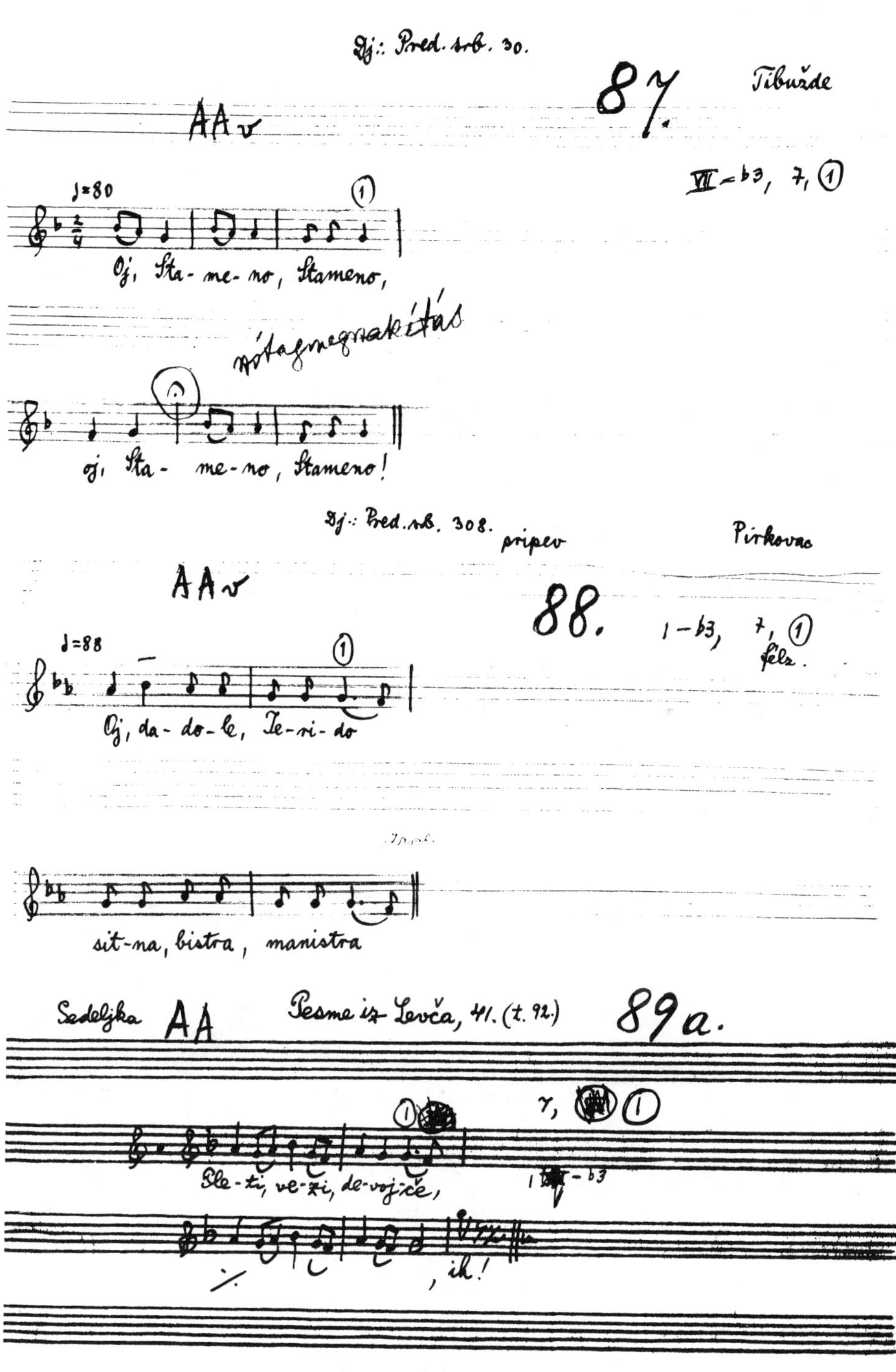
Dj.: Pred. srb. 30.
87.
Tibužde
AAv
VII – b3, 7, ①
♩=80
Oj, Sta- me- no, Stameno,
oj, Sta- me- no, Stameno!
Dj.: Pred. srb. 308.
pripev
Pirkovac
AAv
88.
1 – b3, 7, ①
♩=88
Oj, da- do- le, Te- ri- do
sit-na, bistra, manistra
Sedeljka
AA
Pesme iz Levča, 41. (t. 92.)
89a.
Sle- ti, ve- zi, de- vojče,
, ih!

Dj.: Pred. srb. 539. Pavlica

Jeremiás előestéjén

89b.

AA ① 1–63, 7, ①

♩=88

Je-re-mi-ja u po-lje,

bež-te zmi-je u mo-re

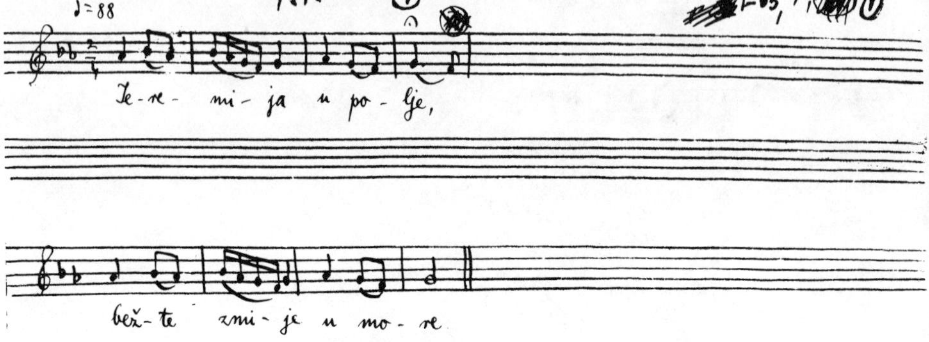

Dj.: Pred. srb. 540. Pavlica

89c. (last)

AAv

1–63 8, ① előbbihez

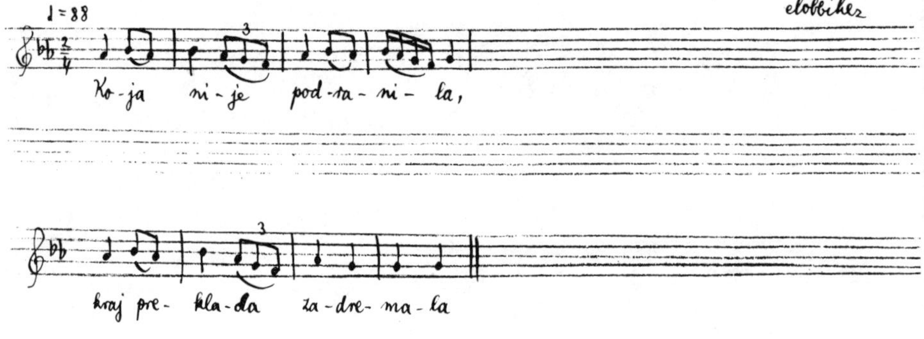

♩=88

Ko-ja ni-je pod-sa-ni-la,

kraj pre-kla-da za-dre-ma-la

Dj.: Pred. srb. 77. Leskovačka okolina

90a.

AAv

① 1–4, 7, ① félz.

♩=66

Cav-te- o mi jer-govan

na Ja-ni-nu plani-nu.

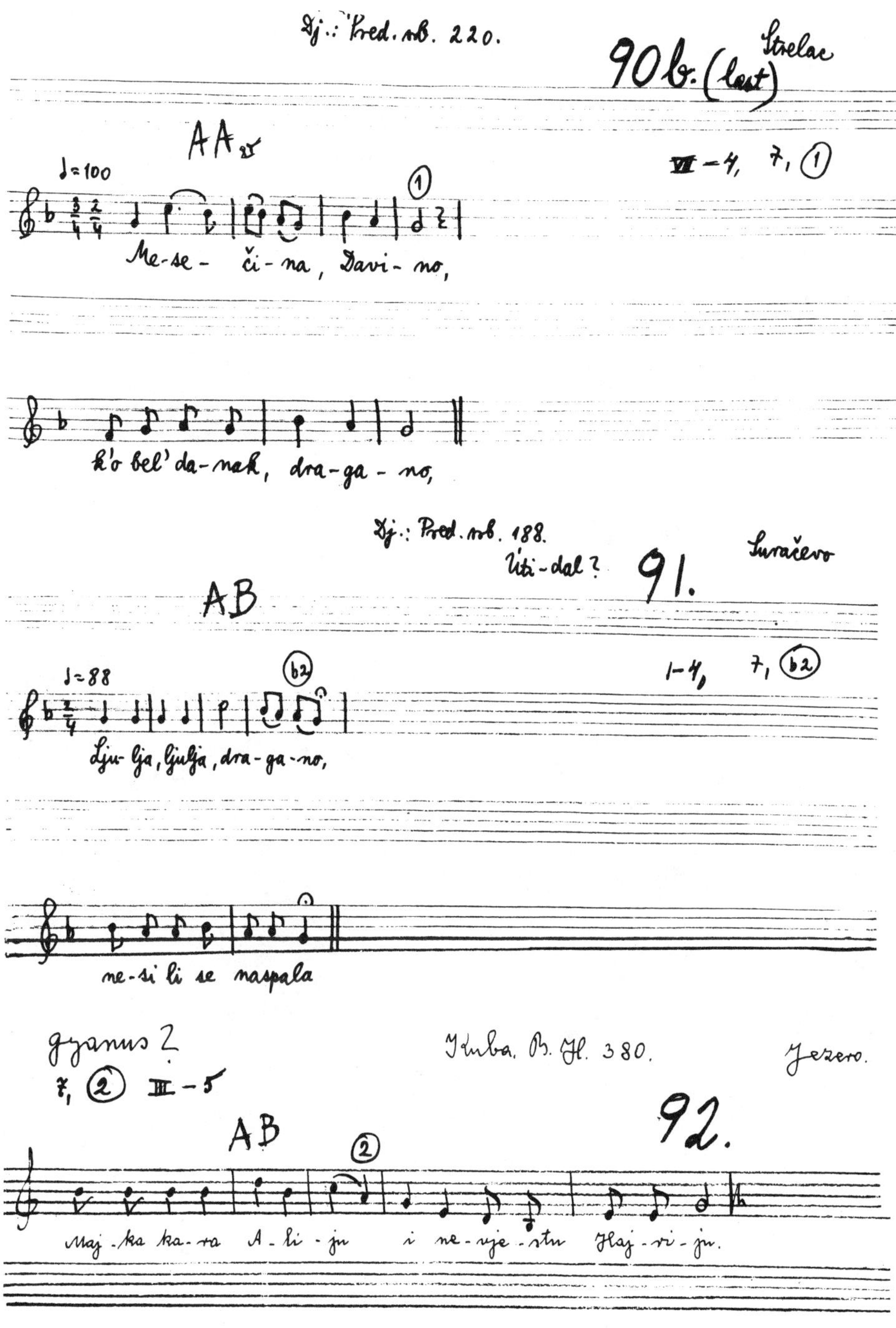
90b.
Strelac
AA
Me-se- či-na, Davi- no,
k'o bel' da-nak, dra-ga- no,
91.
Suračevo
AB
Lju- lja, ljulja, dra-ga-no,
ne-si li se naspala
92.
Jezero.
AB
Maj-ka ka-ra A-li-ju i ne-vje-stu Haj-ri-ju.

772. AA
93.
Moderato.
Sve pšeno sve ze-le-no, sve pšeno
sve ze-le-no,
Kuhač II. 417.
94a.
♩=60.
AB
Pod noć po-djoh niz po-lje
ja-nje mo-je! niz po-lje.
refr.
Kuhač III. 819.
94b.
♩=60
AB
Pripjev.
Pod noć po-djoh niz po-lje.
ja-nje mo-je niz po-lje.

AB félzárlat.
Kuhač II. 480.
94 c. (last)
Iz Bačke.
♩=46.
De - voj-ka plo - vi Du - na-vom - -; de - voj - ka
plo - vi Du - na - vom.
Gy. Var. Kuh. 106.
Kuh. 35. 1060,
AB
Kuba B.H. 675.
95 a.
Allegro moderato
Kreševa.
Šta se ono zeleni pod Daninim pendžerom
šta se ono zeleni pod Daninim pendžerom
Kuba B.H. 754.
95 b. (last)
Moderato.
AB
Blagaj.
Ku - ku - ruzi zeleni, soldat leži
na ze - mi ; ej, kukuruz se
zeleni soldat leži na ze - mi.

Dj: Pred. zb. 542. **96.** Pavlica

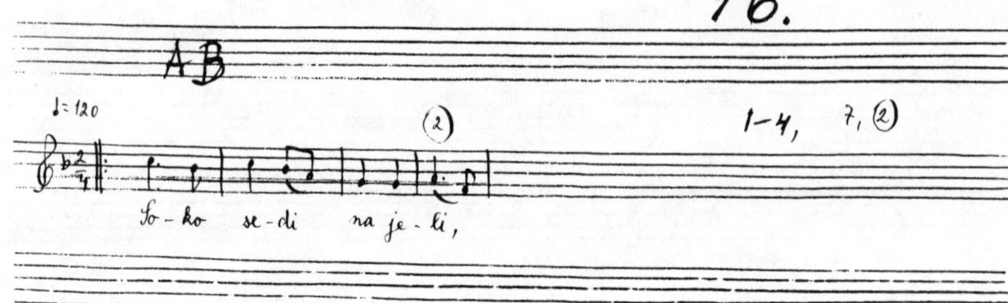

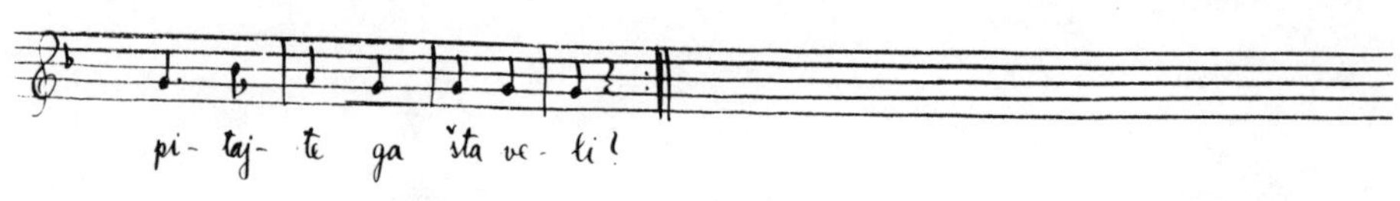

7, (b3) ♭VII – 4 Kuba. B. H. 891. Trebinje

tercelő. AB **97.**

7, (b3) VII – 4 Kuhač 1201. (Na prosidbi) **98a.**

félz. ♩=60. AAv (Lakodalmas) Iz Racvaroša (blizu Pečuha u Baranji).

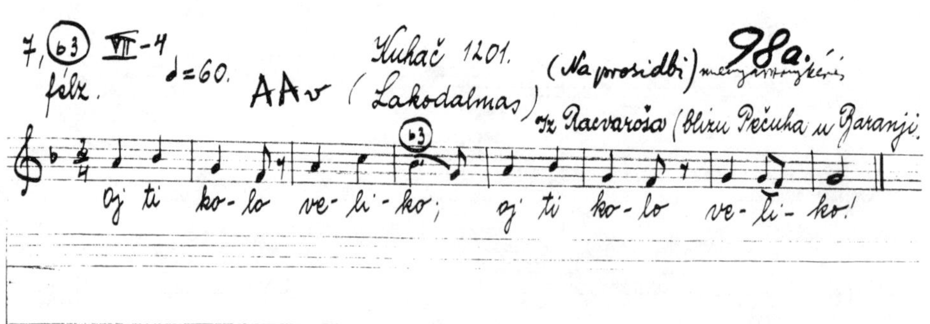

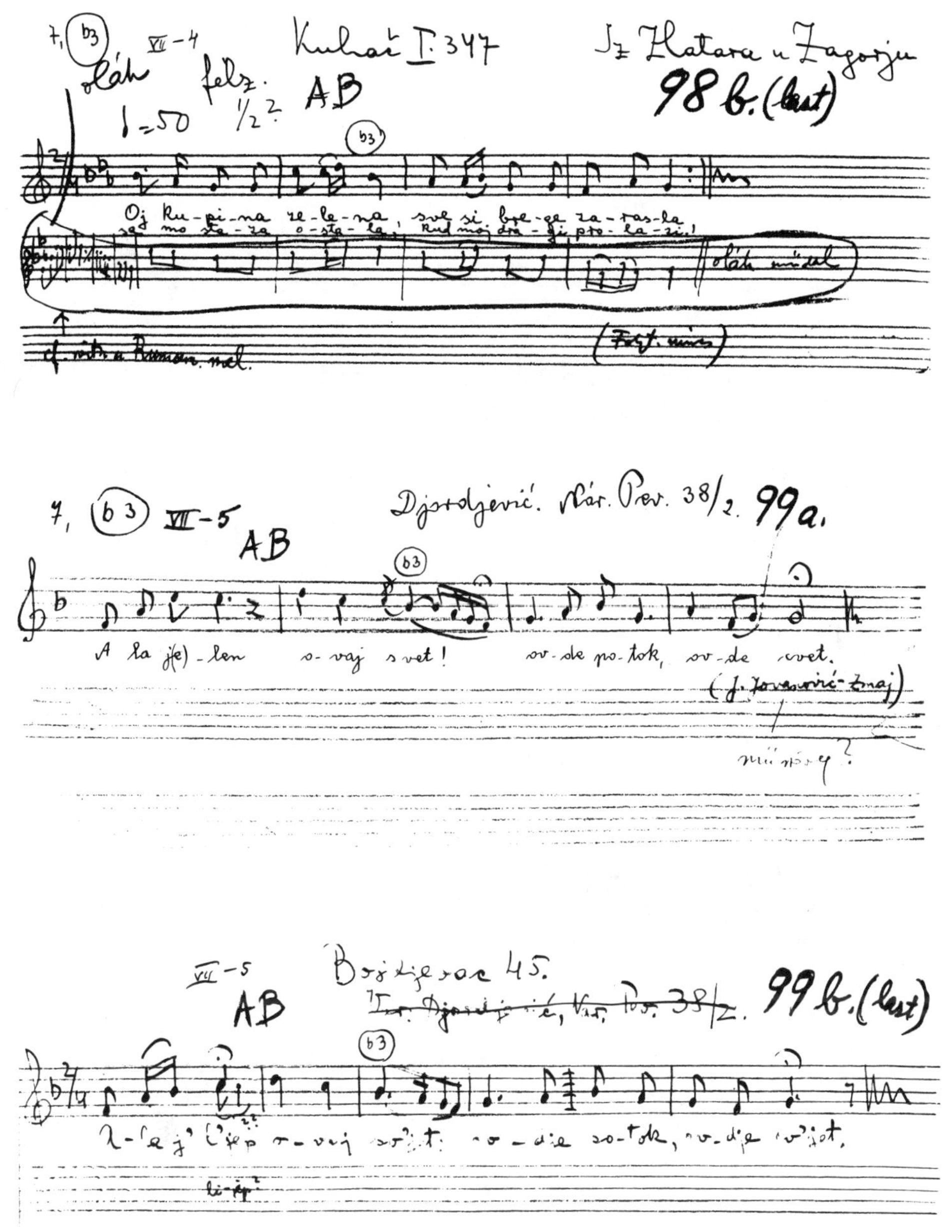

Kuhač I. 347
Iz Hatara u Zagorju
98 b. (last)
AB
J = 50
Oj Kupina zelena, sve si bzege zarasla
Djordjević. Nár. Pev. 38/2.
99a.
AB
A la j(e)-len o-vaj svet! ov-de po-tok, ov-de cvet.
99 b. (last)
AB

Dj.: Pred. sb. 273.
Lázárnapi
Niševci
100.
AB
1–b3, 7, b3
♪ = 152
b3
Ig-raj, ig-raj, laza-re,
la-za-ri-ce de-vojko.
Dj.: Pred. sb. 383.
koleda
Mrzenica
101.
AAv
(8)
1–b3, 7, b3
♩ = 96
b3
Do-dje Bo-žić, ko-le-do
iz pla-ni-ne ko-ledo
Dj.: Pred. sb. 428.
fonó
Mrzenica
102.
AB
1–4, 7, b3
♩ = 92
b3
Mom-če i-de le-di-nom
felr. ?
a de-voj-če gradinom

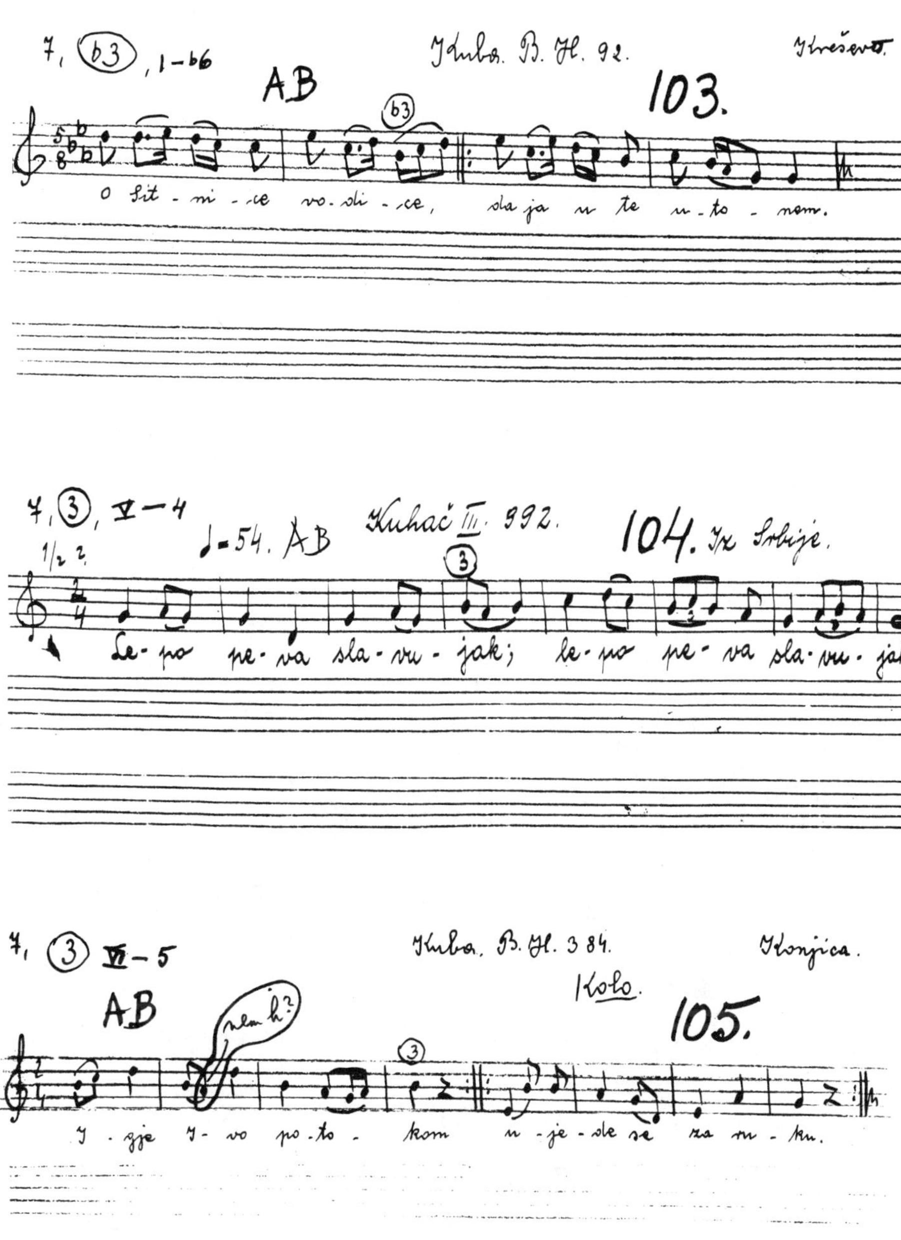
Kuba. B. H. 92.
Kreševo.
AB
103.
O Sit-ni-ce vo-di-ce, da ja u te u-to-nem.
AB
Kuhač III. 992.
104. Iz Srbije.
Le-po pe-va sla-vu-jak; le-po pe-va sla-vu-jak.
Kuba. B. H. 384.
Konjica.
Kolo.
AB
105.

106.
Vlasotinci.
AAv
♩=72
1–4, 7, (4)
Po- djo dole, tam' do-le,
po- djo dole, tam' do-le.
7, (4), phryg! A5Av
1/2 dallam?
szöveg: Barcsai!
Kuba. XII. 6.
107.
Pirot
Po-še-ta se Mi-haj mlad kroz Bu-di-ma be-o grad
Skeleton:
7, (5) 1-7
AB
Kuba B. H. 164.
108.
Plevlje.
O-ganj go-ri, A-lu-ža o-ganj go-ri,
ja-go-do.

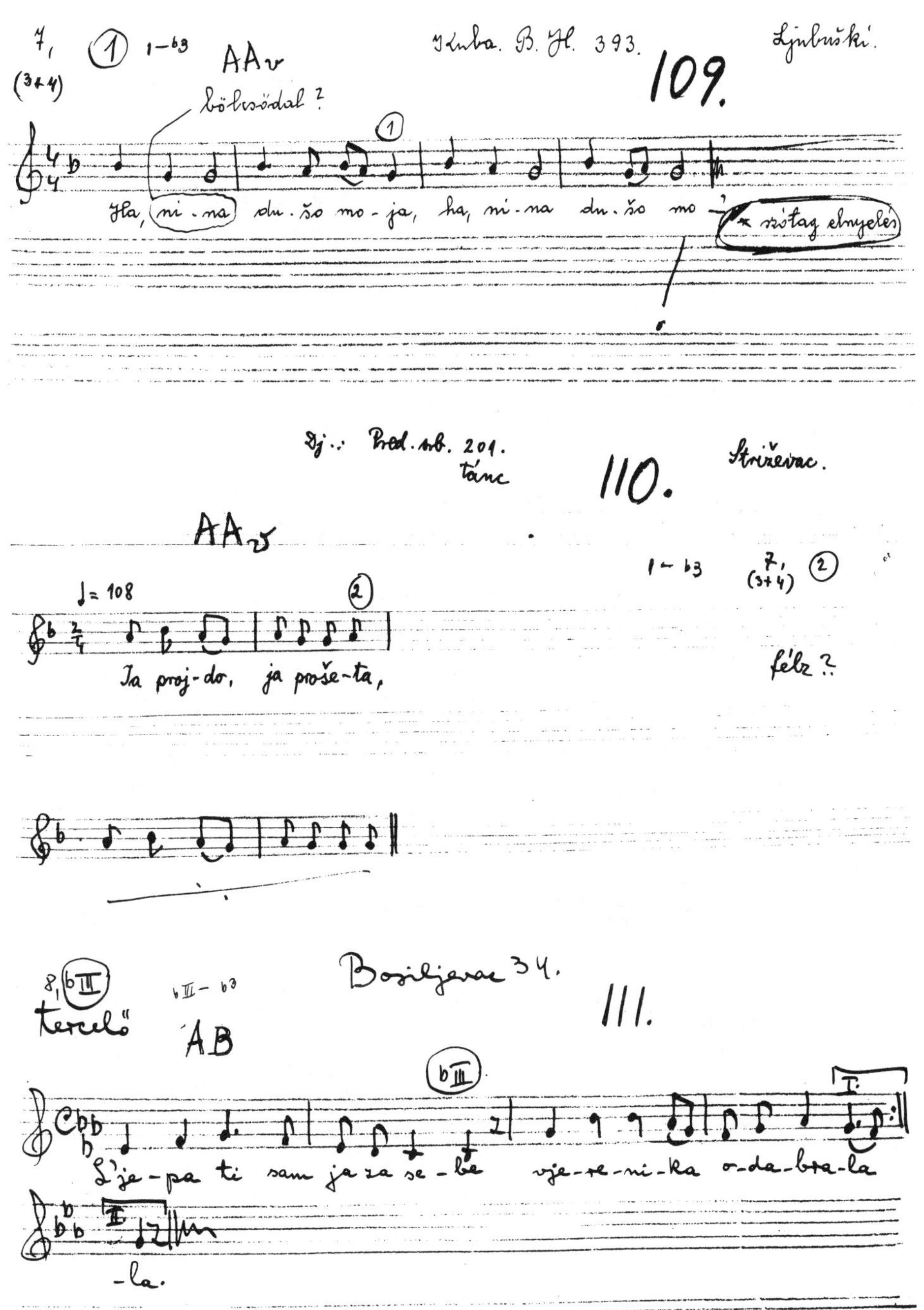
109.
Ljubuški.
AAv
bölcsődal ?
Ha, ni - na du - šo mo - ja, ha, ni - na du - šo mo -
szótag elnyelés
110.
Striževac.
táncz
AA
♩= 108
Ja proj - do, ja proše - ta,
félz ?
111.
Bosiljevac 34.
tercelő
AB
L'je - pa ti sam ja za se - be vje - re - ni - ka o - da - bra - la
- la.

8, IV
I – b3
Kuhač II. 489.
112.
Iz Djakovštine.
tercelő.
AB
IV
Zo – ra zo – ri, ro-sa pa-da, medj' go-ra-mi pa – – su sta-da.
Var. Kuba:
Iz kamena vatra sieva
A na konju diva pjeva
8, VI
III – 3
Kuhač I. 185.
113.
Iz Senja.
fél? AB
hol' van ez?
VII
Gdje si, mi-la, ti se ka-ži! te-be srd-ce mo-je tra-ži,
gdje si, mi-la, ti se ka-ži te-be srd-ce mo-je tra-ži.
n. 6.
ritmus!!
Mi? :
Párosat nem találom.
8, VII
tercelő fél?
bVI – 4
Kuhač I. 186.
114.
Iz M. Bistrica.
♩= 66.
VII
Oj Ja-ni-ce, mi-la mo-ja! ne maš mi-ra nit po-ko-ja.

115a.
AA
J=132
Ovde mi su bani dvori, po-moz' Boga domaćinće.
AB
Kuba, BH. 1001
Allegro moderato.
O, ja-vore, zelen bore, oj, o ja-vo-re, zelen bore, oj!
AB
Kuba. BH. 1001
116. Environ de Sarajevo.
Vivo
osta.

Kuba B.H. 807.
Allegro moderato.
117a. Bugojno (Kolo)
Ko j' za Ko-lo, hajd u ko-lo ! Ko j' za ko-lo hajd u ko-lo.
Skeleton
Kuba B.H. 789.
117b. Kljuc (Kolo)
Allegro moderato.
Igra-la se Ka-te-ri-na.
igra-la se Ka-te-ri-na.
Kuba B.H. 484
118. Jeleč. (Kolo)
Allegro
Tanke rasle konoplji-ce, tanke rasle konoplji-ce.

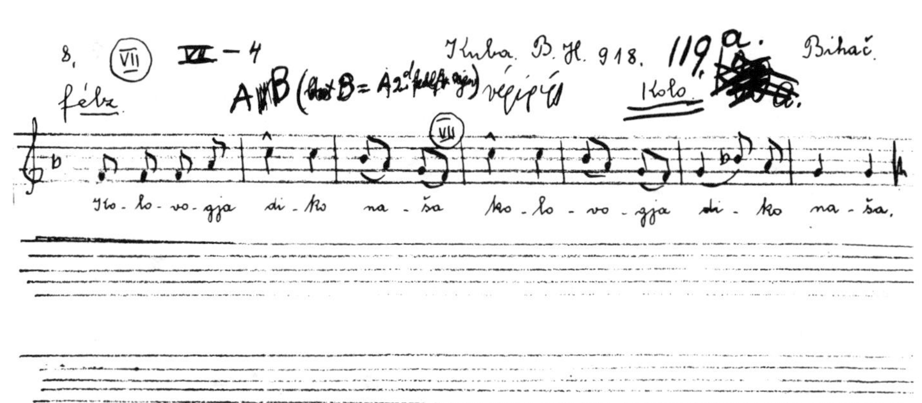
8, VII
Kuba. B. H. 918.
119a.
Bihać.
félz.
Kolo.
Ko-lo-vo-gja di-ko na-ša ko-lo-vo-gja di-ko na-ša.

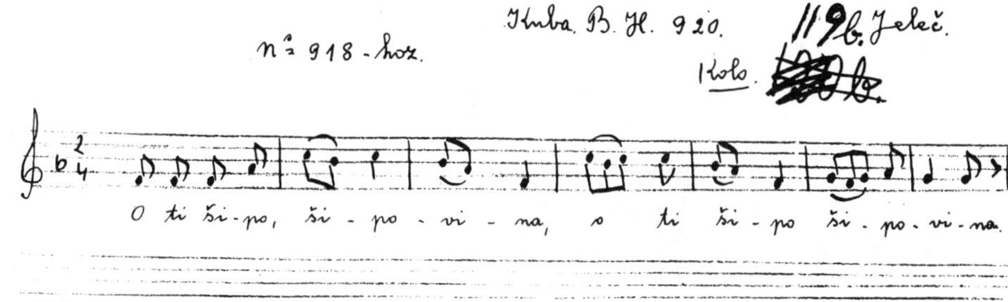
Kuba. B. H. 920.
119b. Jeleč.
n° 918-hoz.
Kolo.
O ti ši-po, ši-po-vi-na, o ti ši-po ši-po-vi-na.

8, VII
Kuba. B. H. 921.
119c. Jeleč
félz.
Si-tan ka-men do ka-me-na, si-tan ka-men do ka-me-na.

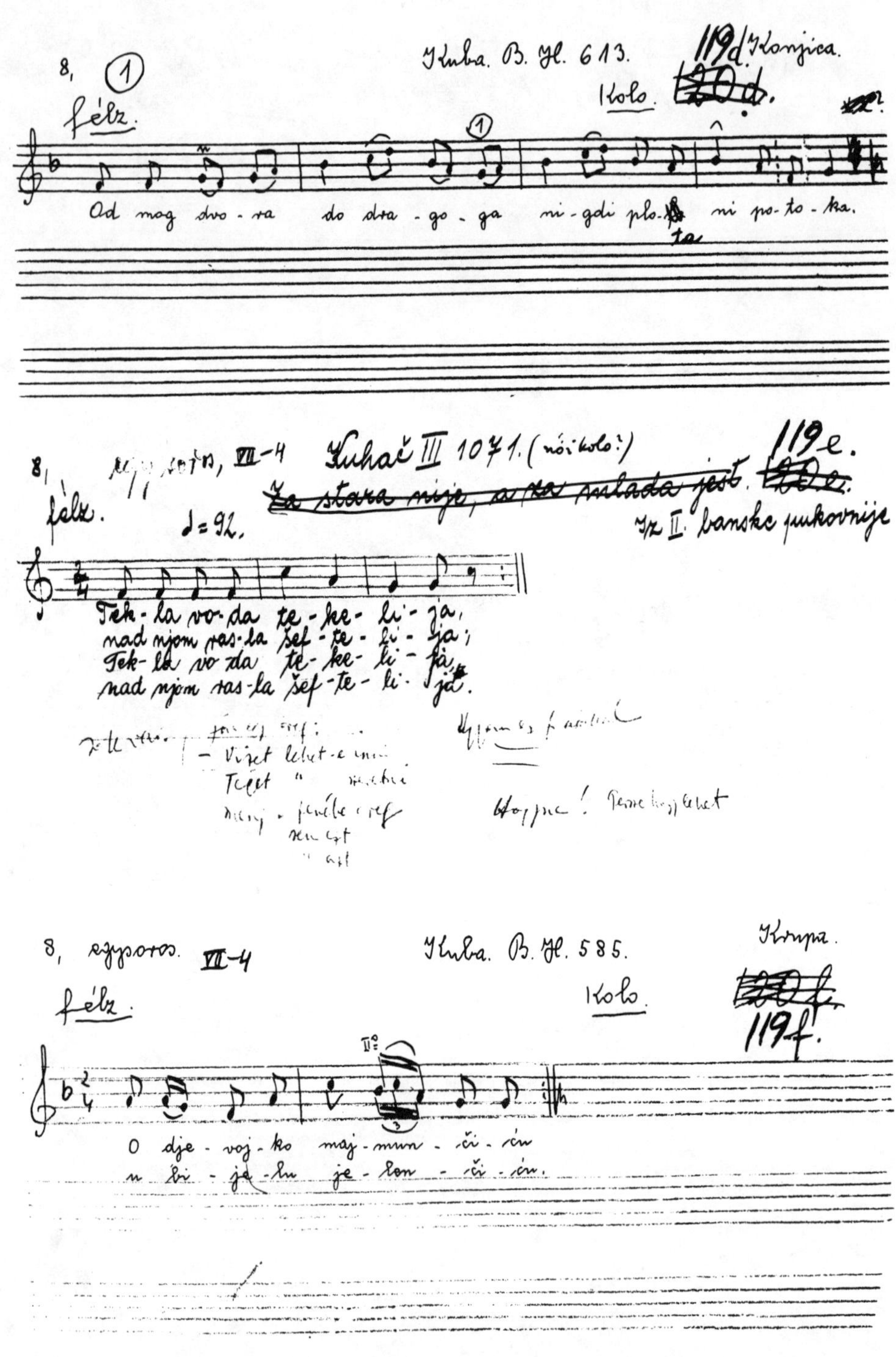
8, (1)
Kuba. B. H. 613.
119d. Konjica.
Kolo.
félz.
Od mog dvo - ra do dra - go - ga ni - gdi plo - ta ni po - to - ka.
8,
Kuhač III 1071. (női kolo?)
119e.
Za stara nije, a za mlada jest.
Iz II. banske pukovnije
félz.
♩= 92.
Tek - la vo - da te - ke - li - ja,
nad njom ras - la šef - te - li - ja;
Tek - la vo - da te - ke - li - ja,
nad njom ras - la šef - te - li - ja.
8, egysoros. VII-4
Kuba. B. H. 585.
Krupa.
Kolo.
félz.
119f.
O dje - voj - ko maj - mun - či - ću
u bi - ja - lu je - len - či - ću.

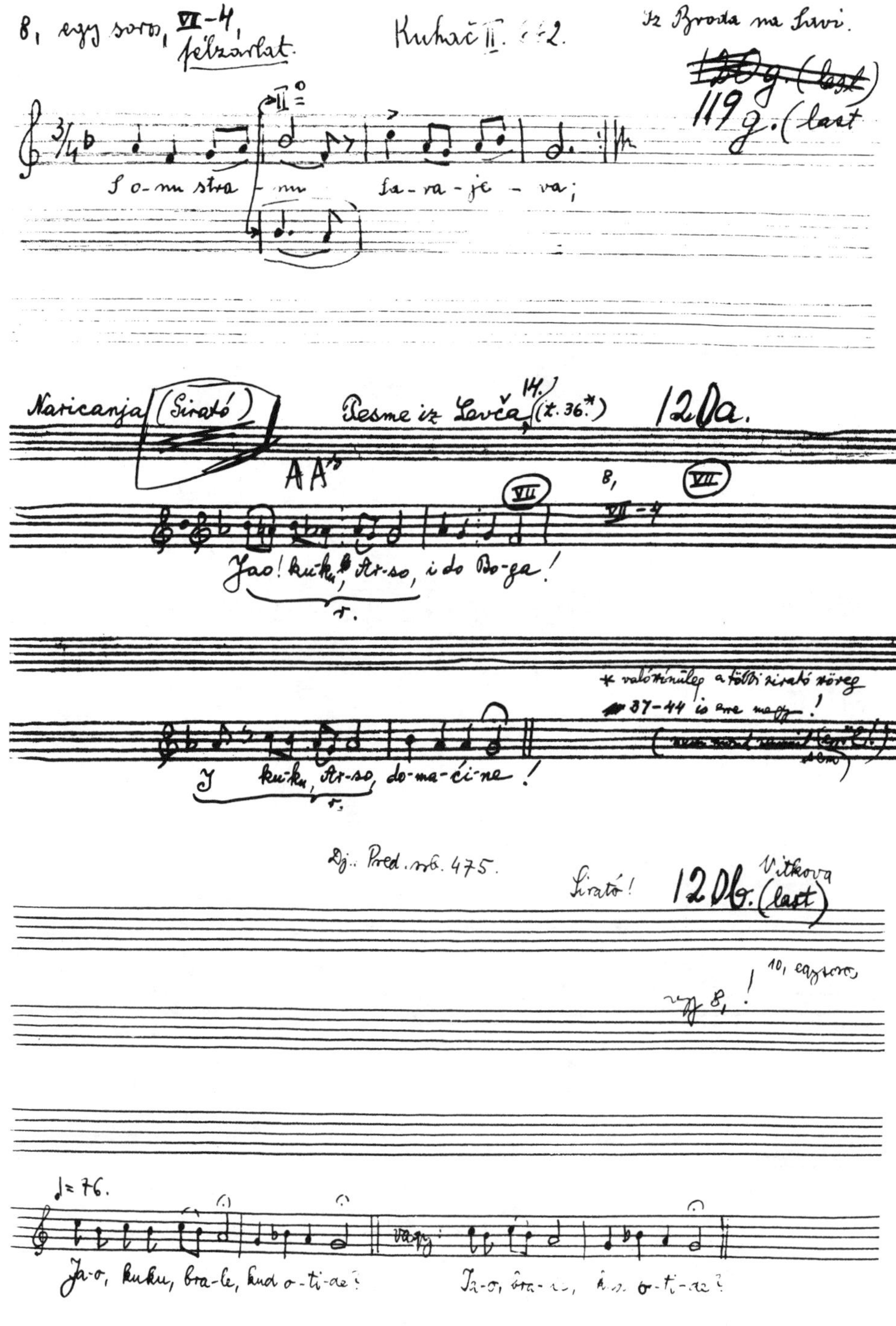
8, egy soros, VI-4, félzárlat.
Kuhač II.
Iz Broda na Savi.
119 g. (last
So-mu stra-nu Sa-ra-je-va;
Naricanja (Sirató)
Pesme iz Levča 14. (t. 36.*)
120a.
AA5
VII
8,
VII-4
Jao! kuku, Ar-so, i do Bo-ga!
* valószínűleg a többi sirató szöveg 37-44 is erre megy!
I kuku, Ar-so, do-ma-ći-ne!
Dj. Pred. sb. 475.
Sirató!
120b. Vitkova (last)
10, egysoros
vagy 8, !
♩= 76.
Ja-o, kuku, bra-te, kud o-ti-de?
vagy:

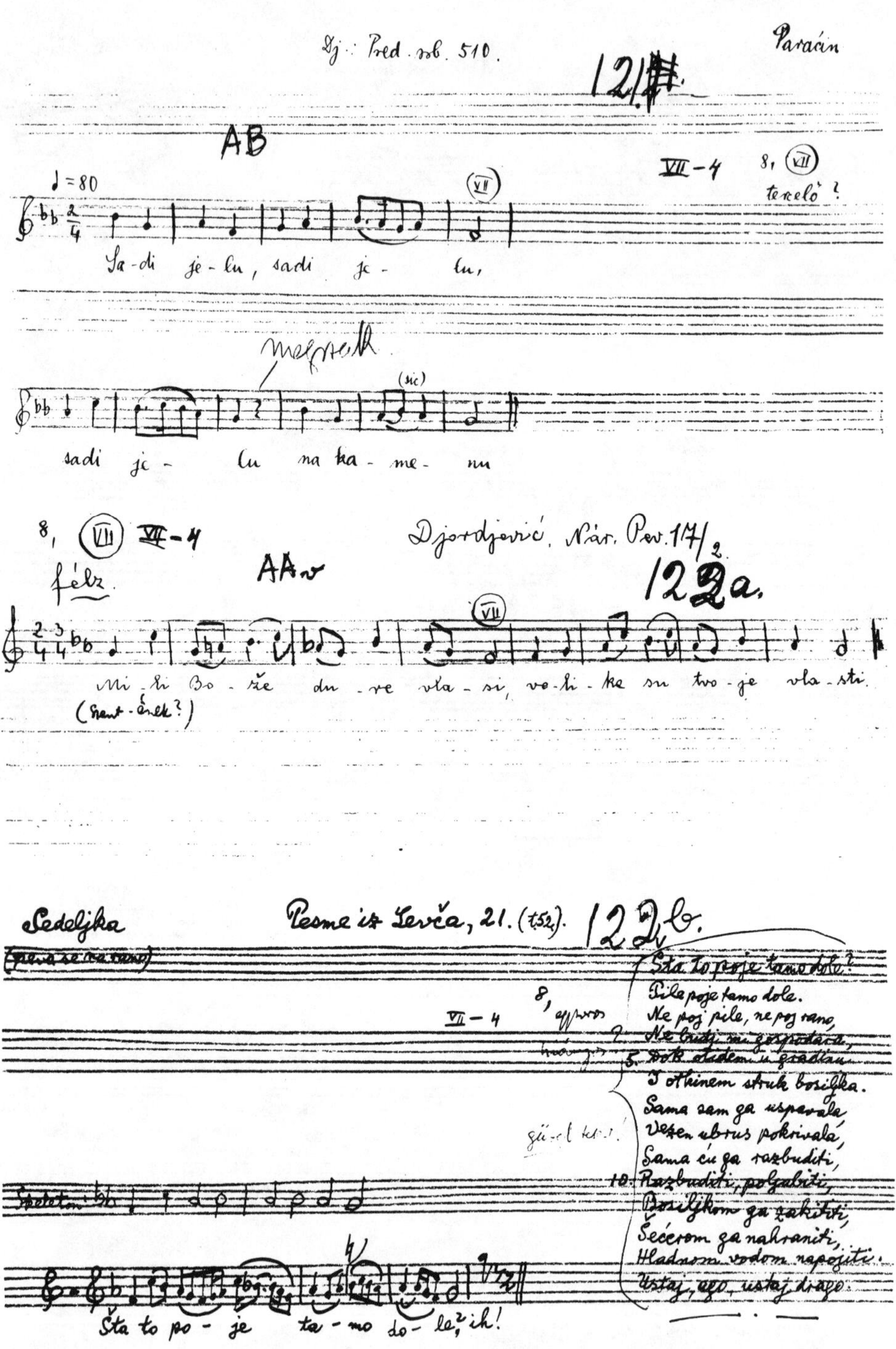
Dj.: Pred. sb. 510.
Paraćin
121.
AB
VII – 4
8, (VII)
♩ = 80
Sa-di je-lu, sadi je- lu,
(sic)
sadi je- lu na ka- me- nu
8, (VII) VII – 4
Djordjević, Nár. Pev. 17/2.
122a.
AAv
félz.
Mi-li Bo-že du-re vla-si, ve-li-ke su tvo-je vla-sti.
Sedeljka
Pesme iz Levča, 21. (t.52).
122b.
VII – 4
Šta to poje tamo dole?
Pile poje tamo dole.
Ne poj pile, ne poj rano,
Ne budi mi gospodara,
5. Dok otidem u gradinu
I otkinem struk bosiljka.
Sama sam ga uspavala,
Vezen ubrus pokrivala,
Sama ću ga razbuditi,
10. Razbuditi, poljubiti,
Bosiljkom ga zakititi,
Šećerom ga nahraniti,
Hladnom vodom napojiti.
Ustaj, ago, ustaj drago.
Šta to po- je ta- mo do- le, ih!

Sedeljka
Pesme iz Levča, 47. (t. 122.)
129c.
Ko- je li je, ko- -je li — je, ih!
8, VII VII-4
félz.
Kuhač III. 1004.
12a.
Iz Hercegovine.
Noć, tamna noć, ♩=50.
Paun (kolo)
Pa- un pa-se, tra-va ra-ste. Moj pa-u- ne — ! siv so-ko-le.
Cf. No 1561 d. e. (Noć, tamna noć)
(8) 8, VII VII-5
Kuba. B. H. 366.
Trnovo.
12b.
félz.
Pa - un pa - se tra - va ra - ste pa - u - ne moj pa - u-
- ne moj!

előbbihez
Játék
Kuhač III. 1007.
Iz Travnika u Bosni.
8, VII
felv.
♩= 42.
Pa-un pa-se, tra-va ra-ste, pa-u-ne moj! pa-u-ne moj! pa-u-ne moj!
Dj.: Pred. sb. 421.
Mrzenica
fonó
123d.
VII-63
8, VII
felv.
♩=96
Kog ćete nam sada da-ti,
daj- te nam daj,
daj- te nam daj!
előbbihez.
Játék
8, 2
felv.
VI-4
Kuhač III. 1006.
Iz Rišna.
Pripjev.
Pa-un trep-ti, da po-le-ti. Pa-u-ne moj! pa-u-ne moj!

Játék
Kuhač III 1005.
123 f.
8, (b3) félz.
♪ = 126.
Iz Risna. (Boka)
Pa-un le-ti da po-le-ti, o pa-u-ne moj, o
pa-u-ne moj!
Dj.: Pred. sb. 96.
Pirot
123 g.
VII-4, 8, 7, 7, (2) (1)
♪ = 116
Paun nase, tra-va ra-ste,
félz.
paun, paun, paun moj,
paun, paun, paun moj!
Dj.: Pred. sb. 187. Keresztvivő
Suračevo
123 h.
♩ = 100
AA 1-2
(10)
8, 10, (1)
Kr-sto-no-še krsto-no-še,
krsto-no-še krsti pone-so-še.

Dj.: Pred. sb. 479. Vitkov..

Dodola **123 i.**

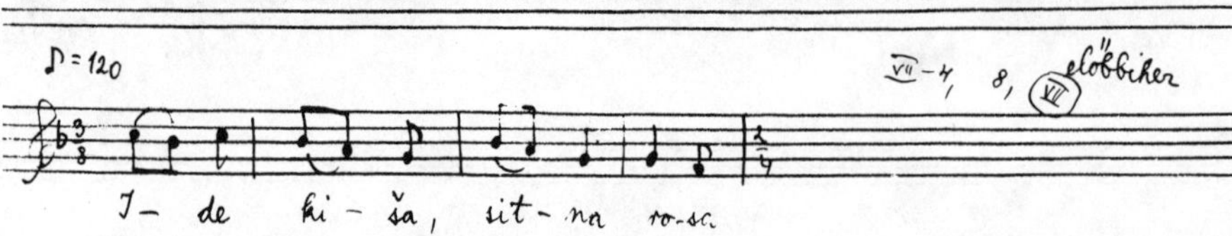

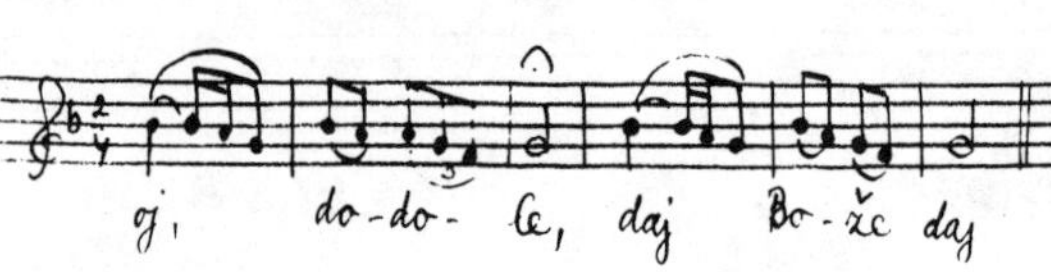

Dj.: Pred. sb. 384. Mozenica.

Uskršnja (?) **123 j.**

1–4 (8) 8, 6, ②

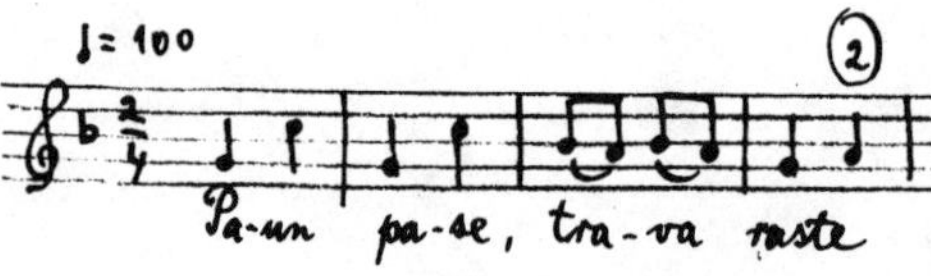

ritm.

Dj.: Pred. sb. 35.

Tibužde

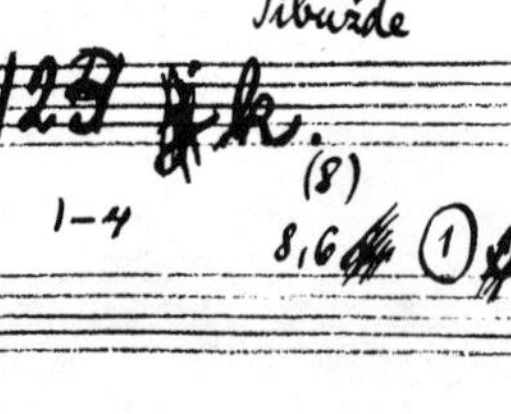

1–4

Dj.: Pred. sob. 173.
keresztvivő
ez is az a prim. fajta
Kalna.
(8)
8, 9. VII
Kr-sti nosim, Bo-ga molim:
Go-spo-di, Go-spodi pomi-luj!
Dj.: Pred. sob. 153.
keresztvivő
Djuštica
(8)
8, 9, 1
Kristi nosim kr-sto-no-ša
Go-spodi, Gospodi pomiluj!
Dj.: Pred. sob. 258.
Mečji Do
keresztvivő
(8)
8, 9, VII
Kr-sto-no-še, kr-sti no-se,
féle.
Go-spodi, Gospodi pomi-luj.

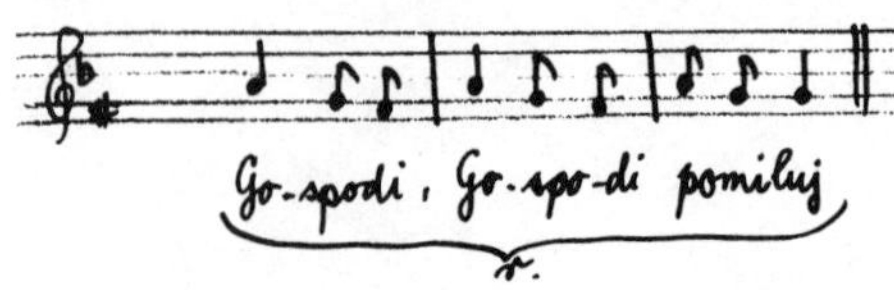

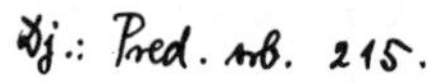

Strelac

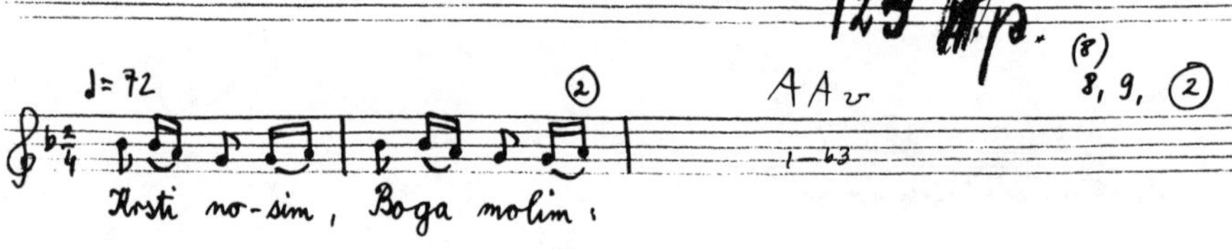

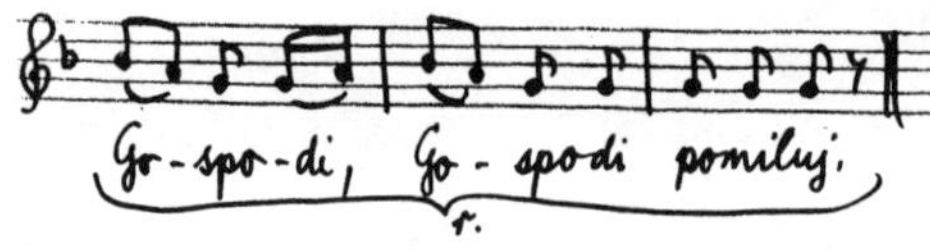

Dj.: Pred. sb. 164.

Topli Do.

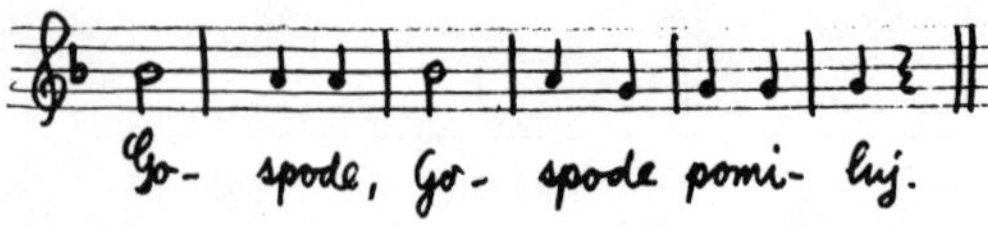

Dj.: Pred. srb. 127.
Keresztjáró napkor
Velika Lukanja
(8)
♩=112
VII
VII – b3
8, 9, VII
AB
Kri-sti nosimo, Bo-ga molimo:
félz.
Go- spode, Go- spode pomi- luj.
Dj.: Pred. srb. 288.
2. sor ritm.
Keresztvivő
Lalinac
VII – b2
(8)
♪=152
VII
8, 6, VII
AB
Oj! Kr-stono-še kr-sti nose,
félz.
Go- spodi pomi- luj!
Dj.: Pred. srb. 478.
2. sor ritm.
Keresztvivő
Vitkova
(8)
♪=120
VII
VII – 4
8, 6, VII
AB
Kr- sto- no- še kr- ste no- se,
félz
Go- spo- di po- mi- luj,

Obredno
Pesme iz Levča, 72.
8, 6,
1 – 5
AB
Kr-sto-no-še Bo-ga mo-le:
Go- -spo- -de po-mi-luj!
Dj.: Pred. srb. 143.
pripev?
Temska
♩= 72
VII – 2, 8, 6,
AB
138-hoz
Lit-no o- do, belo-po – lo,
De – so – le Zu-ji-na.
Dj.: Pred. srb. 23.
Keresztjáró napi?
Tibužde.
♩ = 84
1 – 4
AB
Kri-sti nosim, Bo-ga mo-lim,
Go- spo-de po- mi- luj,
Go - spo- de po- mi- luj,
Go- spo- de za- ra- duj.

Dj.: Pred. srb. 138.
Keresztvivő ?
Temska
ritm.
8,6,6,
félz.
ABC
Kri-sti no-sim, Bo-ga molim,
Go- spo-de, Go- spo-de
po-mi-luj, pomi-luj!
Megint Juž. Srb. 399. Donja Gušterica (Na Kosovu)
mikor a keresztet viszik (?! valószínűleg buzaszentelő)
félz.
ABBv
Hr-sto-no-še Bo-ga mo-le, Go-spo-de po-mi-luj,
Go-spo-de po-mi-luj.
ref.
Dj.: Pred. srb. 233.
Crvena Jabuka
Keresztvivő
u.a. szó gre
8,6,6, > 8,7,6,
Kr-sto-noša Bo-ga moli:
AAvAv
félz.
Go-spodi po-mi luj ni,
Go-spodi po-mi luj.

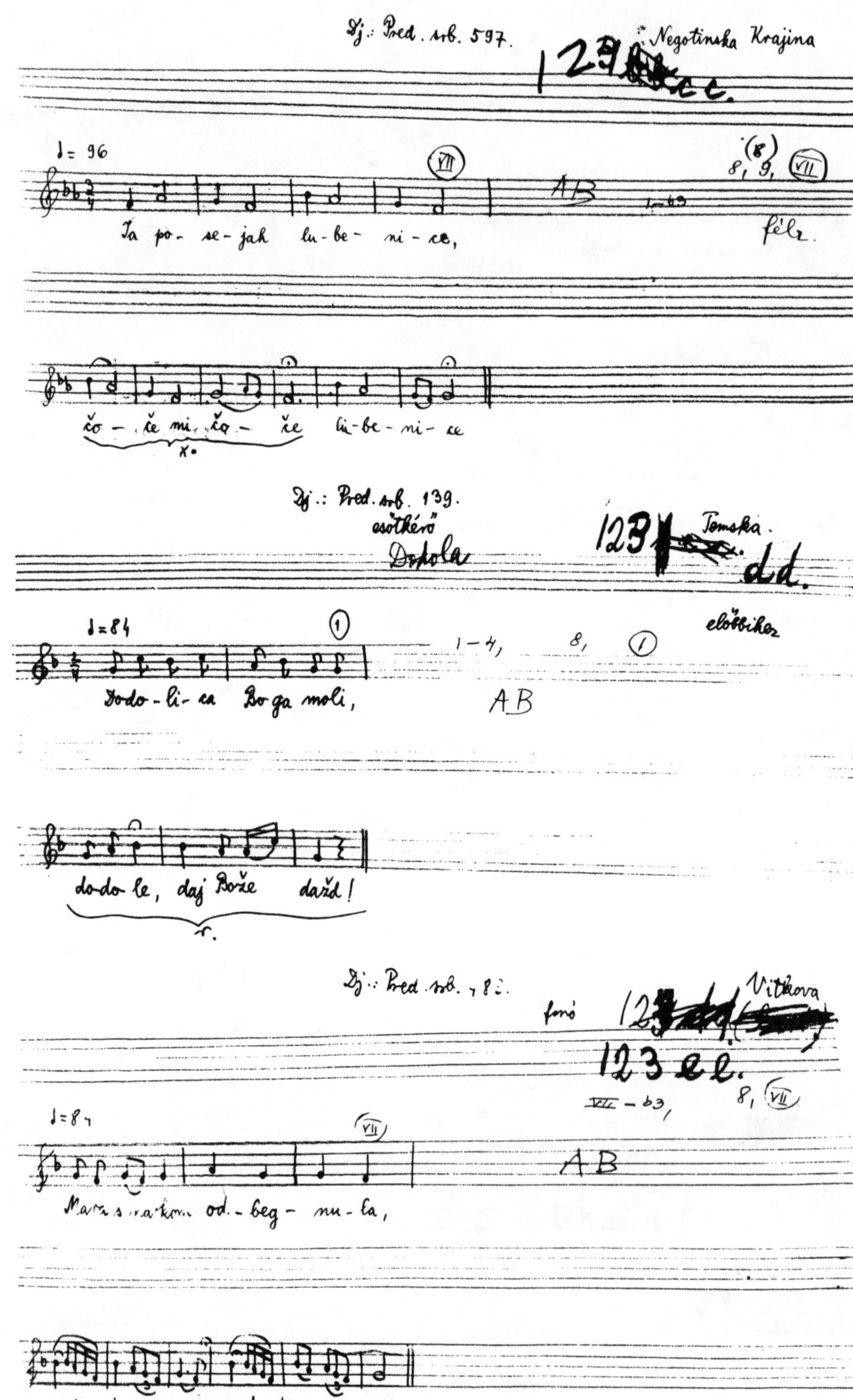

Dj.: Pred. srb. 597.
Negotinska Krajina
123 cc.
♩= 96
8, 9, VII
félz.
Ja po- se- jah lu- be- ni- ce,
ćo- će mi ća- će li-be-ni-ce
Dj.: Pred. srb. 139.
esőthérő
Dodola
123 dd.
Temska
♩=84
1-4, 8, 1
előbbihez
Dodo-li- ca Bo ga moli,
AB
do-do le, daj Bože dažd!
Dj.: Pred. srb.
fonó
123 ee.
Vitkova
8, VII
♩=84
AB
Mara s vrakom od- beg- nu- la,

Dj.: Pred. sob. 406.
fonó
Mrzenica
123 ff.
Po-vr-ve-še rabadži-je
noć, noć tam-na noć
Dj.: Pred. sob. 356.
fonó
Kulina
123 gg.
Sun noć Nejka prese- de-la,
tamna noć, noć, tamna noć
AA 5
Kuhač 1479.
125. Iz Slavonije.
Vakok éneke (= koldusnóta)
O viš-ča-ni mi-la bra-ćo, i viš-jan-ke mi te majke!
Po-da-ruj-te, ob-radujte porad Boga je-di-no-ga,
i rad ča-sa u-mr-lo-ga; i ta-ko vam gospod d'o, i ve-li-ka slava Božja,
i ve-li-ko krsno i - - - - me.
Az elő és utójátékot guslá-n játszotta az énekes. Kuh. egy fokkal feljebb közli az egészet.
Alamizsna kérés

1479.

8, VII VII-5
AB
Kuba. B. H. 846.
Gacko.
125a.
félz.
Kad Mo-ri-će po-hva-ta-še ej b'je-le ru-ke
po-ve-za-še.
8, VII
VII-4
Kuba. B. H. 844.
Jeleč (Svatovska)
Lakodalmas
125b.
AA
Blago sun-cu i mjese-cu aman, a-man i mjesecu!

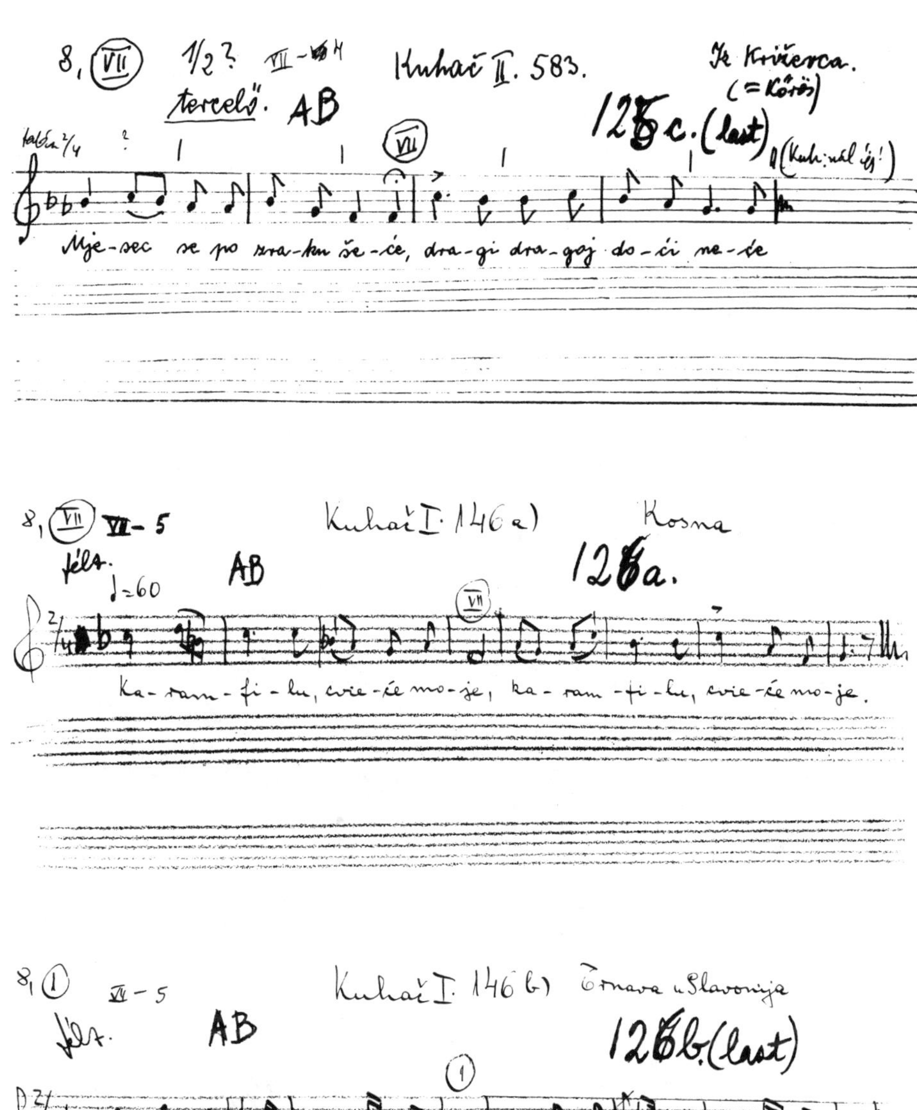

8, (VII) 1/2? VII-4
Kuhač II. 583.
Ik Križevca.
(= Kőrös)
tercelő. AB
12 c. (last)
(Kuh.-nál így!)
Mje-sec se po sra-ku še-će, dra-gi dra-gaj do-ći ne-će
8, (VII) VII-5
Kuhač I. 146 a)
Kosna
félz.
♩=60
AB
12 a.
Ka-ram-fi-lu, cvie-će mo-je, ka-ram-fi-lu, cvie-će mo-je.
8, (1) VI-5
Kuhač I. 146 b)
Črnava u Slavoniji
félz.
AB
12 b. (last)
Ka-ram-fi-lu, cvie-će mo-je; ka-ram-fi-lu cvie-će mo-je.

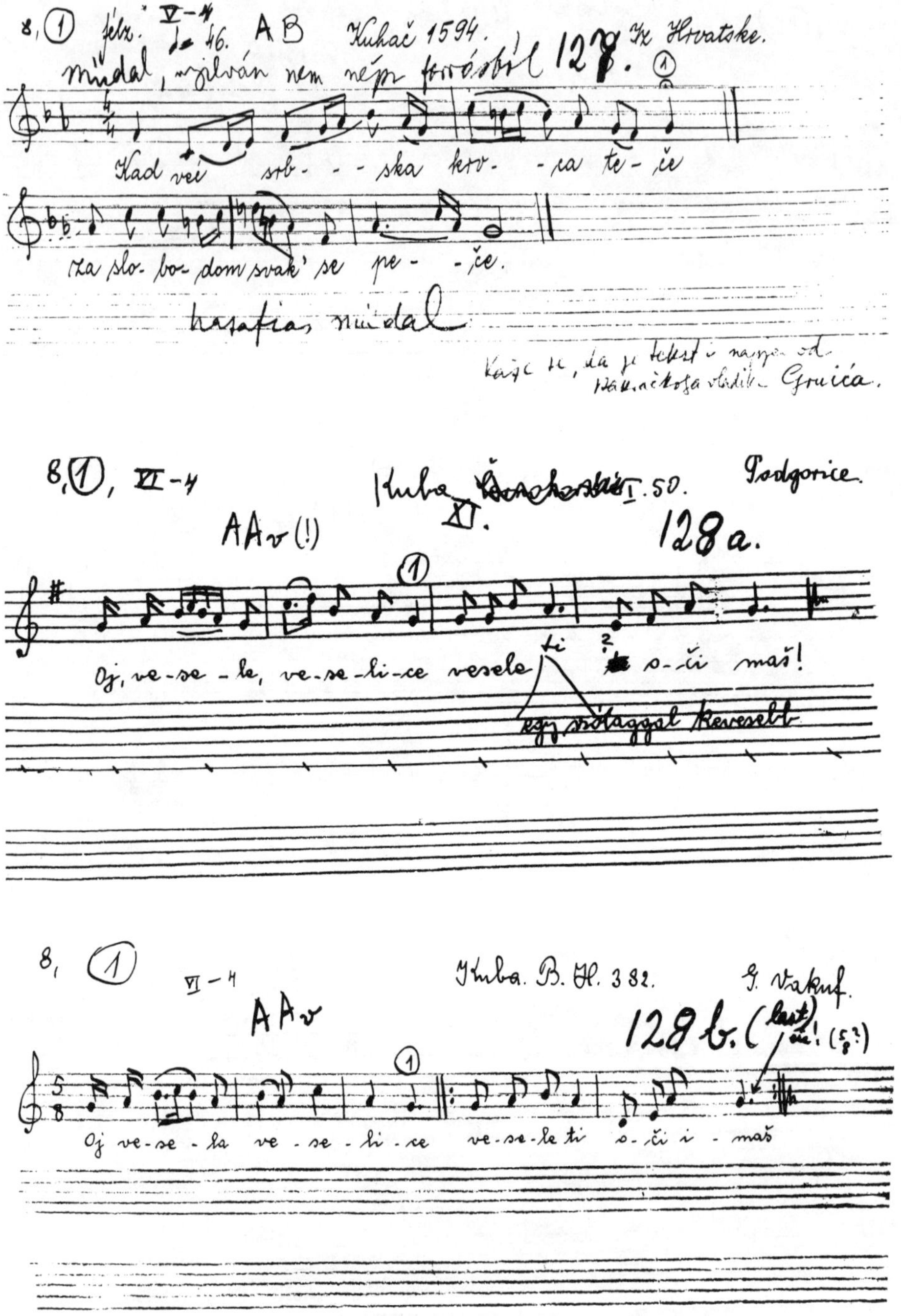
8, ① félz. V-4 ♩=46. AB Kuhač 1594. Iz Hrvatske.
müdal, nyilván nem népi forrásból 127.
Kad već srb- - -ska krv- -ca te- če
za slo- bo- dom svak' se pe- -če.
hazafias müdal
8, ①, VI-4 I. 50. Podgorice
AAv (!)
128 a.
Oj, ve-se-le, ve-se-li-ce vesele ti o-či maš!
egy szótaggal kevesebb
8, ① VI-4 Kuba. B. H. 382. G. Vakuf.
AAv
128 b.
Oj ve-se-la ve-se-li-ce ve-se-le ti o-či i-maš

Dj.: Pred. srb. 21.
Lázárnapi
129a.
Tibužde
№ 19-hez
♩ = 88
Igraj, ripaj naš la- zare,
megnakítás
i-graj, ri- paj naš la- za-re.
Dj.: Pred. srb. 185.
Lázárnaphor
129b.
Suračevo.
♩ = 96
Ov – de li su beli dvo- ri?
Tu- va, tu-va ta de ka- u.
Dj.: Pred. srb. 329.
Na ranilu (?)
129c.
Davidovci
♩ = 84
E, dig' se, majko, će-ru spre-maj,
megnakítás
dig' se, majko, će-ru spremaj,

Dj.: Pred. srb. 330.

Lakodalmas **129d.** Davidovci

AA√

♪ = 152

1 – b3, 10, ① előbbihez

Oj, mili kume, mi-lo-rajsko . cveće,

megfordította

mili oj, kume, milo-raj.. - cve-će

Dj.: Pred. srb. 331.

Lakodalmas **129e.** (last) Davidovci

VII – b2 előbbihez

♩ = 84

Oj, ki-će-na sov-ra redje-na

8, ① VII – b3, AB

Kuba B.H. 459 **130a.**

Klg. Allegro moderato AB Var. Parry ① Ljubinje.

Pl. 35 72 – 3

mf

Ko-nja ve-že Jo-van be-že, ko-nja veže

Jo-van be-že.

Kuba B.H. 767.
Allegro moderato.
Prozor. 130 b.
Lov lovi-o Muharem beg, ko lovi-o
Muharem beg.
Kuba. BH. 1841.
Kalinovik. Kolo
Vivo
Refrain
I-grali se vrani konji Hoj, vamo, hoj. Djevojčice, da sparamo.
Kuba B.-H. 460.
Allegro moderato
Čapljina
O, ja-blane viso-ko-ga, o jablane
vi-so-ko-ga.

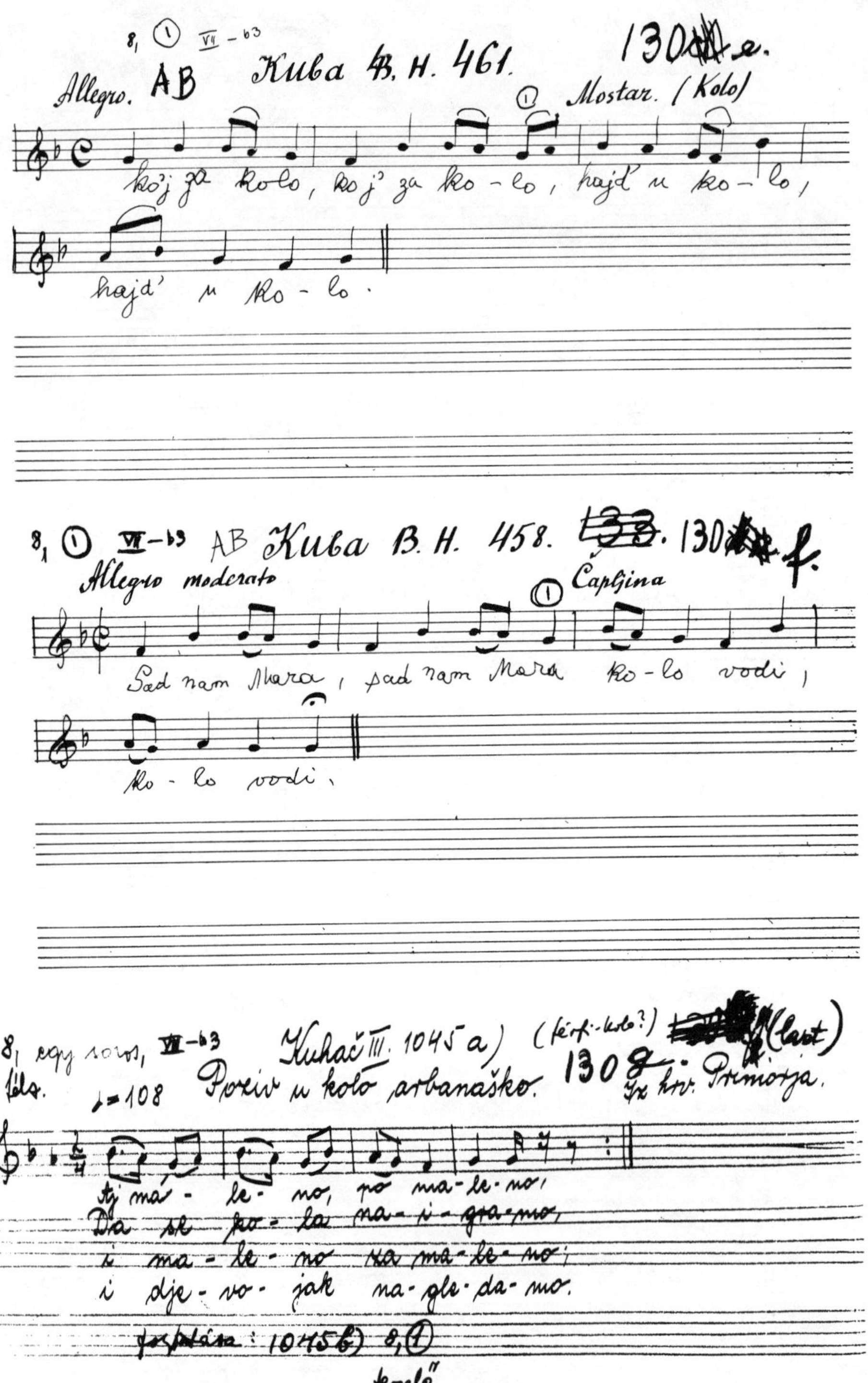

8, ① VII – 63
130
Allegro. AB Kuba B. H. 461.
① Mostar. (Kolo)
koj za kolo, koj za ko - lo, hajd' u ko - lo,
hajd' u ko - lo.
8, ① VII – 63 AB Kuba B. H. 458. 130
Allegro moderato
① Čapljina
Sad nam Mara, sad nam Mara ko - lo vodi,
ko - lo vodi.
8, egy soros, VII – 63 Kuhač III. 1045 a)
Poziv u kolo arbanaško. 130
Iz hrv. Primorja.
♪ = 108
Aj má - le - no, po ma - le - no,
Da se po - la na - i - gra - mo,
i ma - le - no za ma - le - no;
i dje - vo - jak na - gle - da - mo.
1045 b) 8, ①

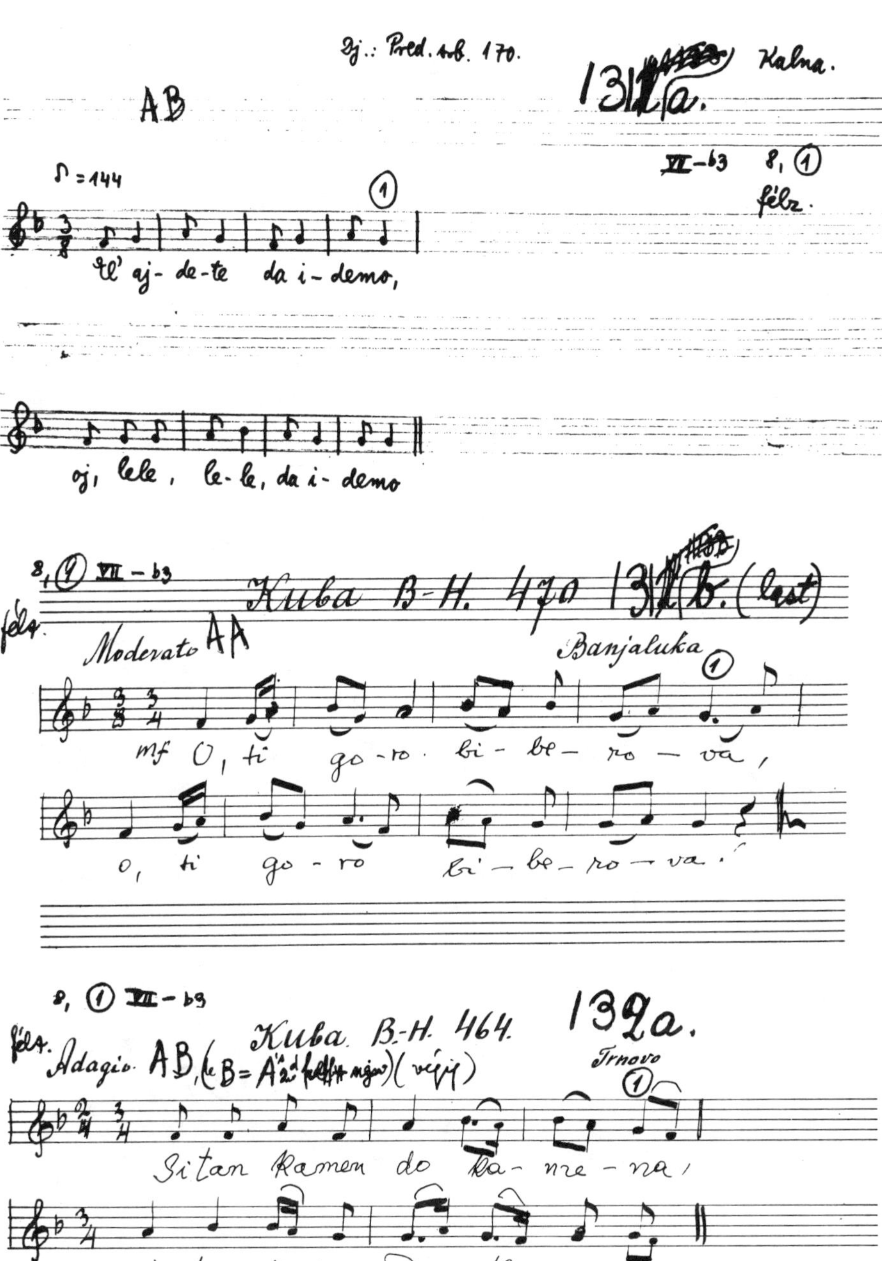

131a.
Kalna.
AB
oj, lele, le-le, da i-demo
Kuba B-H. 470
131b. (last)
Moderato AA
Banjaluka
O, ti go-ro bi-be-ro-va,
o, ti go-ro bi-be-ro-va.
Kuba B-H. 464.
132a.
Adagio. AB
Trnovo
Sitan kamen do ka-me-na,
si-tan kamen do ka-me-na.

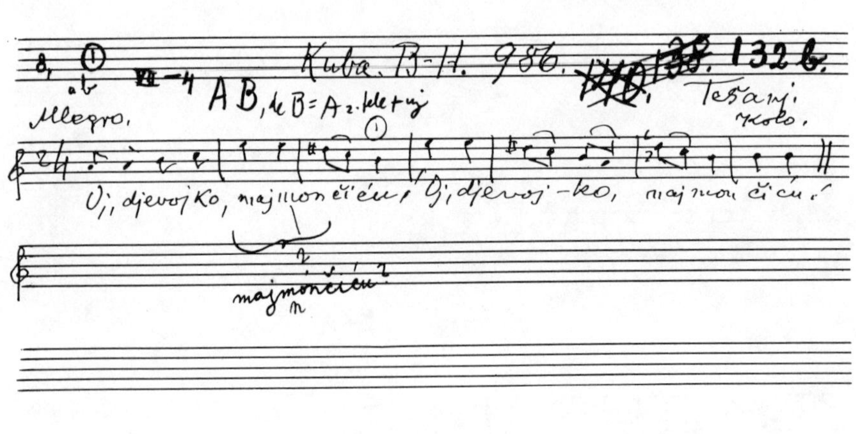
Kuba. B-H. 986.
132 b.
Allegro.
Tešanj kolo.

Kuba B.H. 465
132 c.
Andante
Kalinovik.
Si_tan kamen do ka_me-na,
si_tan kamen do ka_me_na.

132 d.
Kuba B.H. 455
Allegro molto.
Gacko
mf Daj, da jednom za-pje-va-mo, daj, da
jed-nom za-pje-vamo!

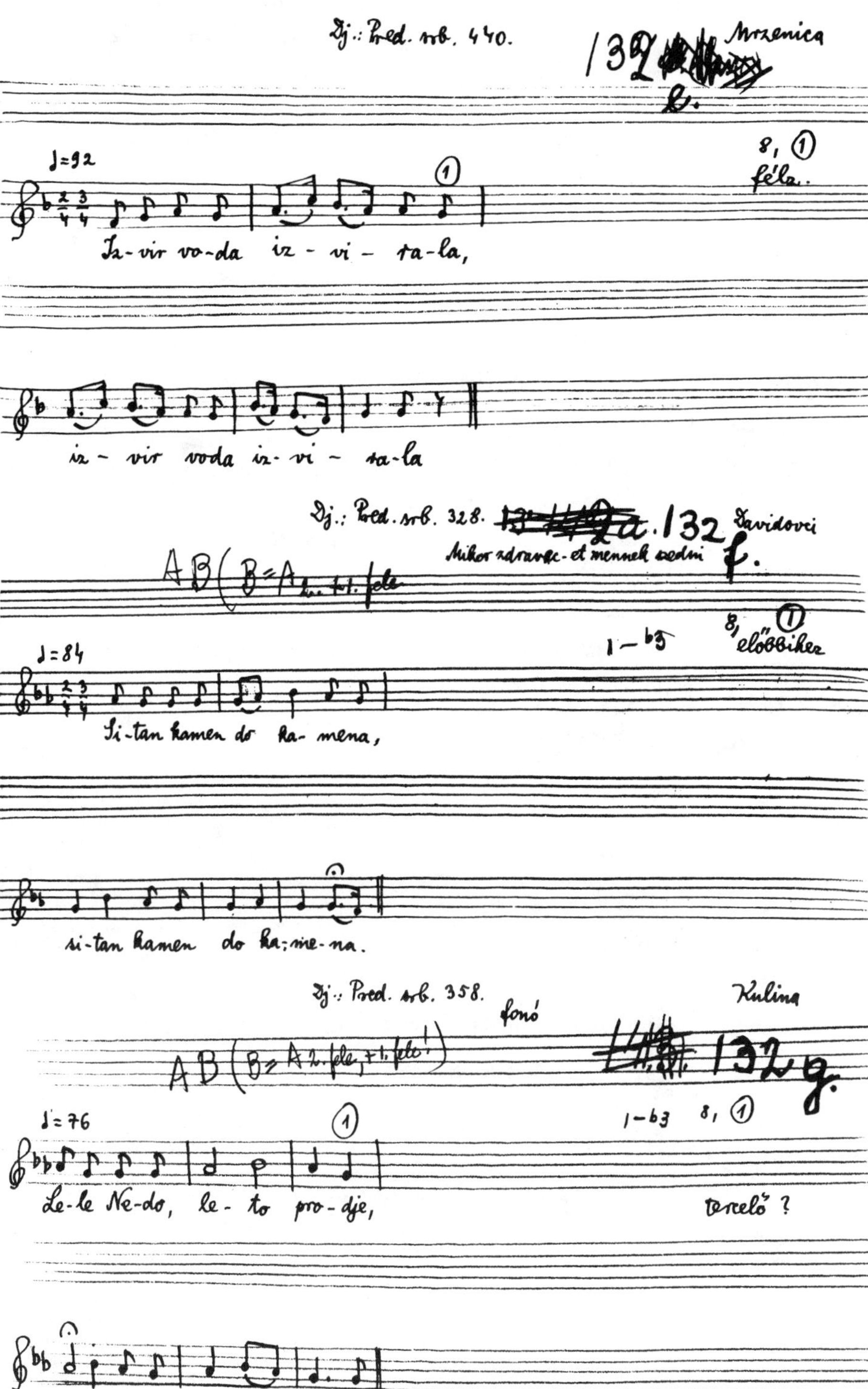

Dj.: Pred. srb. 440.
132 e.
Mrzenica
♩=92
8, (1) féla.
Iz-vir vo-da iz-vi-ta-la,
iz-vir voda iz-vi-ta-la
Dj.: Pred. srb. 328.
a. 132 f.
Davidovci
Mikor zdravec-et mennek szedni
AB (B=A
♩=84
1–b3
8, (1) előbbihez
Si-tan kamen do ka-mena,
si-tan kamen do ka-me-na.
Dj.: Pred. srb. 358.
fonó
Kulina
AB (B=A 2. fele, +1. fele!)
132 g.
♩=76
1–b3 8, (1)
Le-le Ne-do, le-to pro-dje,
terelő?
le-le, Nedo, le-to prodje

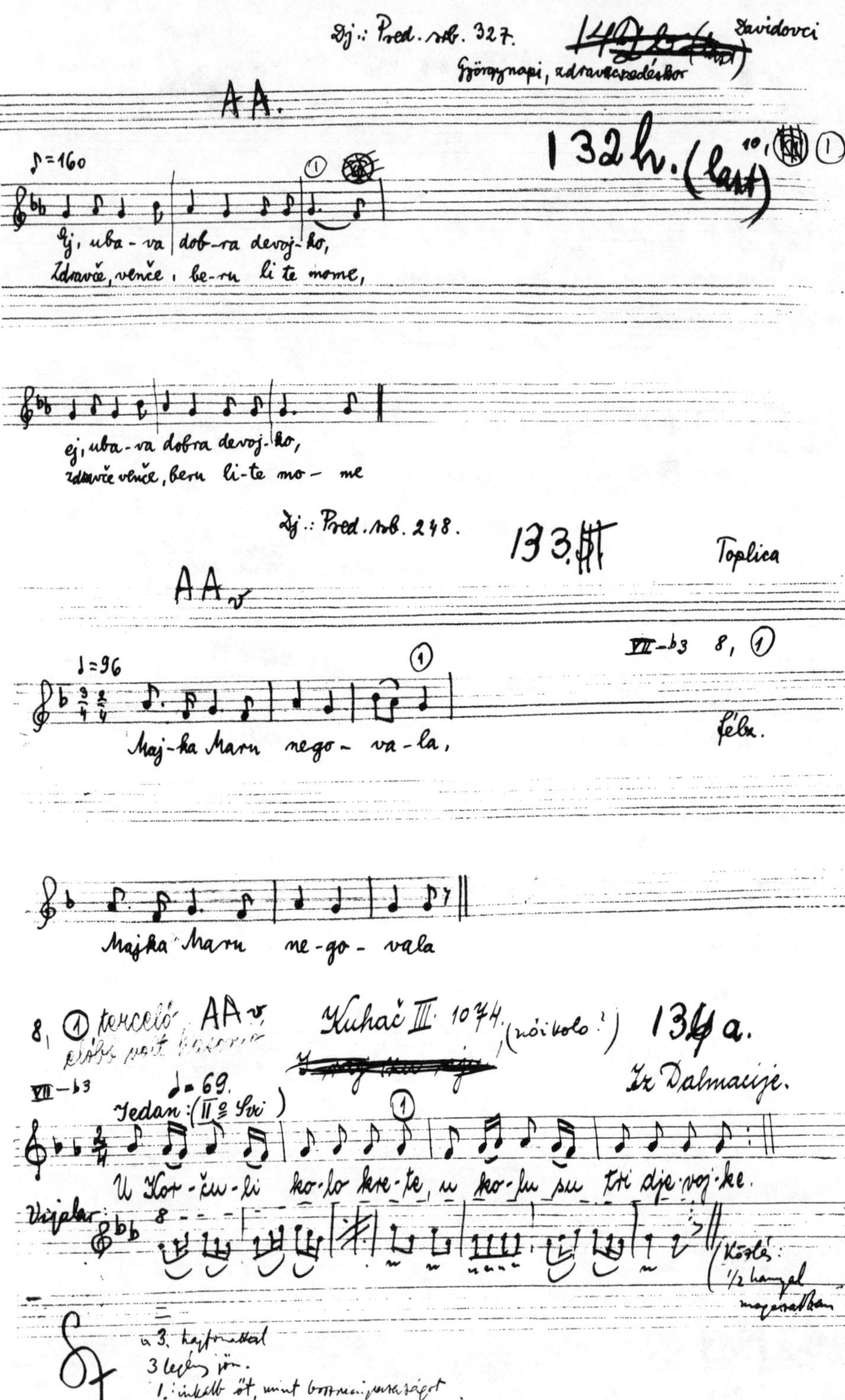

Dj.: Pred. sb. 327.
Davidovci
Györgynapi, zdravecszedéskor
AA.
132 h. (lant)
♪=160
Ej, uba-va dob-ra devoj-ko,
Zdravče, venče, be-ru li te mome,
ej, uba-va dobra devoj-ko,
zdravče venče, beru li-te mo- me
Dj.: Pred. sb. 248.
133.
Toplica
AA
VII-b3 8, ①
♩=96
Maj-ka Maru nego- va-la,
félx.
Majka Maru ne-go- vala
8, ① tercelő
Kuhač III. 1074. (női kolo?)
Iz Dalmacije.
VII-b3
♩=69.
Jedan: (II ≗ Svi)
U Kot-ču-li ko-lo kre-te, u ko-lu su tri dje-voj-ke.
Közlés: 1/2 hanggal magasabban.
3 legény jön.
3.: " " , mint az örök üdvösségét.

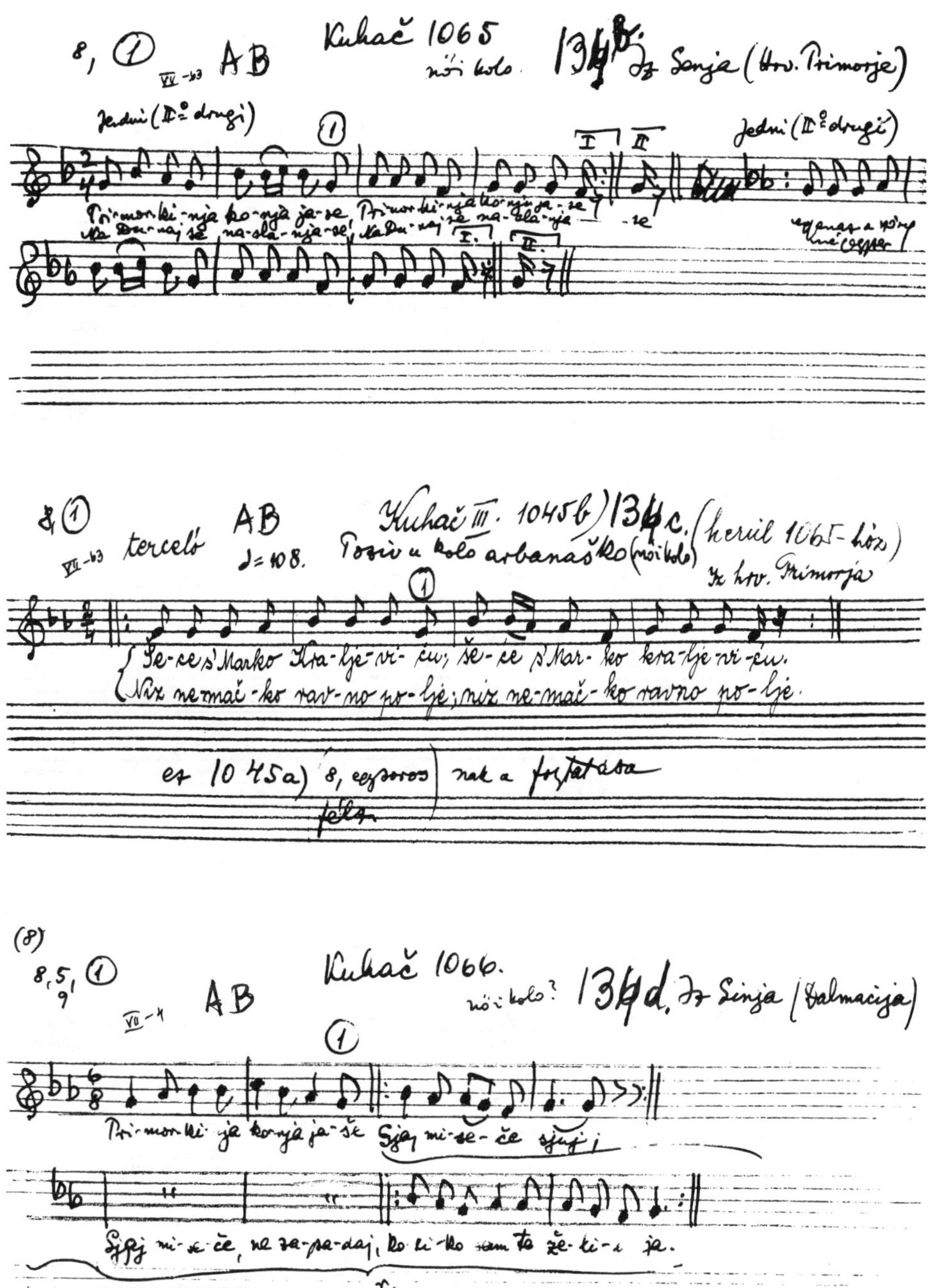
AB
Kuhač 1065
134b. Iz Senja (Hrv. Primorje)
AB
Kuhač III. 1045b) 134c.
Še-ce s' Marko Kra-lje-vi-ću; še-ce s' Mar-ko kra-lje-vi-ću.
Niz ne-mač-ko rav-no po-lje; niz ne-mač-ko ravno po-lje.
AB
Kuhač 1066.
134d. Iz Sinja (Dalmacija)

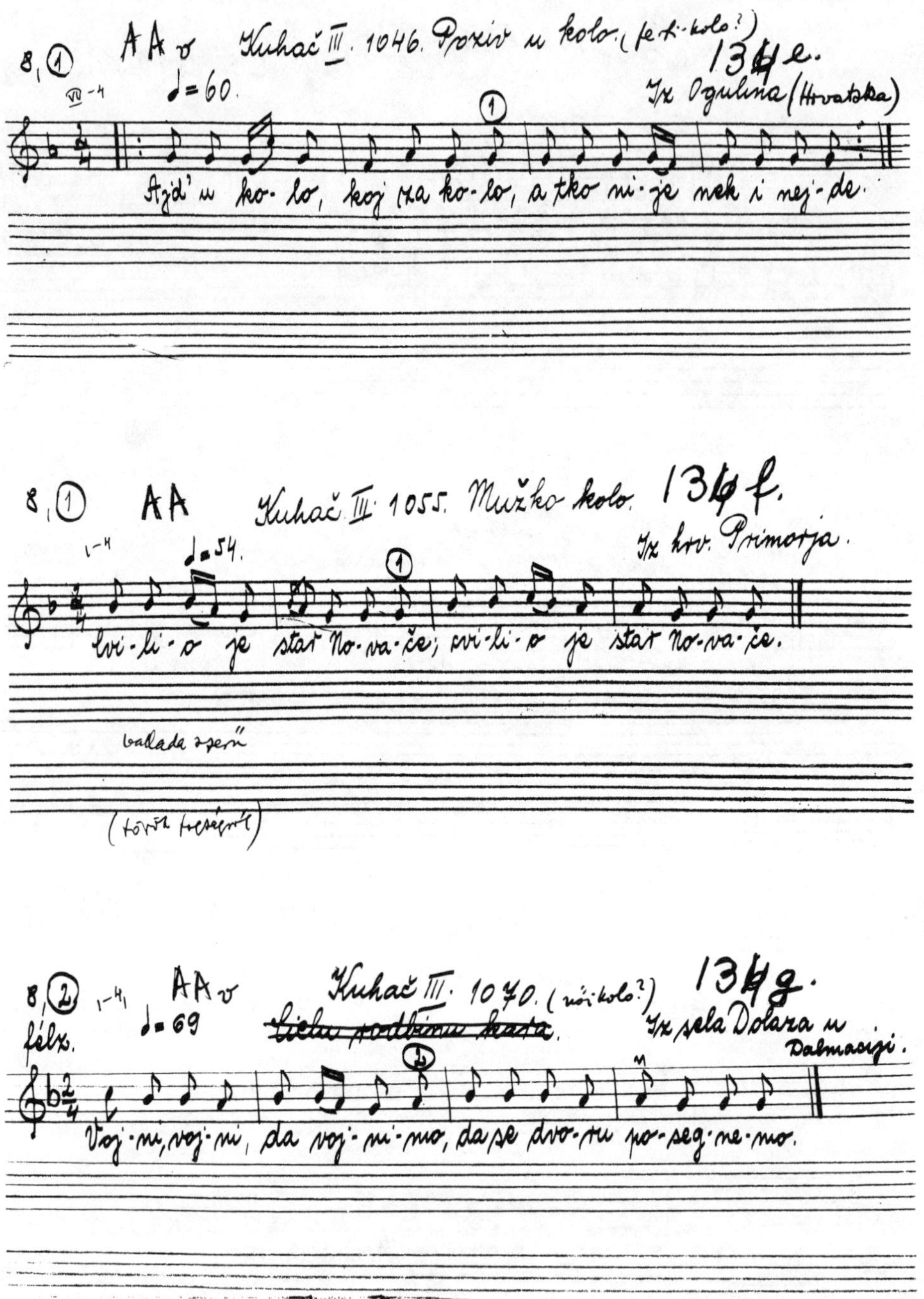
8, ① AA v Kuhač III. 1046. Poziv u kolo. (fetr.-kolo?) 134 e.
♩=60. Iz Ogulina (Hrvatska)
Ajd' u ko-lo, koj zna ko-lo, a tko ni-je nek i nej-de.
8, ① AA Kuhač III. 1055. Mužko kolo. 134 f.
♩=54. Iz hrv. Primorja.
Cvi-li-o je stat No-va-če; cvi-li-o je stat No-va-če.
balada szerű
8, ② 1-4, AA v Kuhač III. 1070. (női-kolo?) 134 g.
félz. ♩=69 Iz sela Dolaza u Dalmaciji.
Voj-ni, voj-ni, da voj-ni-mo, da se dvo-ru po-seg-ne-mo.

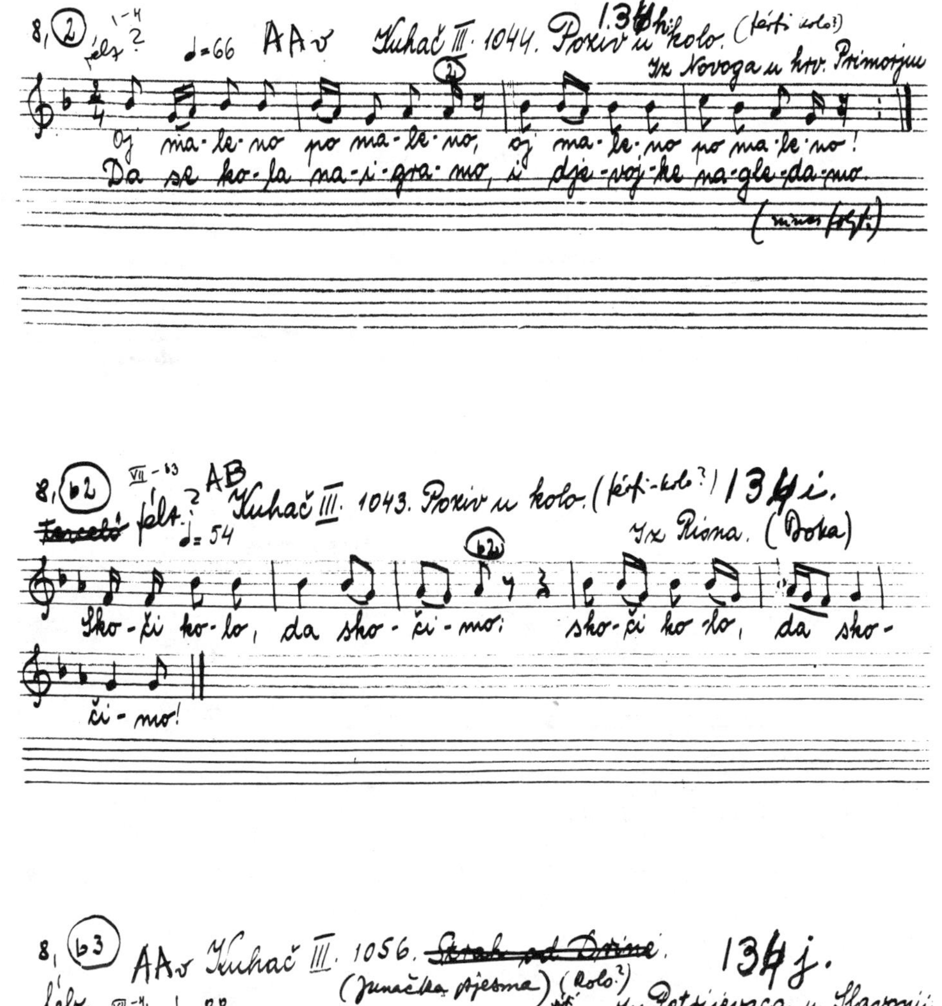

8, (b3) AAv Kuhač III. 1056. ~~Strah od Drine~~. 134j.

(Junačka pjesma) (kolo?)

félz. VII–4, ♩=88. Iz Petrijevaca u Slavoniji

Tur-ski ko-nji Bo-ga mo-le; tur-ski ko-nji Bo-ga mo-le.

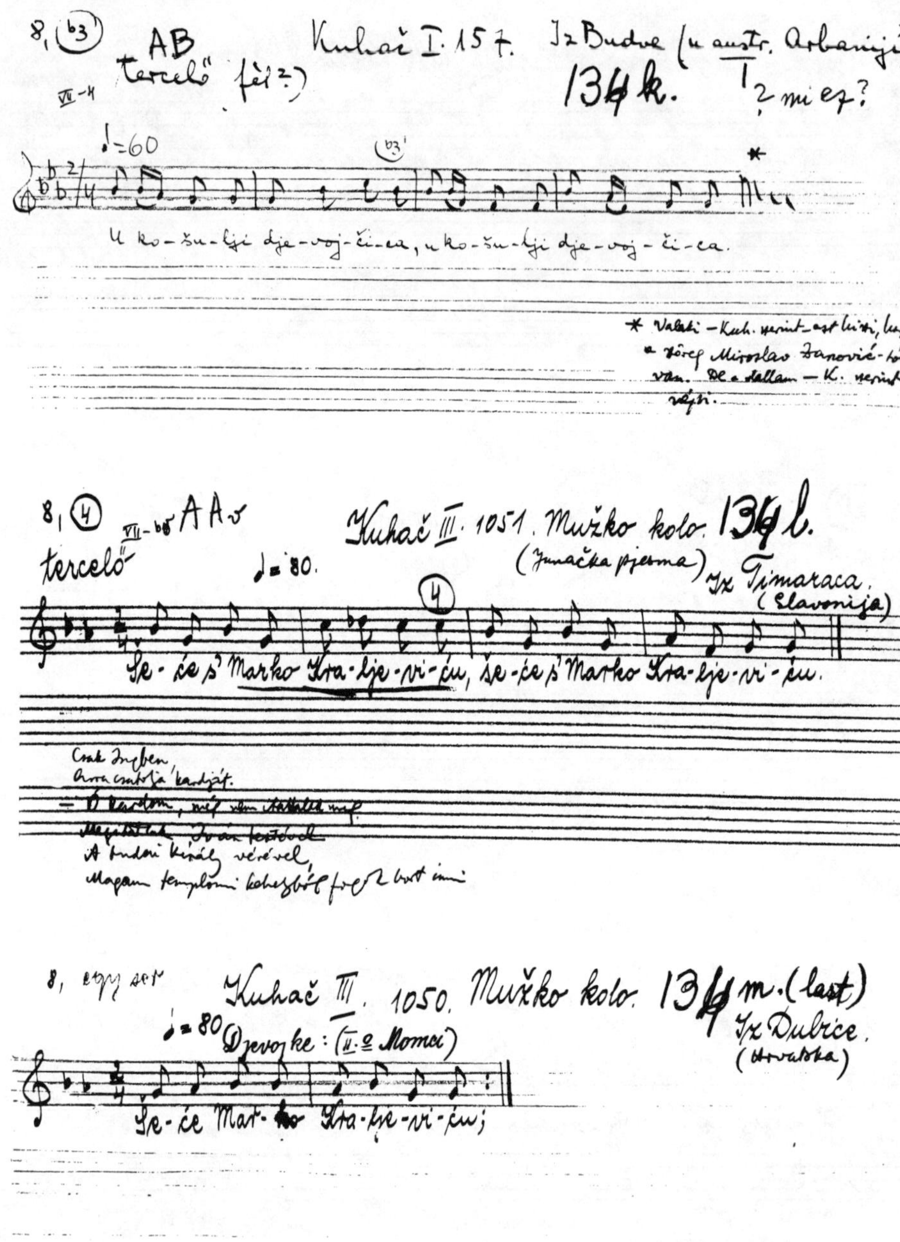
Kuhač I. 157. Iz Budve (u austr. Arbaniji)
134 k.
U ko-šu-lji dje-voj-či-ca, u ko-šu-lji dje-voj-či-ca.
Kuhač III. 1051. Mužko kolo. 134 l.
(Junačka pjesma)
Iz Timaraca (Slavonija)
Še-će s' Marko Kra-lje-vi-ću, še-će s' Marko Kra-lje-vi-ću.
Kuhač III. 1050. Mužko kolo. 134 m.
Iz Dubrice. (Hrvatska)
Še-će Mar-ko Kra-lje-vi-ću;

8, ① AB terceló"
Kuhač II. 529.
Iz Sinja.
VII – b3
♩= 42.
1/2 ?
135a.
Dalmácija ?
Ter da vi-diš ka-ko vru-će go-ri, draga mâ go-spo-je.
(8) 8, ① VII-4 AB
Foča.
135b. (last)
Iz - vir vo - da iz-vir vo - da iz - vi - ra - la,
8, ① VII–4
AA
Manojlović 5.
(narb)
Iz Gračanice-Kosovo.
Allegro moderato
Milutin Popović (student
Što ta bu-na vi-še selo da-do Što ta buna vi-še se-lo
refr.

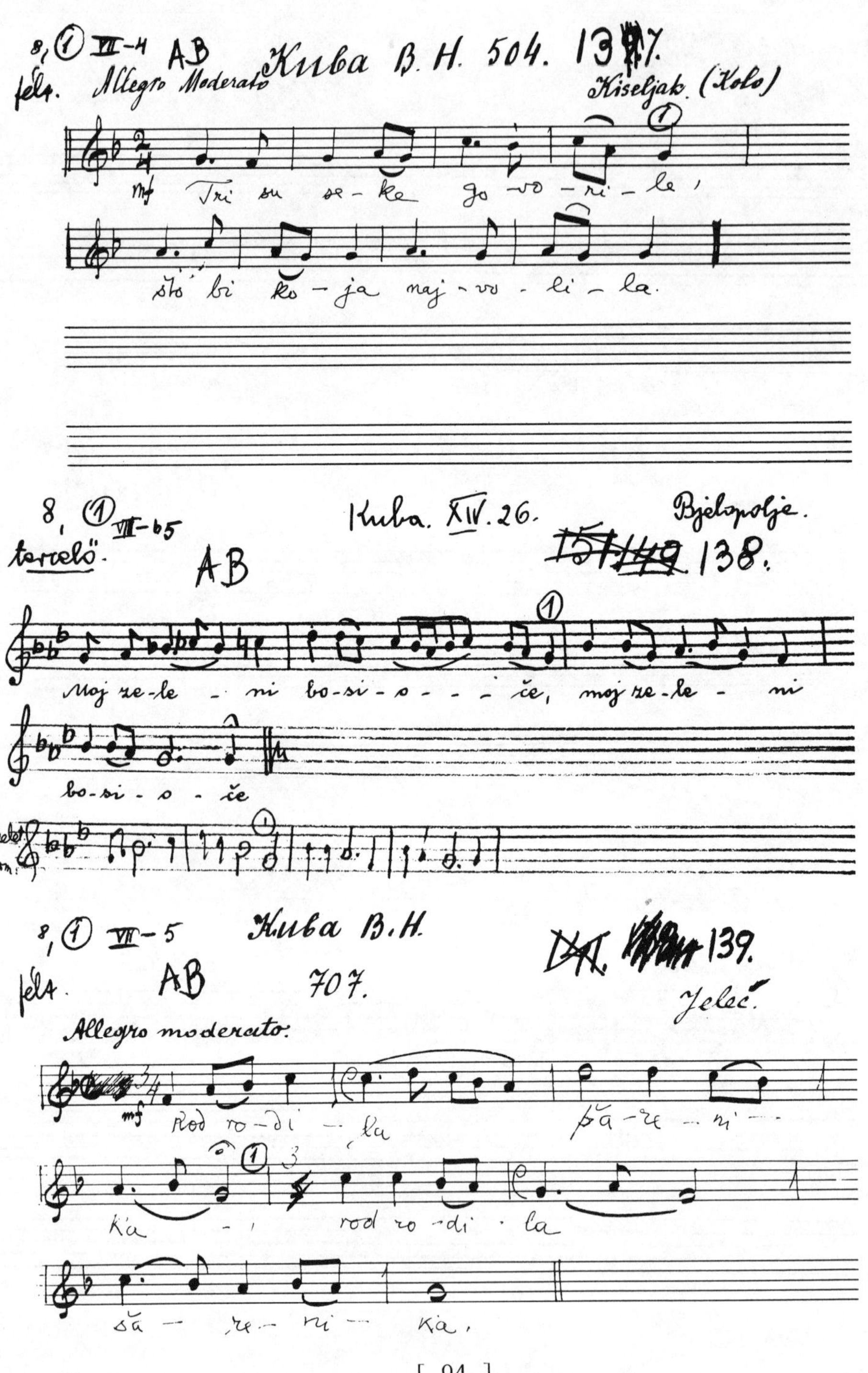

8, ① VII-4 AB
Kuba B. H. 504. 137.
Allegro Moderato
Kiseljak. (Kolo)
Tri su se-ke go-vo-ri-le,
što bi ko-ja naj-vo-li-la.
8, ① VII-65
Kuba. XIV. 26.
Bjelopolje.
AB
138.
Moj ze-le - ni bo-si-o - - - če, moj ze-le - ni
bo-si - o - če
8, ① VII-5
Kuba B. H.
139.
AB
707.
Jeleč.
Allegro moderato.
Rod ro-di - la
ša-re-ni-
ka - rod ro-di - la
ša - re-ni- ka.

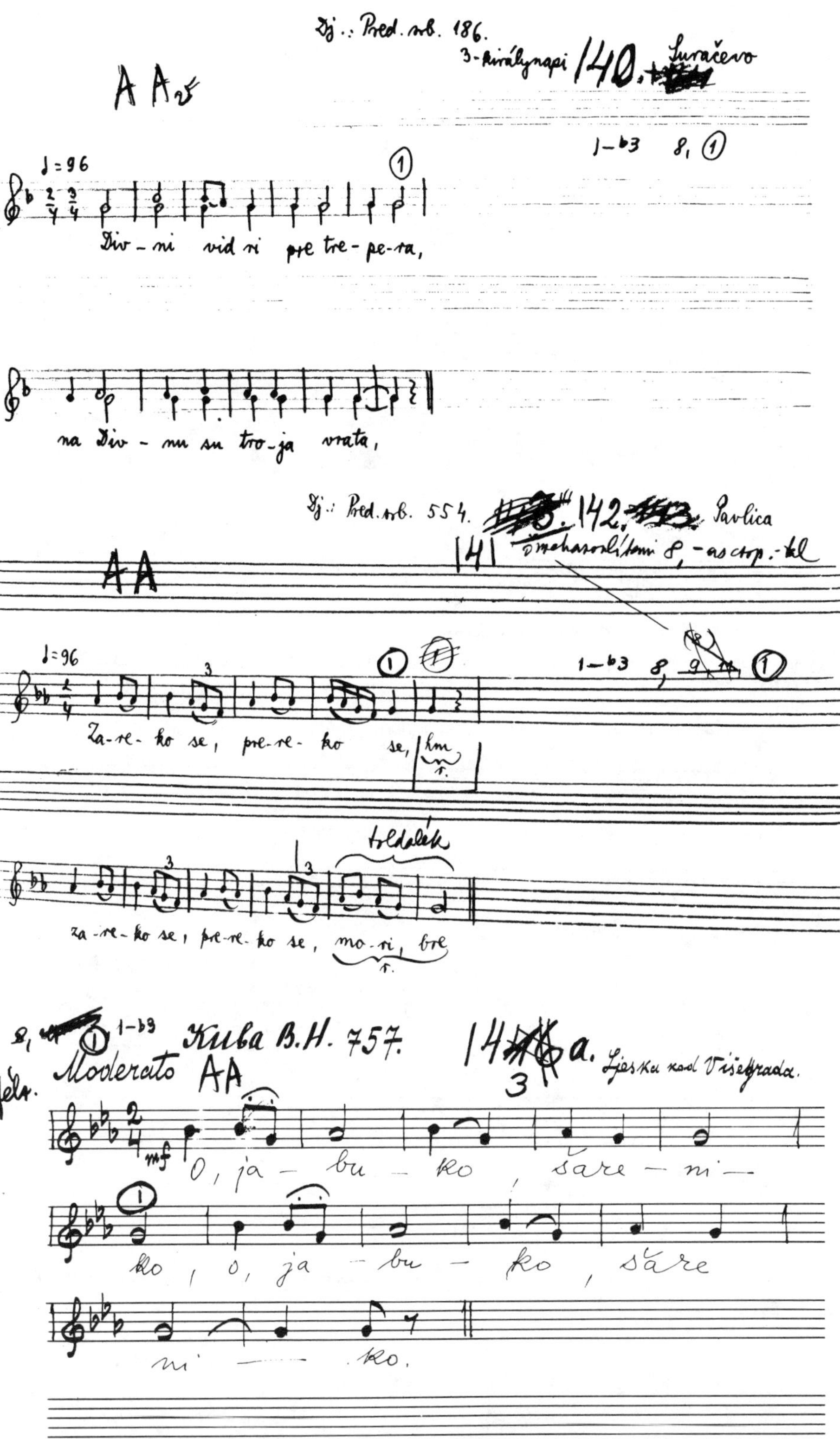

Dj.: Pred. sb. 186.
3-királynapi 140. Juračevo
AA
1—b3 8, ①
♩=96
Div-ni vid ri pre tre-pe-ra,
na Div-nu su tro-ja vrata,
Dj.: Pred. sb. 554. 142. Pavlica
141
AA
♩=96
1—b3 8, ①
Za-re-ko se, pre-re-ko se,
toldalék
za-re-ko se, pre-re-ko se, mo-ri, bre
8, 1-b3 ①
Kuba B.H. 757. 143a. Ljeska kod Višegrada.
Moderato AA
mf
O, ja-bu-ko, šare-ni-ko, o, ja-bu-ko, šare
ni-ko.

8, ① 1–b3
Kuba. B.H. 453
14 b.
3
Allegro moderato
Gacko
mf Oj, so-ko-le, moj so – ko-le,
Oj, so kole, moj so- ko – le,
8, eggoros VII–b3
Kuba B.H. 451
14 c.
3
Andante
Gacko
Oj, neve-ne ——, moj ne- ve – ne!

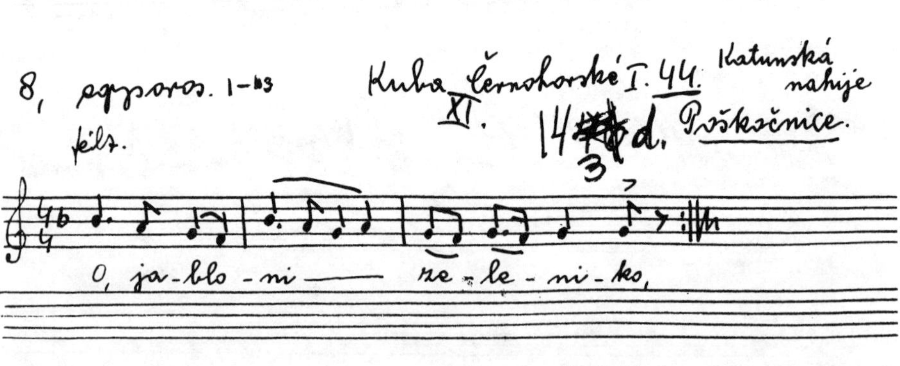
8, eggoros. 1–b3
Kuba Černohorské I. 44.
XI.
Katunská nahije
kilz.
14 d. Pošksčnice.
3
O, ja-blo-ni —— ze-le-ni-ko,

8, egysoros. 1 —b3
félz.
Ford. Juž. Srb. 401.
Donja Gušterica (Na Kosovu)
Tánchívó (húsvétkor, Györgynapkor és Szentháromságnapkor)
143 e. (last)
O - te, dru - ge da i - gra - mo, i ih!
Dj.: Pred. srb. 152.
144-145.
Djuštica
AA
♪ = 152
1–4, 8, ①
Uzmi mene, selja - ni - ne,
ako nećeš meni da uzmeš
Dj.: Pred. srb. 183.
Tánc
146a.
Čorčinci
AB
♩ = 126
1–4, 8, ①
Oj, ti De - no, Kara Deno,
Koj ti dvori si - noć mi - nu?

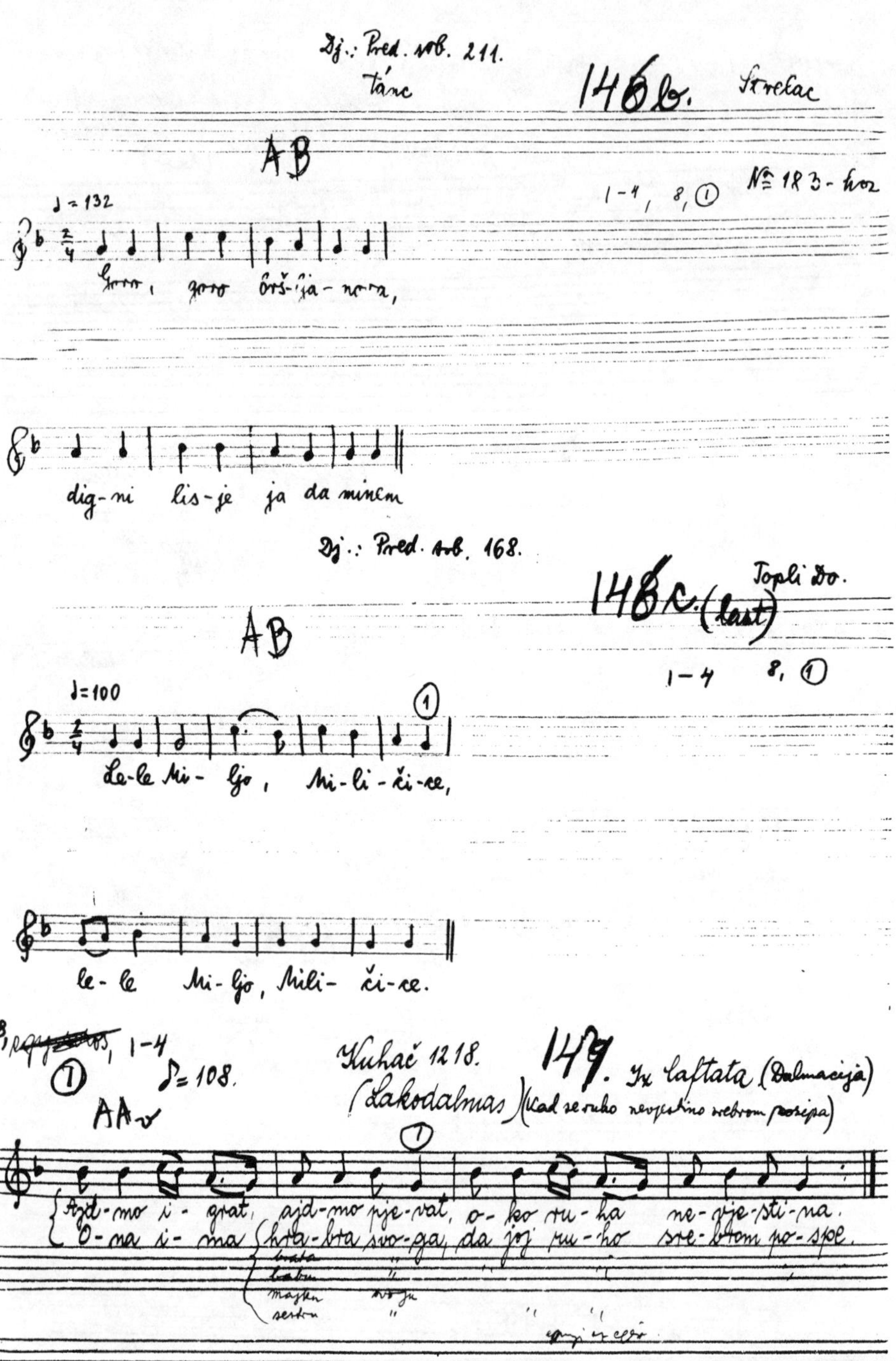

Dj.: Pred. sob. 211.
Tánc
146b.
AB
1-4, 8, ①
♩= 132
Goro, goro Örš-ja-nora,
dig-ni lis-je ja da minem
Dj.: Pred. sob. 168.
146c.
Topli Do.
AB
1-4 8, ①
♩=100
Le-le Mi-ljo, Mi-li-či-ce,
le-le Mi-ljo, Mili-či-ce.
1-4
①
♪= 108.
Kuhač 1218.
147.
(Dalmacija)
(Lakodalmas)
AA
Ajd-mo i-grat, ajd-mo pje-vat, o-ko ru-ha ne-vje-sti-na.
O-na i-ma brata svo-ga, da joj ru-ho sre-brom po-spe.

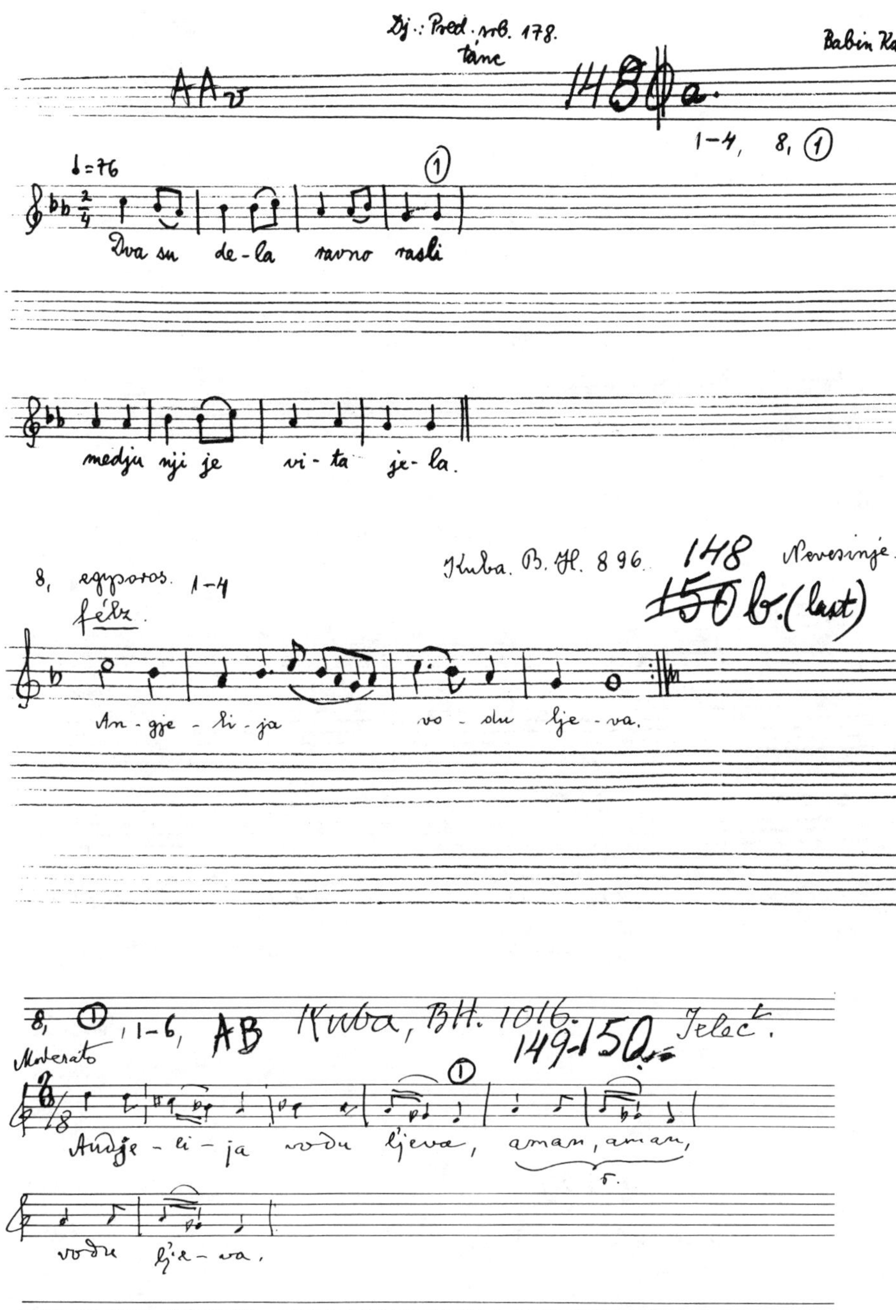
Dj.: Pred. zb. 178.
tane
Babin Kal.
AAv
148 a.
1–4, 8, (1)
♩=76
Dva su de-la ravno rasli
medju nji je vi-ta je-la.
8, egyporos. 1–4
félz.
Kuba. B. H. 896.
148
Nevesinje.
150 b. (last)
An-gje-li-ja vo-du lje-va.
8, (1), 1–6, AB Kuba, BH. 1016.
149-150 a.
Jelec.
Moderato
Andje-li-ja vodu ljeva, aman, aman,
vodu lje-va.

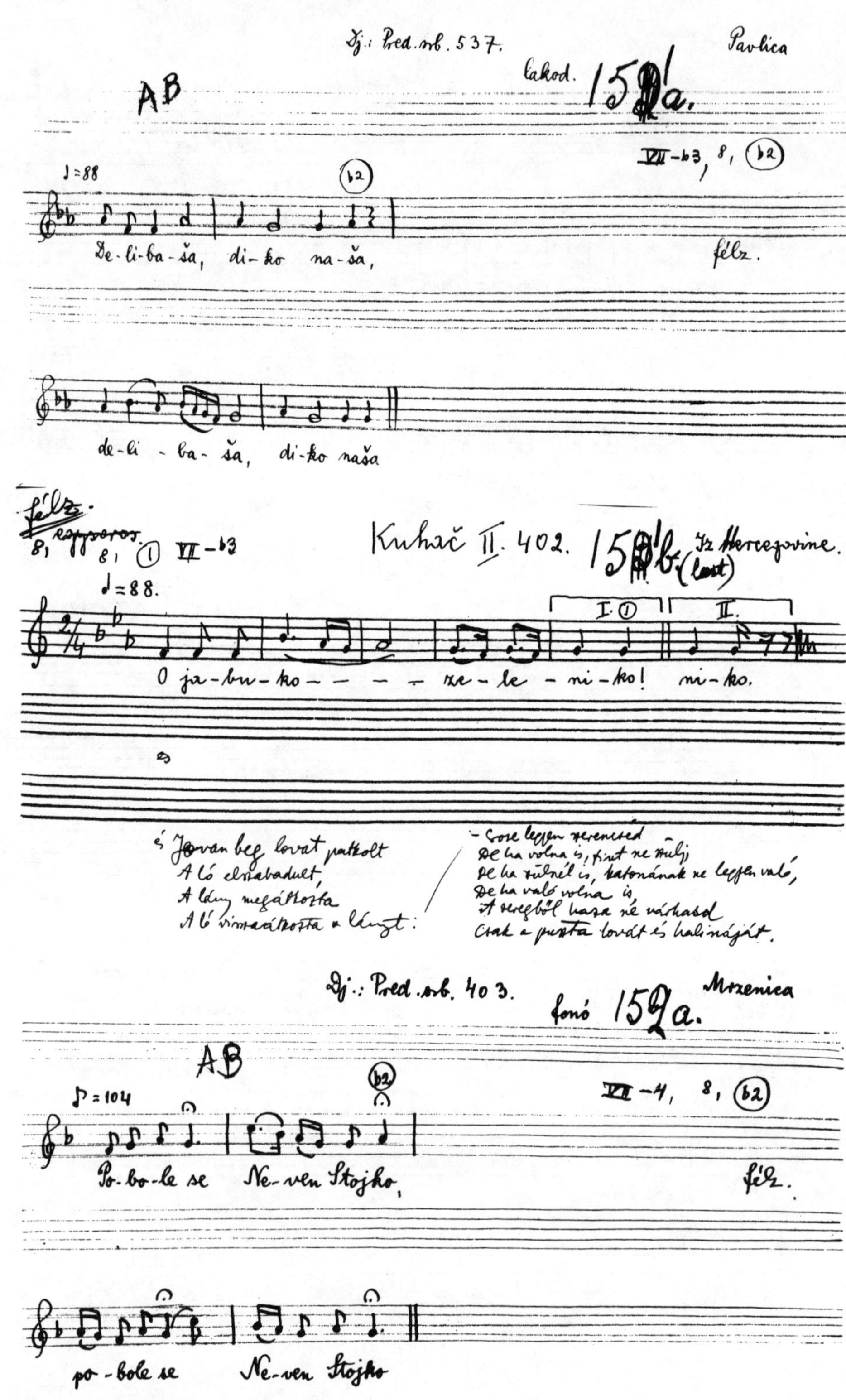

Đj.: Pred. srb. 537.
Pavlica
lakod.
AB
VII–b3, 8, b2
♩=88
De-li-ba-ša, di-ko na-ša,
félz.
de-li - ba- ša, di-ko naša
Kuhač II. 402.
Iz Hercegovine.
VII–b3
♩=88.
O ja-bu-ko - - - - ze-le - ni-ko! ni-ko.
és Jovan beg lovat patkolt
A ló elszabadult,
A lány megátkozta
A ló visszaátkozta a lányt:
– Sose legyen szerencséd
De ha volna is, fiút ne szülj
De ha szülnél is, katonának ne legyen való,
De ha való volna is,
A seregből haza ne várhasd
Csak a puszta lovát és halináját.
Đj.: Pred. srb. 403.
Mrzenica
fonó
AB
♪=104
VII–4, 8, b2
Po-bo-le se Ne-ven Stojko,
félz.
po-bole se Ne-ven Stojko

Dj.: Pred. srb. 306.

Lakodalmas

152b. (last) Pirkovac

VII–b2

8, egy soros!

♪ = 152

Oj, I- li-jo, mlad delijo, Oj, Ilijo, mlad delijo

8, (b2) VII–4

Kuhač. B. H. 115.

Čajniče.

félz.

AB

1553.

(b2)

Što se mo-re za-mu-ti lo gol-na za-no za-mu-ti-lo,

što se mo- što se mo — ?!!

sic!

Dalopj strófakezdés

Dj.: Pred. srb. 40.

154. Krivača

AB

VI–b5 8, (b2)

félz.

♩ = 88

(b2)

Mori, Janče, Mori, Janče,

Zagor-janče, Zagor-janče.

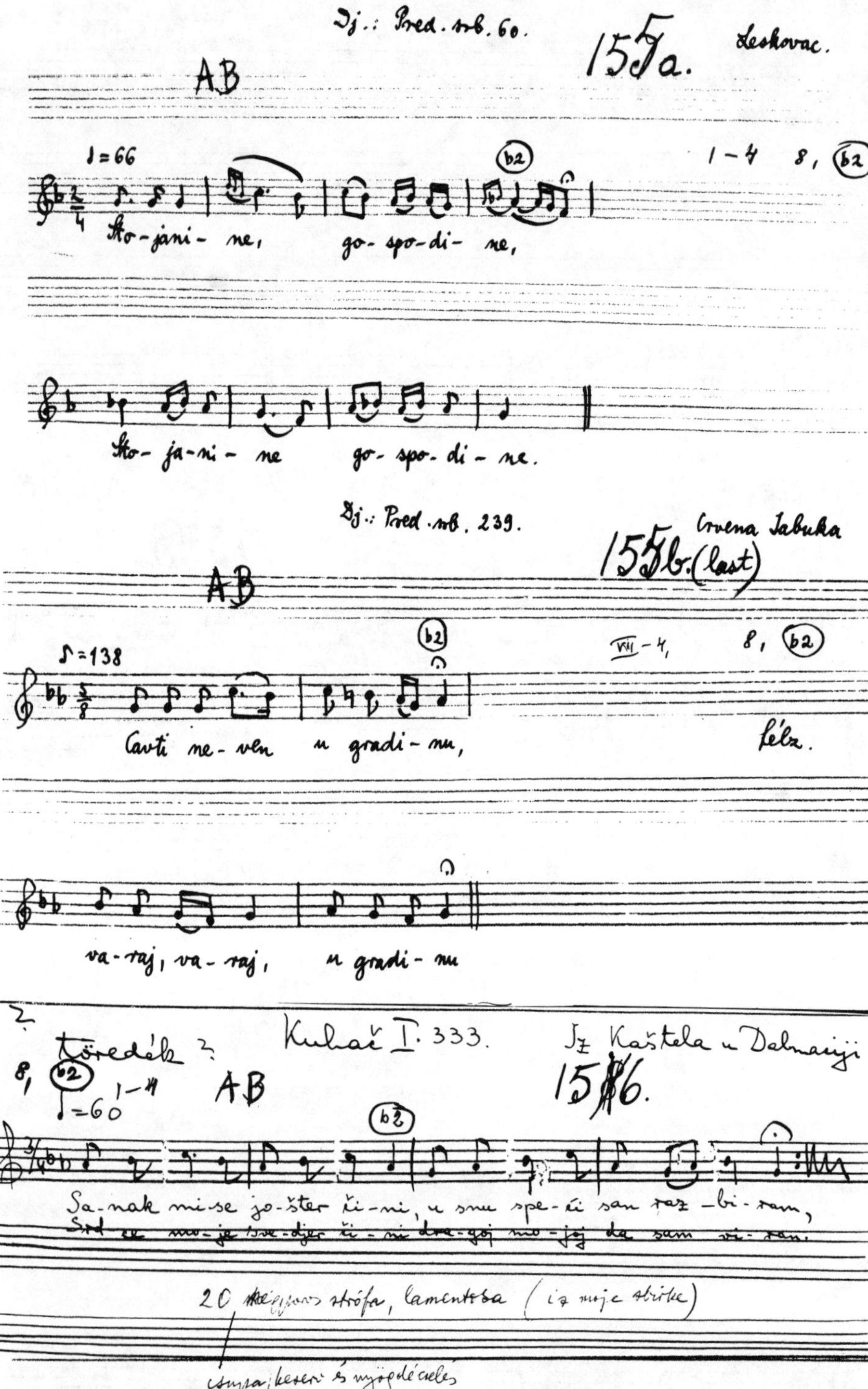

Dj.: Pred. srb. 60.
155a.
Leskovac.
AB
♩=66
b2
1–4 8, b2
Sto-jani-ne, go-spo-di-ne,
Sto-ja-ni-ne go-spo-di-ne.
Dj.: Pred. srb. 239.
Crvena Jabuka
155b. (last)
AB
♪=138
b2
VII–4, 8, b2
Cavti ne-ven u gradi-nu,
félz.
va-raj, va-raj, u gradi-nu
Töredék ?
Kuhač I. 333.
Iz Kaštela u Dalmaciji
156.
8, b2
♩=60 1–4
AB
b2
Sa-nak mi se jo-šter či-ni, u snu spe-ći san raz-bi-ram,
strófa, lamentoso
csupa keserv és nyögdécselés
mű-

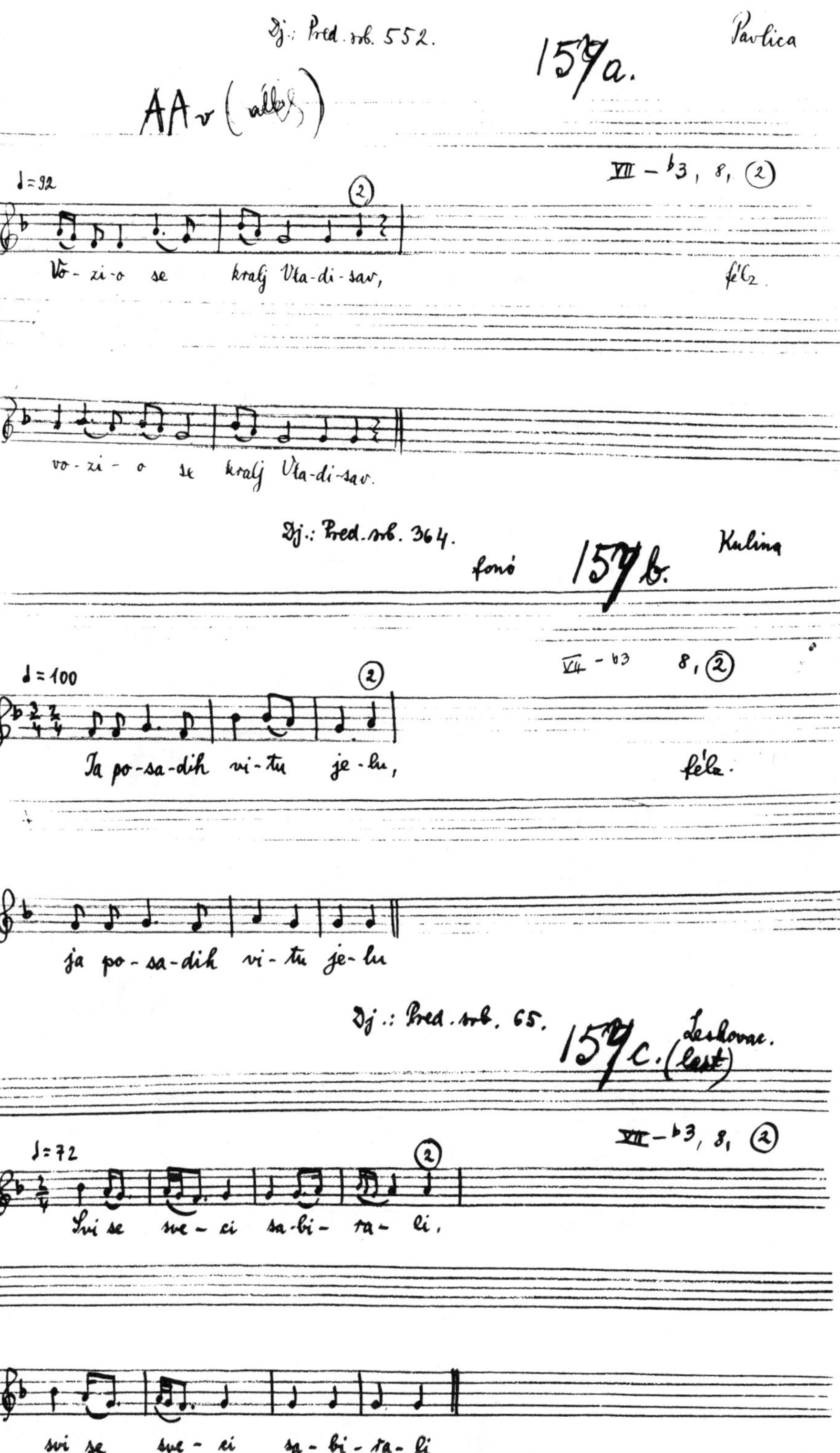
Dj.: Pred. zb. 552.
157a.
Pavlica
AAv (válto.)
♩=92
VII – ♭3, 8, ②
Vo- zi-o se kralj Vla-di-sav,
félC2.
vo-zi-o se kralj Vla-di-sav.
Dj.: Pred. zb. 364.
fonó
157b.
Kulina
♩=100
V4 – ♭3 8, ②
Ja po-sa-dih vi-tu je-lu,
féle.
ja po-sa-dih vi-tu je-lu
Dj.: Pred. zb. 65.
157c.
Leskovac.
♩=72
VII – ♭3, 8, ②
Svi se sve-ci sa-bi-ra-li,
svi se sve-ci sa-bi-ra-li

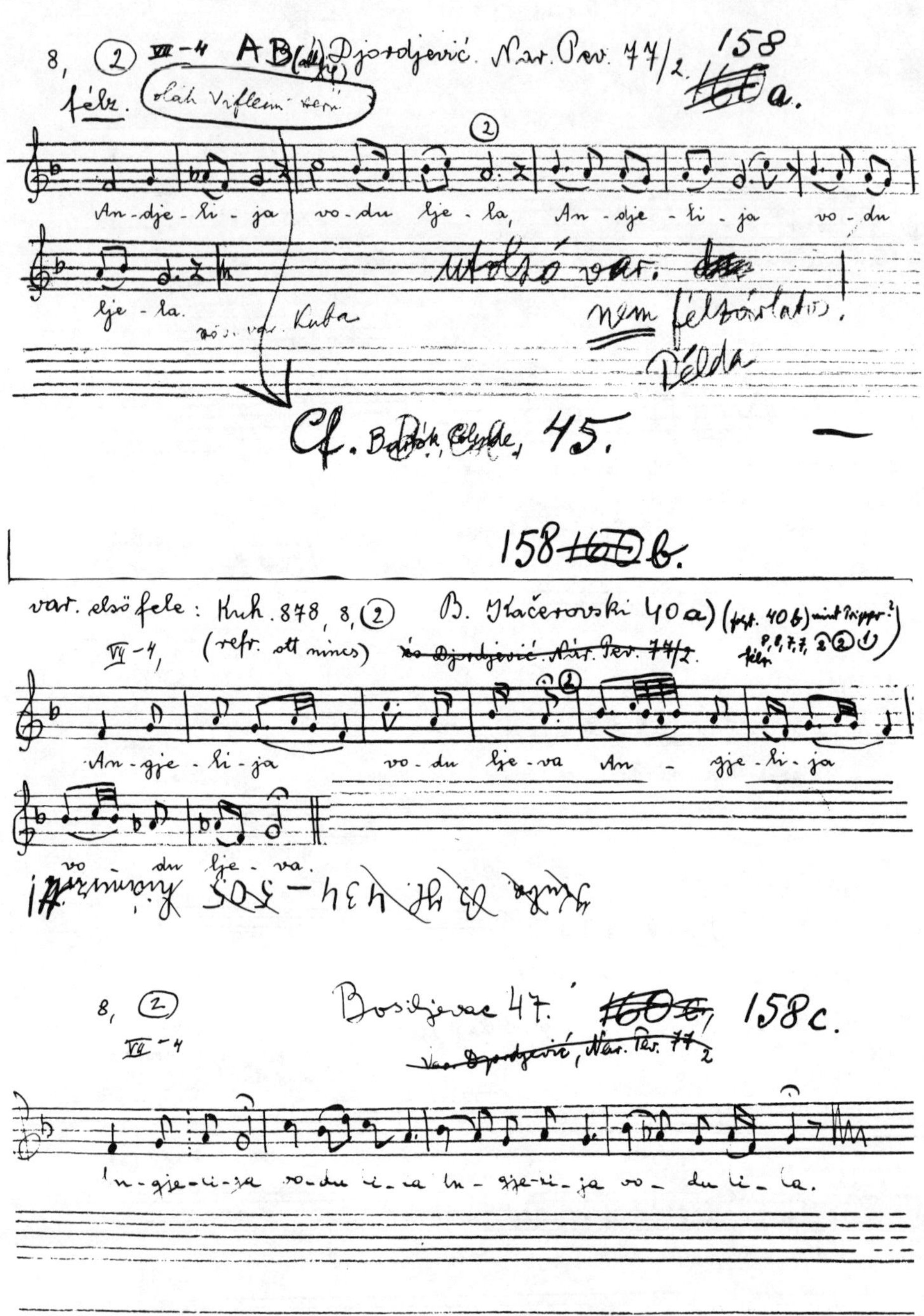

158 a.
Djordjević Nar. Pev. 77/2.
Cf. Bartók, Colinde, 45.
158 b.
Kuh. 878
B. Tkačerovski 40a)
158c.
Bosiljevac 47.

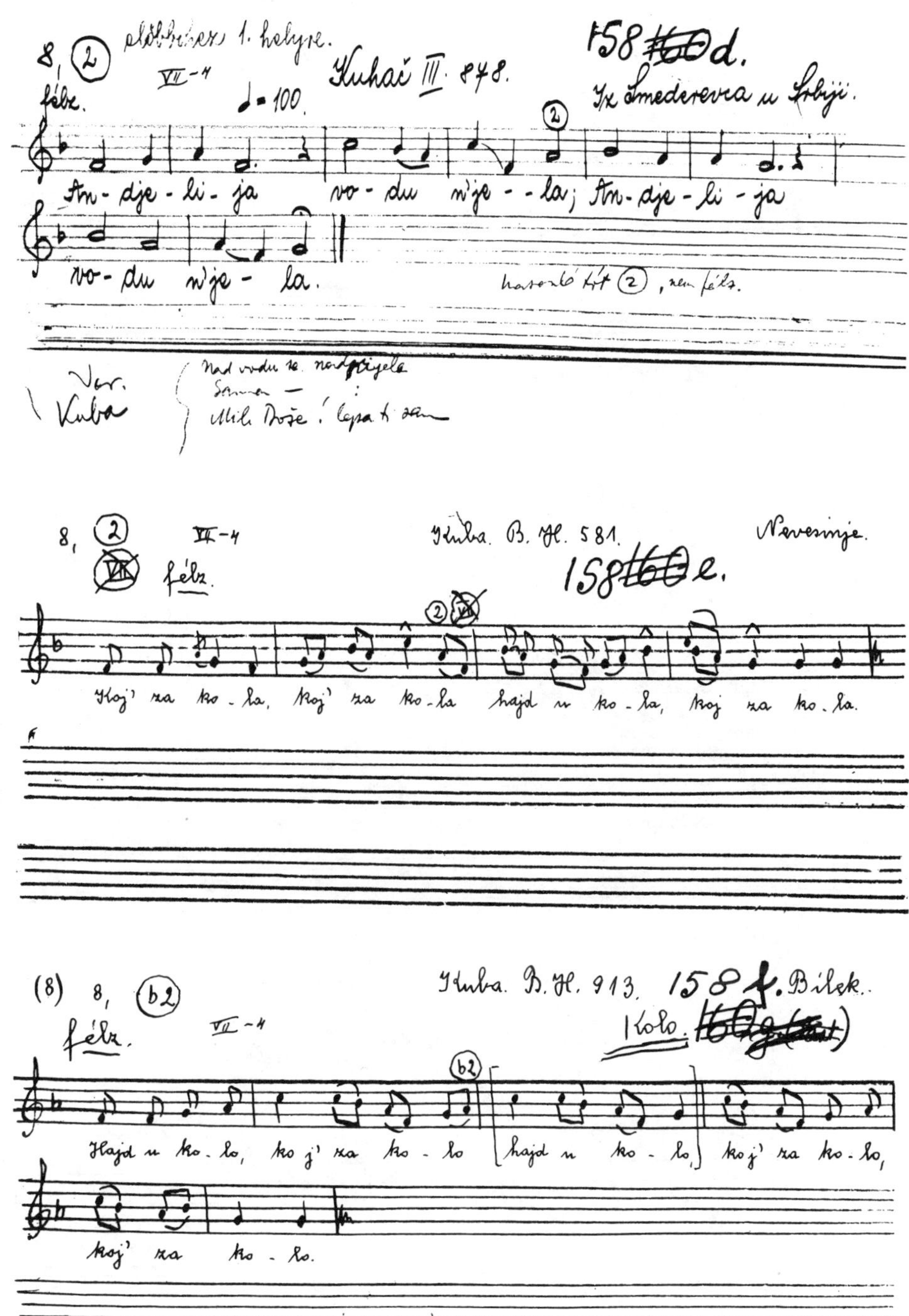
8, (2)
VII-4
Kuhač III. 848.
158 d.
Iz Smedereva u Srbiji.
félz.
♩= 100.
An-dje-li-ja vo-du nje--la; An-dje-li-ja vo-du nje-la.
Var. Kuba
8, (2) VII-4
Kuba. B. H. 581.
Nevesinje.
158 e.
félz.
Koj' za ko-la, koj' za ko-la hajd u ko-la, koj za ko-la.
(8) 8, (b2) VII-4
Kuba. B. H. 913. 158 f. Bilek.
Kolo.
félz.
Hajd u ko-lo, koj' za ko-lo hajd u ko-lo, koj' za ko-lo, koj' za ko-lo.

8, ③ ♩= 46. Kuhač III. 877. ~~160f.~~ 158 g. Iz Biograda. (Last) 1c

harsonló köt: ②

Po-še-ta-la be-la bu-la, po- - - - še- ta - - - - - - la be- la bu- la. Prijejev A-man, a-man.

Néregette magát a virben: Mi szép vagyok!

8, ② VII – 5 AB Kuba B. H. 159 ~~161~~ a.

félt. (oláh lakodalmas!) ① 719.

Allegretto. Trebinje. ②

Po - dne zo - ri a ja drijemam a za ru čak ni - šta ne - znam.

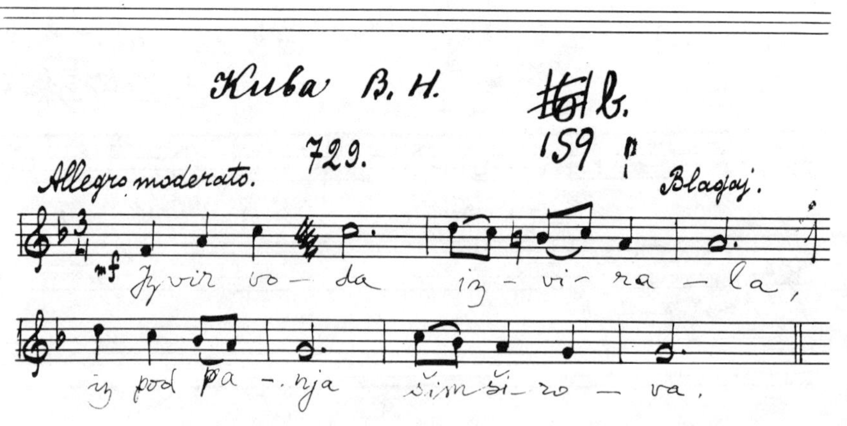

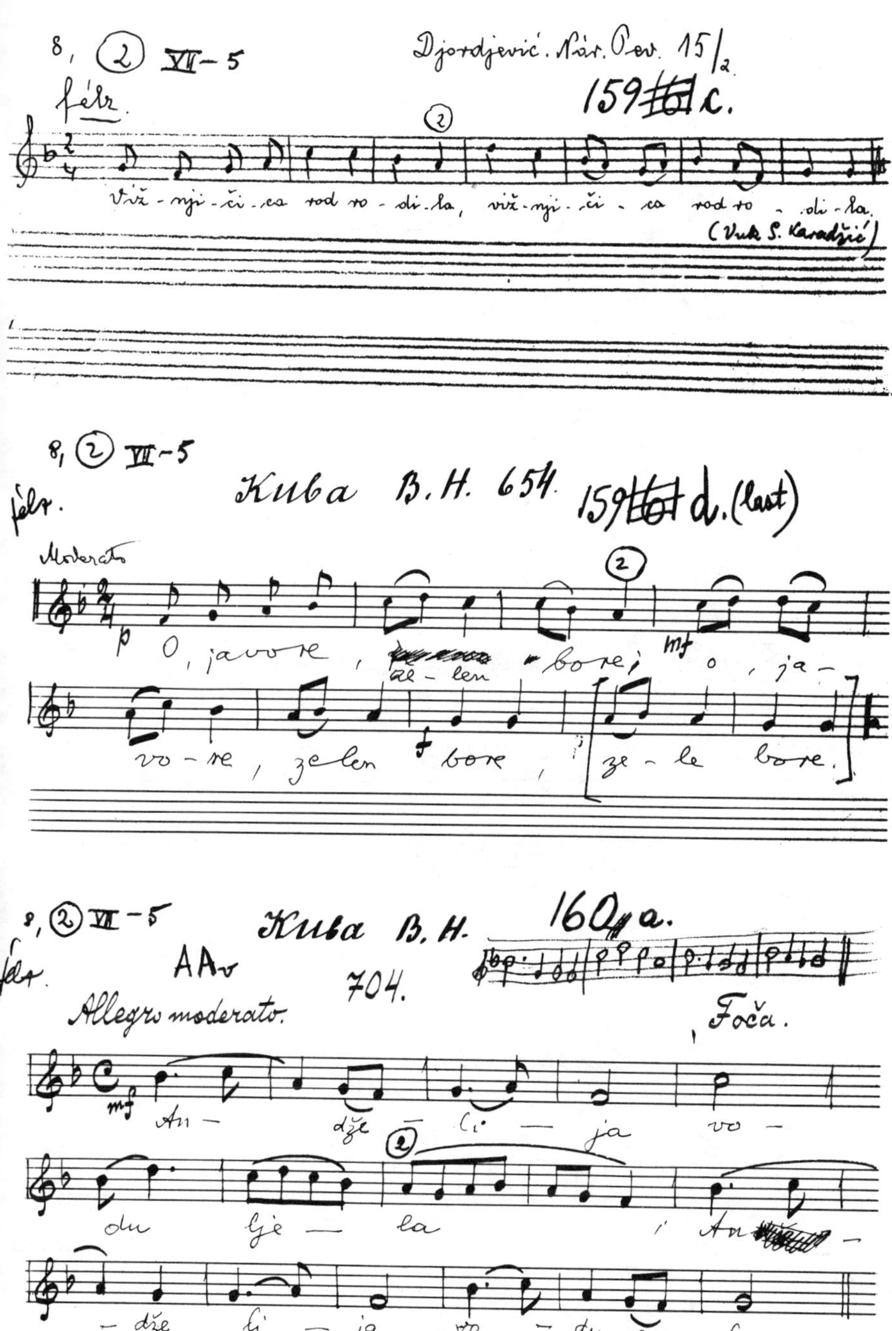

8, (2) VII–5
Djordjević. Nár. Pev. 15/2.
félr.
159 c.
viž-nji-či-ca rod ro-di-la, viž-nji-či-ca rod ro-di-la.
(Vuk S. Karadžić)
8, (2) VII–5
félr.
Kuba B.H. 654.
159 d. (last)
Moderato
O, javore, zelen bore, o, ja-vo-re, zelen bore, ze-le bore.
8, (2) VII–5
Kuba B.H.
160 a.
félr.
AAv
704.
Allegro moderato.
Foča.
An – dže – li – ja vo – du lje – la, An – dže li – ja vo – du lje – la,

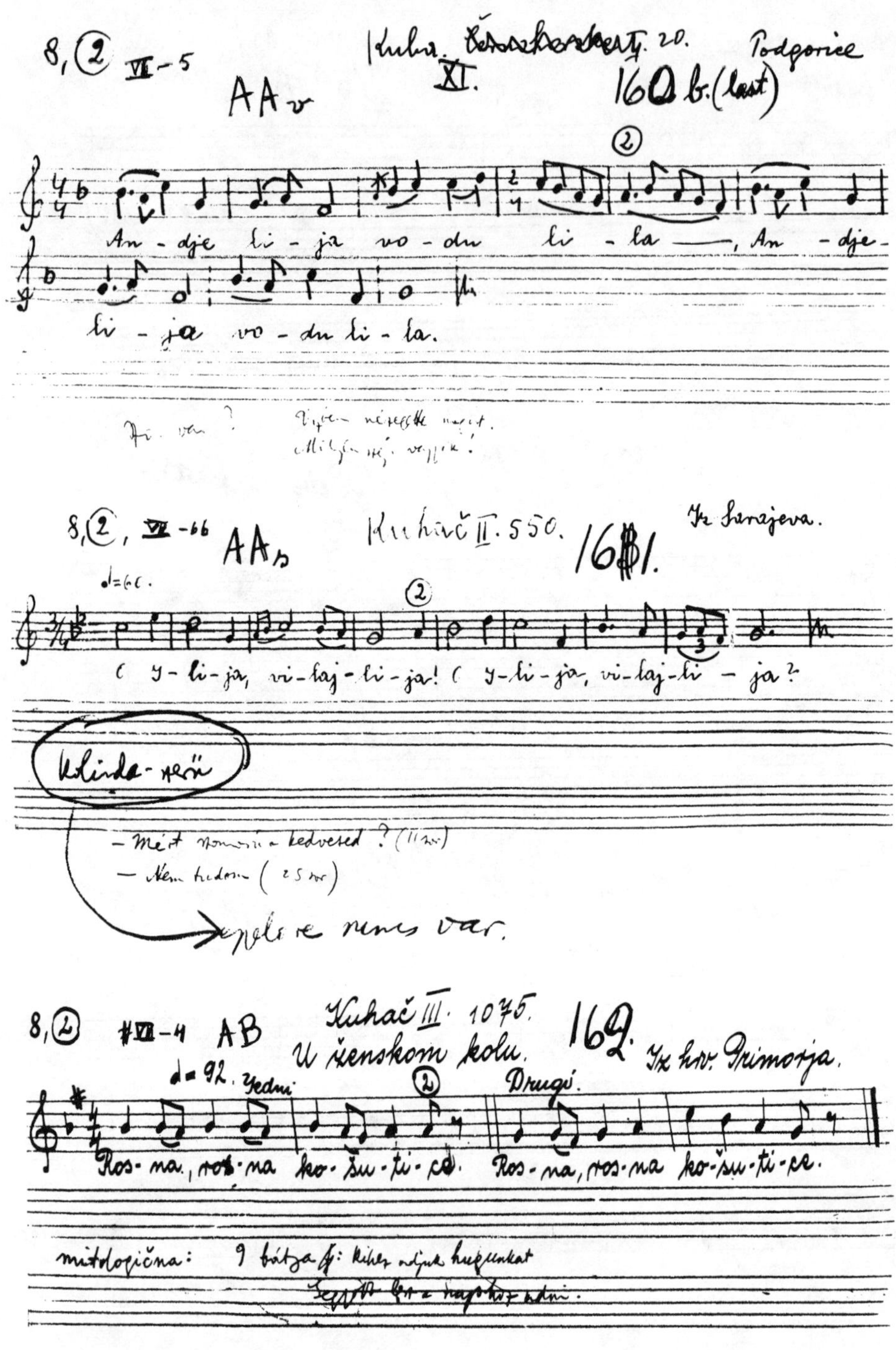

8, ② VI–5
Podgorice
AA
XI.
160 b.(last)
An-dje li-ja vo-du li-la, An-dje-li-ja vo-du li-la.
8, ②, VII–66
AA
Kuhač II. 550.
Iz Sarajeva.
O I-li-ja, vi-laj-li-ja! O I-li-ja, vi-laj-li-ja?
8, ② #VII–4 AB
Kuhač III. 1075.
U ženskom kolu.
162.
Iz hrv. Primorja.
♩= 92.
Ros-na, ros-na ko-šu-ti-ce. Ros-na, ros-na ko-šu-ti-ce.
mitologična:

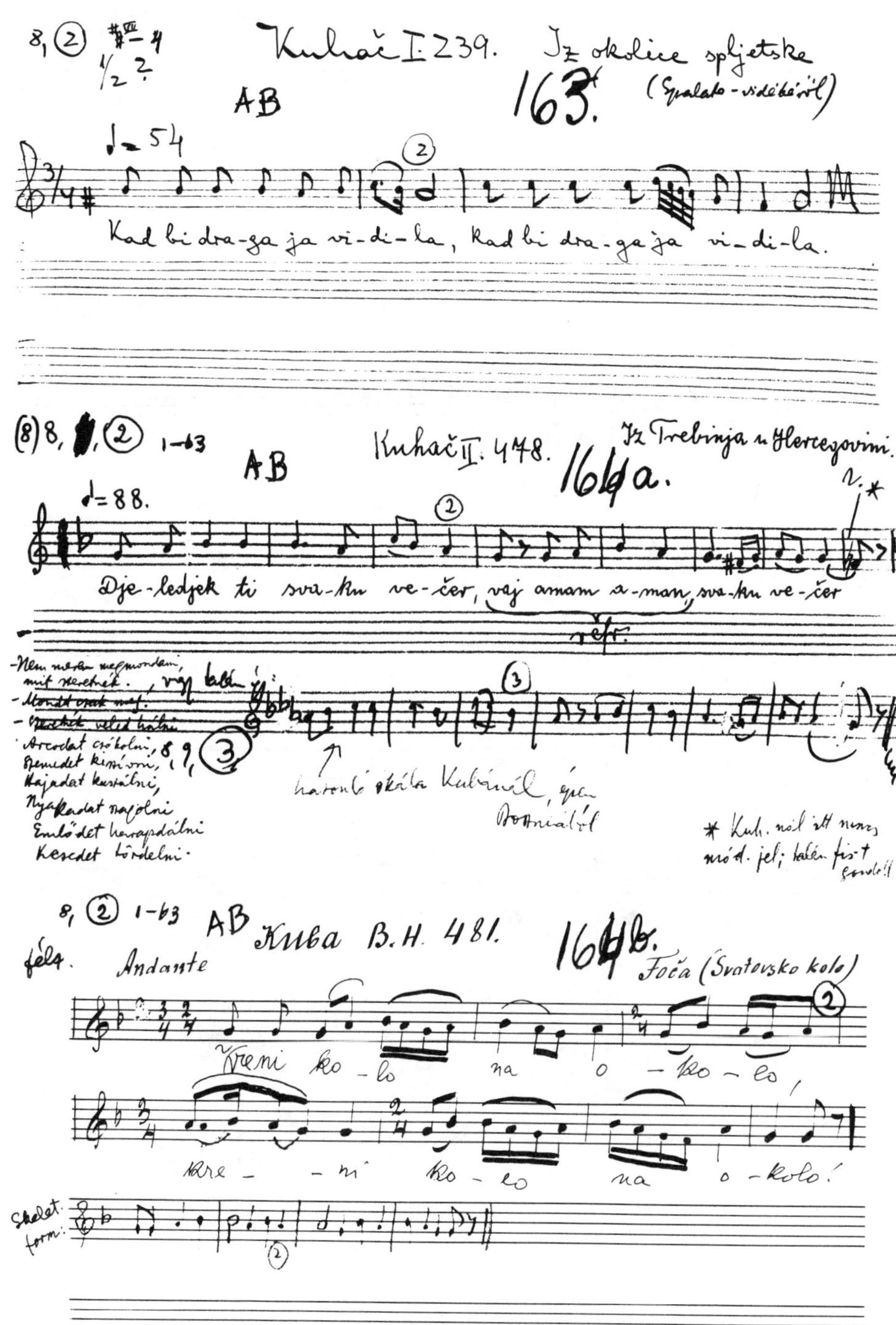

Kuhač I. 239. Iz okolice spljetske
163.
(Spalato-vidékéről)
AB
Kad bi dra-ga ja vi-di-la, kad bi dra-ga ja vi-di-la.
AB
Kuhač II. 478.
Iz Trebinja u Hercegovini.
164a.
Dje-ledjek ti sva-ku ve-čer, vaj amam a-man, sva-ku ve-čer
refr.
AB
Kuba B.H. 481.
164b.
Andante
Foča (Svatovsko kolo)
Kreni ko-lo na o-ko-lo,
Kre-ni ko-lo na o-kolo!
Skelet. form:

Dj.: Pred. zb. 274/a)
Lázárnapi
Niševci
♪=152
Mori, Ve-no, Ve-ni-či-ce,
mori, Ve-no, Ve-ni-či-ce.
Dj.: Pred. zb. 227.
tánc.
Crvena Jabuka
♩=132
Oj, ti, Cveto, mori, oj, ti, Cveto,
le - po cveće, mori le-po cveće
Kuba. B. H. 388.
Goražde.
arabos
O dje-voj-ko dži-džo mo-ja, o dje-voj-ko dži-džo mo-ja!
ili: na dži-dža-la te i.t.d.

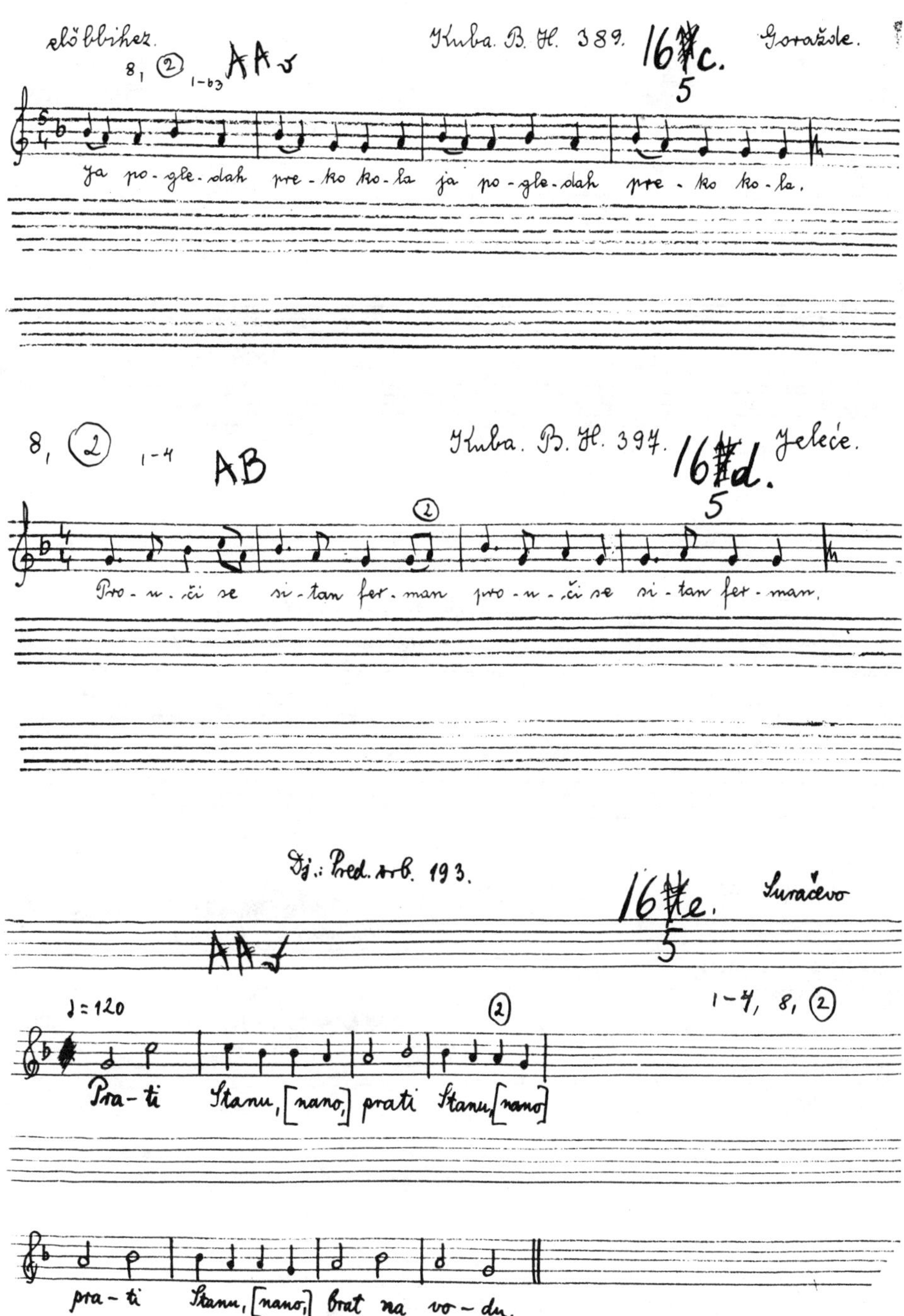

Kuba. B. H. 389.
16#c.
5
Goražde.
8, ② 1–6 3 AA
Ja po-gle-dah pre-ko ko-la ja po-gle-dah pre-ko ko-la.
8, ② 1–4 AB
Kuba. B. H. 397.
16#d.
5
Jeleće.
Pro-u-či se si-tan fer-man pro-u-či se si-tan fer-man.
Dj.: Pred. srb. 193.
16#e.
5
Suračevo
AA
♩= 120
1–4, 8, ②
Pra-ti Stanu, [nano,] prati Stanu, [nano]
pra-ti Stanu, [nano,] brat na vo-du.

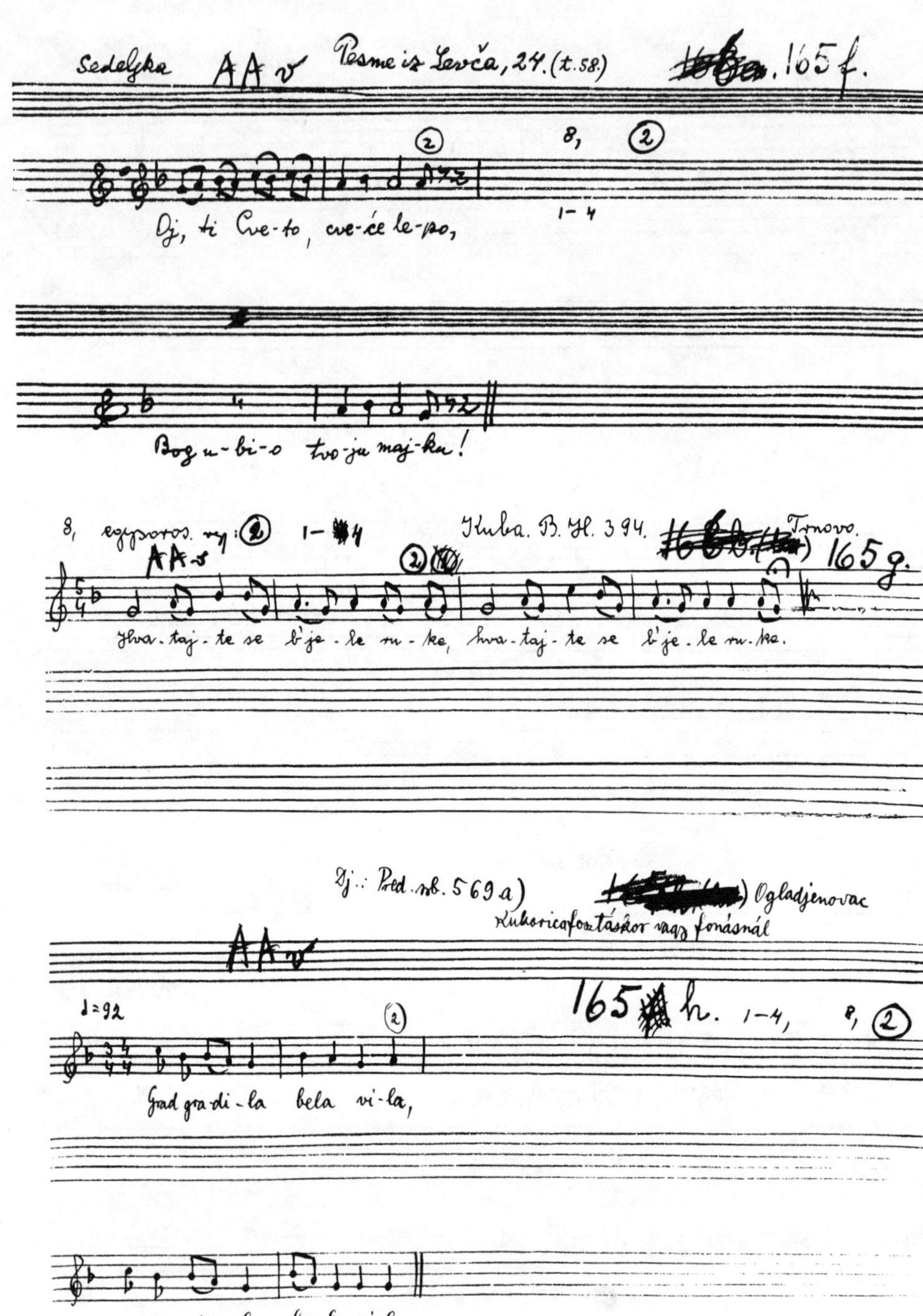
Sedeljka AA v Pesme iz Levča, 24. (t. 58) 165 f.
8, ②
1–4
Oj, ti Cve-to, cve-će le-po,
Bog u-bi-o tvo-ju maj-ku!
8, egyszeres. vagy: ② 1–4
Kuba. B. H. 394. Trnovo. 165 g.
AA-5
Hva-taj-te se b'je-le ru-ke, hva-taj-te se b'je-le ru-ke.
Vj.: Pred. zb. 569 a) Ogladjenovac
Kukoricafosztáskor vagy fonásnál
AA v
165 h. 1–4, 8, ②
♩=92
Grad gra-di-la bela vi-la,
grad gra-di-la be-la vi-la

8, egysoros 1–63
Kuhač III. 1068.
= 120.
Kad se hvata žensko kolo.
16 5 i.
Jedni (II.-o Drugi)
Iz Budve u austr. albaniji
Fa- taj-te se, b'je-le ru-ke;
8, egysoros. 1–63
Kuba. B. H. 385.
Nevesinje.
16 5 J. (last)
O dje-voj-ko cr-no o-ko,
Dj.: Pred. srb. 172.
Koleda. 166–16 Kalna
AB
1–4, 8, ②
= 104
Oj, kole-do, moj ko- le-do,
félz.
oj, ko- le-do, moj ko- le-do.

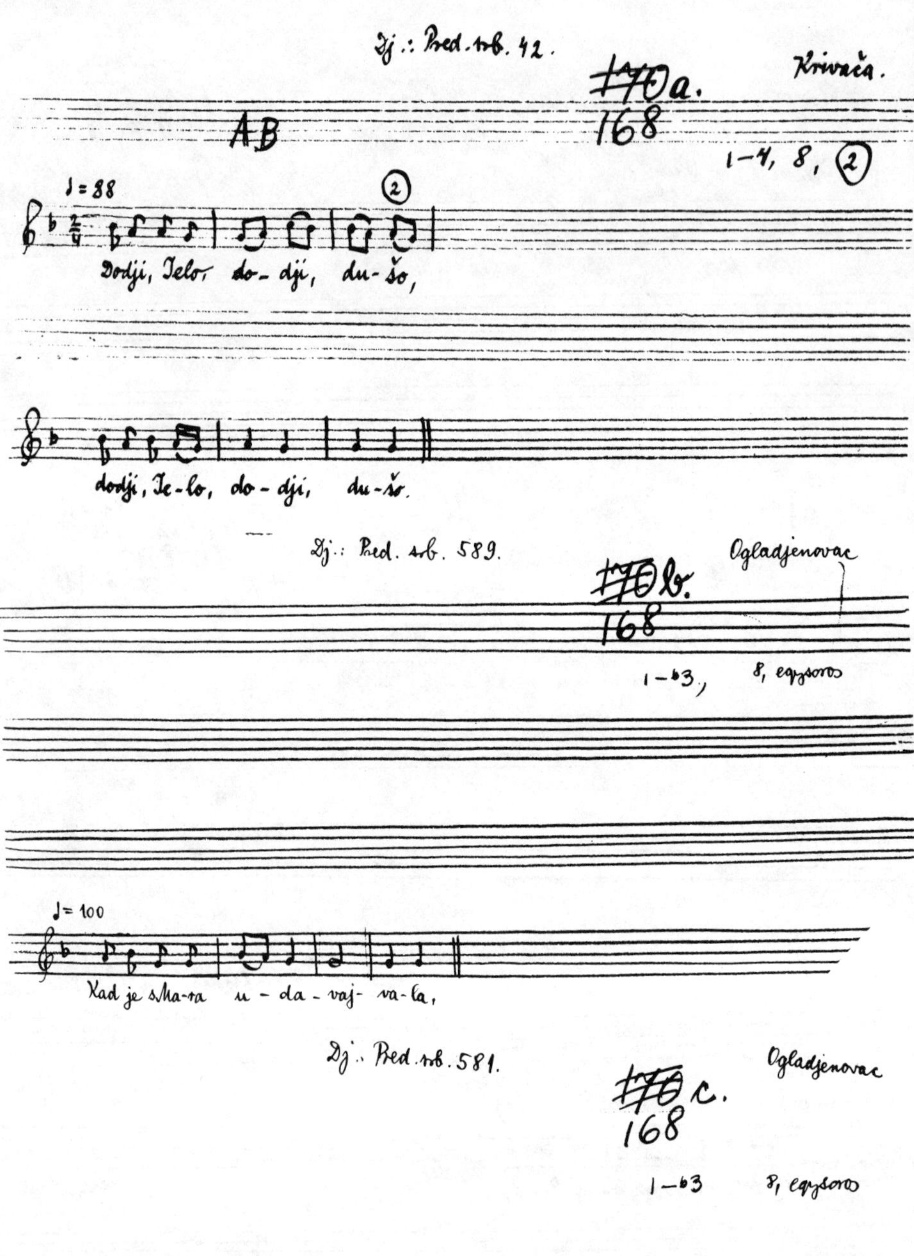

♩= 100

Oj, na gra-du Ca-ri-gra-du, oj, na gra-du Ca-ri-gra-du.

Dj.: Pred. srb. 413.
fonó 168 d.
Mrzenica
1–13 8, egysoros
♩=96
Civriv-rivriv mačak se-di
Dj.: Pred. srb. 516.
Levač.
168 e. (last)
1–4 8, egysoros félz.
♩=60
Ko-je li-je, ko-je li-je
Dj.: Pred. srb. 26.
Esőkérő
169.
Tibužde
AB
♩= 84
1–4, 8, ②
Po-do-li-ce Bo-ga moliv,
félz.
oj, do-do-le, mi-li Bo-že

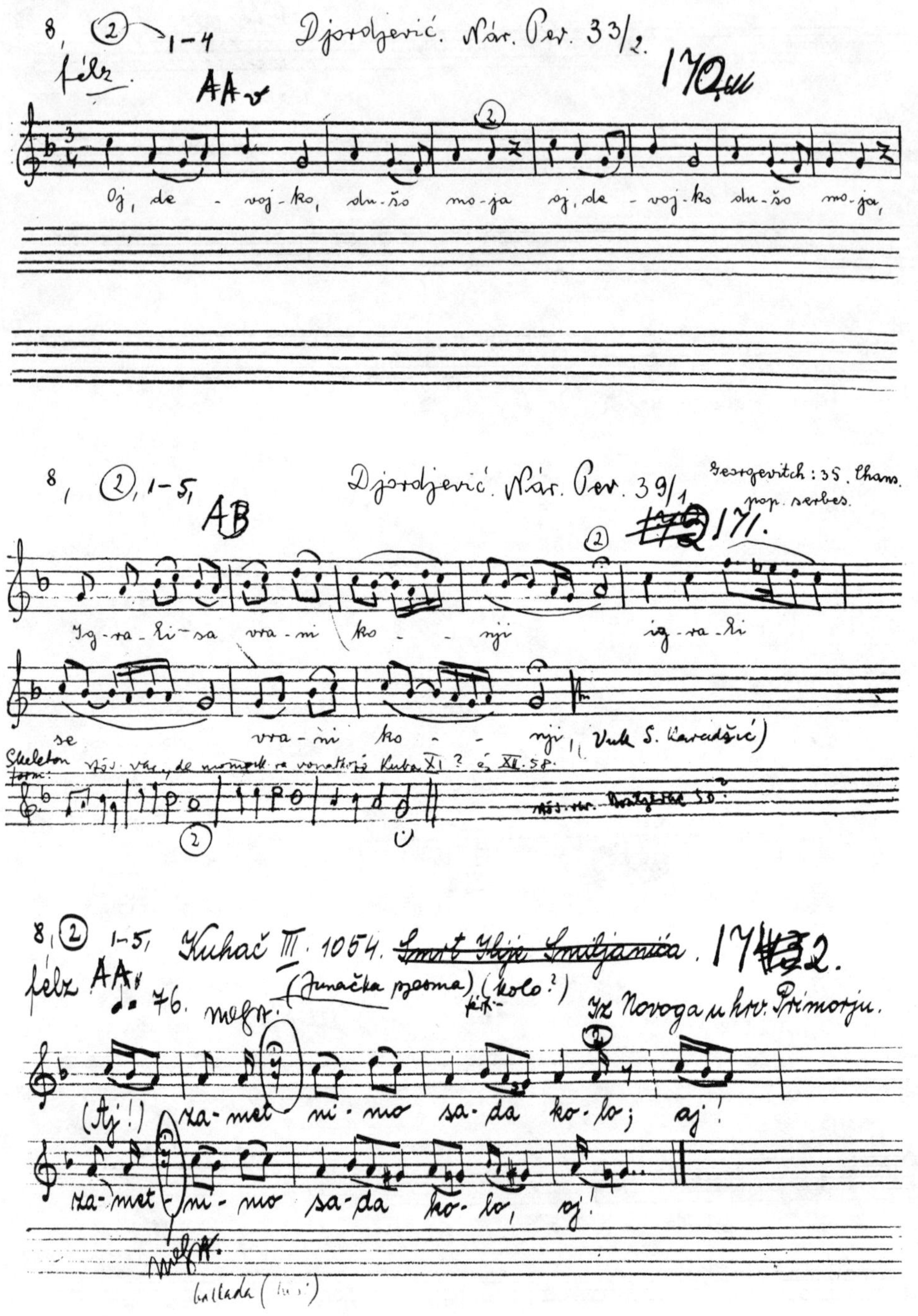
Djordjević. Nár. Pev. 33/2.
170
AA
Oj, de-voj-ko, du-šo mo-ja oj, de-voj-ko du-šo mo-ja,
Djordjević. Nár. Pev. 39/1
Georgevitch: 35. Chans. pop. serbes.
171.
AB
Ig-ra-li-sa vra-ni ko-nji ig-ra-li
se vra-ni ko-nji
Vuk S. Karadžić)
Skeleton form:
Kuhač III. 1054.
(Junačka pjesma) (kolo?)
Iz Novoga u hrv. Primorju.
(Aj!) za-met-ni-mo sa-da ko-lo; aj!
za-met-ni-mo sa-da ko-lo, aj!
ballada

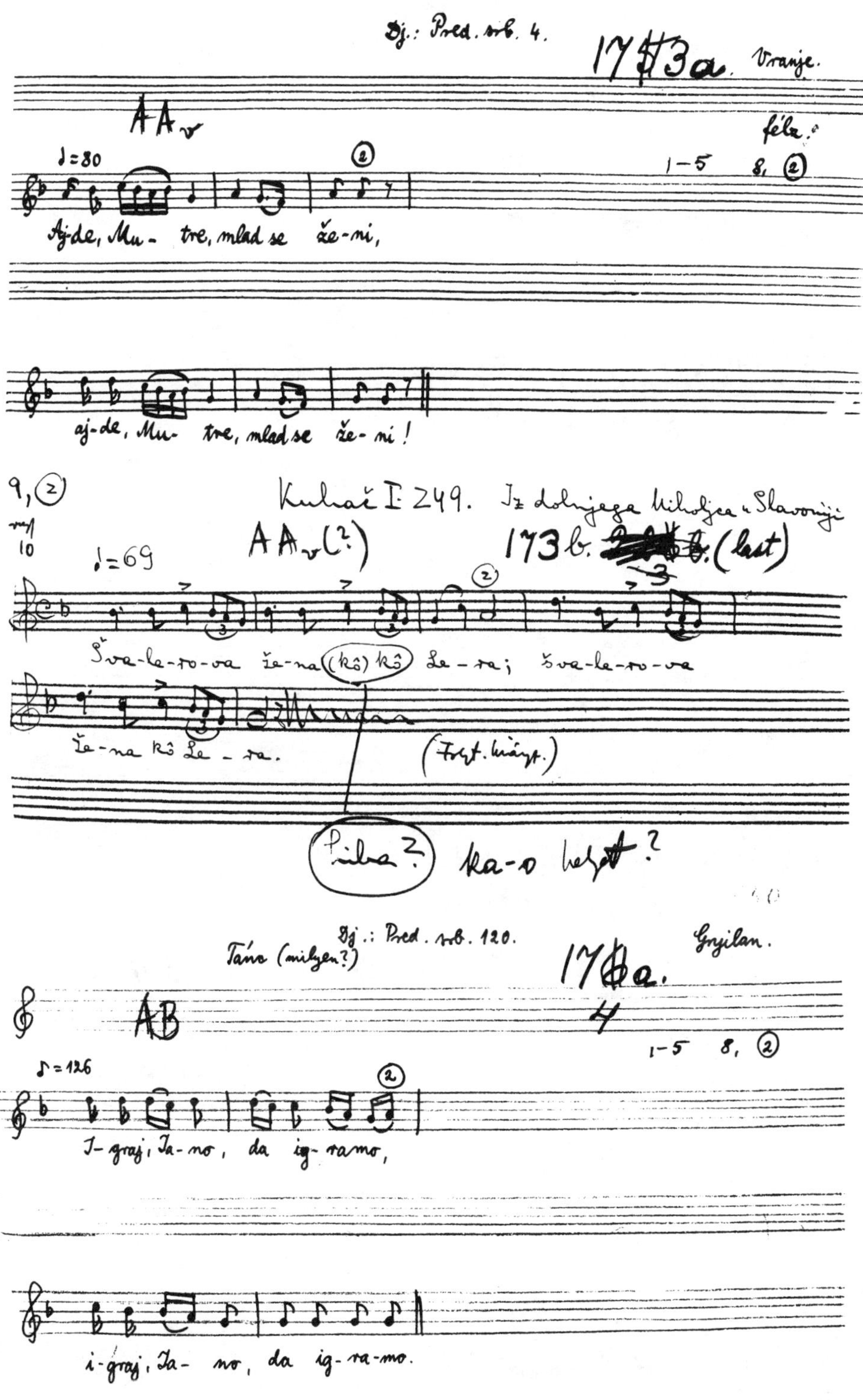

Dj.: Pred. sb. 4.
173a.
Vranje.
AAv
1–5 8, ②
Ajde, Mu- tre, mlad se že-ni,
aj-de, Mu- tre, mlad se že-ni!
9, ②
Kuhač I. 249. Iz dolnjega Miholjca u Slavoniji
AAv (?)
173b.
(last)
Šva-le-ro-va že-na (kô) kô Le-ra; šva-le-ro-va
že-na kô Le-ra.
Dj.: Pred. sb. 120.
Gnjilan.
173a.
AB
1–5 8, ②
I-graj, Ja-no, da ig-ramo,
i-graj, Ja-no, da ig-ra-mo.

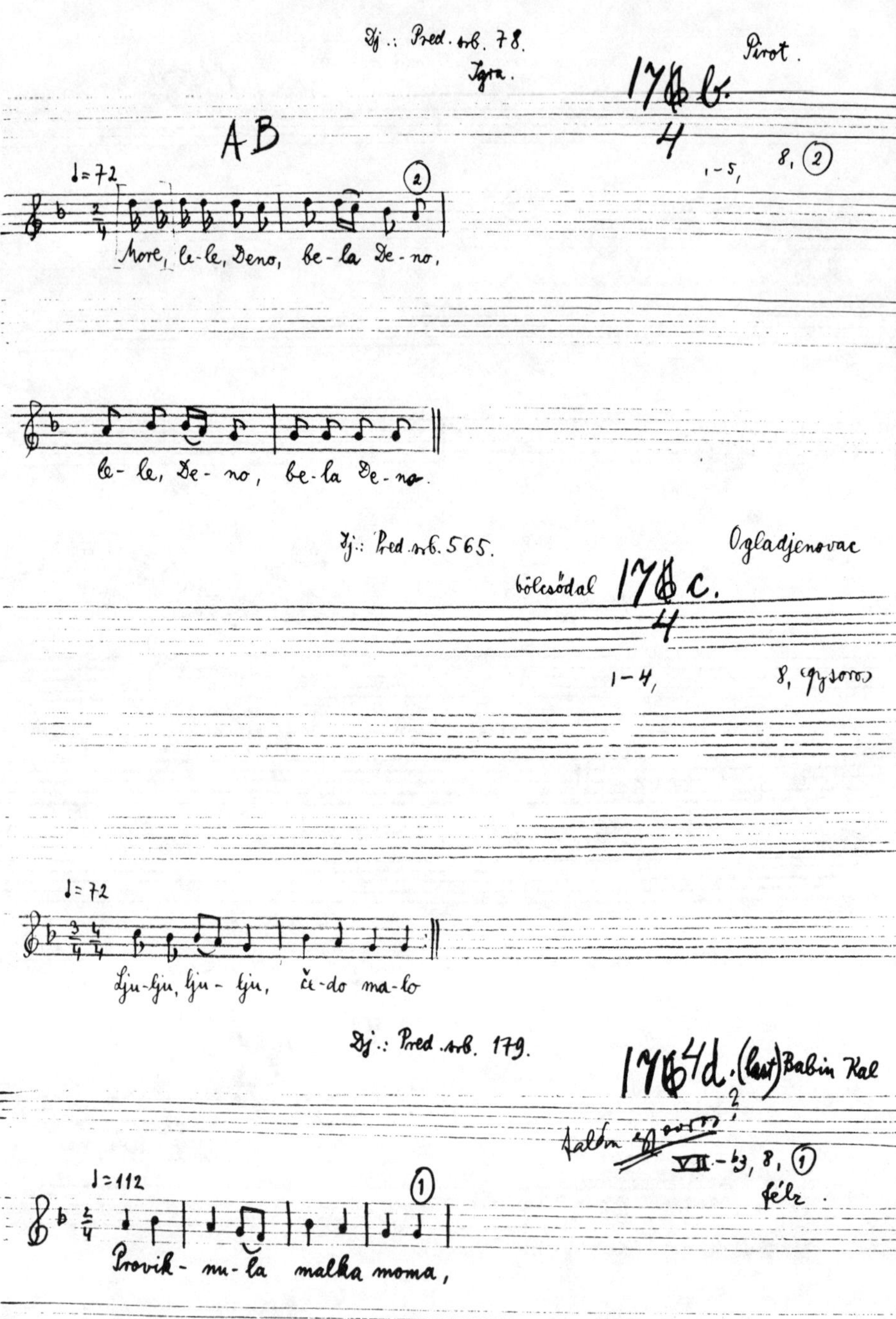

kroz So- vi-ju niz čar-ši-ju

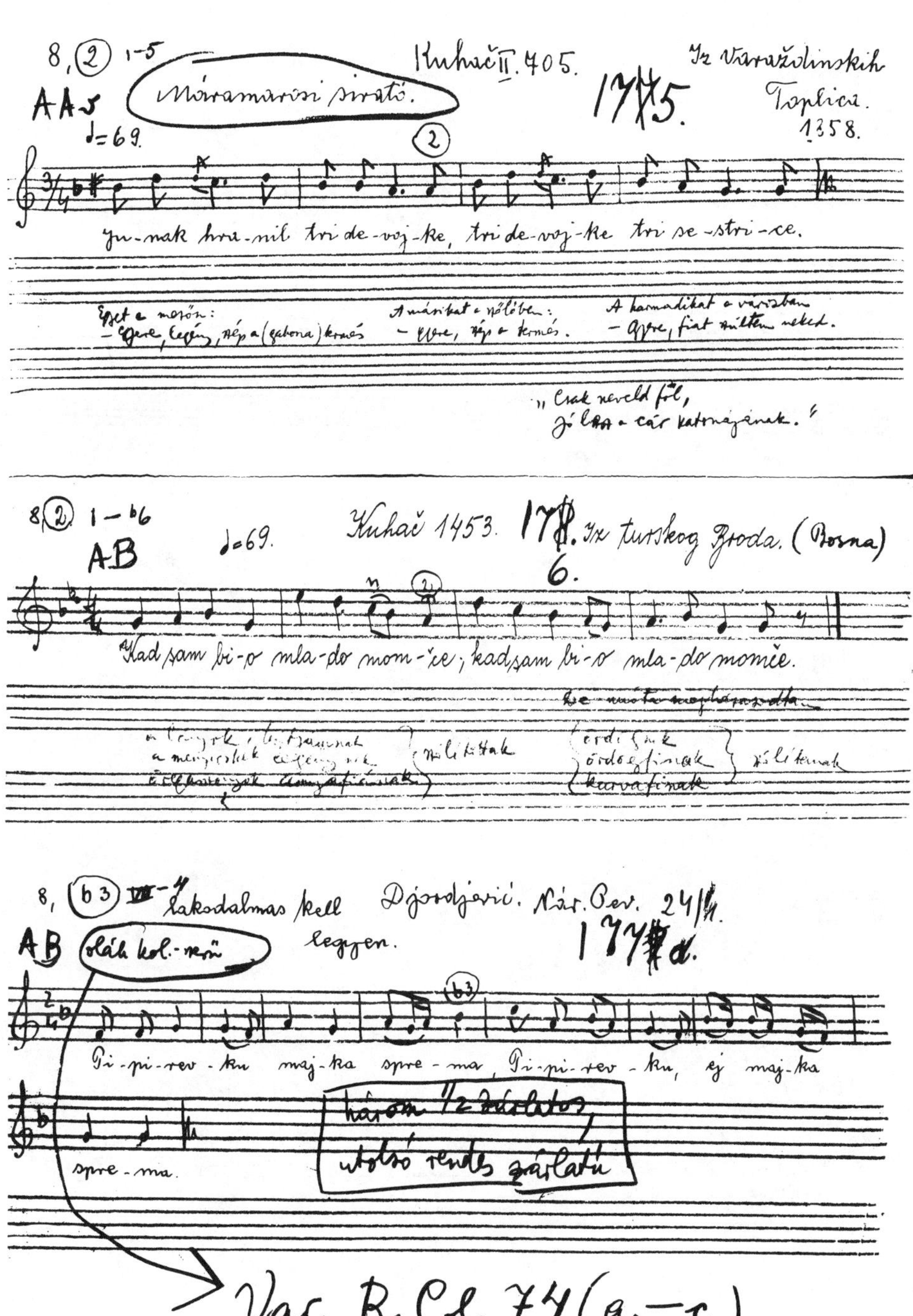
8, (2) 1-5
AA5
Máramarosi sirató.
Kuhač II. 405.
Iz Varaždinskih Toplica.
1358.
♩=69
Ju-nak hra-nil tri de-voj-ke, tri de-voj-ke tri se-stri-ce.
8, (2) 1-b6
AB
♩=69
Kuhač 1453.
Iz turskog Broda. (Bosna)
Kad sam bi-o mla-do mom-če, kad sam bi-o mla-do momče.
8, (b3) VII-4
Lakodalmas kell leggyen.
Djordjević. Nár. Pev. 24/4.
AB
Pi-pi-rev-ku maj-ka spre-ma, Pi-pi-rev-ku, ej maj-ka
spre-ma.
három 1/2 zárlatos,
utolsó rendes zárlatú
Var. B. Col. 74 (a.–c.)

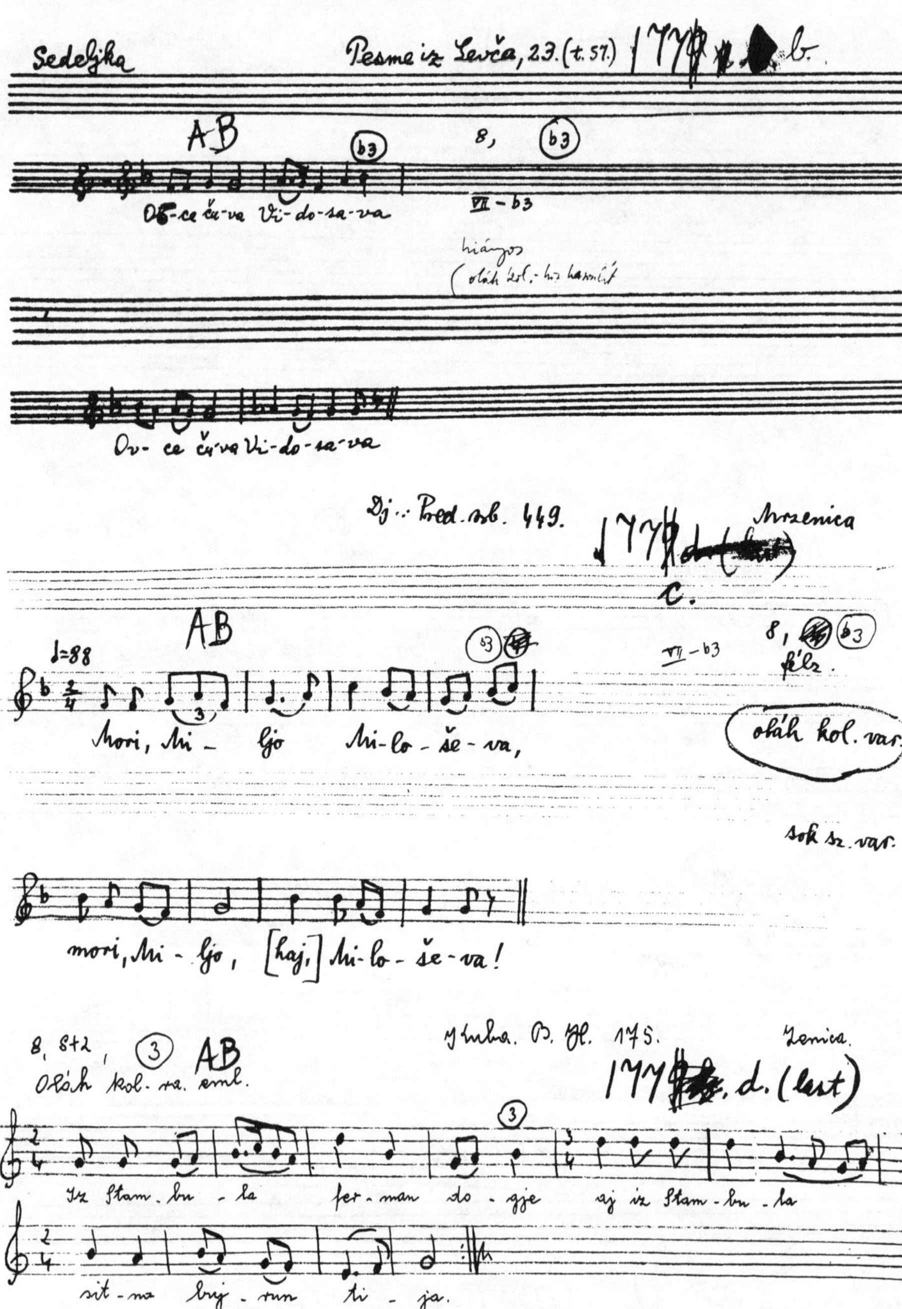
Sedeljka
Pesme iz Levča, 23. (t. 57.)
b.
AB
b3
8,
Ov-ce ču-va Vi-do-sa-va
VII – b3
Ov- ce ču-va Vi-do-sa-va
Dj.: Pred. zb. 449.
Mrzenica
c.
AB
♩=88
b3
8,
VII – b3
félz.
Mori, Mi- ljo Mi-lo-še-va,
oláh kol. var.
sok sz. var.
mori, Mi-ljo, [haj,] Mi-lo-še-va!
8, 8+2, 3 AB
Oláh kol. va. eml.
Kuba. B. H. 175.
Zenica.
d. (last)
3
Iz Stam-bu-la fer-man do-gje aj iz Stam-bu-la
sit-na buj-run ti-ja.

8, (b3) VII – 4 Kuba B.H. 822.
AB
Andante.
Maglaj (uspavanka)
O, bešiko, zlato moje, i u
be – ši čedo mo – je!
8, (b3) VII – 4
Kuba XII. 59.
179.
Pirot?
pent. AB. phryg?
Oj, Ma-ri - - - če, oj, ru - bi - - - če što si
gla-vu pre-vr-za - - la?
180a.
Leskovac.
AB
♪ = 116
1 – 4,
8, (b3)
(sic)
Oj, neve-ne še-sto-re-de,
oj, ne-ve-ne še - sto-re-de.

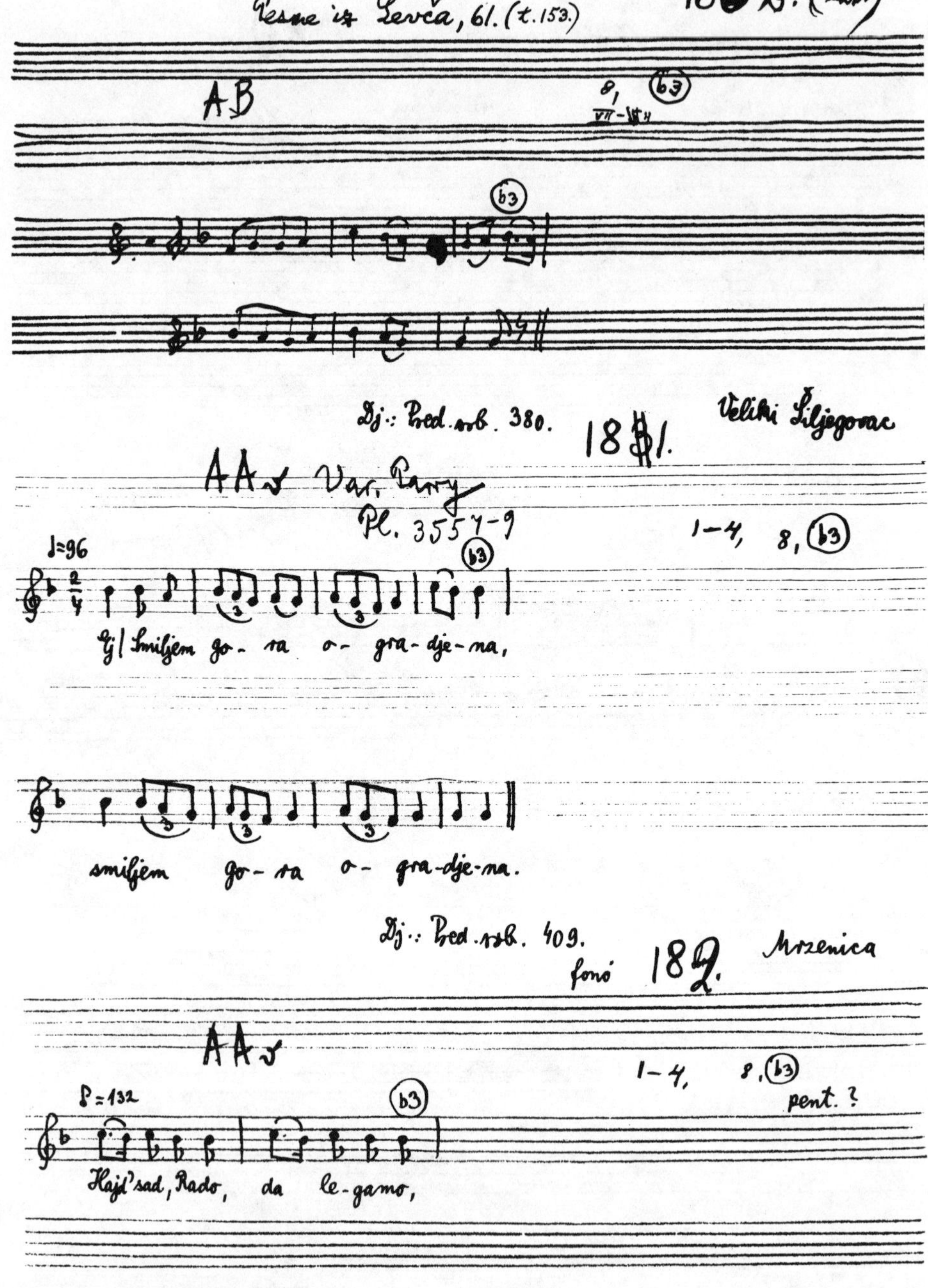
Pesme iz Levča, 61. (t. 153.)
180 b. (last)
AB
Dj.: Pred. zb. 380.
181.
Veliki Šiljegovac
AA v Var. Parry
Pl. 3557-9
1-4, 8, b3
Ej! Smiljem go- ra o- gra- dje- na,
smiljem go- ra o- gra-dje-na.
Dj.: Pred. zb. 409.
fono 182.
Mrzenica
AA v
1-4, 8, b3
pent. ?
Hajd' sad, Rado, da le- gamo,
hajd' sad, Rado, da le- gamo.

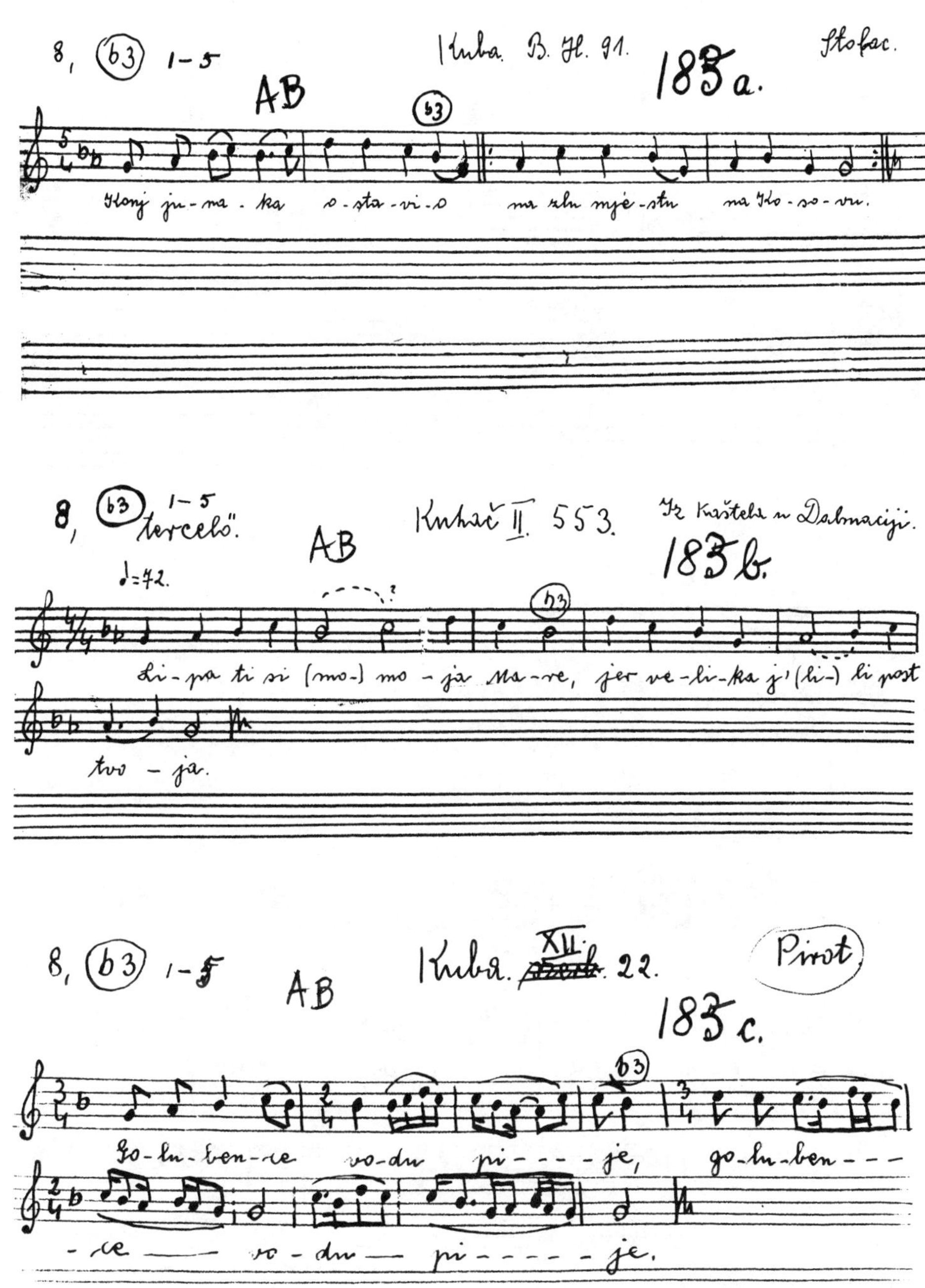

8, (b3) 1–5
Kuba. B. H. 91.
183a.
Stolac.
AB
(b3)
Konj ju-na-ka o-sta-vi-o na zlu mje-stu na Ko-so-vu.
8, (b3) 1–5 „tercelö".
Kuhač II. 553.
Iz Kaštela u Dalmaciji.
AB
183b.
♩=72.
(b3)
Li-pa ti si (mo-) mo-ja Ma-re, jer ve-li-ka j' (li-) li post
tvo-ja.
8, (b3) 1–5
Kuba. XII. 22.
Pirot
AB
183c.
(b3)
Go-lu-ben-ce vo-du pi- - - -je, go-lu-ben- - -
-ce — vo-du — pi- - - - -je.

8, (b3) VII – 5
Kuba. Horvát I. 10.
Podvinja Sl.
AB
183d.
(b3)
Ka-ran-fi-lu, cve-će mo-je, ka-ran-fi-lu,
cve-će mo-je.
Dj.: Pred. srb. 63.
183e.
Leskovac
AB
♩= 76
(b3)
1–5
8, (b3)
Slavej pi-le, ne poj ra- no,
slavej pi- le ne poj ra- no.
8, (b3)
1–5
tercelő?
or phryg.? AB
Kuba. XII. 50.
Vrčice.
183f.
(b3)
Viš-viš-nji-ca — rod ro-di-la — viš-viš-nji-
-ca rod ro-di-la.
Skeleton form:

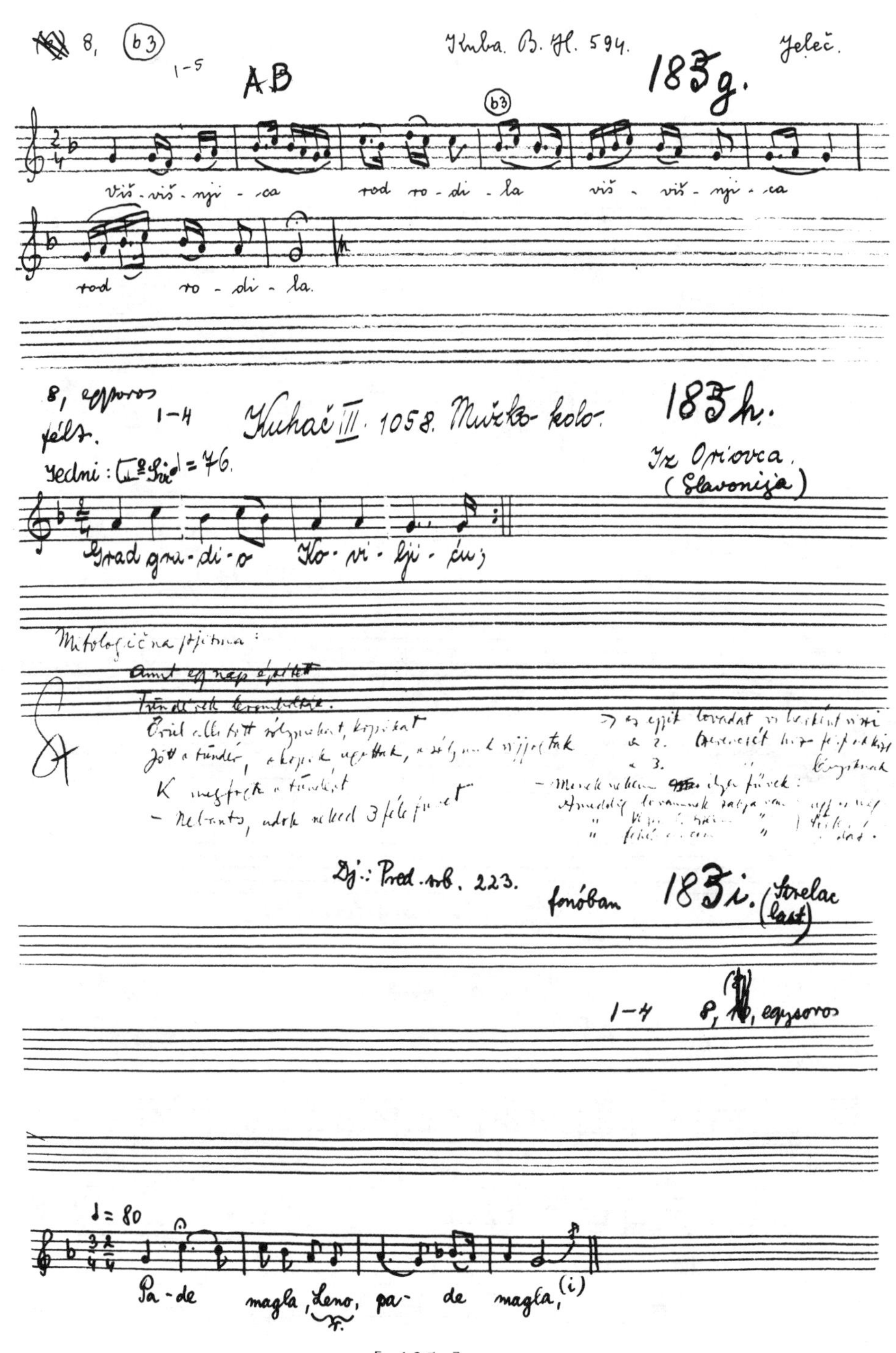
8, (b3)
Kuba. B. H. 594.
Jeleč.
1-5
AB
183g.
(b3)
viš-viš-nji-ca rod ro-di-la viš-viš-nji-ca
rod ro-di-la.
8, egysoros félz.
1-4
Kuhač III. 1058. Mužko-kolo.
183h.
Iz Oriovca. (Slavonija)
Grad gra-di-o Ko-vi-lji-ću;
Mitologična pjesma:
Dj.: Pred. zb. 223.
fonóban
183i.
Strelac (last)
1-4
8, egysoros
♩= 80
Pa-de magla, Leno, pa- de magla, (i)

Dj.: Pred. zb. 134.
Velika Lukanja
AA
1–5 8, b3
♩=96
Pri-pi-rev-ku majka češ-lja,
Pri-pi-rev-ku maj-ka češ-lja.
8, b3 1-5,
AB
Kuba. B.H. 233.
Stolac.
(=XIII. 51)*
Si-noć sam ti do-la-ži-----o ej si-noć sam ti
do-la-ži------o.
* with text: */Ja golube, moj golube :/
73
8, b3 1–5
Kuba. XII. 4.
Pirot.
AB
Adagio. pentat.
Sla-vulj pi---le, ne poj ra-----no,
sla-vulj pi-le, ne poj ra----no.

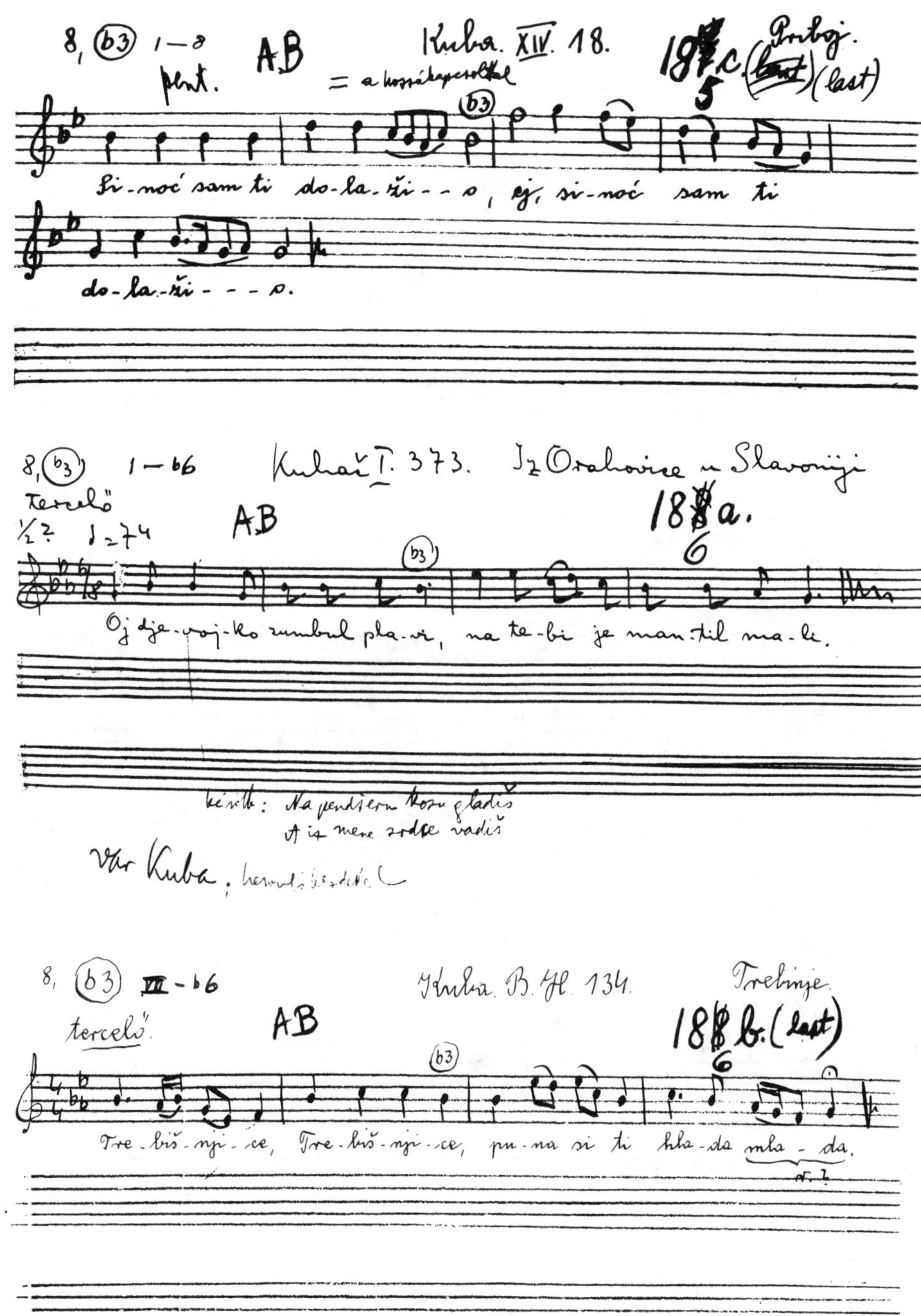
8, (b3) 1—8
AB
Kuba. XIV. 18.
(last)
Si-noć sam ti do-la-ži-- o, ej, si-noć sam ti
do-la-ži--- o.
8, (b3) 1—b6
Kuhač I. 373. Iz Orahovice u Slavoniji
AB
18 a.
Oj dje-voj-ko zumbul pla-vi, na te-bi je man-til ma-li.
Var Kuba
8, (b3) VII-b6
tercelő
Kuba. B. H. 134.
Trebinje.
AB
18 b. (last)
Tre-biš-nji-ce, Tre-biš-nji-ce, pu-na si ti hla-da mla-da.

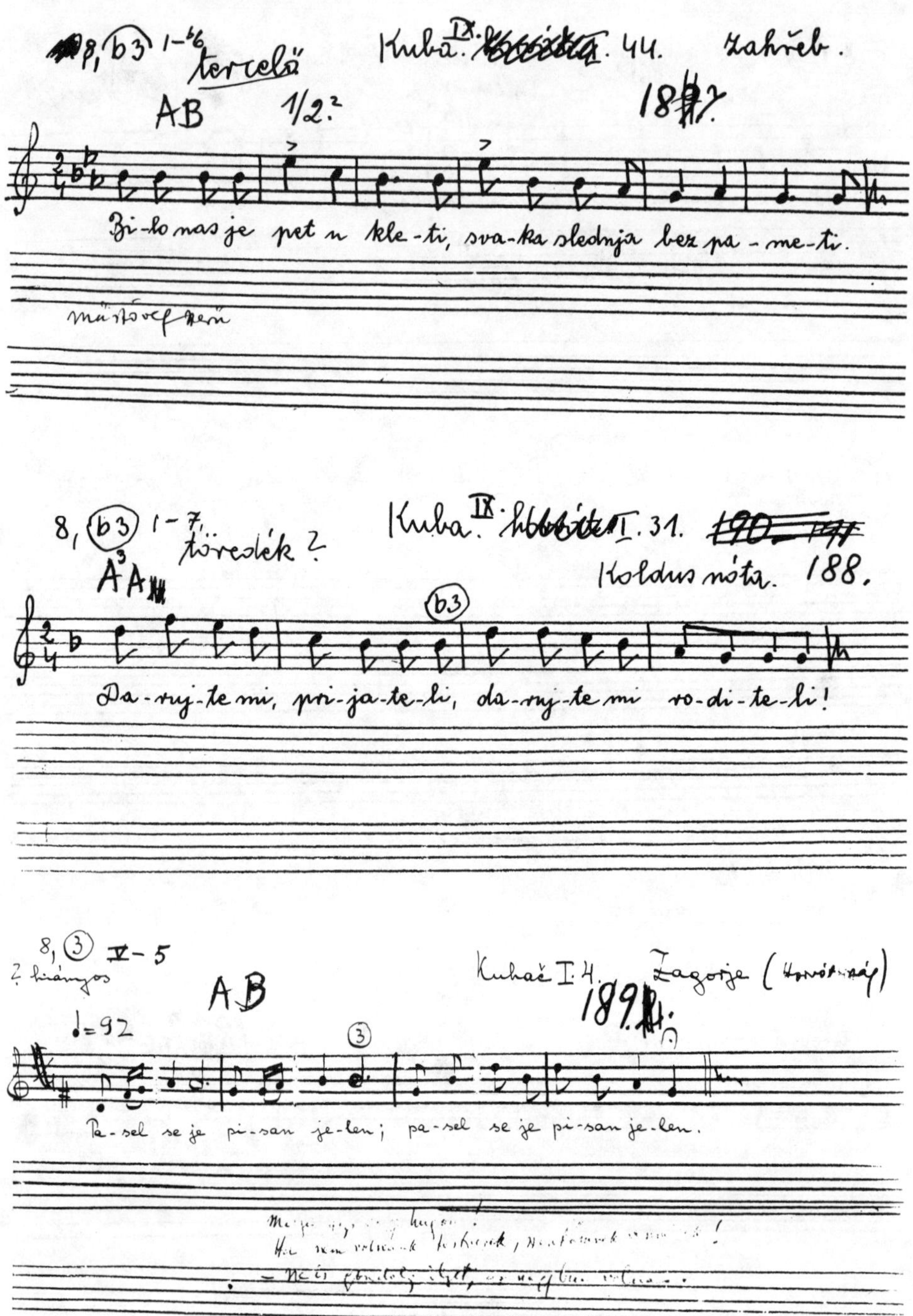

8, b3 1–6 tercelő
Kuba. IX. 44. Zahreb.
AB 1/2.
Bi-lo nas je pet u kle-ti, sva-ka slednja bez pa-me-ti.
8, b3 1–7. töredék?
Kuba. IX. I. 31.
Koldus nóta. 188.
Da-ruj-te mi, pri-ja-te-li, da-ruj-te mi ro-di-te-li!
8, 3 V–5
? hiányos
AB
♩=92
Kuhač I. 4.
Zagorje
Pa-sel se je pi-san je-len; pa-sel se je pi-san je-len.

8, ③ VII – 5
Kuba. B. H. 927.
Ljubinje.
AB
190.
Pu-če puš-ka le-de-nja-ča sa čar-da-ka le-re-vi-ca
8, ③ #VII – 3
Kuhač III. 1117.
♩= 120 · AA
Poskočnica.
194 a.
fót arató vijlesmtő
O-ganj go-ri v gornjen se-lu; o-ganj go-ri v gornjen se-lu.
Okol ognja kolo igra.
U kolu je nješto lipo
Nešto lipo neženjeno
Tri leta ni razčešano stb.
?!
Dj.: Bed. srb. 93.
194 b.
Pirot
1–2
8, egysoros
♪ = 126
Oj, ti Deno, Kara-De-no.

Pavlica
AA
1–4 8, ③
So-ne stra-ne vode Sa-ve
mi-la mo-ja, vo-de Sa-ve.
8, ③ 1–5
AB
Kolo.
Bihač.
Oj dje-voj-ko a-ža-li-jo, dra-gi ti se raz-bo-li-o.
8, ③ 1–5
AB
Bihać
O ja-vo-re ze-len bo-re o ja-vo-re ze-len bo-re.

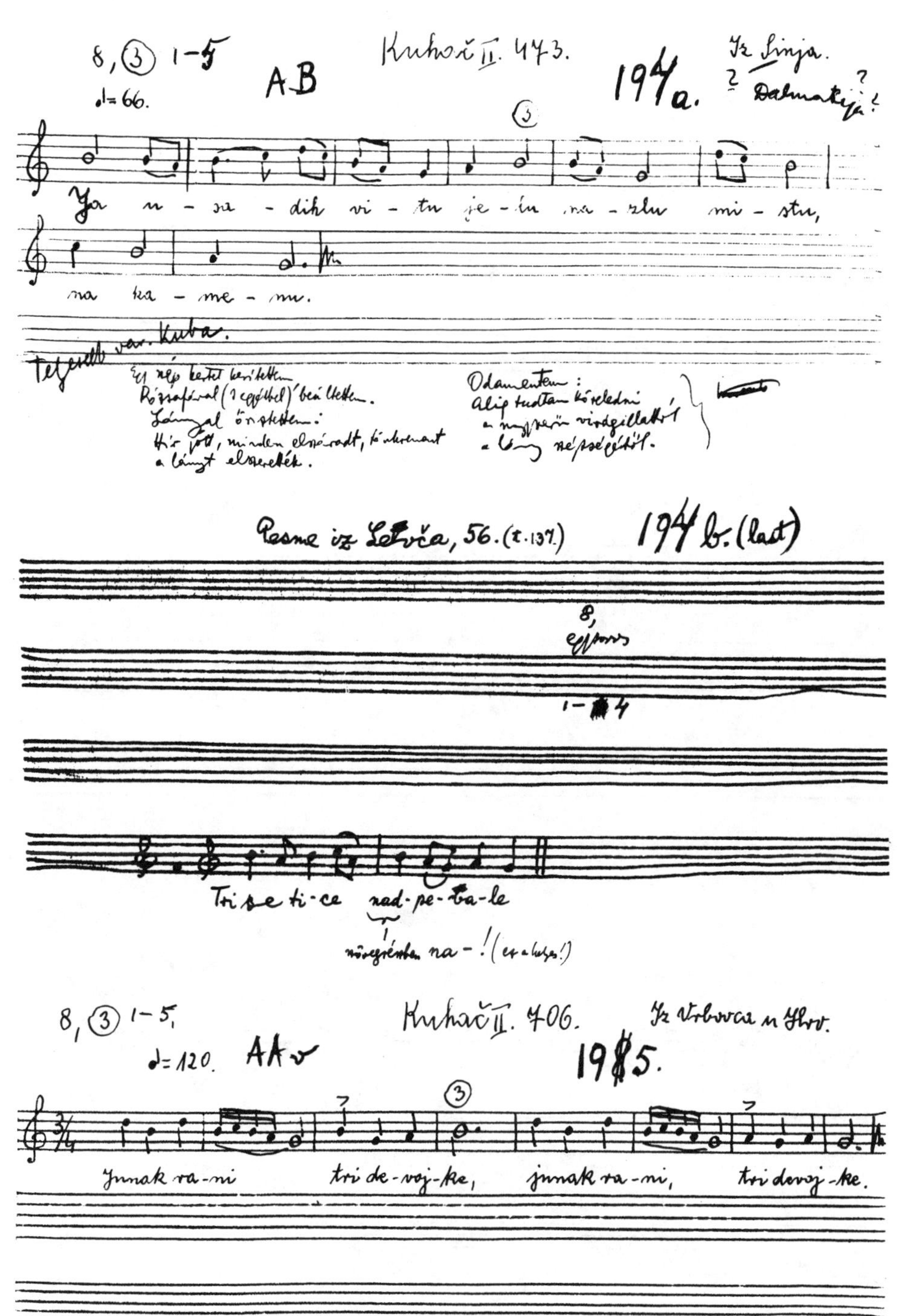

Kuhač II. 473.
Iz Sinja.
AB
194a.
Dalmatija
Odamentem
194 b.
Kuhač II. 706.
Iz Vrbovca u Hrv.
AA
Junak ra-ni tri de-voj-ke, junak ra-ni, tri devoj-ke.

8, (3) 1–6
AB
Kuba. B. H. 376.
Višegrad.
19/6a.
O dje - voj - ko i - me slat - ko, što je vr'je - me ta - ko krat - ko?
előbbihez.
8, (3) 1–6
AB
Kuba. B. H. 374.
Foča.
19/6b.
Ž - vo no - ćas tre - ća ve - čer ka - ko še - ćem pod tvoj pen - džer
előbbihez.
1–6 8, (3)
Kuba. B. H. 378.
Plevlje.
AB
19/6c.
O ja - bu - ko ša - re - ni - ko, što s'to - li - ko rod ro - di - la?

Allegretto. AB
Kuba. B.H. 1123
Metelka.
8, ③ V-5
Kuhač II. 487.
Od medje Medjumurske u Štajerskoj.
♩=60.
AB
le-pa Vi - da ple-je pro - so ra-no, ra - no med ro-sja-mi.
10, ③
Kuba. B. H. 374.
Sarajevo.
AB
(last)
vi-no pi - ju dva mi-la ja - ra - - na, ej vi-no pi - ju
dva mi-la ja - ra - na.

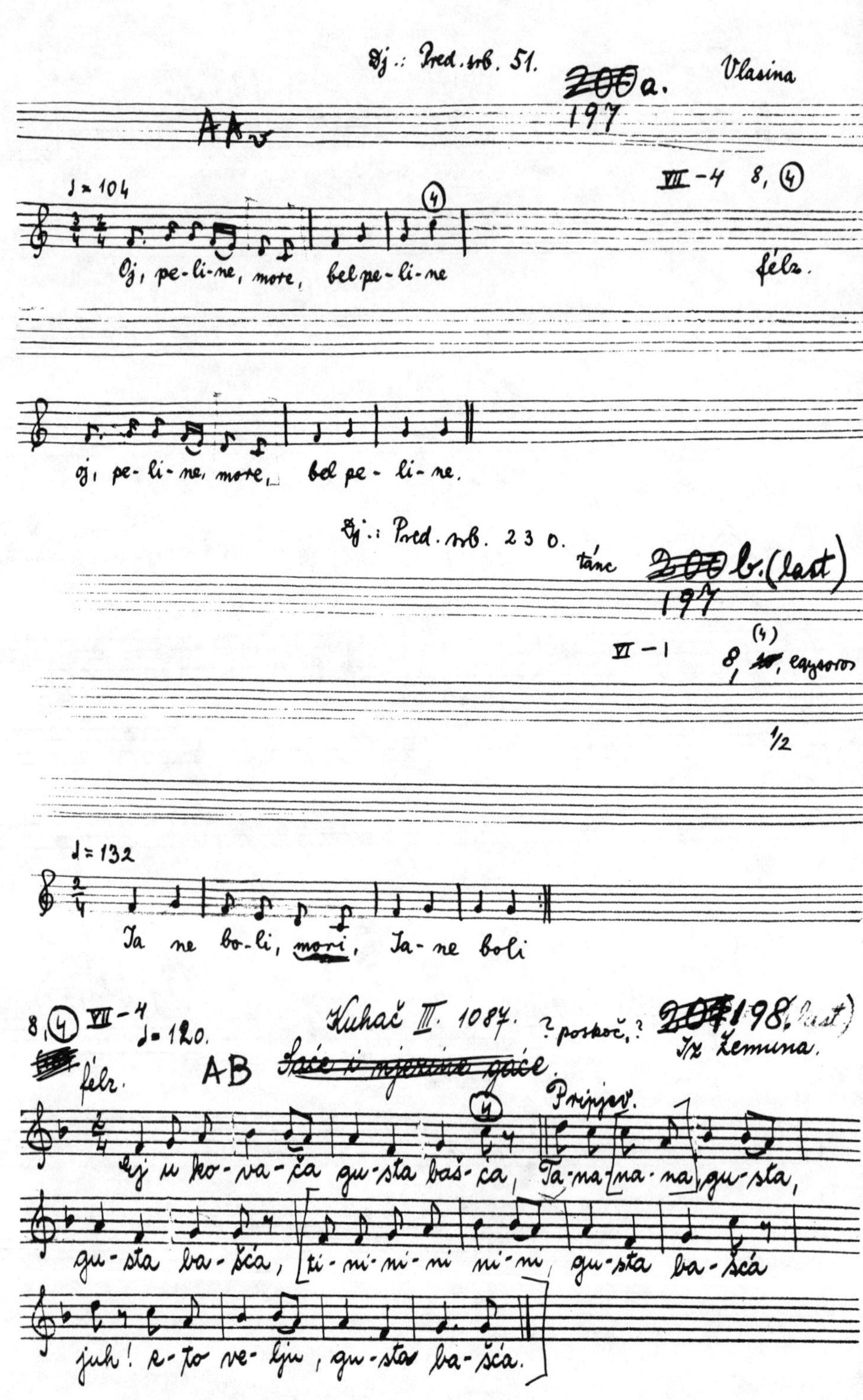

Dj.: Pred. zb. 51.
200 a.
197
Vlasina
AAv
VII -4 8, (4)
♩= 104
Oj, pe-li-ne, more, bel pe-li-ne
félz.
oj, pe-li-ne, more, bel pe-li-ne.
Dj.: Pred. zb. 230.
tánc
200 b. (last)
197
VI -1
8, (4), egysoros
1/2
♩= 132
Ja ne bo-li, mori, Ja-ne boli
8, (4) VII -4
♩= 120.
Kuhač III. 1087.
? poskoč. ?
198. last
Iz Zemuna.
félz.
AB
Pripjev.
Oj u ko-va-ča gu-sta baš-ča, Ta-na-na-na gu-sta,
gu-sta ba-šča, ti-ni-ni-ni ni-ni, gu-sta ba-šča
juh! e-to ve-lju, gu-stas ba-šča.

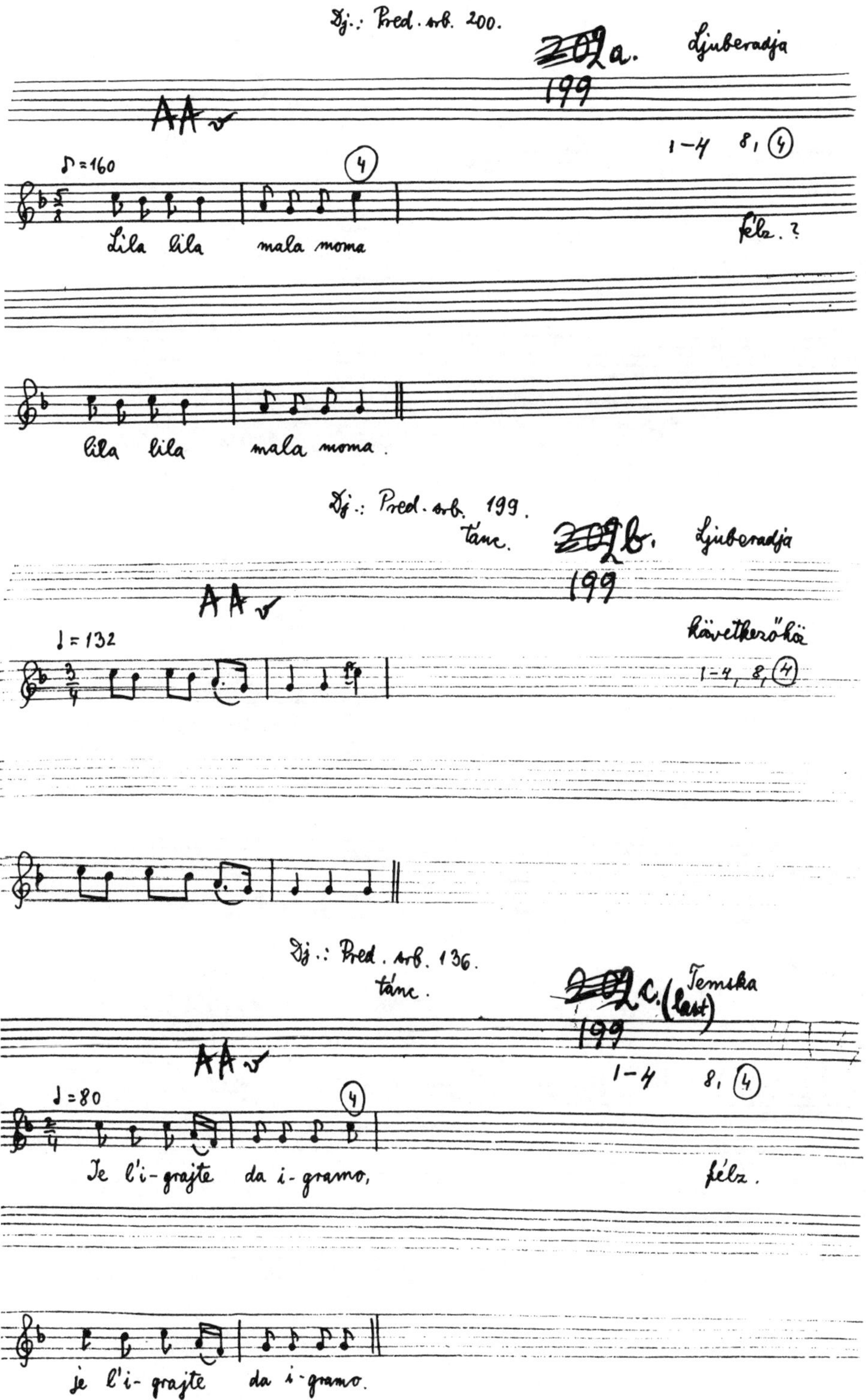
Dj.: Pred. srb. 200.
202a. Ljuberadja
199
AA
♪ = 160
1–4 8, (4)
Lila lila mala moma
félz. ?
lila lila mala moma.
Dj.: Pred. srb. 199.
tánc.
202b. Ljuberadja
199
AA
♩ = 132
1–4, 8, (4)
Dj.: Pred. srb. 136.
tánc.
202c. Temska (last)
199
AA
1–4 8, (4)
♩ = 80
Je l'i-grajte da i-gramo,
félz.
je l'i-grajte da i-gramo.

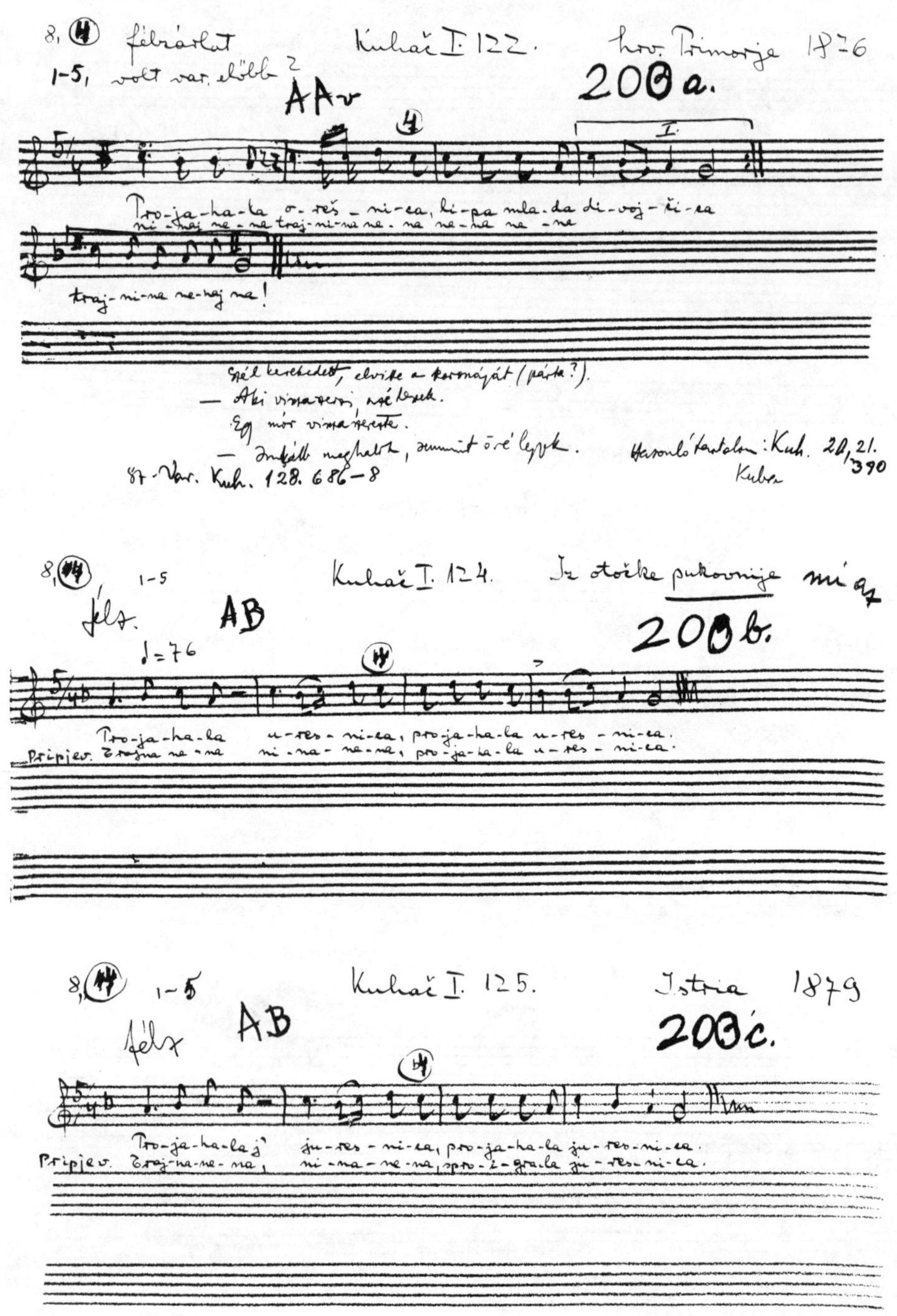

Kuhač I. 122.
Hrv. Primorje 1876
AAv
200a.
Pro-ja-ha-la o-reš-ni-ca, ki-pa mla-da di-voj-či-ca
Kuhač I. 124.
AB
200b.
♩=76
Pro-ja-ha-la u-res-ni-ca, pro-ja-ha-la u-res-ni-ca.
Pripjev.
Kuhač I. 125.
Istria 1879
AB
200c.
Pripjev.

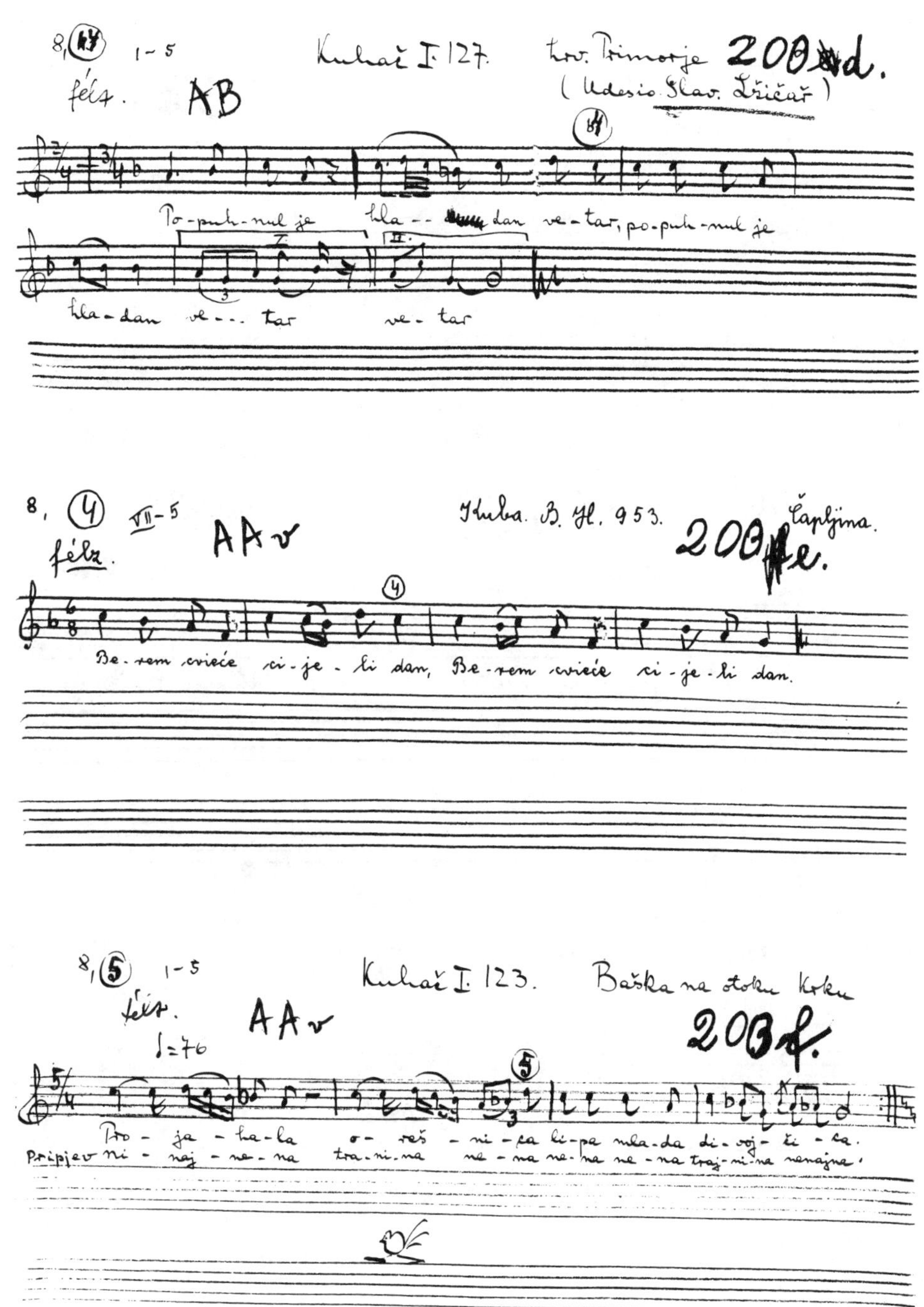
1–5
Kuhač I. 127.
AB
Po-puh-nul je hla-- dan ve-tar, po-puh-nul je
hla-dan ve-- tar ve-tar
VII–5
AAv
Kuba. B. H. 953.
Čapljina.
Be-rem cvieće ci-je-li dan, Be-rem cvieće ci-je-li dan.
1–5
Kuhač I. 123.
Baška na otoku Krku
AAv
♩=76
Pro-ja-ha-la o-reš-ni-ca li-pa mla-da di-voj-či-ca.
Pripjev ni-naj-ne-na tra-ni-na ne-na ne-na ne-na traj-ni-na nenajne.

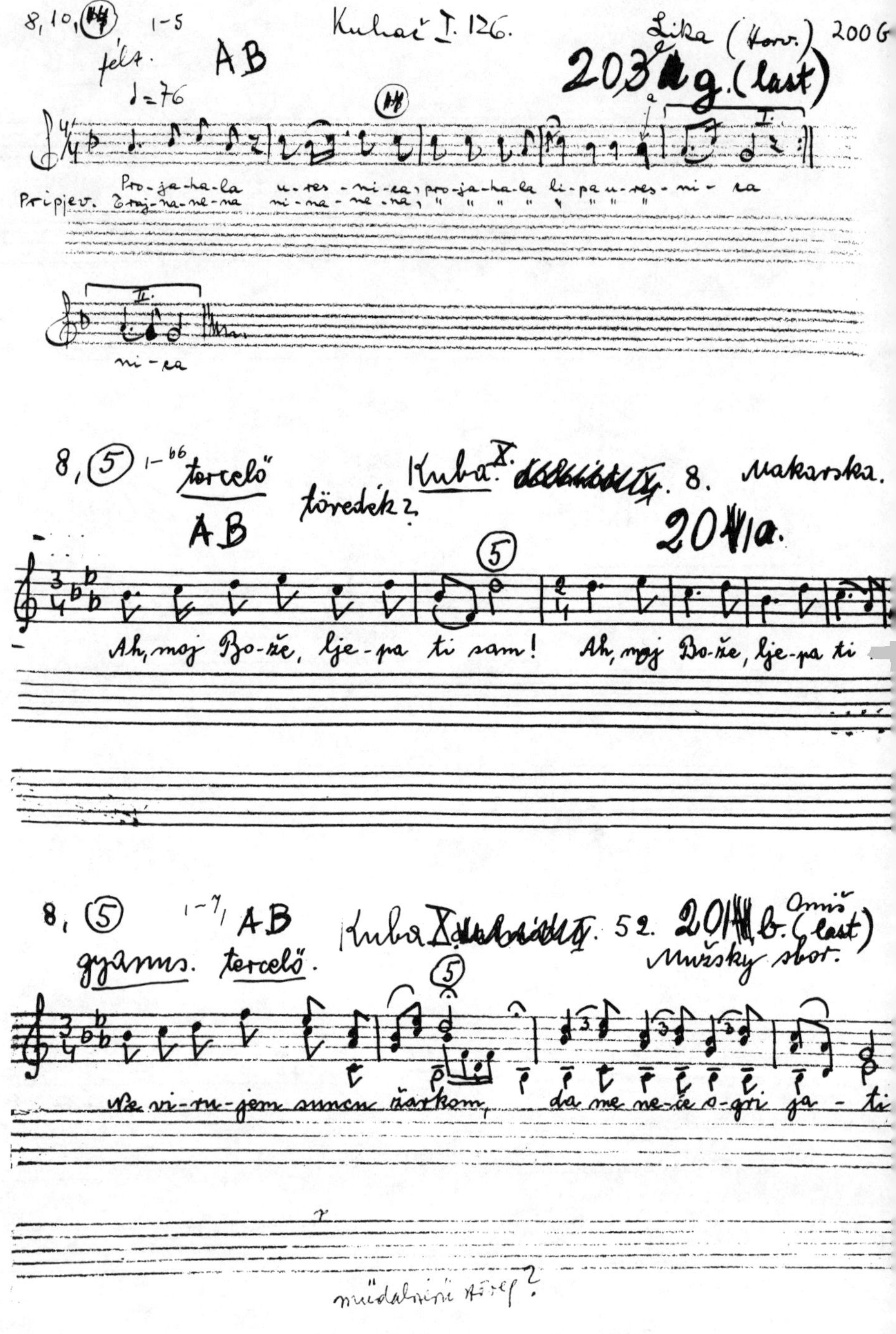

Kuhač I. 126.
Lika (Horv.)
AB
203 g. (last)
Pro-ja-ha-la u-res-ni-ca, pro-ja-ha-la li-pa u-res-ni-ca
Pripjev. Traj-na-ne-na ni-na-ne-na,
ni-ca
tercelő
töredék?
Kuba X. 8. Makarska.
AB
201a.
Ah, moj Bo-že, lje-pa ti sam! Ah, moj Bo-že, lje-pa ti
AB
Kuba X. 52.
201b. (last)
Omiš
gyanus. tercelő.
Mužsky sbor.
Ne vi-ru-jem suncu žarkom, da me ne-će o-gri-ja-ti

töredék. AA
Kuhač II. 45.
Iz Kolnofa u Šopronjskoj županiji.
202.
d = 56.
Lakodalmas (pálinka-iváskor)
Crnoljevica
AB
203.
d = 126
E! Na dve granće dve ja-bu-će
na-pi se ğu-tu ra-ći-ju!
töredék
tercelő
AA
Kuhač 1380.
204.
Iz Senja
(Hrv. Primorje)
d = 76.
Haj-de-mo ku-ći zo-ra je-, haj-de-mo ku-ći zo-ra, zo-ra
je.

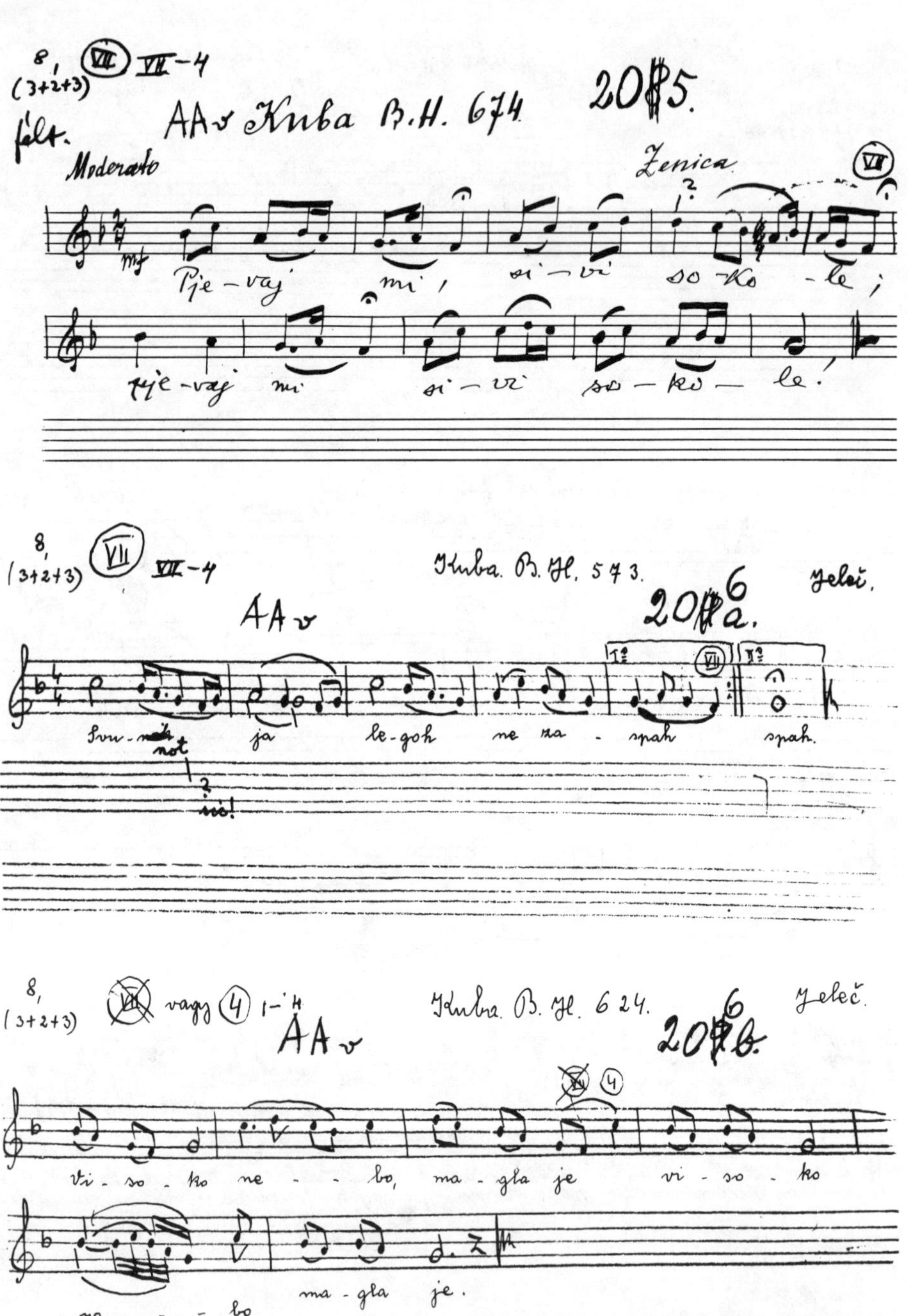

AA v Kuba B.H. 674
2085.
Zenica
Moderato
Pje-vaj mi, si-vi so-ko-le;
pje-vaj mi si-vi so-ko-le.
Kuba. B. H. 573.
Jelač.
AA v
Snu-ja le-goh ne za-spah spah.
Kuba. B. H. 624.
Jeleč.
AA v
Vi-so-ko ne-bo, ma-gla je vi-so-ko
ne-bo ma-gla je.

8, (3+2+3)
félz.
előbbihez
AA v BB v
Kuba. B. H. 625.
Jajce
Is - tr - goh stru - - čak sa zem - lje lje da - doh
ga dra - gom kraj se - be kraj se - be

8, (3+2+3)
VII - 5
Kuba B. H.
AB 721.
Bihać
Andante
Ši - roko po - lje, kraj nema; du - boka
rje ka, kraj ne - ma

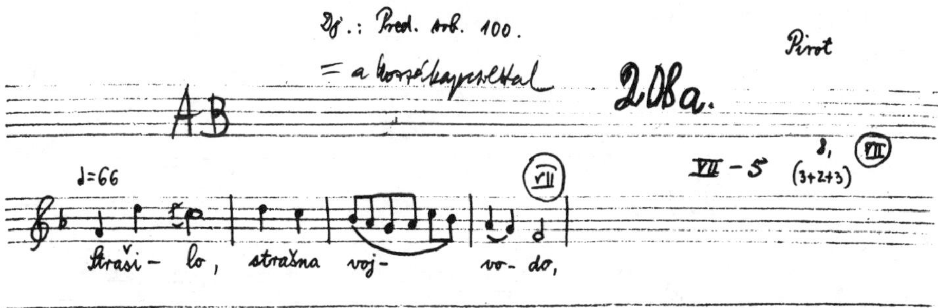
Pirot
AB
♩=66
VII - 5
8, (3+2+3)
Straši - lo, strašna voj - vo - do,

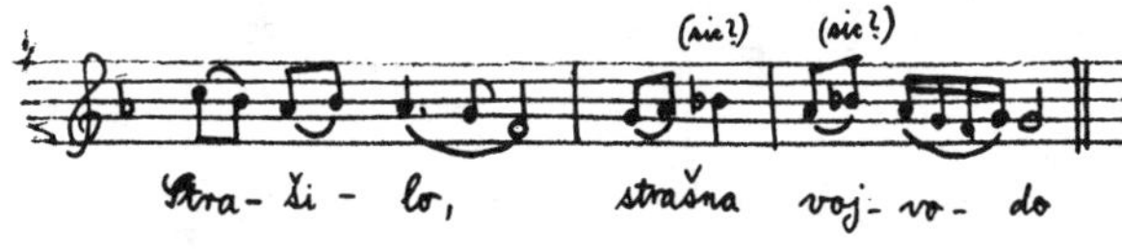
(sic?)
(sic?)
Stra - ši - lo, strašna voj - vo - do

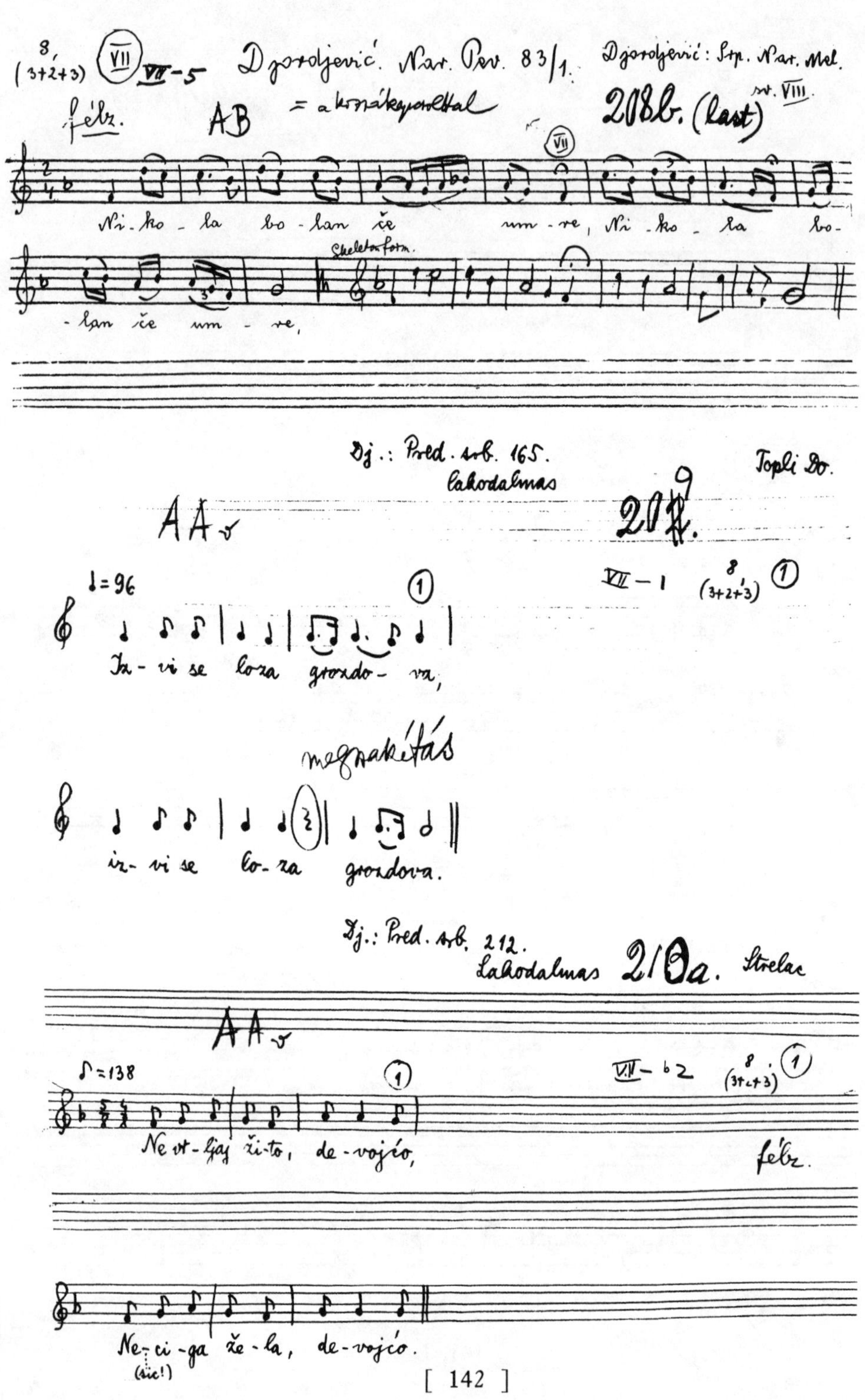
Djordjević. Nar. Pev. 83/1.
Djordjević: Srp. Nar. Mel.
208b. (last)
AB
félz.
Ni-ko-la bo-lan če um-re, Ni-ko-la bo-lan če um-re,
Skeleton form.
Dj.: Pred. srb. 165.
Lakodalmas
Topli Do.
209.
AA
♩=96
Iz-vi se loza grozdo-va,
megrakítás
iz-vi se lo-za grozdova.
Dj.: Pred. srb. 212.
Lakodalmas
210a.
Strelac
AA
♪=138
Ne vr-ljaj ži-to, de-vojćo,
félz.
Ne-ci-ga že-la, de-vojćo.
(sic!)

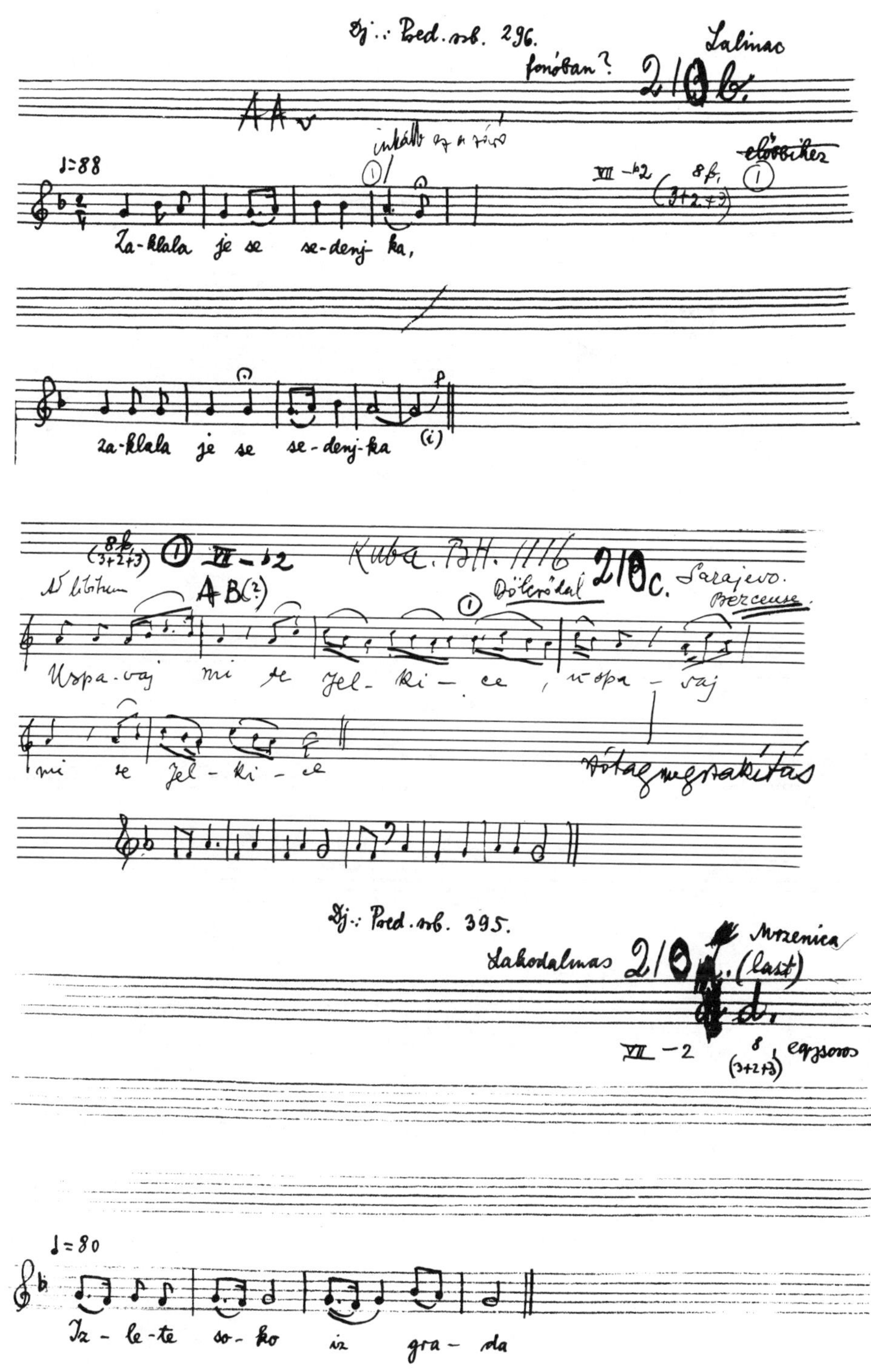

Dj.: Pred. sb. 296.
Lalinac
fonóban?
210b.
AA
♩=88
VII – b2
8 f.
(3+2+3)
Za-klala je se se-denj-ka,
za-klala je se se-denj-ka (i)
(8 f. 3+2+3)
VII – b2
Kuba. BH. 1116
210c.
Sarajevo.
Bölcsődal
Berceuse
AB(?)
Uspa-vaj mi se Jel-ki-ce, uspa-vaj
mi se Jel-ki-ce
Dj.: Pred. sb. 395.
Lakodalmas
210d.
(last)
VII – 2
8
(3+2+3)
egysoros
♩=80
Iz-le-te so-ko iz gra-da

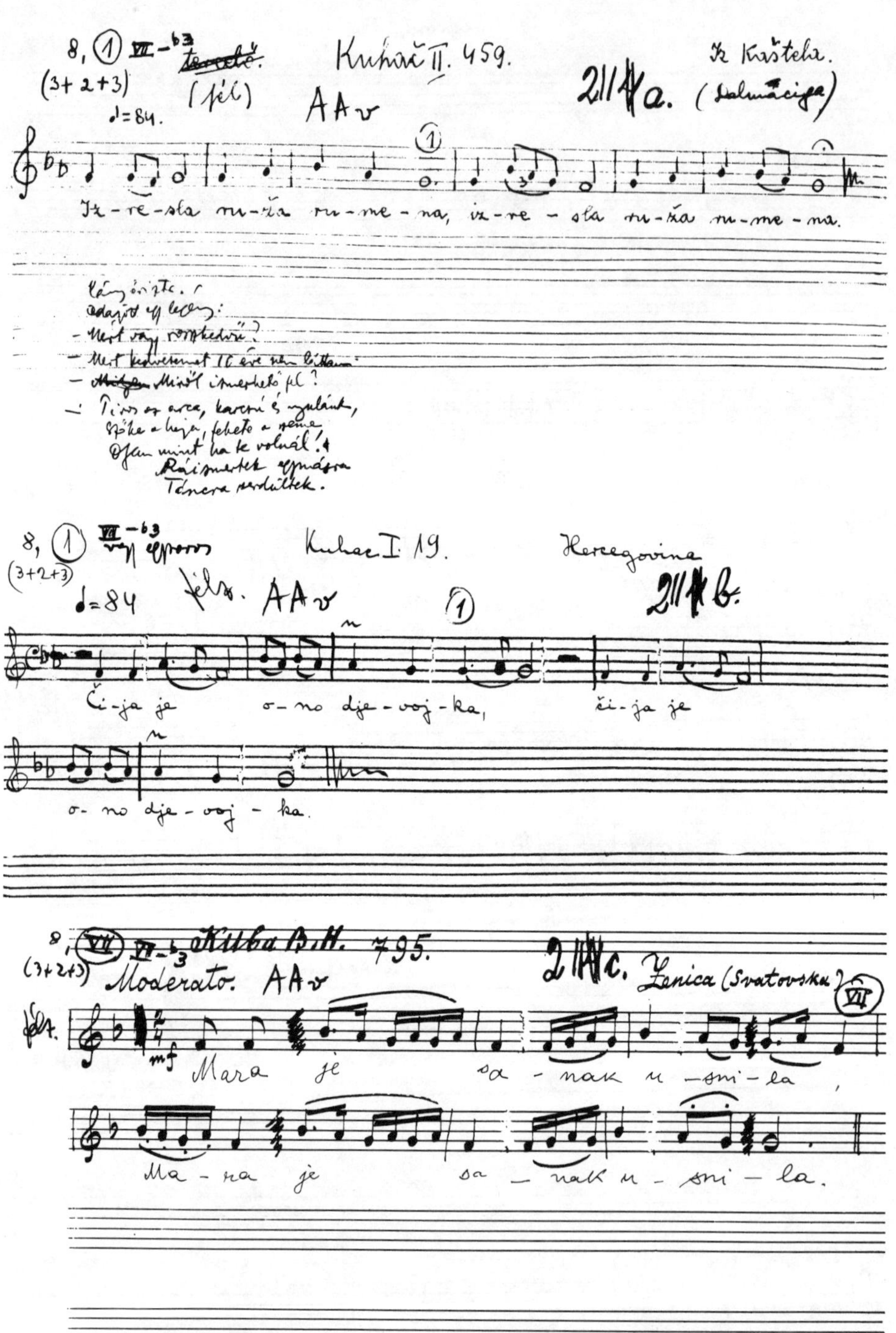
Kuhač II. 459.
Iz Kaštela.
211/a. (Dalmacija)
AAv
Iz-re-sla ru-ža ru-me-na, iz-re-sla ru-ža ru-me-na.
Kuhač I. 19.
Hercegovina
211/b.
AAv
Či-ja je o-no dje-voj-ka, či-ja je o-no dje-voj-ka.
Moderato. AAv
211/c. Ženica (Svatovska)
Mara je sa-nak u-sni-la, Ma-ra je sa-nak u-sni-la.

214 d.
Temska
(last)
AB(?)
VII – b3
8, (3+2+3)
Goro le go-ro zele- na,
goro le go-ro ze-le-na.
212 a.
Kuba B.-H. 450
AA
Rogatica
mf
212 b. (last)
Krupa (Svatovska)
Moderato.
mf

Kuba B.H. 479.
Moderato
Trnovo.
mf
Djevoj-ko moja Gje po-
to, dje-voj- ko, moja
Gje- po- to-!

Kuba B.H. 463
Andante AA
Ženica
Planino moja, sta-ri- no, lele,
pla-ni-no mo-ja, sta-ri- no!

Kuba B.-H. 467.
Moderato
ABBA
Kalinovik.
mf
Pod onom go-rom ze - le-nom,
ze - le-nom, pod onom gorom
Cf. № 1049!

Kuba B.H. 489.
214c.
Moderato AB
Čajniče.
Planino, moja starino, [lele], planino,
moja sta-ri-no.
Kuba B.H. 466.
214d.
Andante AA
Kalinovik.
Momče mi prodje kroz se-lo
momče mi pro-gje kroz se- kroz se-lo.
lo
Kuba B.H. 490
214e. (last)
Allegro AB
U Vakuf. (Kolo)
Aj, Po-savlje, ravno polje; aj, Posavlje,
ravno polje.

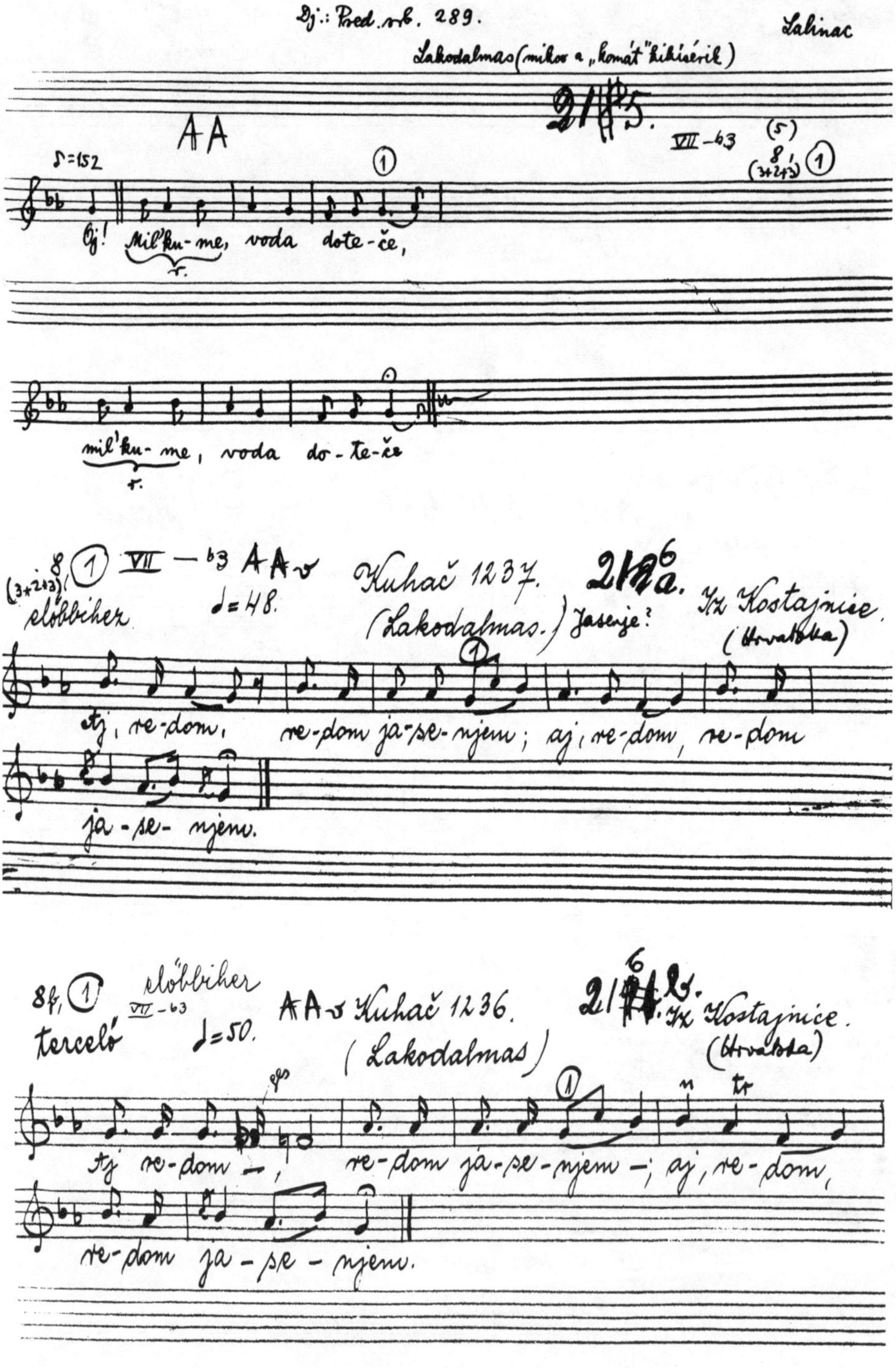

Dj.: Pred. vb. 289. Lalinac

Lakodalmas (mikor a „komát" kikísérik)

21/5.

AA

♪=152 VII–b3 (5) 8, (3+2+3) (1)

Oj! Mil'ku-me, voda dote-če,

mil'ku-me, voda do-te-če

8, (3+2+3) (1) VII — b3 AA∨ Kuhač 1237. 21/6a. Iz Kostajnice.

előbbihez ♩=48. (Lakodalmas.) Jasenje? (Hrvatska)

Oj, re-dom, re-dom ja-se-njem; aj, re-dom, re-dom

ja-se-njem.

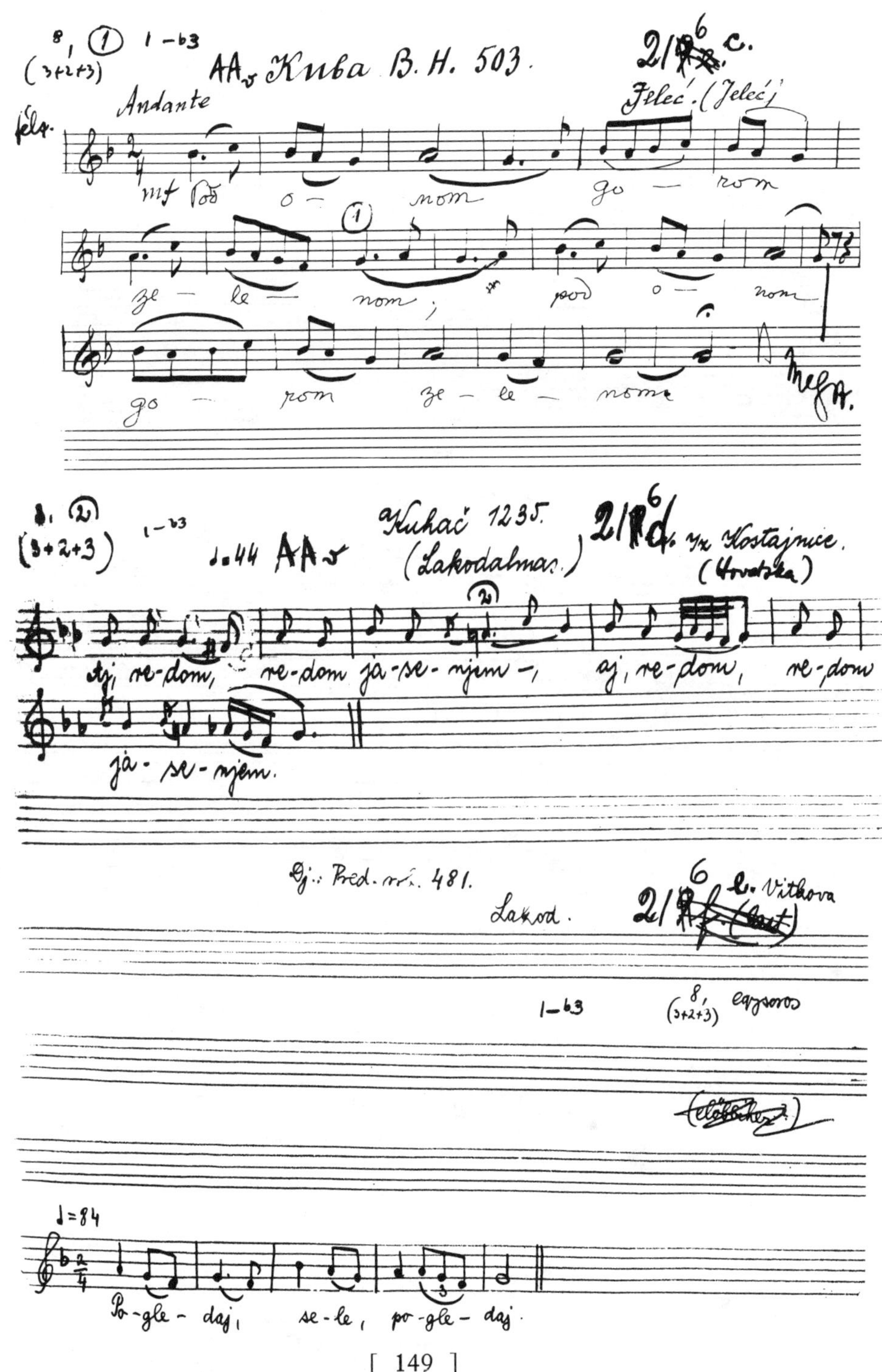

Kuba B. H. 503.
Andante
Jelec (Jelec)
Pod o - nom go - rom ze - le - nom; pod o - nom go - rom ze - le - nom.
Kuhač 1235.
(Lakodalmas)
Kostajnice.
♩= 44
Aj, re-dom, re-dom ja-se-njem, aj, re-dom, re-dom ja-se-njem.
Lakod.
Vitkova
♩= 84
Po-gle-daj, se-le, po-gle-daj.

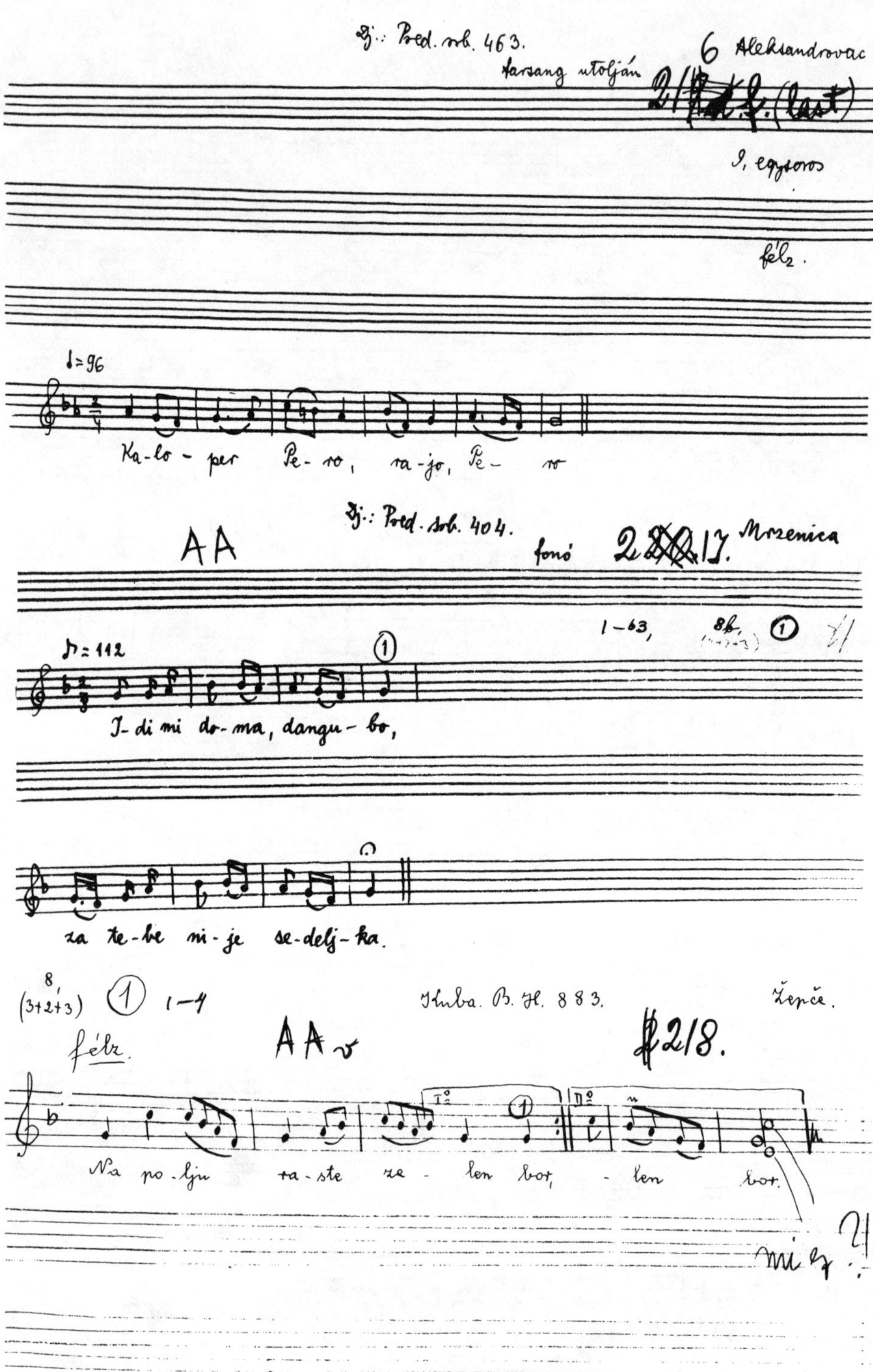
Pred. sob. 463.
farsang utolján
6 Aleksandrovac
I. egysoros
félz.
♩= 96
Ka-lo - per Pe - ro, ra - jo, Pe - ro
Pred. sob. 404.
AA
fonó
Mrzenica
1–63,
♪= 112
I - di mi do - ma, dangu - bo,
za te - be ni - je se - delj - ka.
(3+2+3)
1–4
Žepče.
félz.
AA
2/8.
Na po - lju ra - ste ze - len bor, - len bor.
mi ez?!

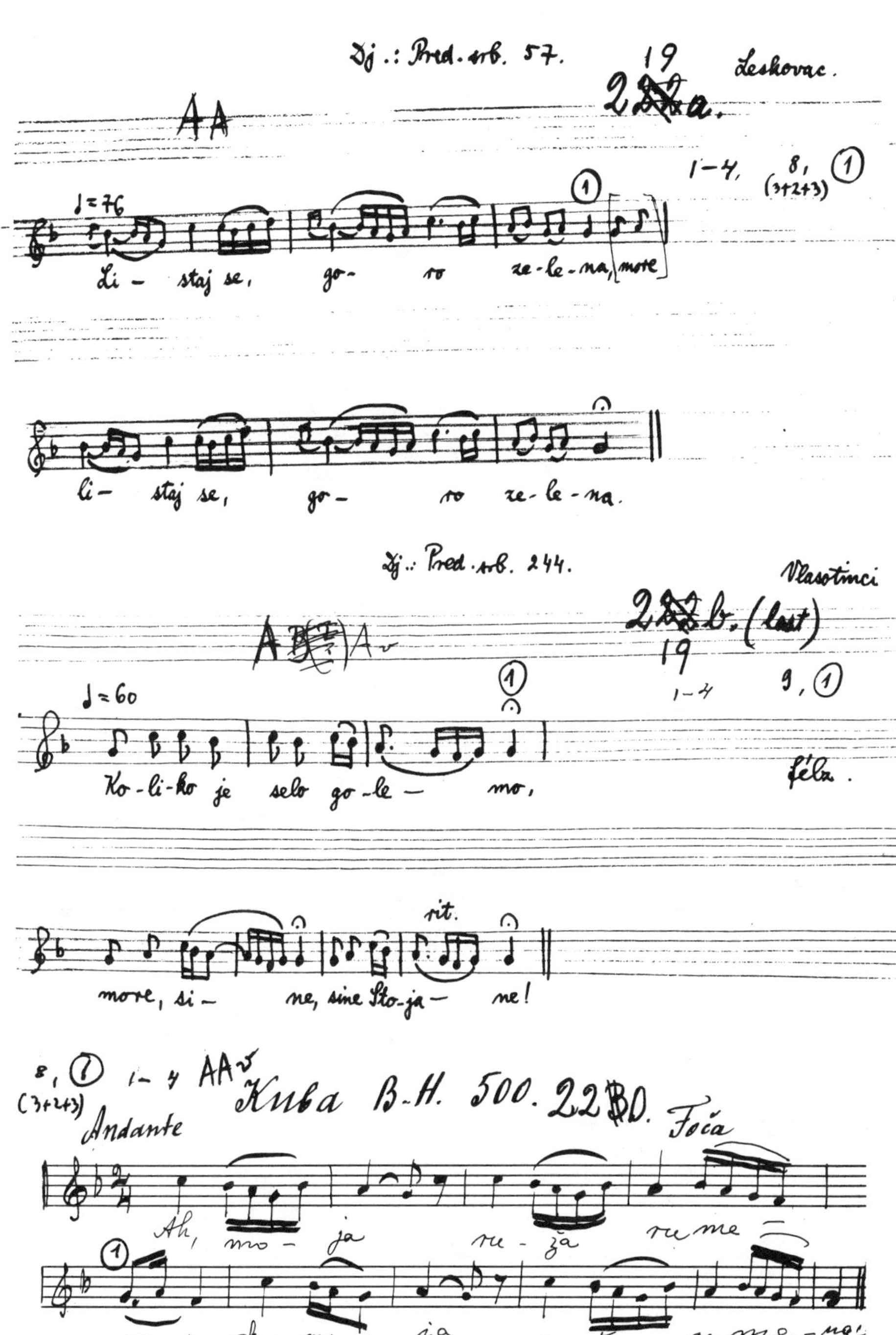
Dj.: Pred. srb. 57.
19
Leskovac.
22a.
AA
1–4, 8, (3+2+3) ①
♩=76
Li – staj se, go – ro ze-le-na, [more]
li – staj se, go – ro ze-le-na.
Dj.: Pred. srb. 244.
Vlasotinci
22b. (last)
19
1–4
9, ①
♩=60
Ko-li-ko je selo go-le – mo,
félz.
rit.
more, si – ne, sine Sto-ja – ne!
8, ① 1–4 AAv
(3+2+3)
Kuba B.-H. 500. 22b.
Foča
Andante
Ah, mo – ja ru – ža ru-me –
na; ah, mo – ja ru – ža ru-me-na

8, (3+2+3) ① 1-5
AA
Kuba B.H.
703.
Moderato.
Čajniče.
O, mo - je ma - lo gle - da - nje, o, mo - je ma - lo gle - da - nje.
8, ① 1-5 ♩=50. (3+2+3)
AB
Kuhač III. 1073.
U ženskom kolu.
Iz otočke pukovnije.
Kada se j' Pavle ženja še gospodu svate skuplja še.
8, (3+2+3) ① 1-5
Kuba. B.H. 200.
Ljubinje.
Pod o-nom go - - rom ze-le-nom i o-nom vi-šom pla - ni - nom.

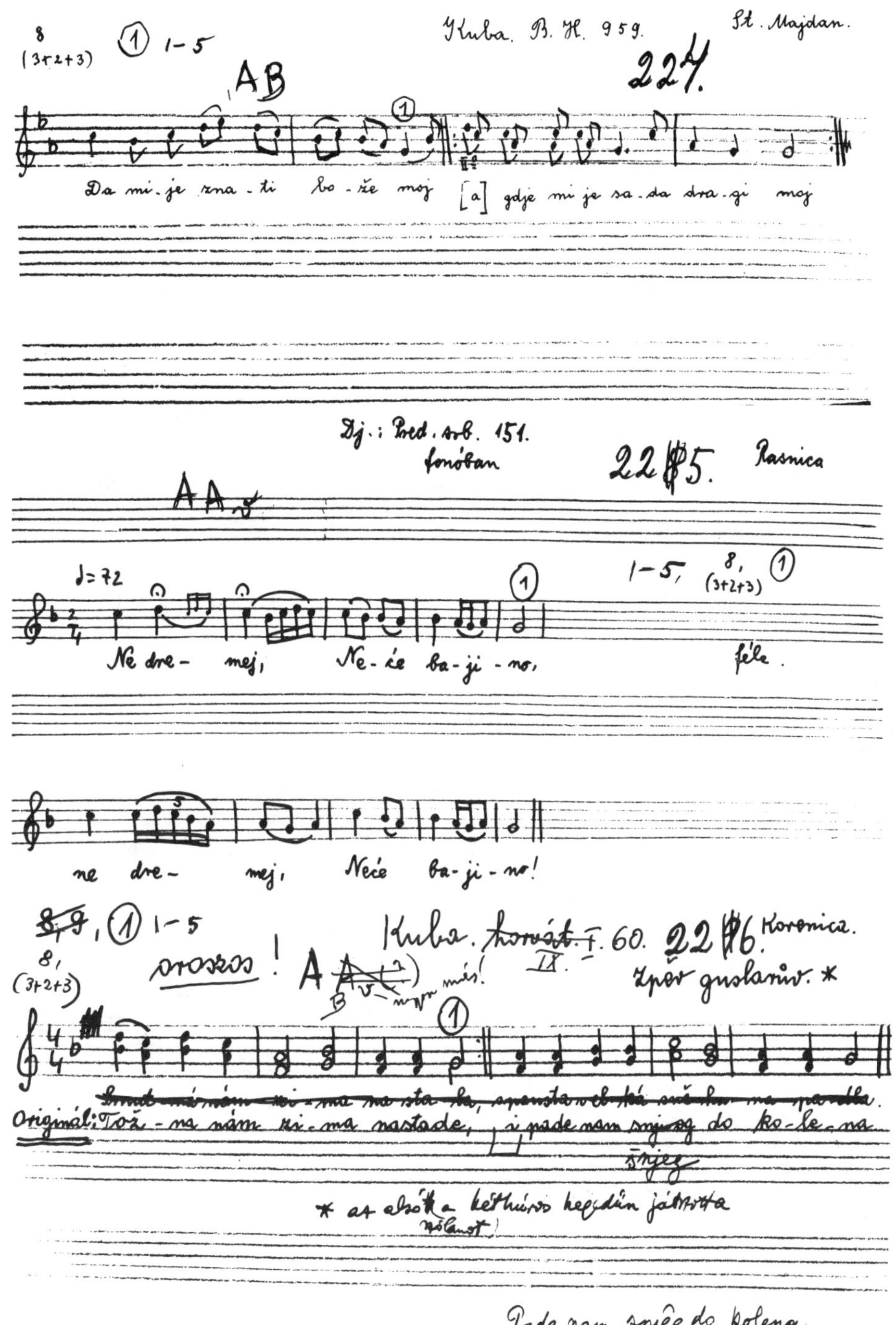

Kuba. B. H. 959.
St. Majdan.
224.
Da mi je zna - ti bo - že moj [a] gdje mi je sa - da dra - gi moj
Dj.: Pred. srb. 151.
fonóban
Rasnica
Né dre- mej, Ne - će ba - ji - no, féle.
ne dre- mej, Neće ba - ji - no!
Korenica.
Original: Tož - na nám zi - ma nastade, i pade nam snjeg do ko - le - na
Pade nam snjêg do kolena

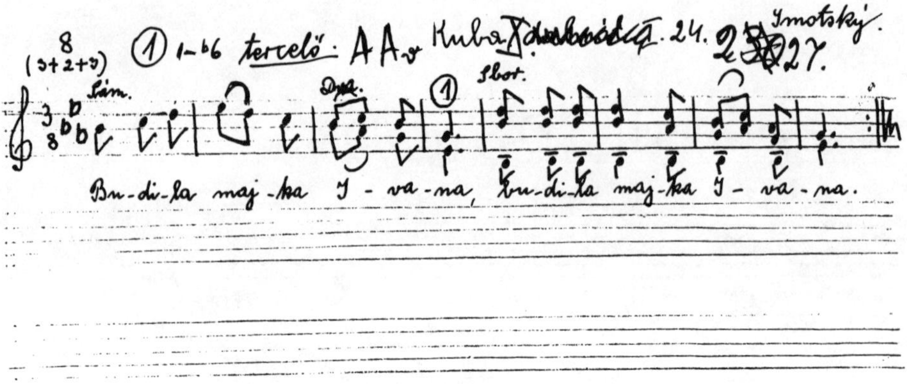

8 (3+2+3)
① 1–b6 tercelő AAv
Kuba 24. 227.
Imotski.
Bu-di-la maj-ka I-va-na, bu-di-la maj-ka I-va-na.

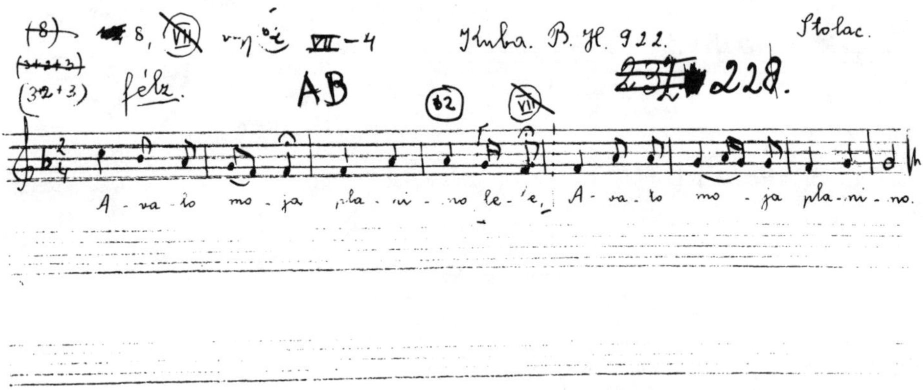

8, VII – 4
Kuba. B. H. 922.
Stolac.
(3+2+3) félz.
AB
228.
A-va-to mo-ja pla-ni-no le-'e, A-va-to mo-ja pla-ni-no.

8, b2 1–4
Kuhač II. 457.
Od otoka Hvara.
(3+2+3) tercelő.
AAsv
♩. = 100.
229a.
Da mi je zna-ti, Bo-že moj, gdi se na-la--zi dra-gi moj!

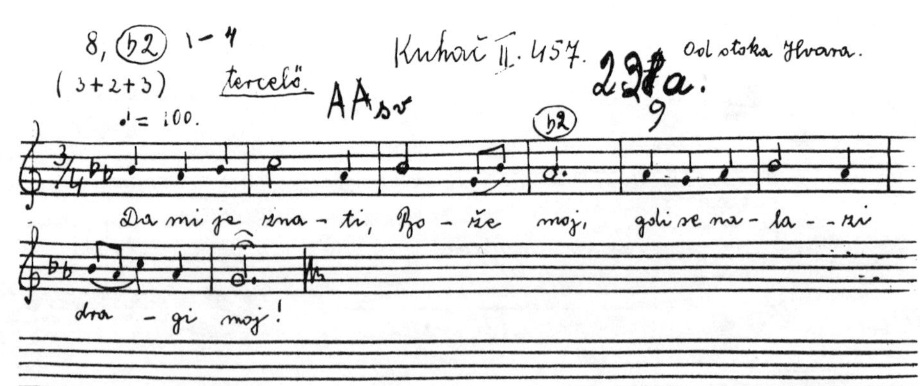

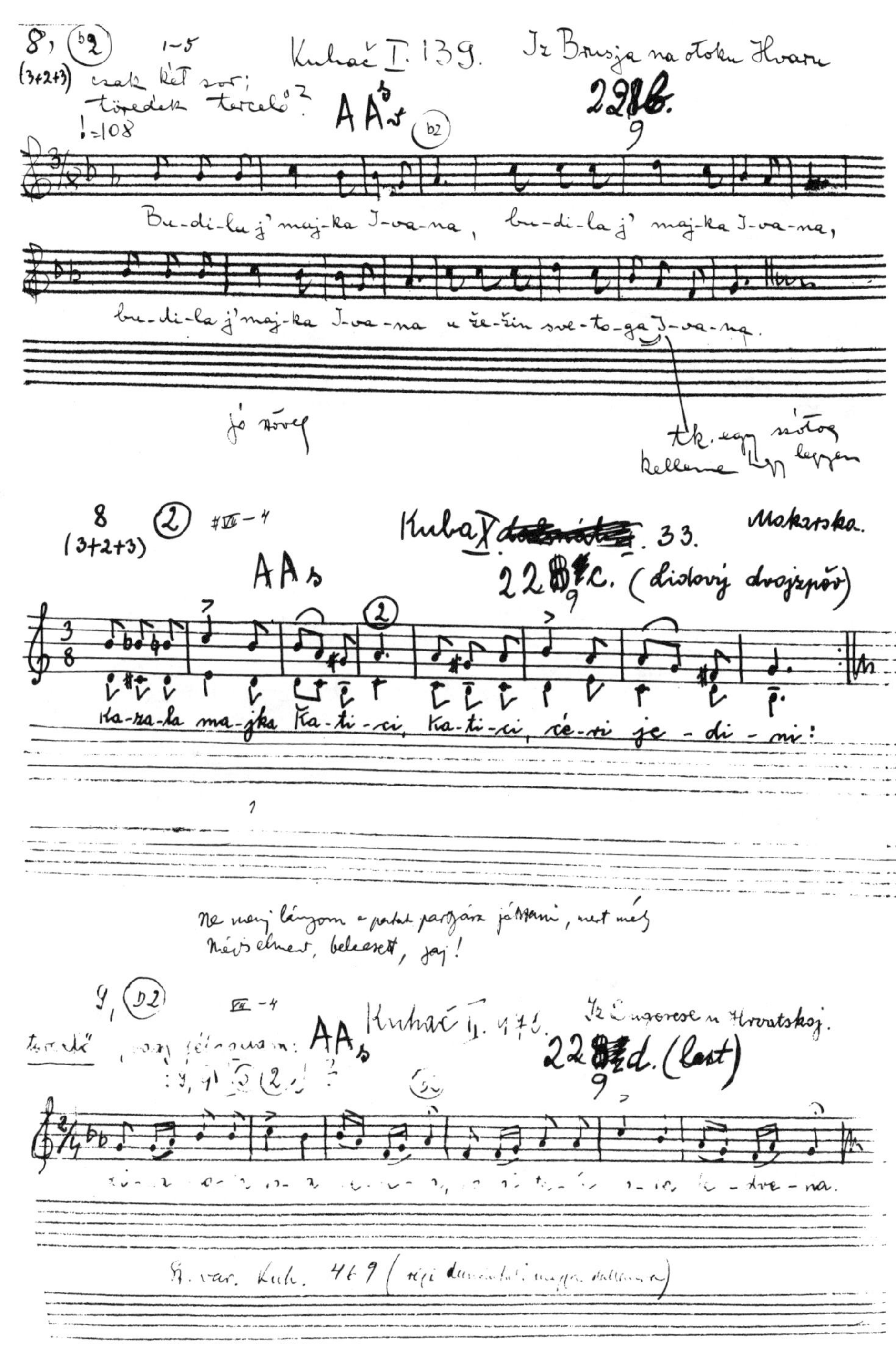

Kuhač I. 139. Iz Brusja na otoku Hvaru
AA
228b.
Bu-di-la j' maj-ka I-va-na, bu-di-la j' maj-ka I-va-na,
bu-di-la j' maj-ka I-va-na u če-čin sve-to-ga I-va-na.
jó szöveg
Kuba X. 33. Makarska.
AA
228c.
Ka-za-la ma-jka Ka-ti-ci, Ka-ti-ci, će-ri je-di-ni:
AA
228d.

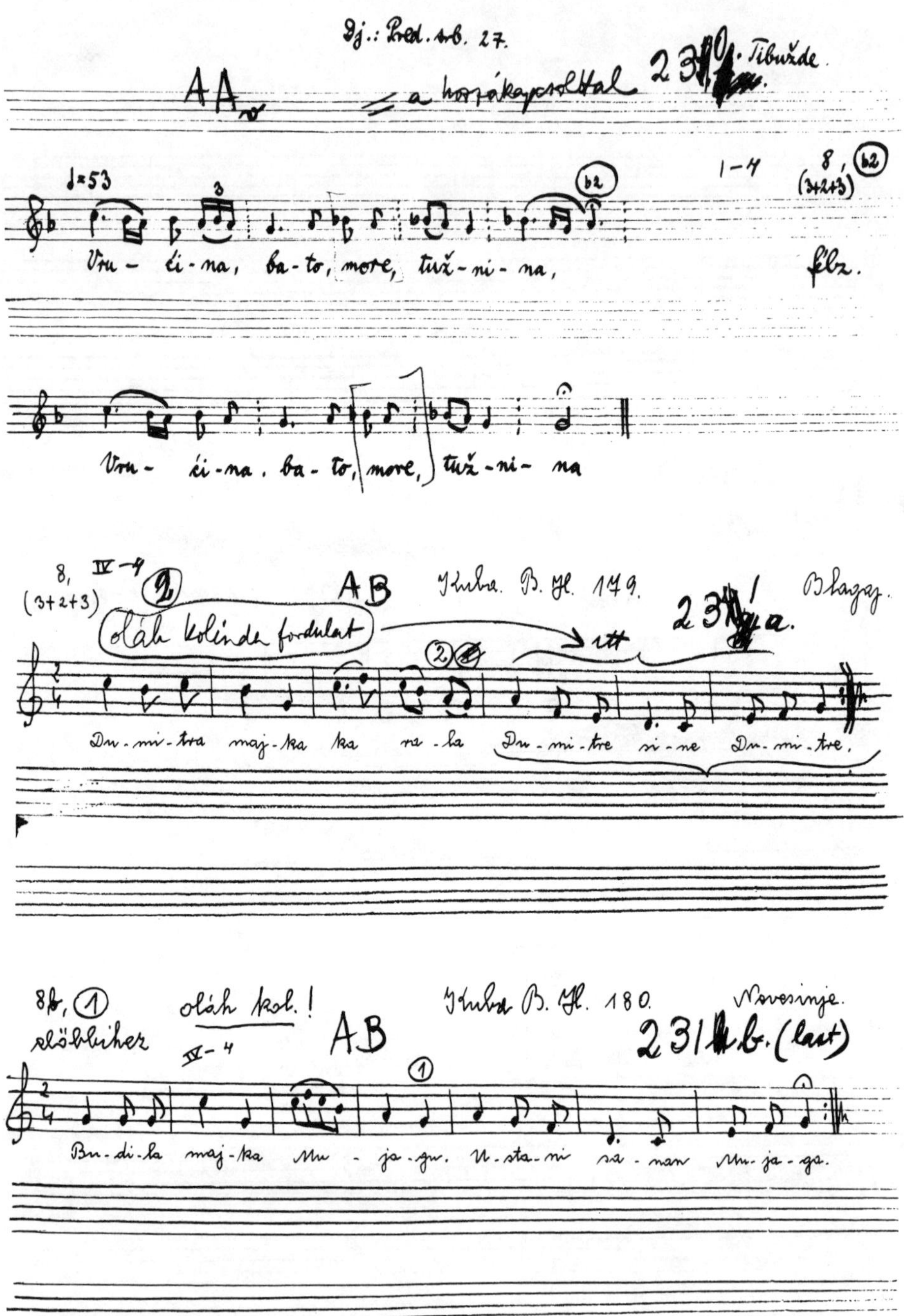

Tibužde
Vru - či - na, ba - to, more, tuž - ni - na,
Vru - či - na, ba - to, more, tuž - ni - na
AB
oláh kolinda fordulat
Blazaj
Du - mi - tra maj - ka ka ra - la Du - mi - tre si - ne Du - mi - tre.
oláh kol.!
AB
Novesinje
Bu - di - la maj - ka Mu - ja - gu. U - sta - ni sa - nan Mu - ja - ga.

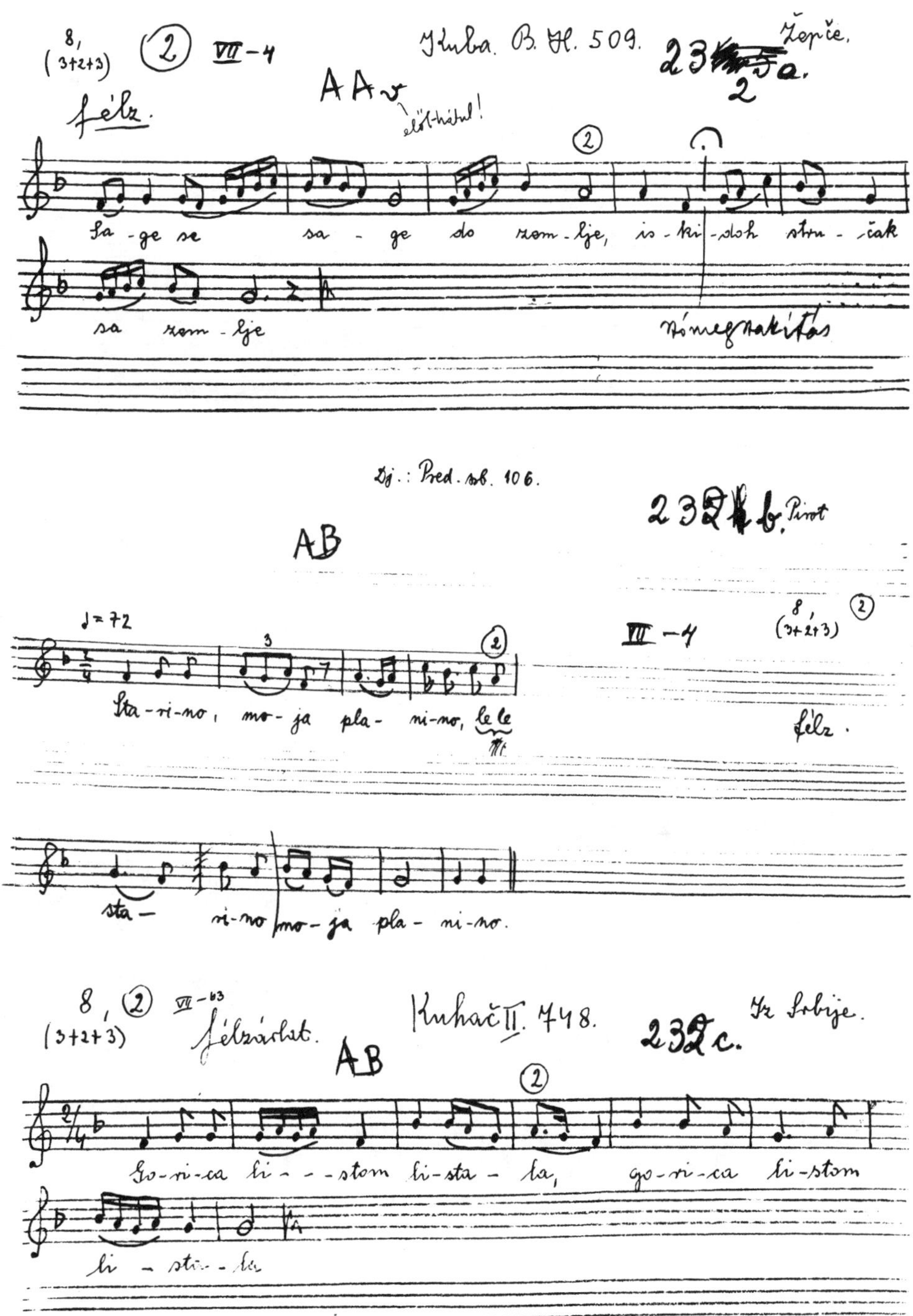
AA
AB
♩= 72
Kuhač II. 748.
Iz Srbije.
AB

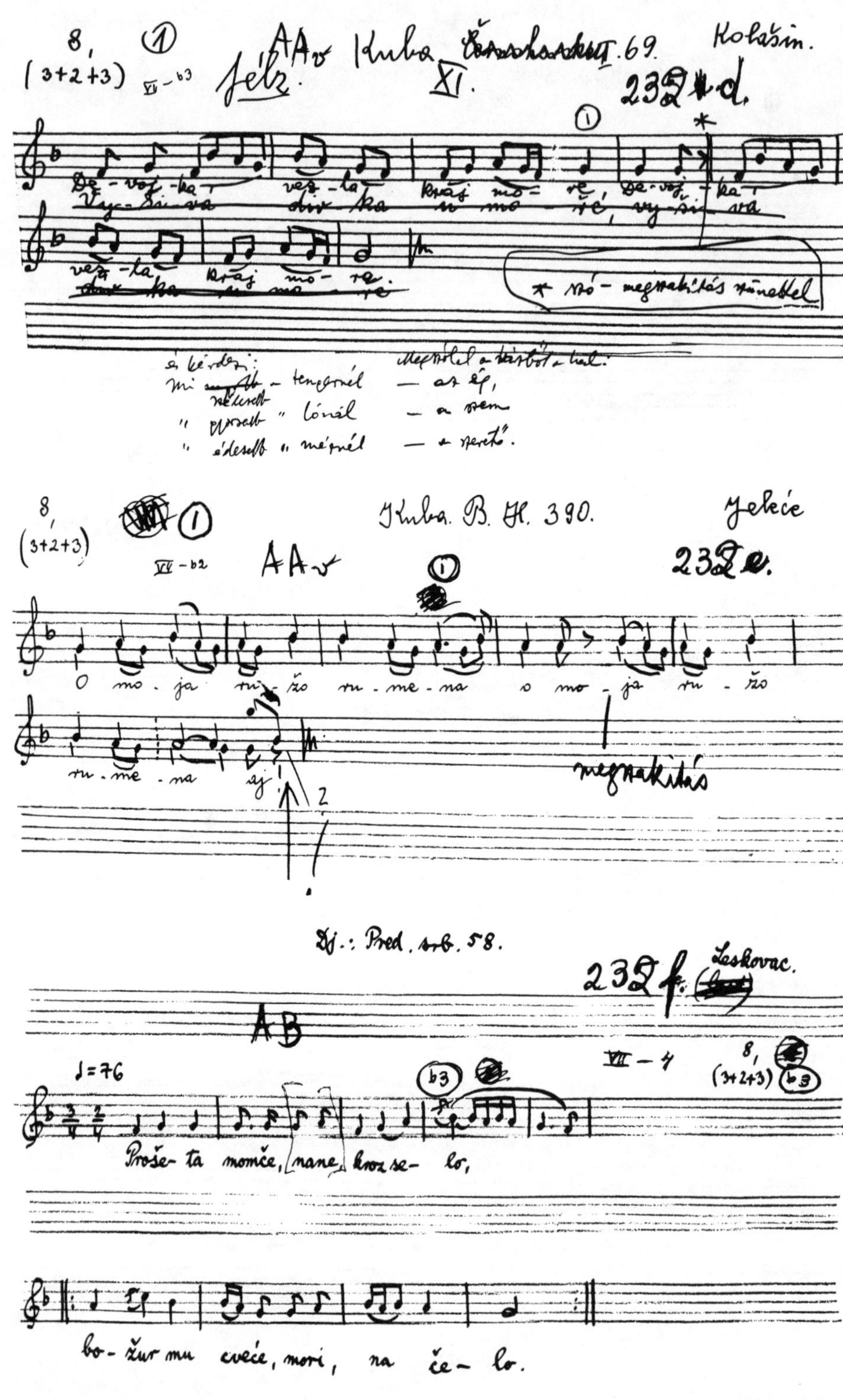

8,
(3+2+3)
Kolašin.
De-voj-ka vez-la kraj mo-re, de-voj-ka
vez-la kraj mo-re
8,
(3+2+3)
Kuba. B. H. 390.
AA
O mo-ja ru-žo ru-me-na o mo-ja ru-žo
ru-me-na aj!
Dj.: Pred. srb. 58.
Leskovac.
AB
♩=76
8,
(3+2+3)
Proše-ta momče, nane, kroz se- lo,
bo-žur mu cveće, mori, na če- lo.

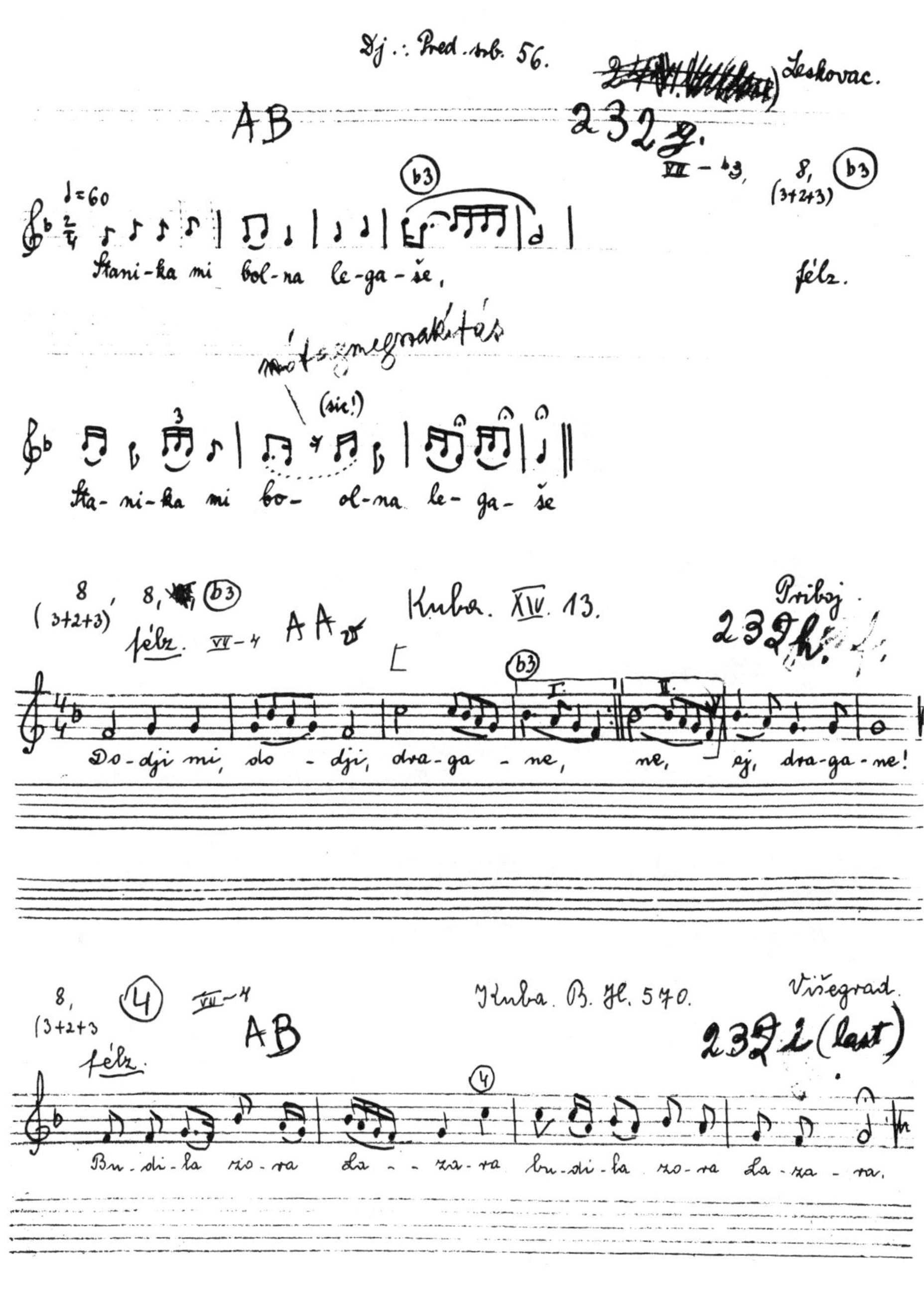
Leskovac.
AB
232g.
Sta-ni-ka mi bol-na le-ga-še,
félz.
(sic!)
Sta- ni- ka mi bo- ol-na le- ga- še
Kuba. XIV. 13.
Priboj
AA
232h.
félz.
Do-dji mi, do - dji, dra-ga - ne, ne, ej, dra-ga-ne!
Kuba. B. H. 570.
Višegrad.
AB
232i (last)
félz.
Bu-di-la zo-ra La- - za-ra bu-di-la zo-ra La-za - ra.

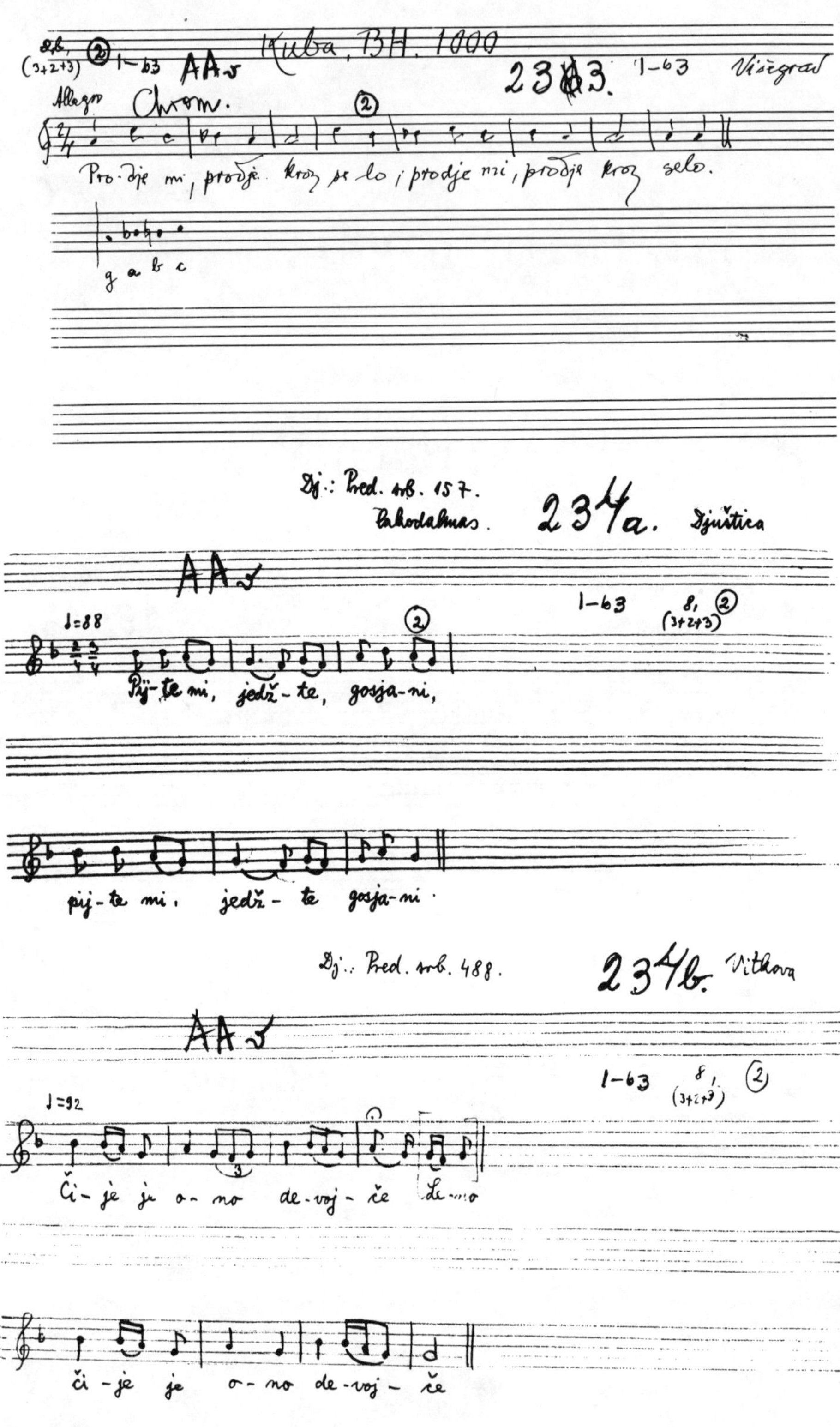
Kuba, BH. 1000
1-63 AA
1-63 Višegrad
Allegro Chrom.
Pro-dje mi, prodje kroz se-lo, prodje mi, prodje kroz selo.
g a b c
Dj.: Pred. srb. 157.
Bakodalmas.
234a. Djuštica
AA
1-63
8, (3+2+3)
Pij-te mi, jedž-te, gosja-ni,
pij-te mi, jedž-te gosja-mi.
Dj.: Pred. srb. 488.
234b. Vitkova
AA
1-63
8, (3+2+3)
Či-je je o-no de-voj-če Le-mo
či-je je o-no de-voj-če

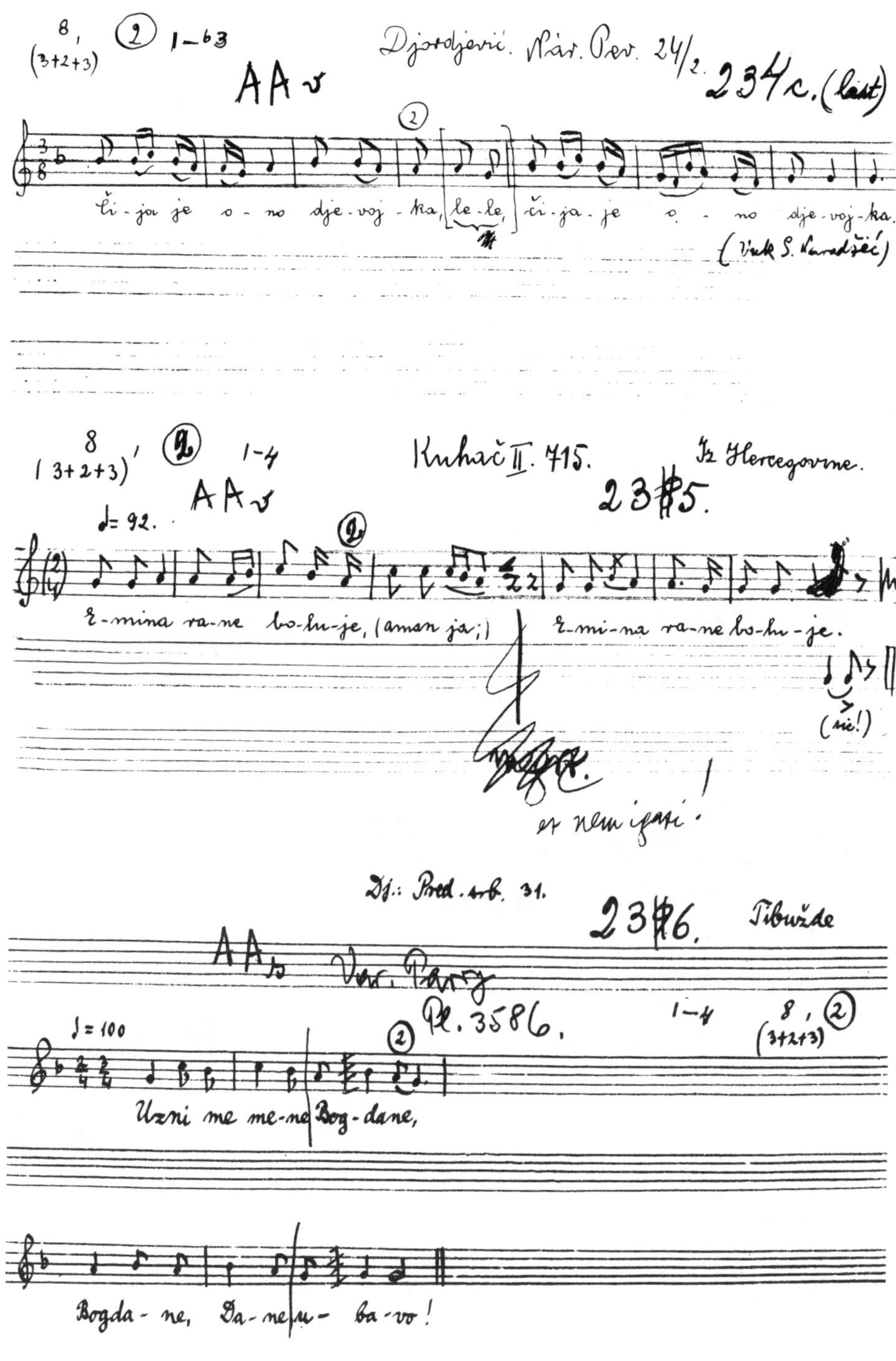

Djordjević. Nár. Pev. 24/2.
234c. (last)
AA
Či-ja je o-no dje-voj-ka, le-le, či-ja je o-no dje-voj-ka.
(Vuk S. Karadžić)
Kuhač II. 715.
Iz Hercegovine.
235.
AA
♩= 92.
E-mina ra-ne bo-lu-je, (aman ja;) E-mi-na ra-ne bo-lu-je.
(sic!)
Dj.: Pred. srb. 31.
236.
Tibužde
AA
Pl. 3586.
♩= 100
Uzni me me-ne Bog-dane,
Bogda-ne, Da-ne-u-ba-vo!

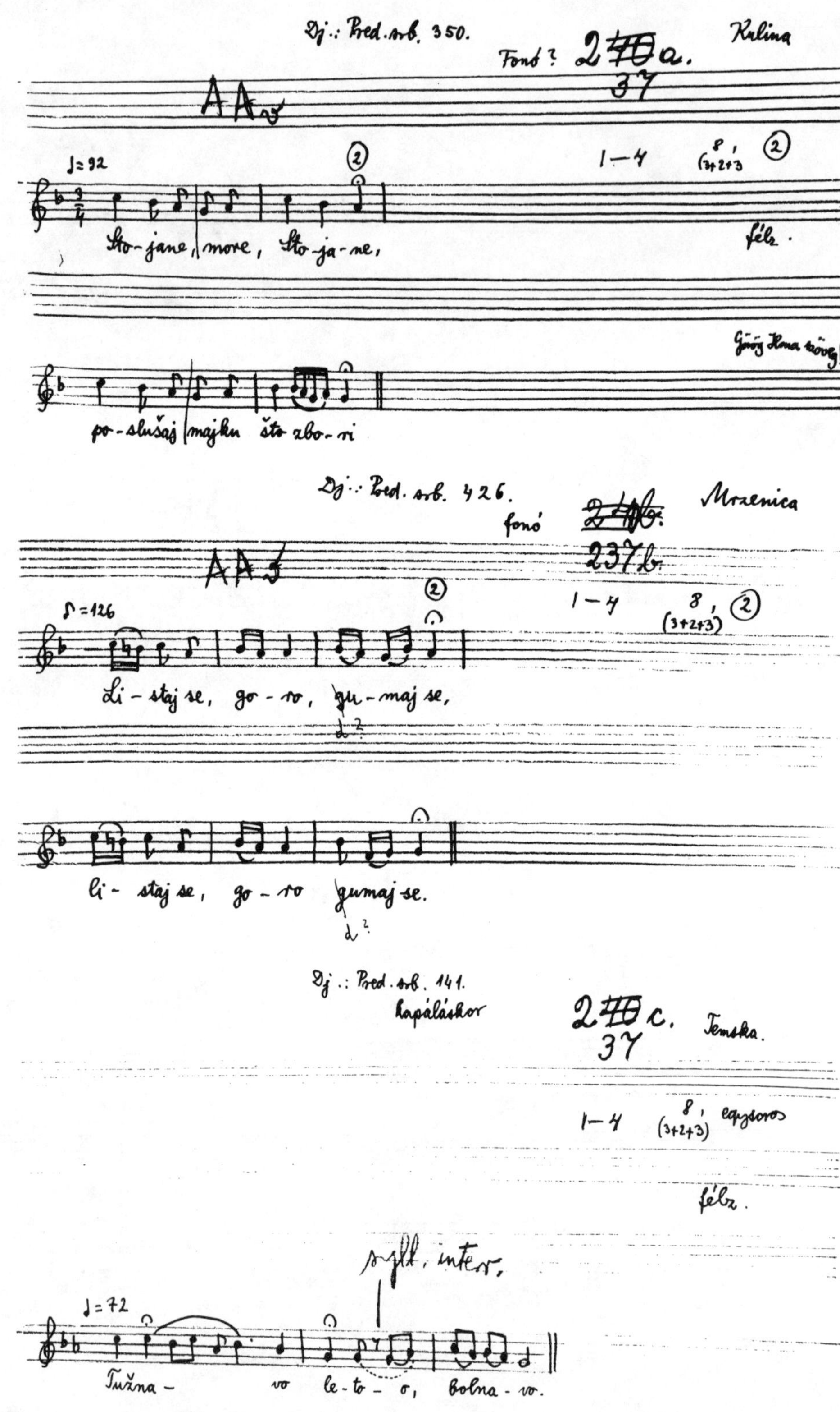

Dj.: Pred. srb. 350.
Fonó? 270a.
37
Kalina
AA
♩= 92
1–4
8, (3+2+3)
félz.
Sto-jane, more, Sto-ja-ne,
György Ilona szöveg!
po-slušaj majku što zbo-ri
Dj.: Pred. srb. 426.
fonó 237b.
Mrzenica
♪=126
1–4
8, (3+2+3)
Li-staj se, go-ro, gu-maj se,
li- staj se, go-ro gumaj se.
Dj.: Pred. srb. 141.
kapáláskor
270c.
37
Temska.
1–4
8, (3+2+3) egysoros
félz.
♩= 72
Tužna- vo le-to-o, bolna-vo.

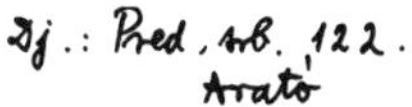

2~~40~~d. Gnjilan
37

8
(3+2+3)
egysoros

Dj.: Pred. szb. 166.
aratáskor

2~~40~~e. Topli Do.
37

1–4 8, (3+2+3) egysoros

félz.

2~~40~~f.
37

Dj.: Pred. szb. 219. Kad se vlači vuna(?) Strelac

8, egysoros
(3+2+3)

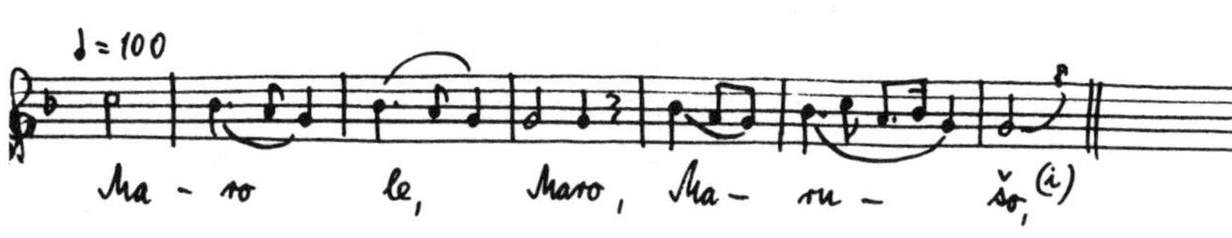

Dj.: Pred. srb 130.
arató 270/37 g. Velika Lukanja

1–4, 8 (3+2+3) egysoros

félz.

♩=80

Na ja- to ti-či le- te-la.

Dj.: Pred. srb. 226.
arató vagy kapáló 270/37 h. Štrelac.

1–4 8, egysoros (3+2+3)

♩=76

Pro- kle-ta da je devoj- ča,(i)

8, egy soros, 1–4 (3+2+3) ♩=50.
Kuhač 1254. (Lakodalmas.) 270/37 i. (last) Iz Slavonije. 9
félz. Jedan (II° Sr.)

Po-mo-zi Bo-že i Go-spo!

jó ki... a ...

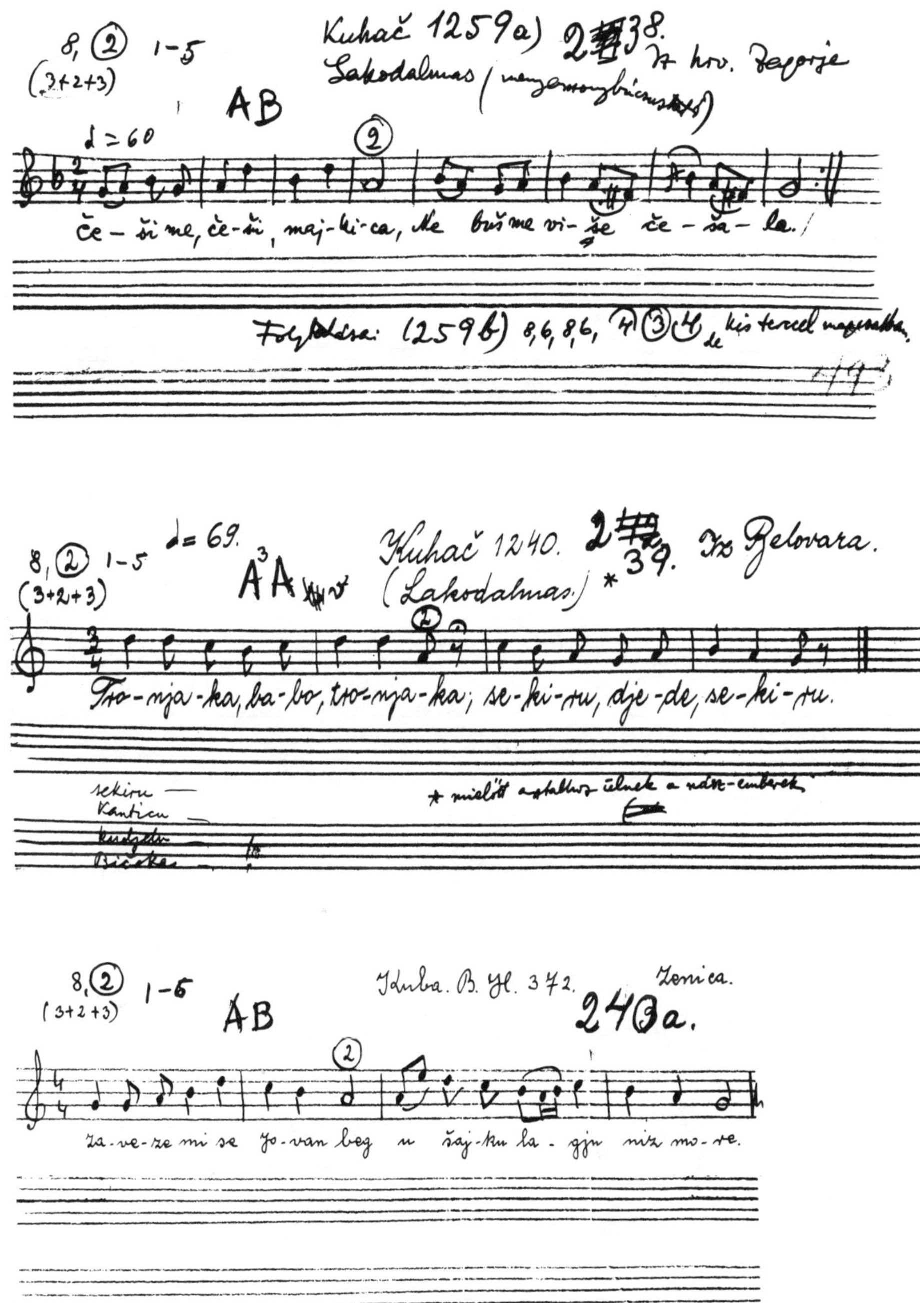
8, (2) 1-5
(3+2+3)
AB
Kuhač 1259a) 238.
Iz hrv. Zagorje
Lakodalmas
♩= 60
Če-ši me, če-ši, maj-ki-ca, ne buš me vi-še če-ša-la.
Folytatása: 1259b) 8,6,8,6,
8, (2) 1-5
(3+2+3)
♩= 69.
Kuhač 1240.
239.
Iz Belovara.
(Lakodalmas)
Tro-nja-ka, ba-bo, tro-nja-ka; se-ki-ru, dje-de, se-ki-ru.
8, (2) 1-5
(3+2+3)
AB
Kuba. B. H. 372.
Zenica.
240a.
za-ve-ze mi se Jo-van beg u šaj-ku la-gji niz mo-re.

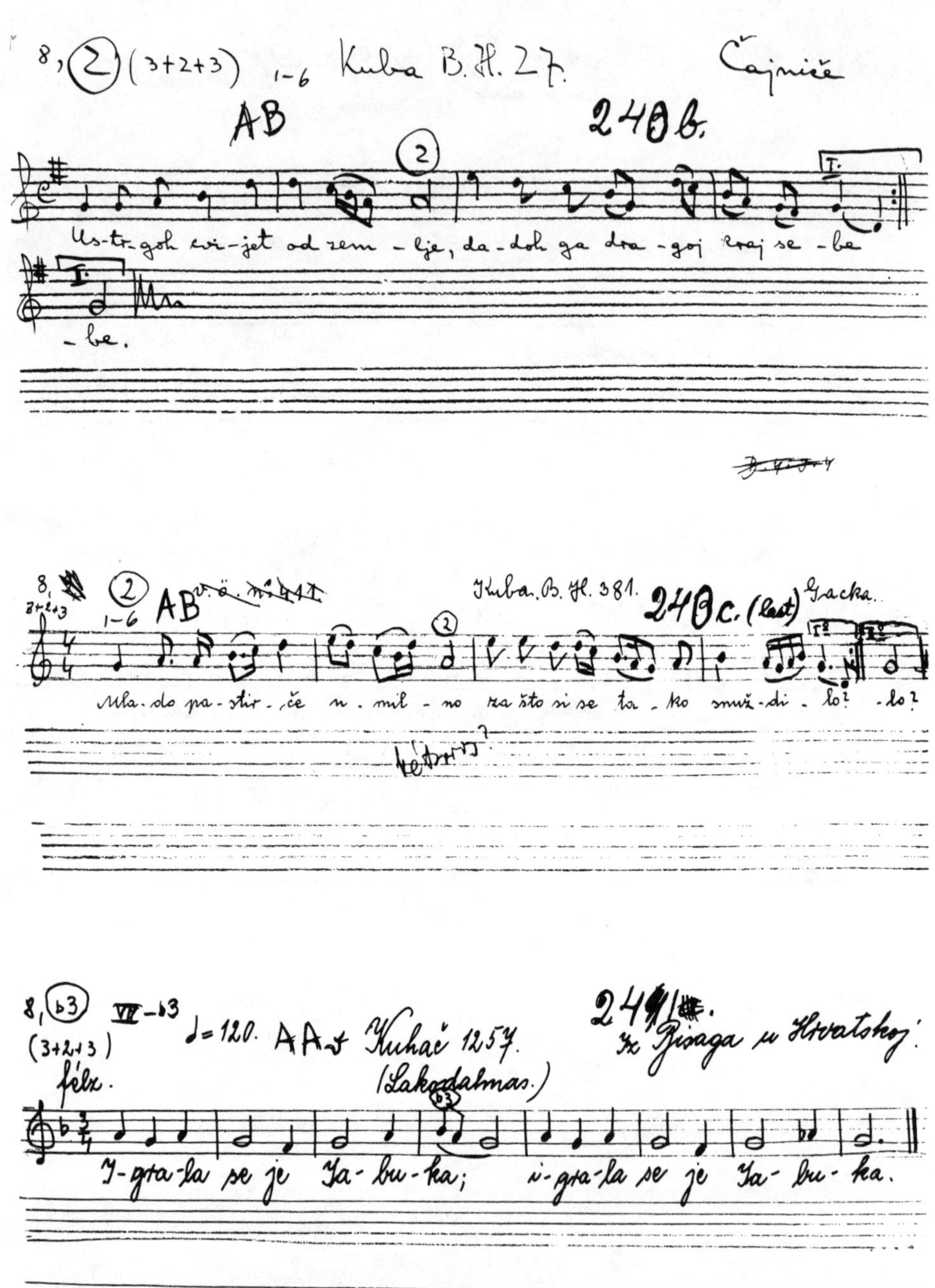
8, (2) (3+2+3) 1-6 Kuba B. H. 27. Čajniče
AB
240b.
Us-tr-goh cvi-jet od zem-lje, da-doh ga dra-goj kraj se-be
-be.
Kuba B. H. 381.
240c.
Gacka.
Mla-do pa-stir-če u-mil-no za što si se ta-ko snuž-di-lo? -lo?
8, (b3) VII-b3 (3+2+3) félz.
♩=120. AA Kuhač 1257. (Lakodalmas.)
241.
Iz Pisaga u Hrvatskoj.
I-gra-la se je Ja-bu-ka; i-gra-la se je Ja-bu-ka.

Kuhač II. 616.
Iz Djakova.
♩=69.
Pod o-nom go-rom ze-le-nom, pod o-nom go-rom ze-le---nom.
Dj.: Pred. sob. 379.
24a.
Veliki Šljegovac.
♩= 112
Spa-val bi a-li ne mogu,
spaval bi áli ne mogu
Dj.: Pred. sob. 249.
24b.
Toplica
♩= 108
Soldat mi prodje kroz se-lo
sol-dat mi prodje, prodje kroz selo.

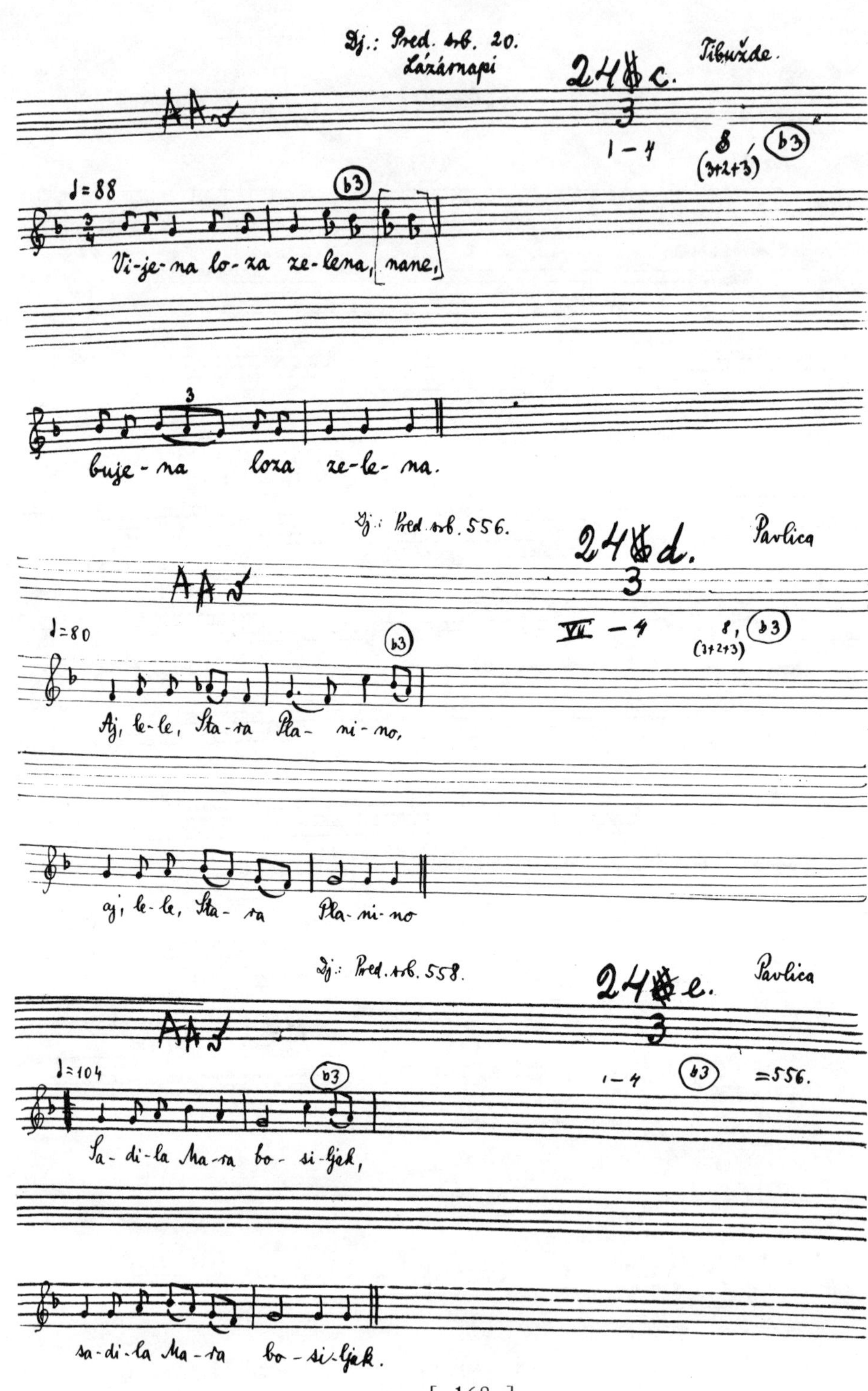
Dj.: Pred. srb. 20.
Lázárnapi
24 c.
3
Tibužde.
1 – 4
8 (3+2+3), b3
♩= 88
b3
Vi-je-na lo-za ze-lena, nane,
buje-na loza ze-le-na.
Dj.: Pred. srb. 556.
24 d.
3
Pavlica
VII – 4
8, (3+2+3) b3
♩= 80
b3
Aj, le-le, Sta-ra Pla- ni-no,
aj, le-le, Sta- ra Pla-ni-no
Dj.: Pred. srb. 558.
24 e.
3
Pavlica
♩= 104
1 – 4
b3
= 556.
b3
Sa-di-la Ma-ra bo- si-ljak,
sa-di-la Ma-ra bo-si-ljak.

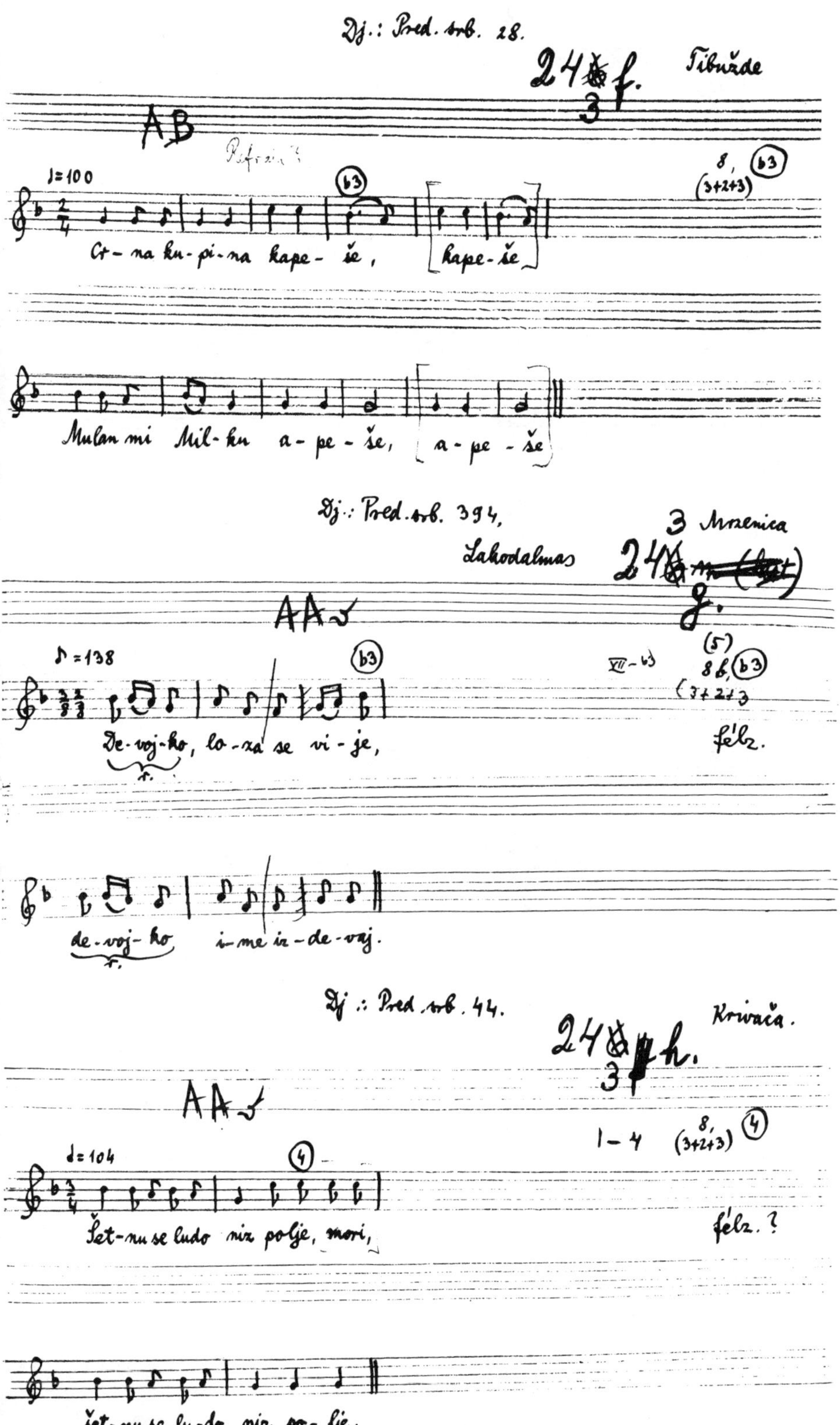
Dj.: Pred. srb. 28.
24 f.
Tibužde
AB
Crna kupina kape- še, kape-še
Mulan mi Milku a-pe-še, a-pe-še
Dj.: Pred. srb. 394,
3 Mrzenica
Lakodalmas
24 g.
AA
De-voj-ko, lo-za se vi-je,
félz.
de-voj-ko i-me iz-de-vaj.
Dj.: Pred. srb. 44.
Krivača.
24 h.
AA
1–4
Šet-nu se ludo niz polje, mori,
félz.?
šet-nu se lu-do niz po-lje.

Kuba B. H. 786.
(3+2+3)
Moderato.
24 i. Brod.
Pje-va-la ti-ca na more.
skeleton form
Dj.: Pred. sb. 175.
séta-üdvözlet?
24 j. Kalna.
1–b3
(3+2+3)
kétszólamú
egysoros
♩=112
Po-še-ta-la Ru-ža Ja-godo.
Dj.: Pred. sb. 311.
Lakodalmas
24 k. Pirkovac.
1–b3
8, (3+2+3)
egysoros
♪=152
Oj, de-ve-re, lo-za se vi-je

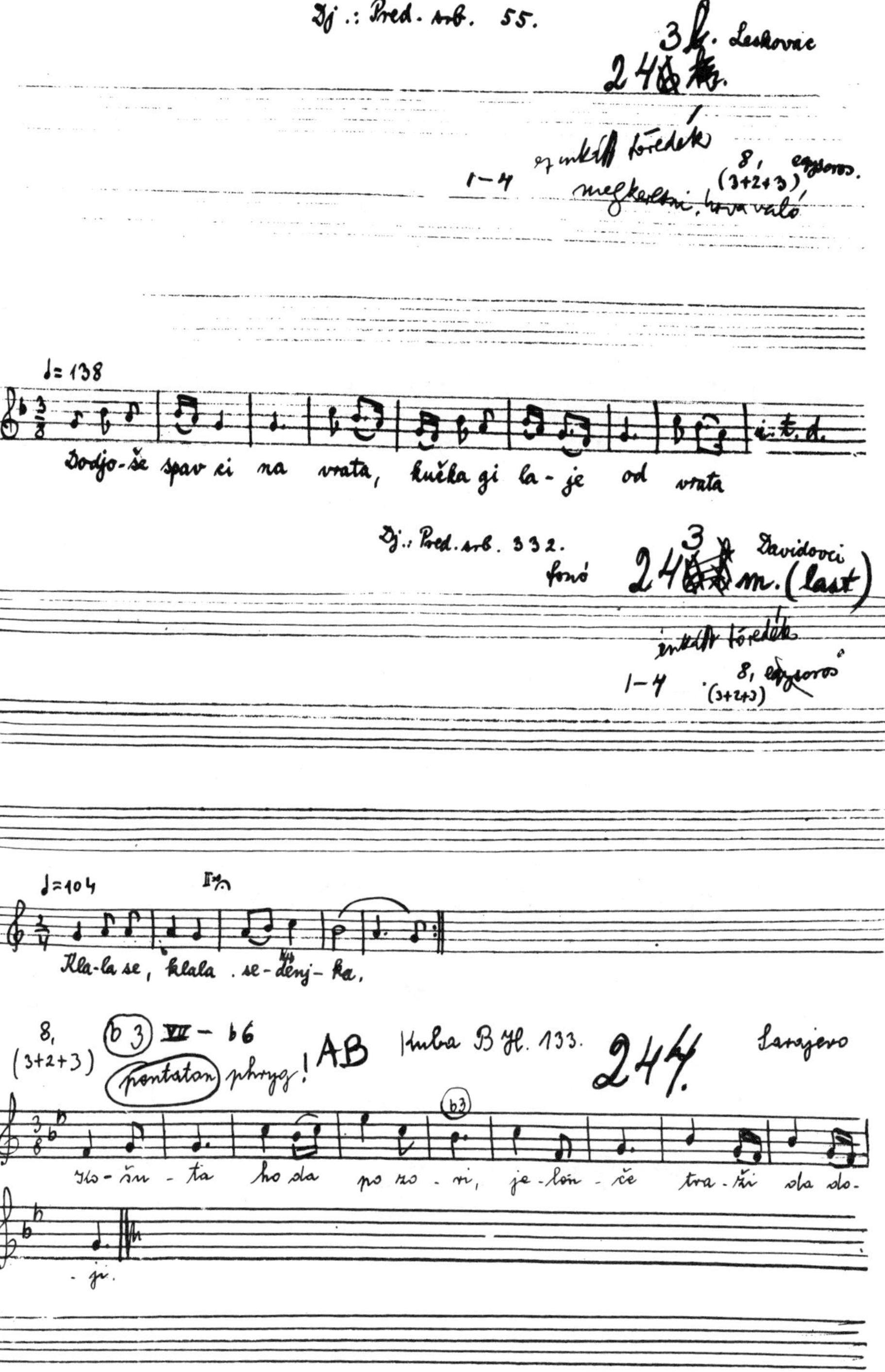

Dj.: Pred. srb. 55.
Leskovac
1–4
8, (3+2+3)
♩= 138
Dodjo-še spav ci na vrata, kučka gi la-je od vrata
Dj.: Pred. srb. 332.
fonó
Davidovci
1–4
8, (3+2+3)
♩= 104
Klala se, klala se-denj-ka,
8, (3+2+3)
pentaton phryg!
AB
Kuba B H. 133.
Sarajevo

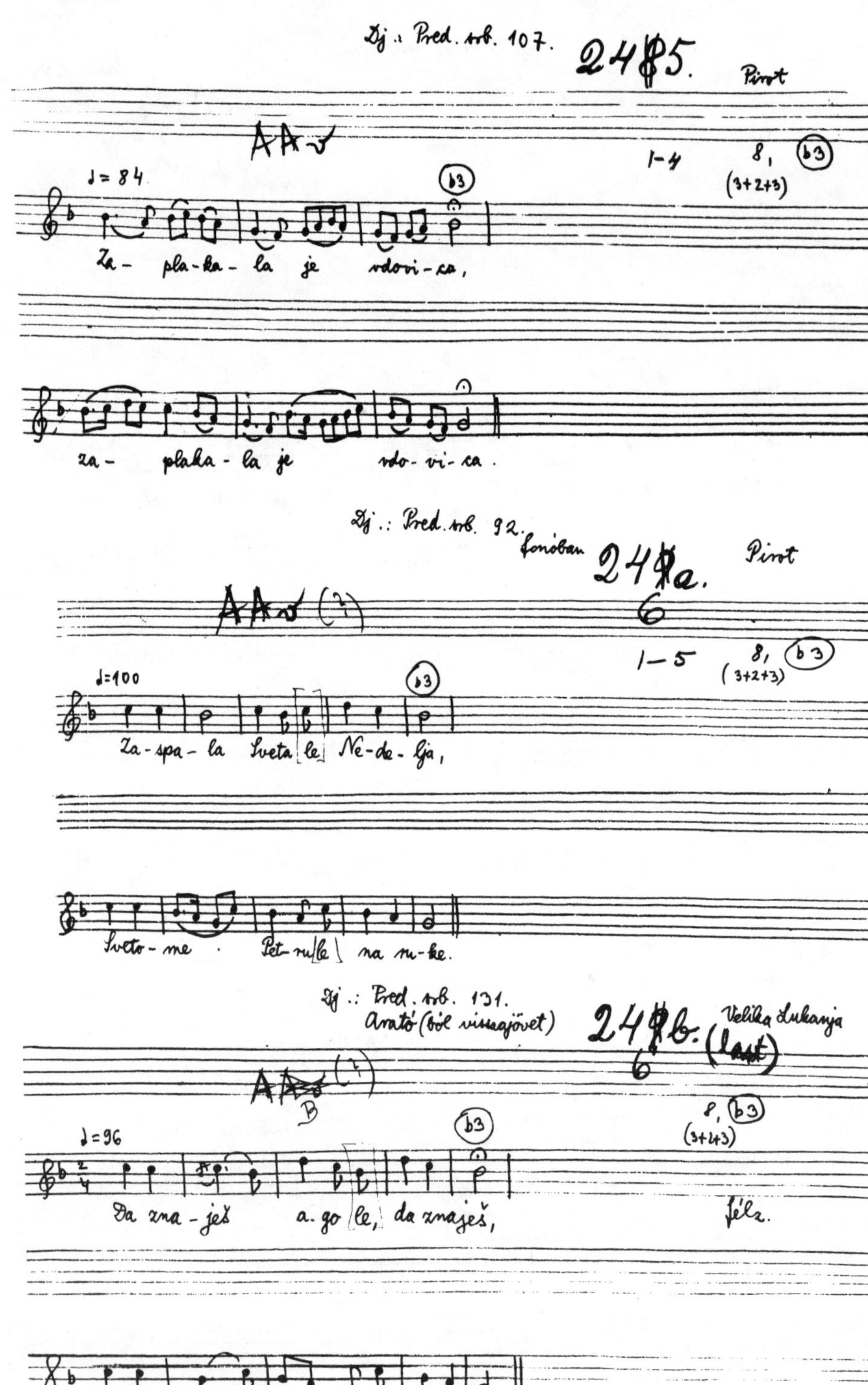

Dj.: Pred. srb. 107.
2485.
Pirot
AA
1-4
8, b3
(3+2+3)
♩= 84
b3
Za- pla-ka- la je udovi-ca,
za- plaka- la je udo- vi- ca.
Dj.: Pred. srb. 92.
fonóban
Pirot
1-5
8, b3
(3+2+3)
♩=100
b3
Za-spa- la Sveta [le] Ne-de- lja,
Sveto- me Pet- ru[le] na ru- ke.
Dj.: Pred. srb. 131.
Arató (ból vissajövet)
Velika Lukanja
8, b3
(3+2+3)
♩=96
b3
Da zna- ješ a- go le, da znaješ,
félz.
da zna- ješ, a- go le, da znaješ.

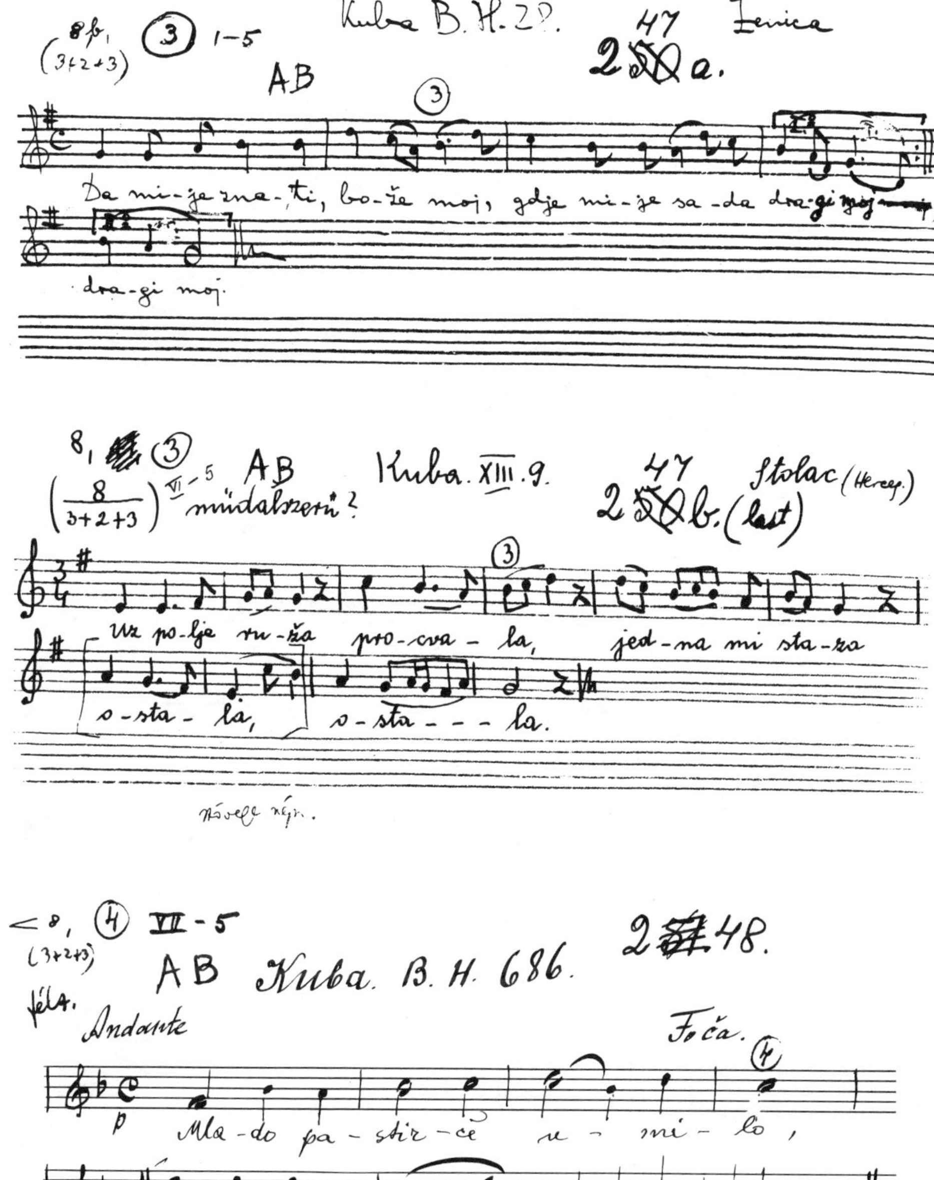

zašto si se ta- ko snuž-di- lo, ?

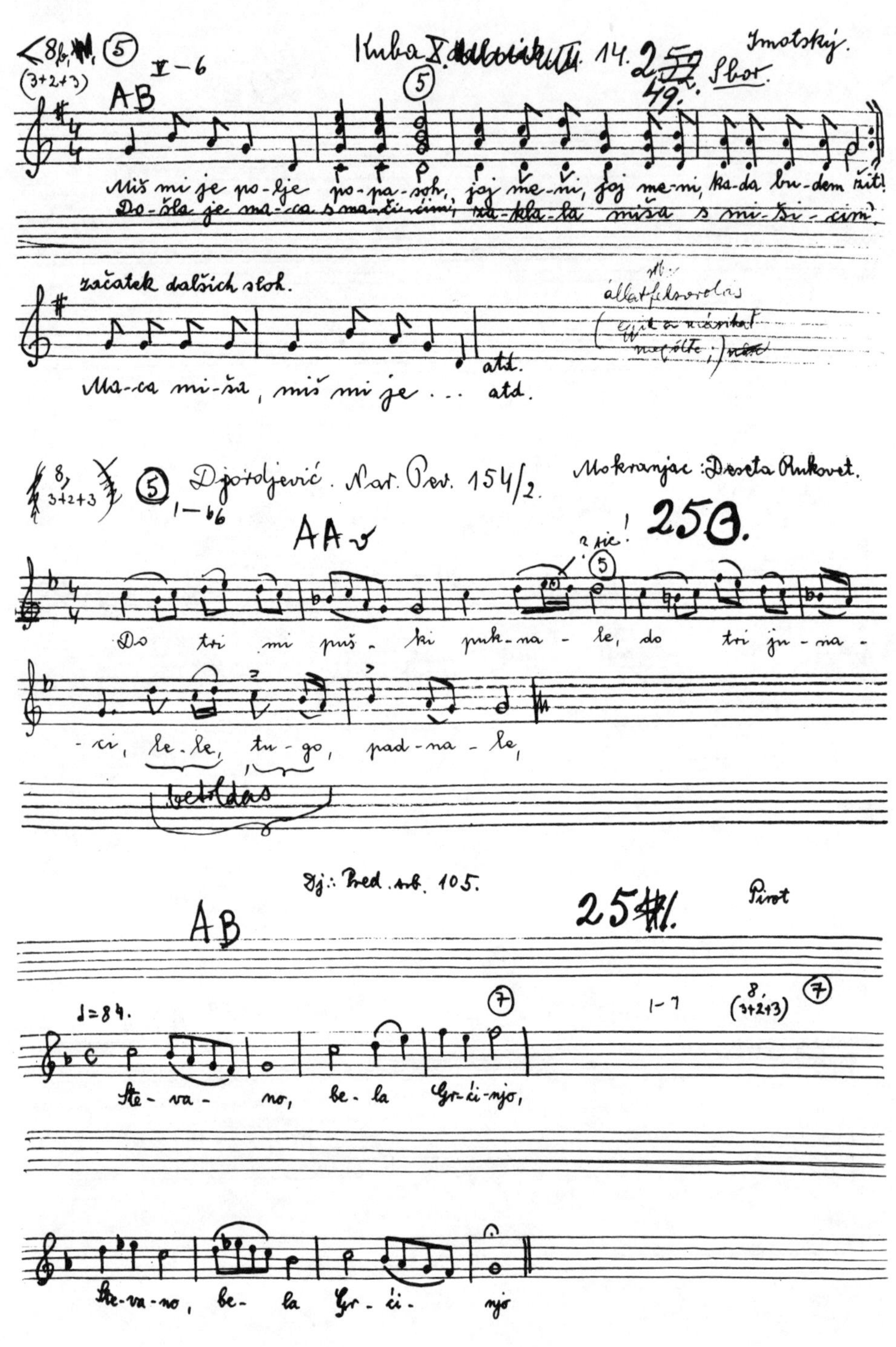
Imotsky.
Sbor.
AB
V–6
Miš mi je po-lje po-pa-soh, joj me-ni, joj me-ni, ka-da bu-dem žit!
Do-šla je ma-ca s ma-či-ćim; za-kla-la miša s mi-ši-ćim.
začatek dalších sloh.
Ma-ca mi-ša, miš mi je ... atd.
atd.
állatfelsorolás
Djordjević. Nar. Pev. 154/2.
Mokranjac: Deseta Rukovet.
AA
250.
Do tri mi puš-ki puk-na-le, do tri ju-na-
-ci, le-le, tu-go, pad-na-le,
Dj.: Pred. srb. 105.
Pirot
AB
♩=84.
Ste-va-no, be-la Gr-či-njo,
Ste-va-no, be-la Gr-či-njo

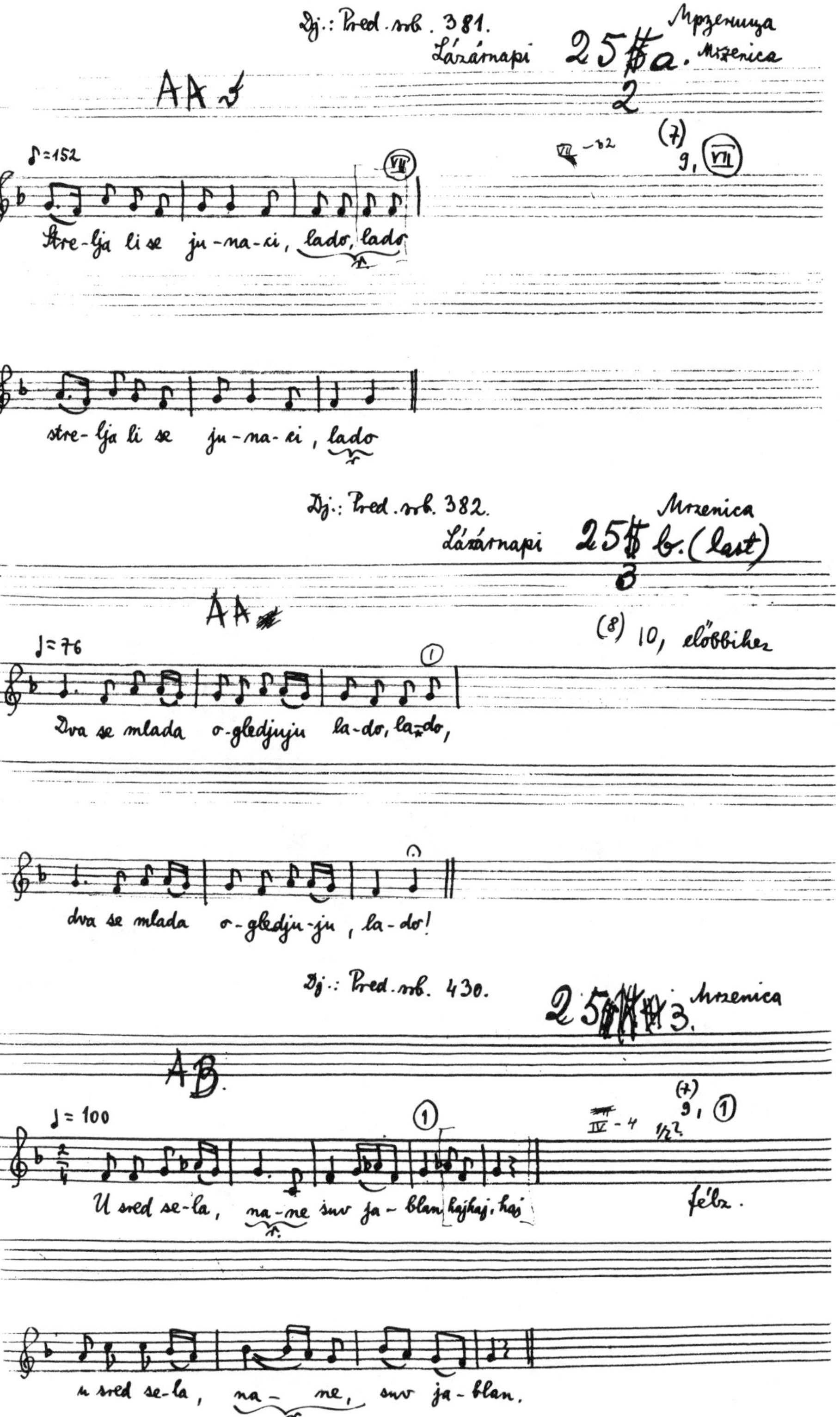
Dj.: Pred. sb. 381.
Мрзеница
Lázárnapi 25 a. Mrzenica
2
AA
(7)
9, VII
♪=152
Stre-lja li se ju-na-ci, lado, lado
stre-lja li se ju-na-ci, lado
Dj.: Pred. sb. 382.
Mrzenica
Lázárnapi 25 b. (last)
3
AA
(8) 10, előbbihez
♩=76
Dva se mlada o-gledjuju la-do, la-do,
dva se mlada o-gledju-ju, la-do!
Dj.: Pred. sb. 430.
25 3. Mrzenica
AB
♩ = 100
U sred se-la, na-ne suv ja-blan hajhaj, haj
félz.
u sred se-la, na- ne, suv ja-blan.

AA
uskršna
Arzenica
Nešto mene zo-ve Ja-go-do,
Jago-do de-vojko, Ja-go-do
AB
Andante
Petrovac.
Ti-ha vo-do ladna! Aj, Duna-vo,
ti-ha vo-do lad-na, aj,
Du-na-vo!
AB
Kuba. B. H. 532.
kolo. 257.
Lipa.
Kad Jo-va-ne, kad ćeš na Do-lja-ne,
kad ćeš na Do-lja-ne?
Should be transposed!

(8)
10, VI
Kuhač III. 1089.
258.
V-2 ♩= 76.
Iz Djakova.
(Slavonija)
AA v
Tur-ci pe-tla, pe-tla u-hva-ti-še, pa ga bi-ju, bi-ju po ta-ba-ni.
10, VI V-4
Hruba. B. H. 174.
Kalinovik.
259.
AA v
Hla-di-la se vi-la i dje-voj-ka. Hla-di-la se vi-la i dje-voj-ka
10, VII ♭VII-4
Hruba. B. H. 264.
Nevešinje.
260a.
falz.
AA v
Mi-sli-la sam, o zlu ne mi-sli-la mi-sli-la sam
o zlu ne mi-sli-la.

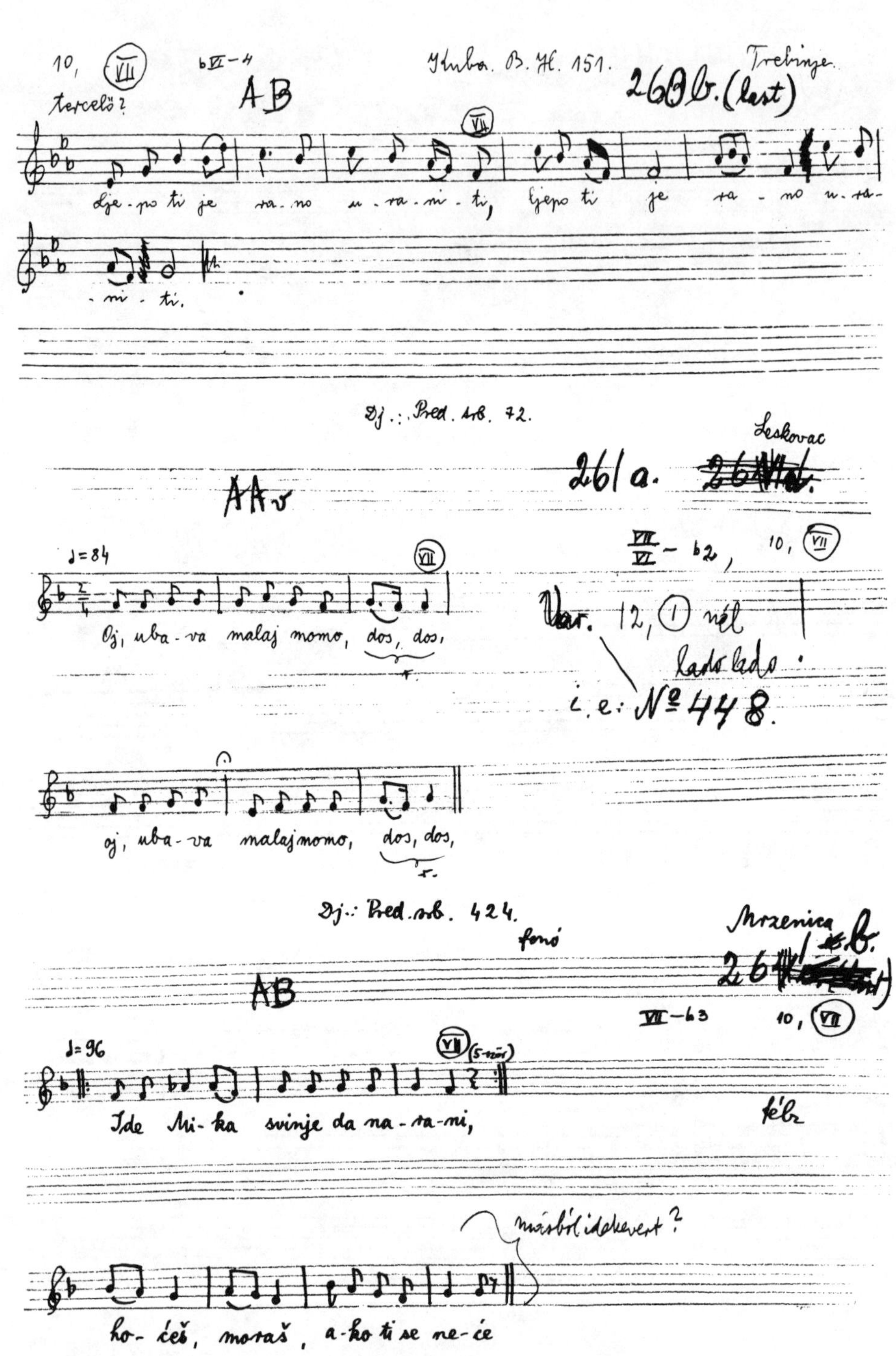

10, (VII) bVI–4
AB
Trebinje
260 b. (last)
tercelő?
lje - po ti je ra - no u - ra - ni - ti, ljepo ti je ra - no u - ra - ni - ti,
Dj.: Pred. sb. 72.
Leskovac
261 a.
AAv
♩=84
VII/VI – b2, 10, (VII)
Oj, uba - va malaj momo, dos, dos,
Var. 12, (1) vél
i. e.: № 448.
oj, uba - va malajmomo, dos, dos,
Dj.: Pred. sb. 424.
fonó
Mrzenica
AB
VII – b3 10, (VII)
♩=96
Ide Mi - ka svinje da na - ra - ni,
ho - ćeš, moraš, a - ko ti se ne - će

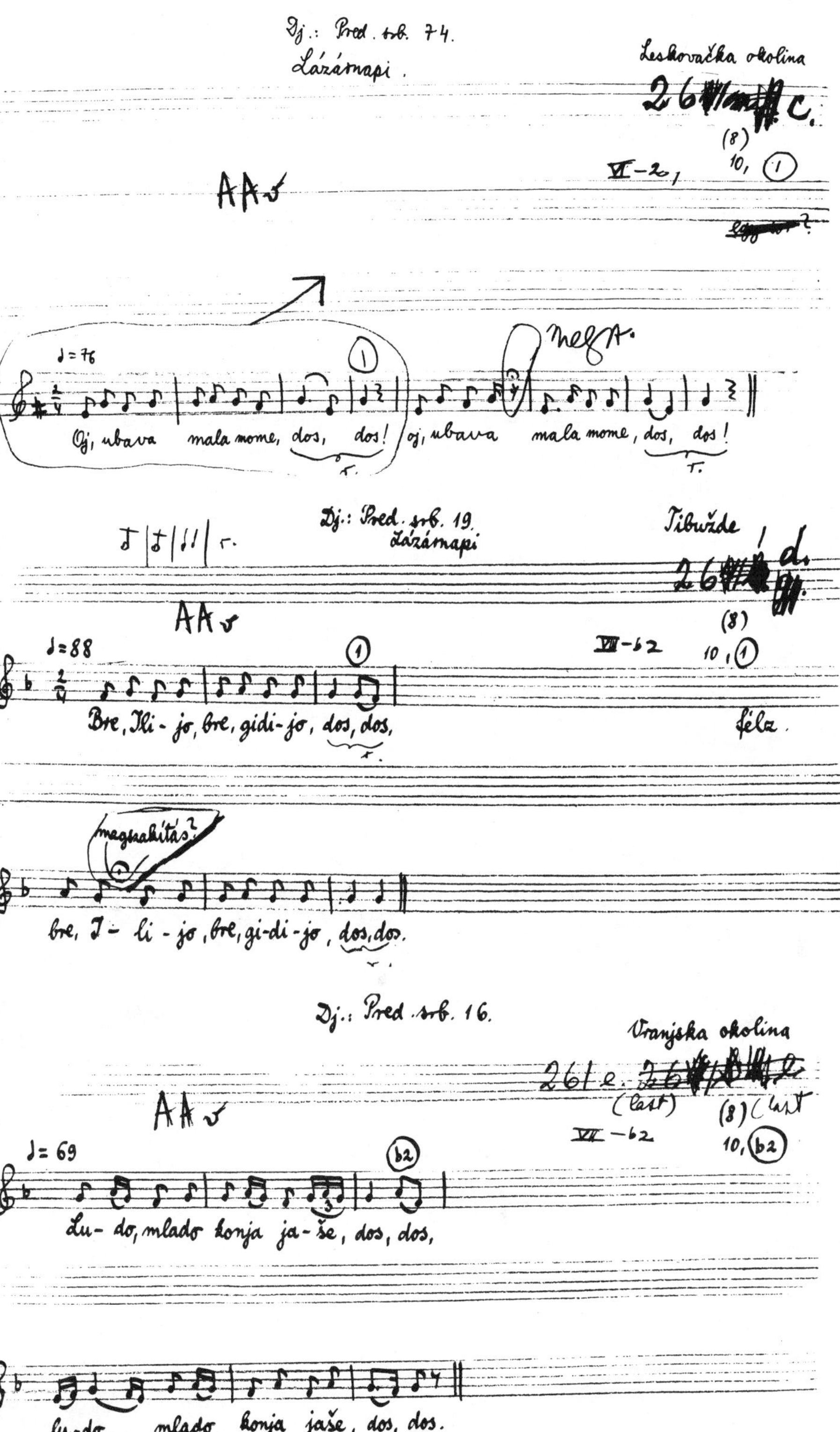

Dj.: Pred. srb. 74.
Lázámapi.
Leskovačka okolina
26 c.
(8)
VI-2, 10, (1)
AA
♩= 76
Oj, ubava mala mome, dos, dos! oj, ubava mala mome, dos, dos!
meg A.
Dj.: Pred. srb. 19.
Lázámapi
Tibužde
26 d.
AA
(8)
♩=88
VII-62
10, (1)
Bre, Ili-jo, bre, gidi-jo, dos, dos,
félz.
magasítás?
bre, I- li - jo, bre, gi-di-jo, dos, dos.
Dj.: Pred. srb. 16.
Vranjska okolina
26 e.
(last)
(8) (last
AA
VII-62
♩= 69
10, (b2)
Lu- do, mlado konja ja- še, dos, dos,
lu-do, mlado konja jaše, dos, dos.

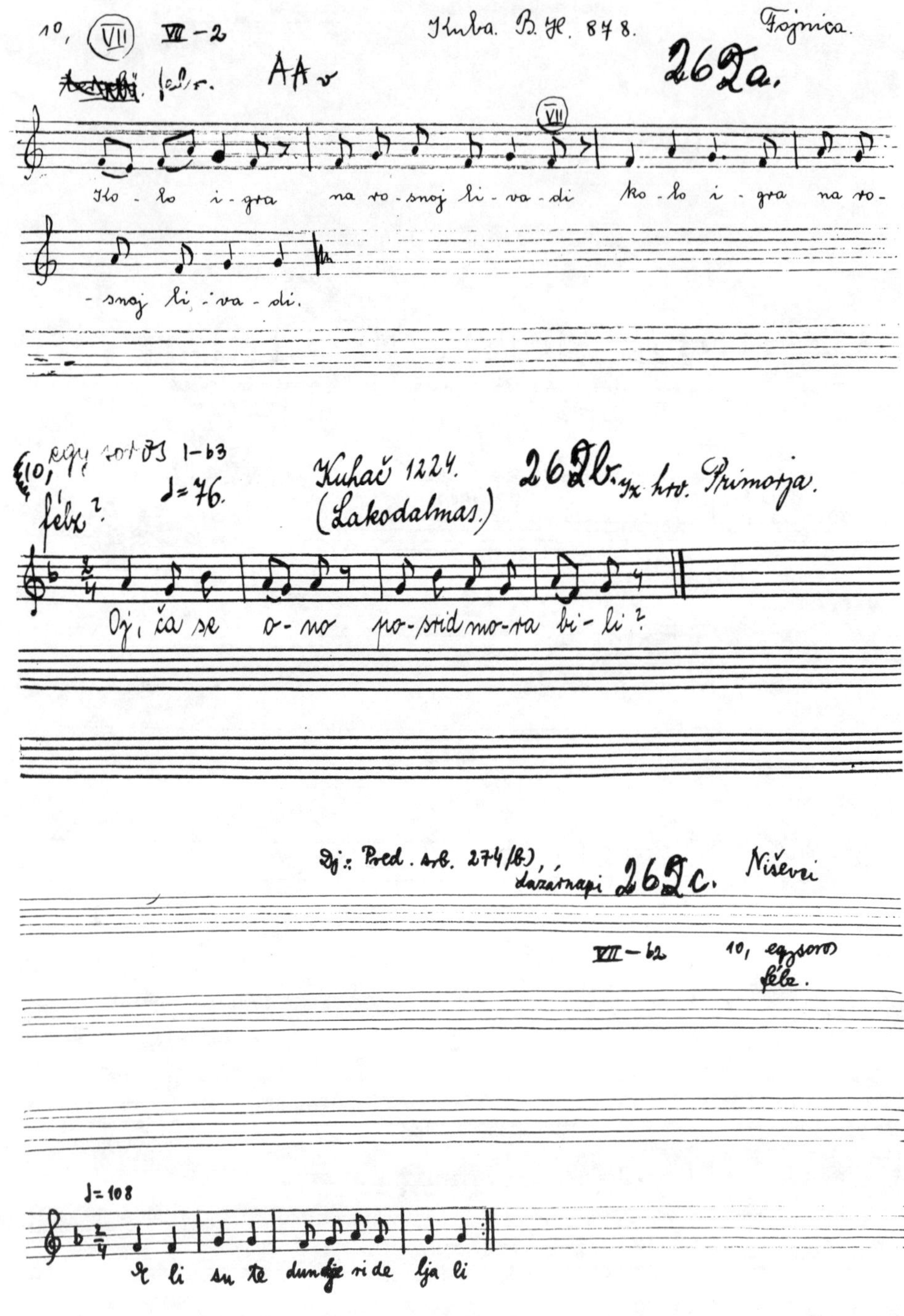
Kuba. B.H. 878.
Fojnica.
262a.
Ko - lo i - gra na ro - snoj li - va - di ko - lo i - gra na ro - snoj li - va - di.
Kuhač 1224.
(Lakodalmas.)
262b.
Oj, ča se o - no po - srid mo - ra bi - li?
262c.
Niševci
♩= 108

Dj.: Pred. sb. 272.
Lázárnapi (érkezéskor, induláskor)
Niševci
262d.
♩= 108
Bog po-moga kuć-ni doma-ći-ni!
Kuba B.H. 775
262e.
Parežević.
Allegro
Ka ke
Kuhač 1364
Slavonje.
262f.
♩= 112
AA
Pij, pij, bra-te, na dnu ti je zla-to, pij, pij, do kape, makar osta bez kape.

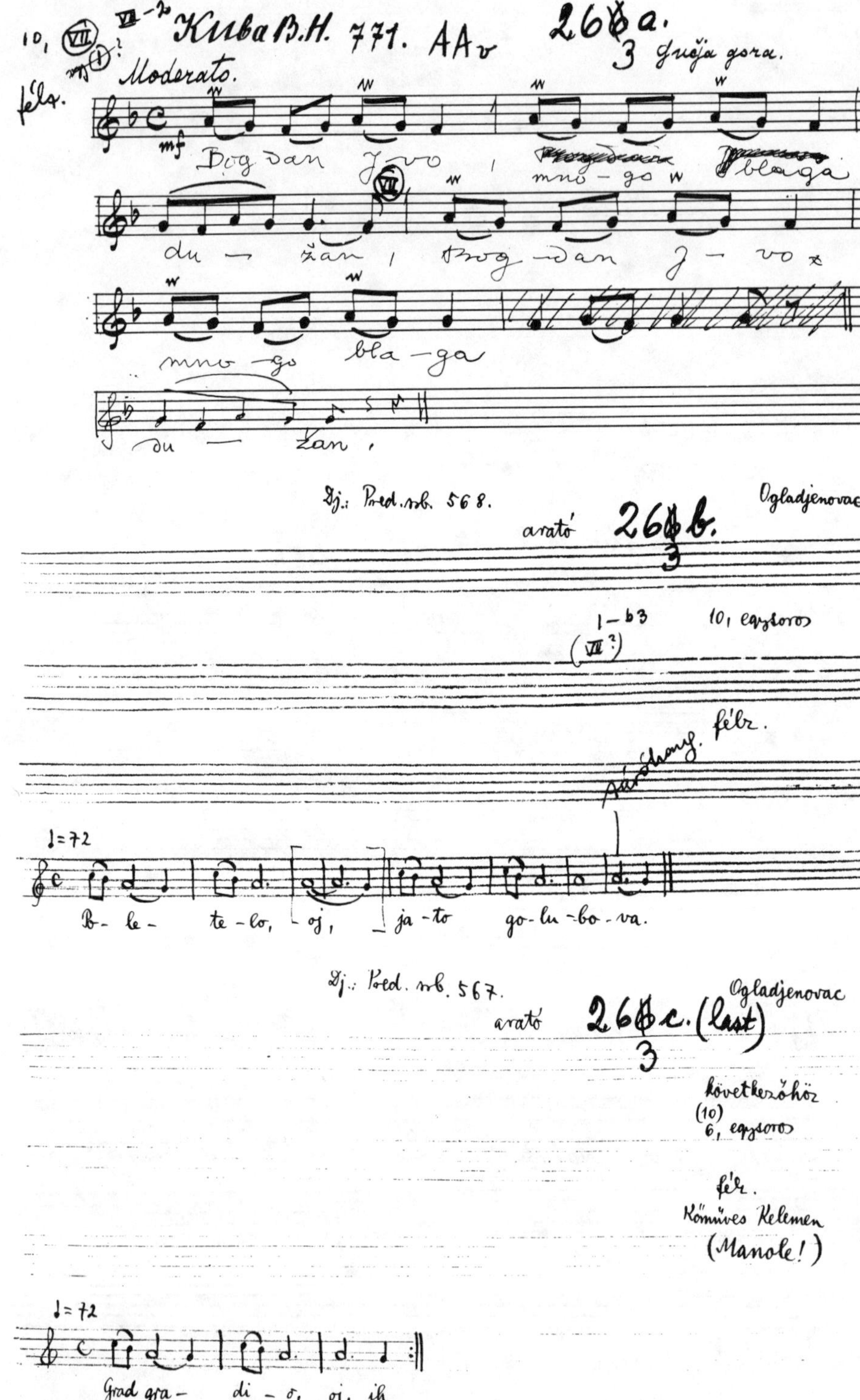

10, VII
Kuba B.H. 771. AAv
26 a.
3 Gučja gora.
Moderato.
félz.
mf
Bog dan Jo vo mno-go bla-ga
du – žan, Bog-dan J-vo
mno-go bla-ga
du — žan.
Dj.: Pred. srb. 568.
Ogladjenovac
arató 26 b.
3
10, egysoros
félz.
♩=72
B- le- te-lo, oj, ja-to go-lu-bo-va.
Dj.: Pred. srb. 567.
Ogladjenovac
arató 26 c. (last)
3
következőhöz
(10)
6, egysoros
félz.
Kőműves Kelemen
(Manole!)
♩=72
Grad gra- di-o, oj, ih

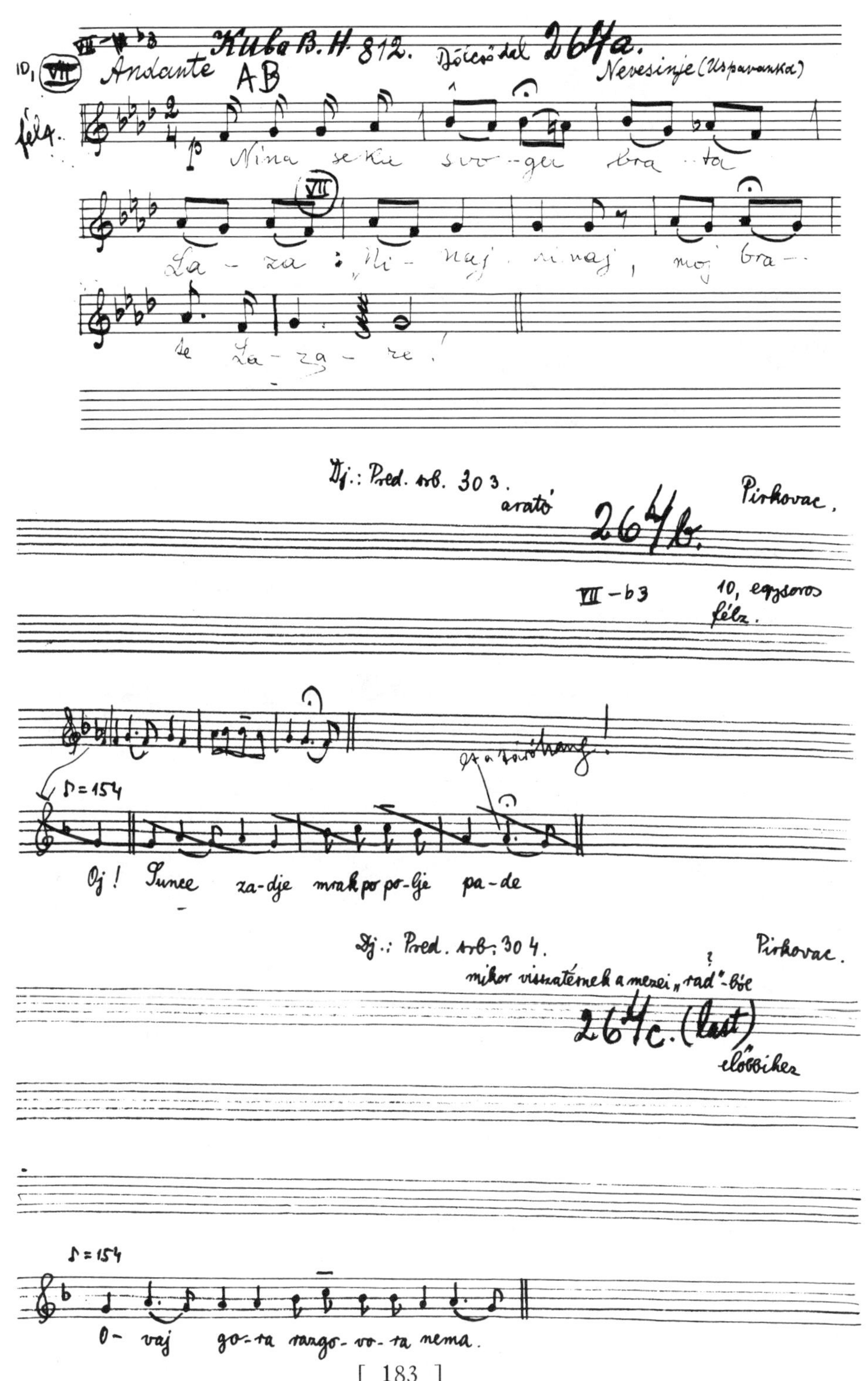
Kuba B.H. 812.
264a.
Nevesinje (Uspavanka)
Andante
AB
Nina seki svo-ga bra-ta
La-za: Ni-naj, ninaj, moj bra-
te La-za-re!
Dj.: Pred. srb. 303.
arató
264/b.
Pirkovac.
VII – b3
10, egysoros félz.
♪ = 154
Oj! Sunce za-dje mrak po po-lje pa-de
Dj.: Pred. srb. 304.
Pirkovac.
264c.
előbbihez
♪ = 154
O- vaj go-ra
nema.

Bilek.
(Herceg.)
Dvi-je se - - - ke bra-ta ne-i-ma-le dvije se-ke
bra-ta ne-i-ma-le.
Furcsa ballada: Két lánynak nem volt bátyja
Moderato. Kuba B.H. 811.
Čapljina
Zmaj pre-le-će mo-ra
na Du-na-vo i pro-ne-se
pod kri-lom dje-voj-ku,
Moderato Kuba B.H. 804.
Nevesinje.
Si-noć pa-še
u Mostar pa-do-še, pa-ša-li-je
o-ko-lo Mo-sta-ra.

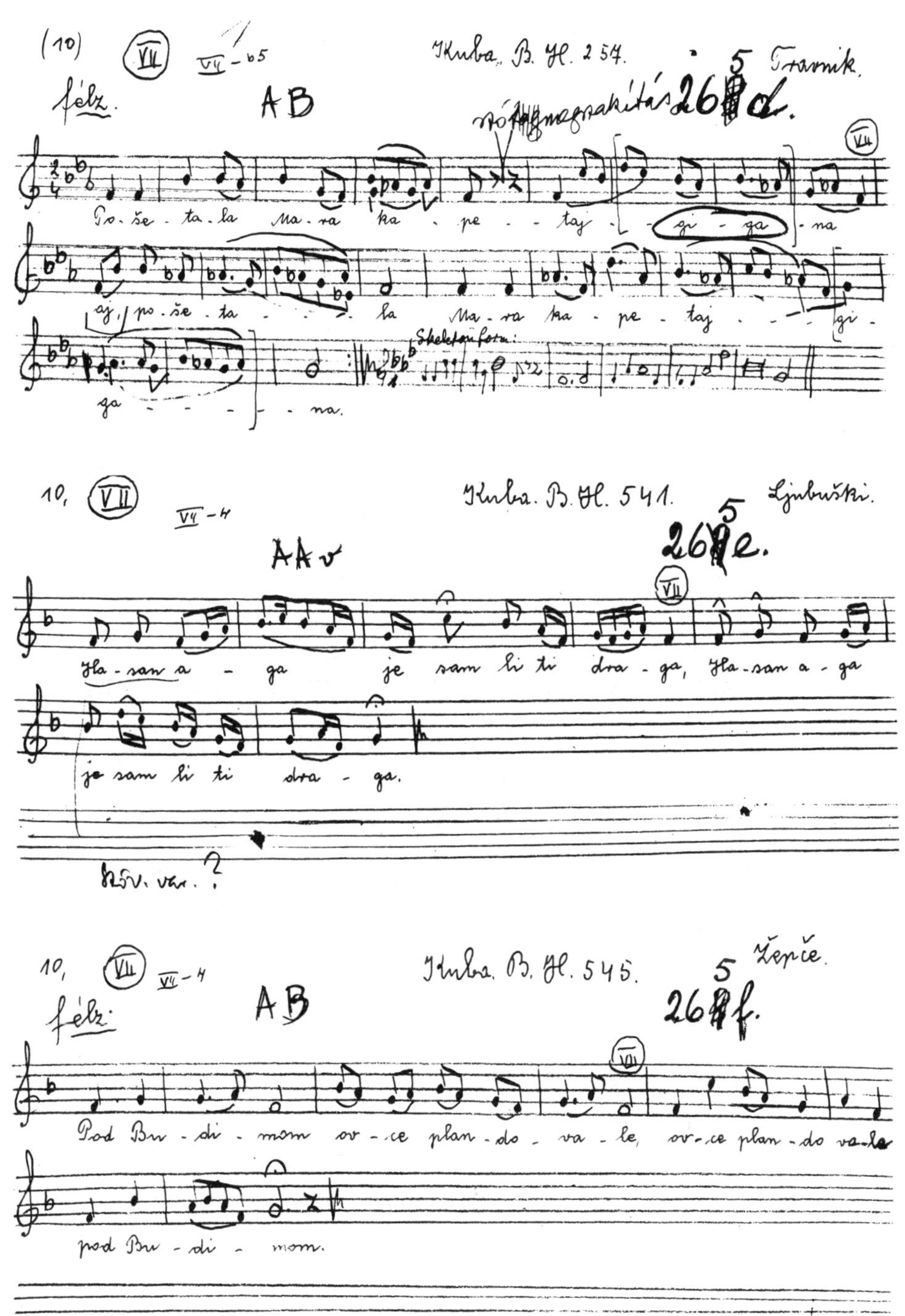
(10) VII VII-65 Kuba. B. H. 254. 5 Travnik.
félz. AB
26d.
Po-še-ta-la Ma-ra ka-pe--taj-[-gi-ga]-na
aj, po-še-ta----la Ma-ra ka-pe-taj---gi-
ga----]--na.
Skeletonform:
10, VII VII-4 Kuba. B. H. 541. 5 Ljubuški.
AAv
26e.
Ha-san a-ga je sam li ti dra-ga, Ha-san a-ga
je sam li ti dra-ga.
10, VII VII-4 Kuba. B. H. 545. 5 Žepče.
félz. AB
26f.
Pod Bu-di-mom ov-ce plan-do-va-le, ov-ce plan-do va-le
pod Bu-di-mom.

10, VII VII –b3
AB
Kuba. B. H. 533.
26 5 g.
Mostar.
félz.
Ti - ha no - ći sjaj - na mje - se - či - na, ti - ha no - ći
sjaj - na mje - se - či - na.
10, VII VI –b3
Kuba. B. H. 571.
Jajce.
AB
26 5 h.
félz.
Dri - na vo - do, što si se po - nje - la, Dri - na vo - do
što si se po - nje
10, VII VI –b3
AB Kuba B. H. 472
26 5 i.
félz. Andante
Doboj.
Ninaj, si - ne - e - e u va -
rak - li be - ši, ninaj, sine,
u va - rak - li be - ši!

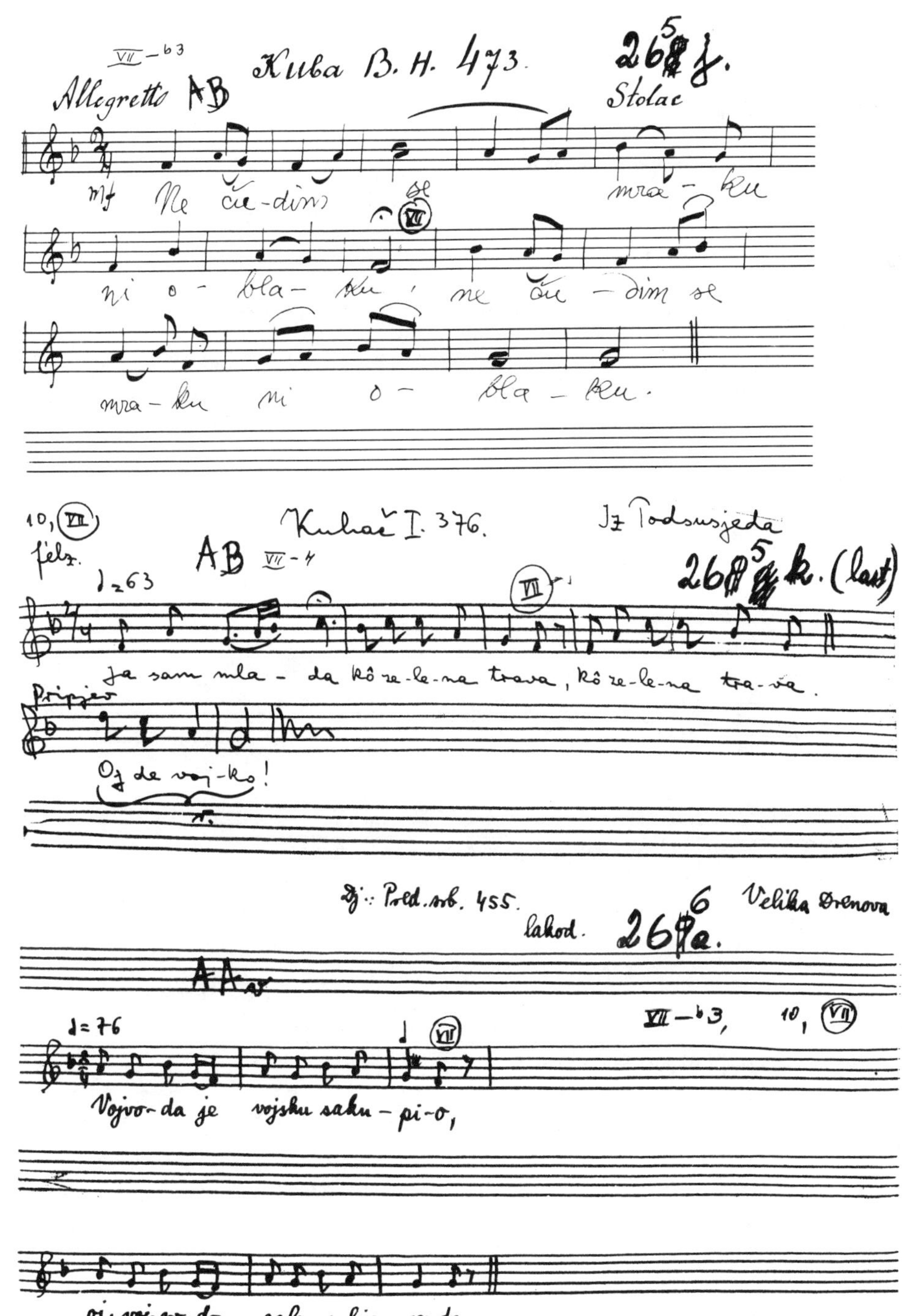
Kuba B. H. 473.
265 j.
Allegretto AB
Stolac
Ne ču-dim se mra-ku ni o-bla-ku, ne ču-dim se mra-ku ni o-bla-ku.
Kuhač I. 376.
Iz Podsusjeda
AB
268 k. (last)
Ja sam mla-da kô ze-le-na trava, kô ze-le-na tra-va.
Pripjev
Oj de voj-ko!
Dj.: Pred. sb. 455.
Velika Drenova
lakod.
266 a.
AA
Vojvo-da je vojsku saku-pi-o,
oj, voj-vo-do, zelena li-vado.

Sedéljka
AAv
Pesme iz Levča, 32. (t. 77. 81.)
Po-kraj pu-ta ro-di-la ja-bu-ka,
10, VII VII-b3
AAv
Juž. Srb. 404.
Donja Gušterica (Na Kosovu)
családi ünnepi.
félz.
Ej, u či-je se zdrav-lje vi-no pi-je, -je.
10, VII VII-4
AAv
Foča.
félz.
Sa-ra-je-vo du-go a ši-ro-ko, -go a ši-ro-ko!

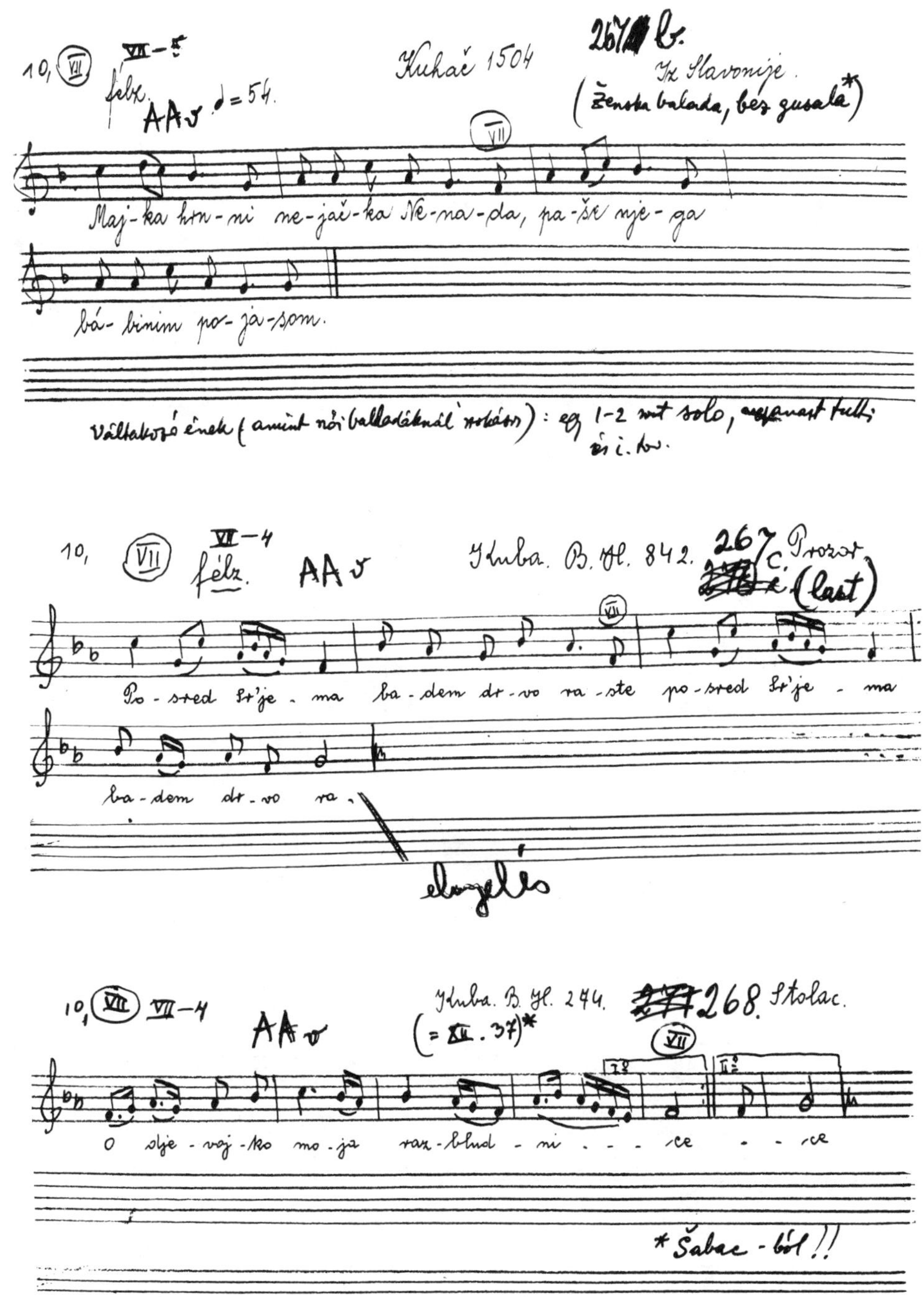
Kuhač 1504
Iz Slavonije.
(ženska balada, bez gusala*)
Maj-ka kni-ni ne-jač-ka Ne-na-da, pa-šr nje-ga
bá-binim po-ja-som.
Ikuba. B. H. 842.
Prozor
Po-sred Srje-ma ba-dem dr-vo ra-ste po-sred Srje-ma
ba-dem dr-vo ra-
Ikuba. B. H. 274.
268. Stolac.
O slje-voj-ko mo-ja raz-blud-ni-ce-ce
* Šabac-ból!!

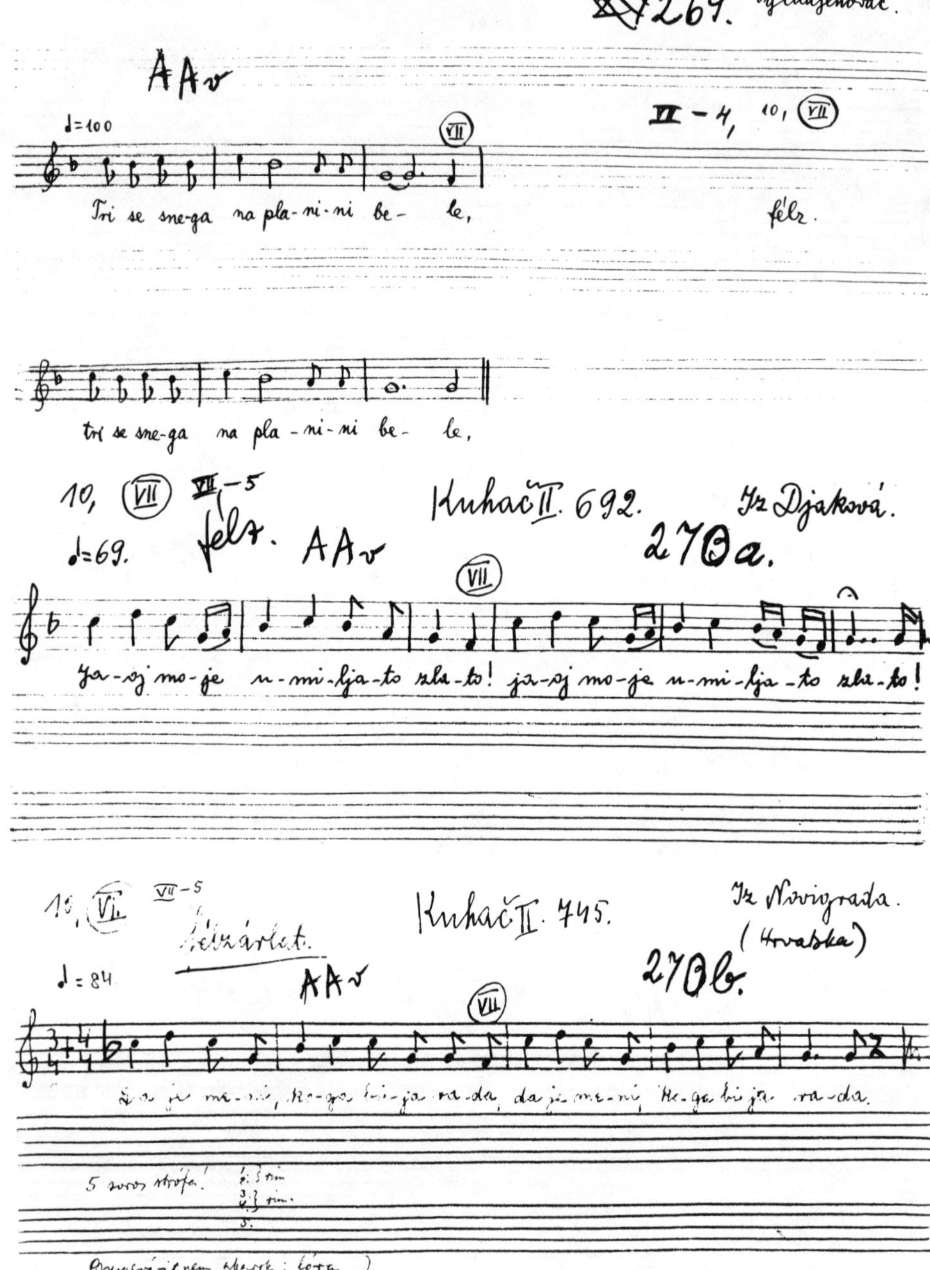
Zj.: Ried. sb. 587.
269. Ogladjenovac.
AAv
II – 4, 10, VII
Tri se sne-ga na pla-ni-ni be- le,
félz.
tri se sne-ga na pla-ni-ni be- le,
10, VII VII–5
félz.
Kuhač II. 692.
Iz Djakova.
270a.
AAv
Ja-oj mo-je u-mi-lja-to zla-to! ja-oj mo-je u-mi-lja-to zla-to!
VII–5
Kuhač II. 745.
Iz Novigrada. (Hrvatska)
270b.
AAv
5 soros strófa!

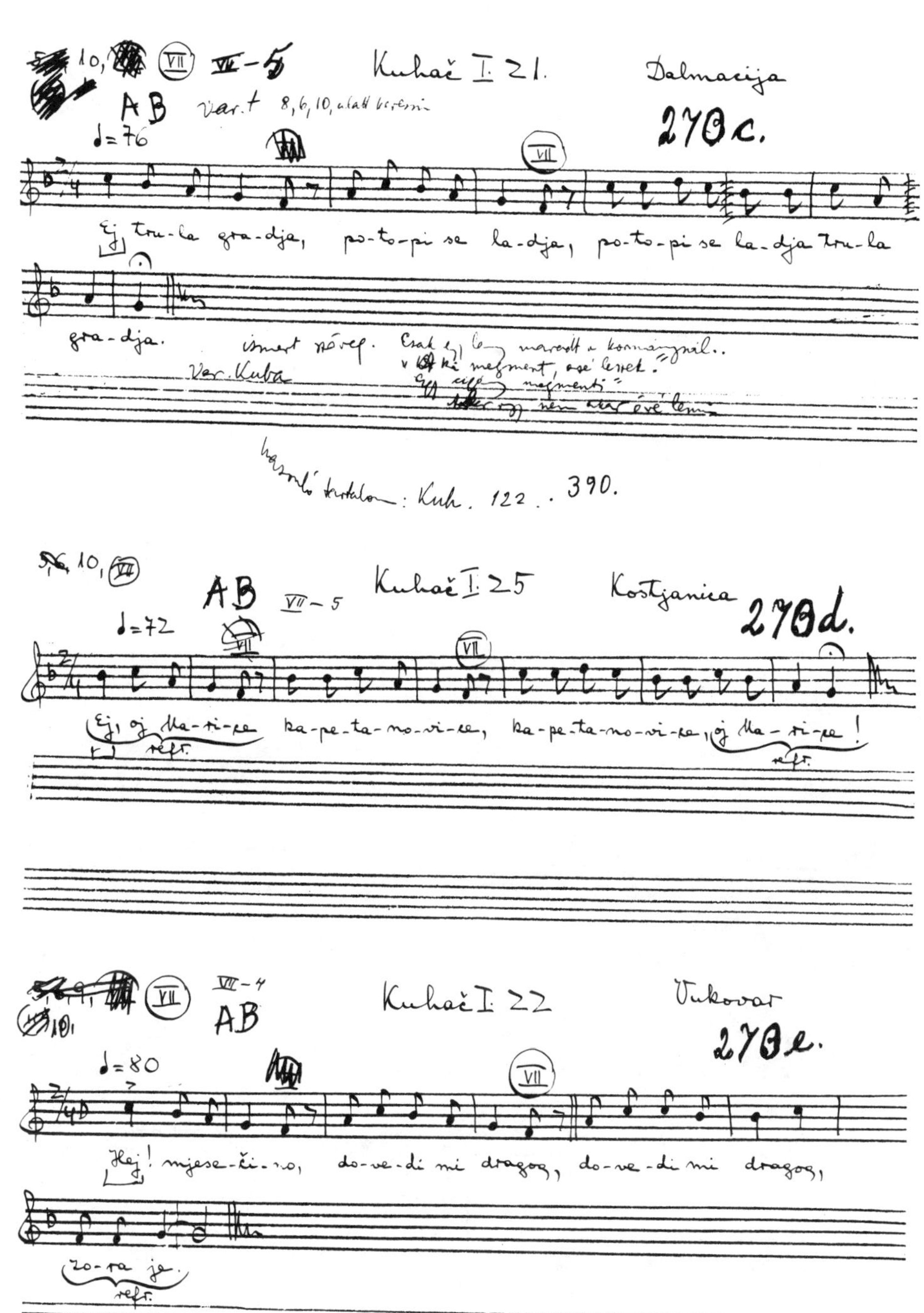
Kuhač I. 21.
Dalmacija
AB
♩=76
270c.
Ej, tru-la gra-dja, po-to-pi se la-dja, po-to-pi se la-dja tru-la gra-dja.
Var. Kuba
Kuh. 122 .. 390.
Kuhač I. 25
Kostjanica
AB
♩=72
270d.
Ej, oj Ma-ri-ce ka-pe-ta-no-vi-ce, ka-pe-ta-no-vi-ce, oj Ma-ri-ce!
refr.
Kuhač I. 22
Vukovar
AB
♩=80
270e.
Hej! mjese-či-no, do-ve-di mi dragog, do-ve-di mi dragog,
zo-ra je.
refr.

VII-4
Kuhač I. 23. Nuštra Slavonija
Nušter 2 nuštor?
270 f. (last)
♩= 80
Ej mje-se-či-no, do-ve-di mi dra-gog, do-ve-di mi dra-gog, oj!
do-ve-di mi dra-gog, oj!
VII-5 AB
Kuba B.H. 745.
271a.
Foča.
Andante
Sunce sja-še ki-ša raz-sje-ja-še, ej, sunce sja-še, ki-ša raz-sje-ja-še
AB VII-5
Kuba B.H. 746.
271b.
Foča.
Moderato
Sunce sja-še, kiša rosi-ja-še, alaj, sunce sja-še, ki-ša rosi-ja-še

Kuba B.-H.
730.
27/c.
Andante.
Žepče
So-ko le-ti iz nad
Sara-je-va.
Kuba B.H.
731.
27/d.
Andante.
Žepče.
Dva pre-bje-ga go-ru
pre-bje-go-še, dva pre-bje-ga
go-ru pre-bje-go-še
10, eggyoros. VII–5
Kuba B. H. 244.
Plevlje.
27/e.
Skeleton form:

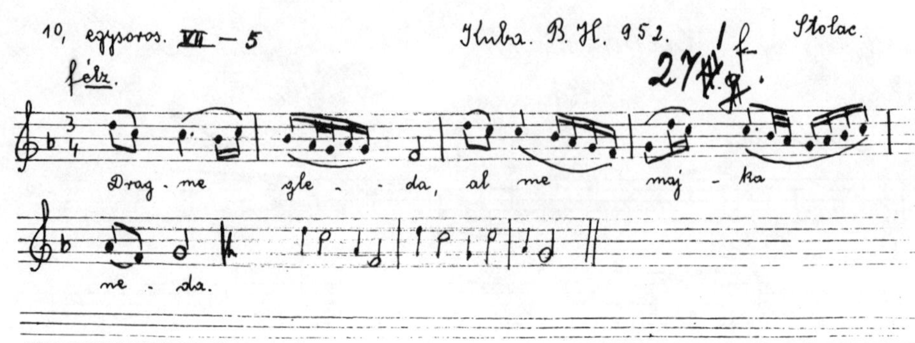
10, egysoros. VII — 5
Kuba. B. H. 952.
Stolac.
félz.
Drag - me gle - - da, al me maj - ka
ne - da.

10, egysoros. VI — 4
Juž. Srb. 412.
Prizren.
(lant)
Što je le - po pod noć po - gle - da - - - ti,

10, VII — 5 AB
Kuba B. H. 670.
27#2.
Allegro.
St. Majdan.
VII
mf
Oj, Sa-vi - ce, tiha vodo, ladna, oj, Sa-vio,
sfz.
tiha vo-do lad —

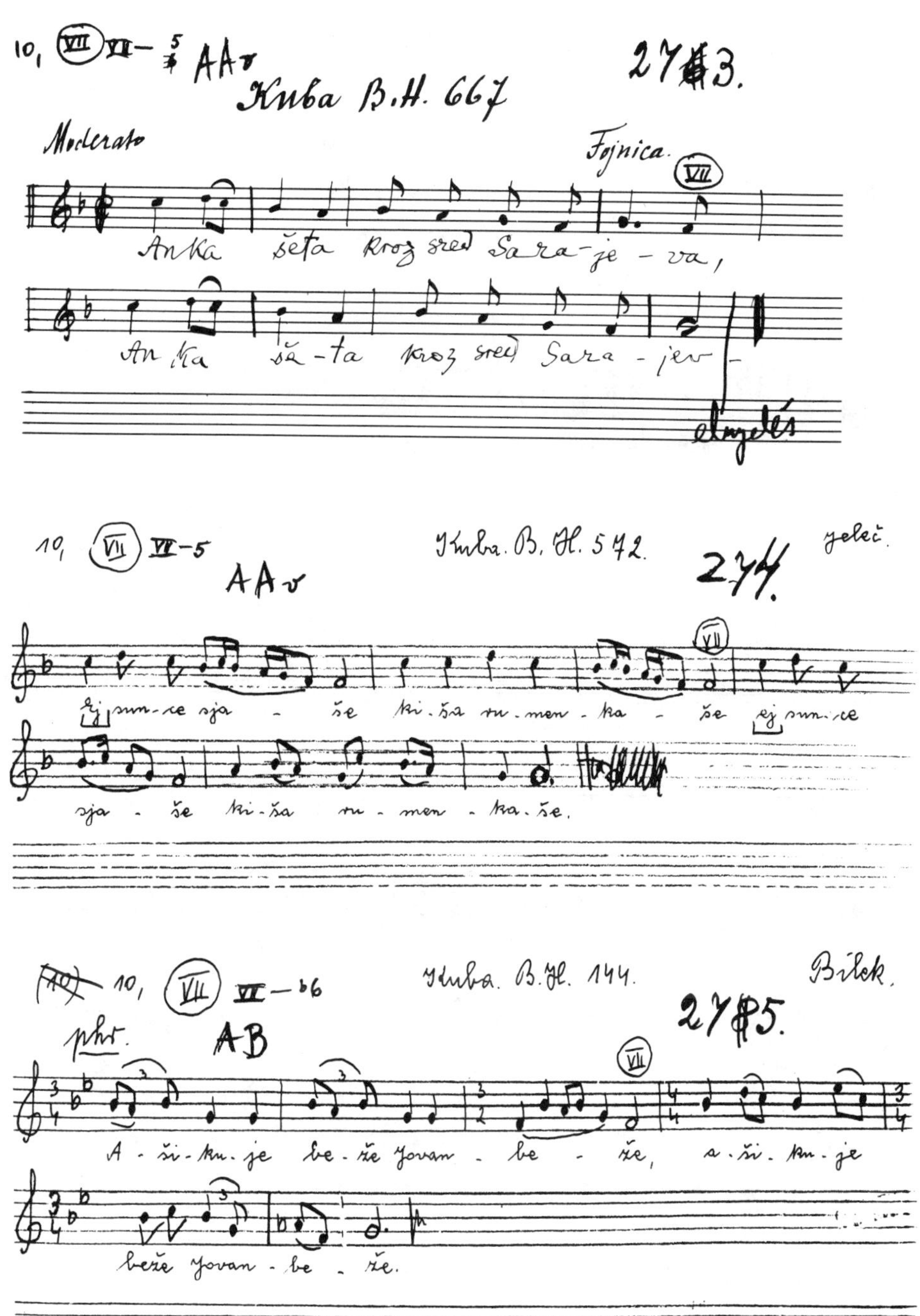
10, VII VII – 5/4 AAv
Kuba B.H. 667
2743.
Moderato
Fojnica.
Anka šeta kroz sred Sa-ra-je-va,
An-ka ša-ta kroz sred Sara-jev-
elnyelés
10, VII VII–5
Kuba. B. H. 572.
274.
Jeleč.
AAv
Ej sun-ce sja - še ki-ša ru-men-ka - še ej sun-ce
sja - še ki-ša ru - men - ka-še.
10, VII VII – b6
Kuba. B.H. 144.
Bileć.
2745.
phr.
AB
A-ši-kn-je be-že Jovan - be - že, a-ši-kn-je
beže Jovan - be - že.

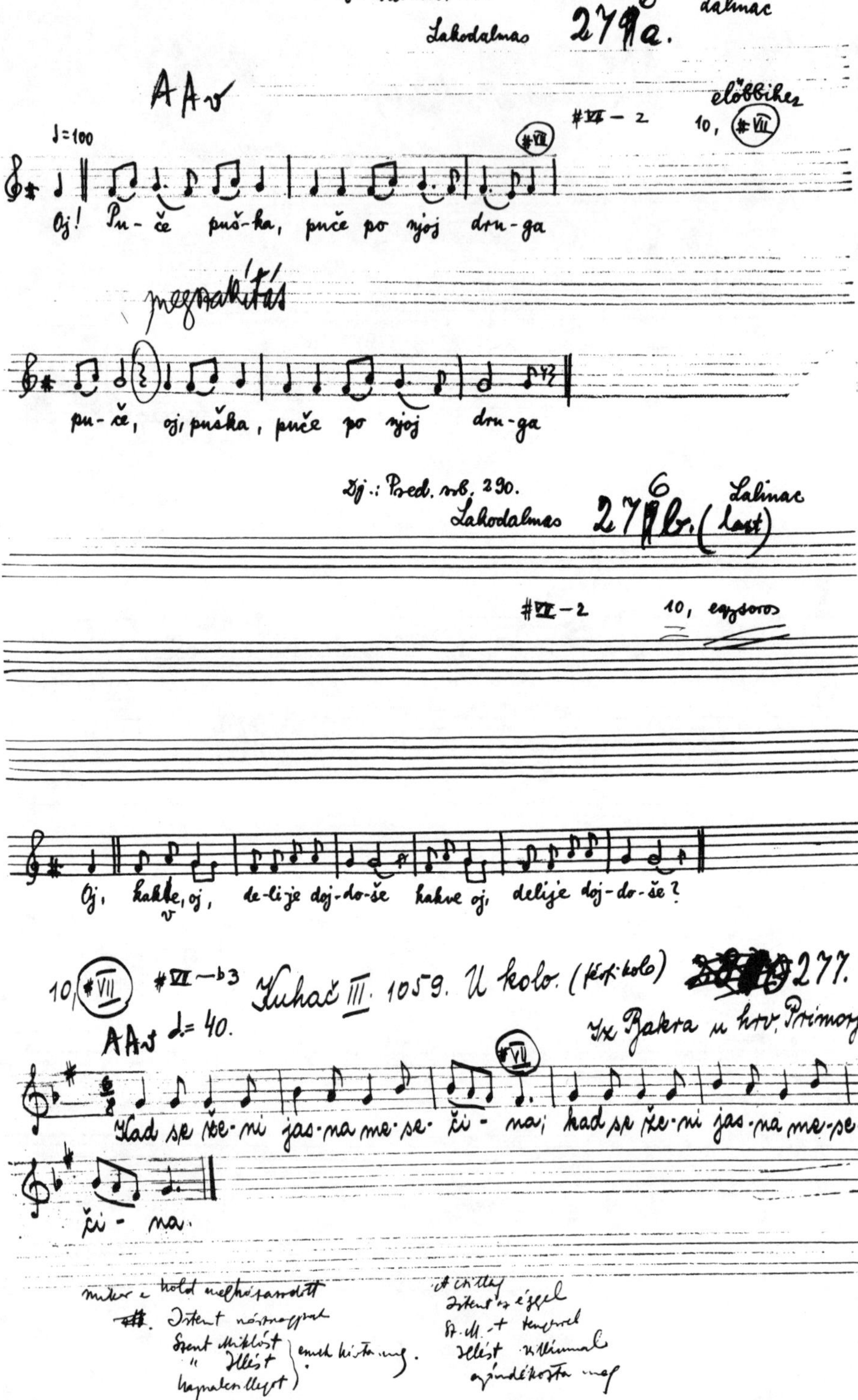

Dj.: Pred. zb. 291.
Lakodalmas 279a. Lalinac
AAv
#VII
#VII – 2 10, #VII elöbbihez
Oj! Pu-če puš-ka, puče po njoj dru-ga
megrakítás
pu-če, oj, puška, puče po njoj dru-ga
Dj.: Pred. zb. 290.
Lakodalmas 279b. (last) Lalinac
#VII – 2 10, egysoros
Oj, kakve, oj, de-li-je doj-do-še kakve oj, delije doj-do-še?
10, #VII #VII – b3 Kuhač III. 1059. U kolo. (férfi kolo) 277.
AAv 𝅗𝅥.= 40.
Iz Bakra u hrv. Primorju
Kad se že-ni jas-na me-se-či-na; kad se že-ni jas-na me-se-či-na.

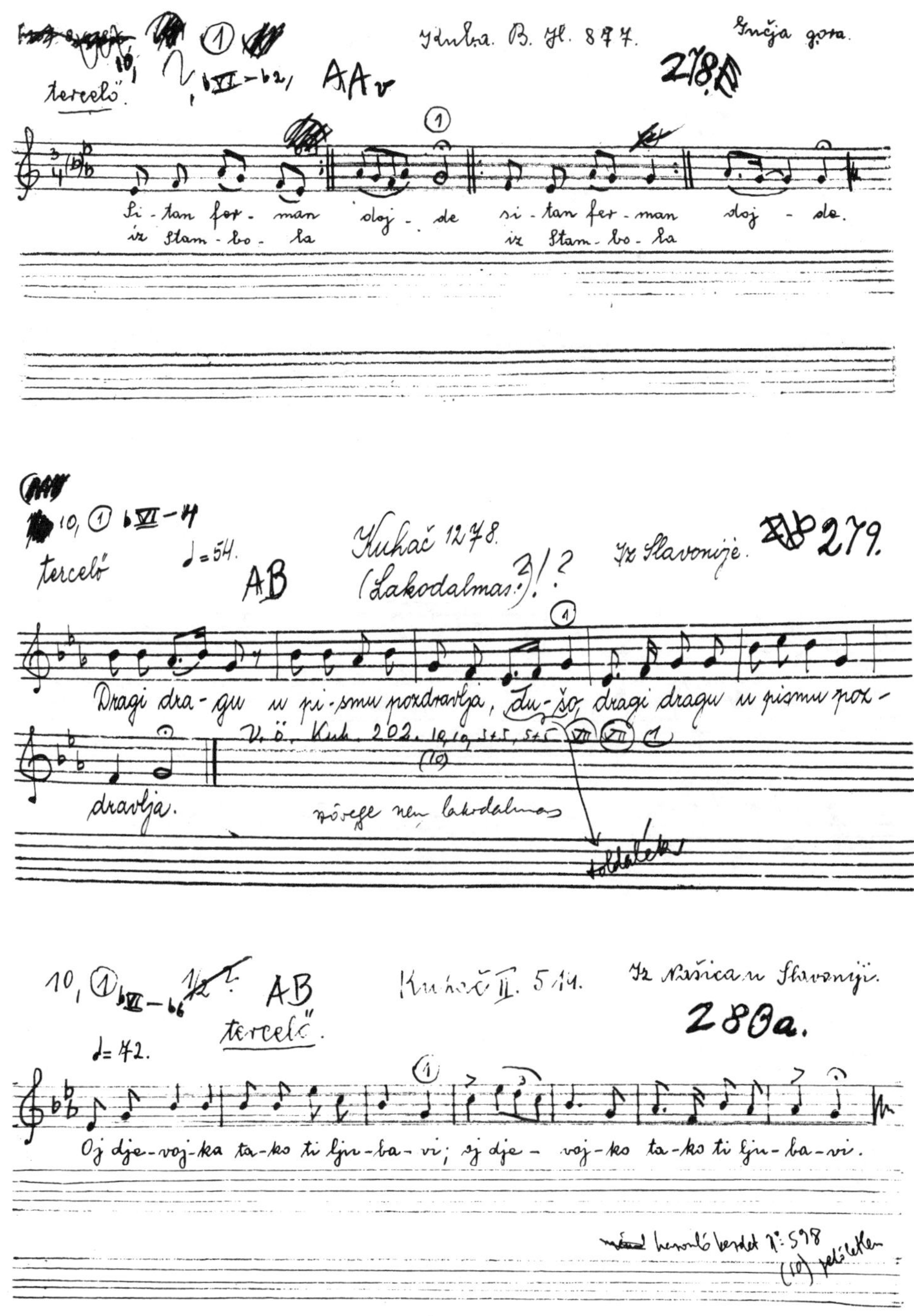

tercelő
AAv
Kuba. B. H. 877.
Gnčja gora.
278.
Si-tan fer-man doj-de si-tan fer-man doj-de.
iz Stam-bo-la iz Stam-bo-la
10, ① bVI–4
tercelő
♩=54.
AB
Kuhač 1278.
(Lakodalmas?)!?
Iz Slavonije.
279.
Dragi dra-gu u pi-smu pozdravlja, du-šo, dragi dragu u pismu poz-dravlja.
10, ① bVI–b6
AB
tercelő
♩= 72.
Kuhač II. 514.
Iz Našica u Slavoniji.
280a.
Oj dje-voj-ka ta-ko ti lju-ba-vi; oj dje-voj-ko ta-ko ti lju-ba-vi.

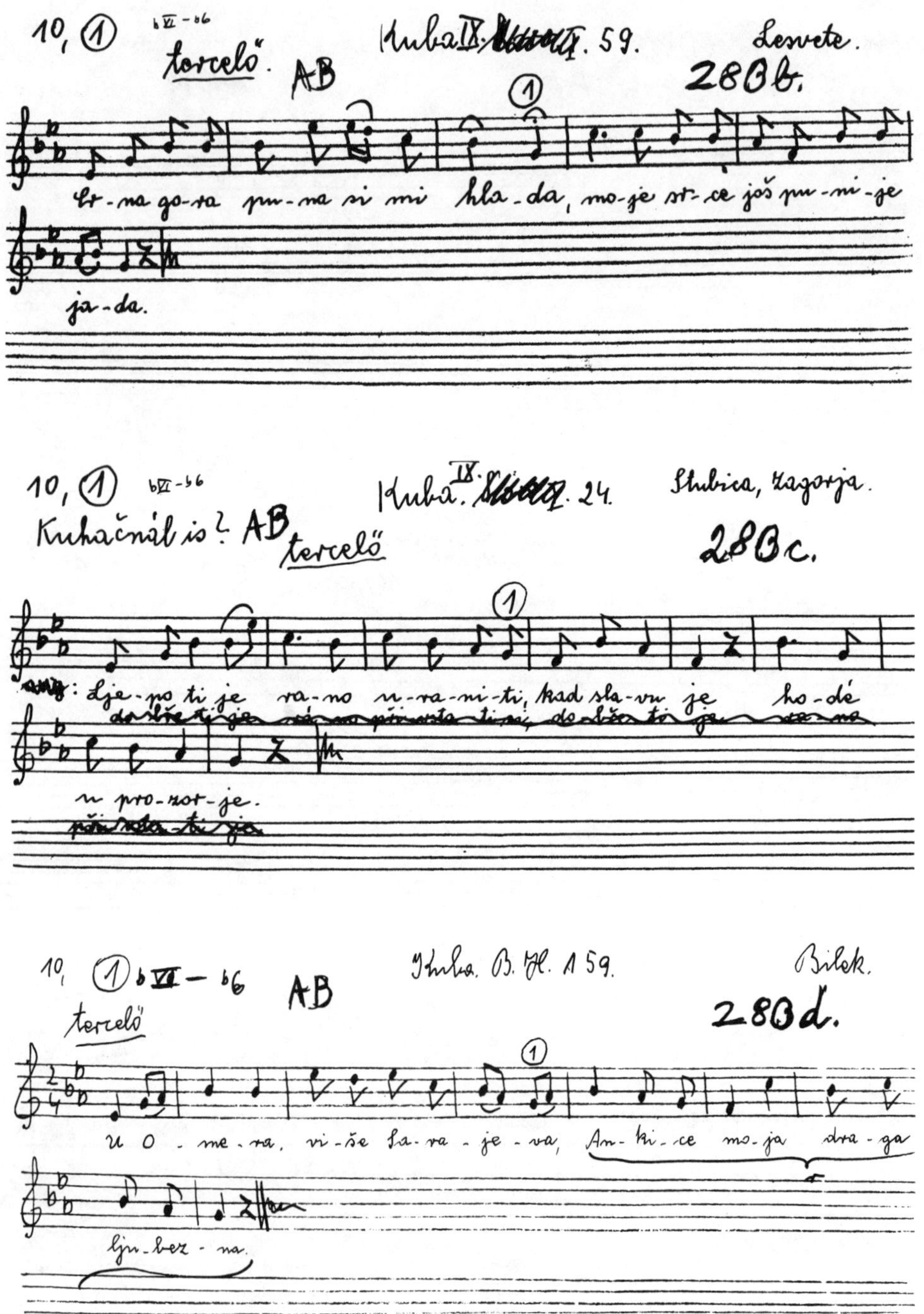
10, ① bVI - b6
tercelő. AB
Kuba IX. 59. Lesvete.
280b.
Cr-na go-ra pu-na si mi hla-da, mo-je sr-ce još pu-ni-je ja-da.
10, ① bVI - b6
Kuba IX. 24. Stubica, Zagorja.
AB tercelő
280c.
Lje-po ti je ra-no u-ra-ni-ti, kad sla-vu je ho-dé u pro-zor-je.
10, ① bVI — b6 AB
tercelő
280d.
u O-me-ra, vi-še Sa-ra-je-va, An-ki-ce mo-ja dra-ga lju-bez-na.

(10) 10, (2) VII–7 AB
Kuba. B. H. 64.
Stolac.
előbbihez.
280e.
O dje - voj - ko, mo - ja raz - blud - ni - ce, do - bro li te
bi - jah raz - blu - - di - - - o.
(10) 10, (2) VII–7
Kuba. B. H. 65.
Trebinje.
előbbihez.
AB
280f.
Je - li ti tu ga i ne - vo - lja, dra - ga, jel' ti tu - ga i ne -
vo - lja dra - ga.
(10) 10, (2) VII–7
Kuba. B. H. 66 (B. H. 4)
Stolac.
előbbihez.
AB
280g. (last)
jel' ti tu ga i ne vo lja dra - gi jel' ti tu ga i ne
vo lja dra - gi.
ez hiányzik, lehetne is!

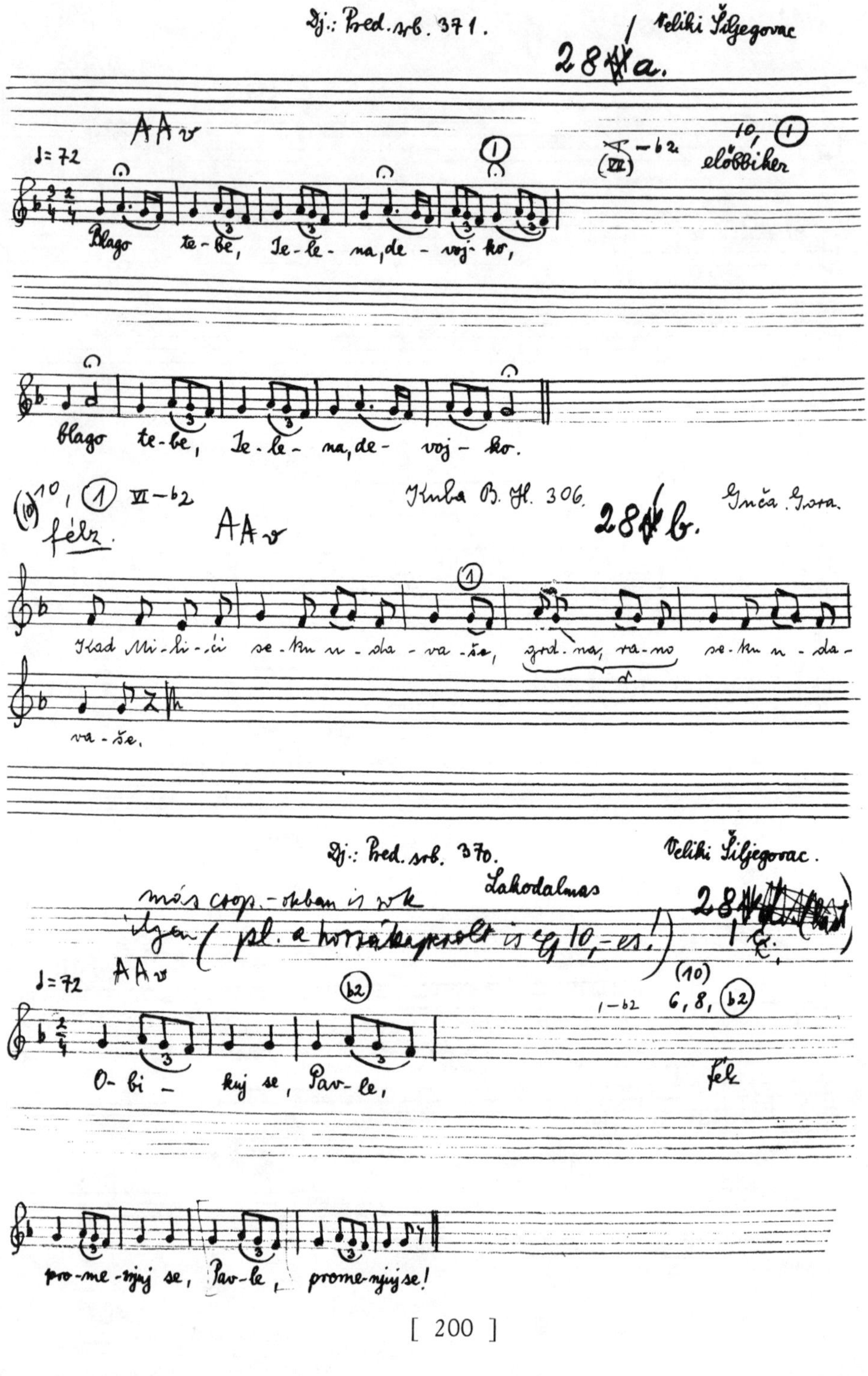

Dj.: Pred. srb. 371. | Veliki Šiljegovac

28 a.

AA v

♩= 72 ① (VII) – b2 10, ① előbbiker

Blago te-be, Je-le-na, de-voj-ko,

blago te-be, Je-le-na, de-voj-ko.

(10) 10, ① VI – b2 félz.

Kuba B. H. 306. Guča Gora.

28 b.

AA v

①

Kad Mi-li-ci se-ku-u-da-va-še, gro-na, ra-no se-ku-u-da-va-še.

Dj.: Pred. srb. 370. Veliki Šiljegovac.

Lakodalmas

más csop.-okban is sok ilyen (pl. a horsákapcsolt is egy 10,-es!)

28 c.

(10) 6, 8, (b2) 1 – b2

♩= 72 AA v (b2)

O-bi-kuj se, Pav-le,

félz

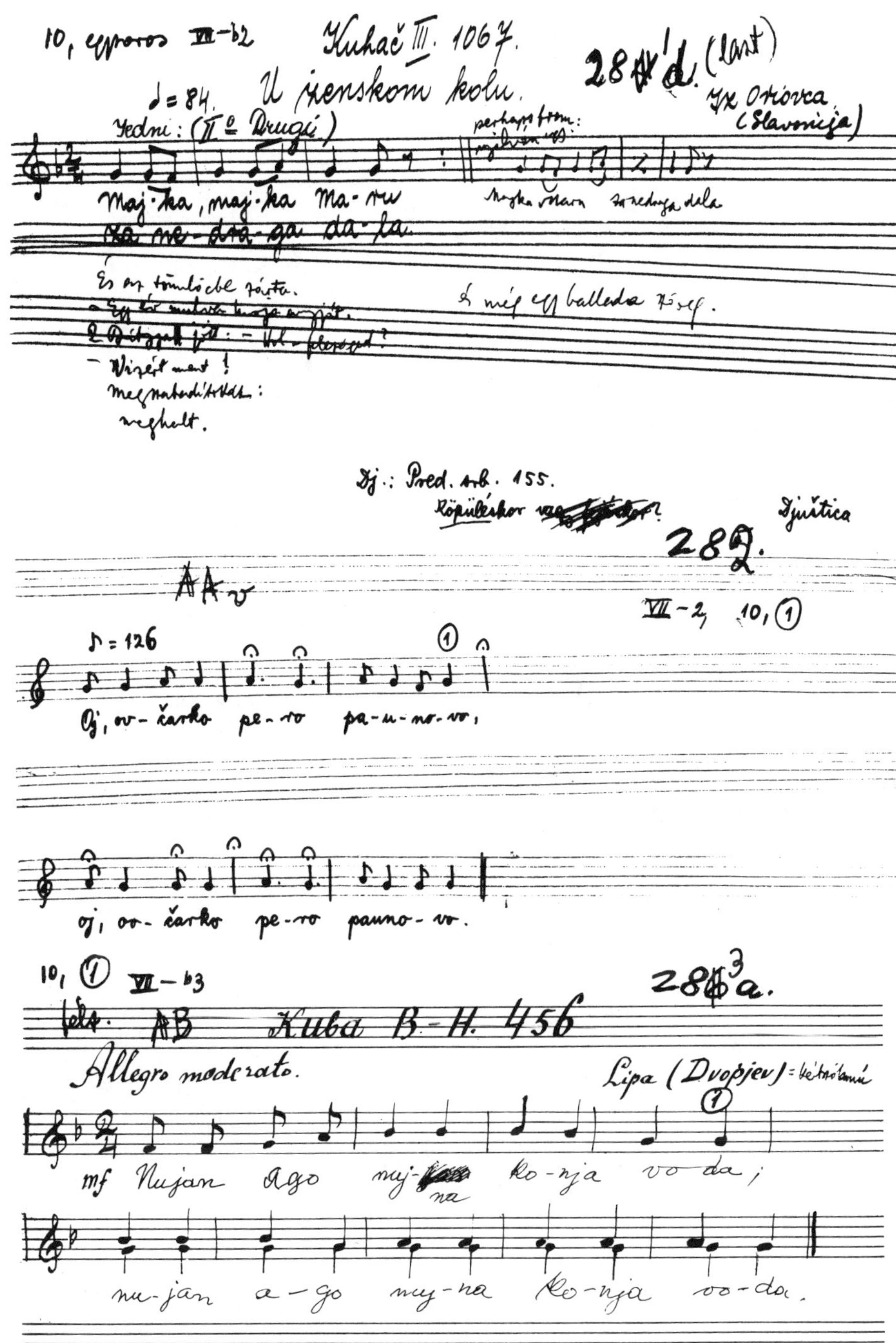
Kuhač III. 1067.
U ženskom kolu.
♩= 84.
Oriovca (Slavonija)
Maj-ka, maj-ka Ma-ru
za ne-da-ga da-la.
Dj.: Pred. srb. 155.
Djuštica
♪ = 126
Oj, ov-čarko pe-ro pa-u-no-vo,
oj, ov-čarko pe-ro pauno-vo.
Kuba B-H. 456
Allegro moderato.
Lipa (Dvopjev)
mf Nujan ago nuj-na ko-nja vo-da;
nu-jan a-go nuj-na ko-nja vo-da.

10, ① VII – 4
fél4. Allegretto AB
Kuba B.H. 497
28c³b.
Petrovac. ①
Konj zelenko rosnu travu pasu,
Konj ze-len-ko rosnu travu pasu

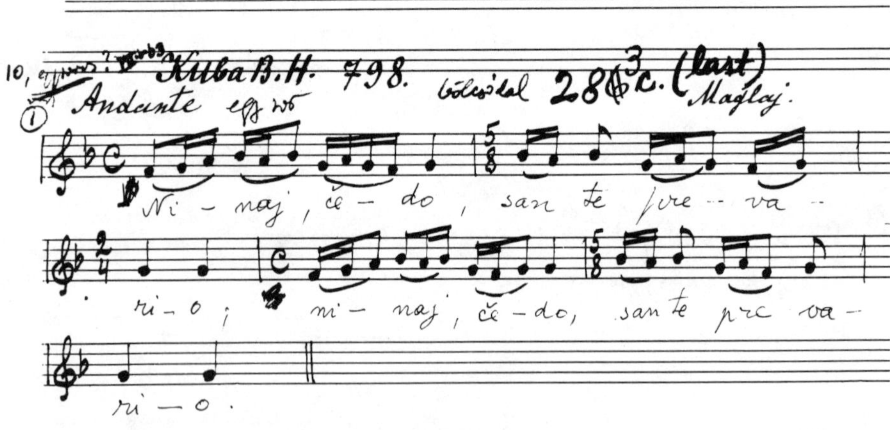
Kuba B.H. 798.
Andante
bölcsődal
28c³c.
Maglaj.
Ni – naj, če – do, san te pre – va –
ri – o; ni – naj, če – do, san te pre va –
ri – o.

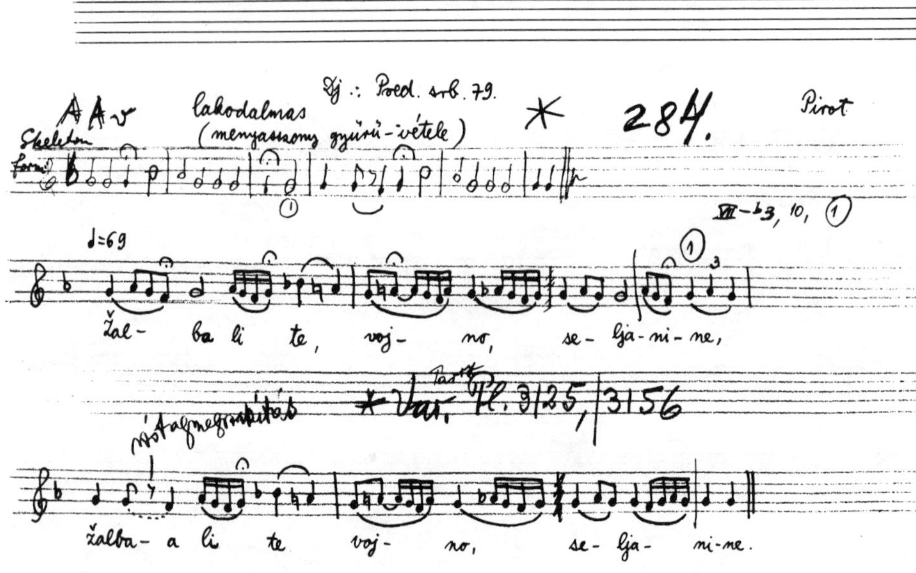
AAv
lakodalmas
(menyasszony gyűrű-vétele)
Dj.: Pred. srb. 79.
284.
Pirot
Skeleton form
VII – b3, 10, ①
♩=69
Žal- ba li te, voj- no, se- lja-ni-ne,
Var. Pl. 3125, 3156
žalba- a li te voj- no, se- lja- ni-ne.

Vivo
Kuba. B.H. 7/19.
Lipa u Bihaće.
Kolo. Dvoglasno.
Driema mi se, spava-la bi, maj- ko, driema mi se,
spava-la bi, maj- ko.
Kuba. B. H. 311.
Žepče.
I-mam dra-gu, al' je na da-le-ku, i-mam dra-gu, al' je na
da-le-ku.
Kuba. B. H. 544.
Petrovac.
ko-nja vo- - - da.

10, (1) VII – 4
Kuba. B. H. 914.
6
Čapljina.
28 c.
félz.
AA
mi-sliš dra-ga da ne ha-jem za te, aj mi-sliš dra-ga ha da ne ha-jem za te.
megállás
előbbihez: VII – 4
Kuba. B. H. 916.
6
Čapljina.
28 d.
félz.
AA
Znaš ne-vje-ro ka-ko si se kle-o aj znaš ne vje-ro kad si mi se kle-o?
megáll.
10, (4) VII – 4
Kuba. B. H. 915.
6
Nevesinje.
28 e.
félz.
AA előbbihez
O-no mad-ne u pe-tak u po-dne aj o-no mlad-ne u pe-tak u pod-ne.
megáll.

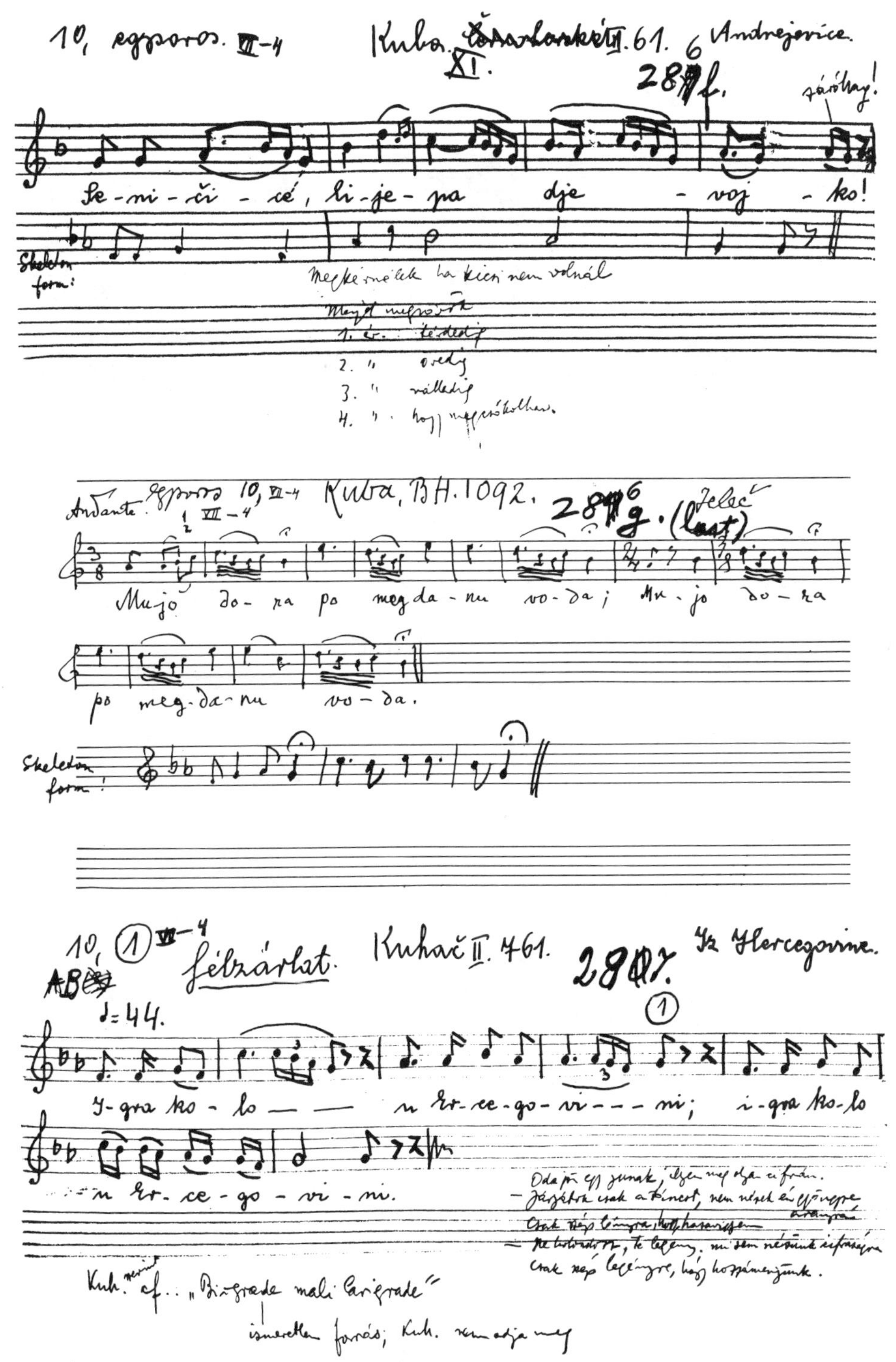
10, egyszeros. VII–4
Kuba XI. 61. 6 Andrejevice.
287f.
Se-mi-či-cé, li-je-pa dje-voj-ko!
Skeleton form:
Andante. egyszeres 10, VII–4 Kuba, BH. 1092. 287g. Jelec
Mujo do-ra po meg-da-nu vo-da; Mu-jo do-ra po meg-da-nu vo-da.
Skeleton form:
10, ① VII–4 félzárlat. Kuhač II. 461. 287h. Iz Hercegovine.
♩= 44.
I-gra ko-lo — — u Er-ce-go-vi- - - ni; i-gra ko-lo u Er-ce-go-vi-ni.

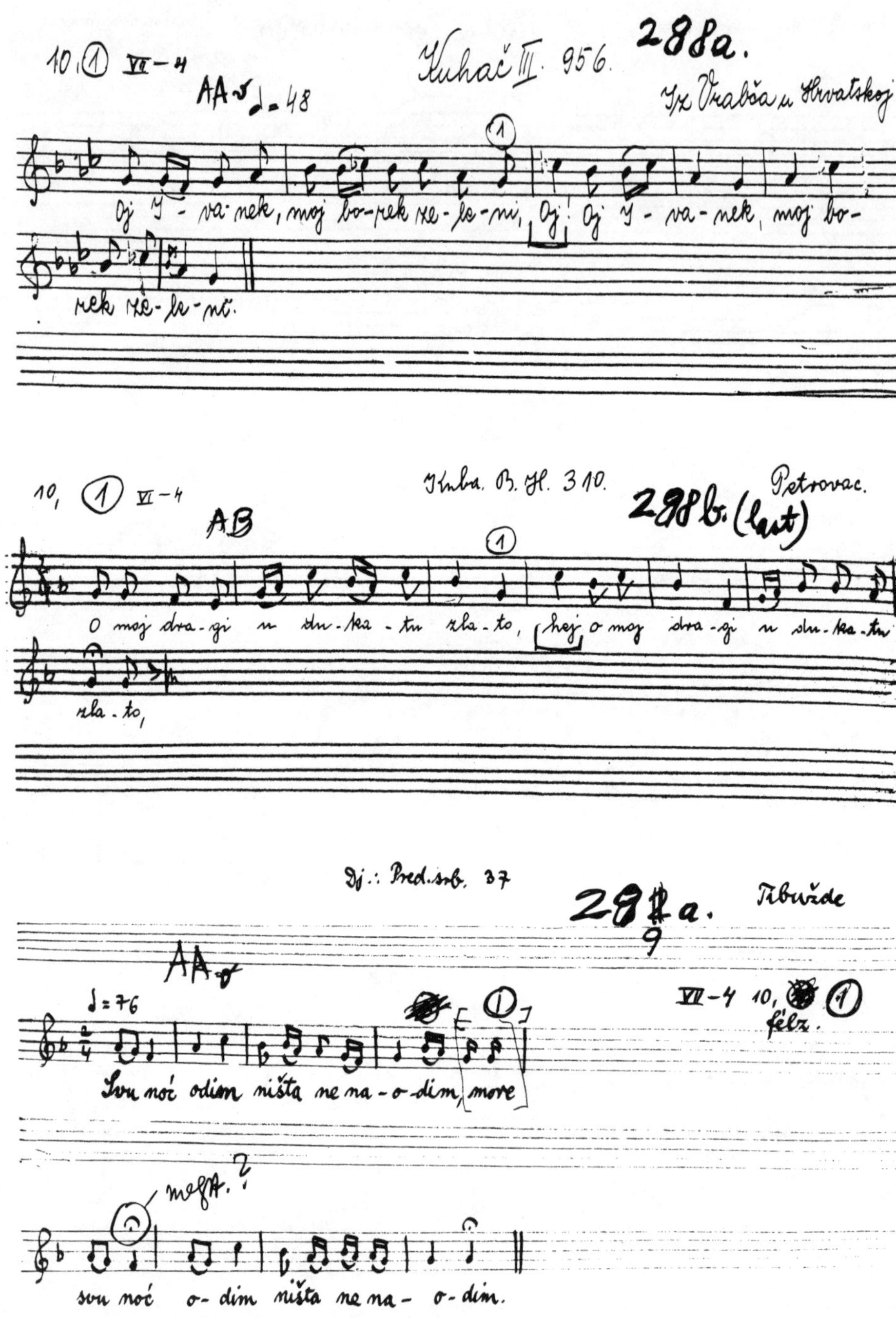
10, ① VII – 4
Kuhač III. 956.
288a.
AA
♩ = 48
Iz Vrabča u Hrvatskoj.
Oj I - va-nek, moj bo-rek ze-le-ni, Oj Oj I - va-nek, moj bo-
rek ze-le-ni.
10, ① VII – 4
Kuba. B. H. 310.
288b. (last)
Petrovac.
AB
O moj dra-gi u du-ka-tu zla-to, hej o moj dra-gi u du-ka-tu
zla-to,
Dj.: Pred.srb. 37
289a.
AA
♩ = 76
VII – 4 10, ①
félz.
Svu noć odim ništa ne na-o-dim, more
svu noć o-dim ništa ne na-o-dim.

Lento
Kuba B.H. 803.
289 b.(last)
Fojnica.
Po že-lala kralji-ca gospo-ja.
Kuhač 1222.b)
(Lakodalmas)
Iz Bačke
290a.
ku- - me, za ra-na ju- - na-ci, za ra-
na nam ku-mu do-ve- - -di-te.
za - ran
előtte: Kuh. (222a)
félz.
Kuba. B. Ha. 909.
(Bölcsődal)
290b.(last)
Ključ.
(Uspavanka)
Spa-vaj lju-bo u tan-koj be-ši-ci spa-vaj lju-bo
u tan-koj be-ši-ci.

Kuhač I. 304.
Iz Srbije
AAv
291.
Znaš li, du - šo, kad si mo-ja bi - - la; znaš li du - šo,
kad si mo-ja bi-la.
Pirot.
(ćilimarska)
292a.
AB
♩= 108
De-voj-ća se Bo-gu po-mo-li- la,
de-voj-ća se Bogu po-mo- li- la
Djordjević. Nar. Pev. 85/1.
292b. (last)
AAv
Ej, či-ja fru-la ža-lo-sti-vo svi-ra, ej, či-ja fru-la ža-lo-
-sti-vo svi-ra?

10, ① VII–4 AAv Kuba B.H. 494. 293.
Allegro moderato
Kupa ①
mf
Oj, naran-če, narančice moja;
oj, na-ranče, na-ran-či-ce moja!
10, ① VII–4 Kuba B.H. 628. 294.
AB
Bihać.
①
p
Soko bi-ra, gdje će na-ći mf mi-ra,
so-ko bi-ra, gdje će
mf
na-ći mi-ra?
10, ① VII–4 AB Kuba B.H. 501. 295.
Moderato
Petrovac.
①
mf
Djevoj-ka je tugjina bratila,
djevoj-ka je tugjina bra-ti-la.

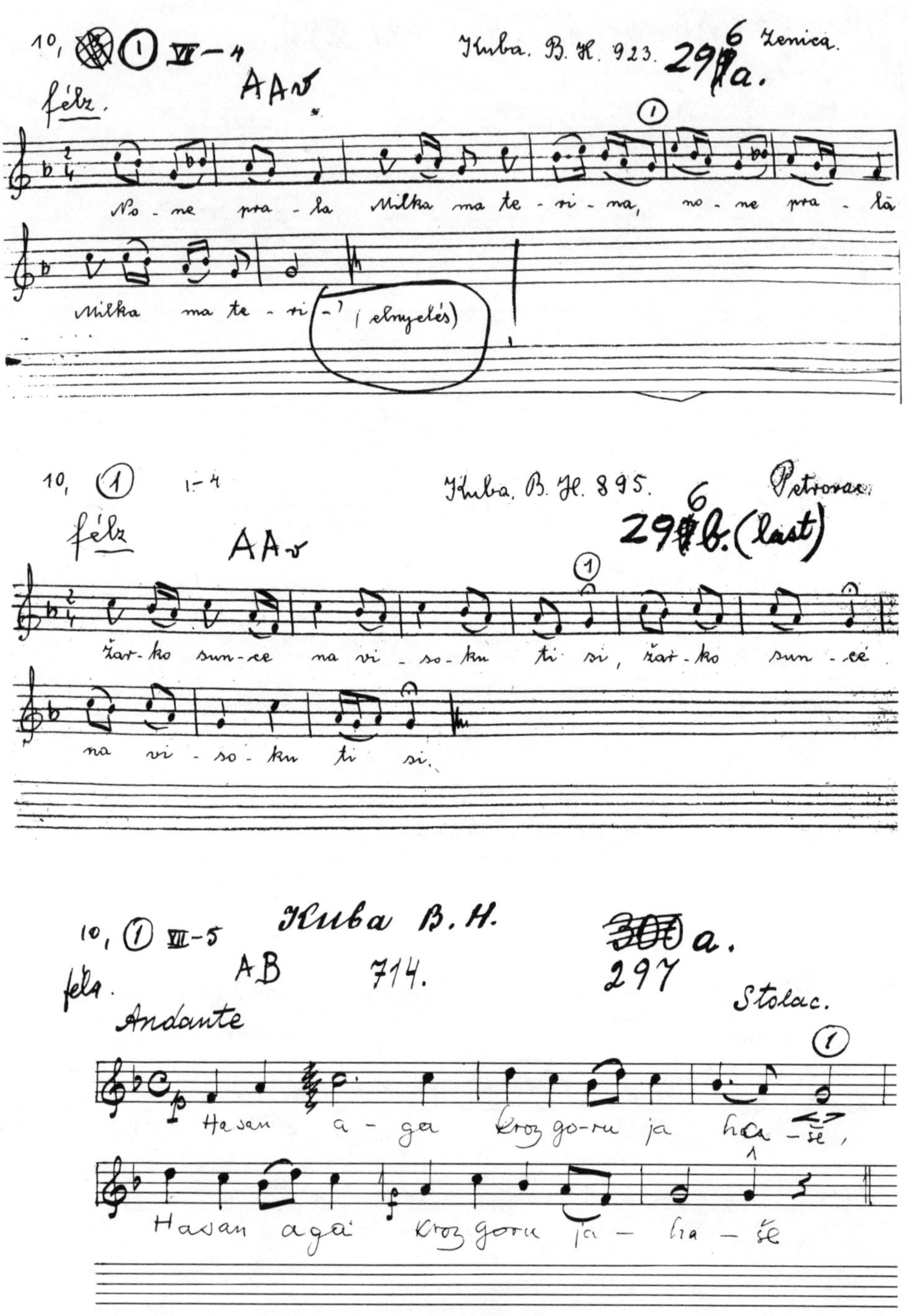

Kuba. B. H. 923.
Zenica.
félz.
AAv
No-ne pra-la Milka ma te-ri-na, no-ne pra-la
Milka ma te-ri-
(elnyelés)
Kuba. B. H. 895.
Petrovac.
félz
AAv
(last)
žar-ko sun-ce na vi-so-ku ti si, žar-ko sun-ce
na vi-so-ku ti si.
Kuba B. H.
AB
714.
297
Stolac.
félz.
Andante
Hasan a-ga kroz go-ru ja ha-še,
Hasan aga kroz goru ja-ha-še

10. ① VII–5
félz. AB
Kuhač II. 645.
297
Iz Žumberka.
(Hrvatska)
Sva se si-la na Francu-za sbi-la, ej —! sva se si-la na Francuza sbi-la.
10, ① VII–5
félz.
Kuba. B. H. 610.
Trnovo.
c. (last)
297
Drag me gle-da al' me maj-ka ne-da, drag me gle-da, al me maj-ka ne-da.
10, ① VII–5
előbbihez.
AB
Kuba. B. H. 946.
Nevesinje.
298.
Ra-njen da-zo u pla-ni-ni le-ži sve mu gla-va u cr-noj zem-lji te-ži.
* Var. Parry
Pl. 3197–3200 (és nem közölt 3235)

10, ① VI–5
féls.
AA Kuba B.-H. 436.
299.
Moderato
Banjaluka ①
Ko – nja kuje zla – to Muhareme.
Ko – nja kuje zla – to Mu-hareme.
10, ① VII-16
Juž. Srb. 419.
300.
Peć.
tercelő.
AB
Györgynapi reggeli hinta-dal.
①
Što je le – po ra-no u-ra-ni-ti, što je le – po
ra-no u-ra-ni – – ti.
10, ① VI–7
Kuba. B. H. 222.
Plevlje.
(félz?) pent.? AAv
①
Ej, ku-ći lo-lo dosta si se lo-lo Ej, ku-ći lo-lo
dosta si se lo – lo.

AB
Bihač.
Teš-ko gra-du, ko-jim pa-ša proj-de, ej teš-ko gra-du,
ko-jim pa-ša proj'
(elnyelés)
Kuba. B.H. 1002.
Višegrad
Allegro
draga dušo moja!
g a b c
Kuba, B.H. 999
Višegrad
Allegro
Kolo
Ovce čuva Niko i Nikola

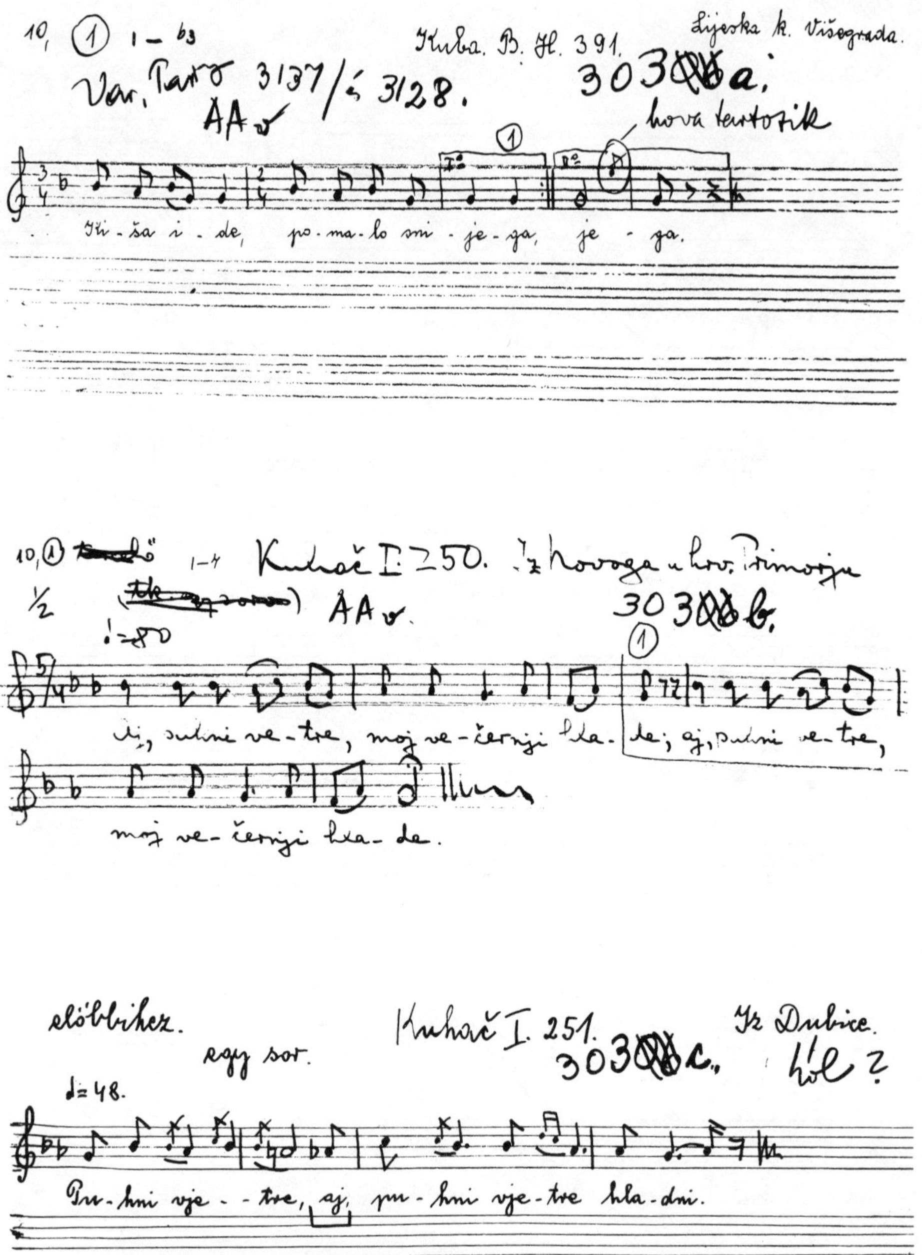

Kuba. B. H. 391.
Lijeska k. Višegrada.
303 a.
hova tartozik
Kuhač I. 250.
303 b.
Aj, suhni ve-tre, moj ve-černji hla-de; aj, suhni ve-tre,
moj ve-černji hla-de.
előbbihez.
egy sor.
Kuhač I. 251.
Iz Dubice.
303 c.
hol?
Pr-hni vje--tre, aj, pr-hni vje-tre hla-dni.

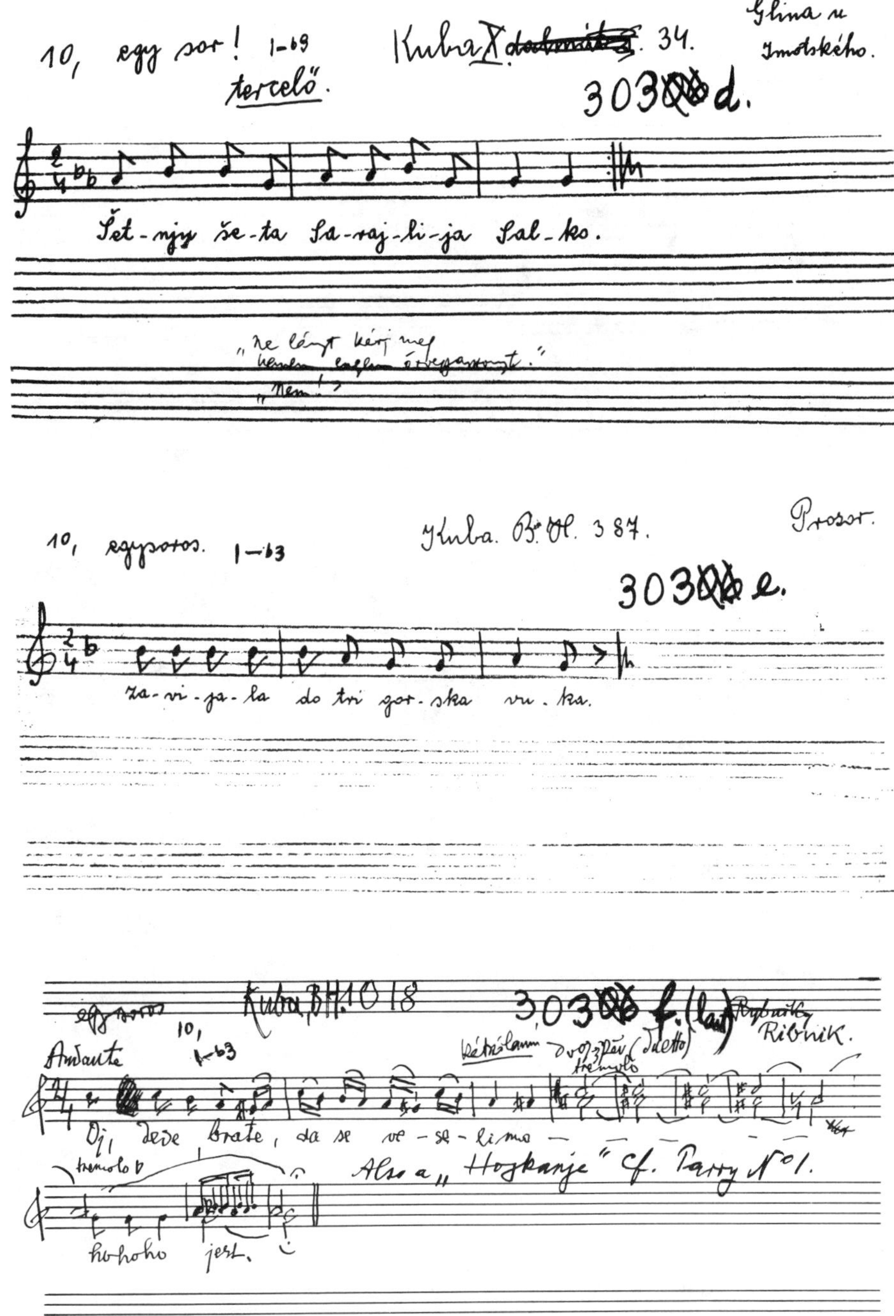
10, egy sor! 1–63
tercelő.
Kuba X. 34.
Glina u Imotského.
303 d.
Šet-njy še-ta Sa-raj-li-ja Sal-ko.
10, egysoros. 1–63
Kuba. B. H. 387.
Prosor.
303 e.
za-vi-ja-la do tri gor-ska vu-ka.
Kuba BH. 1018
303 f.
Ribnik.
Andante
10, 1–63
Oj, dede brate, da se ve-se-li-mo
tremolo
hohoho jest.
Also a „Hojkanje" cf. Parry No 1.

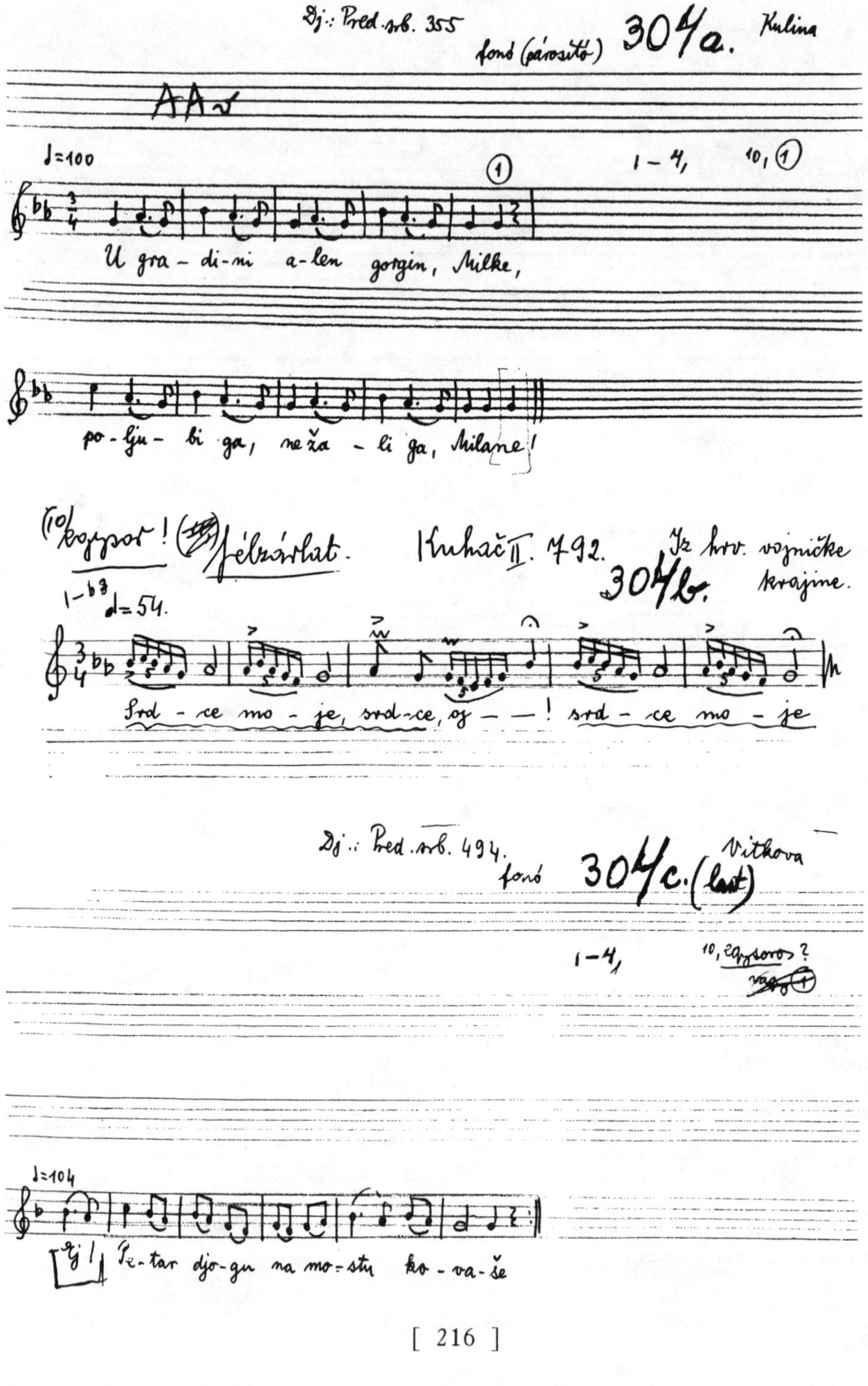

Dj.: Pred. srb. 355 fonó (párosító) 304/a. Kulina

AA v

♩=100 ① 1–4, 10, ①

U gra-di-ni a-len gorgin, Milke,

po-lju-bi ga, ne ža-li ga, Milane!

(10) kopor! félzárlat. Kuhač II. 792. Iz hrv. vojničke krajine. 304/b.

1–b3 ♩=54.

Srd-ce mo-je, srd-ce, oj — — ! srd-ce mo-je

Dj.: Pred. srb. 494. fonó 304/c. (lassú) Vitkova

1–4, 10, 2 ?

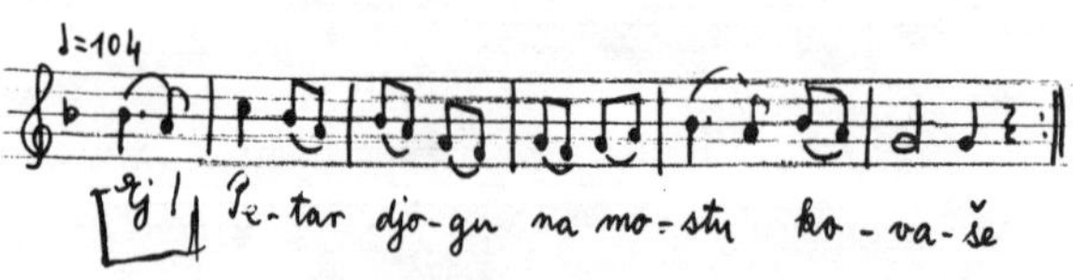

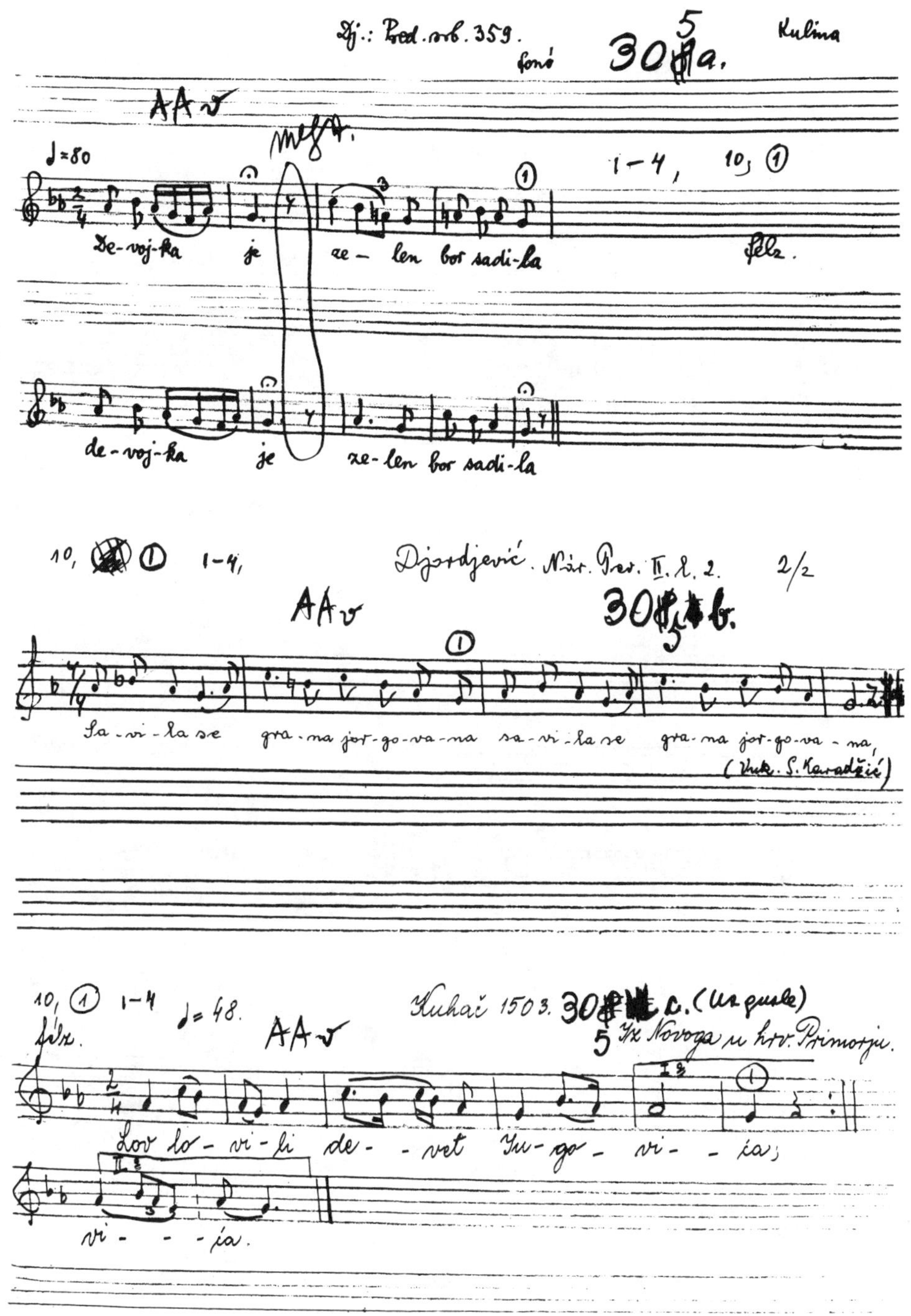

De-voj-ka je ze-len bor sadi-la
de-voj-ka je ze-len bor sadi-la
Sa-vi-la se gra-na jor-go-va-na sa-vi-la se gra-na jor-go-va-na,
(Vuk. S. Karadžić)
Lov lo-vi-li de-vet Ju-go-vi-ja;
vi-ja.

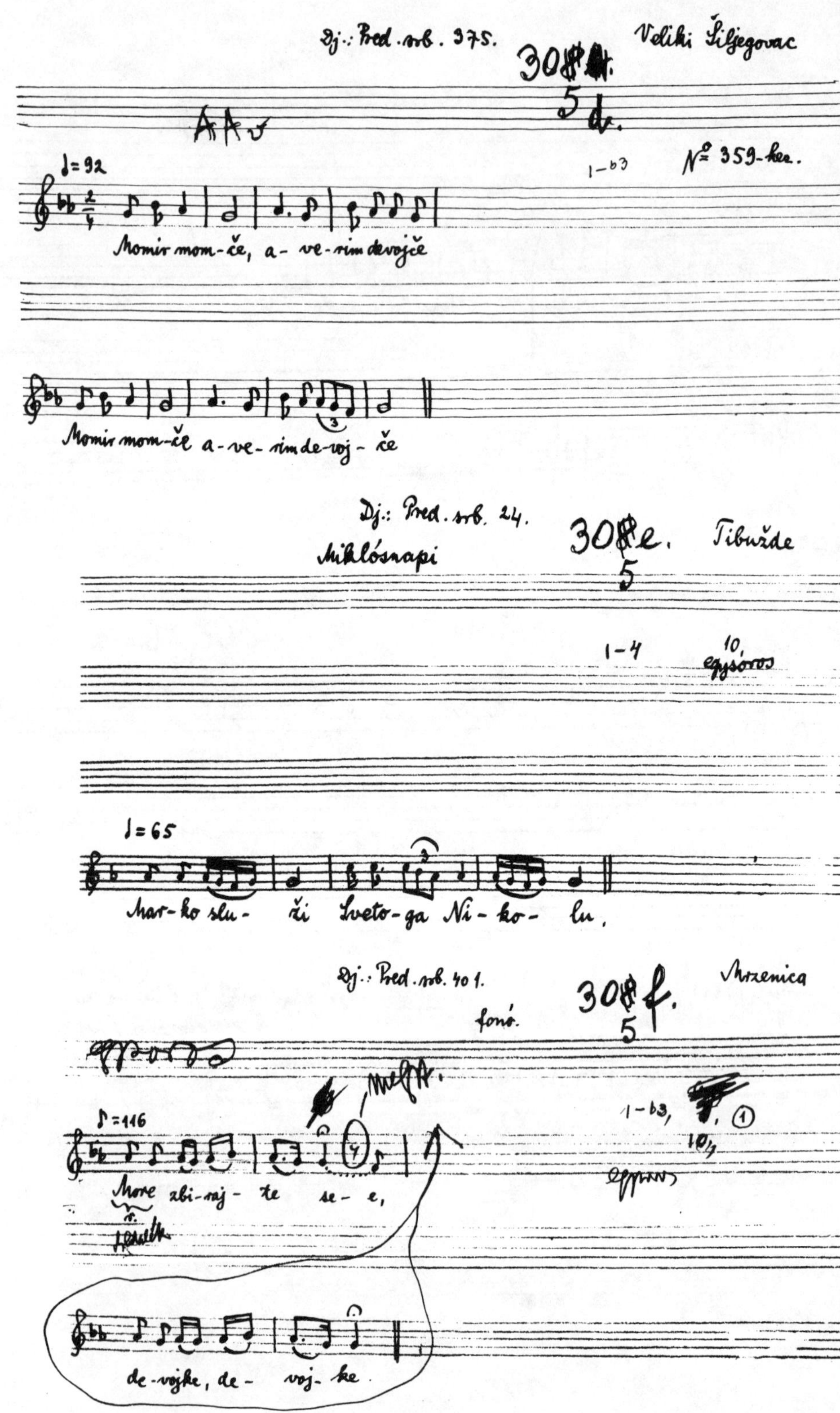
Dj.: Pred. srb. 375.
Veliki Šiljegovac
308d.
5
Nº 359-kee.
♩=92
Momir mom-če, a- ve-rim devojče
Momir mom-če a-ve-rim de-voj-če
Dj.: Pred. srb. 24.
Miklósnapi
308e.
5
Tibužde
1-4
egysoros
♩=65
Mar-ko slu- ži Sveto-ga Ni- ko- lu.
Dj.: Pred. srb. 401.
308f.
5
Mrzenica
fonó.
♪=116
1-b3,
More zbi-raj- te se- e,
de-vojke, de- voj- ke.

Dj.: Pred. srb. 579. **308g.** Ogladjenovac

5

1–6a, 10, egysoros vagy (1)

félz.

♩ = 100

O-tud i-du tro-ja ko-la sa-ma

Dj.: Pred. srb. 584. **308h.** Ogladjenovac.

5

№ 579-hez.

♩ = 100

Hva-li-o se ple-ti-ko-sa Pav-le

Dj.: Pred. srb. 590. **308i.** Ogladjenovac.

5

= 584!

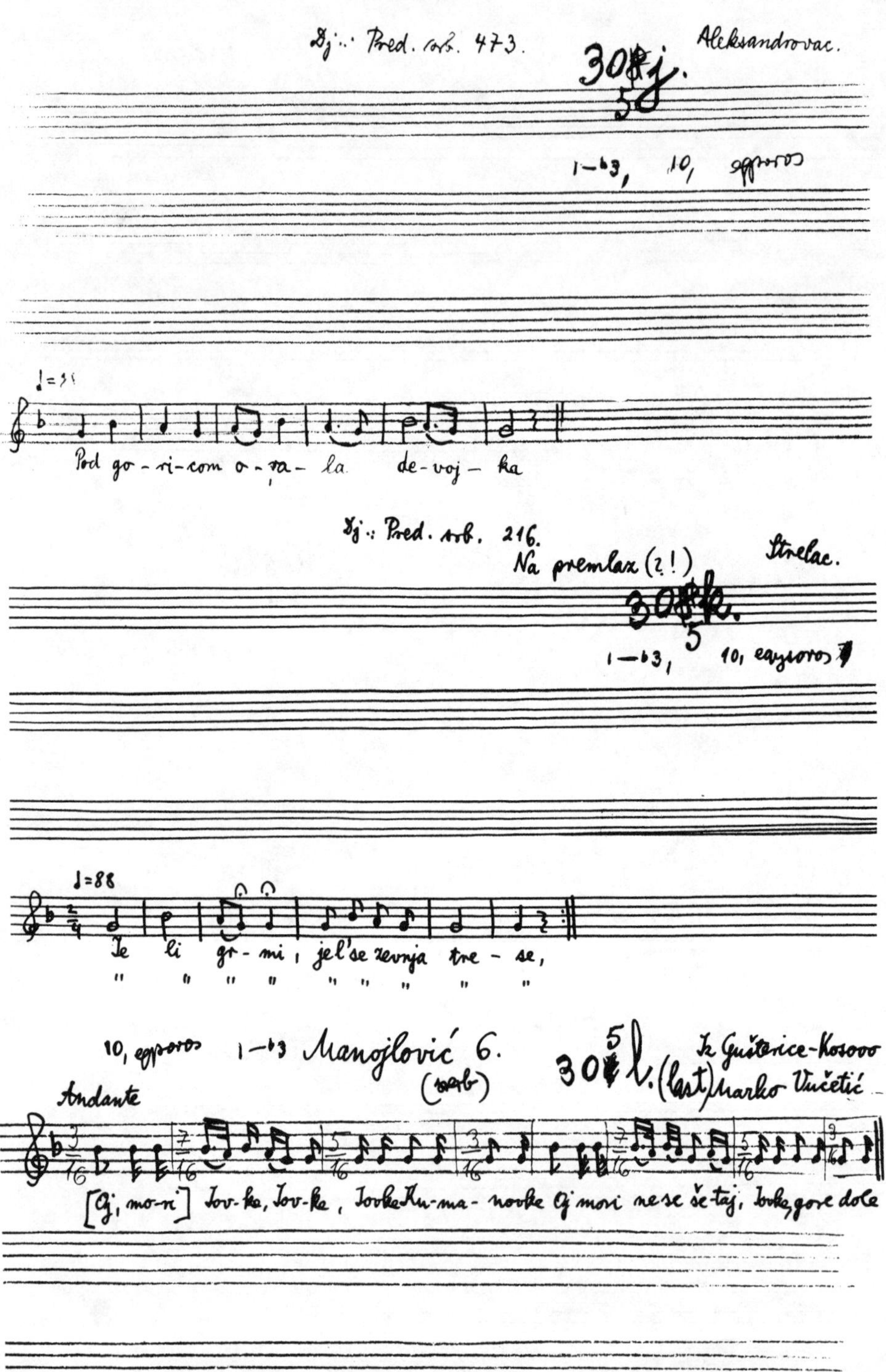

Aleksandrovac.
Pod go-ri-com o-ra-la de-voj-ka
Na premlaz (?!)
Strelac.
Je li gr-mi, jel'se zevnja tre-se,
Manojlović 6.
Andante
Iz Guštarice-Kosovo
Marko Vučetić
[Oj, mo-ri] Jov-ke, Jov-ke, Jovke Ru-ma-novke Oj mori ne se šetaj, Jovke, gore dole

Dj.: Pred. srb. 222.
fonóban 30/6 Strelac
AB
♩=96
1–4, 10, (1)
Zbirajte se mome, na se-denj-ću,
megállt.
zbirajte se, mo- me, na se-denjću,(i)
Dj.: Pred. srb. 25.
Lakodalmas.
3107 Tibužde
AA
♩=72
1–4, 10, (1) félz.
Na-trag, na-trag ki-će-ni sva-to-vi,
megáll.
na- trag, na-trag ki-će-ni svato-vi.
10, (1) AA 1–4
K. BH. 1006.
3108
Allegro moderato.
Lipa u Bihaće.
Kolo.
Sva noć sam se premo- li- la maj- ci, Sva noć sam se
pre- mo- li- la maj- ci.
g b c d

Goražda.
309 a.
félz.
AAv
Što no nej - ma od Dri - ne ve - dri - ne, što no
nej - ma od Dri - ne ve - dri - ne?
Aleksandrovac
farsang utóján
AAv
♩= 104
O - će je - ža da se že - mi, je - žo,
o - će je - ža da se že - mi, je - žo
74
495. Utekla je.
Iz sriemskih Karlovaca.
Larghetto ♩ = 60.
No - ćas mi je u - te - kla dje - voj - - - - ka,
no - ćas mi je u - te - kla dje - voj - ka.
(Nastavka tekstu ne imam.)

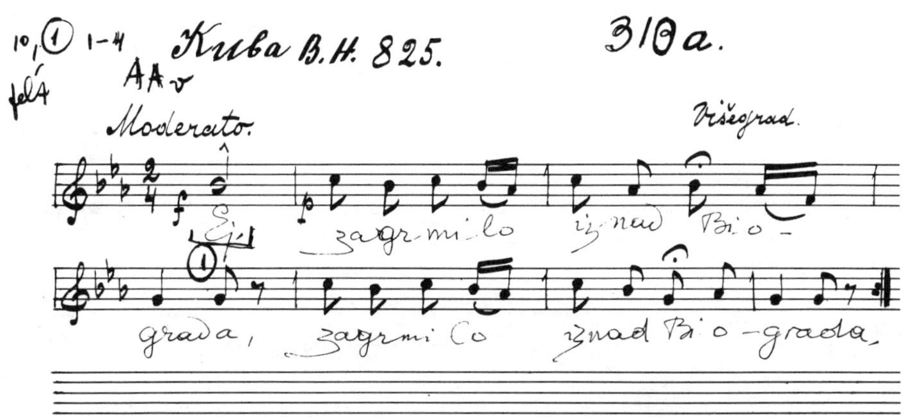
10, ① 1-4
AAv
Kuba B.H. 825.
310a.
Moderato.
Višegrad.
Ej! zagrmilo iznad Bio-
grada, zagrmilo iznad Bio-grada.

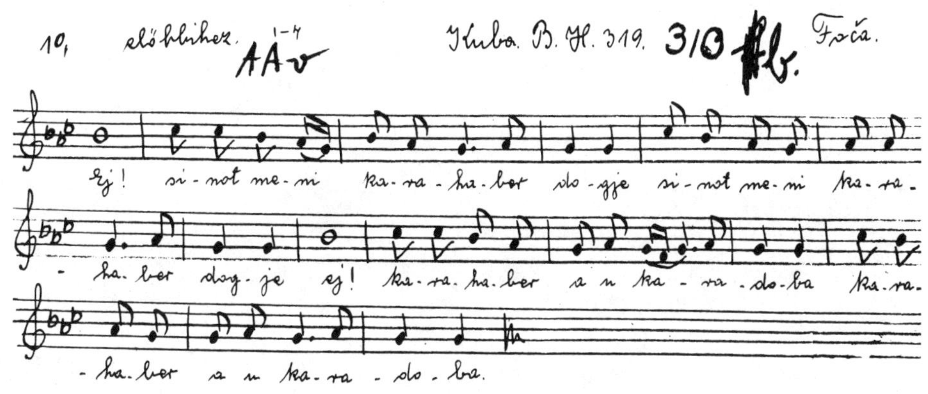
10, előbbihez. 1-4
AAv
Kuba B.H. 319.
310 b.
Foča.
Ej! si-not me-ni ka-ra-ha-ber do-gje si-not me-ni ka-ra-
-ha-ber dog-je ej! ka-ra-ha-ber a u ka-ra-do-ba ka-ra-
-ha-ber a u ka-ra-do-ba.

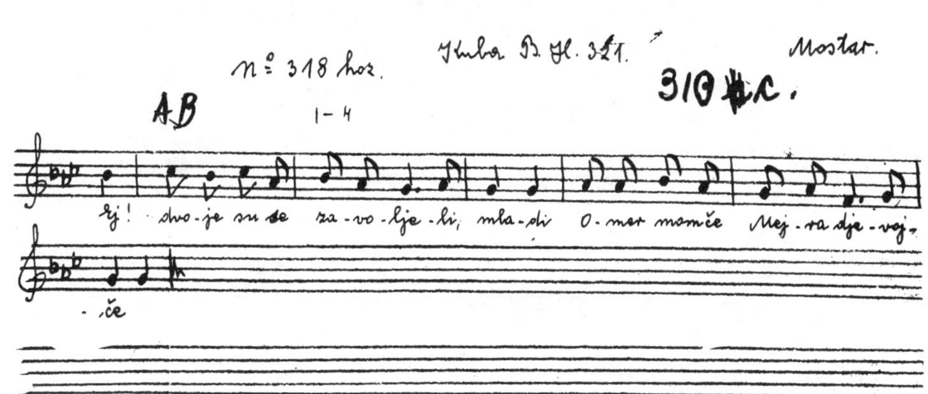
N° 318 hoz.
Kuba B.H. 321.
Mostar.
310 c.
AB
1-4
Ej! dvo-je su se za-vo-lje-li, mla-di O-mer momče Mej-ra dje-voj-
-če

Dj.: Ired. rb. 580.

310 d.

Ogladjenovac

AA

1–4,

félz.

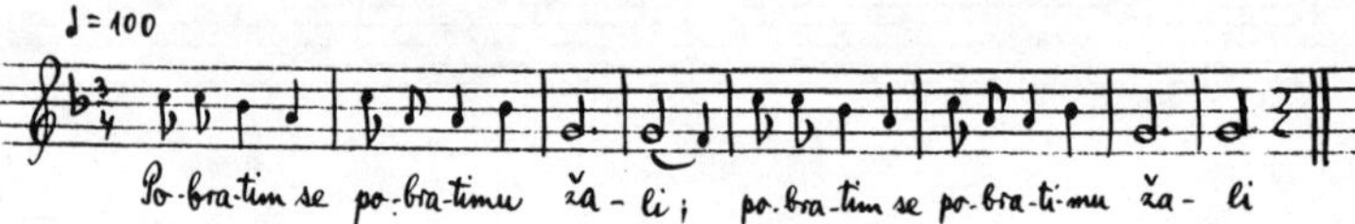

Dj.: Ired. rb. 578.

310 e.

Ogladjenovac

AA

1–4,

10, egysoros vagy (1) ?

félz.

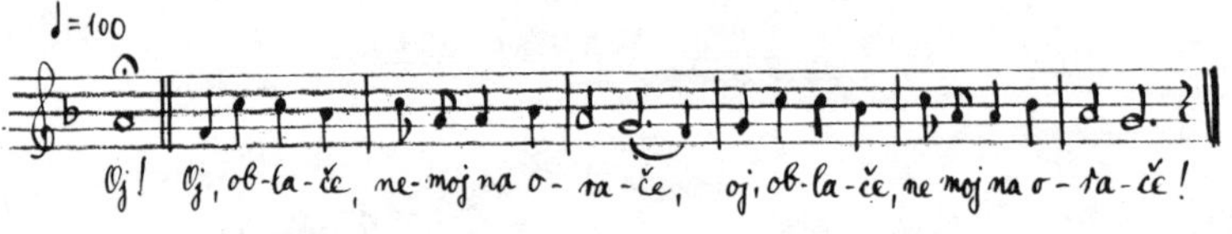

10, egysoros. 1–4

Kuba. B. H. 398. 310 f.

Goražde.

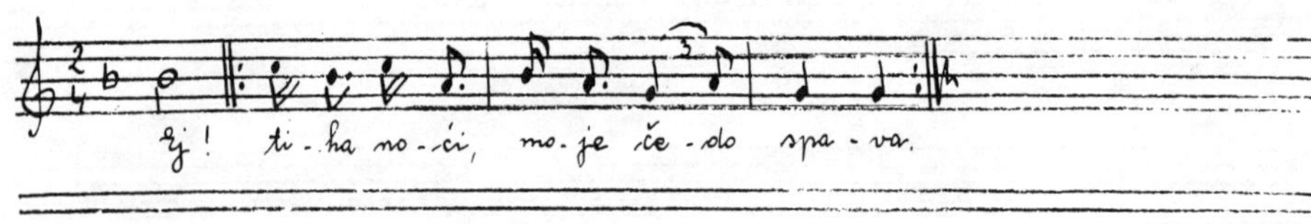

10, egysoros, 1-4,
Kuba B. H. 2.
310 g.
Bugojno
I.
II.
U Mo-sta--ru dva nova du- ća-na ća-na.
10, egysoros, 1-4
Kuba B. H. 318.
310 h.
Višegrad.
Ej! u O-me-ra vi še Sa-ra-je-va.
Dj.: Pred srb. 569 b)
310 i. (last)
Ogladjenovac
1-4, 10, egysoros
Za ovim dolazi:
Do-ve-la vi- la [pre-mud-ru La-tin-ku.

10, (1) 1–b4
Kuba. B. H. 329.
Petrovac.
31/a.
AAv
Svu noj sam se pre-mo-li-la maj-ci svu noj sam se
pre-mo-li-la maj-ci!

10, (b2) VII–b4
Kuba. B. H. 330.
31/b. ?
AAv
Moj dil-be-re po-gle-daj i me-ne, moj dil-be-re
po-gle-daj i me-ne.

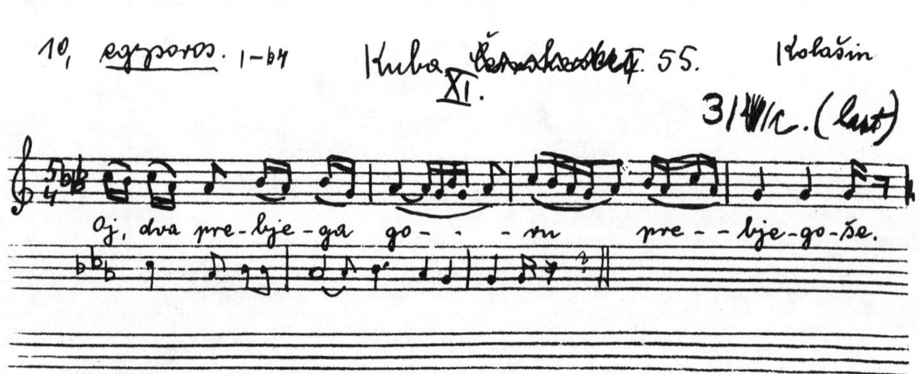
10, 1–b4
Kolašin
XI.
31/c. (last)
Oj, dva pre-bje-ga go- -ru pre- -bje-go-še.

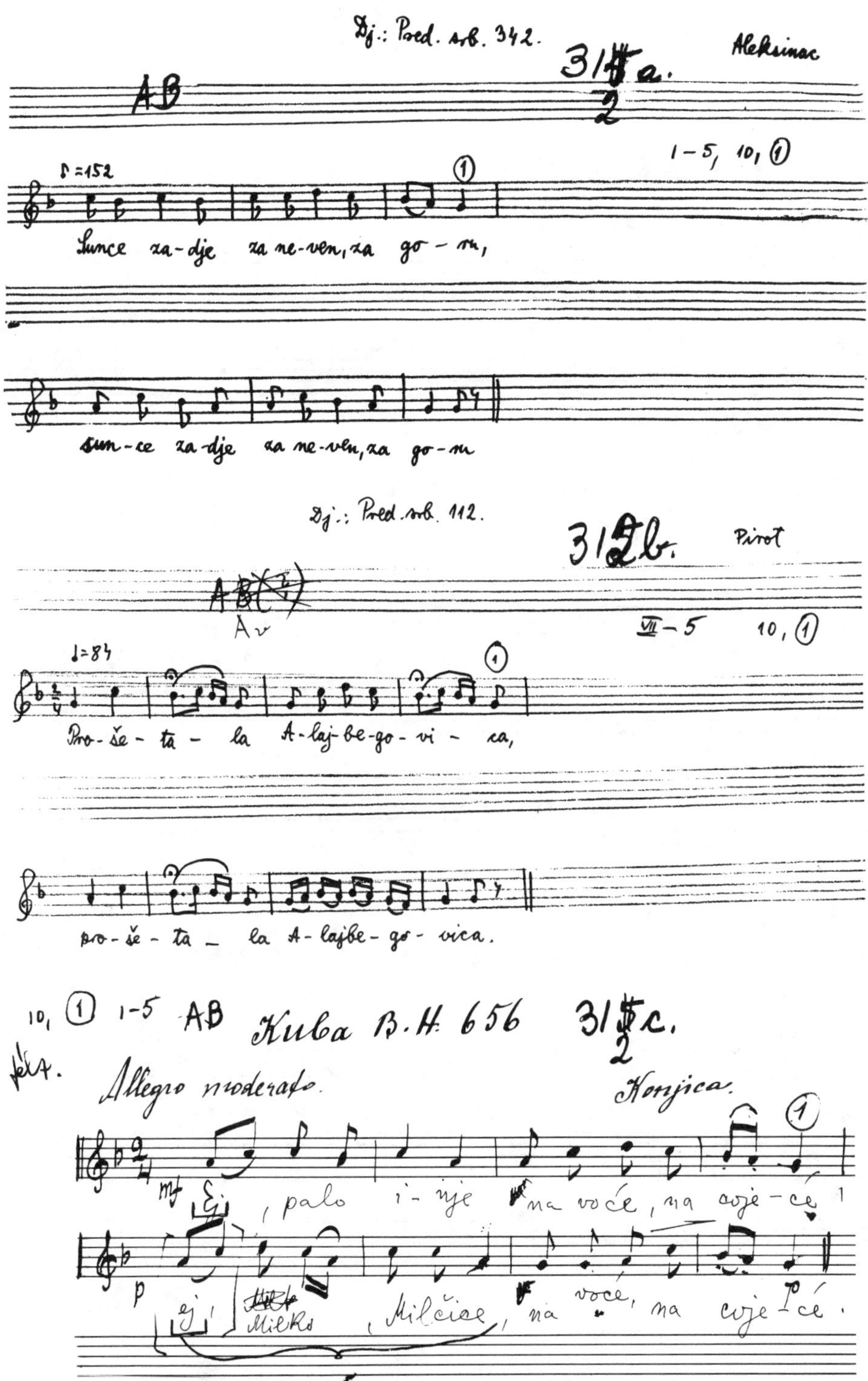

Dj.: Pred. zb. 342.
Aleksinac
AB
1–5, 10, (1)
Sunce za-dje za ne-ven, za go-ru,
sun-ce za-dje za ne-ven, za go-ru
Dj.: Pred. zb. 112.
Pirot
Pro-še-ta-la A-laj-be-go-vi-ca,
pro-še-ta-la A-lajbe-go-vica.
10, (1) 1-5 AB
Kuba B.H. 656
Allegro moderato.
Konjica.
palo i-nje na voće, na coje-će
na voće, na coje-će.

Djordjević. Nár. Pev. 36/2.
AA
-Ej, pa-de i-nje na cve-će na vo-će, ej, Mil-ka, Mil-či-ce, na
cve-će na vo-će
B. Kačerovski. 41.
félz.
AB
Cr-ne o-či u dra-ga-na mo-ga, ka-ko sam ih pre-go-re-
-ti mo-gla!
Kuhač III. 882.
félz. AB
Iz Kapele kod Belovara.
Še-ta-la se Ana kraj Du-na-va; še-ta-la se Ana kraj Du-
na-va.
Mili Bože, prelijepa je Ana:

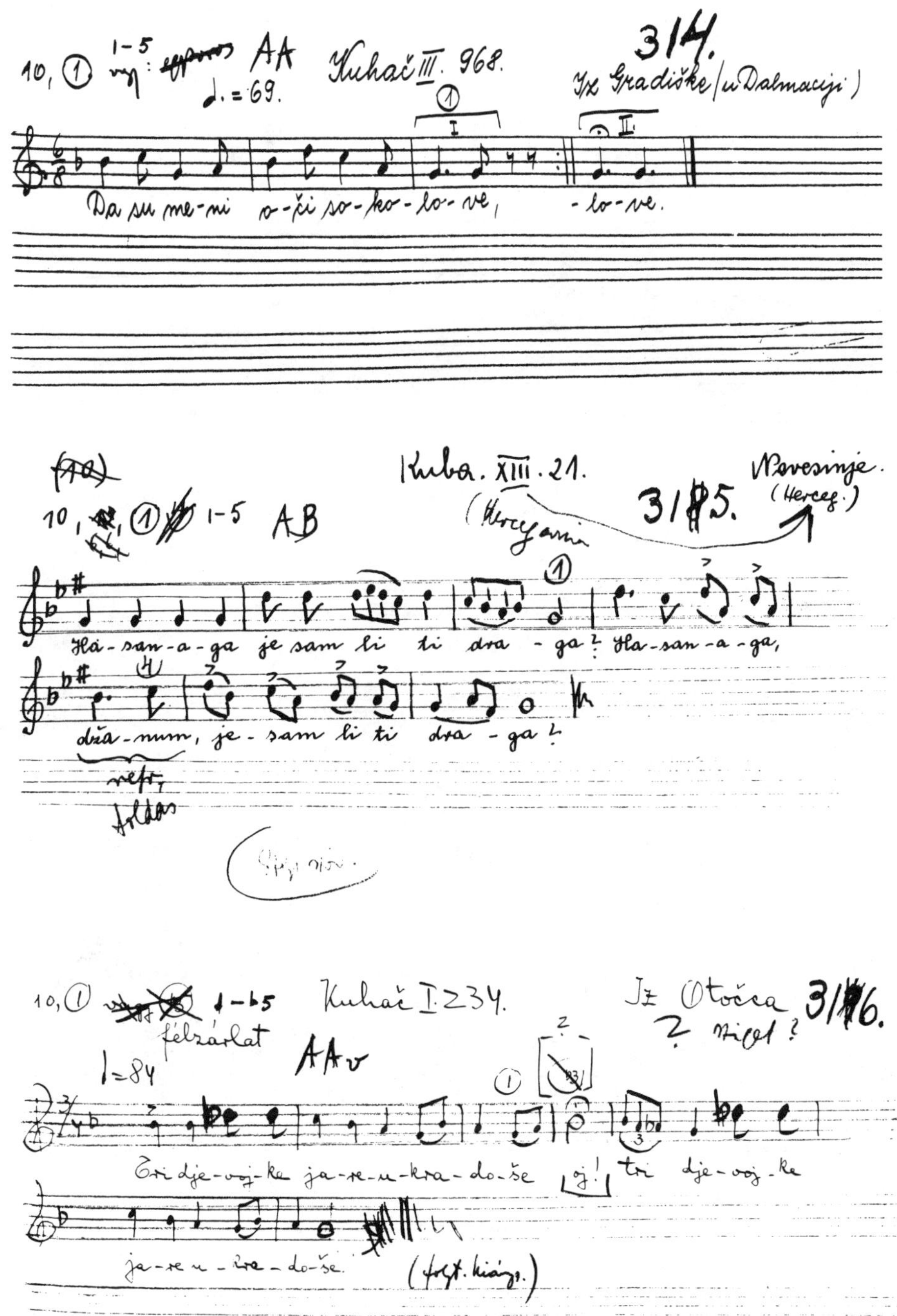
10, ① 1–5 AA Kuhač III. 968. 314. Iz Gradiške (u Dalmaciji)
♩. = 69
Da su me-ni o-či so-ko-lo-ve, -lo-ve.
Kuba. XIII. 21. Nevesinje. (Herceg.)
10, ① 1–5 AB 315.
Ha-san-a-ga je sam li ti dra-ga? Ha-san-a-ga,
dža-num, je-sam li ti dra-ga?
10, ① 1–b5 Kuhač I. 234. Iz Otočca ? 316.
félzárlat AAv
♩=84
Tri dje-voj-ke ja-re-u-kra-do-še oj! tri dje-voj-ke
ja-re-u-kra-do-še.

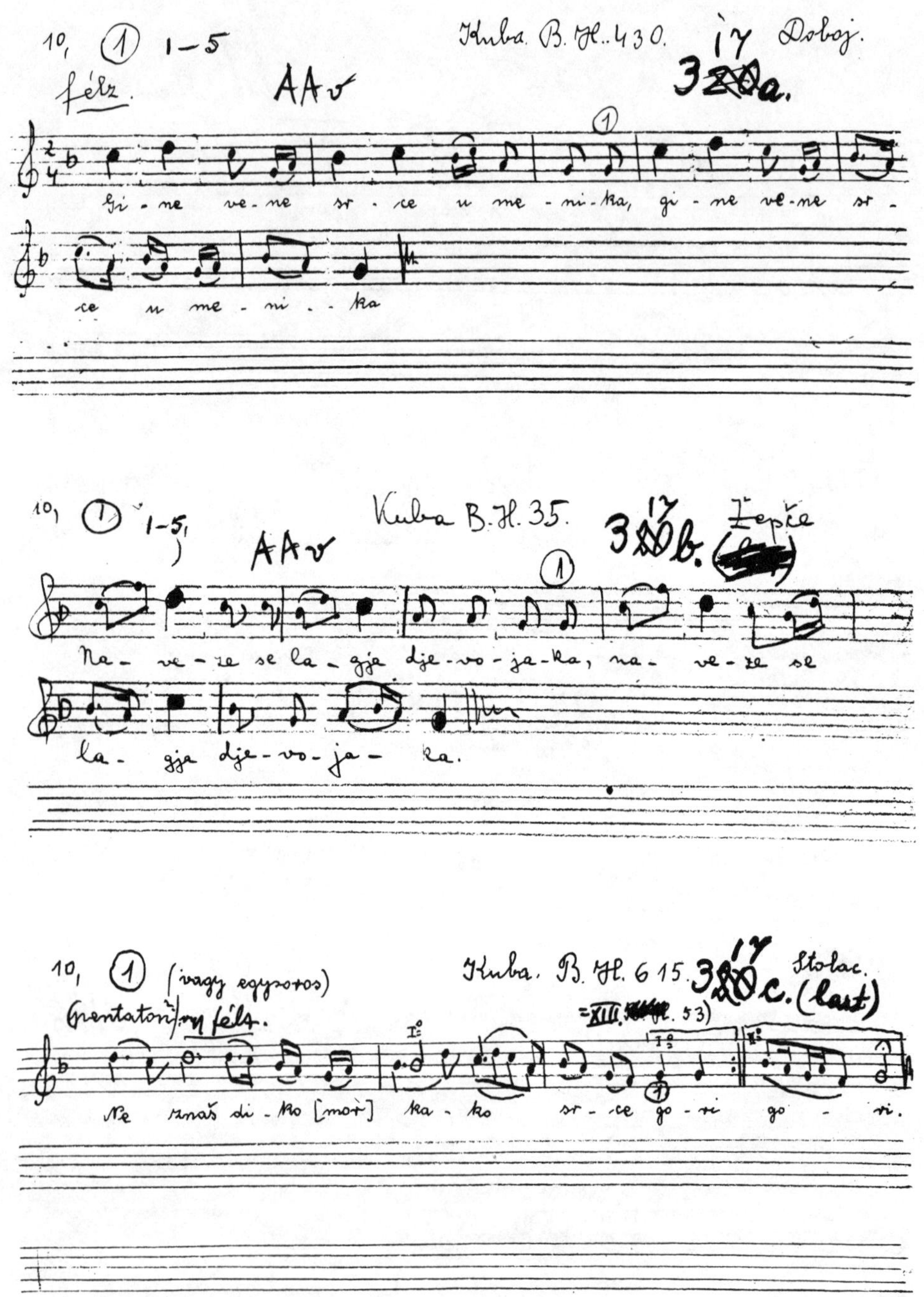
10, (1) 1–5
Kuba. B. H. 430.
Doboj.
félz.
AAv
Gi - ne ve - ne sr - ce u me - ni - ka, gi - ne ve - ne sr -
ce u me - ni - ka
10, (1) 1–5,
Kuba B. H. 35.
Žepče
AAv
Na - ve - ze se la - gja dje - vo - ja - ka, na - ve - ze se
la - gja dje - vo - ja - ka.
10, (1) (vagy egysoros)
Kuba. B. H. 615.
Stolac.
félz.
Ne znaš di - ko [moř] ka - ko sr - ce go - ri go - ri.

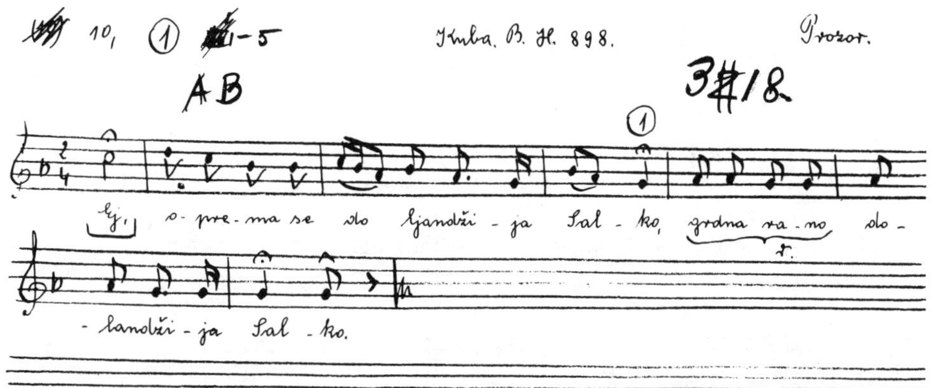
10, ① 1-5
Kuba. B. H. 898.
Prozor.
AB
3#18.
Ej, o-pre-ma se do Ljandži-ja Sal-ko, grdna ra-no do-
-landži-ja Sal-ko.

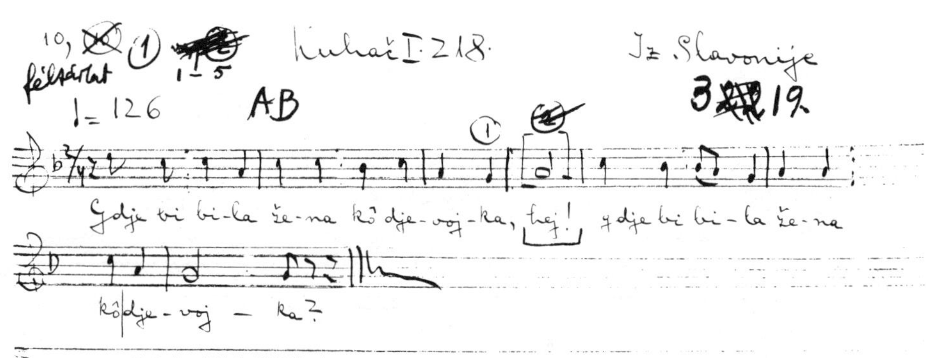
10, ① 1-5
Kuhač I. 218.
Iz Slavonije
♩= 126
AB
3 19.
Gdje bi bi-la že-na kõ dje-voj-ka, hej! gdje bi bi-la že-na
kõdje-voj-ka?

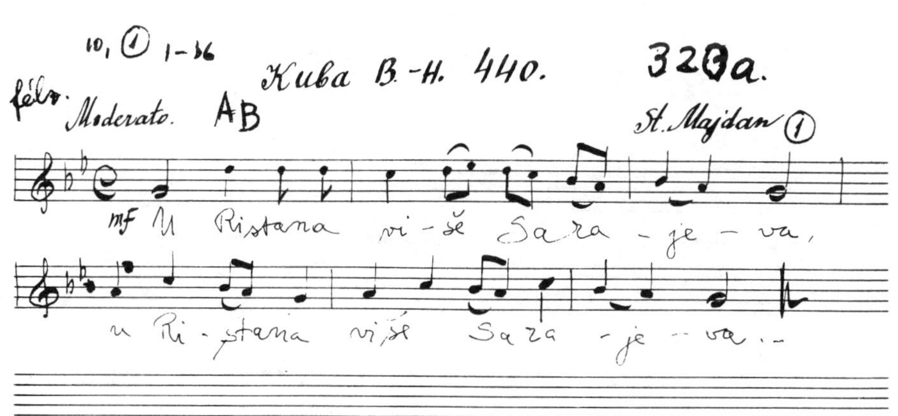
10, ① 1-36
Kuba B.-H. 440.
320a.
Moderato.
AB
St. Majdan ①
mf U Ristana vi-še Sa-ra-je-va,
u Ri-stana više Sa-ra-je-va...

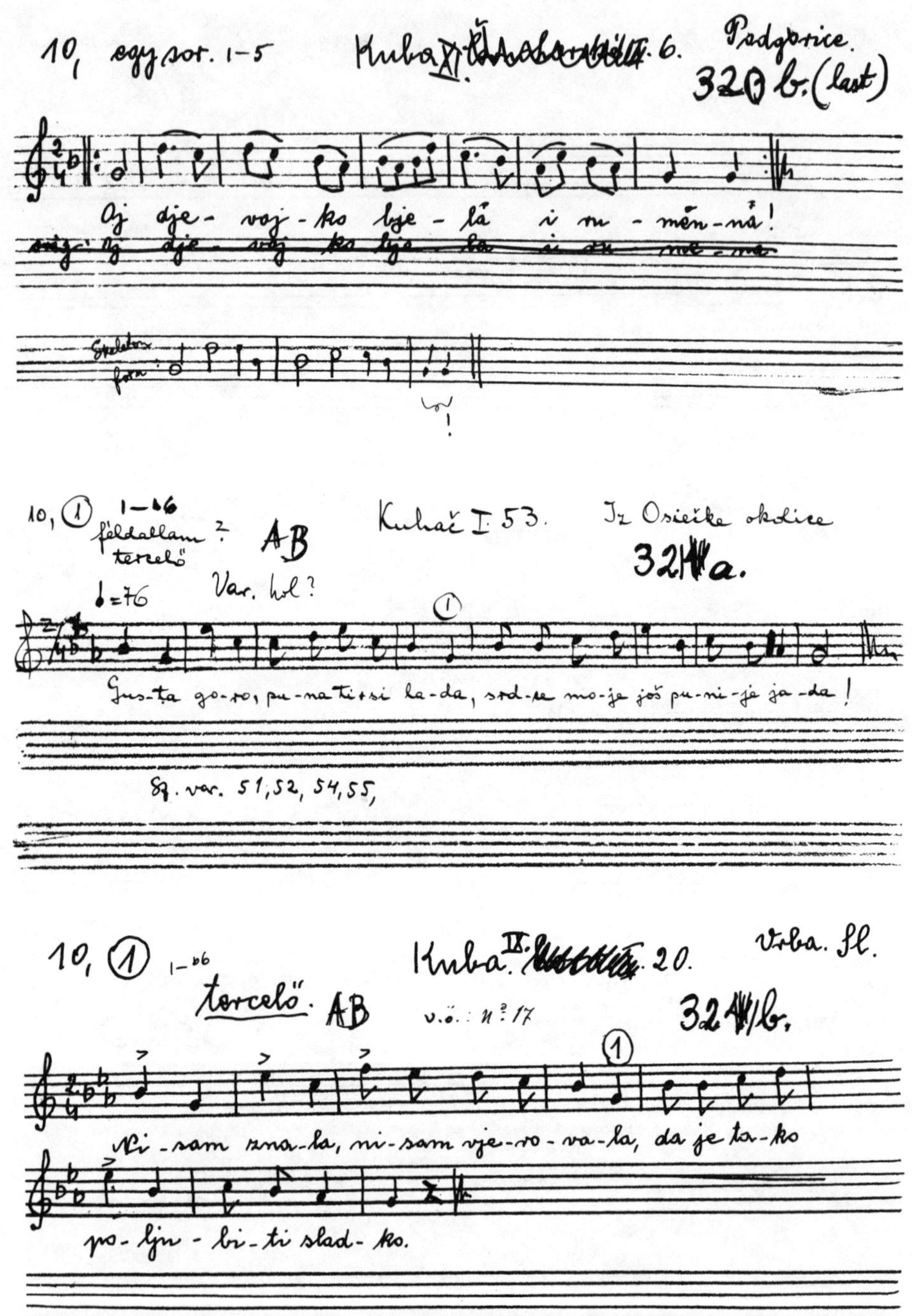
10, egy sor. 1–5
Kuba XI. 6.
Podgorice.
320 b. (last)
Oj dje- voj - ko bje - lā i ru - mēn-nā!
Skeleton form:
10, (1) 1–b6
féldallam? tercelő
AB
Kuhač I. 53.
Iz Osiečke okolice
321 a.
♩=76
Var. hol?
Gus-ta go-ro, pu-na ti si la-da, srd-ce mo-je još pu-ni-je ja-da!
Sz. var. 51, 52, 54, 55,
10, (1) 1–b6
Kuba. IX. 20.
Vrba. Sl.
tercelő. AB
v. ö.: N.º 17
324 b.
Ni-sam zna-la, ni-sam vje-ro-va-la, da je ta-ko
po-lju-bi-ti slad-ko.

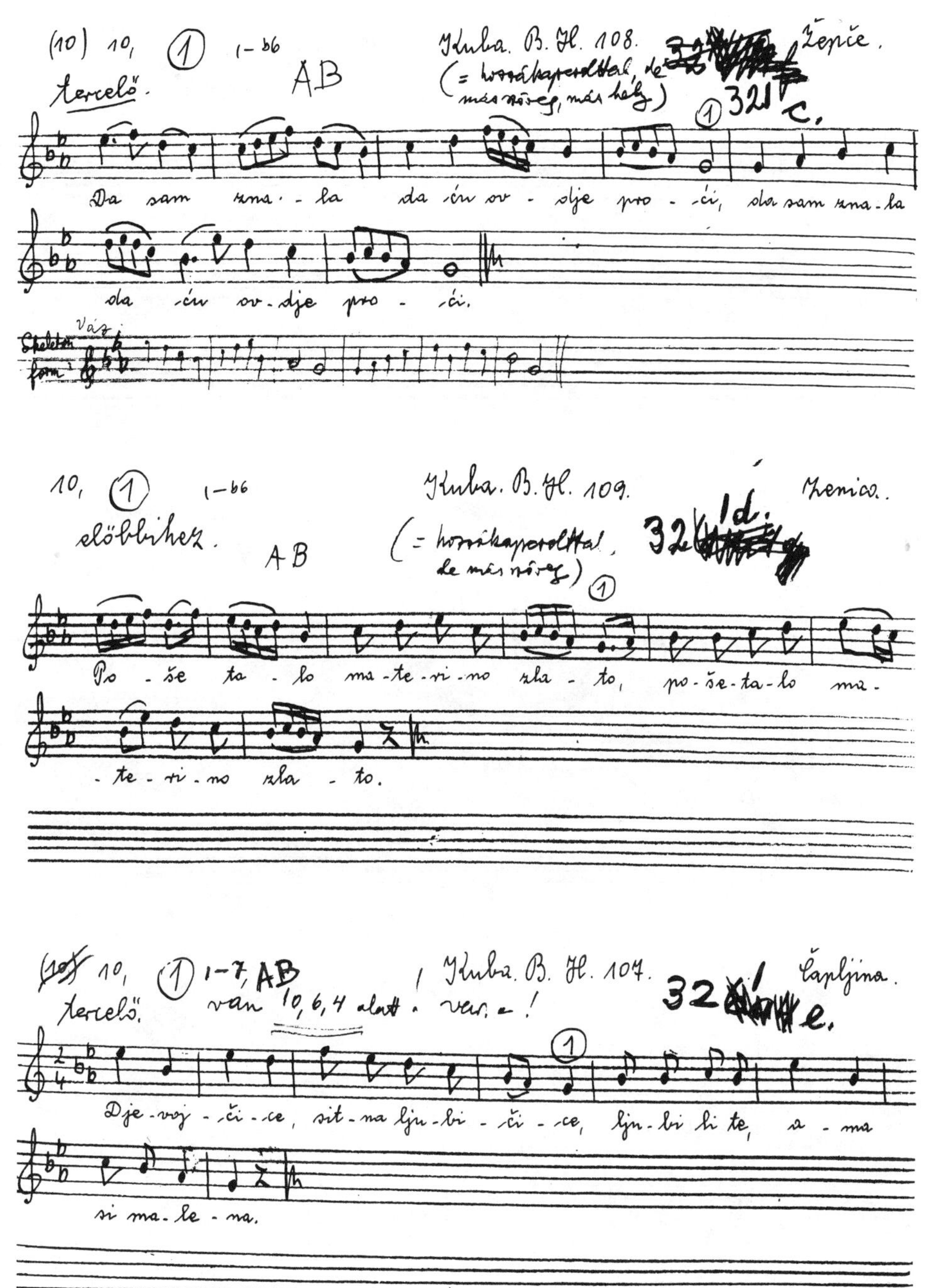

(10) 10, ① 1–66
AB
Kuba. B. H. 108.
Žepče.
Da sam zna - la da ću ov - dje pro - ći, da sam zna - la
da ću ov - dje pro - ći.
10, ① 1–66
AB
Kuba. B. H. 109.
Zenica.
Po - še ta - lo ma - te - ri - no zla - to, po - še - ta - lo ma -
- te - ri - no zla - to.
10, ① 1–7, AB
Kuba. B. H. 107.
Čapljina.
Dje - voj - či - ce, sit - na lju - bi - či - ce, lju - bi li te, a - ma
si ma - le - na.

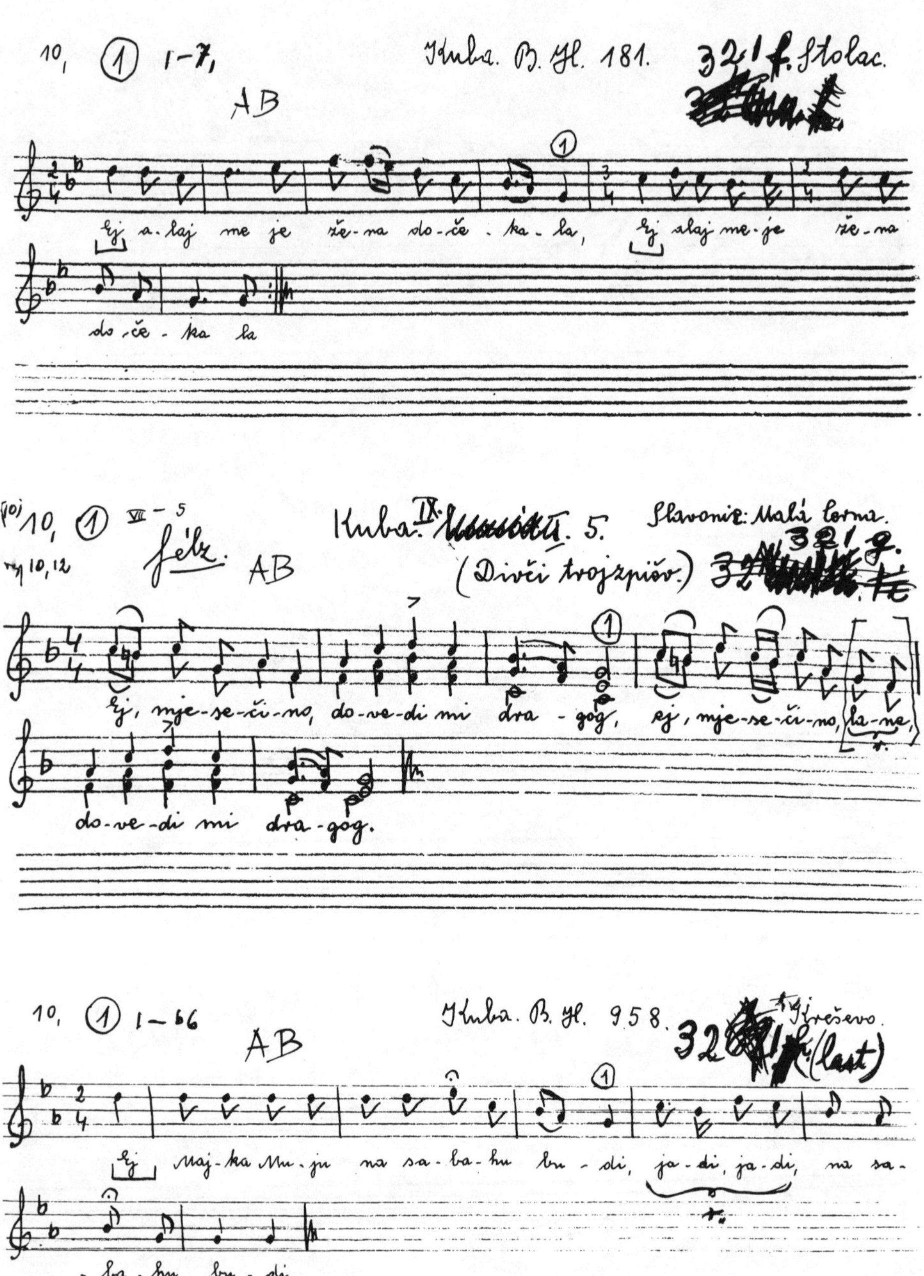
10, ① 1–7, Kuba. B. H. 181. 321 f. Stolac.
AB
Ej a-laj me je že-na do-če-ka-la, Ej alaj me-je že-na
do-če-ka la
10, ① VII – 5 Kuba. IX. 5. Slavonia
félz. AB (Divči trojzpiev) 321 g.
Ej, mje-se-či-no, do-ve-di mi dra-gog, ej, mje-se-či-no, la-ne,
do-ve-di mi dra-gog.
10, ① 1–66 Kuba. B. H. 958. 321 (last)
AB
Ej Maj-ka Mu-ju na sa-ba-hu bu-di, ja-di, ja-di, na sa-
-ba-hu bu-di.

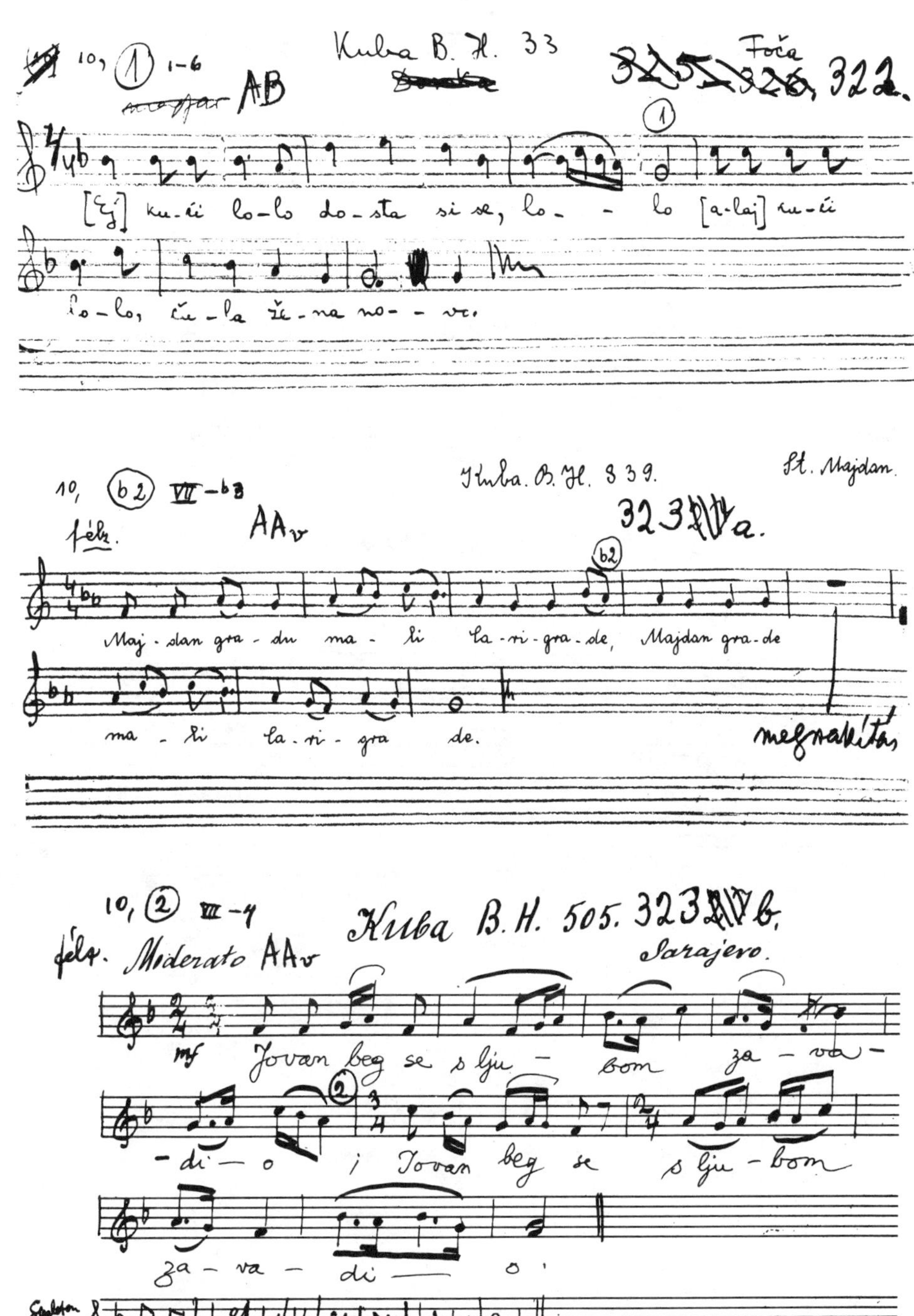
10, ① 1–6
Kuba B. H. 33
Foča
322.
AB
①
[Ej] ku-ći lo-lo do-sta si se, lo- - lo [a-laj] ku-ći
lo-lo, ću-la ži-na no- - vo.
10, (b2) VII–b3
Kuba. B. H. 339.
St. Majdan.
félz.
AAv
(b2)
Maj-dan gra-du ma-li la-ri-gra-de, Majdan gra-de
ma-li la-ri-gra de.
10, ② VII–4
Kuba B.H. 505.
félz. Moderato AAv
Sarajevo.
mf
Jovan beg se s lju- bom za-va-
-di-o i Jovan beg se s lju-bom
za-va-di-o.
Skeleton form:

10, b2 VI – b3
Kuba, BH. 1004
323c. (last)
Lipa u Bihaće.
Allegro moderato. AAv
Rumen Gjure, da se ne va-ra-mo; rumen Gjure,
oj, da se ne va – ka – mo!
Kromatikus
Skeleton form:
10, b2 tipus 2 Kuba XI. 23. Andrejevice
VI – 4 AB félzárlat.
Po-še-ta-la ja-go-da na vo-di, po-še-ta-la
Ja-go-da na vo-di.
Dj.: Sred. zb. 68.
32 a.
5
Leskovac.
AAv
♩=69
VII – 4, 10, b2
Svu noć o-do, ni-šta ne u-kra-do, more,
féle.
svu noć o-do, ništa ne u-kra-do.

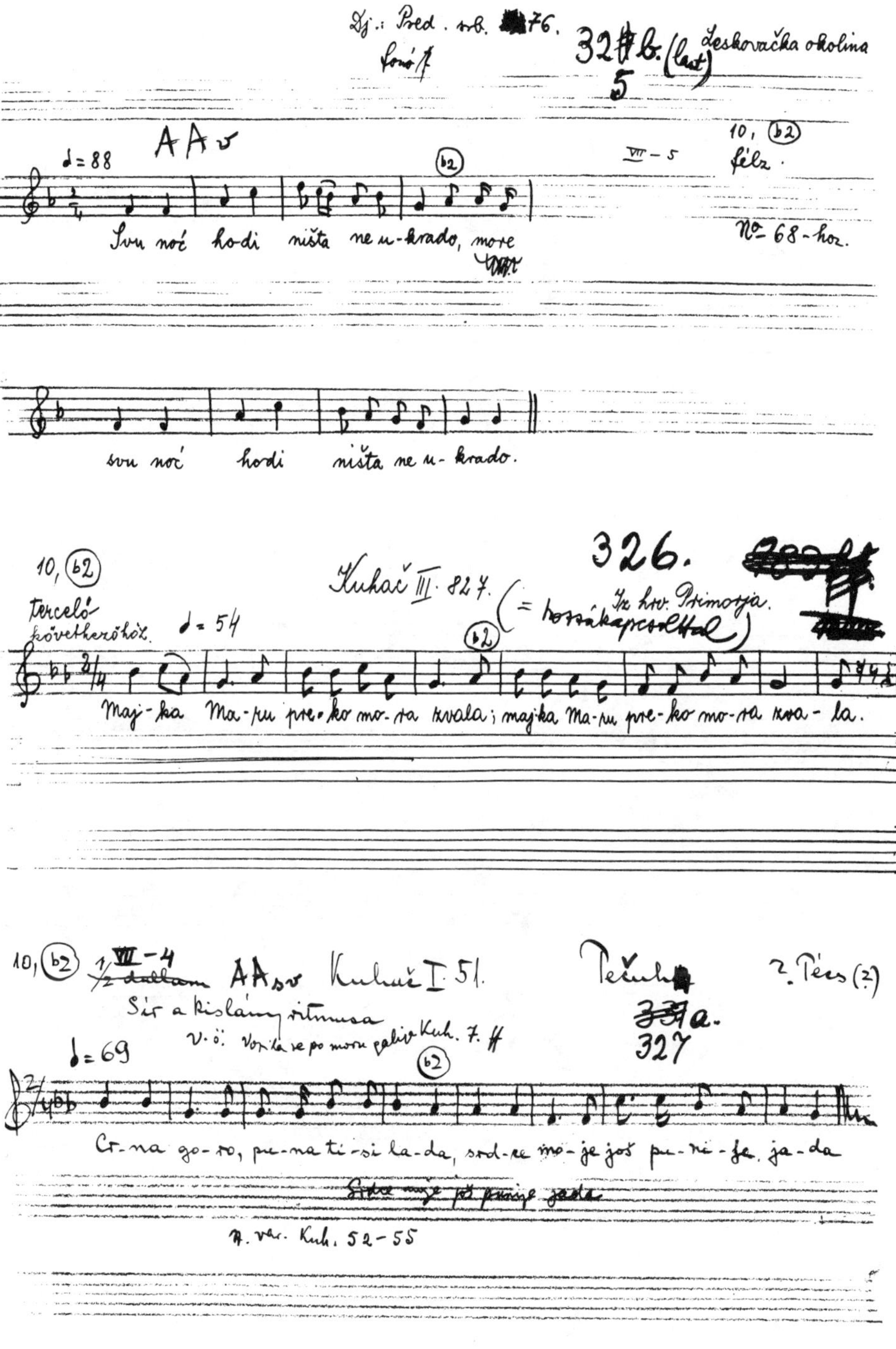
Dj.: Pred. srb. 76.
fonó
32#b. (lat)
5
Leskovačka okolina
AAv
10, (b2)
félz.
No 68-hoz.
Svu noć hodi ništa ne u-krado, more
svu noć hodi ništa ne u-krado.
326.
10, (b2)
Kuhač III. 827.
Iz hrv. Primorja.
Maj-ka Ma-ru pre-ko mo-ra zvala; maj-ka Ma-ru pre-ko mo-ra zva-la.
10, (b2)
AAv Kuhač I. 51.
Pečuh
Z. Pécs (?)
327
Crna go-ro, pu-na ti-si la-da, srd-ce mo-je još pu-ni-je ja-da
Var. Kuh. 52-55

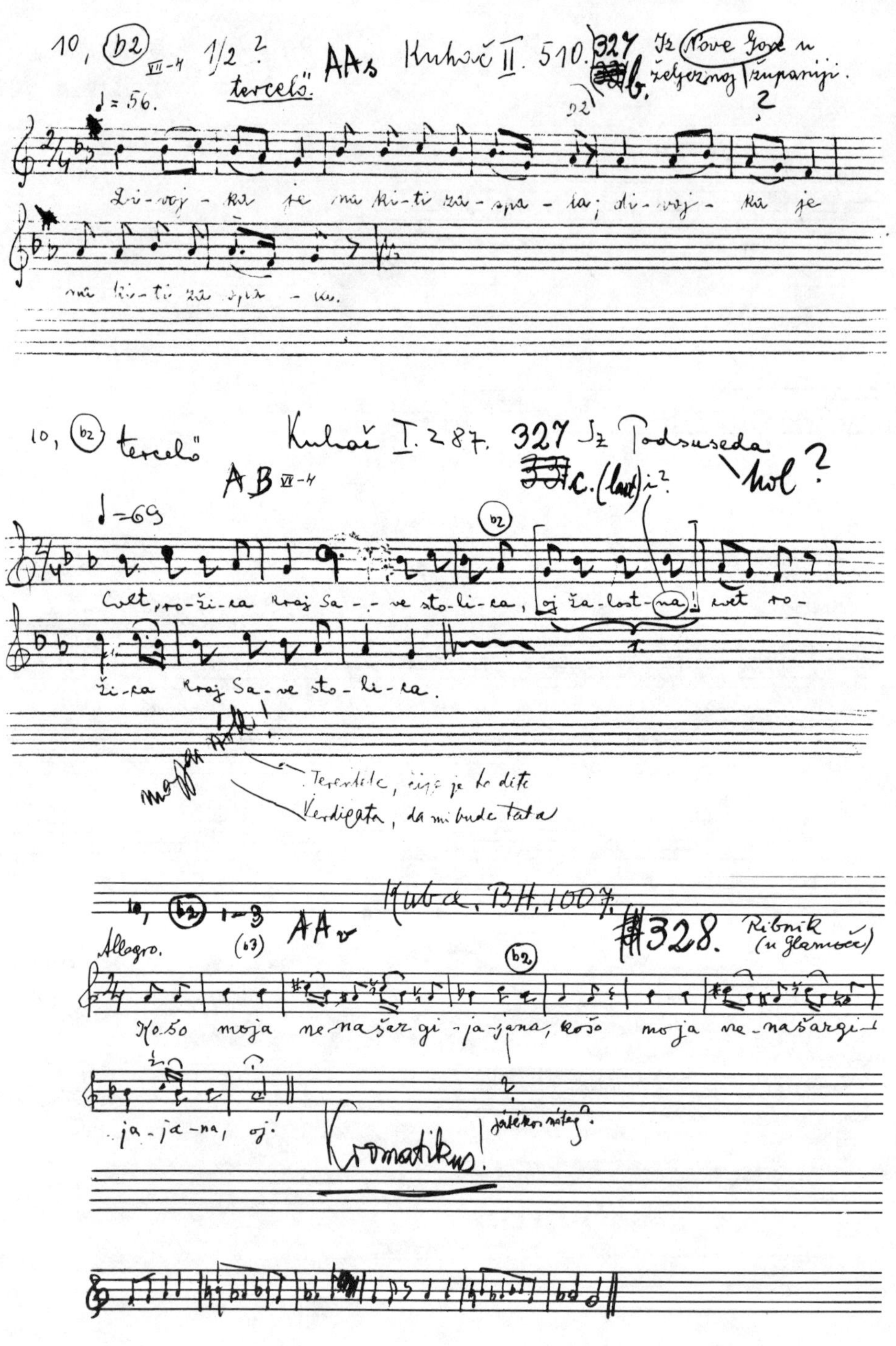

Kuhač II. 510.
327
Kuhač I. 287.
327
Allegro.
328.
Kromatikus!

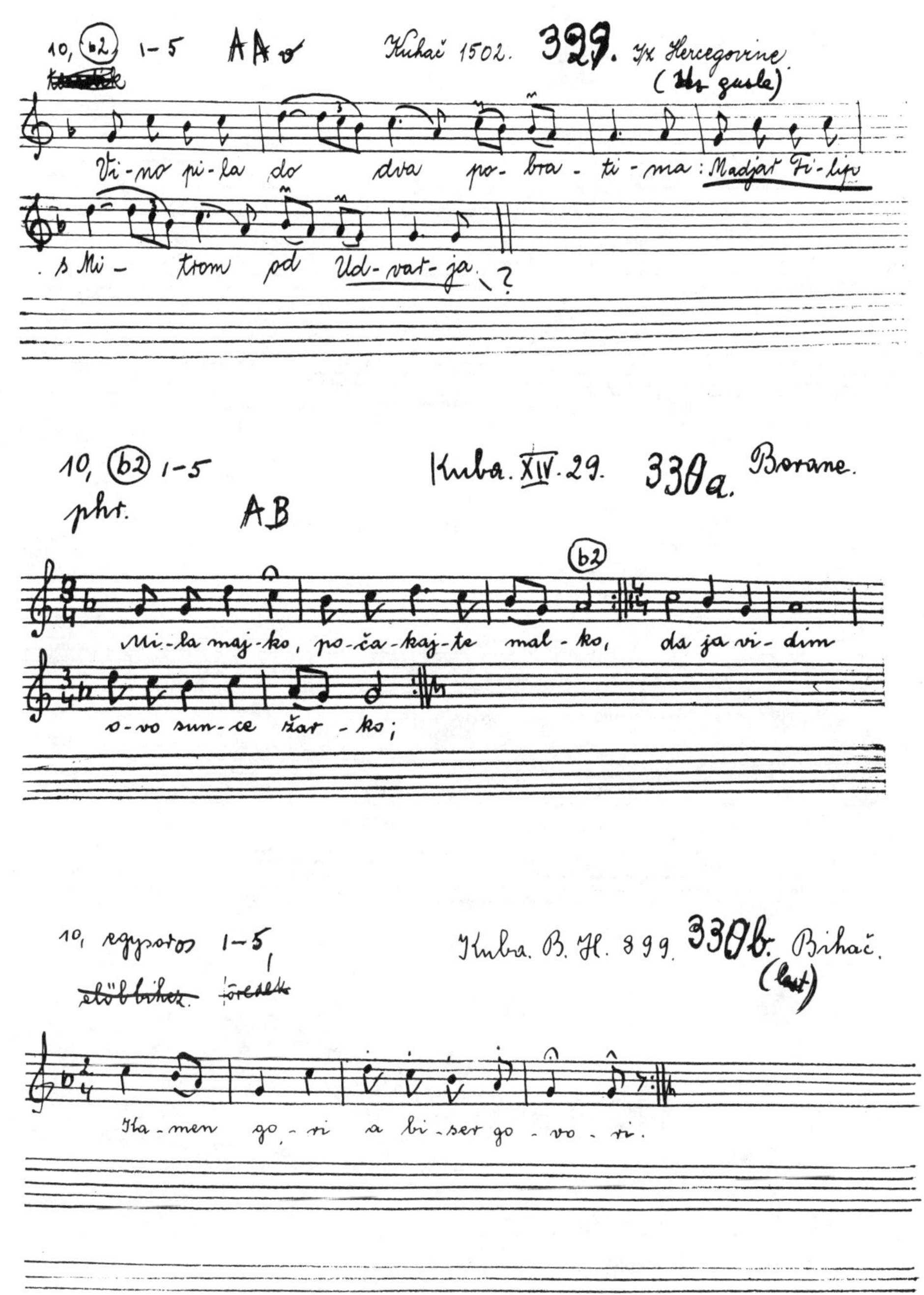
10, (b2) 1–5 AA
Kuhač 1502.
329.
Iz Hercegovine
(uz gusle)
Vi-no pi-la do dva po-bra-ti-ma: Madjar Fi-lip
s Mi-trom pd Ud-var-ja ?
10, (b2) 1–5
phr.
AB
Kuba. XIV. 29.
330a.
Borane.
(b2)
Mi-la maj-ko, po-ča-kaj-te mal-ko, da ja vi-dim
o-vo sun-ce žar-ko;
10, egysoros 1–5,
Kuba. B. H. 899.
330b.
Bihač.
Ka-men go-ri a bi-ser go-vo-ri.

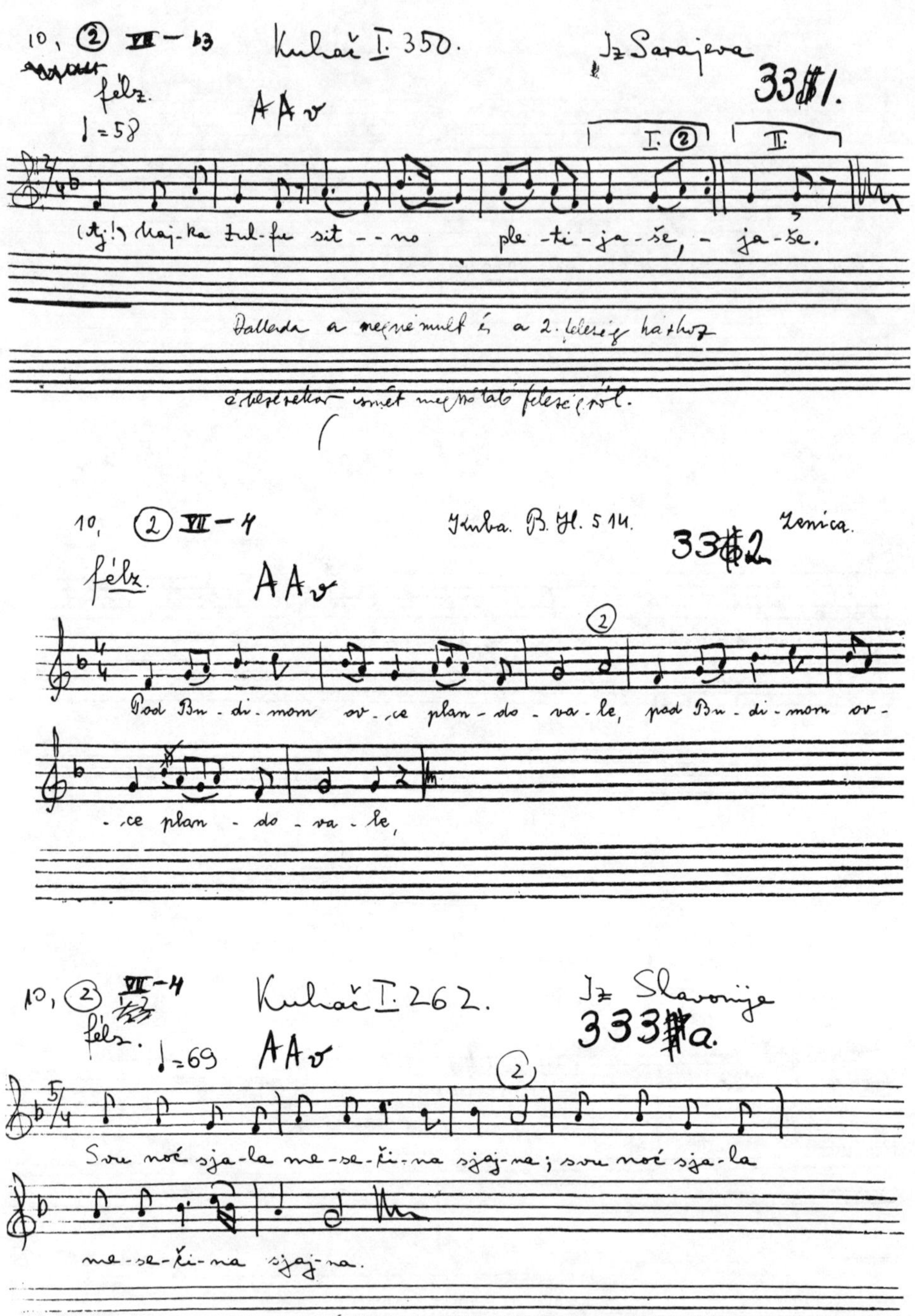
10, ② VII – b3
Kuhač I. 350.
Iz Sarajeva
33#1.
félz.
AAv
♩=58
I. ②
II.
(Aj!) Maj-ka Zul-fe sit - - no ple-ti-ja-še, - ja-še.
10, ② VII – 4
Kuba. B. H. 514.
Zenica.
félz.
AAv
②
Pod Bu-di-mom ov-ce plan-do-va-le, pod Bu-di-mom ov-
-ce plan-do-va-le,
10, ② VII – 4
Kuhač I. 262.
Iz Slavonije
333#a.
félz.
♩=69
AAv
②
Svu noć sja-la me-se-či-na sjaj-na; svu noć sja-la
me-se-či-na sjaj-na.

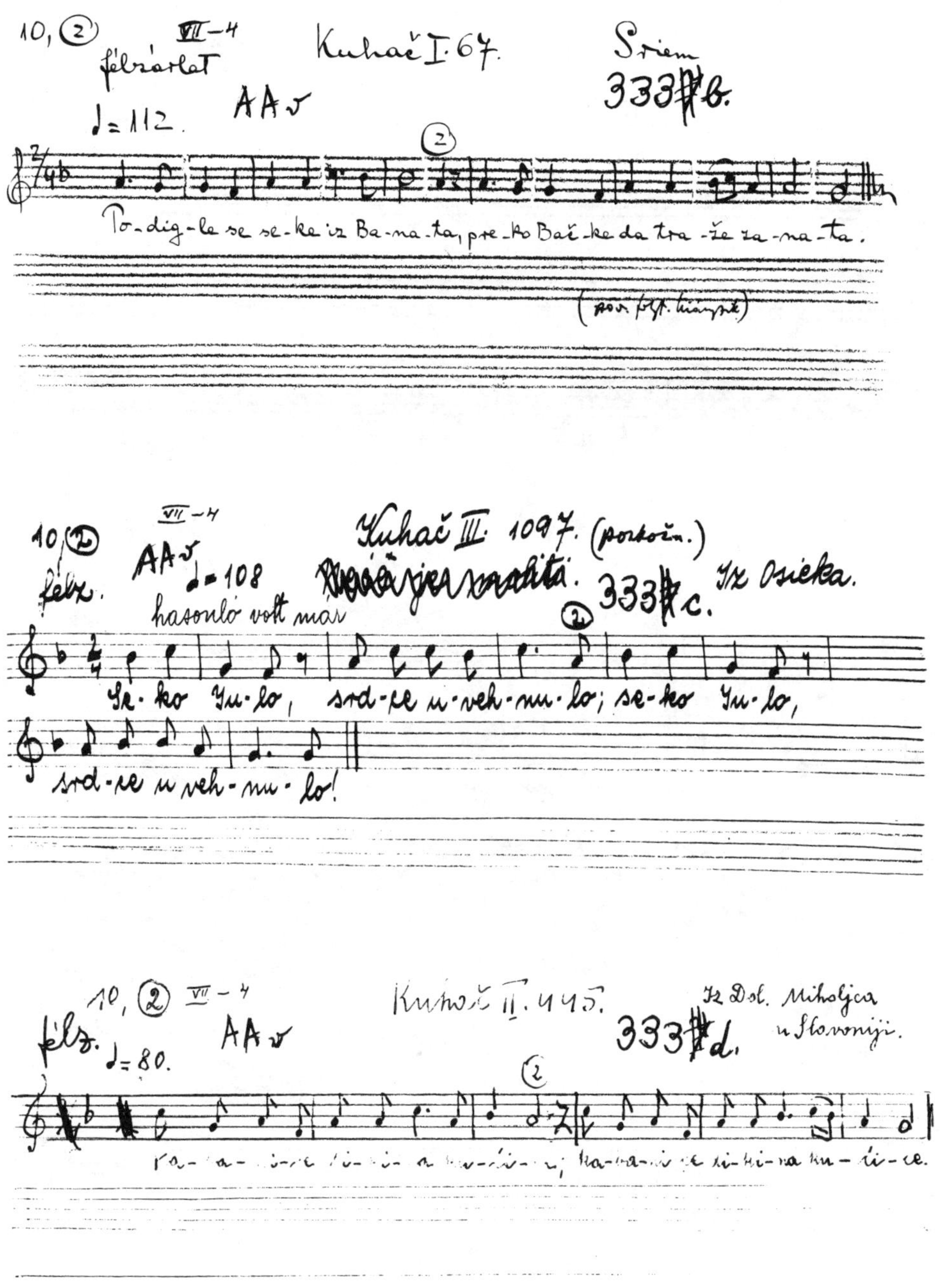
10, ② VII–4
félzárlat
Kuhač I. 67.
Sriem
333#b.
AA
♩= 112.
Po-dig-le se se-ke iz Ba-na-ta, pre-ko Bač-ke da tra-že za-na-ta.
10, ② VII–4
félz.
AA
♩= 108
Kuhač III. 1097. (poskočn.)
333#c.
Iz Osieka.
hasonló volt már
Se-ko Ju-lo, srd-ce u-veh-nu-lo; se-ko Ju-lo,
srd-ce u veh-nu-lo!
10, ② VII – 4
félz.
♩= 80.
AA
Kuhač II. 445.
333#d.
Iz Dol. Miholjca u Slavoniji.

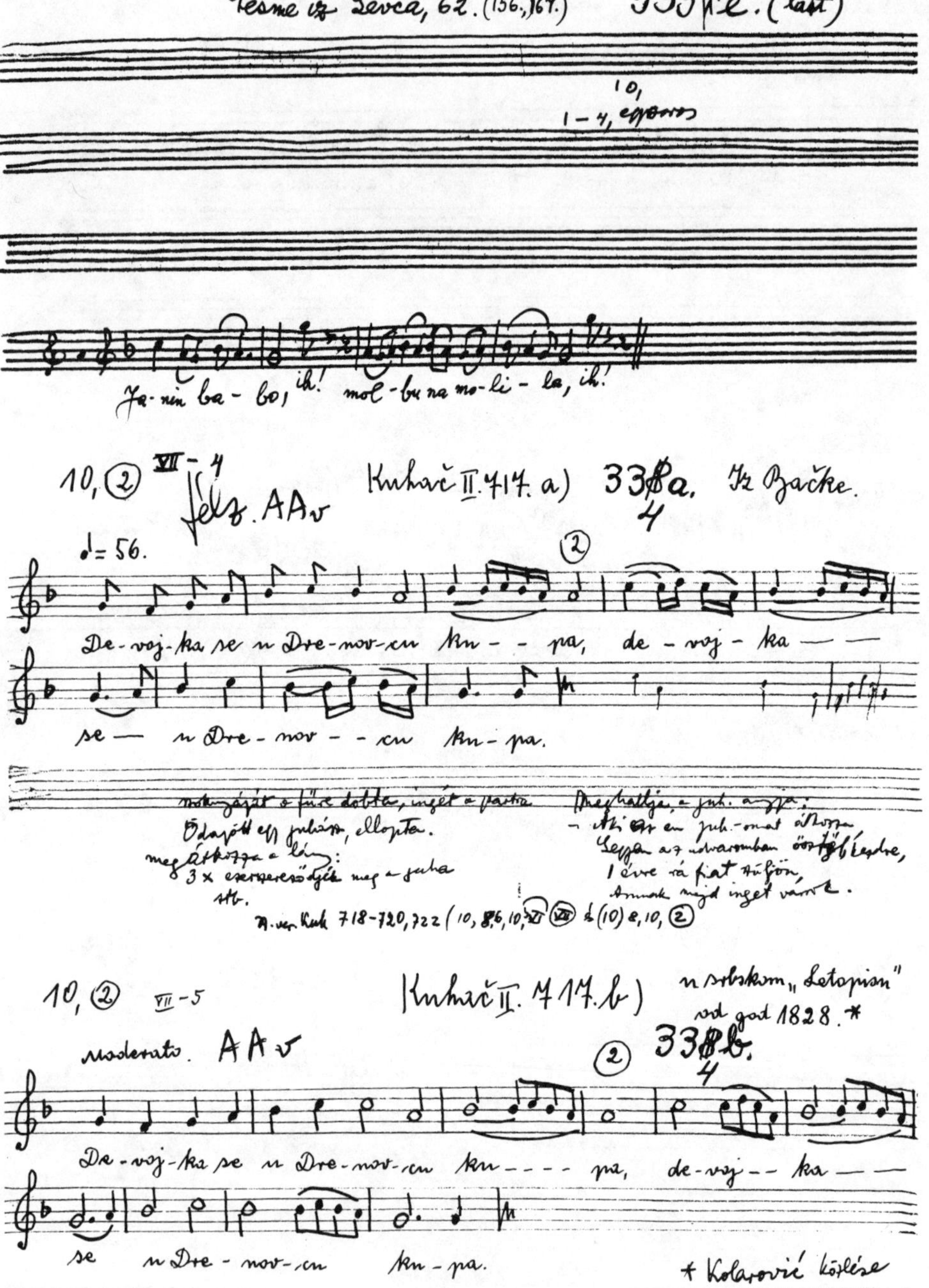

Pesme iz Levča, 62. (156., 167.)
333 e. (last)
10,
1 – 4,
Ja-nin ba - bo, ih! mol - bu na mo - li - la, ih!
10, ② VII – 4
AAv
Kuhač II. 417. a)
338a. Iz Bačke.
♩= 56.
De - voj - ka se u Dre - nov - cu ku - - pa, de - voj - ka — se — u Dre - nov - - cu ku - pa.
10, ② VII – 5
Kuhač II. 417. b)
u srbskom „Letopisu" od god. 1828. *
Moderato. AAv
338b.
De - voj - ka se u Dre - nov - cu ku - - - pa, de - voj - - ka — se u Dre - nov - cu ku - pa.
* Kolarović közlése

Stoj- ne, mo- me, mo- me, mori,
Ka-ra-dač- ko-va, mo - me.
Kuhač III. 1132 a)
335a.
Pljeskavica
Iz Pančeva.
Hej, Ti-čo Gli-šo! ne-va-lja ti rad-nja, hej ne-ka, ne-ka
po-pra-vit će se-ka.
Sedeljka
Pesme iz Levča, 33. (t. 78.)
335b.
De-voj-ka se vr-lo do-bro da-la,

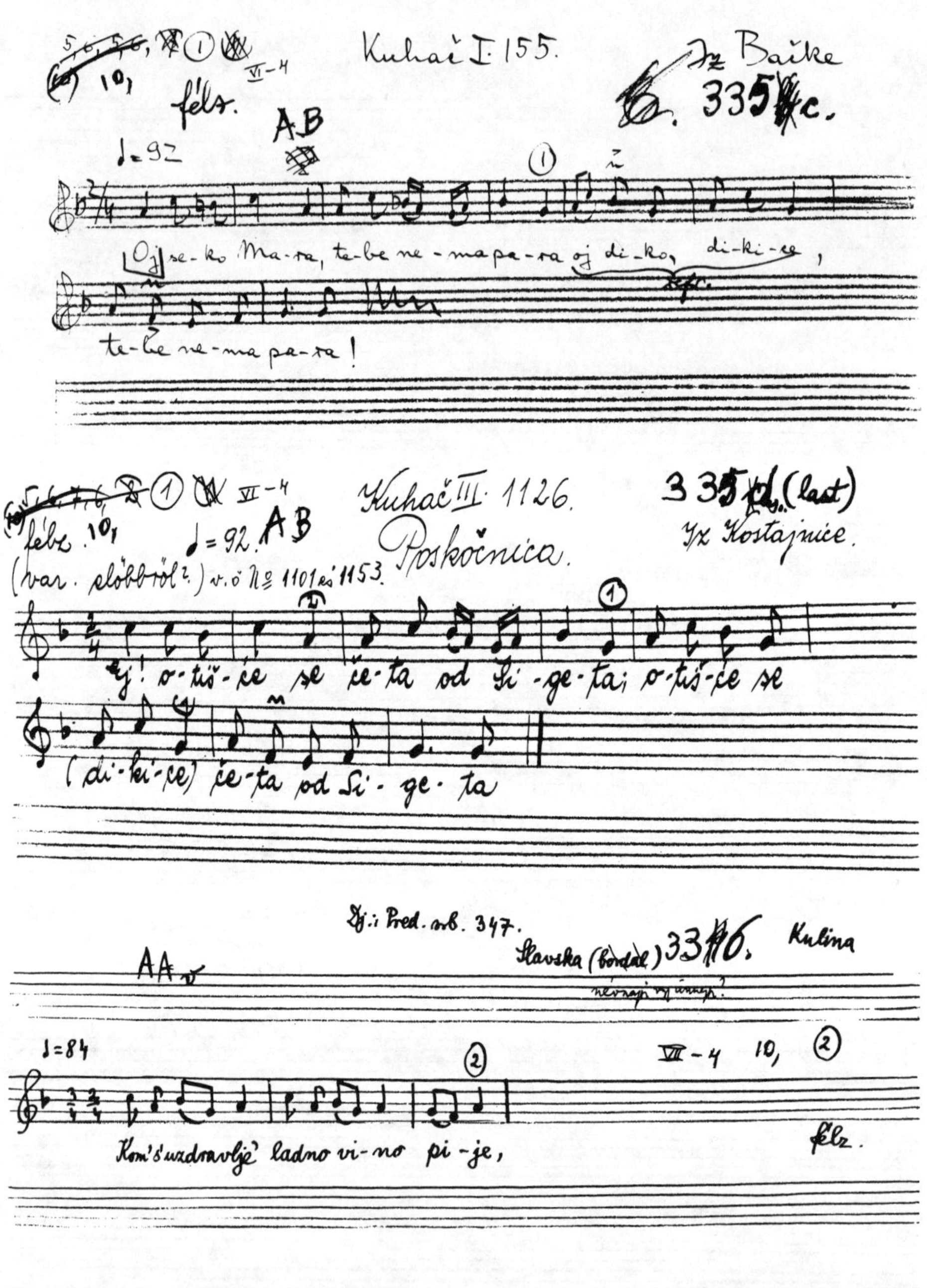

Kuhač I. 155.
Iz Baćke
335 c.
félz.
AB
Oj se-ko Ma-ra, te-be ne-ma pa-ra oj di-ko, di-ki-ce,
te-be ne-ma pa-ra!
Kuhač III. 1126.
335 (last)
Iz Kostajnice.
félz. 10,
AB
Poskočnica.
(var. előbbről?) v.ö. № 1101 és 1153.
Oj! o-tiš-će se če-ta od Si-ge-ta; o-tiš-će se
(di-ki-će) če-ta od Si-ge-ta
Đj.: Pred. zb. 347.
Slavska (bordal) 3316.
Kulina
AA
VII-4
10,
félz.
Kom' s'uzdravlje ladno vi-no pi-je,
kom' s'uzdravlje ladno vi- no pije.

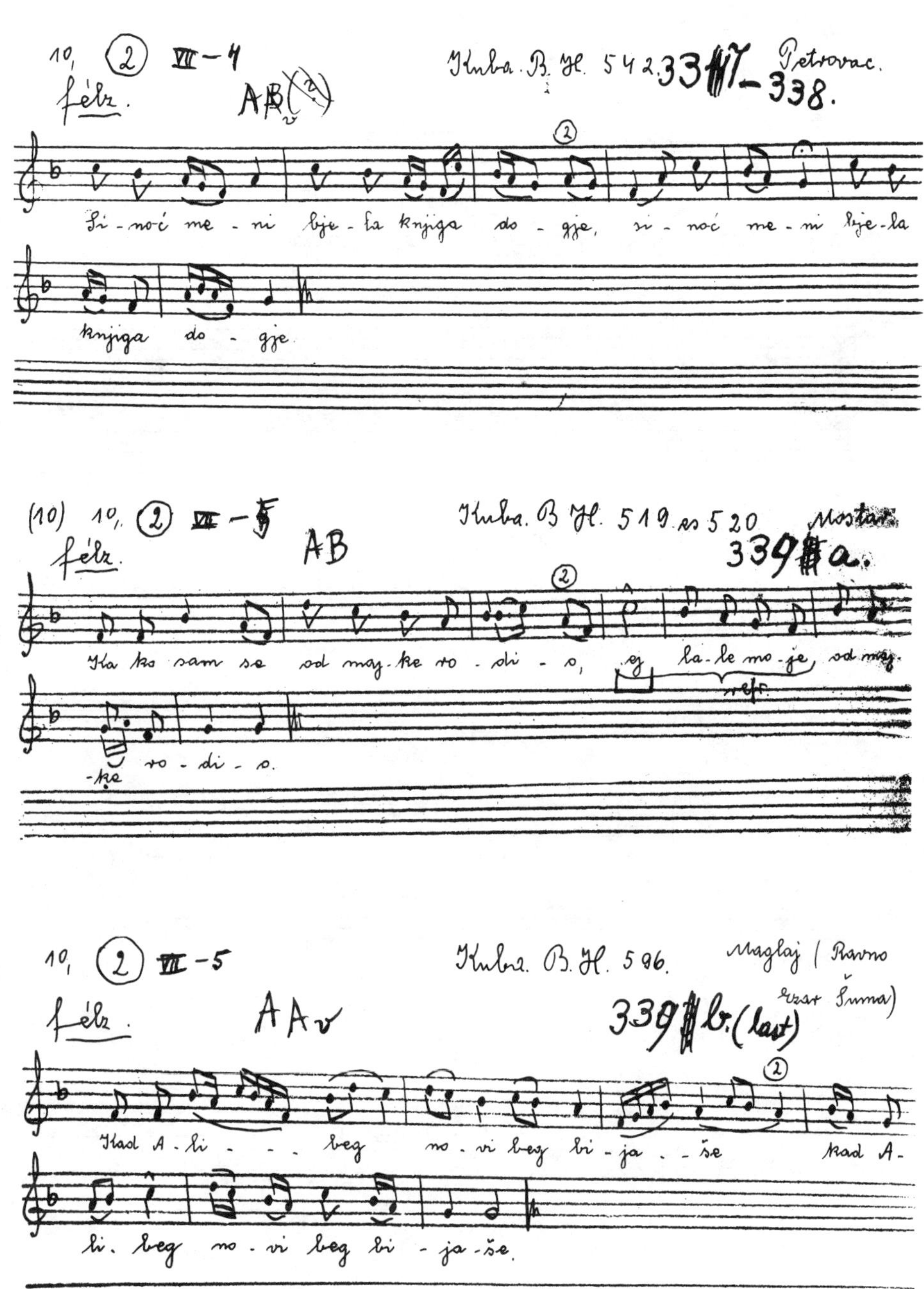

10, (2) VII – 4
Kuba. B. H. 542. 338. Petrovac.
félz.
AB
Si - noć me - ni bje - la knjiga do - gje, si - noć me - ni bje - la
knjiga do - gje.
(10) 10, (2) VII – 5
Kuba. B. H. 519 és 520 Mostar
339 a.
félz.
AB
Ka ko sam se od maj - ke ro - di - o, oj la - le mo - je, od maj -
- ke ro - di - o.
refr.
10, (2) VII – 5
Kuba. B. H. 596. Maglaj (Ravno
339 b. (last)
félz.
AAv
Kad A - li - - - beg no - vi beg bi - ja - - še kad A -
li - beg no - vi beg bi - ja - še.

AB
Allegro moderato Kuba B.-H. 632.
340.
Prozor.
1. O-pre-ma se na Doljane Salko, veće
svoje zla-to na o-ma-ne da-je,
2. Koju veče Salko na Doljane, onu
ve-če zlato upro-še-no.
3. Koju veče Salko sa Doljane,
onu veče zlato u kal-va-tu.
AB
♩= 60.
Kuhač 1541.
(Ženska balada)
Iz Vrbovca u Hrvatskoj.
Še-ta-la se mu-dra Ka-ta-le-na; še-ta-la se mudra Ka-ta-le-na.

Dj.: Pred. srb. 39.
34ɸ2. Rataje.
AB
♩= 104 (sic!)
Što je sjaj-na, Du-de, mese-čina,
što je sjaj-na, Dude, mese-čina,
Kuba B. H. 62.
Nevesinc.
So-ko bi-ra, gdje-će na-ći mi-ra, so-ko bi-ra, gdje će
na-ći mi-ra, hoj!
Kuba XIII. 26.
Stolac. (Herceg.)
So-ko bi-ra, gdje će na-ći mi-ra, oj, so-ko bi-ra,
gdje će na-ći mi-ra, ša-laj!

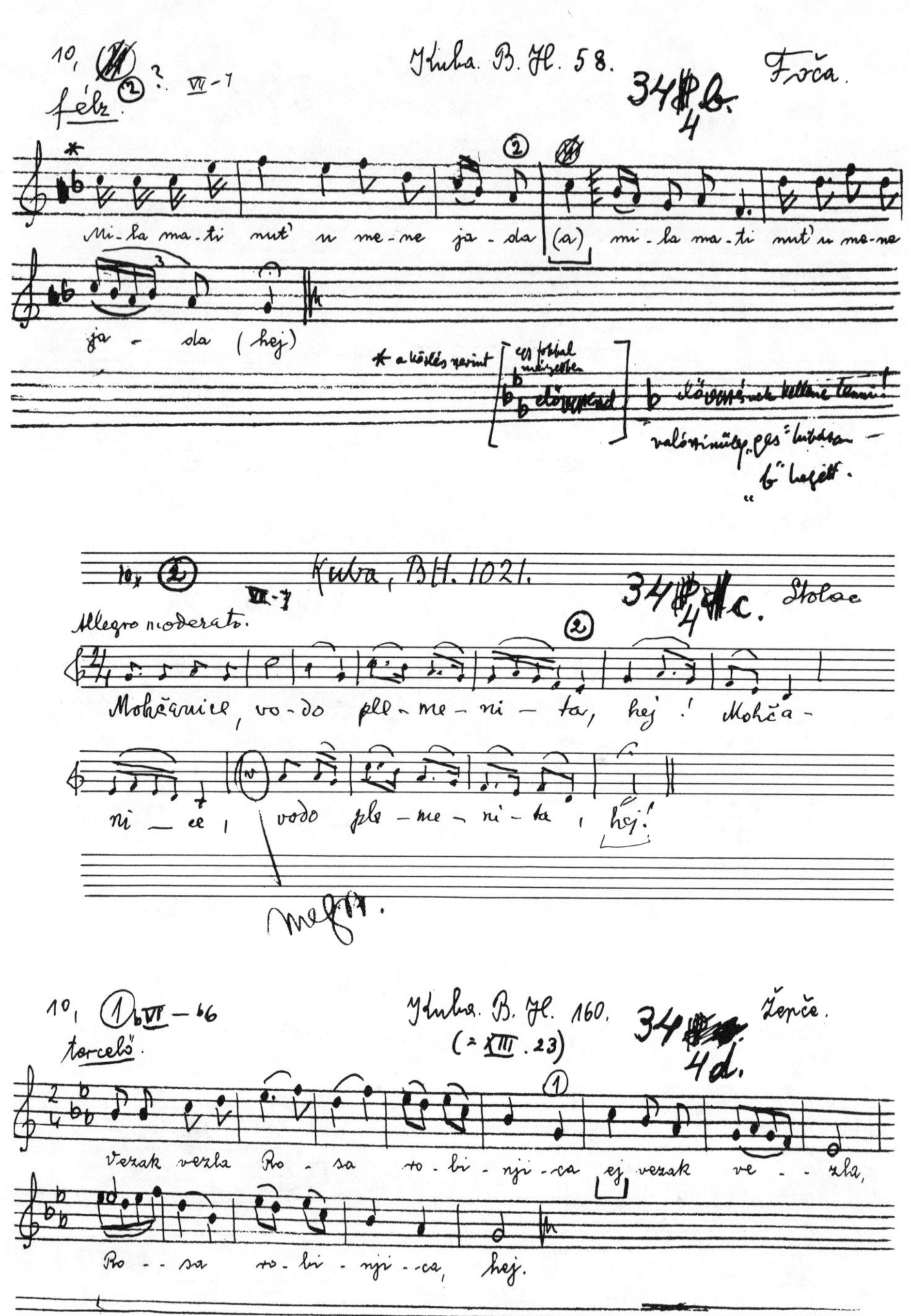

Kuba. B. H. 58.
Foča.
Mi-la ma-ti nut' u me-ne ja-da (a) mi-la ma-ti nut' u me-ne
ja - da (hej)
Kuba, BH. 1021.
Stolac
Allegro moderato.
Mohčanice, vo-do ple-me-ni-ta, hej! Mohča-
ni-ce, vodo ple-me-ni-ta, hej!
Kuba. B. H. 160.
(= XIII. 23)
Žepče.
Vezak vezla Ro-sa ro-bi-nji-ca ej vezak ve-zla,
Ro-sa ro-bi-nji-ca, hej.

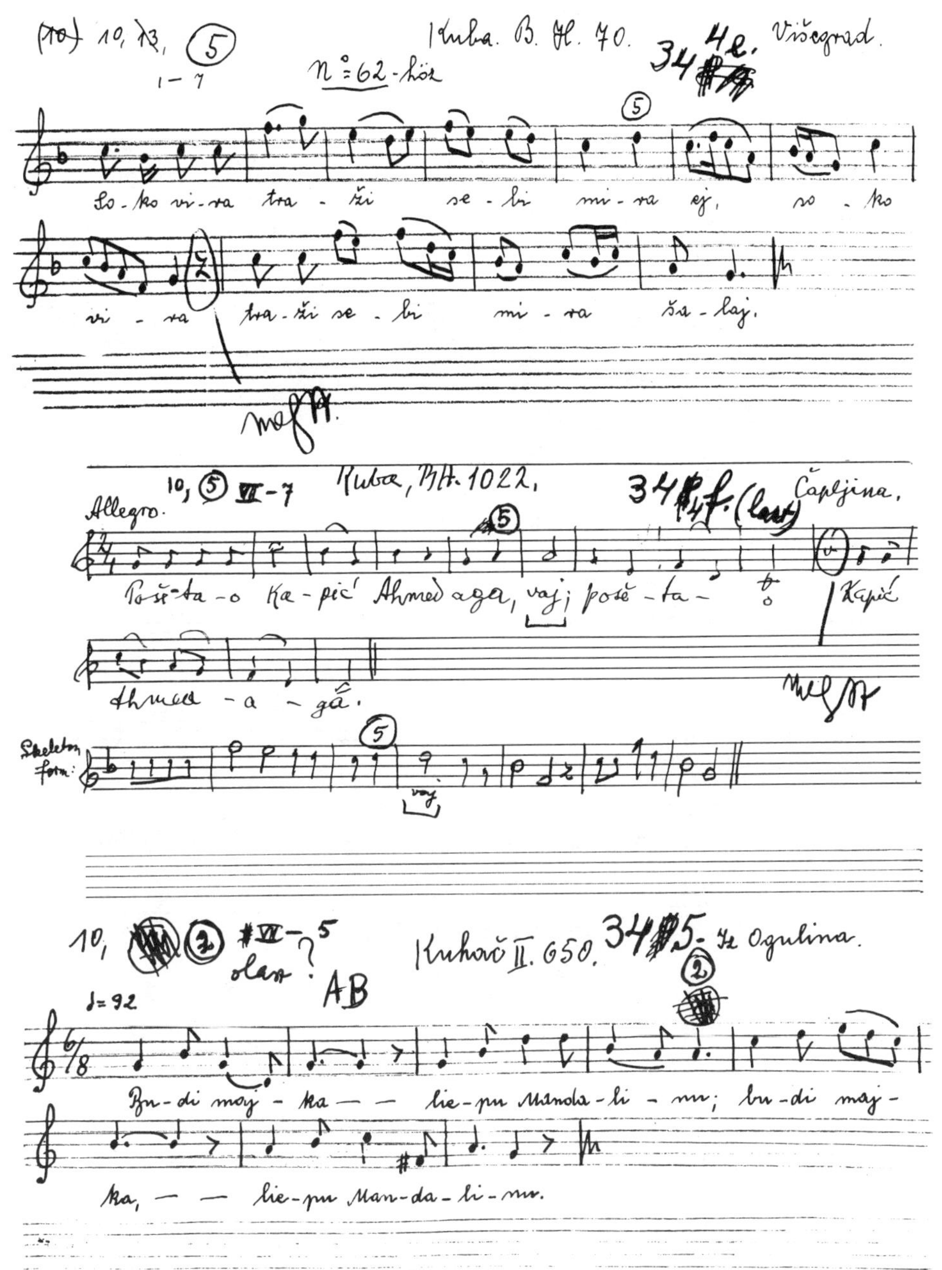

Elrabolt egy török egy lányt.
Kilenc (10) évig raboskodott a lány,
megszökött, hazament.
~~Megfo~~ Vízért ment a kútra
Ott találkozott kedvesével

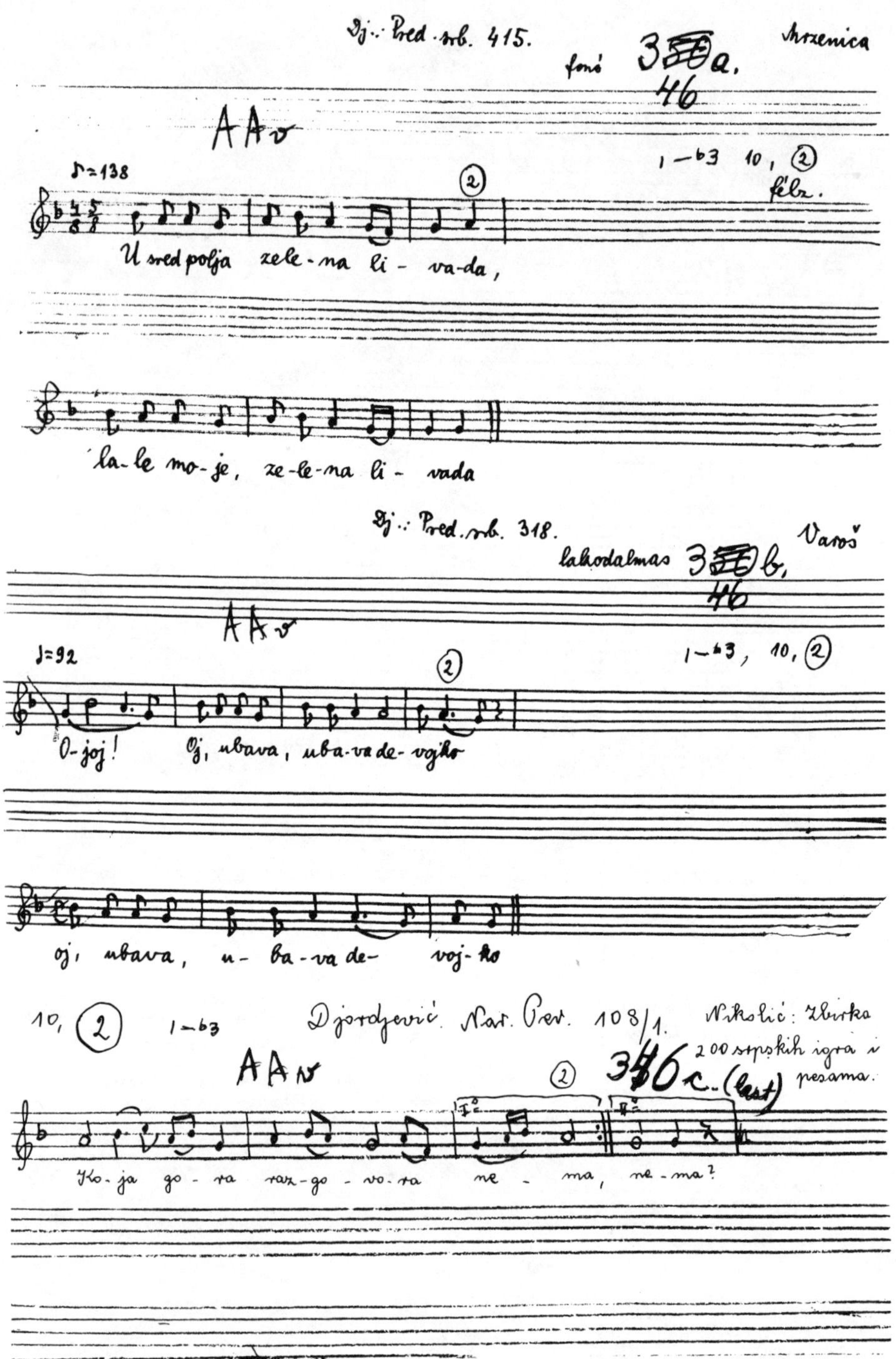
Dj.: Pred. srb. 415.
foná 3a.
46
Arzenica
AAv
♪=138
1–63 10, ②
félz.
U sred polja zele-na li-va-da,
la-le mo-je, ze-le-na li-vada
Dj.: Pred. srb. 318.
lakodalmas 3b.
46
Varoš
AAv
♩=92
1–63, 10, ②
O-joj! Oj, ubava, uba-va de-vojko
oj, ubava, u-ba-va de-voj-ko
10, ② 1–63
Djordjević Nar. Pev. 108/1.
Nikolić: Zbirka 200 srpskih igra i pesama.
AAv
36 c.
Ko-ja go-ra raz-go-vo-ra ne-ma, ne-ma?

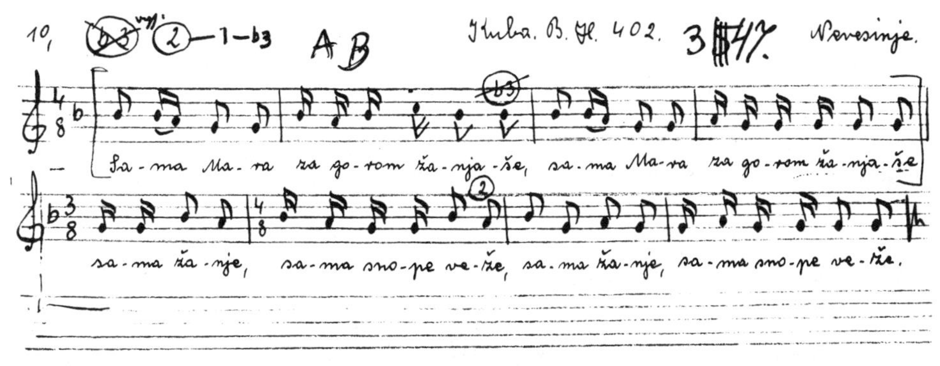
10, (2) — 1 — b3
AB
Kuba. B. H. 402.
347.
Nevesinje.
Sa-ma Ma-ra za go-rom ža-nja-še, sa-ma Ma-ra za go-rom ža-nja-še
sa-ma ža-nje, sa-ma sno-pe ve-že, sa-ma ža-nje, sa-ma sno-pe ve-že.

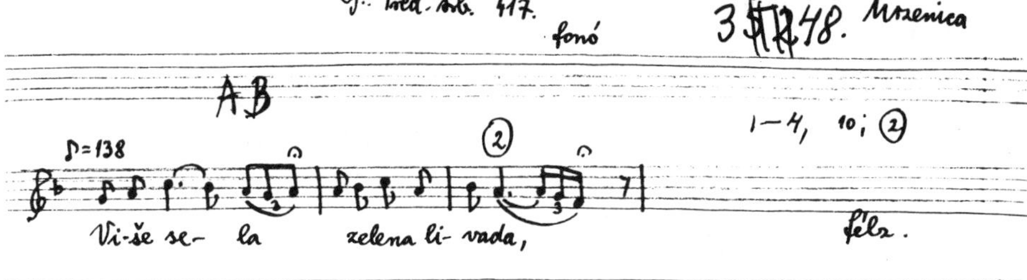
Dj.: Pred. sb. 417.
fonó
348.
Mrzenica
AB
1—4, 10; (2)
♪=138
Vi-še se- la zelena li- vada,
félz.

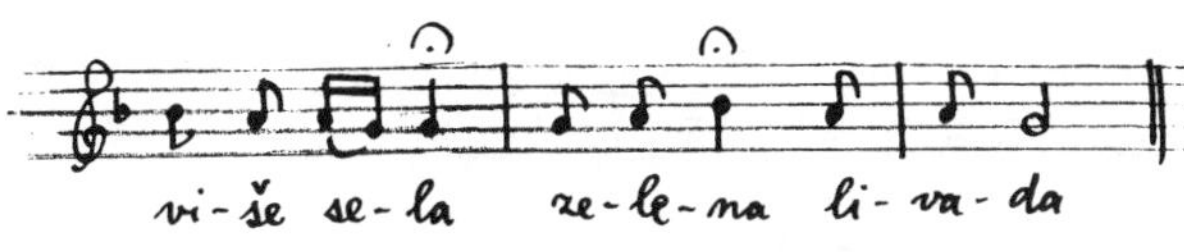
vi-še se-la ze-le-na li-va-da

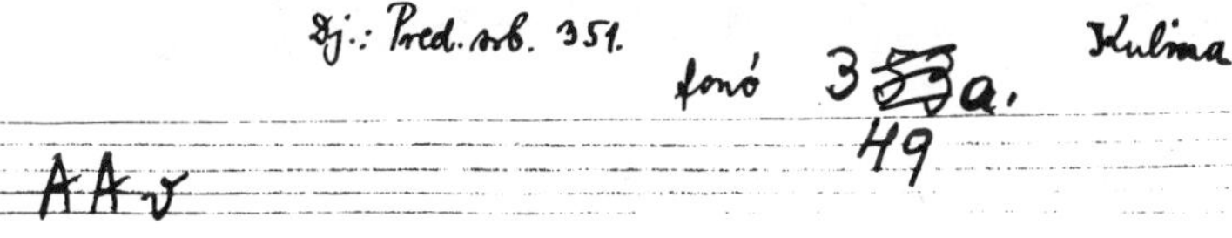
Dj.: Pred. sb. 351.
fonó
349
Kulina
AAv
1 — 4, 10, (2)

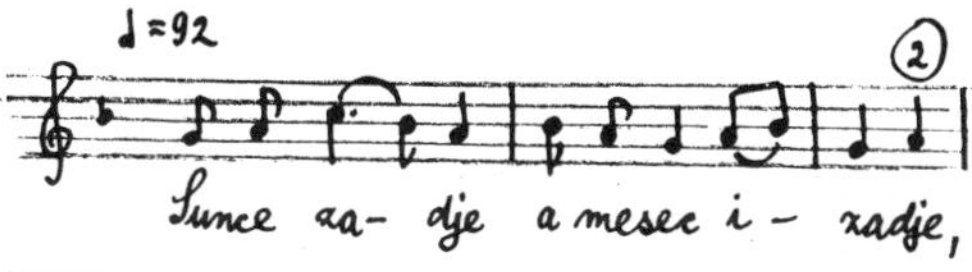
♩=92
Sunce za- dje a mesec i- zadje,

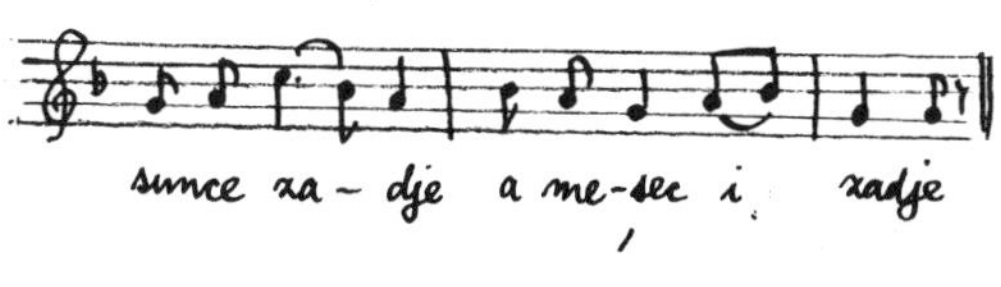
sunce za-dje a me-sec i zadje

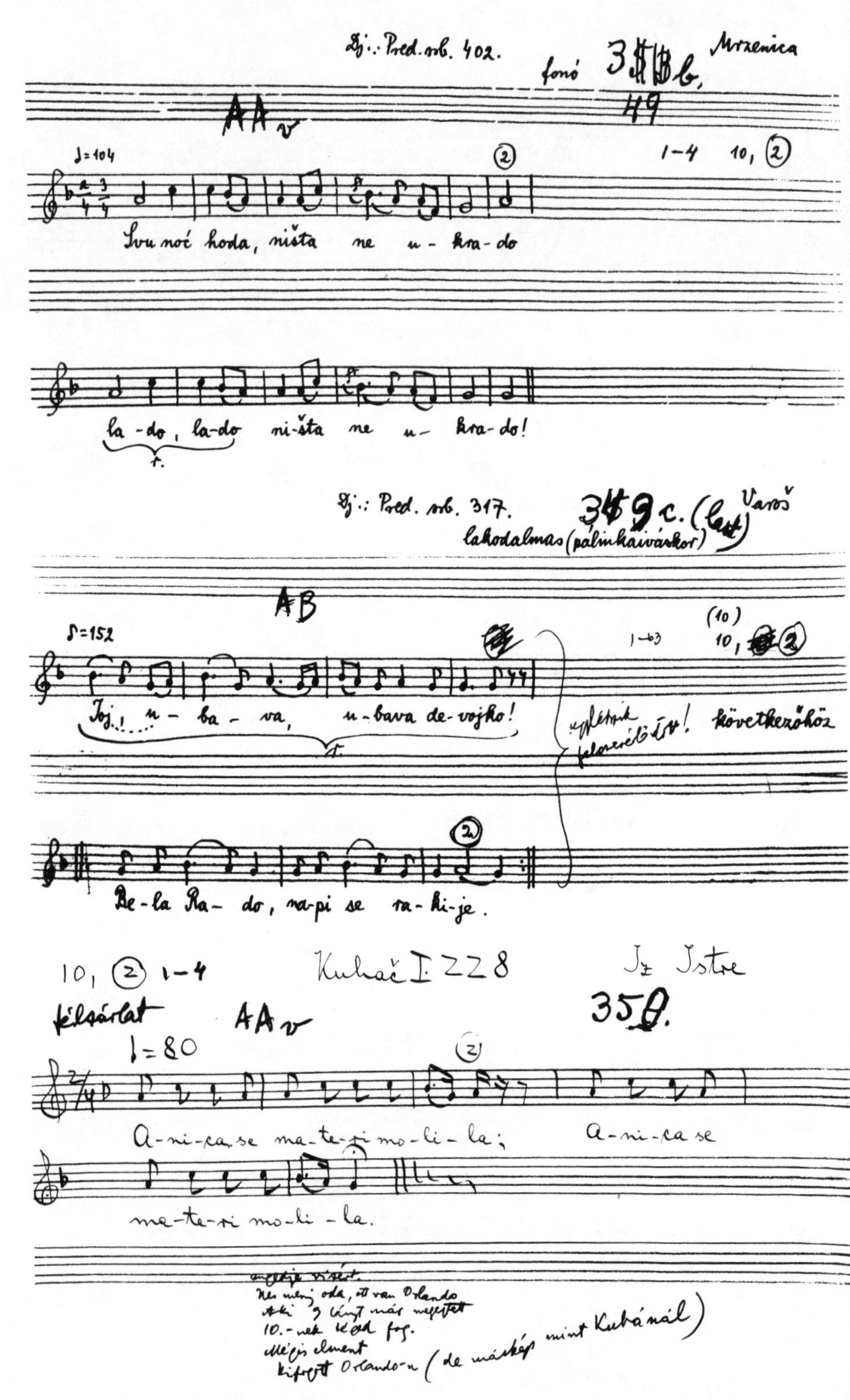
Dj.: Pred. sb. 402.
fonó
Mrzenica
49
AAv
♩=104
1–4 10, ②
②
Sva noć hoda, ništa ne u- kra-do
la-do, la-do ni-šta ne u- kra-do!
r.
Dj.: Pred. sb. 317.
Varoš
lakodalmas (pálinkaiváskor)
AB
♪=152
1–63
(10)
10, ②
Joj, u- ba- va, u-bava de-vojko!
r.
következőhöz
②
Be-la Ra- do, na-pi se ra-ki-je.
10, ② 1–4
Kuhač I. 228
Iz Istre
350.
AAv
♩=80
②
A-ni-ca se ma-te-ri mo-li-la; A-ni-ca se
ma-te-ri mo-li-la.

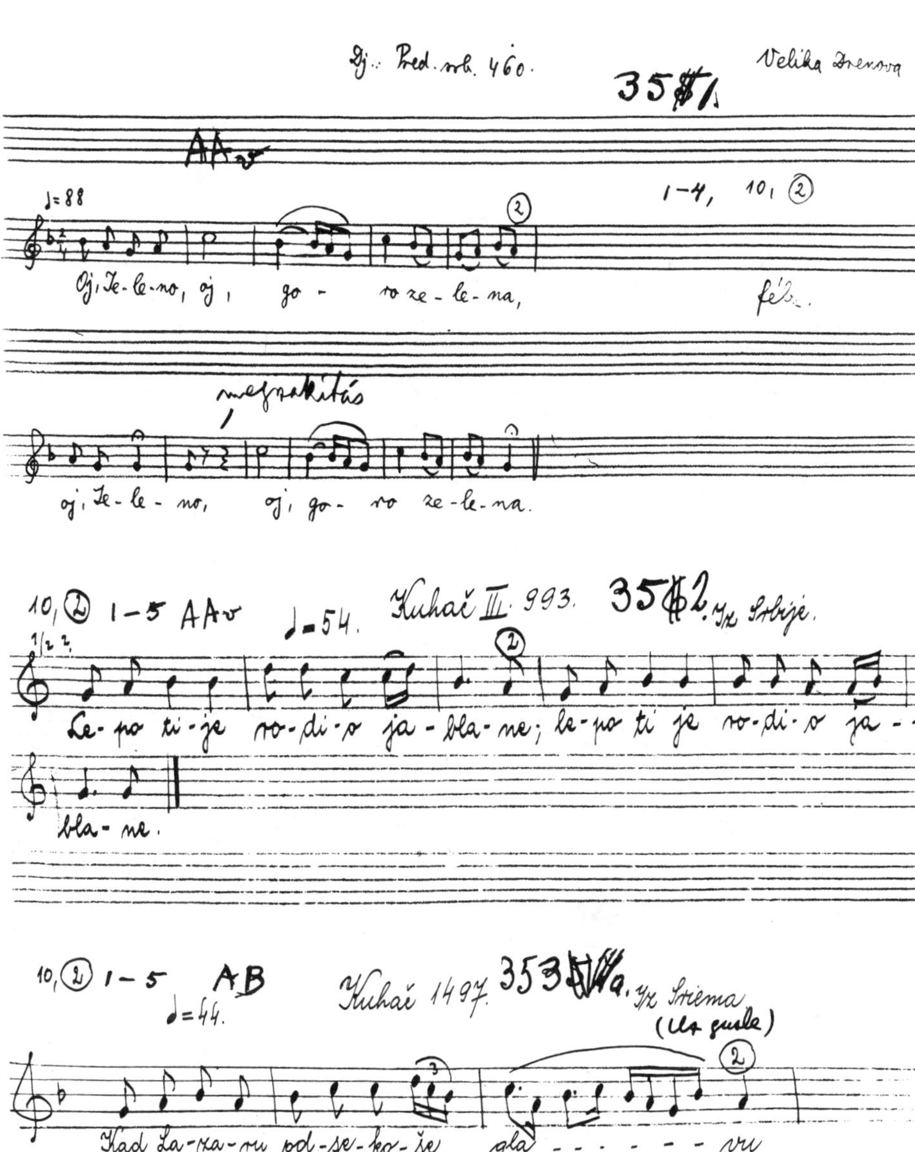

Lázár fejedelem fejének megmentése

10, ② 1–5
Kuhač II. 721.
Iz Djakova.
353#b.
AB
♩=50.
Dje-voj-ka se u Dre-nov-cu ku-pa, dje-voj-ka se u Dre-nov-cu ku-pa.
10, 1–5
Kuba. B. H. 614.
353#c. (last)
A moj dra-gi, je-dan la-fe-dži-ja.
10, ② 1–5
Kuhač I. 390.
Iz otoka Krka
35#4.
AB(?)
♩=100
Vo-zi-la se šaj-ka ma-la bar-ka, vo-zi-la se šaj-ka ma-la bar-ka.
Kuh. 122.
Kuba

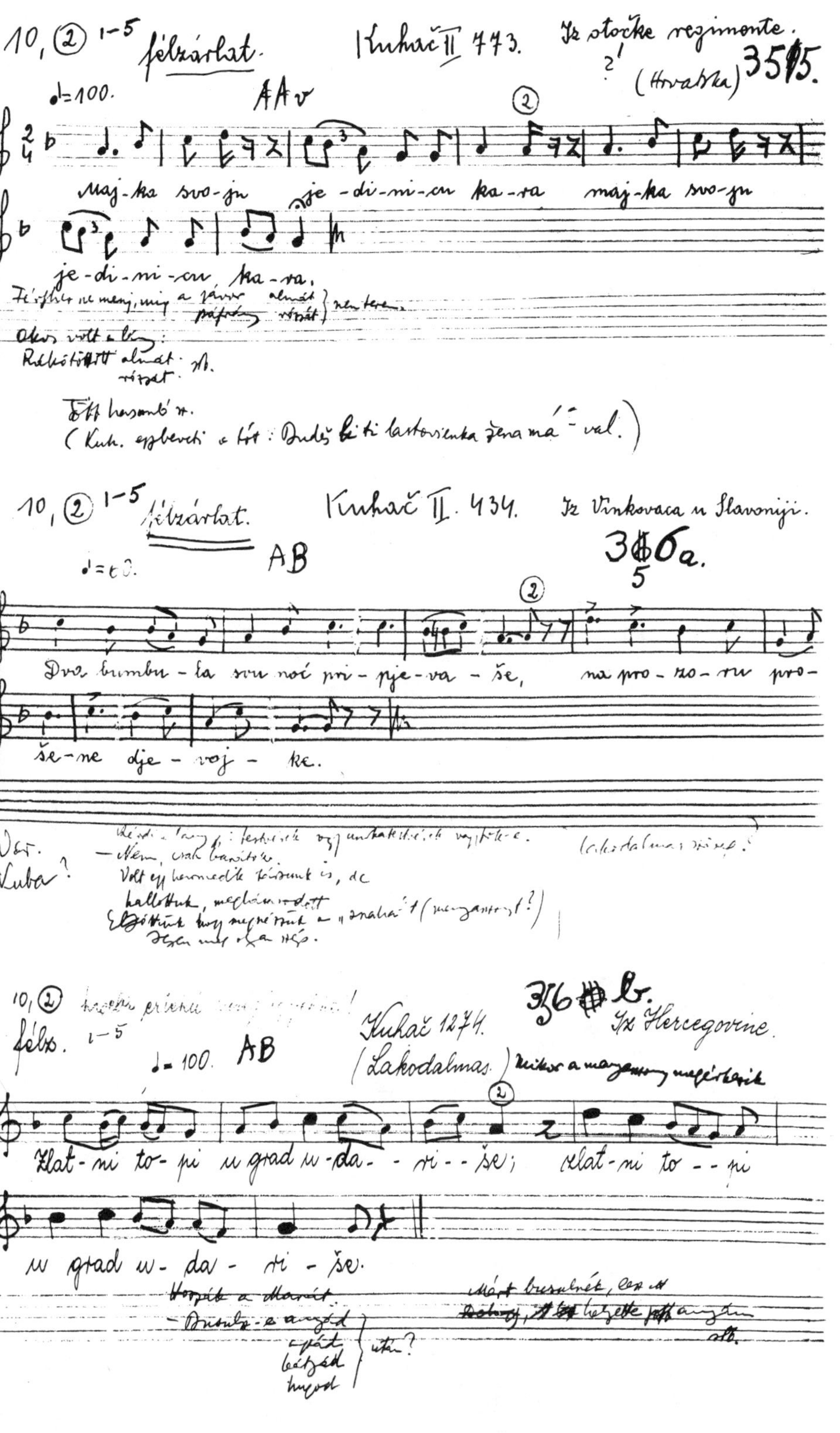
10, ② 1–5 félzárlat.
Kuhač II 773.
Iz stočke regimonte.
(Hrvatska)
♩=100.
Maj-ka svo-ju je-di-ni-cu ka-ra maj-ka svo-ju
je-di-ni-cu ka-ra.
10, ② 1–5 félzárlat.
Kuhač II. 434.
Iz Vinkovaca u Slavoniji.
AB
Dva bumbu-la svu noć pri-pje-va-še, na pro-zo-ru pro-
še-ne dje-voj-ke.
10, ② félz. 1–5
Kuhač 1274.
(Lakodalmas)
Iz Hercegovine.
♩=100. AB
Zlat-ni to-pi u grad u-da-ri-še; zlat-ni to-pi
u grad u-da-ri-še.

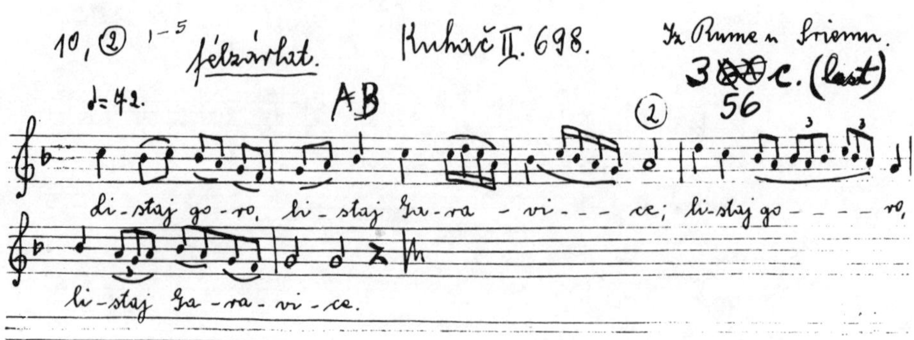
10, ② 1–5 félzárlat. Kuhač II. 698. Iz Rume u Sriemu.
56
AB
li-staj go-ro, li-staj Ga-ra-vi-ce; li-staj go-ro,
li-staj Ga-ra-vi-ce.

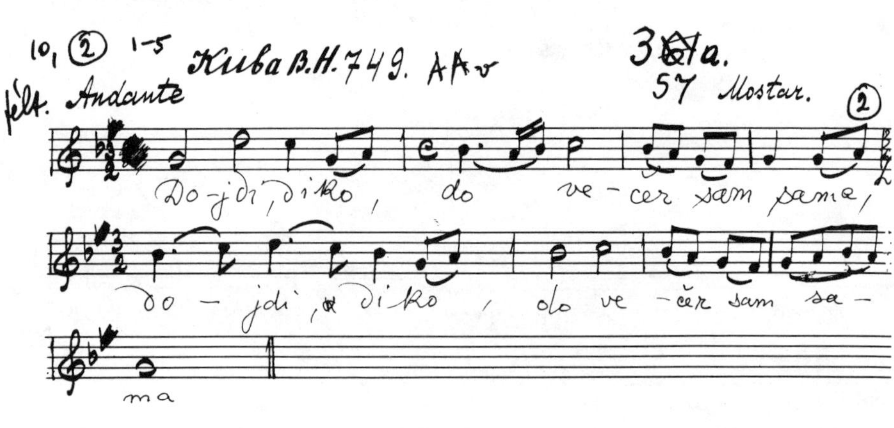
10, ② 1–5 Kuba B.H. 749. AAv
félz. Andante
57 Mostar.
Do-jdi, diko, do ve-čer sam sama,
do-jdi, diko, do ve-čer sam sa-
ma

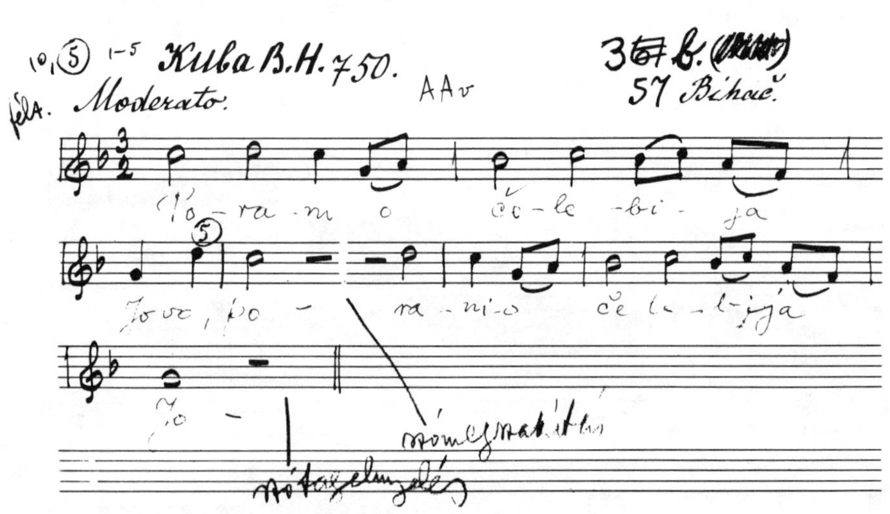
10, ⑤ 1–5 Kuba B.H. 750. AAv
félz. Moderato.
57 Bihać.
Po-ra-ni o če-le-bi-ja
Jovo, po-ra-ni-o če-le-bi-ja
Jo-

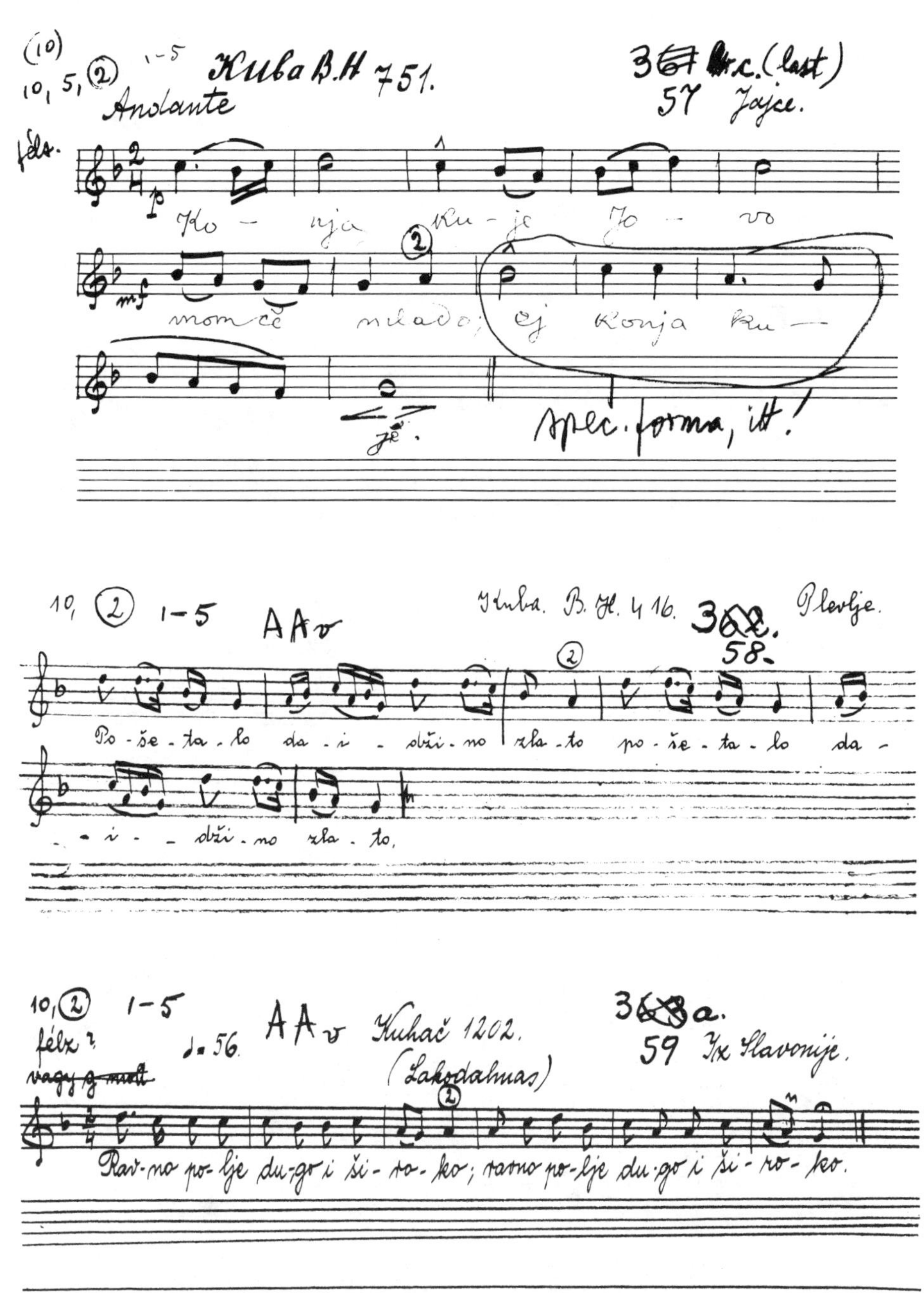

(10)
10, 5, ② 1–5
Kuba B.H 751.
57 Jajce.
Andante
félx.
Ko – nja ku – je Jo – vo
②
mom-če mlado; oj Konja ku –
je.
Spec. forma, itt!
10, ② 1–5 AAv
Kuba. B. H. 416.
58.
Plevlje.
Po-še-ta-lo da-i-dži-no zla-to po-še-ta-lo da-
-i-dži-no zla-to.
10, ② 1–5
félx ?
♩= 56.
AAv
Kuhač 1202.
(Lakodalmas)
59
Slavonije.
Rav-no po-lje du-go i ši-ro-ko; ravno po-lje du-go i ši-ro-ko.

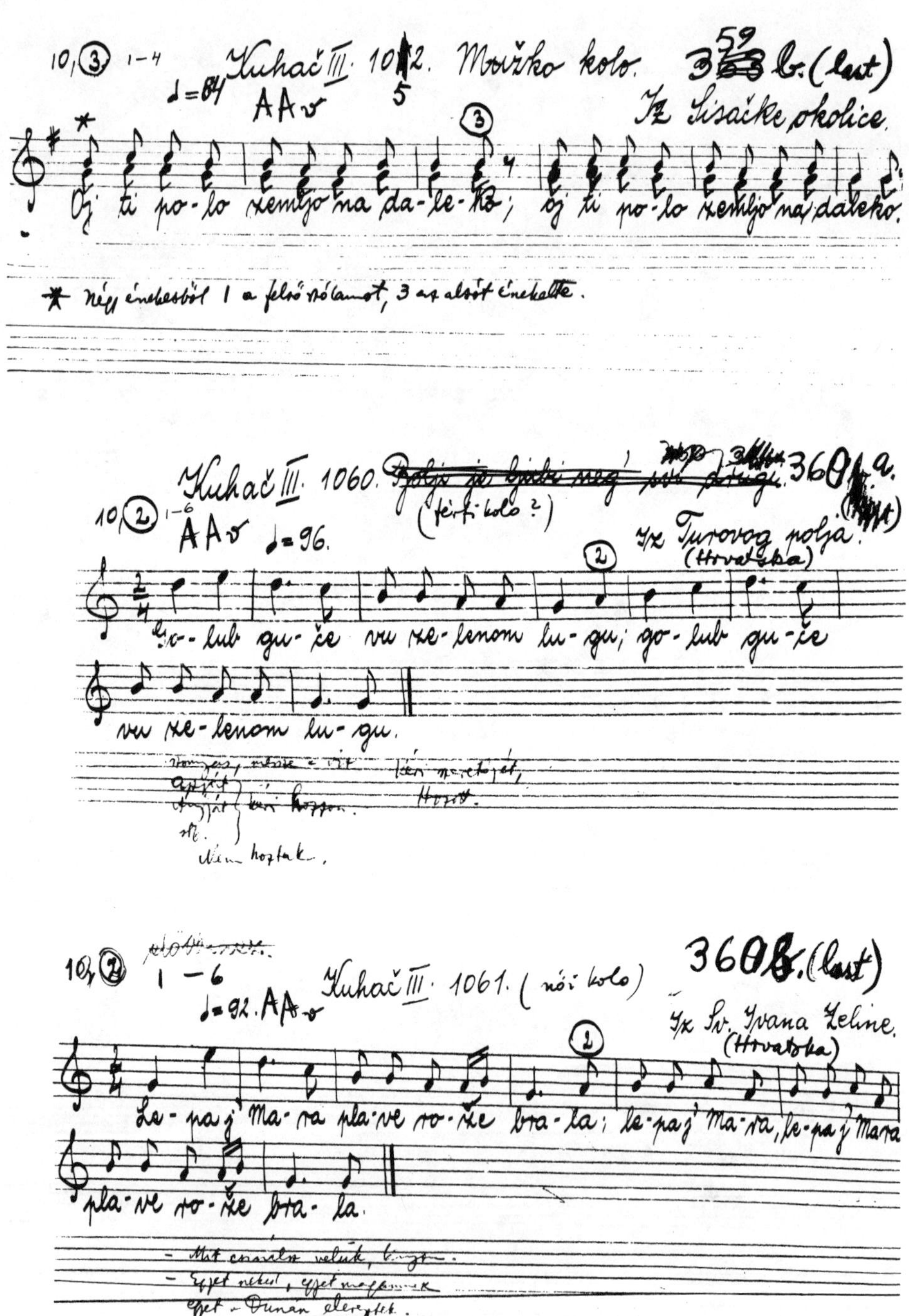
Kuhač III.
Mužko kolo.
Iz Sisačke okolice.
Oj ti po-lo zemljo na da-le-ko; oj ti po-lo zemljo na daleko.
* négy énekesből 1 a felső szólamot, 3 az alsót énekelte.
Kuhač III. 1060.
Iz Turovog polja. (Hrvatska)
Go-lub gu-če vu ze-lenom lu-gu; go-lub gu-če
vu ze-lenom lu-gu.
Kuhač III. 1061. (női kolo)
Iz Sv. Ivana Zeline. (Hrvatska)
Le-pa j Ma-ra pla-ve ro-že bra-la; le-pa j Ma-ra, le-pa j Mara
pla-ve ro-že bra-la.

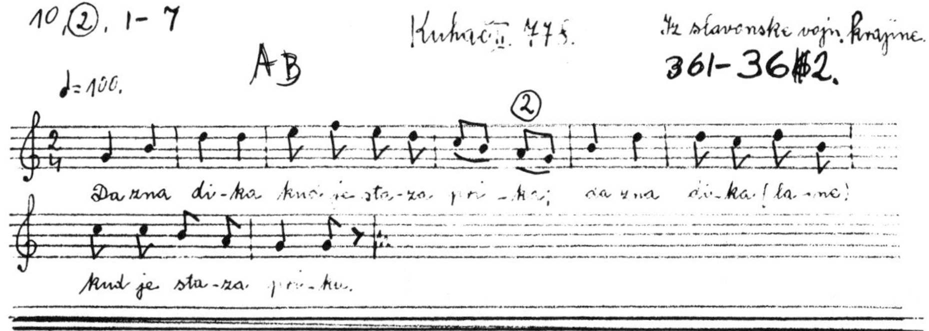
10, ②, 1- 7
Kuhač II. 775.
Iz slavonske vojn. krajine.
AB
♩=100.
②
Da zna di-ka kud je sta-za pri-ka; da zna di-ka (la-ne)
kud je sta-za pri-ka.

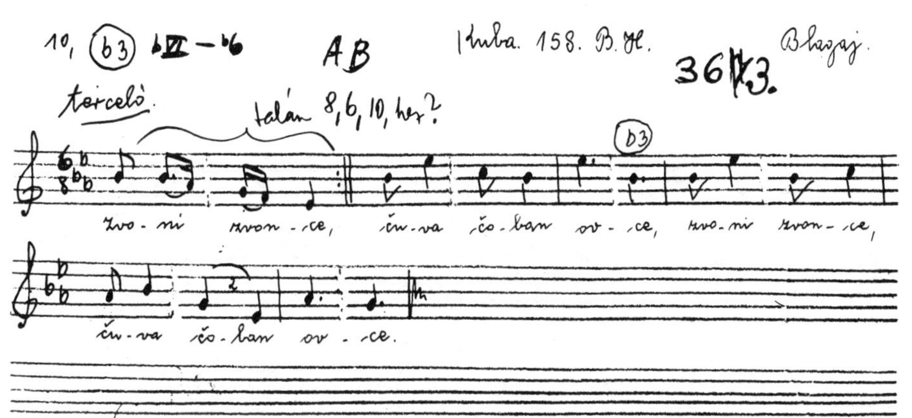
10, b3 bVII – b6
AB
Kuba. 158. B. H.
Blagaj.
tercelő.
talán 8,6,10, hez?
b3
Zvo-ni zvon-ce, ču-va čo-ban ov-ce, zvo-ni zvon-ce,
ču-va čo-ban ov-ce.

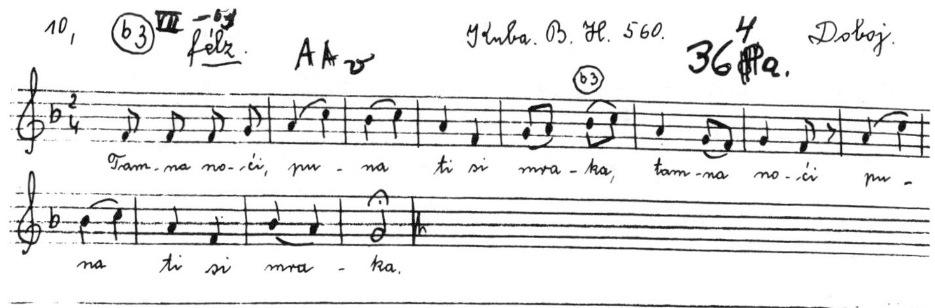
10, b3
félz.
Kuba. B. H. 560.
Doboj.
b3
Tam-na no-ći, pu-na ti si mra-ka, tam-na no-ći pu-
na ti si mra-ka.

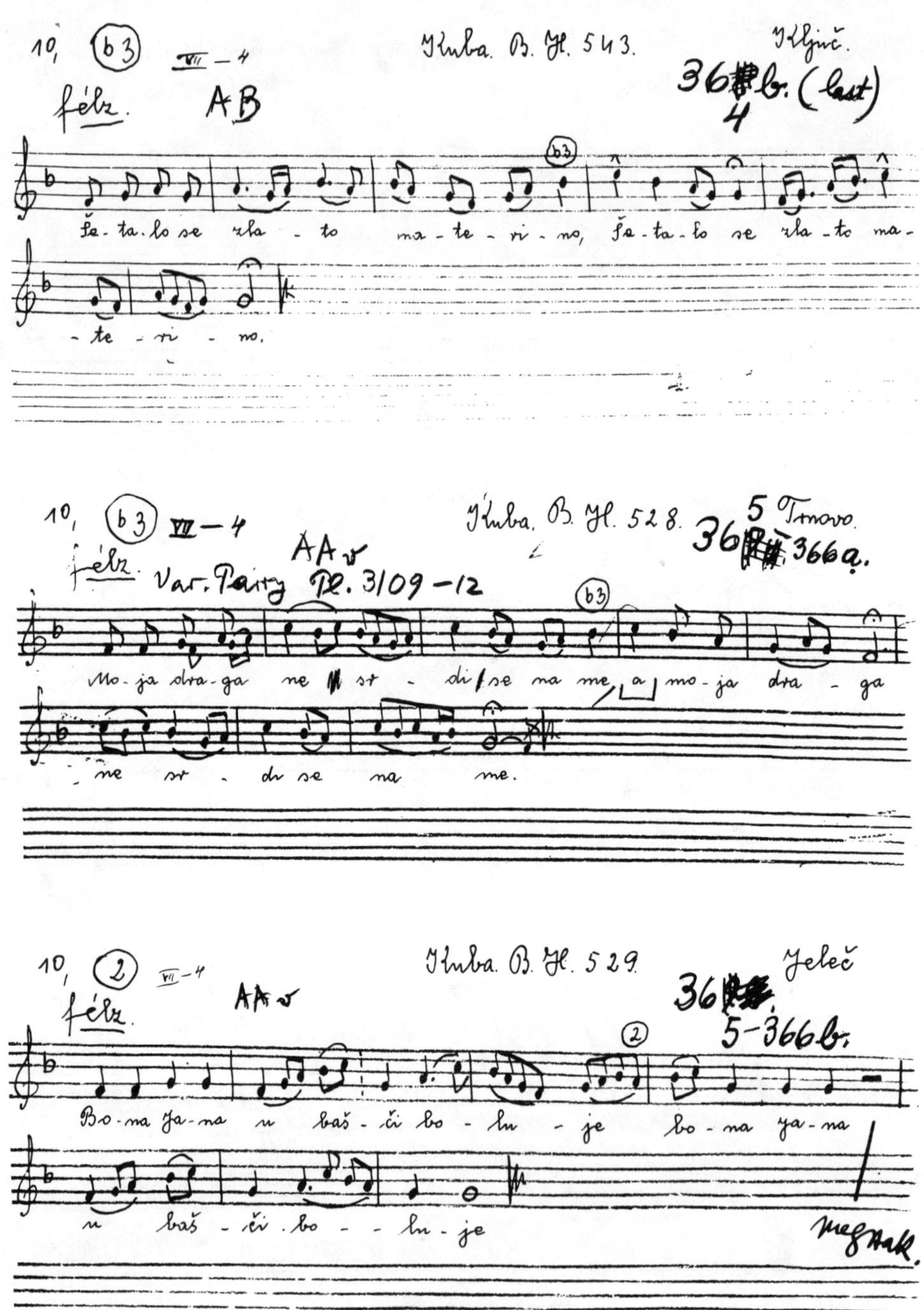
10, b3 VII — 4
félz. AB
36 b. (last)
Ša-ta-lo se zla - to ma - te - ri - no, ša-ta-lo se zla-to ma-
- te - ri - no.
10, b3 VII — 4
5 Trnovo.
félz. AA v
Mo-ja dra-ga ne st - di se na me, a mo-ja dra - ga
ne st - di se na me.
10, 2 VII — 4
Jeleč
félz. AA v
5-366b.
Bo-na Ja-na u baš - či bo - lu - je bo - na ja-na
u baš - čiv bo - - lu - je
megnak.

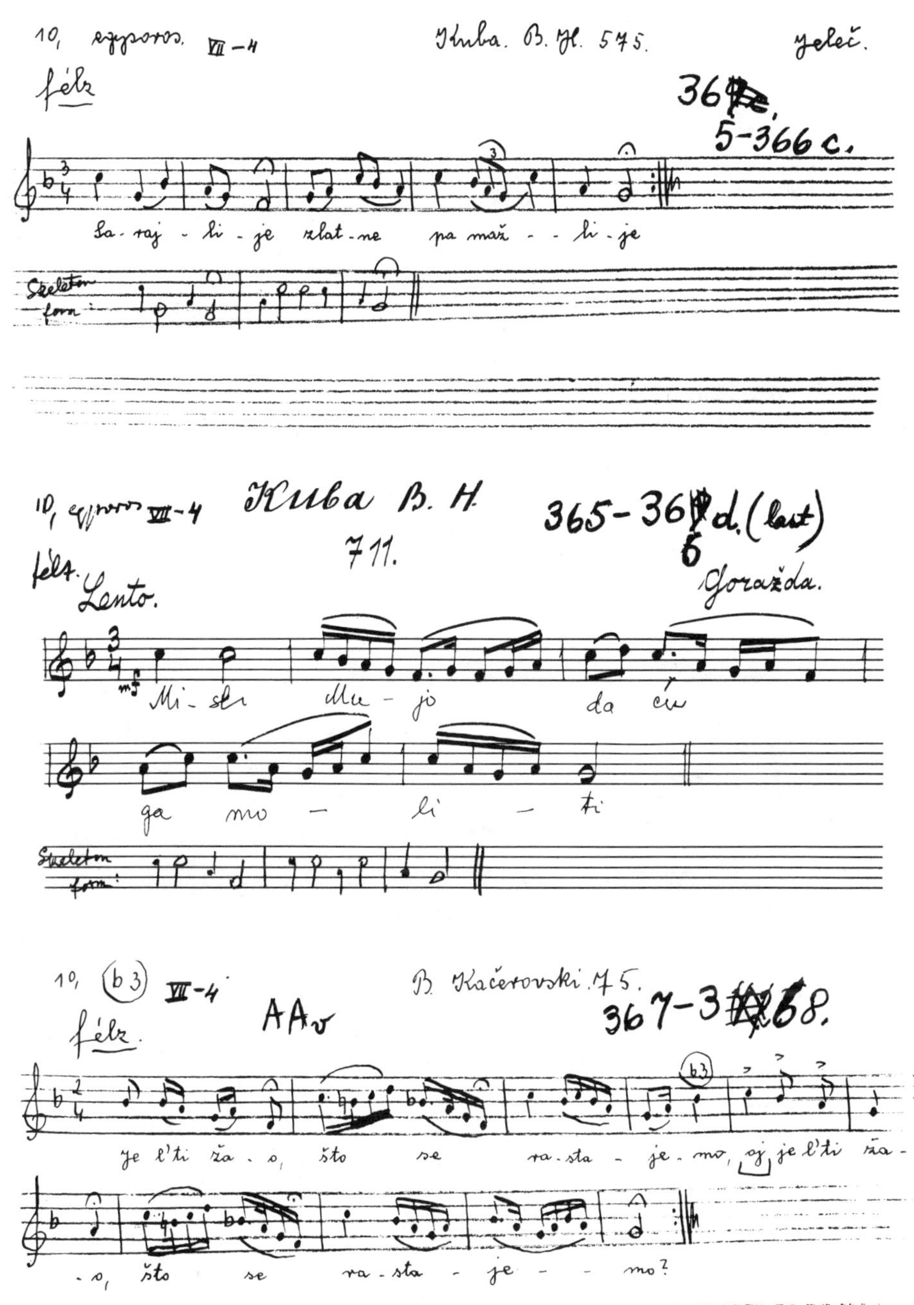
10, egysoros. VII – 4
Kuba. B. H. 575.
Jeleč.
félz
365-366 c.
Sa-raj-li-je zlat-ne pa maž-li-je
Skeleton form:
10, egysoros VII – 4
Kuba B. H. 711.
365-366 d. (last)
félz.
Lento.
Goražda.
Mi-sli Mu-jo da ću ga mo-li-ti
Skeleton form:
10, (b3) VII – 4
B. Kačerovski 75.
AAv
367-368.
félz.
Je l'ti ža-o, što se ra-sta-je-mo, oj je l'ti ža-o, što se ra-sta-je-mo?

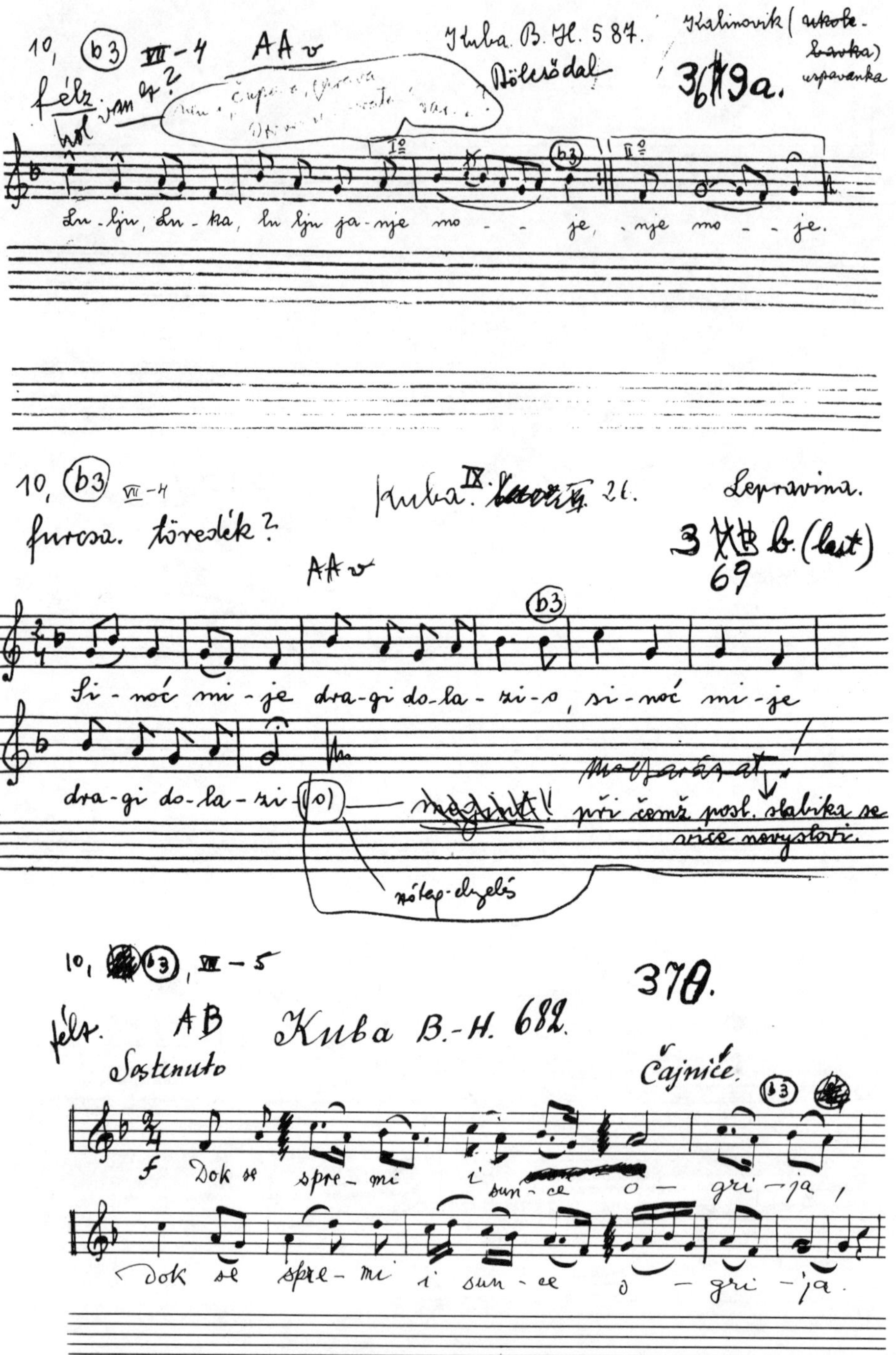
10, (b3) VII–4 AAv
Kuba B. H. 587.
Kalinovik
uspavanka
3679a.
Bölcsődal
Lu-lju, Lu-ka, lu lju ja-nje mo- - je, nje mo- - je.
10, (b3) VII–4
Kuba IX. 26.
Lepravina.
furcsa. töredék?
AAv
69
Si-noć mi-je dra-gi do-la-zi-o, si-noć mi-je
dra-gi do-la-zi-(o)
při čemž posl. slabika se více nevyslovi.
10, (b3), VII – 5
370.
félz.
AB
Kuba B.-H. 682.
Sostenuto
Čajniče.
Dok se spre-mi i sun-ce o-gri-ja,
Dok se spre-mi i sun-ce o-gri-ja.

10, (b3) VII – b6
tercelő
♩= 108.
AAsv
Kuhač 1431.
37/1.
Iz Slavonije.
(b3)
Maj-ka mo-ja o-že-ni me mla-da; maj-ka mo-ja o-že-ni me
mla-da.
10, (b3) VII – 7
phr.
AB
Kuhač B. H. 137.
Mostar.
37/2.
(b3)
L'je-pa ti je u A-la-ge ju-ba,
oj, l'je-po-te joj u svoj Bos-ni ne-ma.
Skeleton form:
Dj.: Pred. sb. 4 14.
Mozenica
fono 37/3.
AAv
1–b3, 10, (b3)
♩= 76
(b3)
Oj, de-vojko ta-na-na ko-nóplјo
oj, de-vojko ta-na-na ko-no-pljo

Dj.: Pred. srb. 363.
fonó
374.
Kulina
AAv
1-4, 10, b3
♩=100
b3
Gorom šeta mla- di Ra-di-vo- je,
félz.
gorom še-ta mladi Radi-vo- je.
Dj.: Pred. srb. 149.
fonóban
375.
Rasnica
AB
1-4, 10, b3
♩=84
b3
Niško po- lje rav-no za o- de- nje,
niš-ko polje rav-no za o- de- nje.
Dj.: Pred. srb. 71.
380a.
76
Leskovac.
AB
1-4, 10, b3
♪=126
félz.
b3
Oj, u-bava, uba-va de- vojko
oj, u-bava, u-ba-va de- vojko.

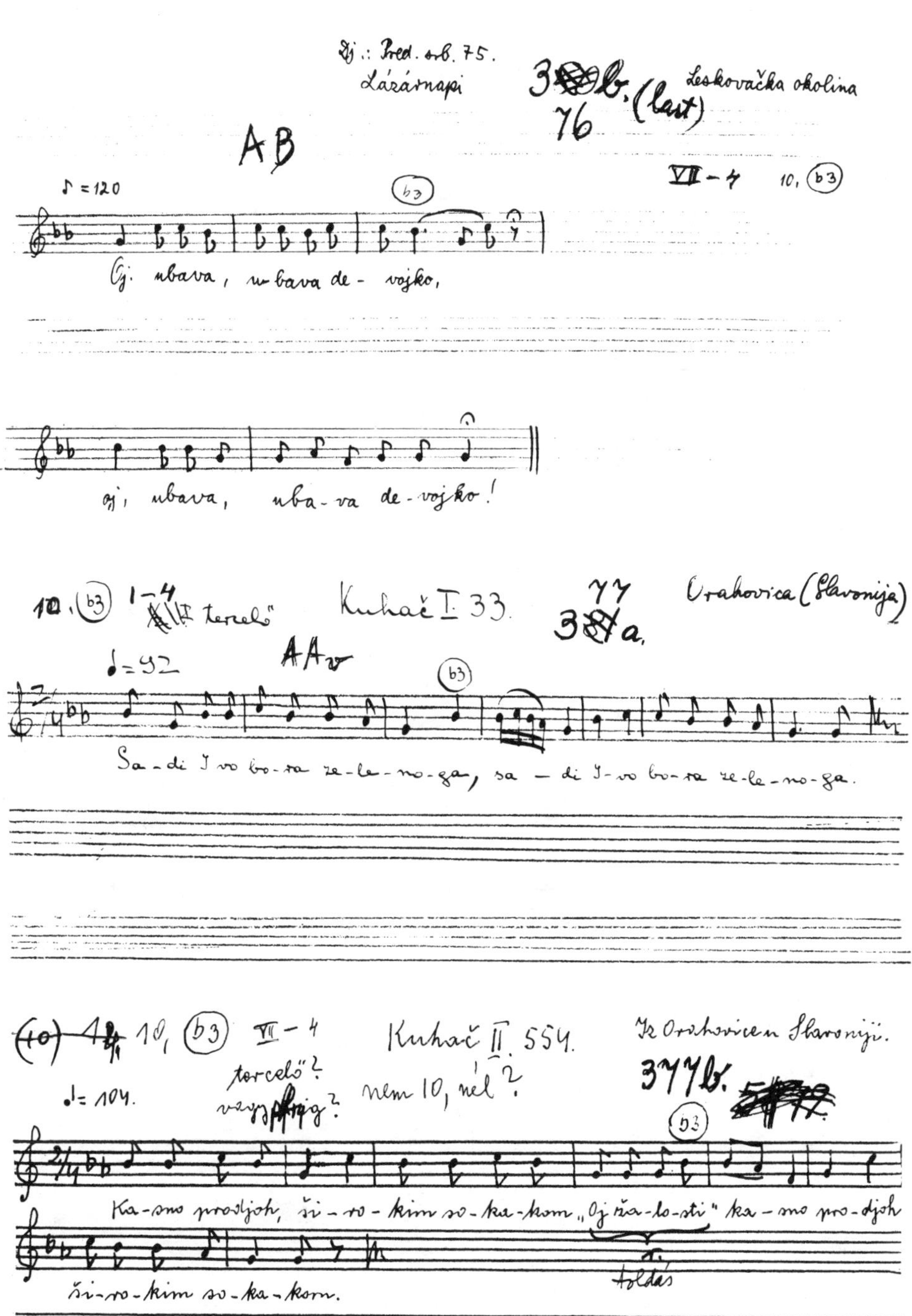

Lázárnapi
Leskovačka okolina
76
AB
VII – 4
10, b3
Oj, ubava, ubava de- vojko,
oj, ubava, uba-va de-vojko!
10, b3
Kuhač I. 33.
77
Orahovica (Slavonija)
Sa-di I-vo bo-ra ze-le-no-ga, sa-di I-vo bo-ra ze-le-no-ga.
10, b3
VII – 4
Kuhač II. 554.
Iz Orahovice u Slavoniji.
377b.
nem 10, vél?
Ka-sno prodjoh, ši-ro-kim so-ka-kom „Oj ža-lo-sti" ka-sno pro-djoh
ši-ro-kim so-ka-kom.
toldás

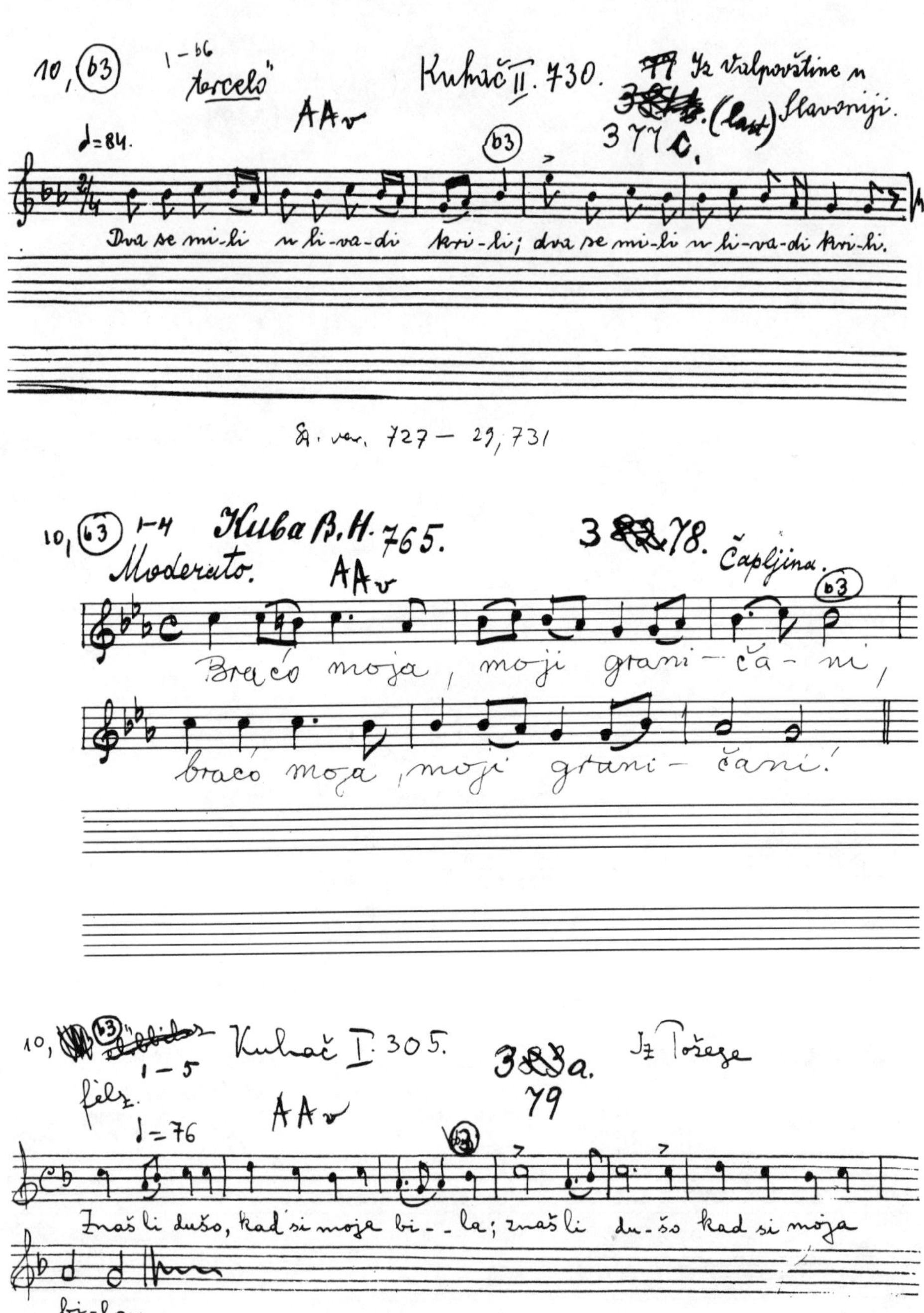
10, (b3) 1–b6 „terceló"
Kuhač II. 730.
Iz Valpovštine u Slavoniji.
AAv
377c.
♩=84.
Dva se mi-li u li-va-di kri-li; dva se mi-li u li-va-di kri-li.
727 — 29, 731
10, (b3) 1–4 Kuba B.H. 765.
378.
Čapljina.
Moderato.
AAv
Braćo moja, moji grani-ča-ni,
braćo moja, moji grani-čani!
10, (b3) Kuhač I. 305.
379a.
Iz Požege
1–5
AAv
♩=76
Znaš li dušo, kad si moja bi-la; znaš li du-šo kad si moja
bi-la.

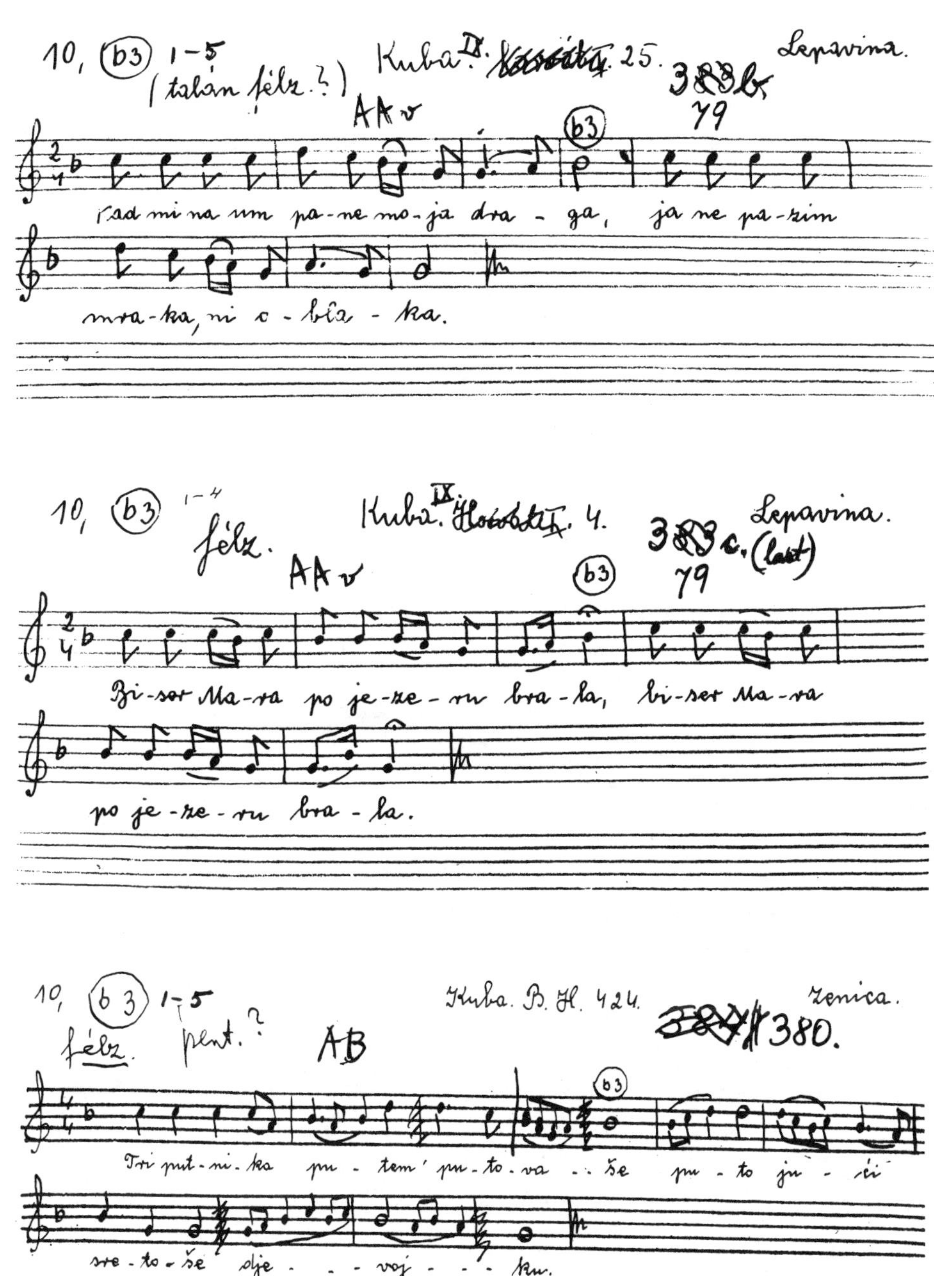
10, (b3) 1–5
(talán félz.?)
Kuba IX. 25.
Lepavina.
79
AA v
(b3)
Rad mi na um pa-ne mo-ja dra-ga, ja ne pa-zim
mra-ka, ni o-bla-ka.
10, (b3) 1–4
félz.
Kuba IX. 4.
Lepavina.
79
AA v
(b3)
Bi-ser Ma-ra po je-ze-ru bra-la, bi-ser Ma-ra
po je-ze-ru bra-la.
10, (b3) 1–5
félz. pent.?
AB
Kuba. B. H. 424.
Zenica.
380.
(b3)
Tri put-ni-ka pu-tem pu-to-va-še pu-to ju-ći
sve-to-še dje-voj-ku.

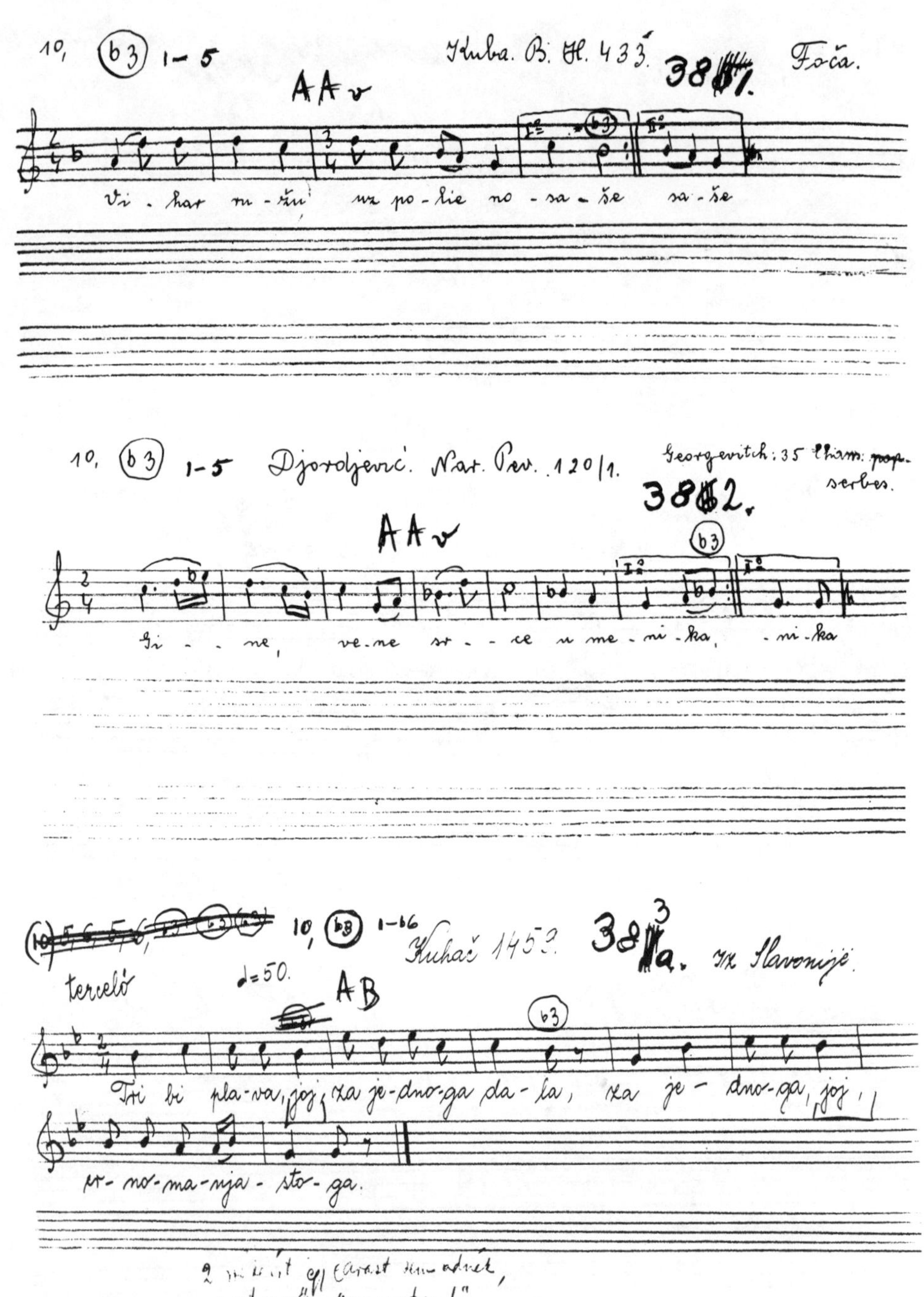
10, (b3) 1–5
Kuba. B. H. 433.
Foča.
AA v
10, (b3) 1–5
Djordjević. Nar. Pev. 120/1.
Georgevitch: 35 Cham. pop. serbes.
AA v
Kuhač 1453
iz Slavonije.
tercelő
AB

10 (b3) 1–♭♭ tercelő. Kuba X. 54. Trogir
AB
Dívčí sbor
(b3)
383 b. (last)
Na-re-sla je tra-va dja-te-li-na. Na-re-sla je
tra-va dja-te-li-na.
10, ③ VII–5 Kuba. BH. 1108. Banjaluka.
AB
Parry var. *
384a.
Grave
gorom jez-di budimski baš-la-ga,
a sa svojom ljubom džuzel U-mi-ha-nom.
* Pl. 3225/3180/3052/3079/3163.
(10) 10, (b3) VII–5 Kuba. B. H. 111. Prozor.
félz.
AB
Putnička.
(b3) 384 b.
Aj žarko sun-ce na vi-so-ku ti si
aj žarko sun-ce, na vi-so-ku, ti si hi hi.
hihi!
Aj
Aj

Kuba B.H.
Andante
Prozor (Uspavanka)
384 c.
Adagio
Kuba. B.H. 1013.
384 d.
Skeleton form:
Kuba. B.H. 173.
Nevesinje.

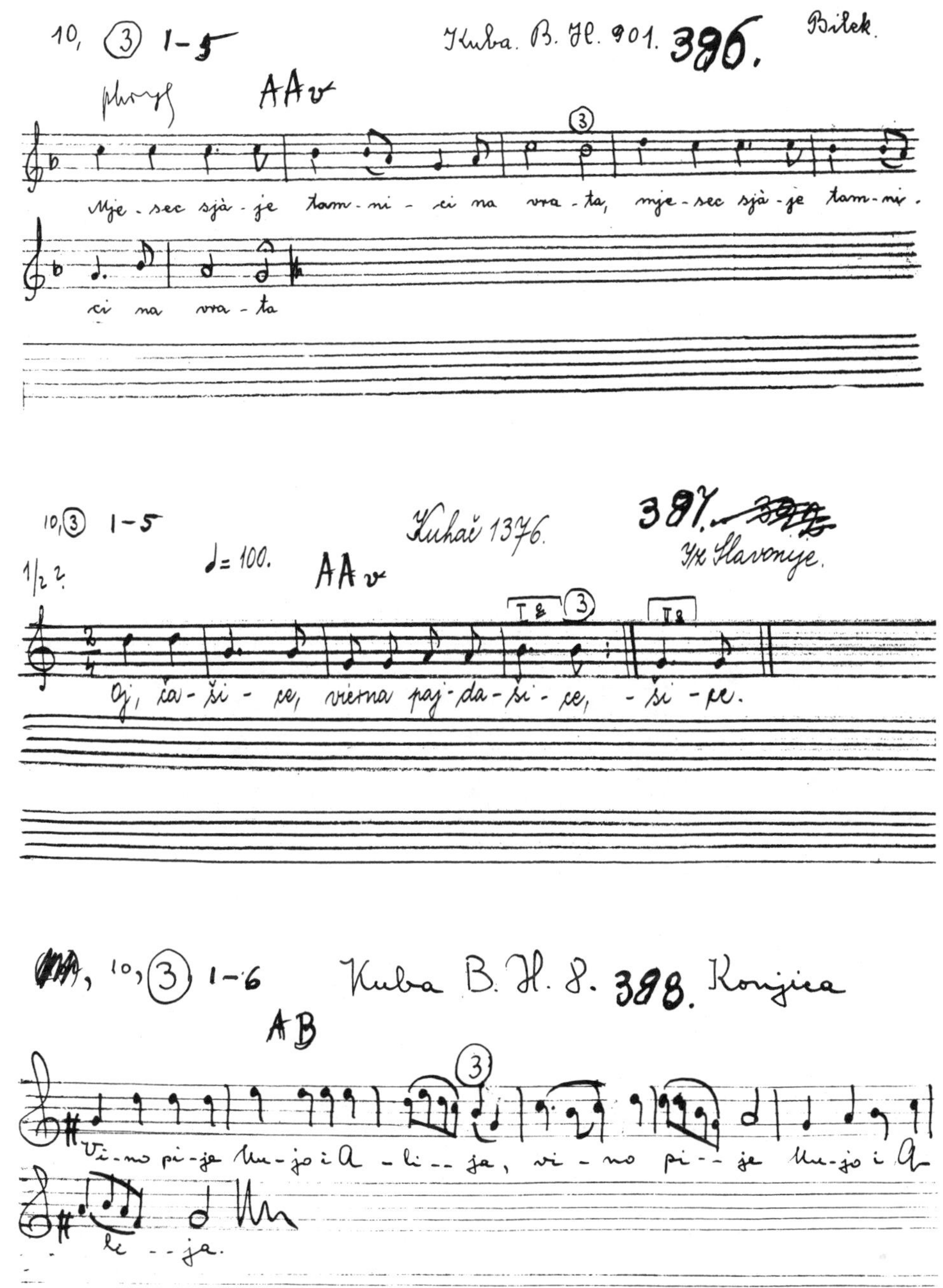
10, ③ 1–5
Kuba. B. H. 901. 386.
Bilek.
AAv
Mje - sec sjà - je tam - ni - ci na vra - ta, mje - sec sjà - je tam - ni -
ci na vra - ta
10, ③ 1–5
Kuhač 1376.
387.
Iz Slavonije.
♩= 100.
AAv
Oj, ćaj - ši - ce, vierna paj - da - ši - ce, - ši - ce.
10, ③ 1–6
Kuba B. H. 8. 388. Konjica
AB
Vi - no pi - je Mu - jo i A - li - - ja, vi - no pi - - je Mu - jo i A -
li - - ja.

J=92.
Kuhač 1435
389.
Iz Hercegovine.
U Mo- sta- ru na no-vom pa-za-ru, u Mo- sta-ru
na no-vom pa-za-ru.
Kuba. B. H. 577.
390a.
Doboj.
Haj-de Ma-ro da ču-va-mo ov-ce haj-de Ma-ro da
ču-va-mo ov-ce.
Kuba. B. H. 565.
390b.
Foča.
Ža-los-no mi na pro-zor-ju cvje-će, ža-los-no mi
na pro-zor-ju cvje-će.

10, (4) VII–4 tipus
félz.
var? hol?
♩= 60.
Kuhač 1518.
390c.
Iz Kamenice u Bosni.
AA
Oj! da je te- - - - bi po-slu-ša-ti po-bre, što go-vo-re
Tur-ci kra-jiš- ni-ci.
(betyárnóta?)
10, (4) VII–4
♩= 132.
Kuhač III. 1092.
390d.
Iz Jaske.
(Hrvatska)
AB
Da sam ma-la ko ze-le-na tra-va, ja bi zna-la, gdje bi ja sta-
ja-la;
10, (4) VII–4
Djordjević. Nar. Pev. 151/2.
Mokranjac: Druga Rukovet.
félz.
var. Kuh 703.
AA
391a.
Smilj smi-lja-na po-kraj vo-de bra-la, smilj smi-
-lja-na po-kraj vo-de bra-la

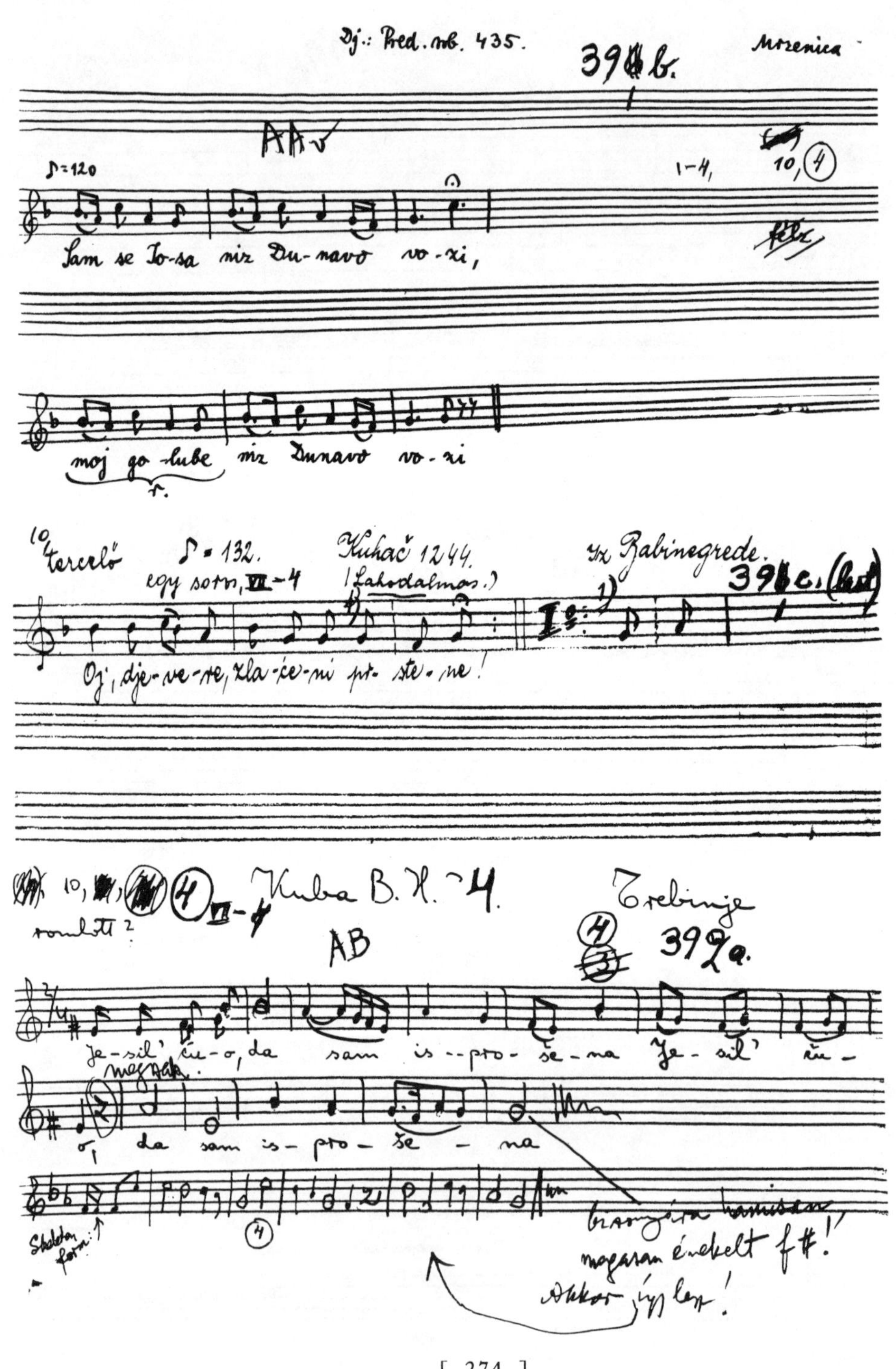

Dj.: Pred. nb. 435.
39a b.
Mrzenica
AA v
♪=120
1–4,
10, (4)
Sam se Jo-sa niz Du-navo vo-xi,
moj go-lube niz Dunavo vo-xi
10 tercelő
♪=132.
Kuhač 1244.
Iz Babinegrede.
egy sorv, VII–4
(Lakodalmas.)
39b c.
Oj, dje-ve-re, zla-će-ni pr-ste-ne!
10,
(4)
VII–4
Kuba B. H. ~4.
Trebinje
AB
(4)
392 a.
Je-sil' ću-o, da sam is-pro-še-na Je-sil' ću-
o, da sam is-pro-še-na
(4)
Akkor így lesz!

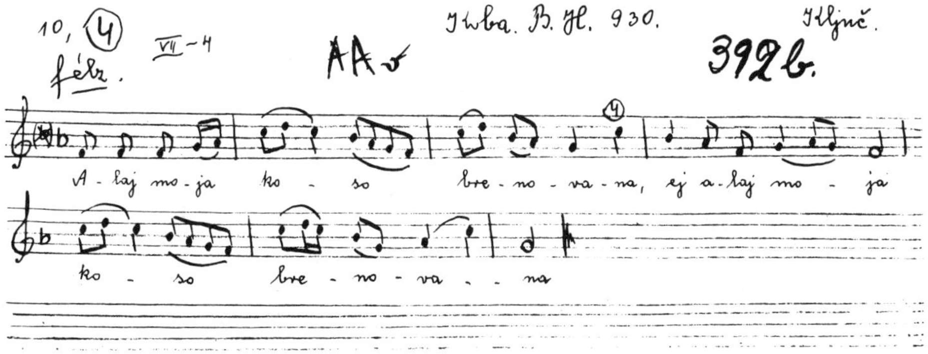

10, (4) VII-4
félz.
AA v
Kuba. B. H. 930.
Iljuč.
392b.
A-laj mo-ja ko-so bre-no-va-na, ej a-laj mo-ja
ko-so bre-no-va-na

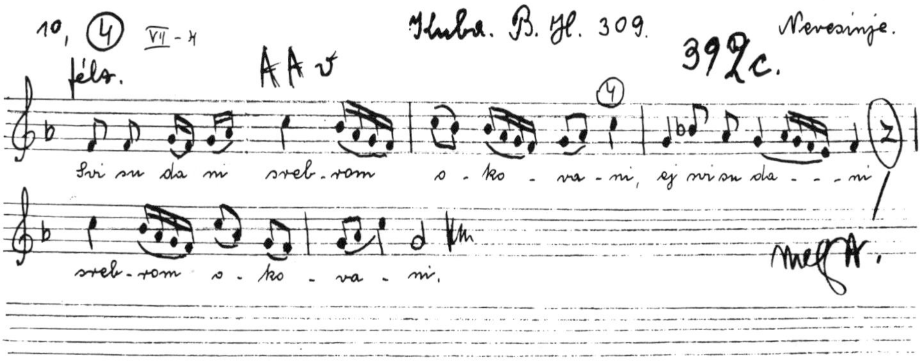

10, (4) VII-4
félz.
AA v
Kuba. B. H. 309.
Nevesinje.
392c.
Svi su da mi sreb-rom o-ko-va-ni, ej svi su da-mi
sreb-rom o-ko-va-ni.

10, (4) VII-4
Kuba. B. H. 599.
Trebinja.
AB
392d. (last)
Vjetar puh-nu o-zgor sa gor-nja-ka, vje-tar puh-nu
o-zgor sa gor-nja-ka.

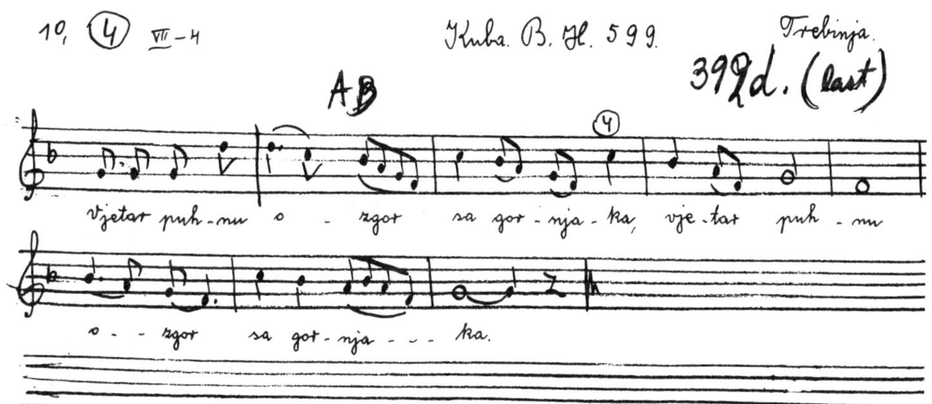

Kuhač 1263.
Iz Zemuna.
(Lakodalmas.)
Od le-gla je po-pa-di-ja, ra-no; od-le-gla je
po-pa-di-ja, ra-a-a-no i-hi-hi-hi, ra-no.
Kuba B.-H. 434
Allegretto
St. Majdan
Men se moja ne-vjè-ruje dra-ga
men se moja ne-vjè-re-je dra-ga.
Kuba B.H. 671.
Allegro
Krupa.
Gorom jašu ki-će-ni svatovi, ej, gorom ja-šu ki-
će ni sva-to-vi.

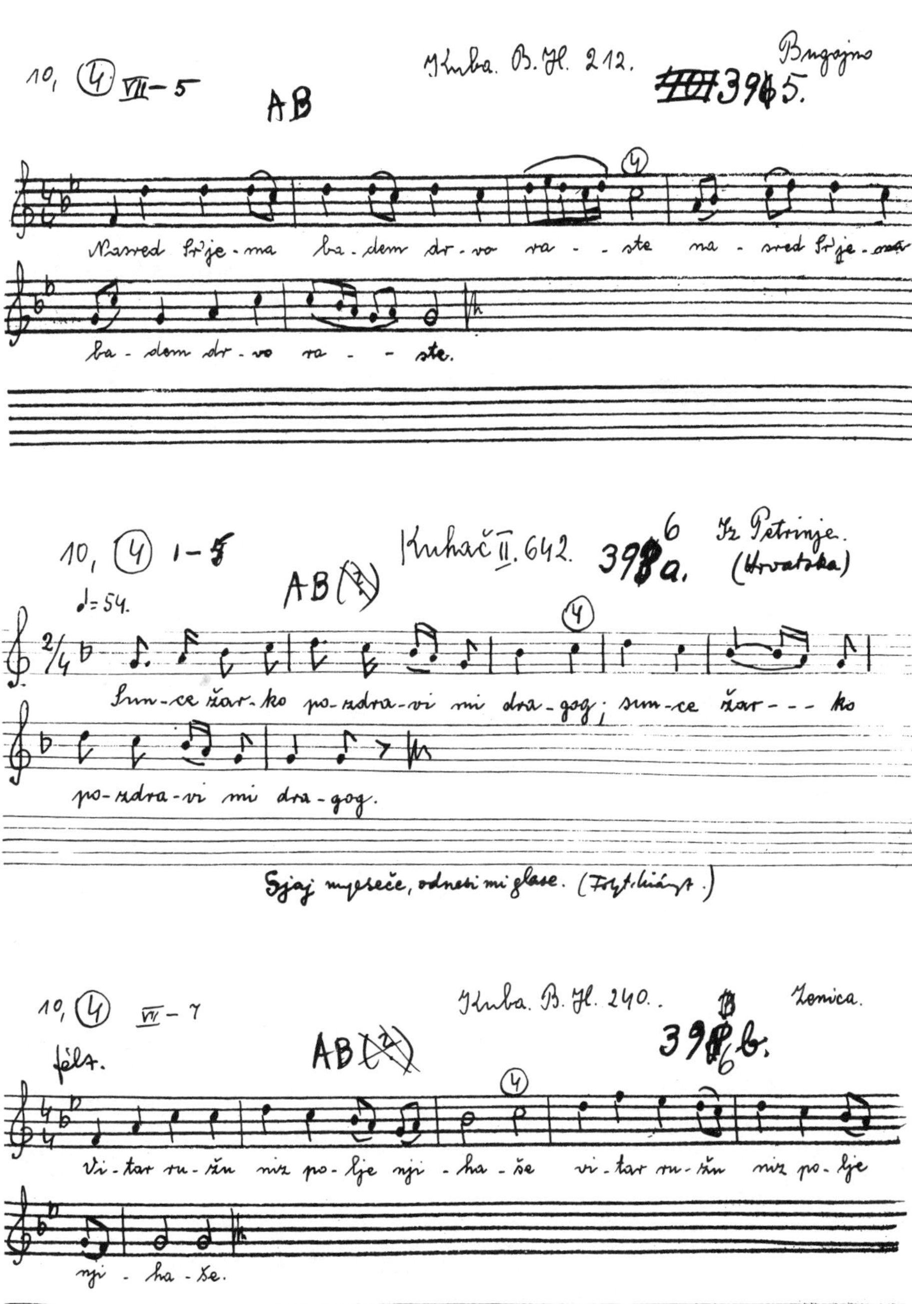
10, (4) VII–5
Kuba. B. H. 212.
3965.
Bugojno
AB
Nasred Srije-ma ba-dem dr-vo ra- - -ste na-sred Srije-ma
ba-dem dr-vo ra- - -ste.
10, (4) 1–5
Kuhač II. 642.
3966a.
Iz Petrinje. (Hrvatska)
AB
♩= 54.
Sun-ce žar-ko po-zdra-vi mi dra-gog; sun-ce žar- - -ko
po-zdra-vi mi dra-gog.
Sjaj mjeseče, odnesi mi glase.
10, (4) VI–7
Kuba. B. H. 240.
Zenica.
3966b.
AB
Vi-tar ru-žin niz po-lje nji-ha-še vi-tar ru-žin niz po-lje
nji-ha-še.

10, ④ 1-7 félz.
Kuba XII/33.
Kragujevac.
39 c. (laut)
AB
④
Bi - stra vo - - do, moj la - djan stu - den - - če, ej, bi - stra
ej bi - stra vo - do, moj la - djan stu - den - če!
10, ④ 1—5
Kuhač 1492.
397.
♩= 80
AB
Iz Boke kotorske. (Boka)
(uz gusle) *
④
Mi - li Bo - že ču - da ve - li - ko - - ga; mi - li
Bo - že - - ču - da ve - li - ko - ga.
Kuba. B. H. 296.
Bänjaluka
397 bis.
előbbihez
10, ⑤ VII — 7
AB
⑤
O Trav - ni - če ma - li la - ri - gra - - - du! Aj!
O Trav - ni - če ma - li la - ri - gra - - - du.

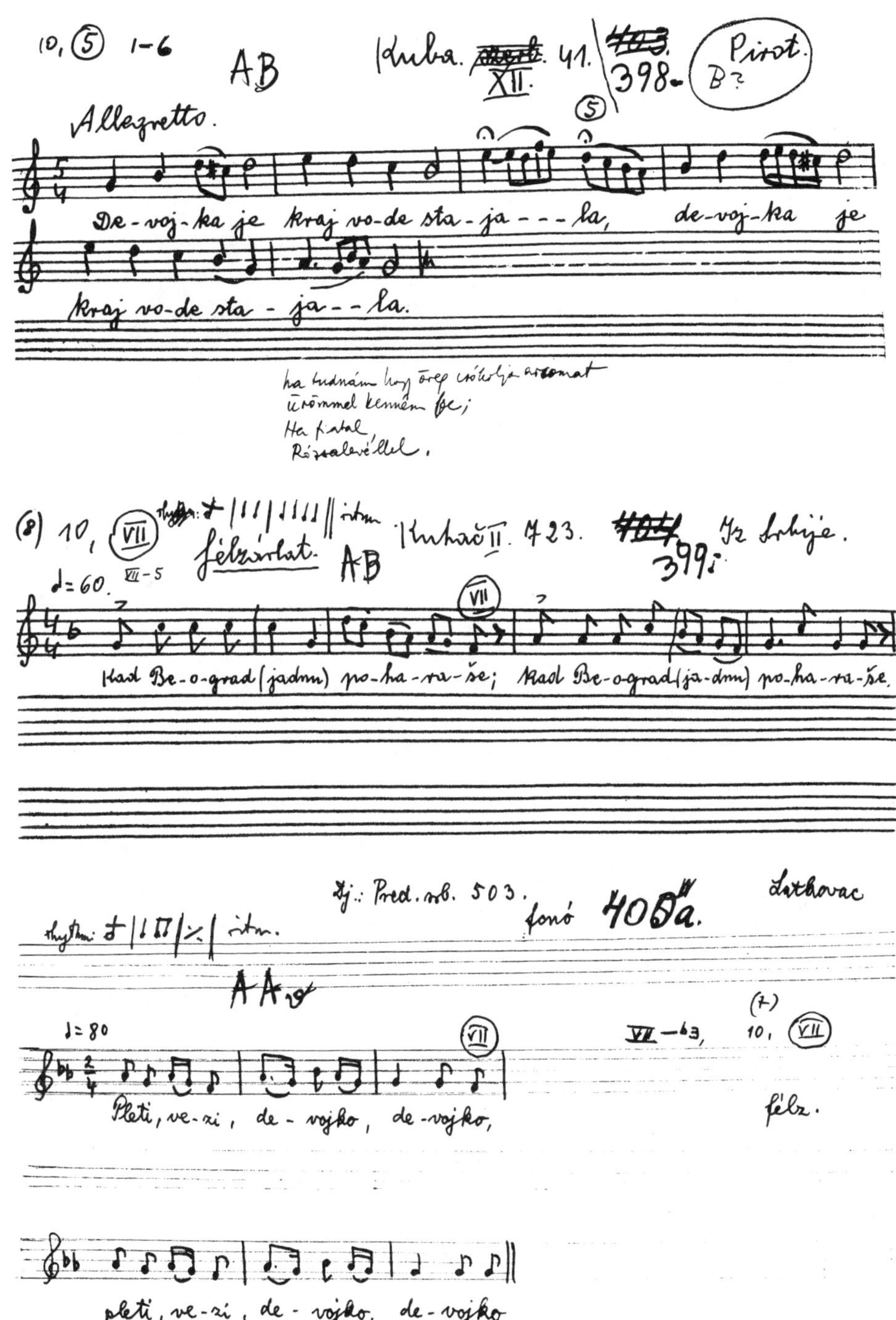
10, 5 1-6
AB
Kuba. XII. 41.
398.
Pirot. B?
Allegretto.
De-voj-ka je kraj vo-de sta-ja---la, de-voj-ka je
kraj vo-de sta-ja--la.
(8) 10, VII
félzárlat.
AB
Kuhač II. 723.
399.
Iz Srbije.
♩=60. VII-5
Kad Be-o-grad (jadnu) po-ha-ra-še; Kad Be-o-grad (ja-dnu) po-ha-ra-še.
Zj.: Pred. zb. 503.
fonó 405a.
AA
♩=80
VII
Pleti, ve-zi, de-vojko, de-vojko,
(7) 10, VII
félz.
pleti, ve-zi, de-vojko, de-vojko

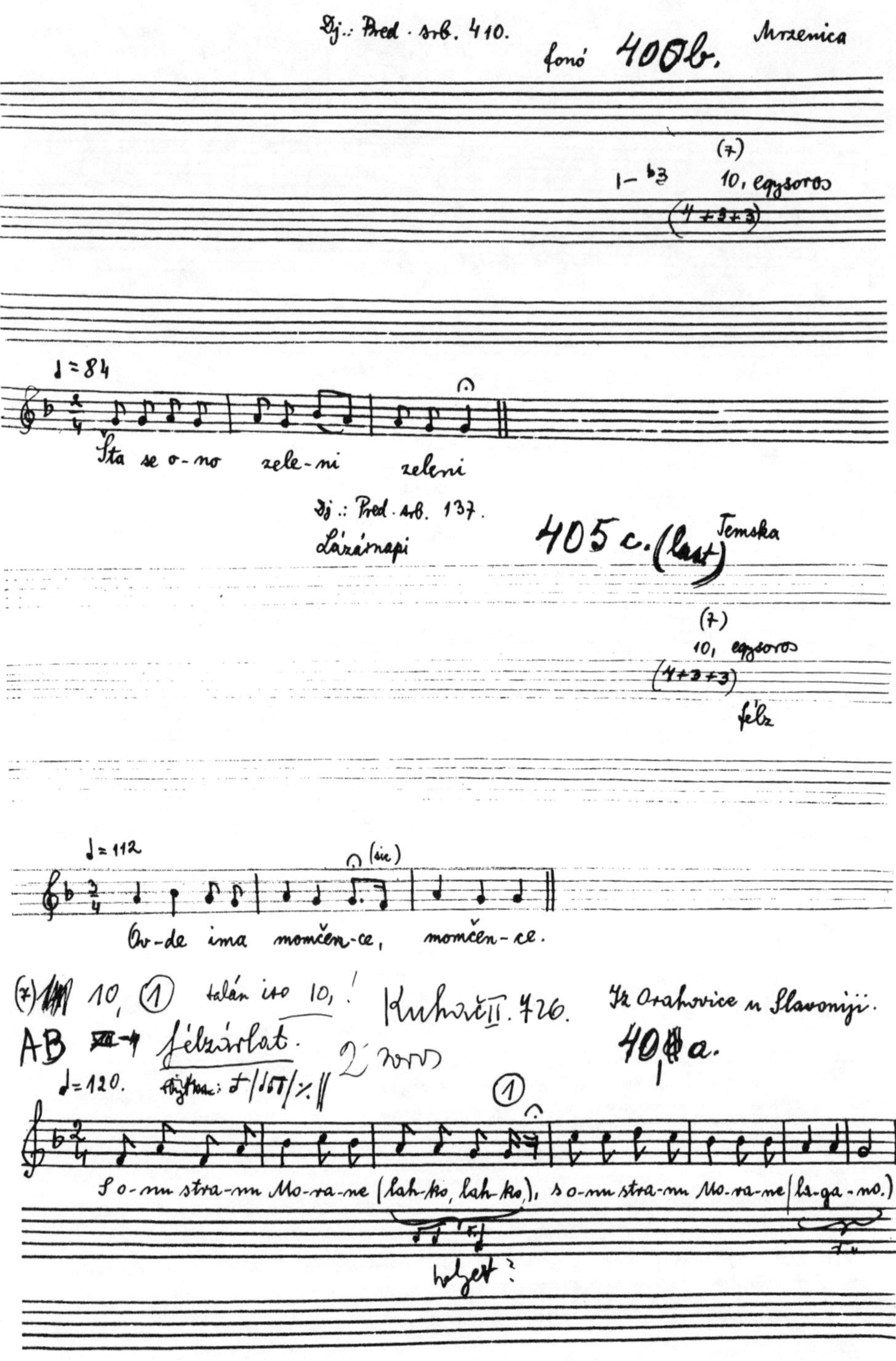
Dj.: Pred. srb. 410.
fonó 400b.
Mrzenica
(7)
10, egysoros
(4+3+3)
♩= 84
Šta se o-no zele-ni zeleni
Dj.: Pred. srb. 137.
Lázárnapi
405 c. (last)
Temska
(7)
10, egysoros
(4+3+3)
♩= 112
(sic)
Ov-de ima momčen-ce, momčen-ce.
(7) 10, ① talán iso 10, !
Kuhač II. 726.
Iz Orahovice u Slavoniji.
AB
félzárlat.
401a.
♩= 120.
①
So-nu stra-nu Mo-ra-ne (lah-ko, lah-ko), so-nu stra-nu Mo-ra-ne (la-ga-no.)
helyett?

(7) 10, (4+3+3) egyetlen sor.
4+3+3
Kuhač II. 579.
Iz lme gore. *
401b. (last)
Oj ja-vo-re, ja-vo-re, ja-vo-re.
* Kuhač
Dj.: Pred. srb. 210.
tánc
402a. Strelac
AB
1-4
10, 1
Te-če re-ka, tedeno, tedeno
te-če re-ka, le-de-no, ledeno
Dj.: Pred. srb. 231.
tánc
Crvena Jabuka
AB
402b.
(7)
10, 1
Po-tam, povam Sto-jane, Stojane,
po-tam, povam, Stojane, Stojane

Đj.: Pred. srb. 474. **402c.** Aleksandrovac

AB

№ 231-hez.

♩= 104

1–4 (7) 10, ①

Garvan grok-će na je-li, na je-li

pi-taj te ga šta ve-li, šta ve-li

Dj.: Pred. srb. 340. **402d.** Aleksinac

Gyermekjáték

1–4, (7) 10, egysoros

félz. ?

♩= 112

Oj, ja-vo-re, ja-vore, ja-vo-re!

Dj.: Pred. srb. 518. Adrani

Jeremiás előestéjén.

402e. (last) a következőhöz

♩= 112

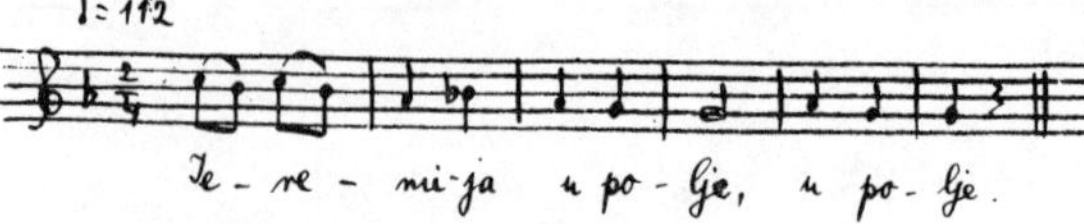

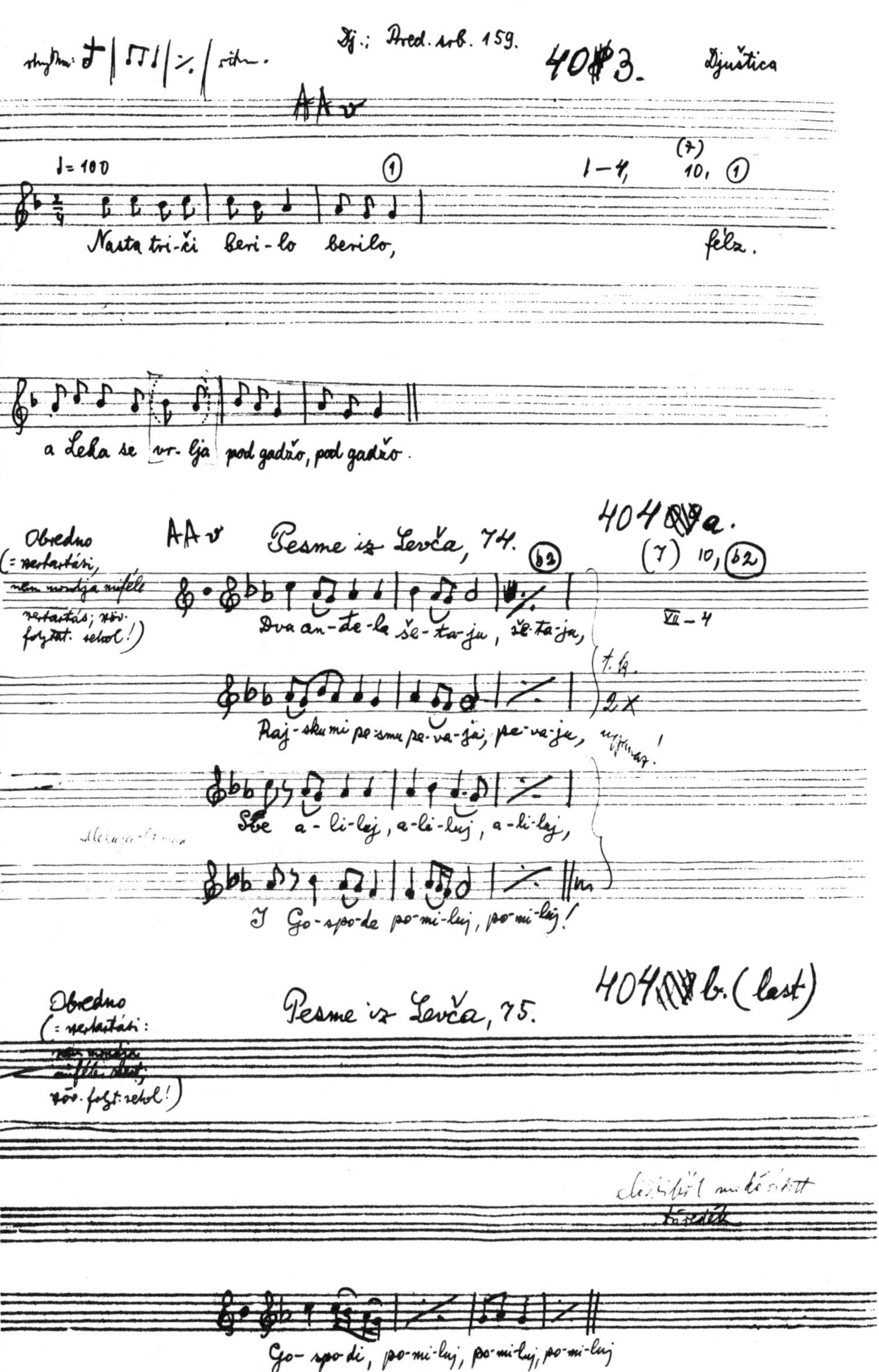

Dj.: Pred. sob. 159.
4083.
Djuštica
AA v
♩= 100
1–4,
10,
Nasta tri-či beri-lo berilo,
félz.
a Leka se vr- lja pod gadžo, pod gadžo.
404a.
Obredno
AA v
Pesme iz Levča, 74.
10,
Dva an-đe-la še-ta-ju, še-ta-ju,
Raj-sku mi pe-smu pe-va-ju, pe-va-ju,
2x
Sve a-li-luj, a-li-luj, a-li-luj,
I Go-spo-de po-mi-luj, po-mi-luj!
404b. (last)
Obredno
Pesme iz Levča, 75.
Go- spo di, po-mi-luj, po-mi-luj, po-mi-luj

(7)10, (b3) bVI–4
tercelő.
fél 2. AB
Kuhač II. 738.
4105.
Iz Risna.
(Arbanija)
Momčič i-de stran-či-com, strančicom, za-ki-ćen je gran-čicom,
gran-či-com.
AB
(7) 10, (4)
Kuhač II. 766.
Iz Miholjanaca u Kopriv podžupaniji.
4106. (Hrvatska)
emlékeztet.
1/2.
félre
Kaj se s-no ze-le-ni, ze-le-ni pod dra-gi-nih pon-dže-ri, pon-dže-ri.
Dj.: Pred. sob. 505.
Latkovac
AA
Baba tikve pro-da-vala, tandara trup
féla.
helyett
baba tikve prodava-la tandara truptruptrup

Dj.: Pred. srb. 405.
fonó
♩=104
Po-ra-ni-la tanka I-va, zorole, zoro
po-ra-ni-la tanka I-va, aj, zoro-le!
Kuhač II. 505.
Iz sriemskog Karlovca.
408.
Je si l' bi-o ta-mo go-re u dvo-ru, je si l' čuo šta o me-ni go-vo-ru.
Djordj. Nar. Pev. 191/2
Georgevitch: 35
Chans. pop. serbes.
409.
Šta se ču-je i-za gra-da, dju-do, dju-do, ej!
šta se ču-je i-za gra-da, mo-re, dju-di-jo?

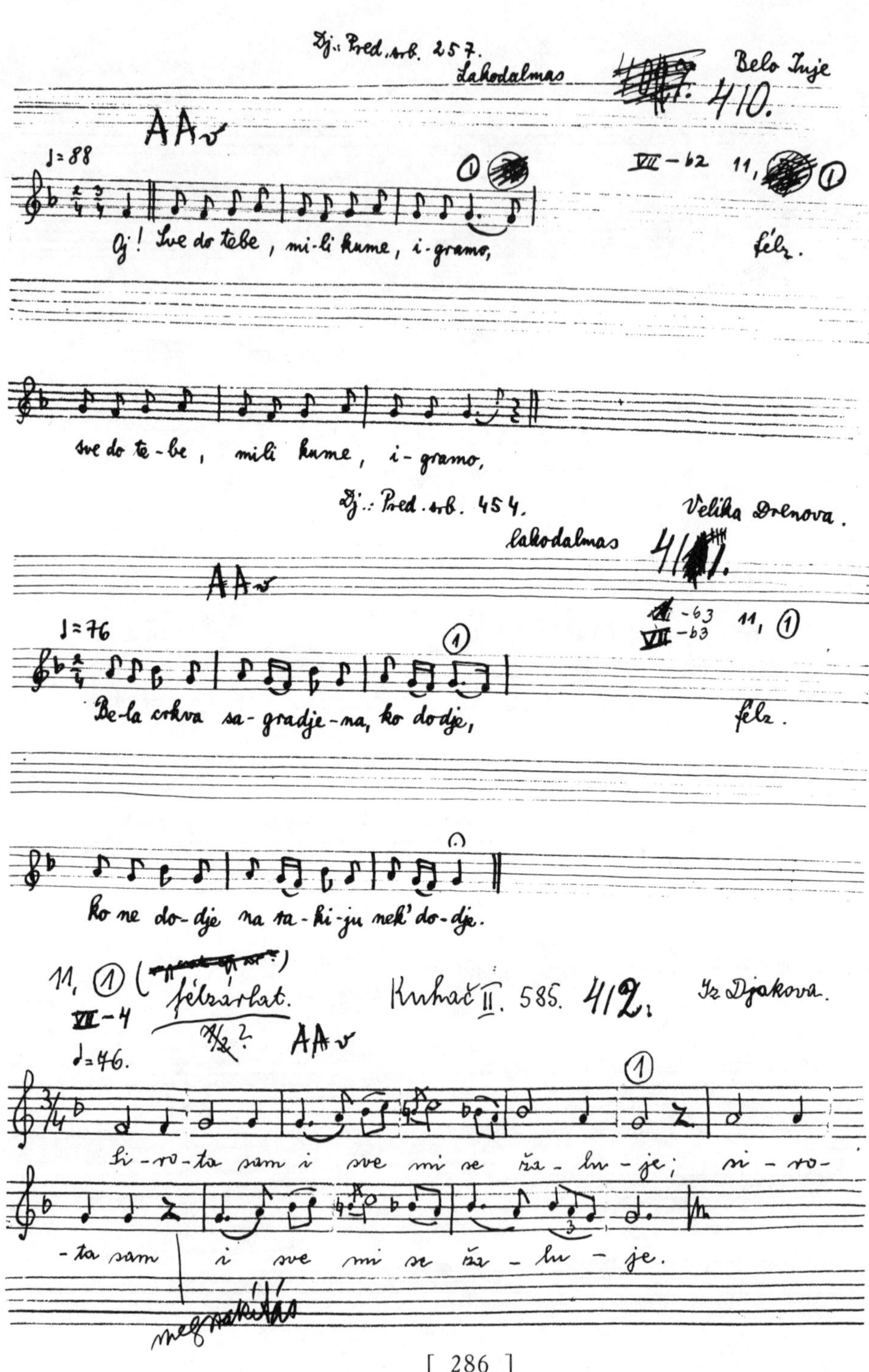

Dj.: Pred. srb. 257.
Lakodalmas
410.
AA
♩= 88
VII – b2 11, ①
Oj! Sve do tebe, mi-li kume, i-gramo,
félz.
sve do te-be, mili kume, i-gramo,
Dj.: Pred. srb. 454.
Velika Drenova.
Lakodalmas
411.
AA
♩= 76
VII – b3 11, ①
Be-la crkva sa-gradje-na, ko dodje,
félz.
Ko ne do-dje na ta-ki-ju nek' do-dje.
11, ① (
félzárlat.
VII – 4
Kuhač II. 585.
412.
Iz Djakova.
AA
♩= 46.
Si-ro-ta sam i sve mi se ža-lu-je; si-ro-
-ta sam i sve mi se ža-lu-je.

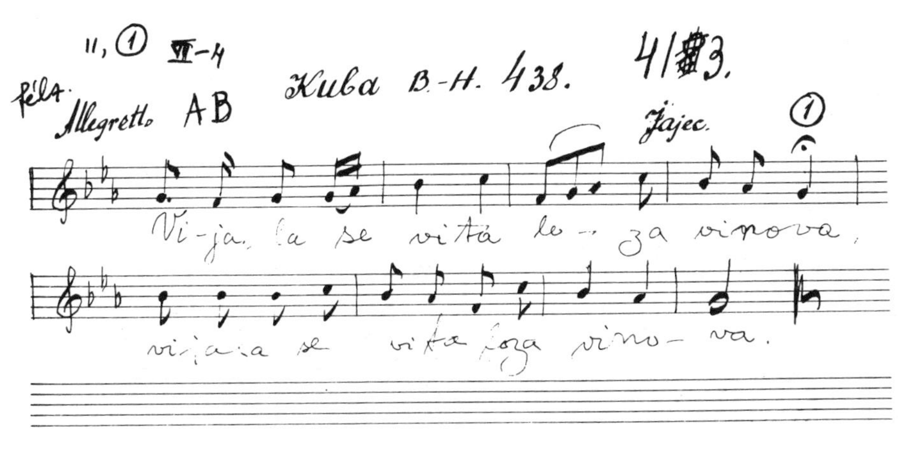

11, ① VII–4
Kuba B.-H. 438.
413.
félA.
Allegretto AB
Jajec.
①
Vi-ja-la se vita lo-za vinova,
vi-ja-la se vita loza vino-va.

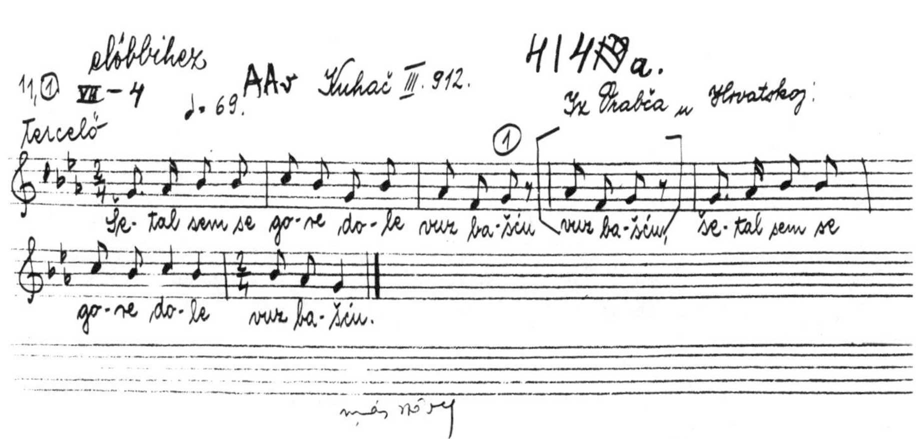

előbbihez
414a.
11, ① VII–4
♩= 69.
AAv Kuhač III. 912.
Iz Prabča u Hrvatskoj.
Tercelő
①
Še-tal sem se go-re do-le vuz ba-šču vuz ba-šču, še-tal sem se
go-re do-le vuz ba-šču.
más nővel

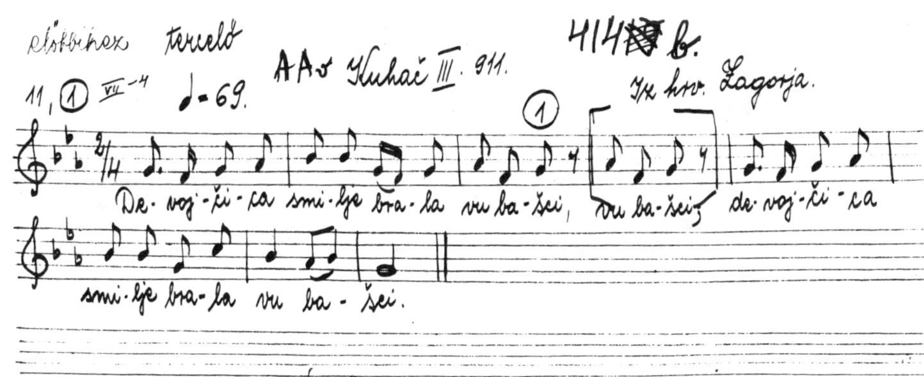

előbbihez tercelő
414b.
AAv Kuhač III. 911.
11, ① VII–4
♩= 69.
Iz hrv. Zagorja.
①
De-voj-či-ca smi-lje bra-la vu ba-šči, vu ba-šči, de-voj-či-ca
smi-lje bra-la vu ba-šči.
más nővel

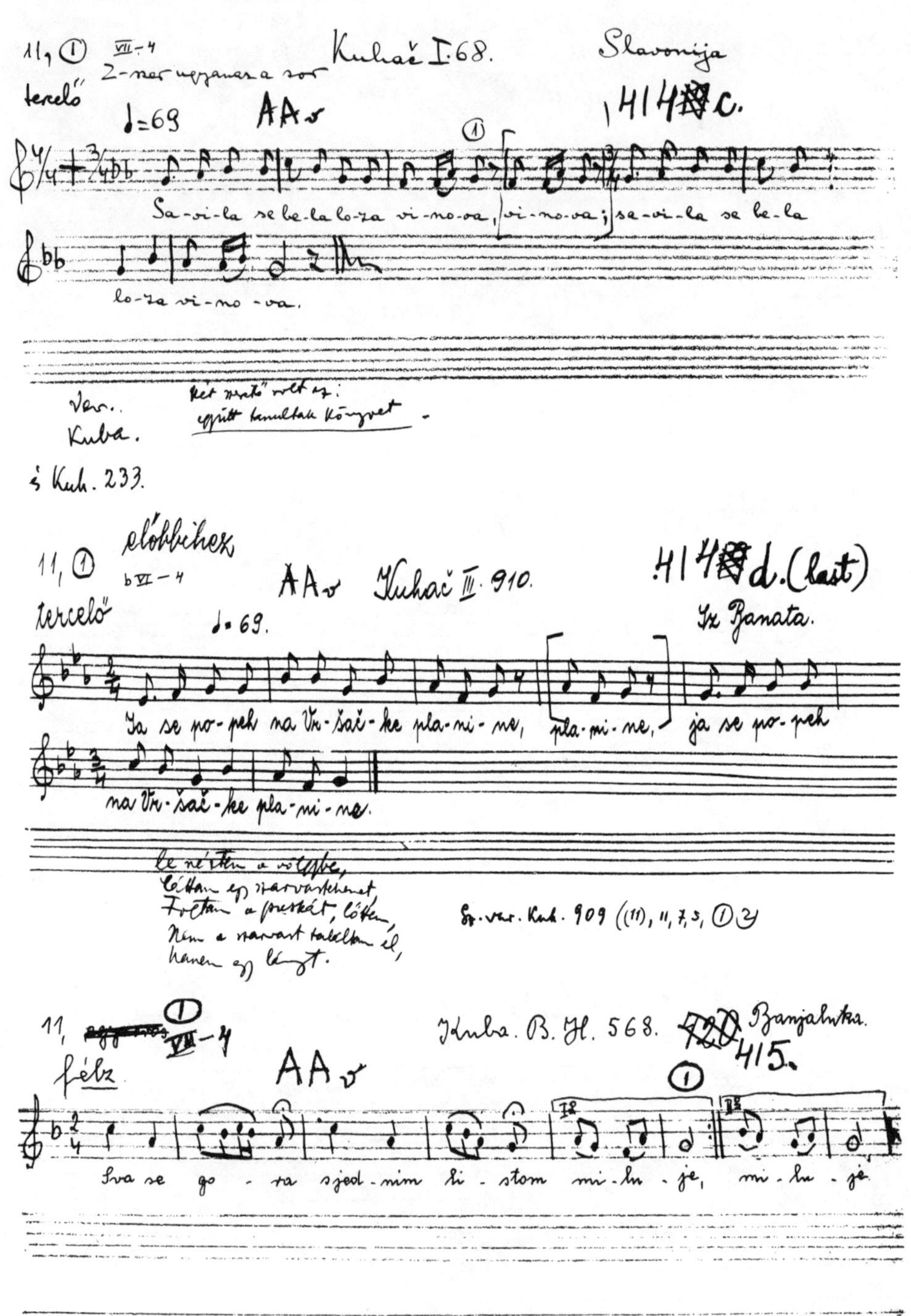

Kuhač I. 68.
Slavonija
terelő
♩=69
AA
414 c.
Sa-vi-la se be-la lo-za vi-no-va, vi-no-va; sa-vi-la se be-la
lo-za vi-no-va.
Kuba.
előbbihez
terelő
AA
Kuhač III. 910.
Iz Banata.
♩=69.
Ja se po-peh na Vr-šač-ke pla-mi-ne, pla-mi-ne, ja se po-peh
na Vr-šač-ke pla-mi-ne.
Kuba. B. H. 568.
Banjaluka.
415.
AA
Sva se go-ra sjed-nim li-stom mi-lu-je, mi-lu-je.

Kuba. B. H. 322.
4416. Čajniče.
Po-le-ti - la dva bi-je-la go-lu - - - ba pa su pa - la
na dva bo - - ra ze - le - - na,
Andante Kuba B. H. 813.
4417. Jeleč.
Po-le-će-la dva bi-je-la goluba,
po - le-će-la dva bi-je-la goluba
Dj.: Pred. sb. 181.
4418. Babin Kal.
♩=84
Cavti bo-žur na plani-na, Le-po-le
ot-ki-ni ga, miri-ši ga Dragole
Var. Parry No 14.
Cf. 592, 679.

Kuba B.H. 764. AA
419.
Glamoč.
Moderato.
Sva se go – ra jednim
lis – tom milu – je ; sva se
go – ra jed nim lis – tom milu je

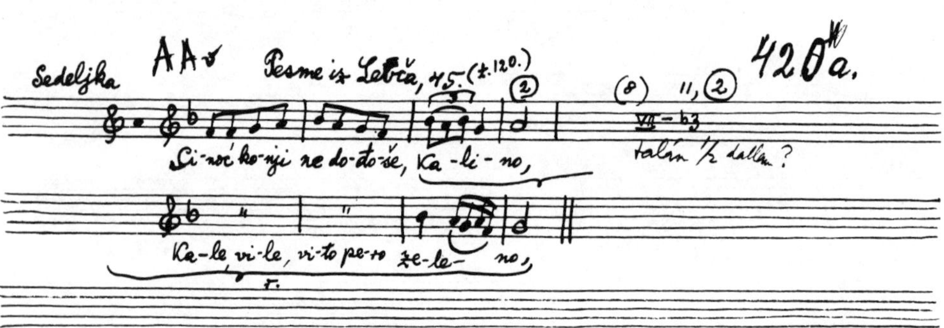
Sedeljka
AA
Pesme iz Lebča, 45.
420a.
Ci-noć ko-nji ne do-do-še, Ka-li-no,
Ka-le, vi-le, vi-to pe-ro ze-le- no,

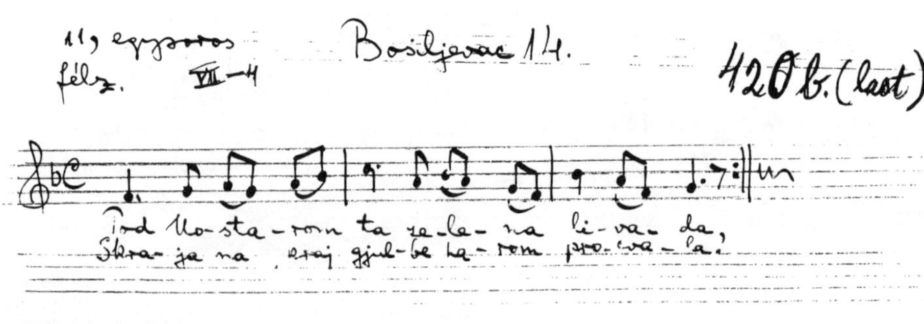
Bosiljevac 14.
420b. (laut)
Pod Ho-sta-rom ta ze-le-na li-va-da,

Sedeljka
AAv Pesme iz Lebča, 35. (t. 80.)
42/a.
Ej, loj zeču-va pa-ra-čin-ka de-voj-ka,
11, (2)
III – b3
talán fél?
, ih!
Dj.: Pred. srb. 29.
42/b. Tibužde.
1 – b3
11,
egy sor
♩= 100
Refrain?
Cr-no groj-ze gar-ba-ni-to, Stojno le,
o-be-ri ga, na-zo-bu se, Mula-ne!
Dj.: Pred. srb. 444.
42/c. Mrzenica (last)
1 – b3
11, egysoros
♩=88
Mene maj-ka jednu i-ma, te i-ma.

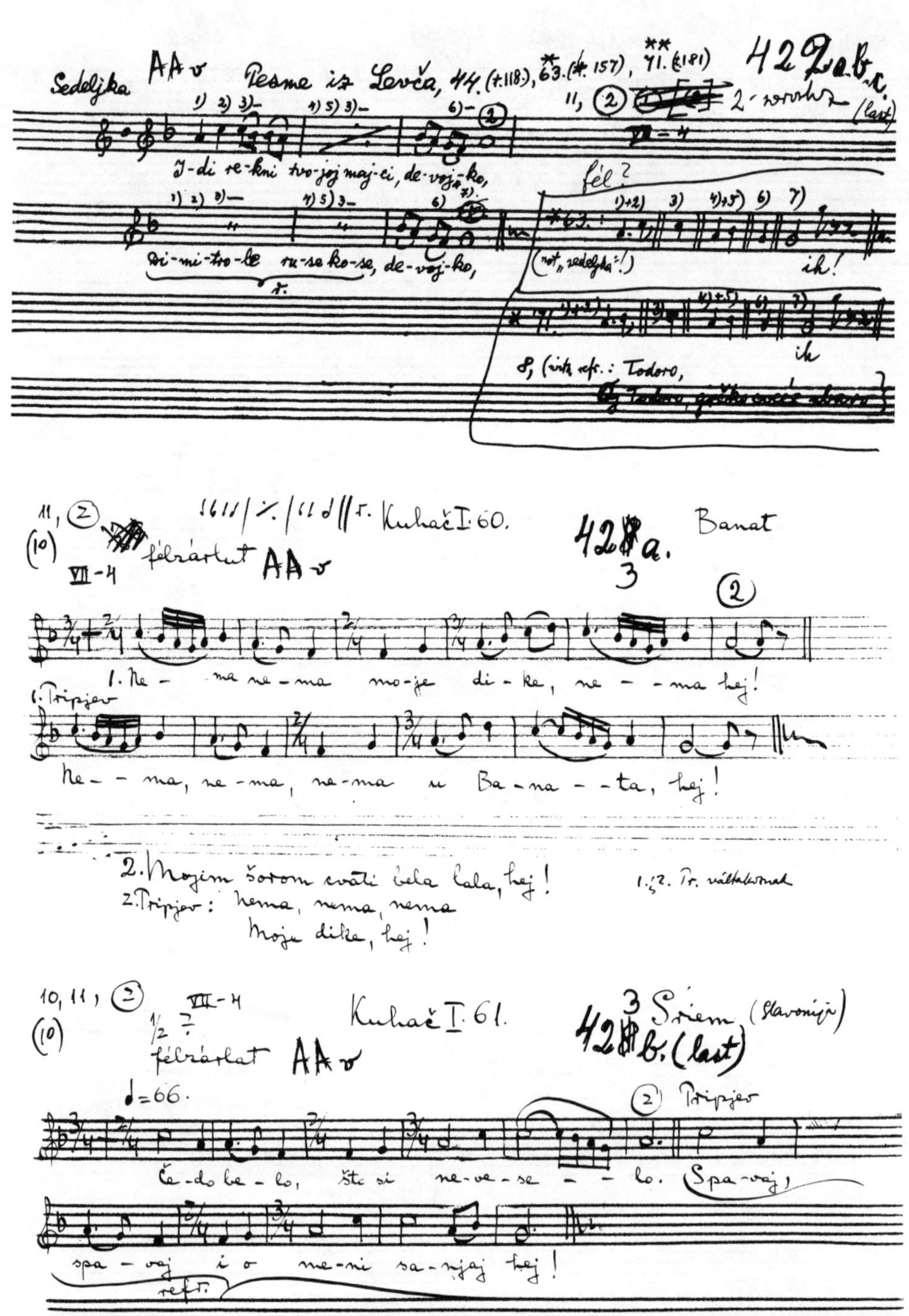
Sedeljka
Pesme iz Levča, 44.
I-di re-kni tvo-joj maj-ci, de-voj-ko,
Di-mi-tro-le ru-se ko-se, de-voj-ko,
Kuhač I. 60.
Banat
félzárlat
1. Ne-ma ne-ma mo-je di-ke, ne-ma hej!
Ne-ma, ne-ma, ne-ma u Ba-na-ta, hej!
2. Mojim šorom cvati bela lala, hej!
2. Tripjer: nema, nema, nema
Moja dike, hej!
Kuhač I. 61.
Sriem (Slavonija)
félzárlat
Če-do be-lo, što si ne-ve-se-lo. Spa-vaj,
spa-vaj i o ne-ni sa-njaj hej!
Tripjer

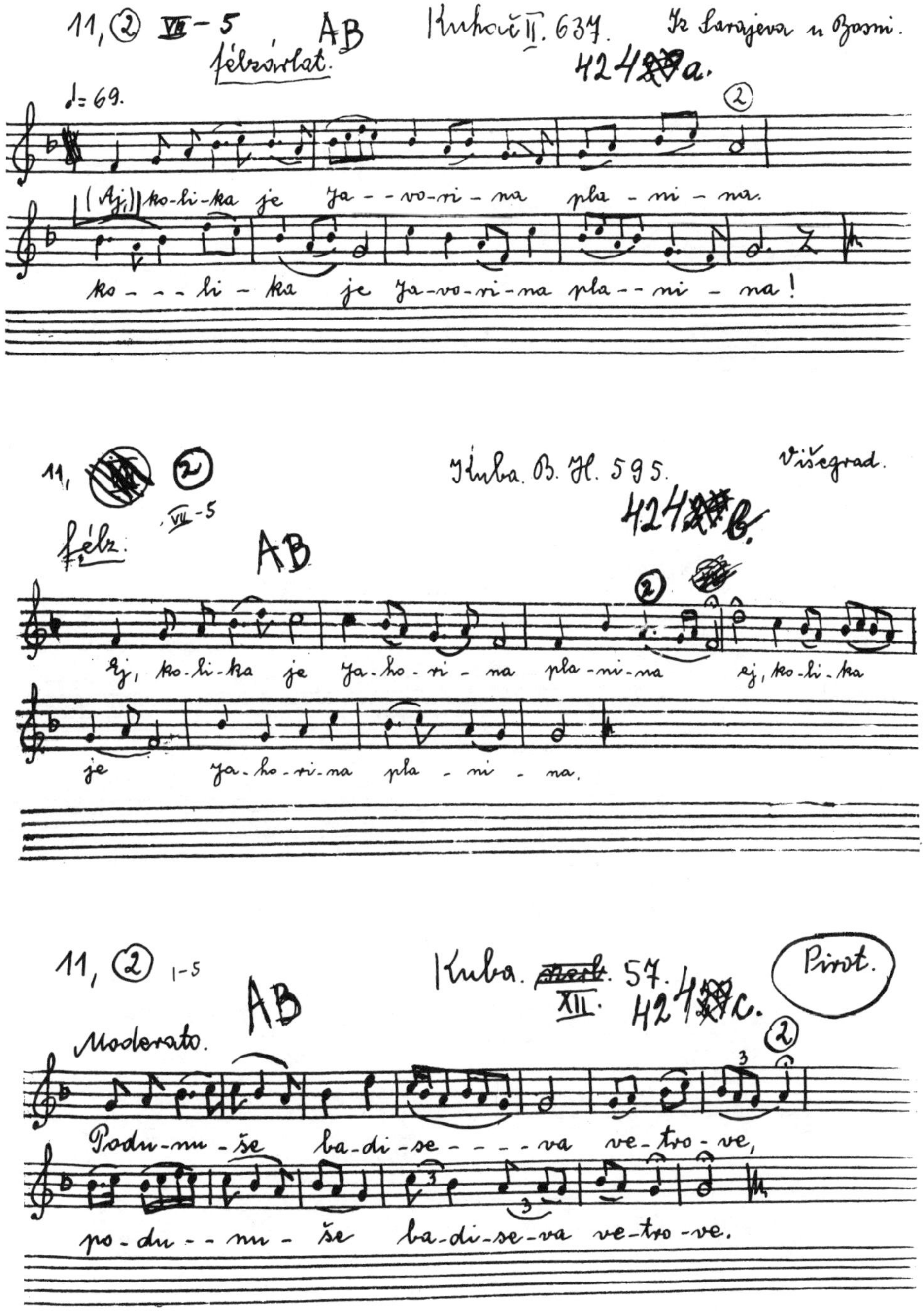

11, ② VII – 5 AB Kuhač II. 637. Iz Sarajeva u Bosni.

félzárlat. 424 a.

♩= 69. ②

(Aj,) ko-li-ka je Ja--vo-ri-na pla-ni-na.

ko---li-ka je Ja-vo-ri-na pla--ni-na!

11, ② VII-5 Kuba. B. H. 595. Višegrad.

félz. AB 424 b.

②

Ej, ko-li-ka je Ja-ho-ri-na pla-ni-na ej, ko-li-ka

je Ja-ho-ri-na pla-ni-na.

11, (2) VII-5 Djordjević. Nar. Pev. 155/2. (last)
AB
Ej, po-du-nu-še sa-ba-zor-ski ve-tro-vi ej, po-
-du-nu-še sa-ba-zor-ski ve-tro-vi.
Var. Kuba
11, (2) VII-5 Djordjević. Nár. Pev. 7/1.
félz.
AB
Sa-vi-la se be-la lo-za vi-no-va, sa-vi-la se be-la lo-za
vi-no-va. (Vuk. S. Karadžić)
11, (2) VII-5 Kuba B.H. 735.
426a.
Andante
AB
Rogatica.
Ka-ran-fil-i se na put pre-
ma i pjeva, ej, Karan-fi-la,
ej, stazom šeće i pla-će.

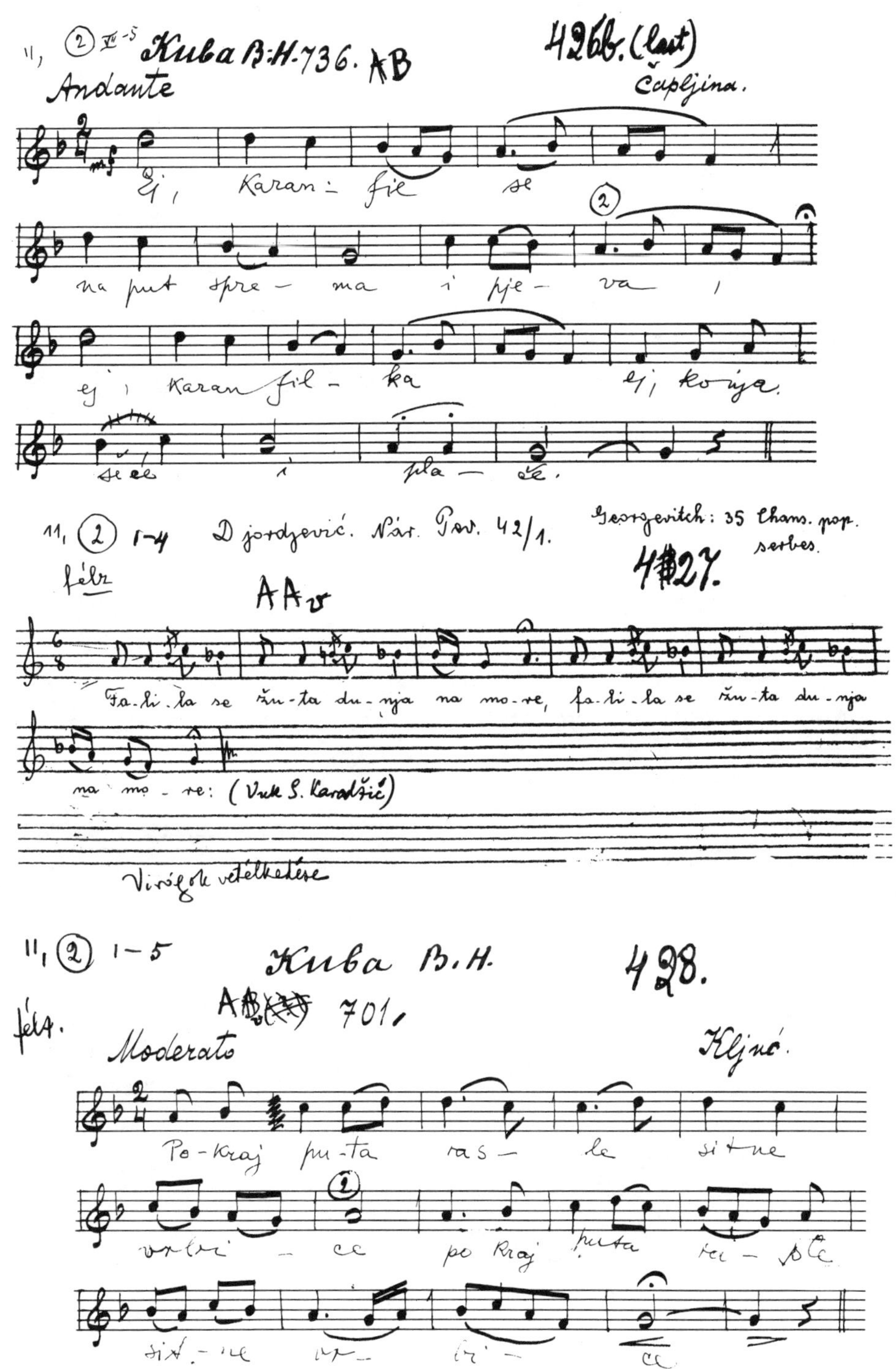

11, ② VII-5 Kuba B:H-736. AB
426bb. (last)
Andante
Čapljina.
Ej, Karan- fil se
na put spre- ma i pje- va,
ej, Karan- fil- ka ej, ko-ja
se će i pla- če.
11, ② 1-4 Djordjević. Nár. Pev. 42/1.
Georgevitch: 35 Chans. pop. serbes.
4@27.
félr
AAv
Fa-li-la se žu-ta du-nja na mo-re, fa-li-la se žu-ta du-nja
na mo-re: (Vuk S. Karadžić)
Virágok vetélkedése
11, ② 1-5
Kuba B.H.
428.
AB 701
félt.
Moderato
Kljuć.
Po-kraj pu-ta ras- le sit-ne
vrbi- ce po kraj puta ra- sle
sit.- ne vr- bi- ce

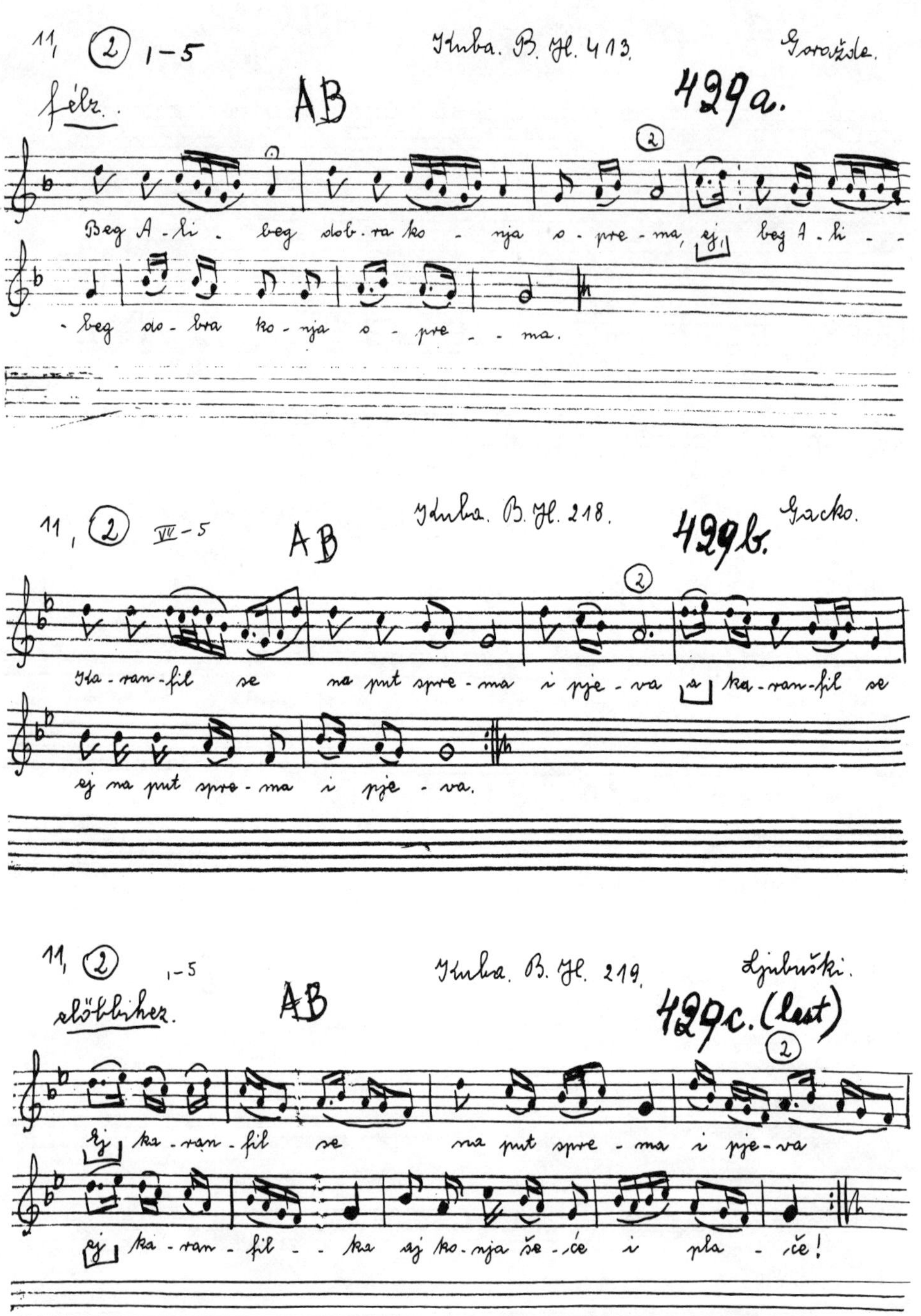
11, (2) 1–5
Kuba. B. H. 413.
Goražde.
félz.
AB
429a.
Beg A - li - beg dob - ra ko - nja o - pre - ma, ej, beg A - li -
- beg do - bra ko - nja o - pre - - ma.
11, (2) VII–5
Kuba. B. H. 218.
Gacko.
AB
429b.
Ka - ran - fil se na put spre - ma i pje - va a ka - ran - fil se
ej na put spre - ma i pje - va.
11, (2) 1–5
Kuba. B. H. 219.
Ljubuški.
előbbihez.
AB
429c. (last)
Ej ka - ran - fil se na put spre - ma i pje - va
ej ka - ran - fil - - ka aj ko - nja še - će i pla - će!

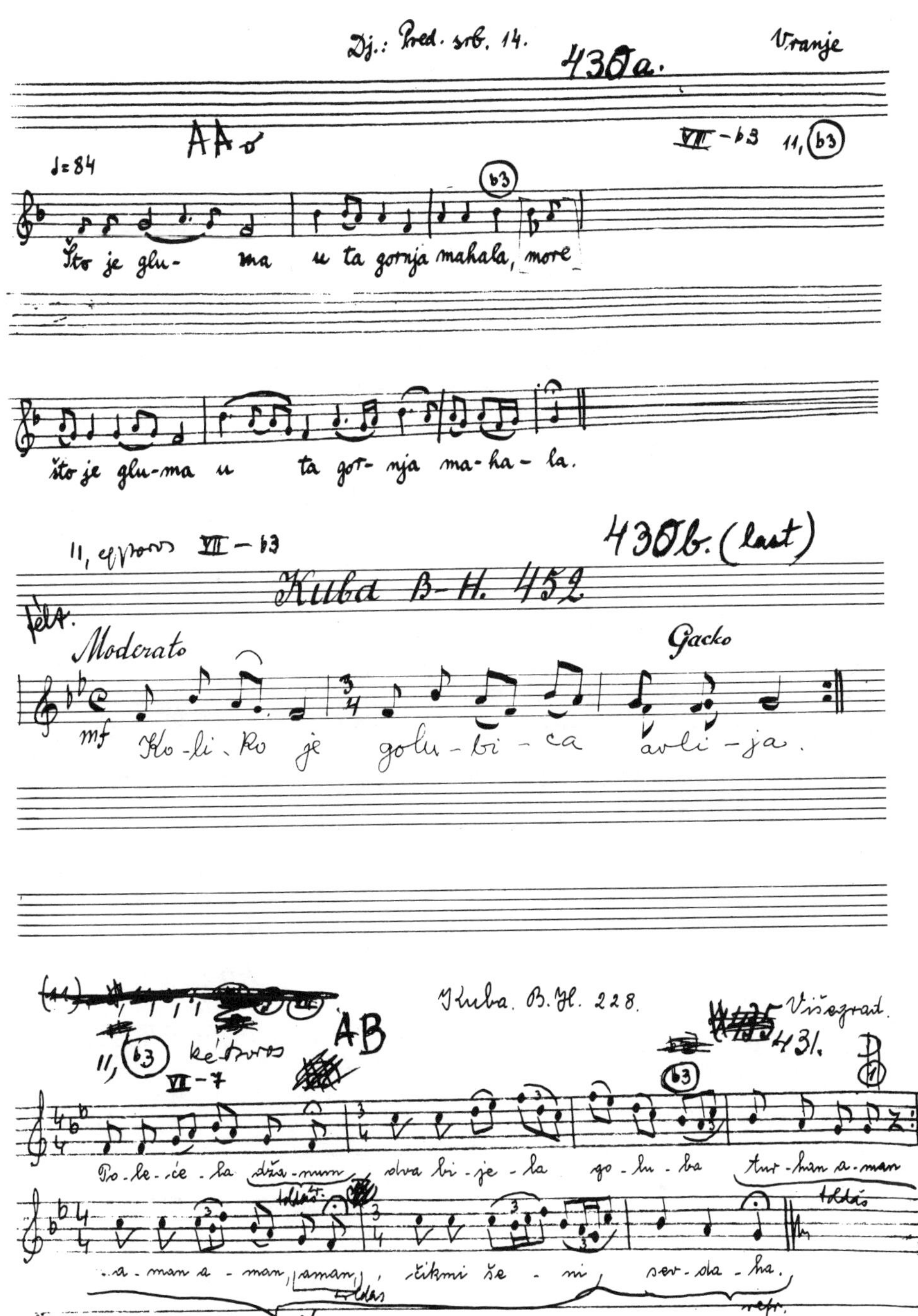

Dj.: Pred. srb. 14.
430a.
Vranje
AA
Što je glu- ma u ta gornja mahala, more
što je glu-ma u ta gor- nja ma-ha- la.
430b. (last)
Kuba B-H. 452
Moderato
Gacko
Ko-li-ko je golu-bi-ca avli-ja.
Kuba. B.H. 228.
Višegrad.
431.
AB
Po-le-će-la dža-num dva bi-je-la go-lu-ba tur-han a-man
a-man a-man, aman, čikmi še-ni sev-da-ha.
refr.

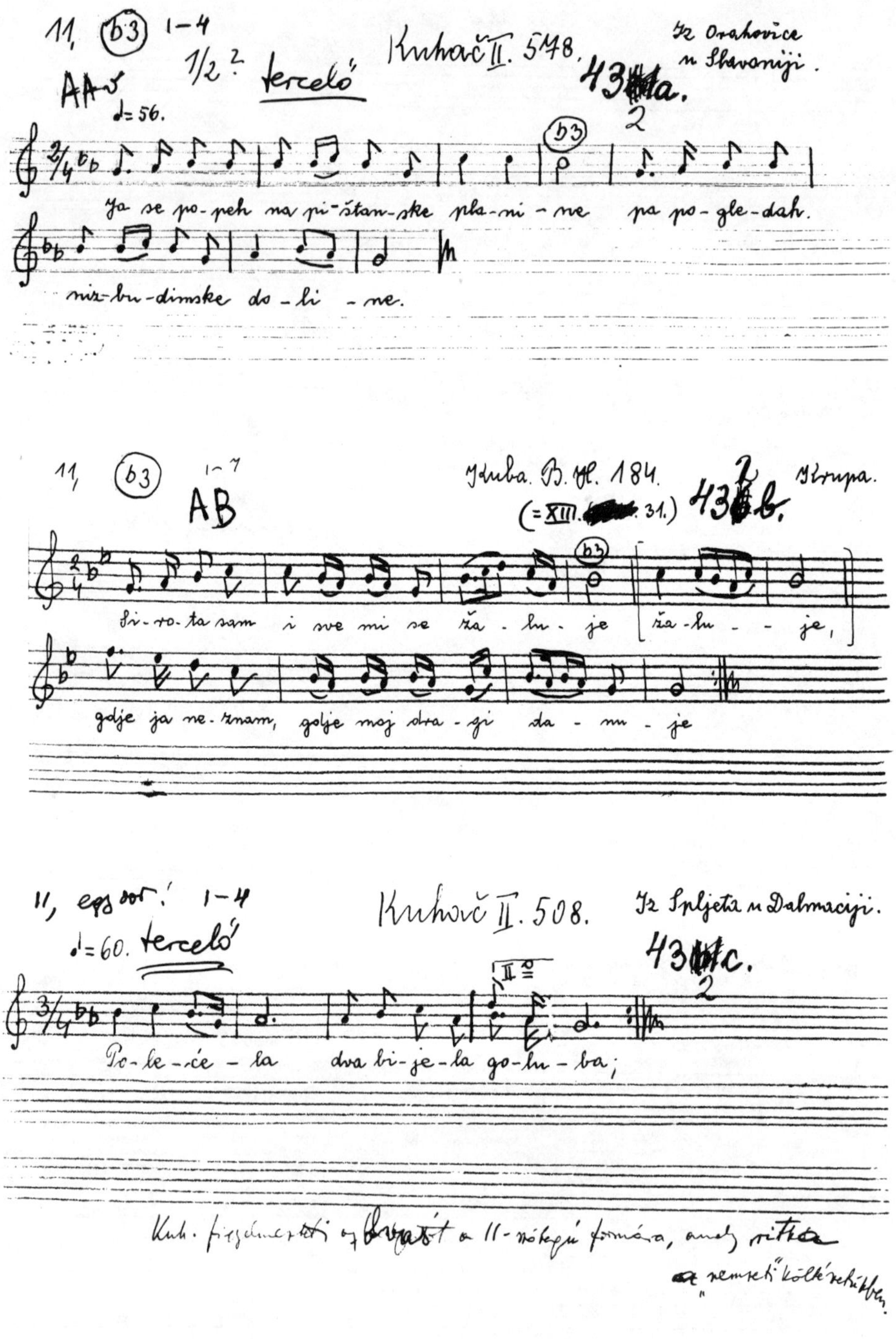
11, b3 1–4
tercelő
Kuhač II. 548.
Iz Orahovice u Slavoniji.
43a.
♩= 56.
Ja se po-peh na pi-štan-ske pla-ni-ne pa po-gle-dah
niz-bu-dimske do-li-ne.
11, b3 1–7
AB
Kuba. B. H. 184.
(= XIII. 31.)
43b.
Krupa.
Si-ro-ta sam i sve mi se ža-lu-je ža-lu-je,
gdje ja ne-znam, gdje moj dra-gi da-nu-je
11, 1–4
♩.= 60. tercelő
Kuhač II. 508.
Iz Spljeta u Dalmaciji.
43c.
Po-le-će-la dva bi-je-la go-lu-ba;

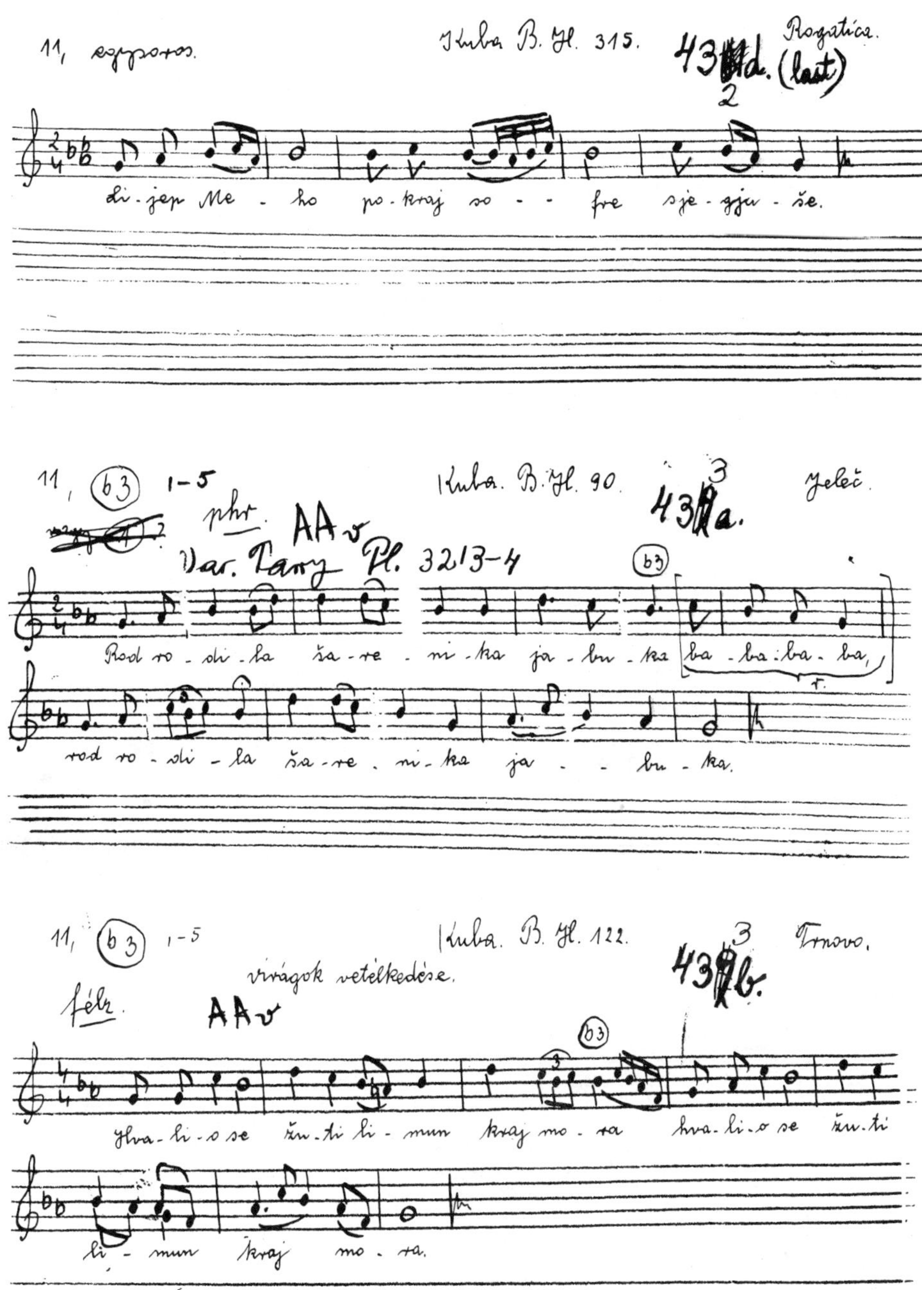
11, egyszeres.
Kuba B. H. 315.
43 d. (last)
Rogatica.
Li-jep Me-ho po-kraj so-fre sje-gju-še.
11, (b3) 1–5
Kuba. B. H. 90.
43 a.
Jeleč.
phr.
AAv
Var. Tary Pl. 3213–4
Rod ro-di-la ša-re-ni-ka ja-bu-ka ba-ba-ba-ba,
rod ro-di-la ša-re-ni-ka ja-bu-ka.
11, (b3) 1–5
Kuba. B. H. 122.
43 b.
Trnovo.
virágok vetélkedése.
félz.
AAv
Hva-li-o se žu-ti li-mun kraj mo-ra hva-li-o se žu-ti
li-mun kraj mo-ra.

11, b3 1–5 Kuba. B. H. 121. 3 Trnovo.
utóbbihoz. AA Virágvetélkedés?
Hva-li-o se žu-ti li-mun kraj mo-ra, a-man, hva-li-
o se žu-ti li-mun kraj mo-ra.
11, b3 1–5 Kuba. B. H. 594. 3 Čapljina.
félz. AA Virág vetélkedés.
Hva-li-o se žu-ti li-mun kraj mo-ra, hva-li-o-se
žu-ti li-mun kraj mo-ra.
11, b3 1–5 Kuhač 1531. Iz Crne Gore
(8) AB
Ja po-se-jah grah po do-lu (perdi-voj); ja po-se-jah grah po dolušah,
ja-di moj!

Andante AB Kuba B.H. 673.
Žepče.
Po-vi-la se bjela loza vi-no-va,
po-vi-la se bje-la loza vi-no-va
vi-no-va
Moderato AA Kuba B.H. 444.
Zenica
Hva-li-o se žu-ti li-man kraj mo-ra, hva-li-o se žu-ti li-mun kraj mo-ra
Kuba. B. H. 604. Sarajevo.
Kraj Mo-sta-ra ta li-va-da ze-le-na Kraj Mo-sta-ra ta li-va-da ze-le-na.

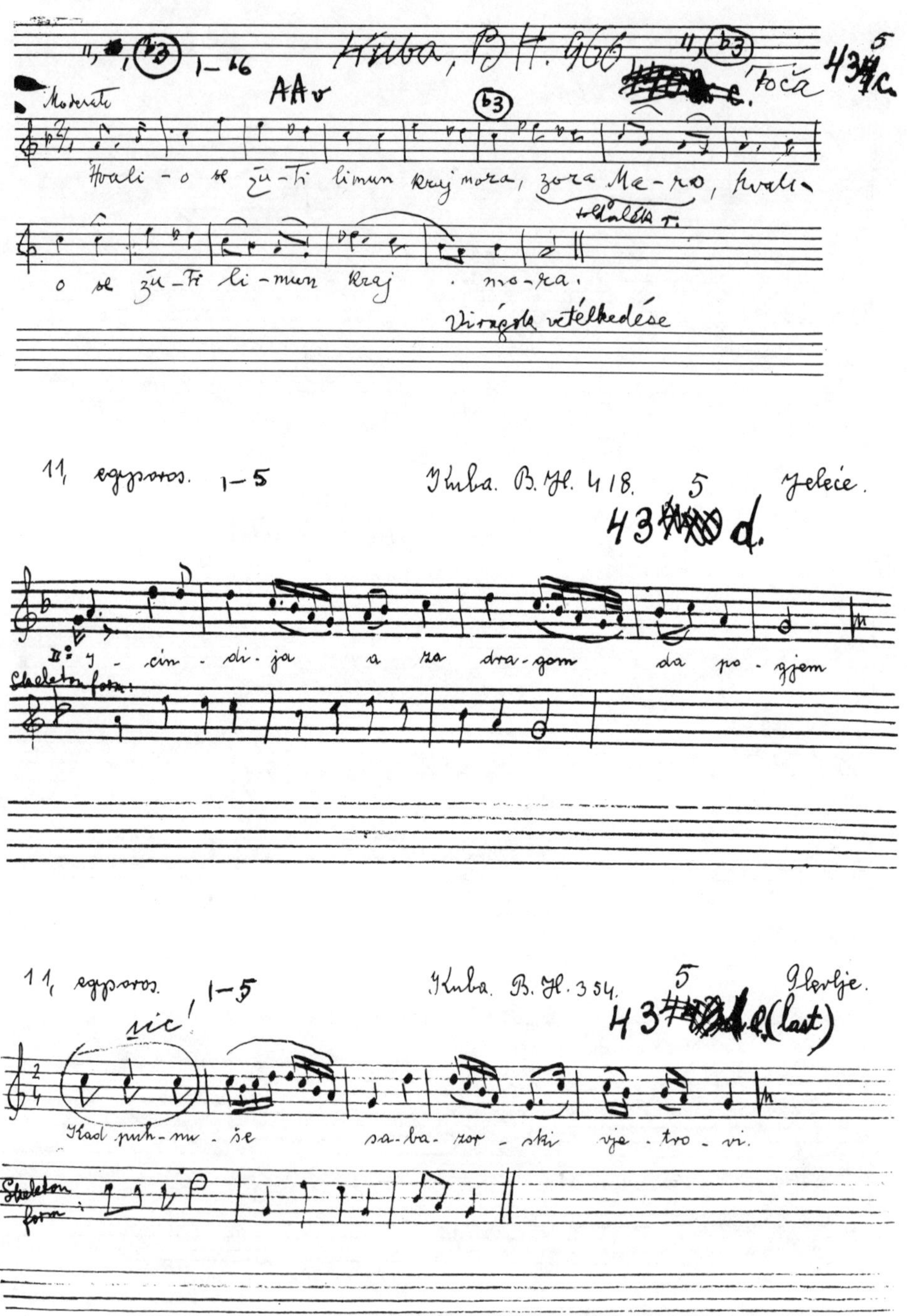
11, 1–16 Kuba, B.H. 466 11, b3 Toča 43 5/c.
AAv
Moderato
Hvali-o se žu-ti limun kraj mora, zora Ma-ro, hvali-o se žu-ti li-mun kraj mo-ra.
Virágok vetélkedése
11, egyporos. 1–5 Kuba. B. H. 418. 5 Jelece. 43 d.
Y-cin-di-ja a za dra-gom da po-jjem
Skeleton form:
11, egyporos. 1–5 Kuba. B. H. 354. 5 Glevlje. 43 (last)
sic!
Kad puh-nu-še sa-ba-zor-ski vje-tro-vi.
Skeleton form:

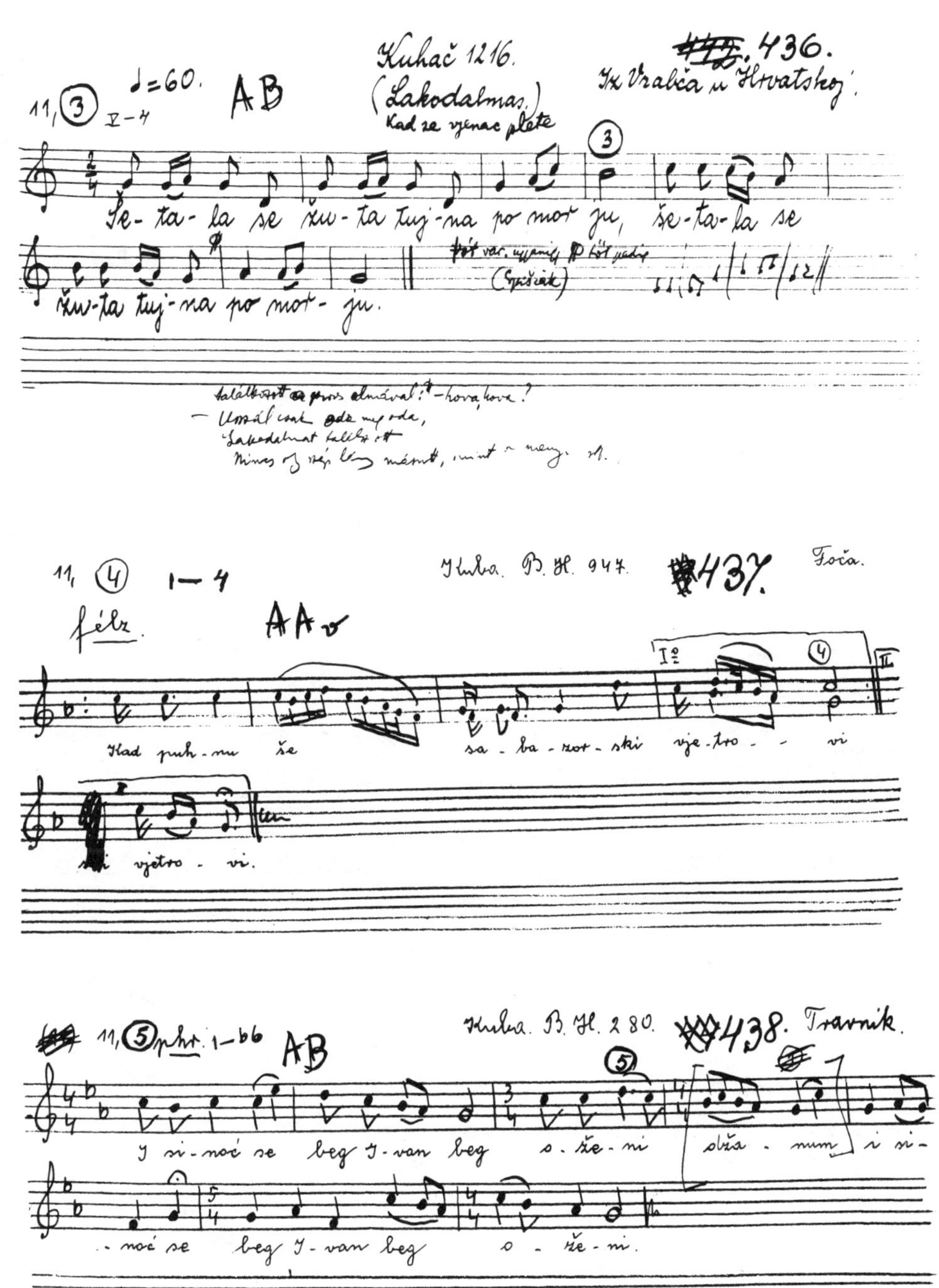
Kuhač 1216.
(Lakodalmas.)
Kad se vjenac plete
436.
Iz Vrabča u Hrvatskoj.
♩=60.
AB
Še-ta-la se žu-ta tuj-na po mor-ju, še-ta-la se
žu-ta tuj-na po mor-ju.
Kuba. B. H. 947.
437.
Foča.
félz.
AA
Kad puh-nu že sa-ba-zor-ski vje-tro-vi
vjetro-vi.
Kuba. B. H. 280.
438.
Travnik.
AB
I si-noć se beg I-van beg o-že-ni
-noć se beg I-van beg o-že-ni.

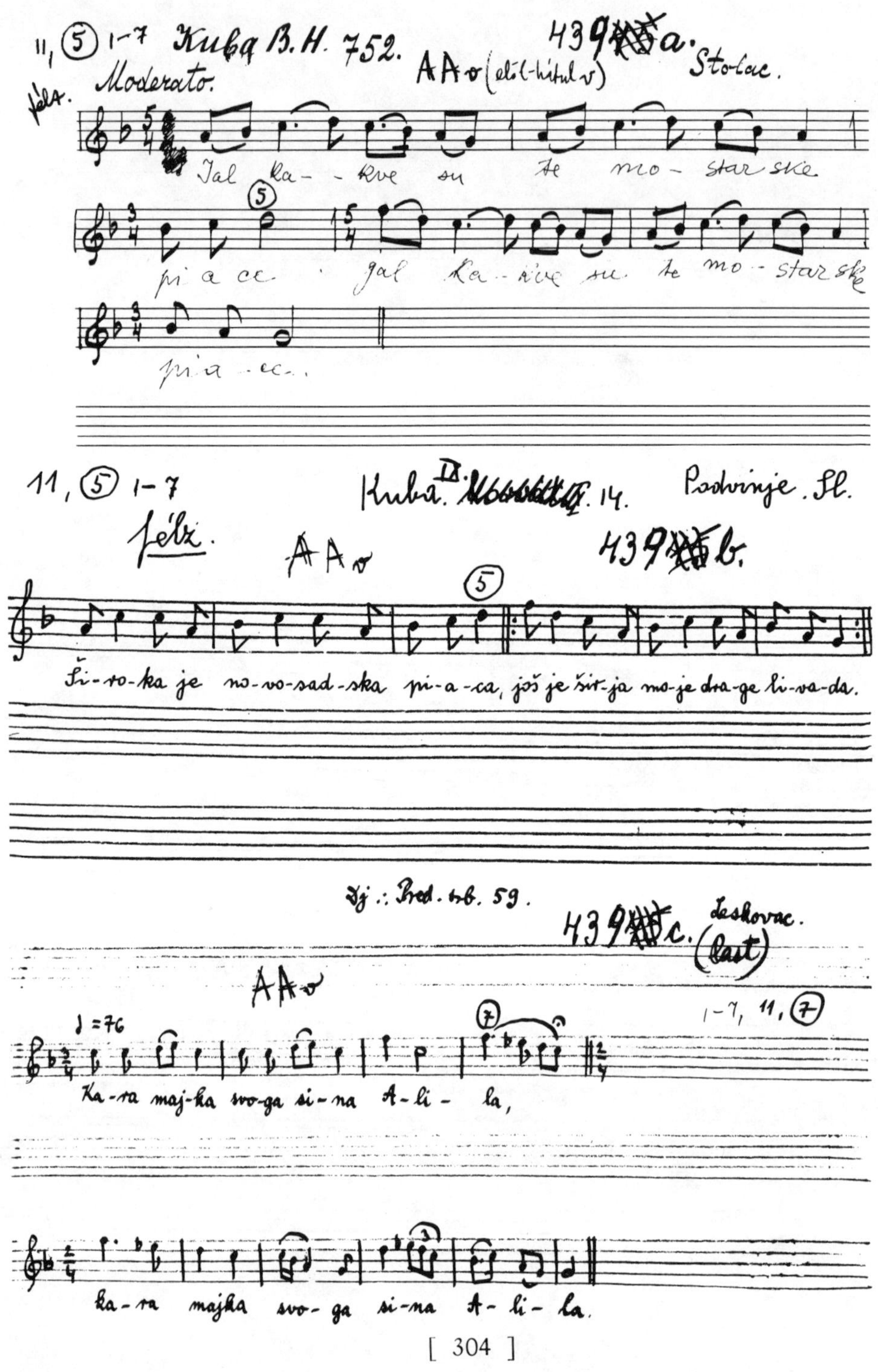
11, ⑤ 1-7 Kuba B.H. 752.
439 a.
Stolac.
Moderato.
Jal ka-kve su te mo-star-ske
pi a ce · jal ka-kve su te mo-star-ske
pi a ce.
11, ⑤ 1-7
Podvinje. Sl.
439 b.
Ši-ro-ka je no-vo-sad-ska pi-a-ca, još je šir-ja mo-je dra-ge li-va-da.
439 c.
1-7, 11, ⑦
Ka-ra maj-ka svo-ga si-na A-li-la,
ka-ra majka svo-ga si-na A-li-la.

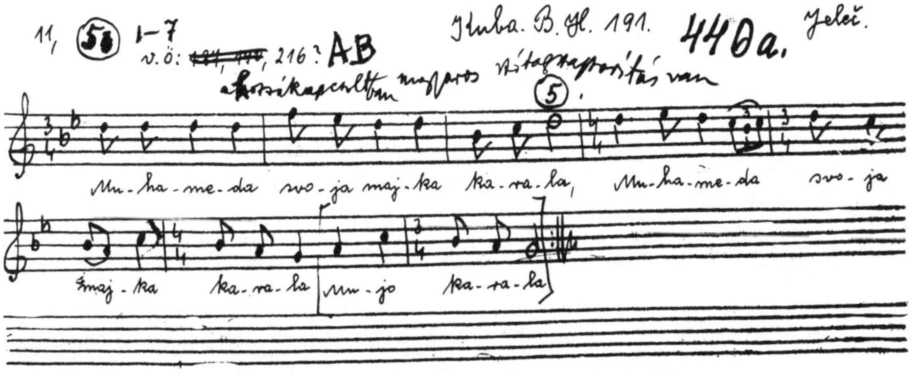

11, (5) 1–7 v.ö: 216? AB

Iluba. B. H. 191. **440a.** Jeleč.

kosszákapcsoltban magyaros sztagrapozitás van (5).

Mu-ha-me-da svo-ja maj-ka ka-ra-la, Mu-ha-me-da svo-ja maj-ka ka-ra-la mu-jo ka-ra-la

előbbihez. AB

Iluba. B. H. 192. **440b. (lent)** Jeleč.

u po-to-ka bi-stra vo-da, šu-ma ze-le-na, u po-to-ka bi-stra vo-da šu-ma ze-le-na.

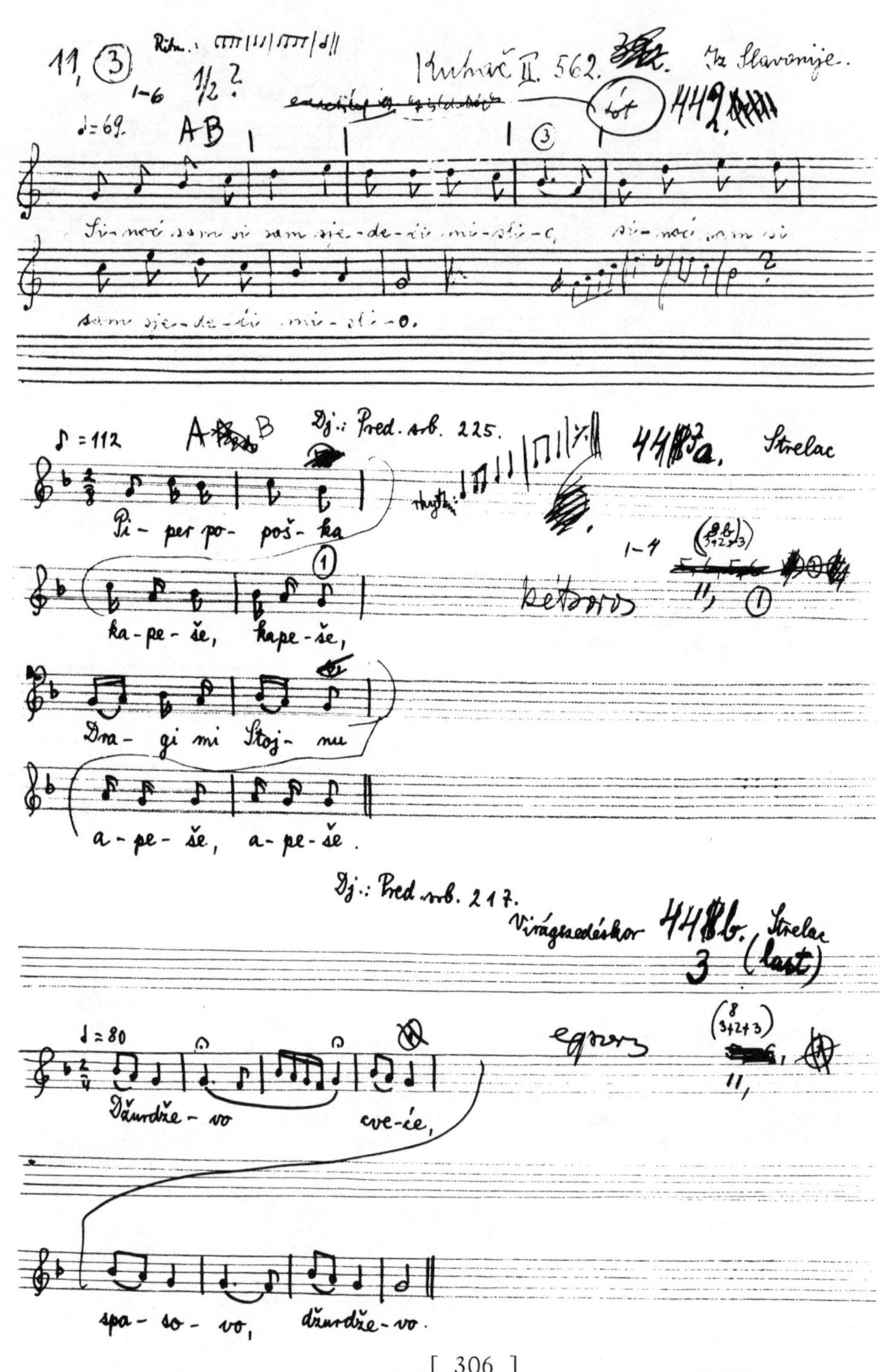

Kuhač II. 562.
Iz Slavonije.
AB
Dj.: Pred. sb. 225.
Strelac
Pi - per po - poš - ka
ka-pe-še, kape-še,
Dra- gi mi Stoj- nu
a - pe - še, a - pe - še.
Dj.: Pred. sb. 217.
Virágszedéskor
Strelac
(last)
spa - so - vo, džurdže - vo.

Djordj. Nar. Pev. 130/2.
444
AB
Či-ja je o-no de-vojka, Ra-du-le, što ra-no ra-ni na vo-du, Ra-du-le,
Kuba. B. H. 840
Nevesinje.
445a.
AAv
u-zo-ri dra-gi rav-ni-ne rav-ni-ne, uz-o-ri dragi ravni-ne rav-ni-ne.
Kuba. B. H. 887.
Mostar (Svatovska)
(Lakodalmas)
445b.
AB
tercelő.
Tes-li džen mi se ne-ni-ha, ne-ni-ha tes-li-džen mi se ne-ni-ha ne-ni-ha.

Kuba B.H. 776. AB 445
Kiseljak.
Allegro moderato
Pri-oni mobu za la-da
za la-da, prioni mobu za la-
da za la-da.
Kuba B.H. 778. AA 445
Ljubuški.
Allegro moderato.
Pod onom gorom ze-le-nom, ze-le-
nom, pod onom gorom ze-le-
nom, ze-le-nom.
Kuba B.H. 779. AB 445
Parežević.
Allegro moderato.
Pri-oni mobu za la-da, za la-
da, prioni mobu za la-da,
za la-da.

Kuba B.H. 782.
AA
Moderato
Nevesinje (Svatovska)
Fes li gjen mi se ne nji - ha,
ne nji - ha, što mu je, šta se
le - li - ja, le - li - ja.
Bosiljevac 33.
AA
Pu-ni ni, pu-ni la-gja-ne, la-gja-ne,
pu-ni ni, pu-ni la-gja-ne, la-gja-ne.
Kuba B.H. 773.
AA
Moderato.
Rogatica.
U zori, dragi, ravni - ne, ravni - ne,
u zori, dragi, ravni - ne, ravnine.

Largo.
Kuba B.H. 780.
Nevesinje.
Planino, mo– ja sta–ri–
no, lele, pla–nino, mo– ja
sta – ri – no!
Moderato
Kuba B.H. 777.
Maglaj.
Pod o – nom gorom ze – le – nom,
pod o – nom gorom zelenom.
Andrejevice.
I Lim vo— i Lim vo-da ne-ma bro-da, i Lim vo–
i Lim vo-da ne-ma bro-da.
cf: No
1396.

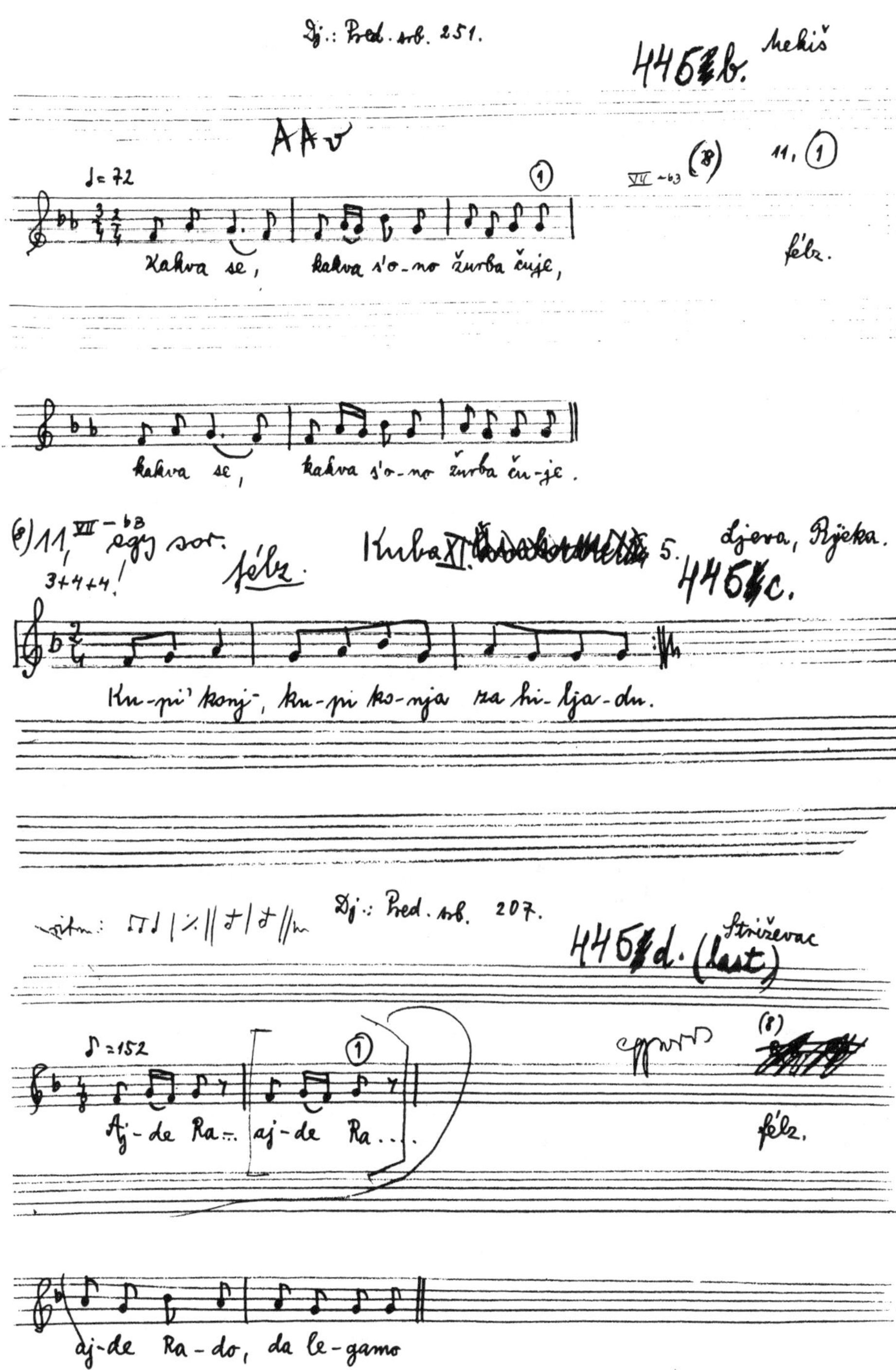
Dj.: Pred. srb. 251.
446b.
AAv
♩= 72
(8) 11, (1)
Kakva se, kakva s'o-no žurba čuje,
félz.
kakva se, kakva s'o-no žurba ču-je.
(8) 11, egy sor.
3+4+4!
félz.
5.
Ljeva, Rijeka.
446c.
Ku-pi' konj-, ku-pi ko-nja za hi-lja-du.
Dj.: Pred. srb. 207.
446d.
Striževac
♪=152
Aj-de Ra-... aj-de Ra...
félz.
aj-de Ra-do, da le-gamo

Dj.: Pred. sb. 550.
4+4+4
AA
Pavlica
(10)
♩ = 100
(4+4+4)
Iz-vi-la se ko-nop-lji-ca tan-ka, tanka,
félz.
iz-vi-la se konop-lji-ca, ne-ka, neka
Dj.: Pred. sb. 262.
Kraljička
4+4+4
AA
előbbihez
(8)
♪ = 152
12, 11,
(4+4+4)
Oj, u-bava mala momo, la-do, lado,
Var. 10, VII nél
(dos, dos)
Cf. i.e.: № 261
oj, u-bava ma-la momo la-doj-lo!
(8) 12, egyporos.
Koj' za ko-lo, koj' za ko-lo hajd u ko-lo

(8) 12,
1-♭3
AA
Kuba. B. H. 267.
Kalinovik.
448
o j - li - ja be - laj - li - ja be - laj - li - ja.
Dj.: Pred. sb. 184.
3- királynapkor
Čerčinci
448d.
AA
♩=138
(8)
10,
VII
U - lezo mo bani dvori, lado, lado,
félz.
u - le - zo mo bani dvori, lado
Dj.: Pred. sb. 283.
Lalinac
kraljička
AA
448
♩=108
(8)
10,
VII
Oj, u-bava mala momo, lado la-do,
félz.
oj, ubava malamomo la-doj- lo!

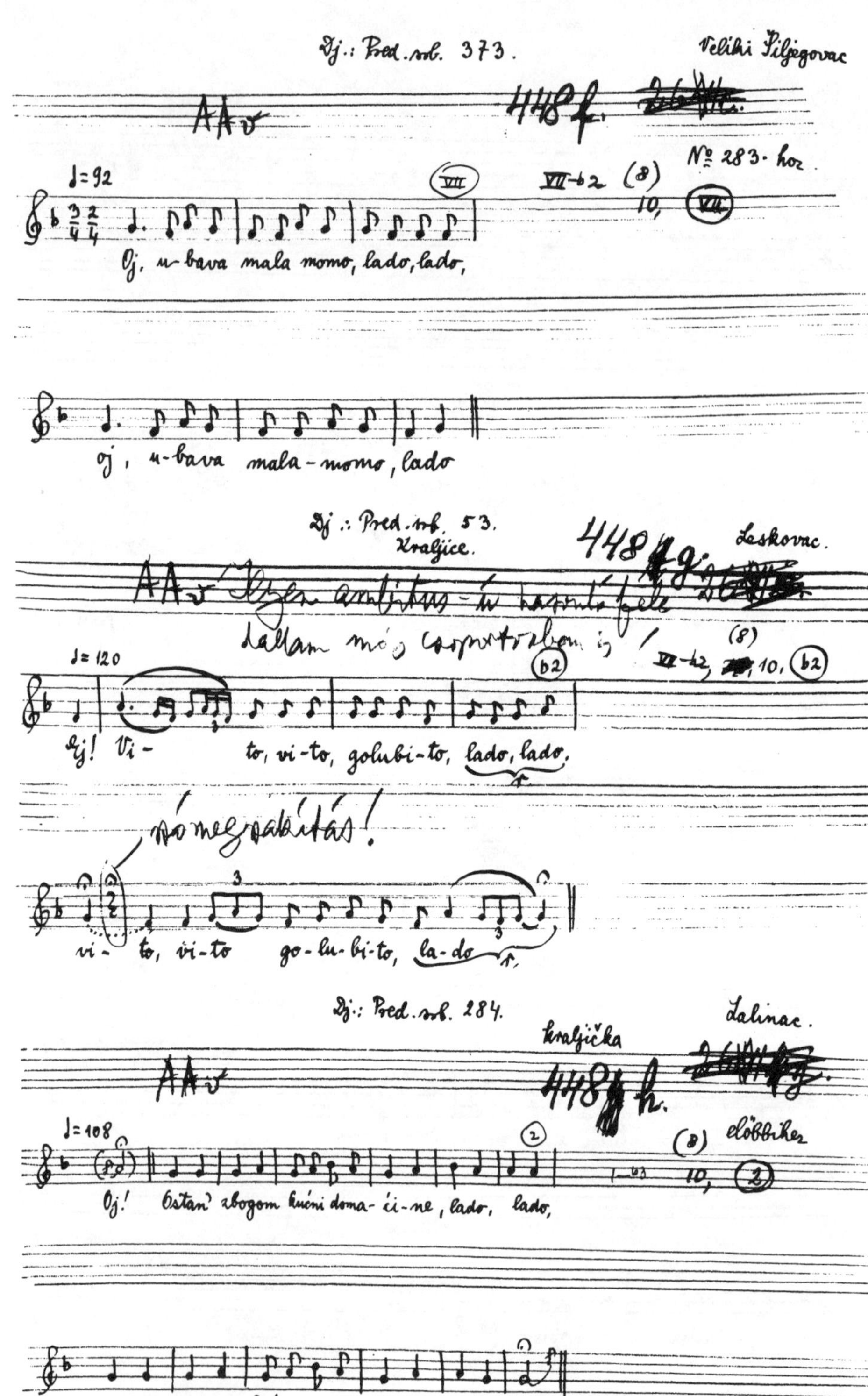

Dj.: Pred. sb. 373.
Veliki Piljegovac
AAv
448 f.
№ 283. hoz
♩=92
VII
VII–b2 (8)
10, VII
Oj, u-bava mala momo, lado, lado,
oj, u-bava mala-momo, lado
Dj.: Pred. sb. 53.
Kraljice.
448 g.
Leskovac.
(8)
♩= 120
b2
10, b2
Ej! Vi- to, vi-to, golubi-to, lado, lado.
vi- to, vi-to go-lu-bi-to, la-do
Dj.: Pred. sb. 284.
Lalinac.
Kraljička
AAv
448 h.
♩= 108
(8)
előbbihez
10, 2
Oj! Ostan' zbogom kućni doma- ći-ne, lado, lado,
o-stan' zbogom kućni doma- ći-ne, la-doj-lo!

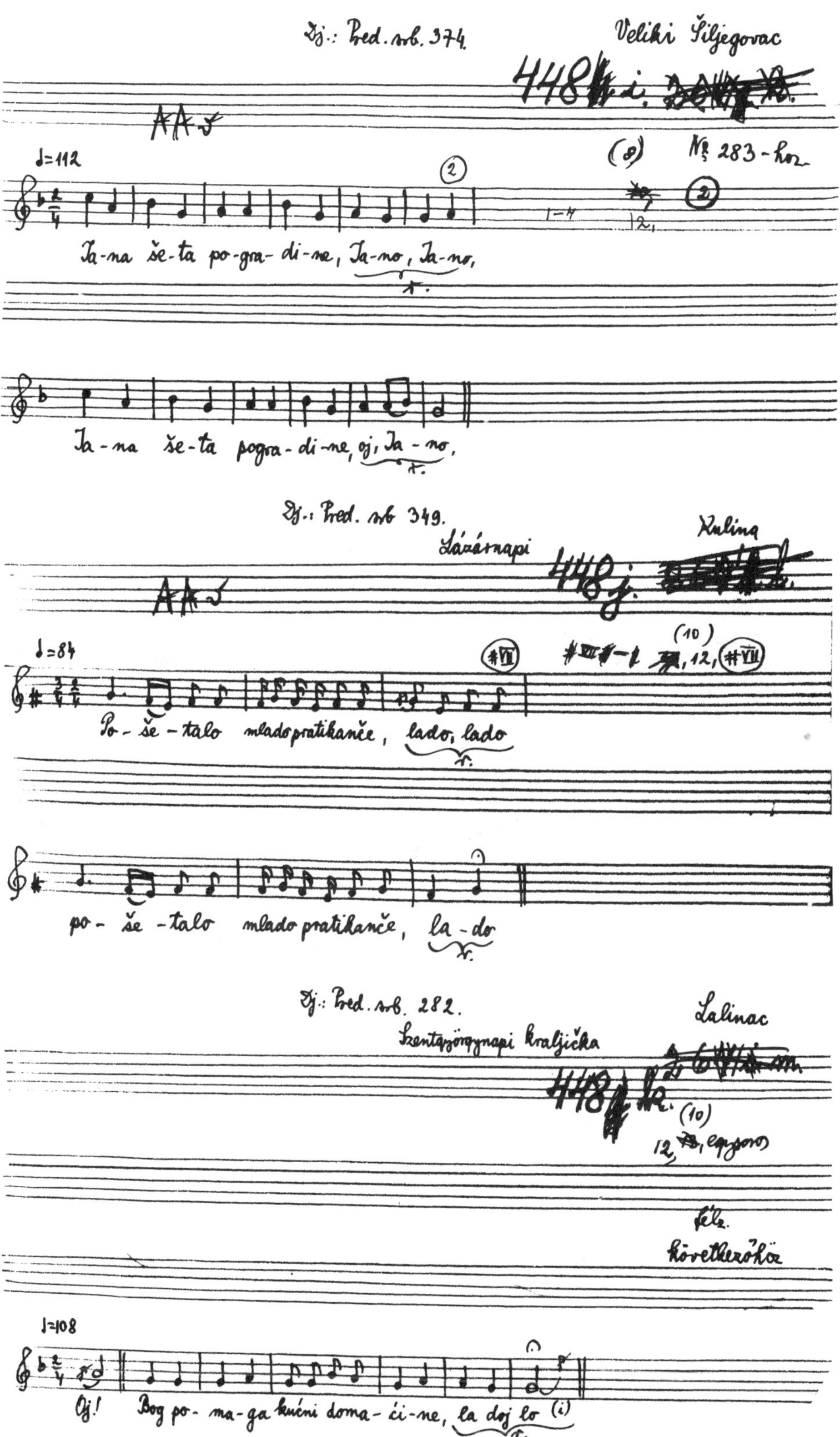

Dj.: Pred. sb. 374.
Veliki Siljegovac
448 i.
№ 283-hoz
♩=112
Ja-na še-ta po-gra-di-ne, Ja-no, Ja-no,
Ja-na še-ta pogra-di-ne, oj, Ja-no,
Dj.: Pred. sb 349.
Kulina
Lázárnapi
448 j.
♩=84
Po-še-talo mlado pratikanče, lado, lado
po-še-talo mlado pratikanče, la-do
Dj.: Pred. sb. 282.
Lalinac
Szentgyörgynapi kraljička
448 k.
12, egyszer
Oj! Bog po-ma-ga kućni doma-ći-ne, la doj lo (i)

Dj.: Pred. srb. 287
Lalinac
kraljička
448 l.
№ 282-kör
(10)
13,
♩=108
Aj! Ko-li-ka je care-va li-va-da, la-doj-lo (i)
(8) 12, egysoros
Kuba. B. H. 386.
Ljubinje.
1–♭3
448 m.
Jo-van be-że, Jo-van be-że ko-nja ve-że.
Dj.: Pred. srb. 232.
Crvena Jabuka
Lázárnapi
(last)
448 m.
VII–♭2
(8)
12, egysoros
félz.
♩=112
Ov-de li su ravni dvori, lado, lado?

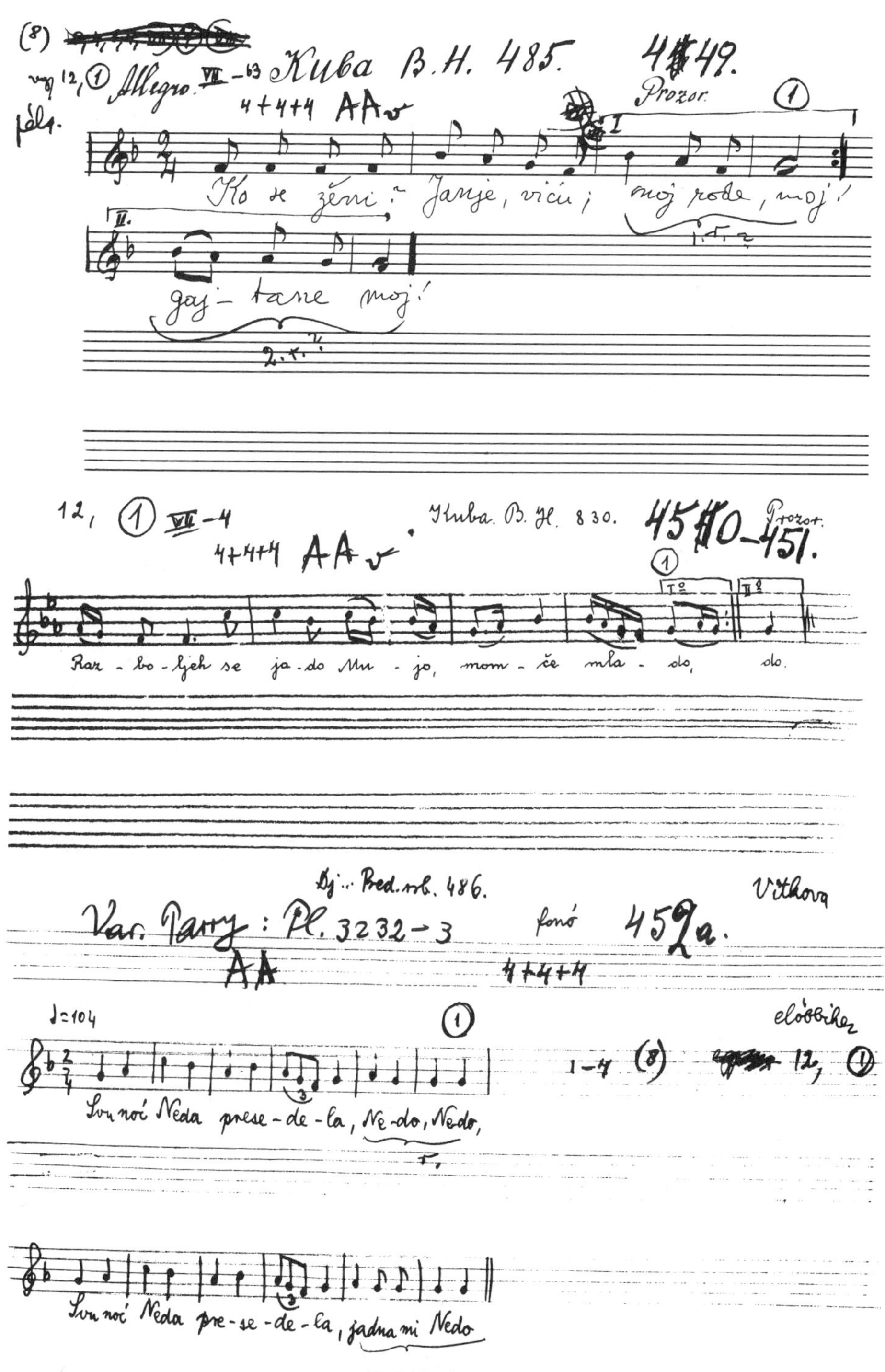
Allegro
Kuba B.H. 485.
449.
Prozor.
4+4+4 AA
Ko se ženi; Janje, viču; moj rode, moj!
gaj-tane moj!
Kuba B. H. 830.
450–451.
Prozor.
4+4+4 AA
Raz-bo-ljeh se ja-do Mu-jo, mom-če mla-do, do.
Pred. sb. 486.
Var. Parry: Pl. 3232–3
fonó
452a.
AA
4+4+4
♩=104
előbbihez
Sinoć Neda prese-de-la, Ne-do, Nedo,
Sinoć Neda pre-se-de-la, jadna mi Nedo

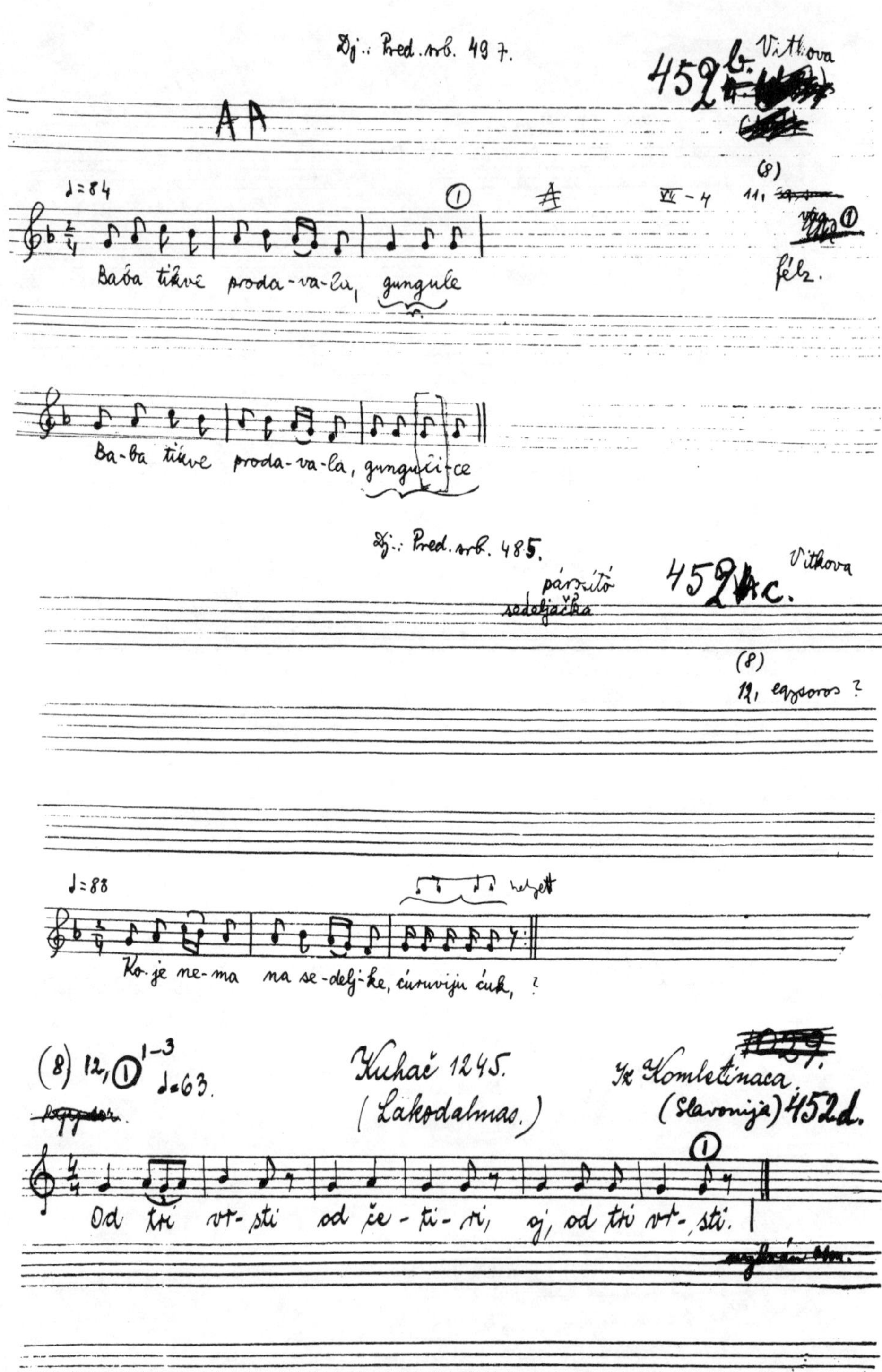

Dj.: Pred. srb. 497.
452 b. Vitkova
AA
♩= 84
VI - 4
(8)
11,
félz.
Baba tikve proda-va-la, gungule
Ba-ba tikve proda-va-la, gunguči-ce
Dj.: Pred. srb. 485.
Vitkova
sedeljačka
452 c.
(8)
12, egysoros ?
♩= 88
helyett
Ko-je ne-ma na se-delj-ke, ćuruviju ćuk, ?
(8) 12, ① 1-3
♩=63.
Kuhač 1245.
(Lakodalmas.)
Iz Komletinaca
(Slavonija) 452 d.
Od tri vr-sti od če-ti-ri, oj, od tri vr-sti.

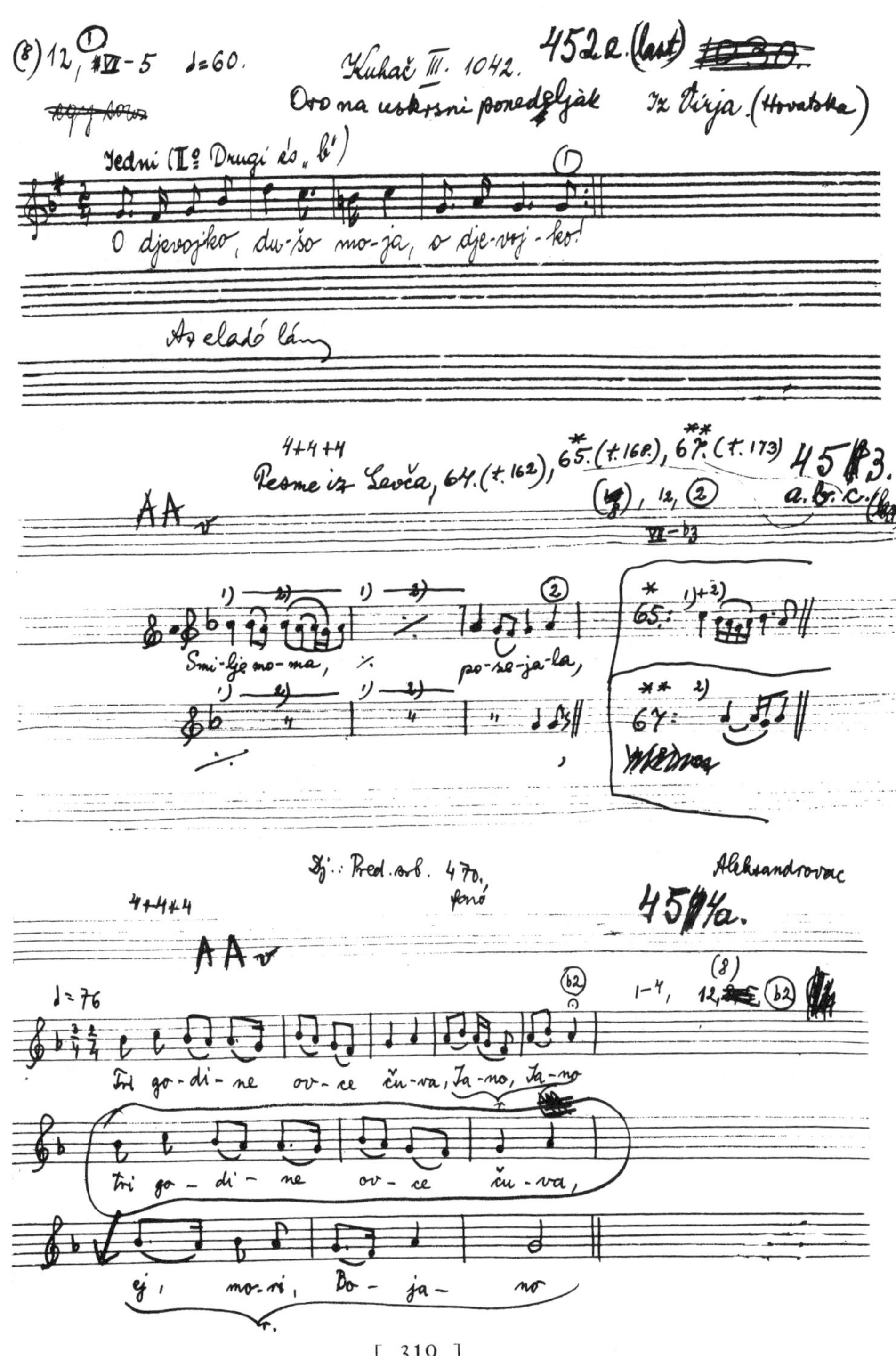
Kuhač III. 1042.
452a.
Oro na uskrsni ponedjeljak
Iz Virja (Hrvatska)
O djevojko, du-šo mo-ja, o dje-voj-ko!
Pesme iz Levča, 64. (t. 162), 65. (t. 168), 67. (t. 173)
a. b. c.
Smi-lje mo-ma, po-se-ja-la,
Dj.: Pred. srb. 470.
Aleksandrovac
J = 76
Tri go-di-ne ov-ce ču-va, Ja-no, Ja-no
Tri go-di-ne ov-ce ču-va,
ej, mo-ri, Bo-ja-no

Sedeljka
AAv
Pesme iz Levča, 43. (t. 117.)
454 b. (last)
Ču-vam ov-ce tri go-di-ne,
Ja-no! Ja-no
Ču-vam ov-ce tri go-di-ne,
Oj, Bo-ja-no!
2. refr.
Bosiljevac 10.
4+4+4
A, B
55
Iz-vir vo-da iz-vi-ra-la, iz-vi ra-la, haj, haj, haj,
haj! Kroz baš-či-cu pro-ti-ca-la pro-ti-ca-la.
Djordjević, Nár. Pev. 37/1.
Stanković.
Iz-vir vo-da iz-vi-ra-la, haj, haj, haj, haj, kroz ba-
šti-cu pro-ti-ca-la, pro-ti-ca-la.

Kuba B. H. 162.
Goražda.
AB
Iz-vir vo-da iz-vi-ra-la iz-vi-ra-la a - vaj, vaj, vaj
Kroz-baš-či-cu pro-tje-ca-la pro-tje-ca-la, tuj mi sje-di
mo-ja dra-ga mo-ja dra-ga a - vaj, vaj, vaj.
egy fokkal fel transzponálni
Kuba X. I. 44.
Omiš.
AB tercelő.
Iz-vir vo-da, izvirala, izvir vo-da, izvirala, izvira - la.
vége
eleje!
egy fokkal feltransp.
Kuba B. H. 793.
Moderato
Ključ.
Iz-vir vo-da iz-vi-ra-la,
jadi jadi, iz-vi- rala,
oj iz-vi- ra - la.

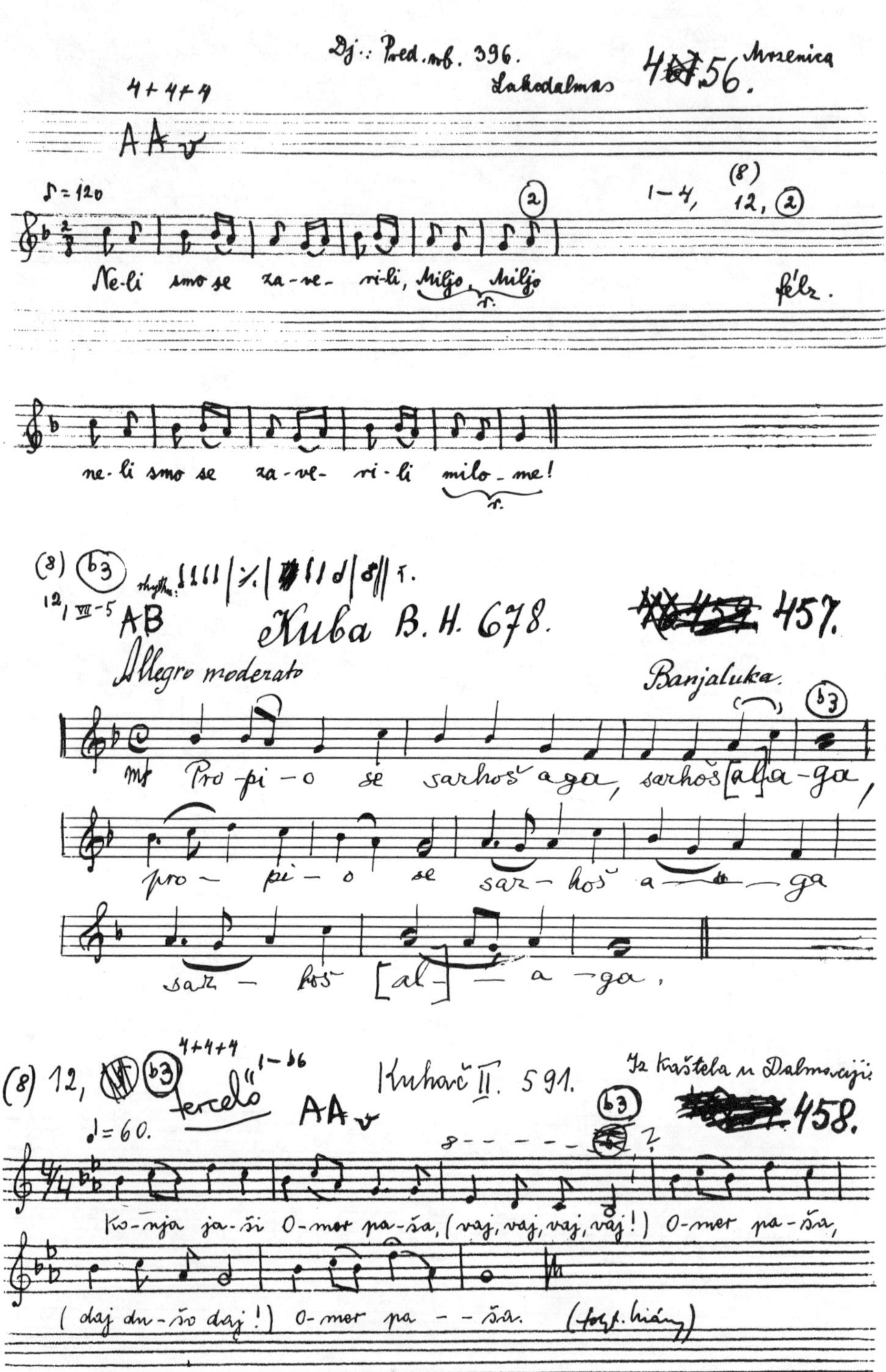
Dj.: Pred.mb. 396.
Lakodalmas
456.
Mrsenica
4+4+4
AA
♪ = 120
1–4, 12, (2)
Ne-li smo se za-ve-ri-li, Miljo, Miljo
félz.
ne-li smo se za-ve-ri-li milo-me!
(8) (b3)
12, VII-5
AB
Kuba B. H. 678.
457.
Allegro moderato
Banjaluka.
Pro-pi-o se sarhoš aga, sarhoš[al]a-ga,
pro-pi-o se sar-hoš a-ga
sar-hoš [al-] a-ga,
(8) 12, (b3)
4+4+4
tercelő
1–b6
Kuhač II. 591.
Iz Kaštela u Dalmaciji.
AA
458.
♩= 60.
Ko-nja ja-ši O-mer pa-ša, (vaj, vaj, vaj, vaj!) O-mer pa-ša,
(daj du-šo daj!) O-mer pa---ša.

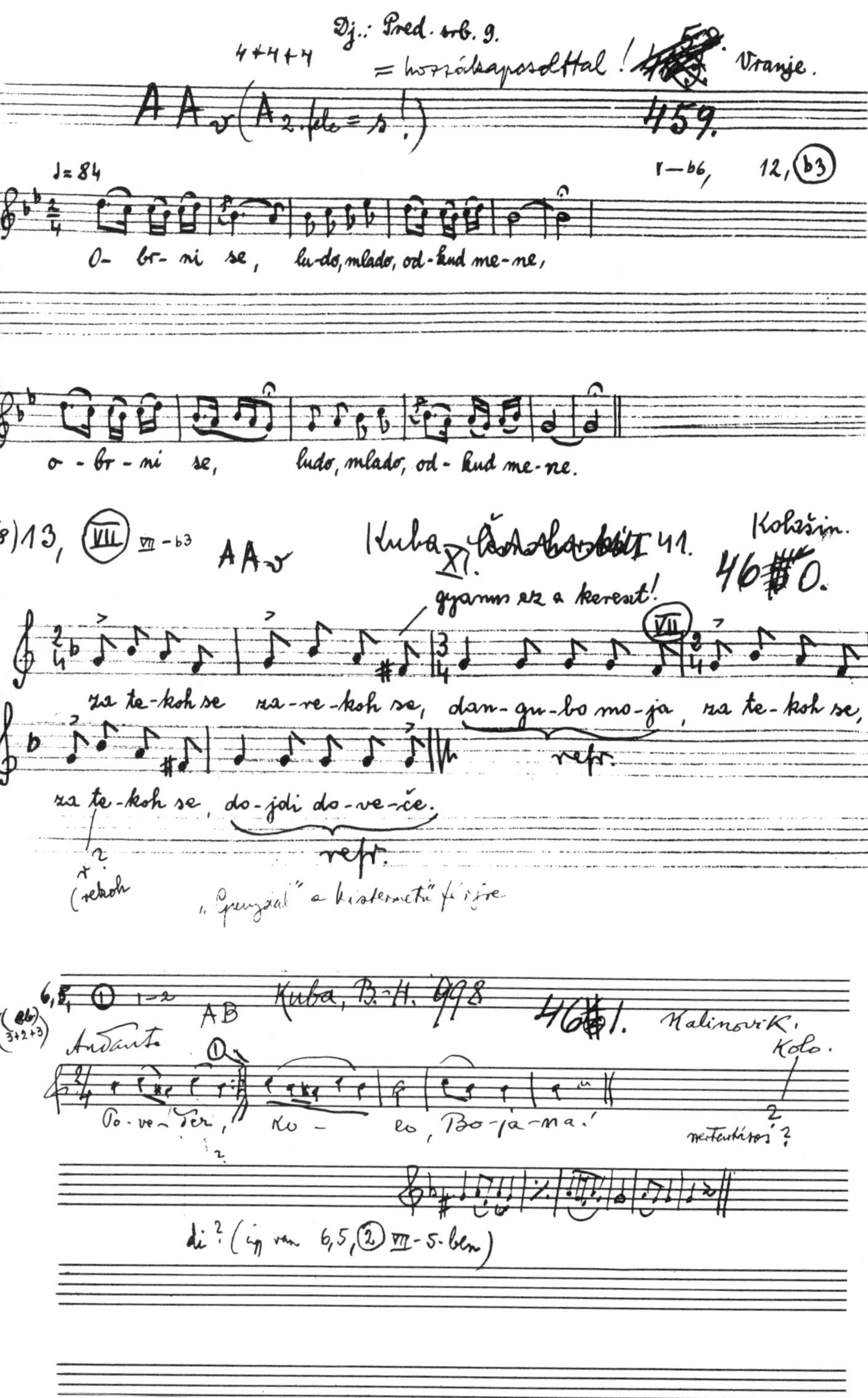
Dj.: Pred. srb. 9.
4+4+4
Vranje.
459.
♩= 84
O- br- ni se, lu-do, mlado, od-kud me-ne,
o - br - ni se, ludo, mlado, od - kud me-ne.
8)13, VII
AAv
Kuba
XI.
41.
Kolašin.
460.
gyanus ez a kereszt!
za te-koh se za-re-koh se, dan-gu-bo mo-ja, za te-koh se,
refr.
za te-koh se, do-jdi do-ve-če.
refr.
(rekoh
AB
Kuba, B.-H. 998
461.
Kalinovik.
Kolo.
Andante

Kuba. B. H. 395.
Trnovo.
AB
Za-pje-vaj, za-pje-vaj si-vi so-ko-le za-pje-vaj za-pje-vaj
si-vi so-ko-le!
Kuhač II. 438.
Iz Berata u Krbaniji
♩=63.
Moj tu-ma-re ku-tja moj, ku-ka da le-ri.
AB
Kuba B.H. 477.
464.
Zenica. (Kolo.)
Moderato.
Plani-ni-co, plani-no,
selo ka-me-ni-to.
transp.
Skeleton form

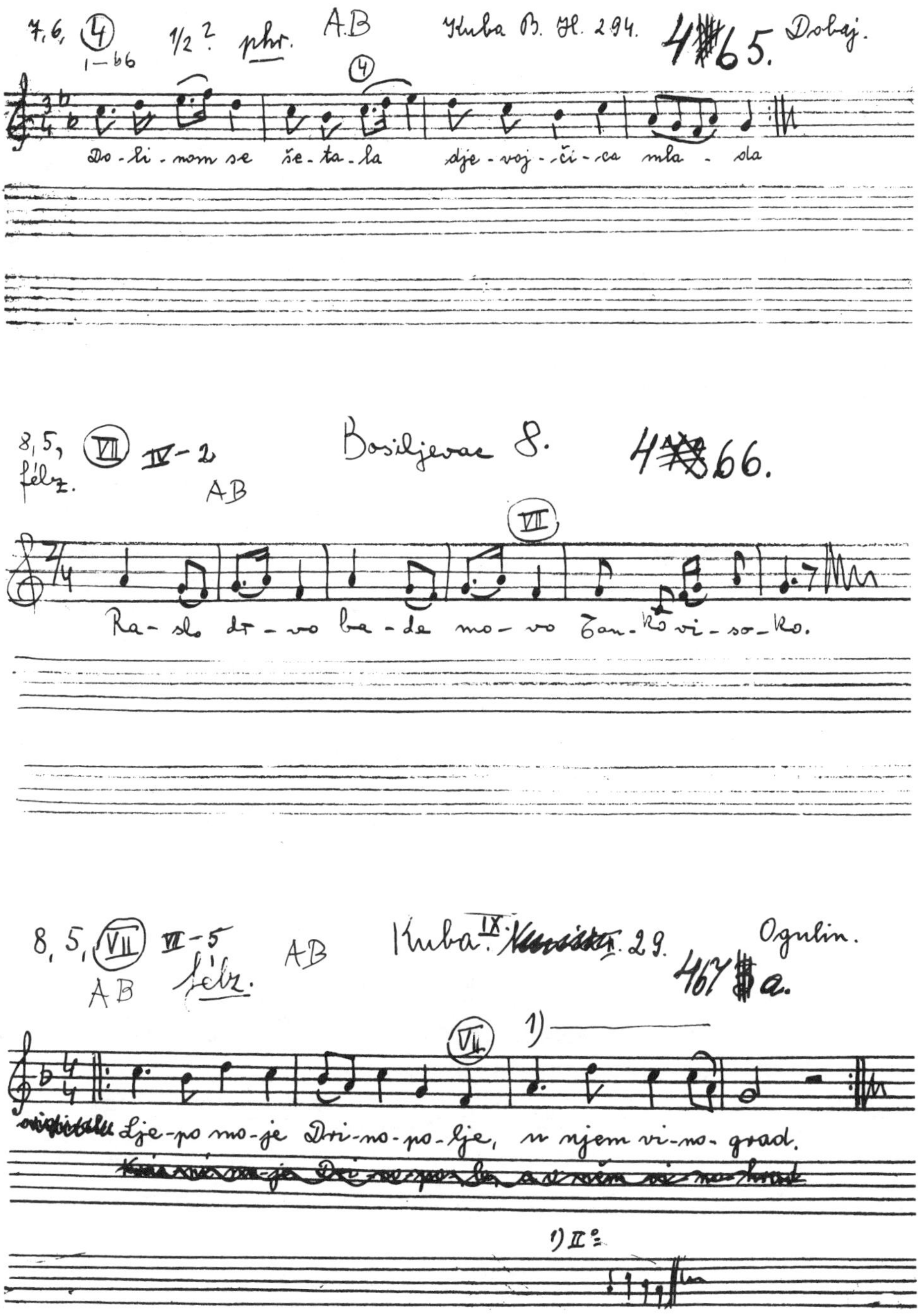
AB
Dobaj.
Do-li-nom se še-ta-la dje-voj-či-ca mla-da
Bosiljevac 8.
AB
Ra-slo dr-vo ba-de mo-vo Zan-ko vi-so-ko.
Ogulin.
AB
Lje-po mo-je Dri-no-po-lje, u njem vi-no-grad.

8, 5, VII VII – 5 AB
Kuba. B. H. 113.
Čajniče
467
phr.
i pa-do-še, pred ma-na-stir Pe-tra sve-to-ga.
Kuba. BH. 989
468.
Allegro
AA
Ljubuški.
Variant.
Nešto otac, nešto mati, a ja nejmam s kim.
preko puta vrlo krasan sin. Čini mi se, mila mati,
da bi mogla s njim.
8, 5, VII – 4
Kuhač III. 1072.
469 – 470.
♩= 69.
AA
Iz Budve u austr. Albaniji
La-re-koh se i za-fa-lih ja do-bar ju-nak.

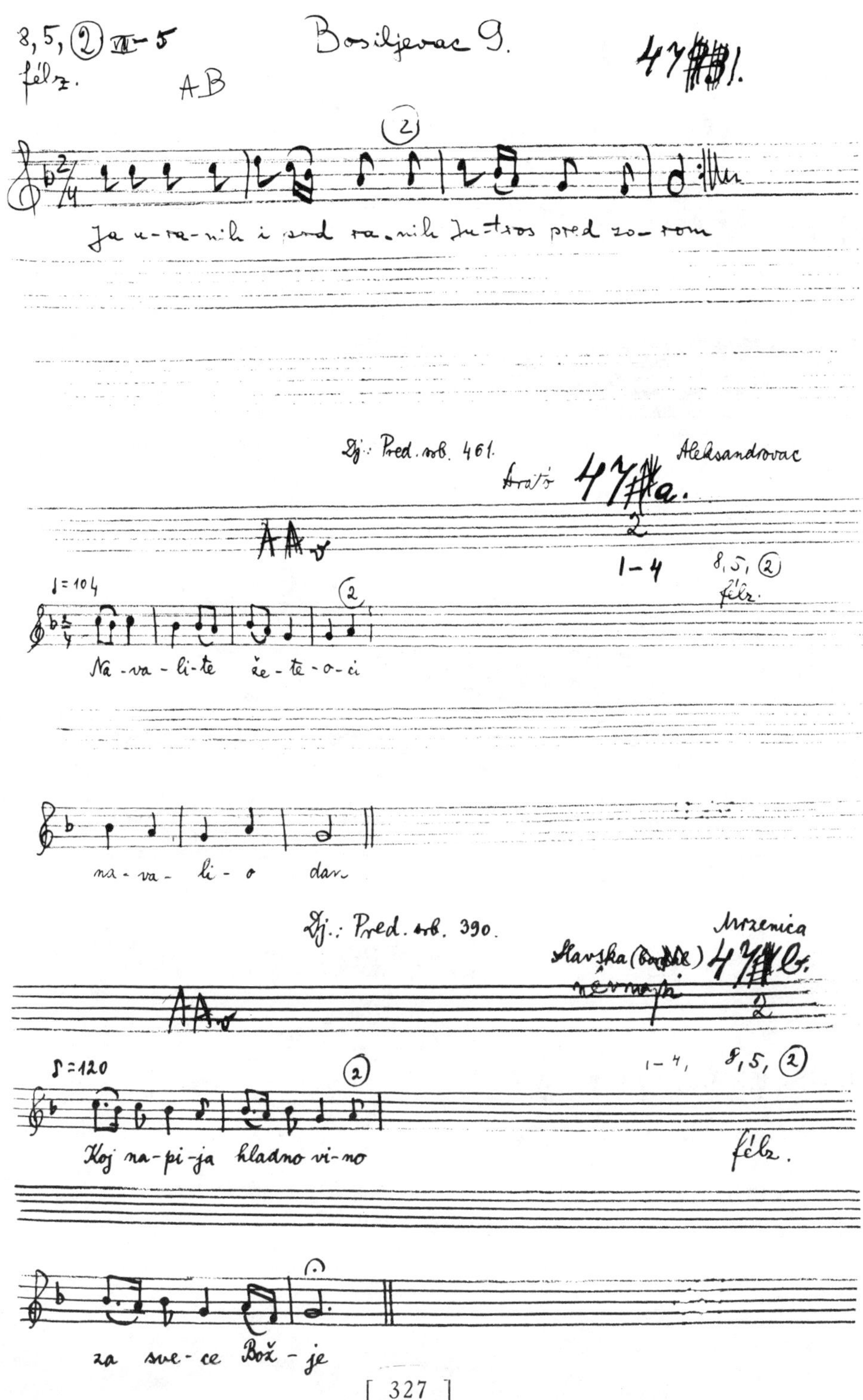
Bosiljevac 9.
47/B1.
Ja u-ra-nih i pred ra-nih Ju-tros pred zo-rom
Aleksandrovac
47/a.
Na-va-li-te že-te-o-ci
na-va-li-o dan
Mrzenica
47/c.
Koj na-pi-ja hladno vi-no
za sve-ce Bož-je

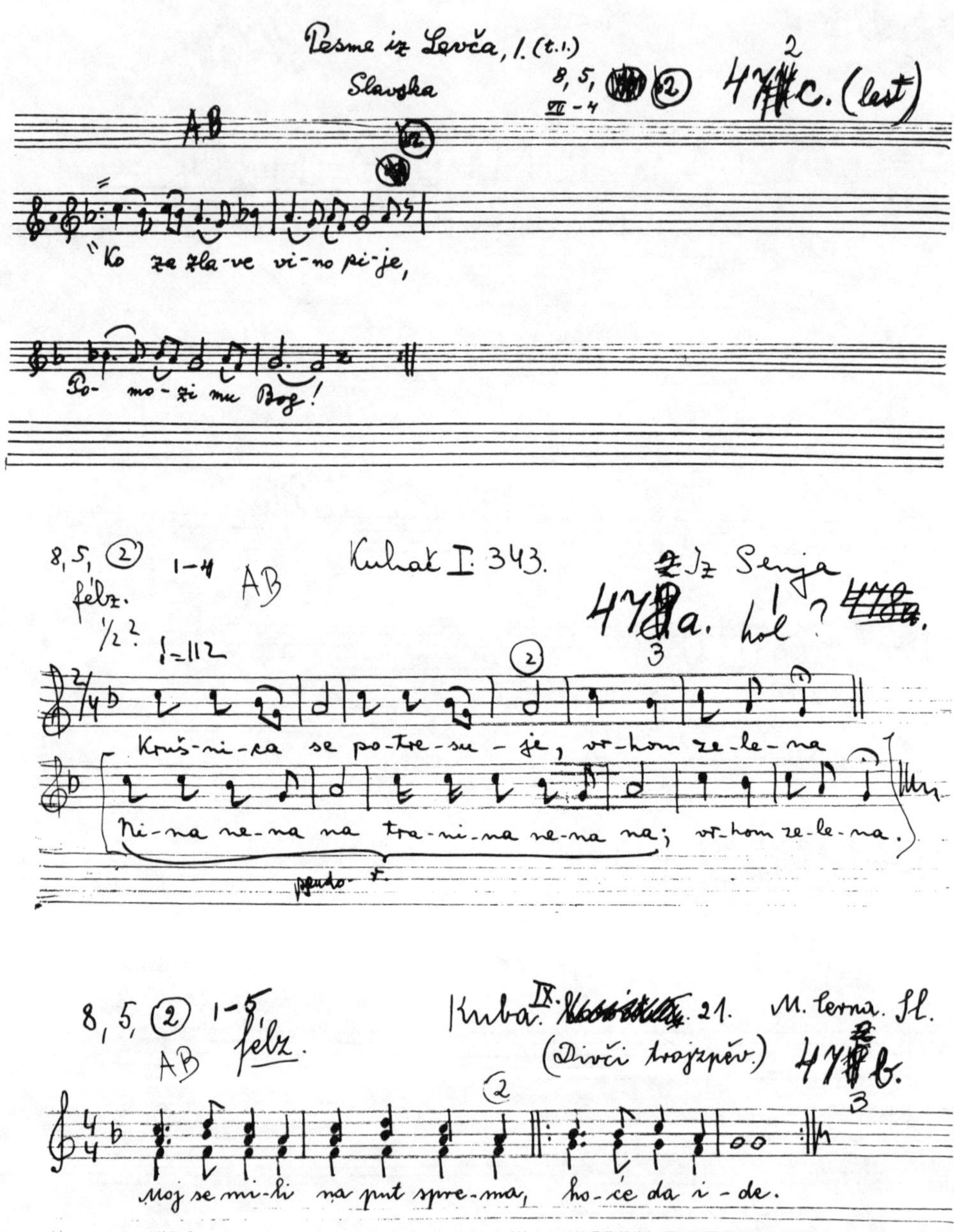

Pesme iz Levča, I. (t.1.)
Slavska
8, 5,
AB
Ko za zla-ve vi-no pi-je,
Po- mo-zi mu Bog!
8, 5, (2) 1–4
félz.
AB
Kuhač I. 343.
Iz Senja
♩=112
Kruš-ni-ca se po-tre-su-je, vr-hom ze-le-na
Ni-na ne-na na tra-ni-na ne-na na; vr-hom ze-le-na.
8, 5, (2) 1–5
félz.
AB
Kuba. IX. 21.
M. Cerna. Sl.
(Dívčí trojzpěv.)
Moj se mi-li na put spre-ma, ho-će da i-de.

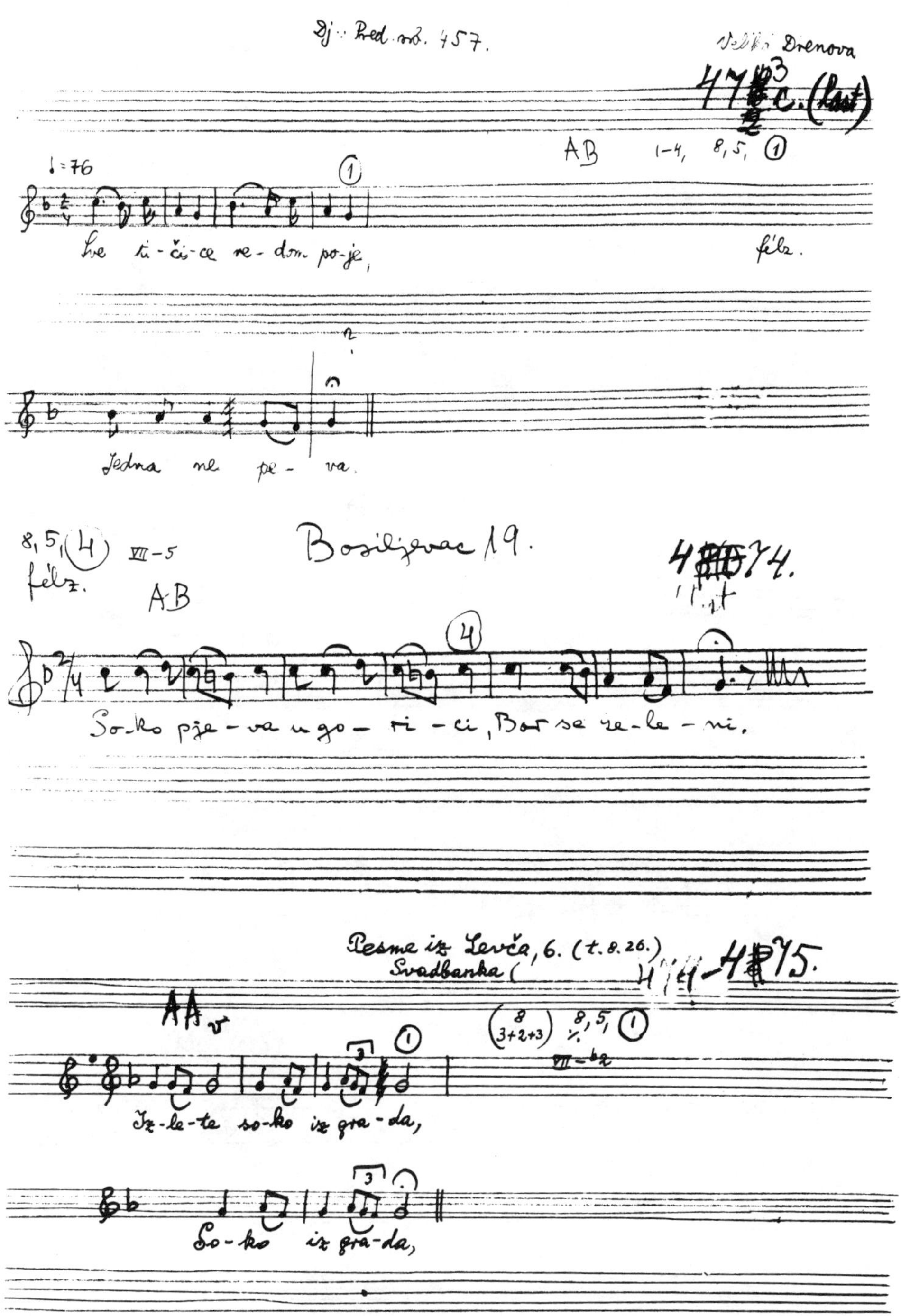
AB
Jedna ne pe-va.
AB
Bosiljevac 19.
So-ko pje-va u go-ri-ci, Bor se ze-le-ni.
Pesme iz Levča, 6.
Svadbanka
AA
Iz-le-te so-ko iz gra-da,
So-ko iz gra-da,

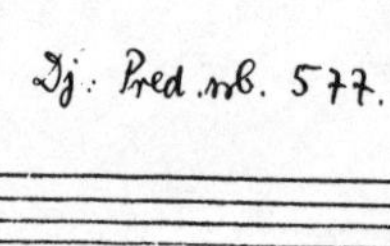

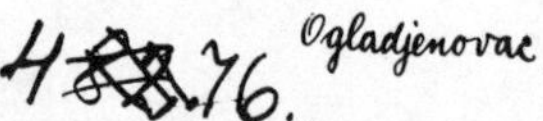

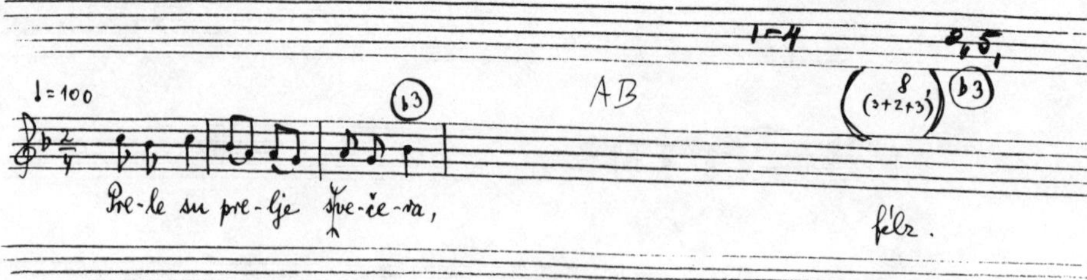

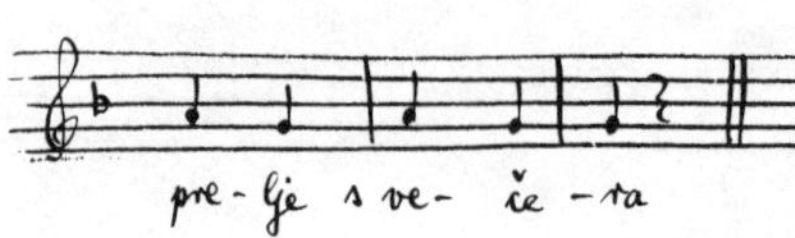

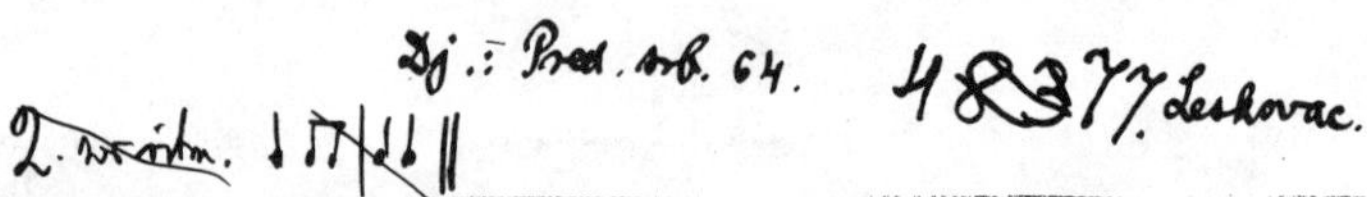

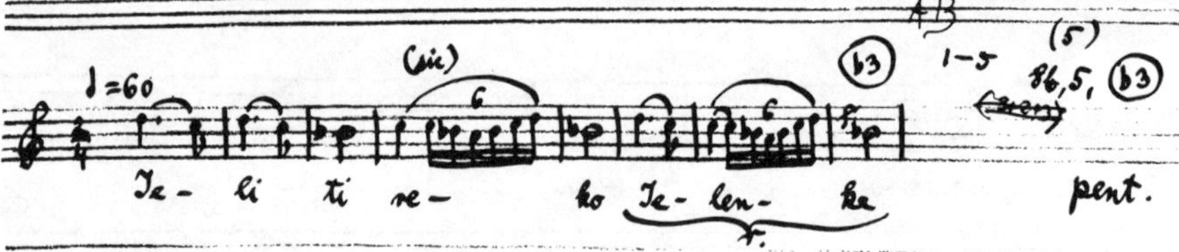

Der- ven da- ču- vaš

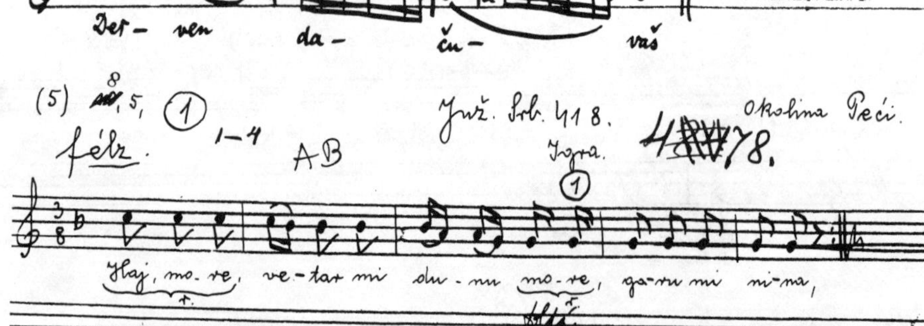

Kuba B.H. 823.
479a.
Largo. AB
Dölésödal
Ključ (Uspavanka)
Li – la, si – ne, li – la, si – ne,
u tan – koj be – ši – ci.
Skeleton form:
Kuba B.H. 809.
479b.
Andante
Doboj (Svatovska)
Zlat – ni to – pi,
zlatni to – pi na gra – du
pu – ko – še
Skeleton form:
Kuba B.H. 770.
479c.
Uspavanka
(Dölésödal)
Andante AB
Doboj (Koljevka)
Spa – vaj, si – ne, spavaj si – ne, san te pre – va – ri – o –

Pred. sb. 352.
fonó H.
479 d.
Kulina
♩=80
VII
AB
VII — b2
(10)
8, 6, VII
Be-ri- te se, berite se,
félz.
rit.
mome na se- delj- ku!
(10) 8,6, VII VII — b2 AB
Kuba B. H. 307.
479 é.
Kiseljak
félz.
Lu-gom leg-la, lu-gom leg-la tra-va dje-te-li-na.
megszakítás
(10) 8,6, VII VII — b2 AB
Kuba B. H. 879:
(Lakodalmas)
Doboj (Svatovska)
félz.
479 f.
Sad se Ma-ra, sad se Ma-ra sva-to-vi-
ma na-da.
megszakítás

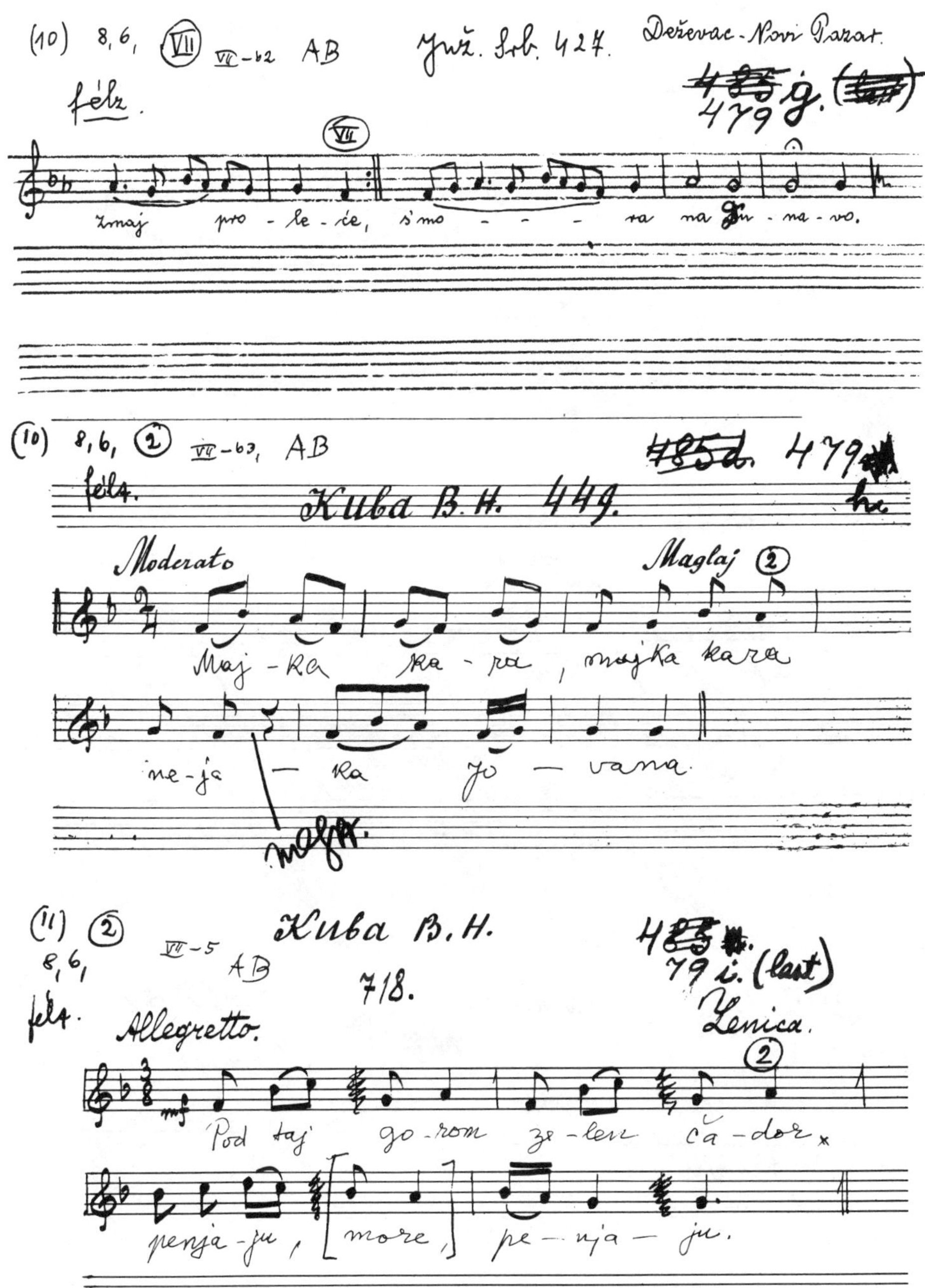

(10) 8, 6, VII VII – 62 AB
Juž. Srb. 427.
Deževac - Novi Pazar.
479 g.
zmaj pro - le - će, s'mo - - - ra na Đu - na - vo.
(10) 8, 6, 2 VII – 63, AB
479
Kuba B. H. 449.
Moderato
Maglaj 2
Maj - ka ka - ra, majka kara
ne - ja — ka jo — vana.
(11) 2 Kuba B. H.
8, 6, VII – 5 AB
718.
79 i. (last)
Zenica.
Allegretto.
Pod taj go - rom ze - len ča - dor
penja - ju, [more,] pe — nja — ju.

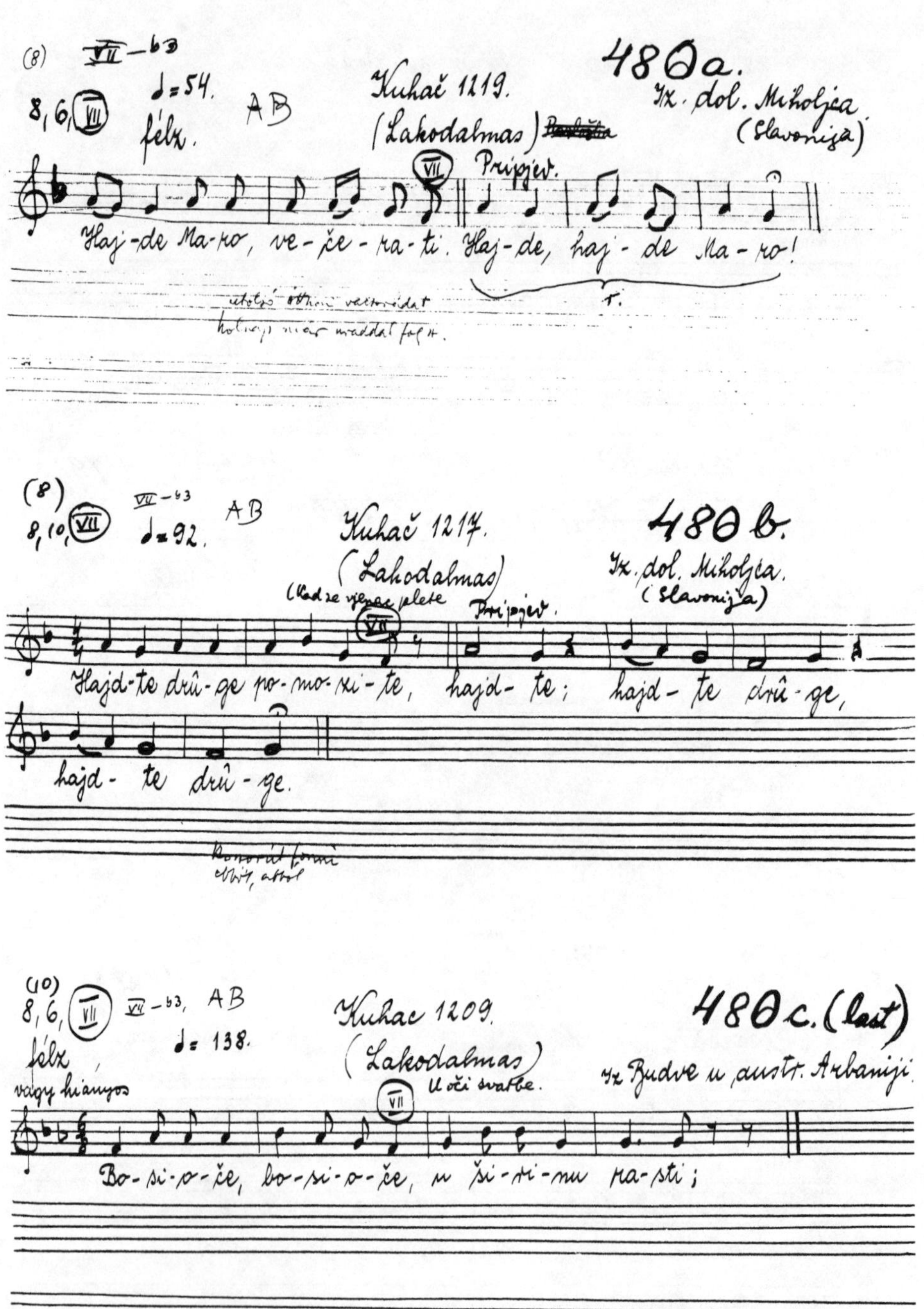

(8) VII–63
480a.
8, 6, VII ♩=54.
félz.
AB
Kuhač 1219.
(Lakodalmas)
Iz. dol. Miholjca
(Slavonija)
VII
Pripjev.
Haj-de Ma-ro, ve-če-ra-ti. Haj-de, haj-de Ma-ro!
(8)
8, 10, VII
VII–63
♩=92.
AB
Kuhač 1217.
480b.
(Lakodalmas)
Iz. dol. Miholjca.
(Slavonija)
(Kad se vjenac plete
VII
Pripjev.
Hajd-te drû-ge po-mo-zi-te, hajd-te; hajd-te drû-ge,
hajd-te drû-ge.
(10)
8, 6, VII
VII–63,
AB
♩= 138.
Kuhač 1209.
480c. (last)
félz
vagy hiányos
(Lakodalmas)
Iz Budve u austr. Arbaniji.
U oči svatbe.
VII
Bo-si-o-če, bo-si-o-če, u ši-ri-nu ra-sti;

8, 6, VII VII—4
Kuba. B. H. 881.
Glamoč.
48/a.
félz. AB
Ve-sel-te se dje-voj-či-ce, ko-je pje-vat zna-te.
8, 6, VII v. ö. 607.
Kuba. B. H. 833.
48/b.
Jeleč.
phr. VII-4 AB
Dje-voj-či-ca vo-du ga-zi, no-ne joj se b'je-le.
mégis „n"!
(10) 8, 6, VII VII—4
Kuba. B. H. 834.
Žepče.
48/c. (last)
félz. AB
U-go-ri-ci u go-ri-ci je-la ne-sje-če-na.

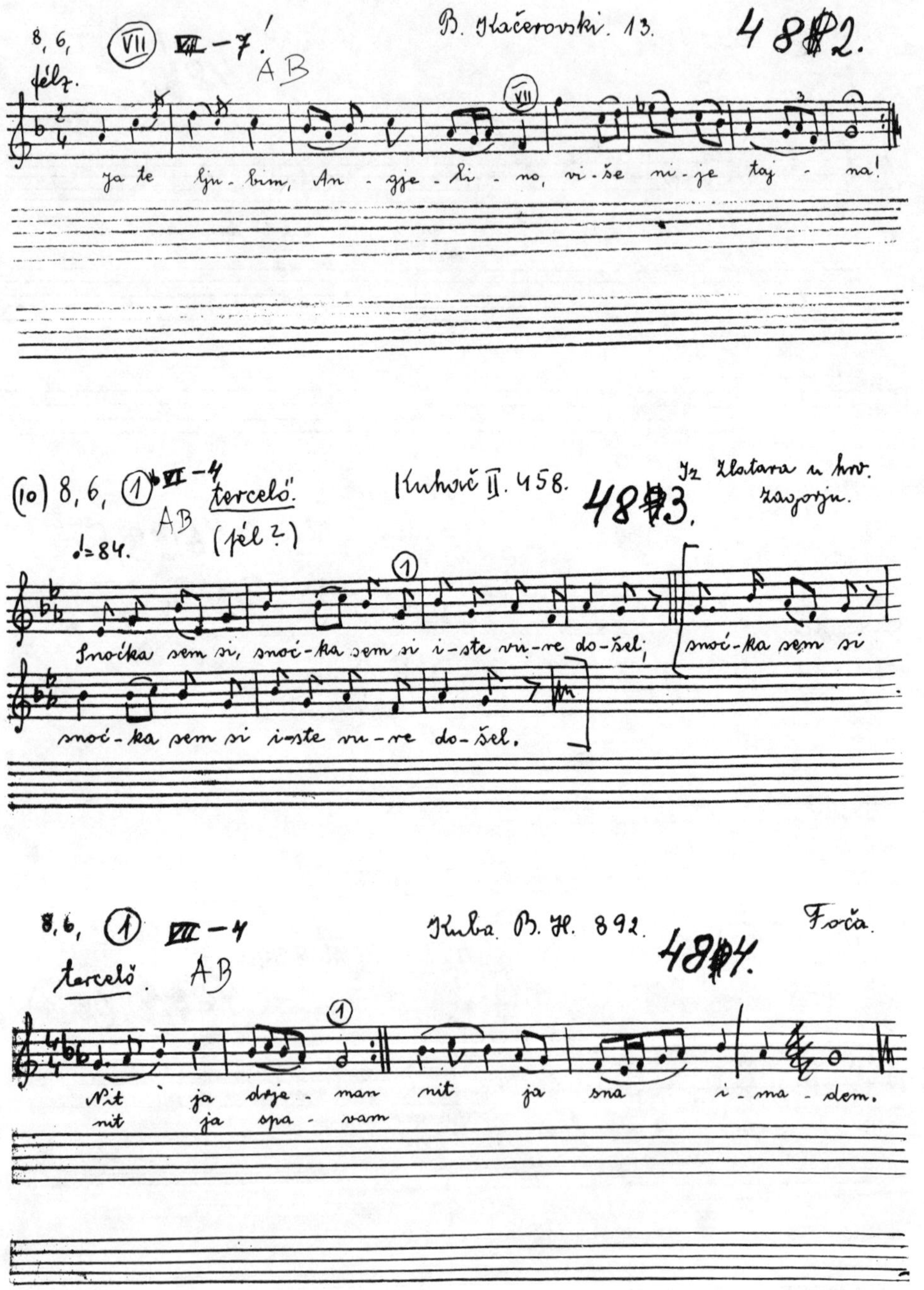

8, 6, VII –7!
AB
B. Kačerovski. 13.
félz.
Ja te lju-bim, An-gje-li-no, vi-še ni-je taj-na!
(10) 8, 6, 1 –4 tercelő.
AB
(fél?)
Kuhač II. 458.
Iz Zlatara u hrv. zagorju.
♩.=84.
Snoćka sem si, snoć-ka sem si i-ste vu-re do-šel; snoć-ka sem si
snoć-ka sem si i-ste vu-re do-šel.
8,6, 1 VII –4
Kuba. B. H. 892.
Foča.
tercelő.
AB
Nit ja dnje-man nit ja sna i-ma-dem.
nit ja spa-vam

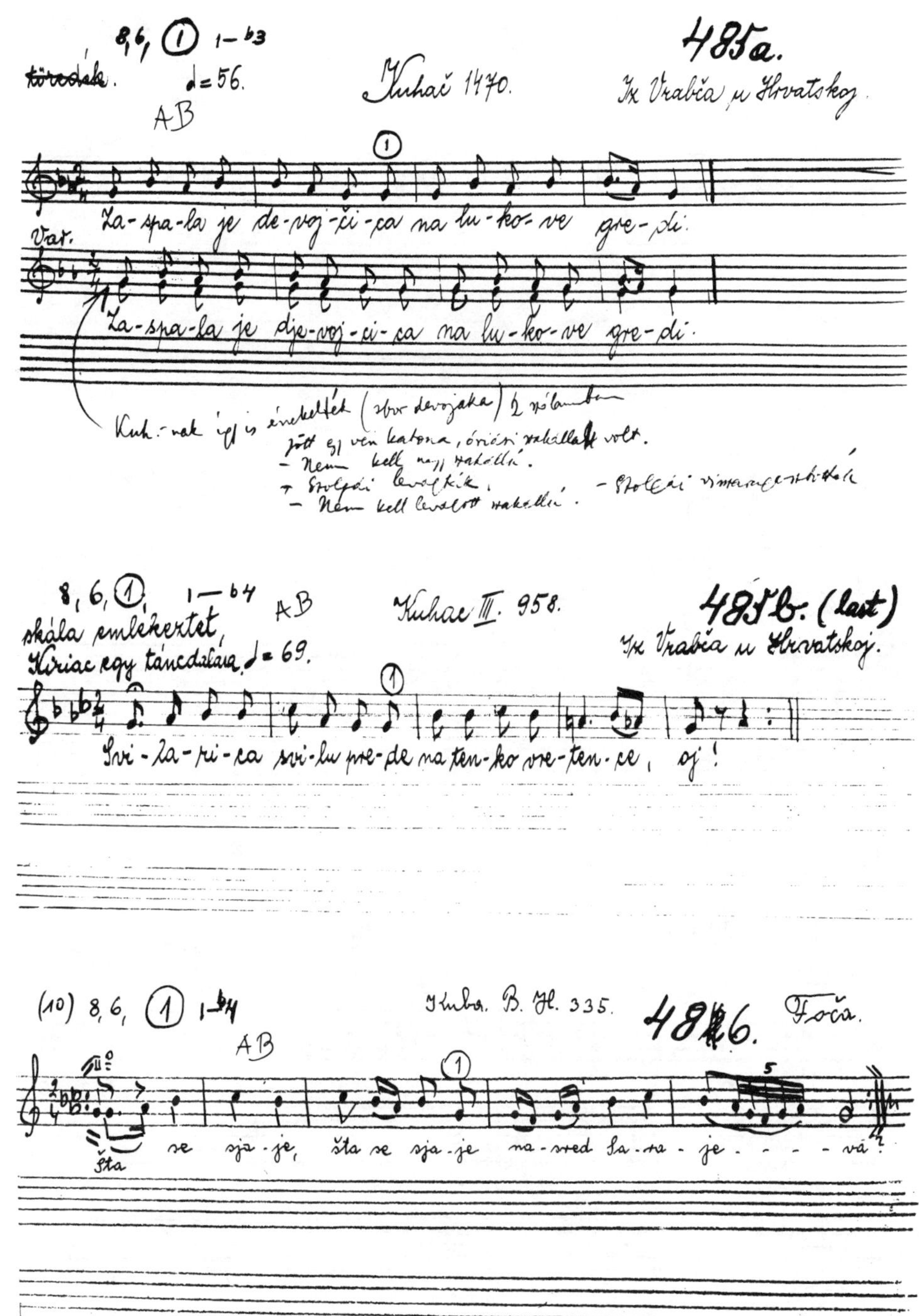

485a.
Kuhač 1470.
Iz Vrabča u Hrvatskoj.
♩=56.
AB
Za-spa-la je de-voj-či-ca na lu-ko-ve gre-di.
Var.
Za-spa-la je dje-voj-či-ca na lu-ko-ve gre-di.
485b. (last)
Kuhač III. 958.
Iz Vrabča u Hrvatskoj.
AB
skála emlékeztet,
Kiriac egy táncdalára ♩= 69.
Svi-la-ri-ca svi-lu pre-de na ten-ko vre-ten-ce, oj!
Kuba. B. H. 335.
Foča.
AB
šta se sja-je, šta se sja-je na-sred Sa-ra-je - - - - vá?

Kuhač I.370.
Iz Kostajnice
(báni kerület)
Je-li ra-no, je-li ra-no, jel' sva-nu-lo dar-no.
Kuhba. B. H. 516.
488a.
Nevesinje.
előbbihez
Hajduk Velj-ko ej, Hajduk Veljko po or-di-ji še-će
Skeleton form:
Kuhba. B. H. 515.
488b.
Stolac.
félz.
Haj-duk Velj-ko ej mo-re, haj-duk Velj-ko kroz or-di-ju še-će.

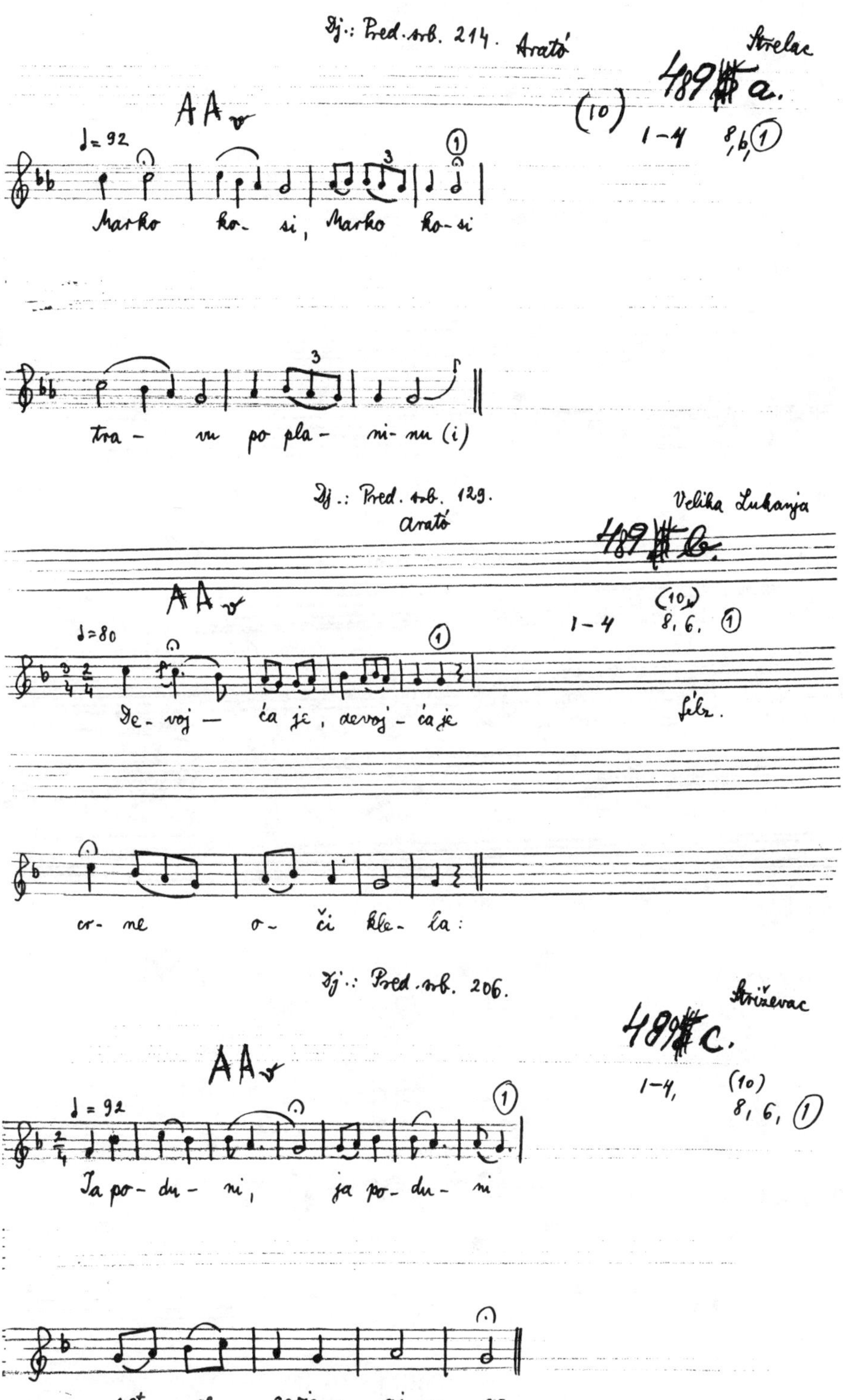
Dj.: Pred. sb. 214. Arató
Střelac
489 a.
(10)
1–4 8,6,①
AA v
♩= 92
①
Marko ko- si, Marko ko- si
tra – vu po pla- ni- nu (i)
Dj.: Pred. sb. 129.
arató
Velika Lukanja
489 b.
(10)
1 – 4 8, 6. ①
AA v
♩=80
①
De- voj – ća je, devoj- ća je
filr.
cr- ne o- či kle- la:
Dj.: Pred. sb. 206.
Strizevac
489 c.
AA v
1–4, (10)
8, 6, ①
♩ = 92
①
Ja po- du- ni, ja po- du- ni
vet re gorja – ni – ne.

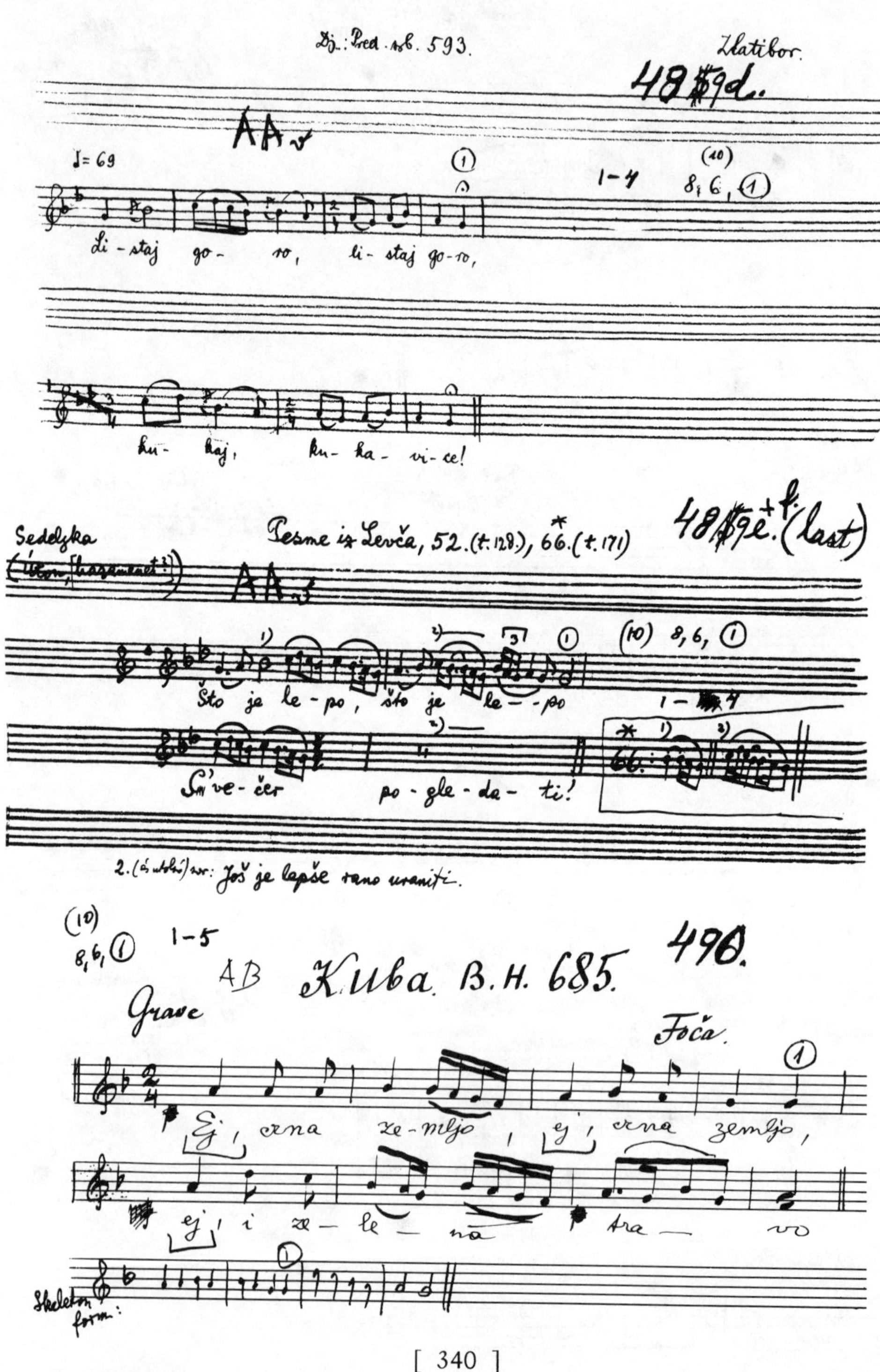
Dj.: Pred. sb. 593.
Zlatibor.
48 §9d.
AA
♩= 69
1–4
(10)
8, 6, ①
Li - staj go - ro, li - staj go-ro,
ku - kaj, ku - ka - vi - ce!
Sedelzka
Pesme iz Levča, 52. (t. 128.), 66. (t. 171)
48 §9e. (last)
AA
(10) 8, 6, ①
Što je le - po, što je le - - po
1–4
Sn' ve - čer po - gle - da - ti!
66.
Još je lepše rano uraniti.
(10)
8, 6, ①
1–5
490.
AB
Kuba. B.H. 685.
Grave
Foča.
Ej, crna ze - mljo, ej, crna zemljo,
ej, i ze - le — na tra — vo
Skeleton form:

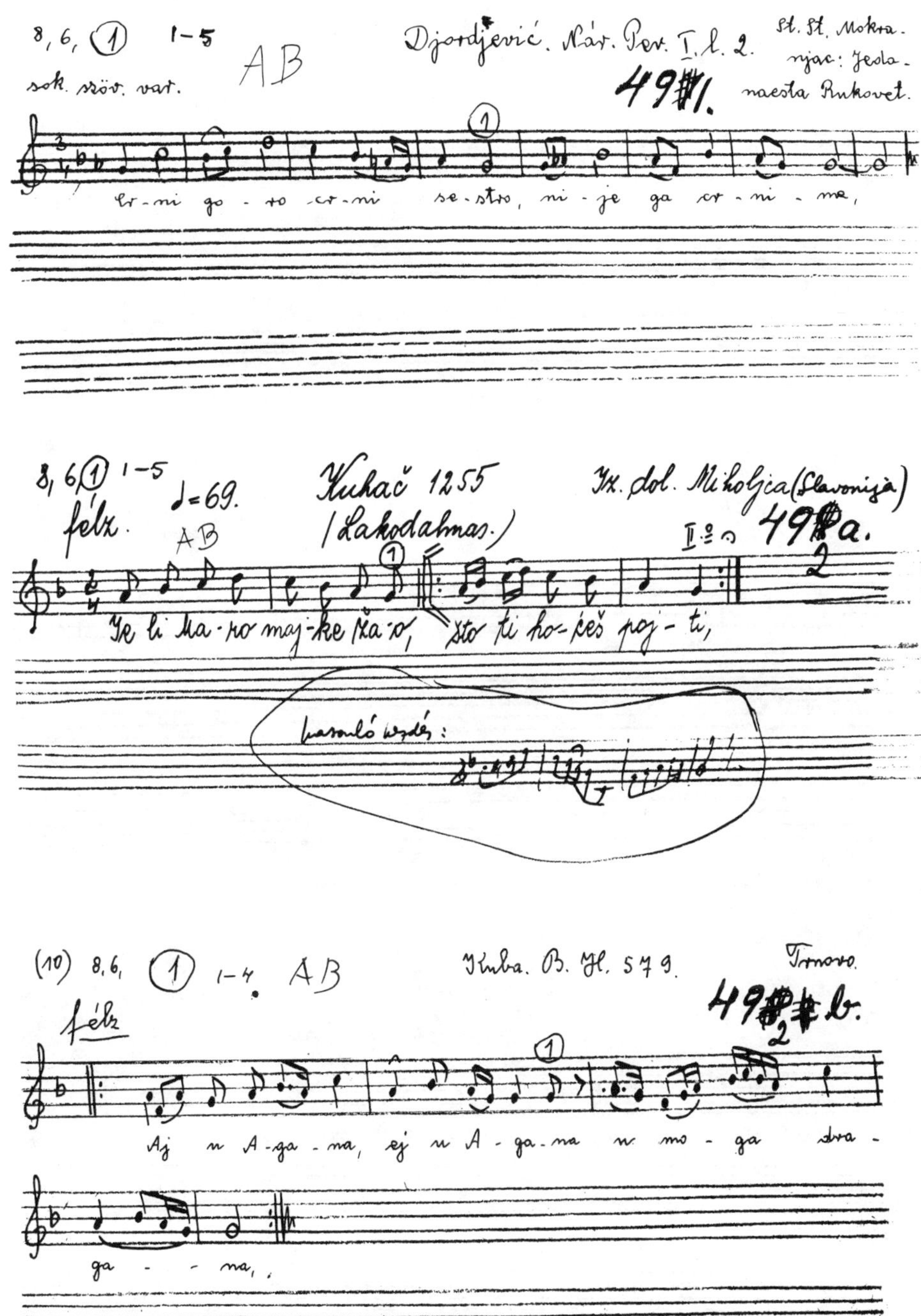

8, 6, ① 1–5
AB
Djordjević. Nár. Pev. I. l. 2.
St. St. Mokranjac: Jedanaesta Rukovet.
sok. szöv. var.
49#1.
Cr-ni go-ro cr-ni se-stro, ni-je ga cr-ni-ma,
8, 6 ① 1–5
♩=69.
Kuhač 1255
(Lakodalmas.)
Iz dol. Miholjca (Slavonija)
félz.
AB
49#a. 2
Je li Ma-ro maj-ke ka-o, što ti ho-ćeš poj-ti,
hasonló végz:
(10) 8, 6, ① 1–4. AB
Kuba. B. H. 579.
Trnovo.
félz
49#2 #b.
Aj u A-ga-na, ej u A-ga-na u mo-ga dra-ga-na,

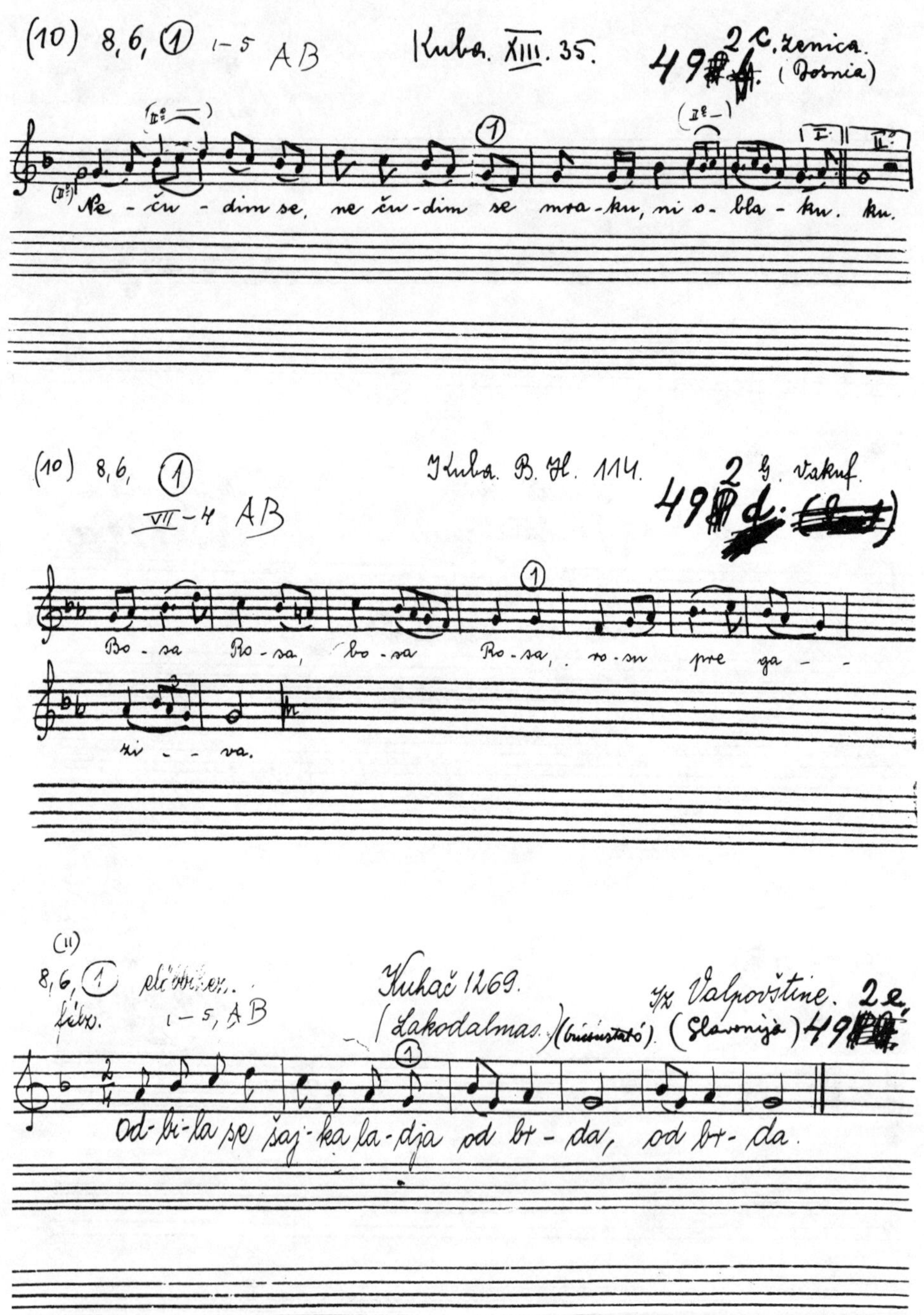

(10) 8,6, ① 1–5 AB
Kuba. XIII. 35.
2 C. zenica.
49
(Bosnia)
Ne - ču - dim se, ne ču-dim se mra-ku, ni o- bla - ku. ku.
(10) 8,6, ①
VII – 4 AB
Kuba. B. H. 114.
2 G. vakuf.
49
Bo - sa Ro - sa, bo - sa Ro - sa, ro - su pre ga - zi - - va.
(11)
8,6, ①
1 – 5, AB
Kuhač 1269.
(Lakodalmas.)
Iz Valpovštine.
(Slavonija) 49
Od-bi-la se šaj-ka la-dja od br - da, od br - da.

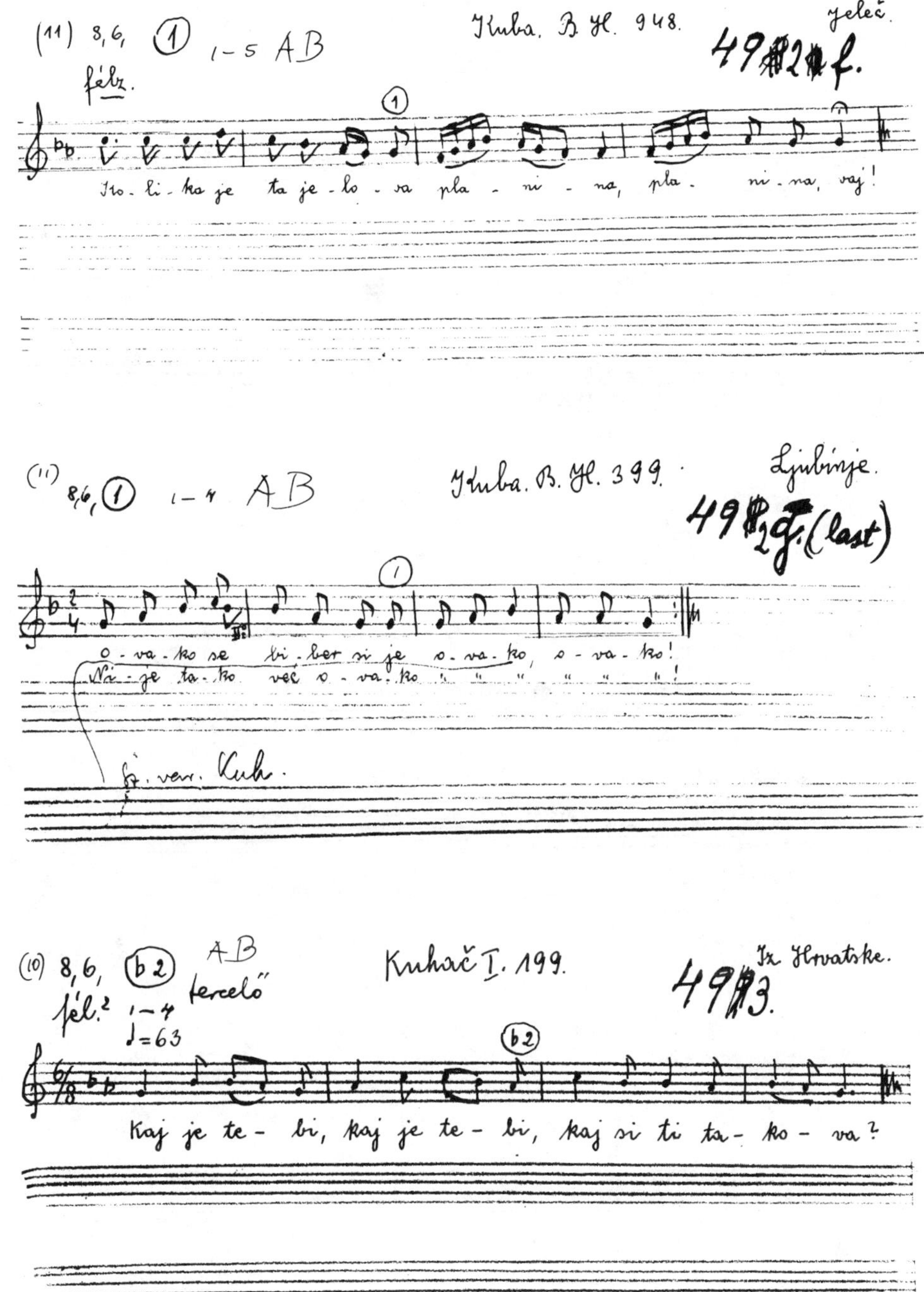
(11) 8,6, (1) 1–5 AB
félz.
Kuba. B. H. 948.
Jeleč.
49#2#f.
(1)
Ito-li-ka je ta je-lo-va pla-ni-na, pla-ni-na, vaj!
(11) 8,6, (1) 1–4 AB
Kuba. B. H. 399.
Ljubinje.
49#2g.(last)
(1)
o-va-ko se bi-ber si je o-va-ko, o-va-ko!
Ná-je ta-ko već o-va-ko " " " " " "!
Jf. var. Kuh.
(10) 8,6, (b2) AB tercelő
fél.2 1–4
♩=63
Kuhač I. 199.
Iz Hrvatske.
49#3.
(b2)
Kaj je te-bi, kaj je te-bi, kaj si ti ta-ko-va?

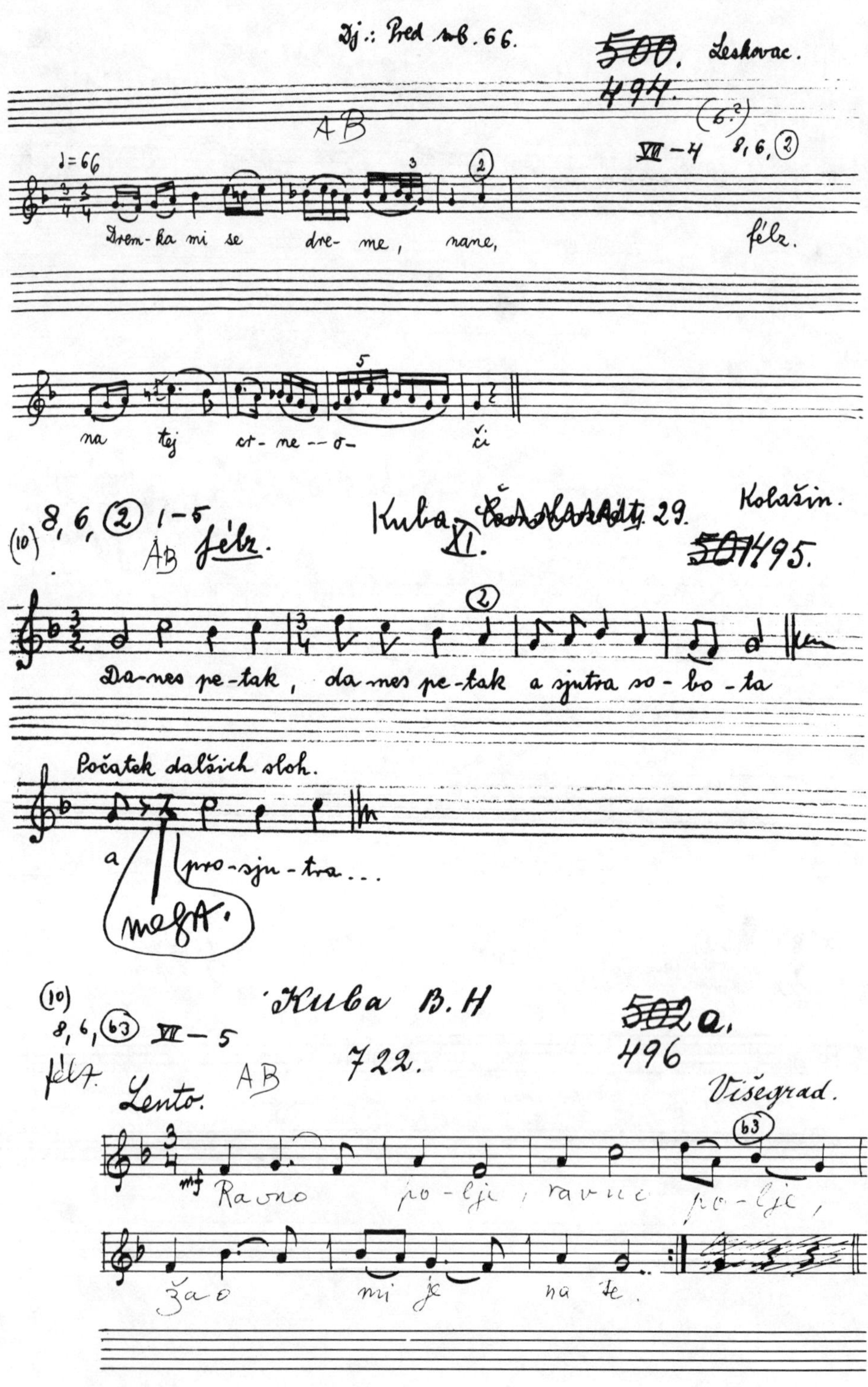
Dj.: Pred nb. 66.
500. Leskovac.
494.
(6²)
AB
VII-4
8, 6, ②
♩=66
Drem-ka mi se dre- me, nane,
félz.
na tej cr- ne -- o- či
(10) 8, 6, ② 1-5
AB félz.
Kuba 29.
XI.
Kolašin.
501 495.
Da-nes pe-tak, da-nes pe-tak a sjutra so- bo - ta
Počatek dalších sloh.
a pro-sju-tra...
meGA.
(10)
Kuba B.H
8, 6, (b3) VII - 5
722.
502 a.
496
félz.
Lento.
AB
Višegrad.
mf
Ravno po-lje, ravno po-lje,
žao mi je na te.

(10) 8, 6, b3 VII – 5
Djordjević. Nár. Pev. 35/2.
496
félz.
AB
Rav - no po - lje, rav - no po - lje, ža - o mi je na te.
8, 6, b3 VII – 5
v. ö: 833
B. H. 607.
Plevlje
497.
félz.
AB
Dje - voj - či - ca vo - du ga - zi no - ne joj se bje - le.
bi - je!
Dj.: Pred. srb. 218.
Kad se vraća sa rada (?!)
Strelac
498.
(10)
8, 6, b3
1–4
AB
félz. ?
♩=100
Stan ju - nače, stan ju - nače
ču - do da gle - da - mo

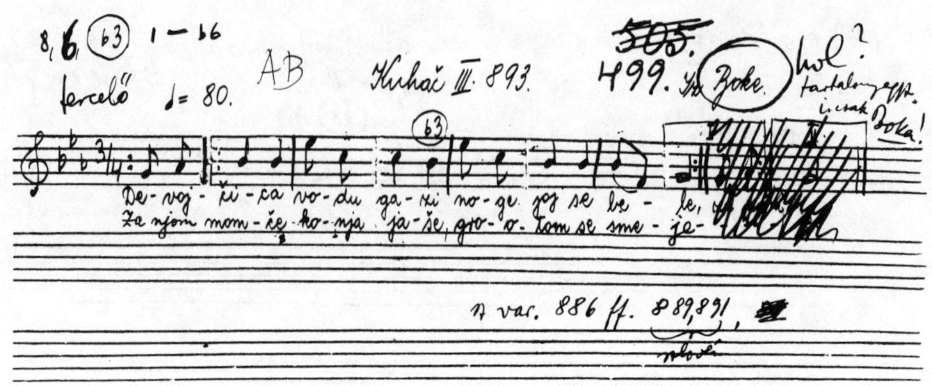
8, 6, b3 1—b6
AB
Kuhač III. 893.
499.
Boka.
♩= 80.
De-voj-či-ca vo-du ga-zi no-ge. joj se be-le,
Za njom mom-če ko-nja ja-še, gro-o. Tom se sme-je-
var. 886 ff. 889, 891,

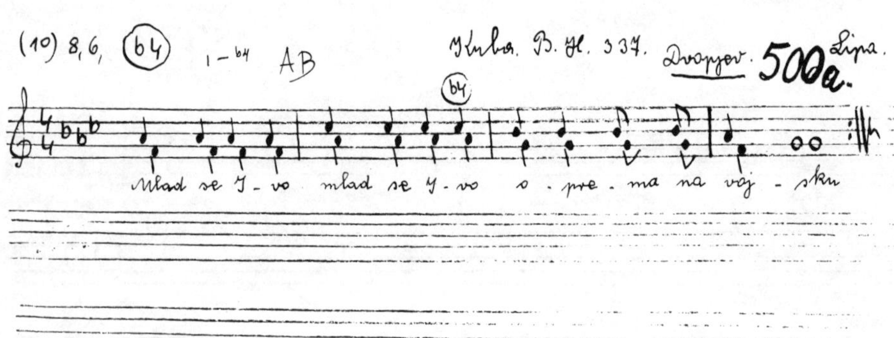
(10) 8, 6, b4 1—b4
AB
Kuhač. B. H. 337.
Dvopjev.
500a.
Lipa.
Mlad se I-vo mlad se I-vo o-pre-ma na voj-sku

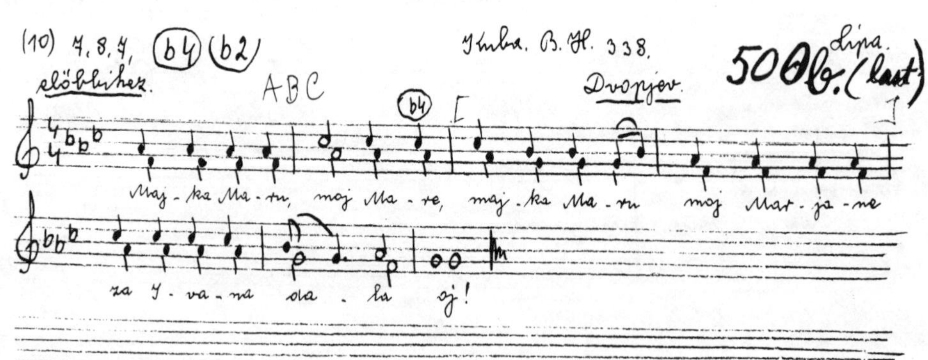
(10) 7, 8, 7, b4 b2
ABC
Kuhač. B. H. 338.
Dvopjev.
500b.
Lipa.
Maj-ka Ma-ru, moj Ma-re, maj-ka Ma-ru moj Mar-ja-ne
za I-va-na da-la oj!

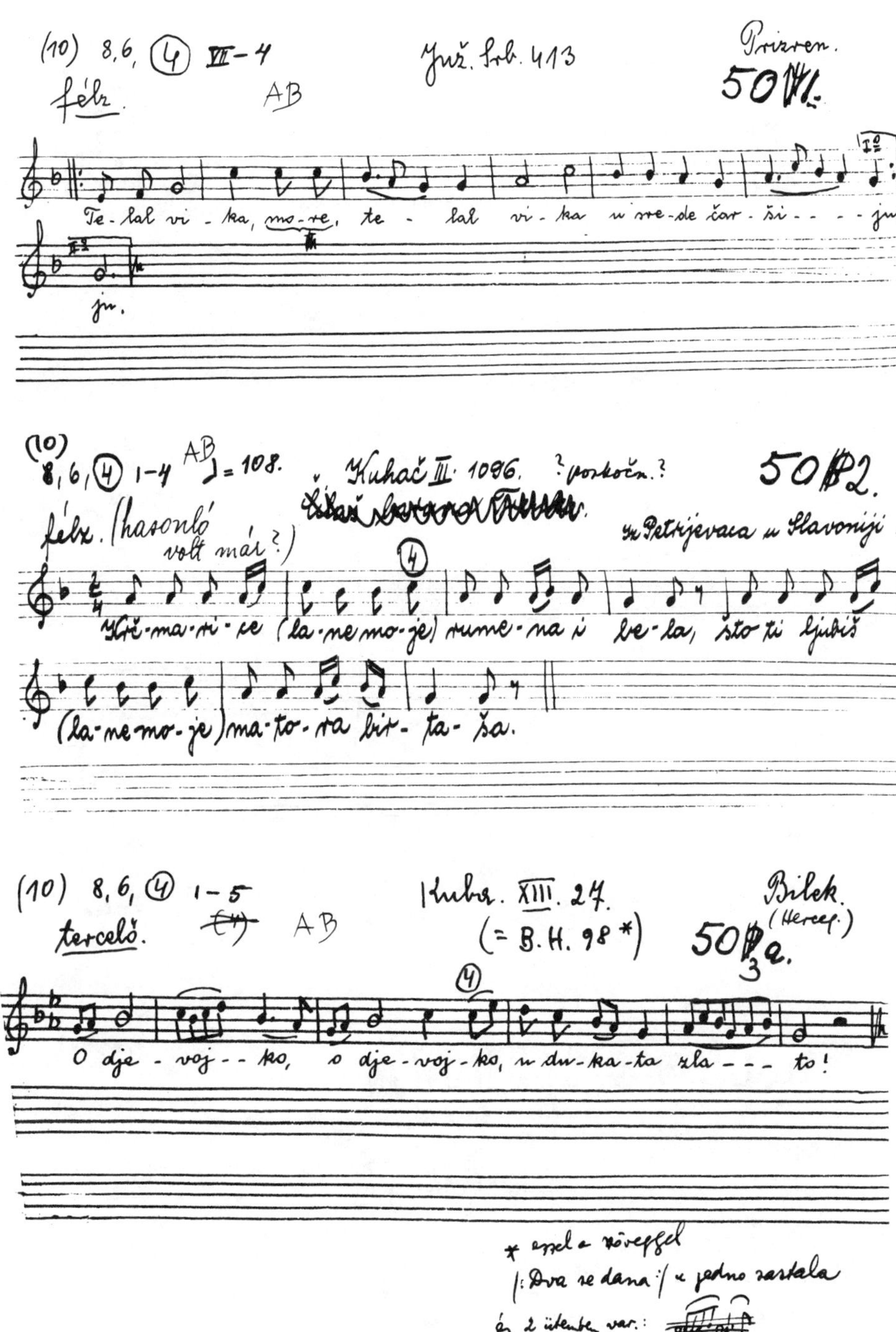
(10) 8,6, ④ VII–4
félz.
AB
Juž. Srb. 413
Prizren.
50VI.
Te-lal vi-ka, mo-re, te-lal vi-ka u sre-de čar-ši---ju,
ju.
(10) 8,6, ④ 1–4
AB
♩= 108.
Kuhač III. 1096.
? poskočn. ?
50VI2.
félz. (hasonló volt már?)
iz Petrijevaca u Slavoniji.
Kće-ma-ri-ce (la-ne mo-je) rume-na i be-la, što ti ljubiš
(la-ne mo-je) ma-to-ra bit-ta-ša.
(10) 8, 6, ④ 1–5
tercelő.
AB
Kuba. XIII. 27.
(= B. H. 98 *)
Bilek.
(Herceg.)
50VI3a.
O dje-voj--ko, o dje-voj-ko, u du-ka-ta zla---to!
* ezzel a szöveggel
|: Dva se dana :| u jedno sastala
és 2 ütemben var.:

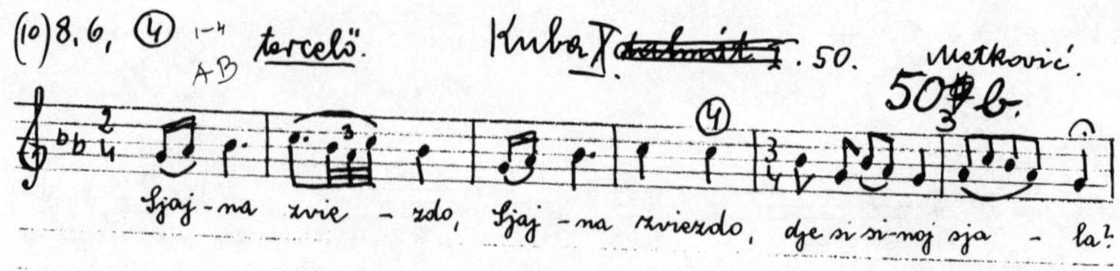
(10) 8, 6, ④ 1–4
AB
tercelő.
Kuba X. 50.
Metković.
50 b.
Sjaj-na zvie - zdo, Sjaj - na zviezdo, dje si si-noj sja - la?

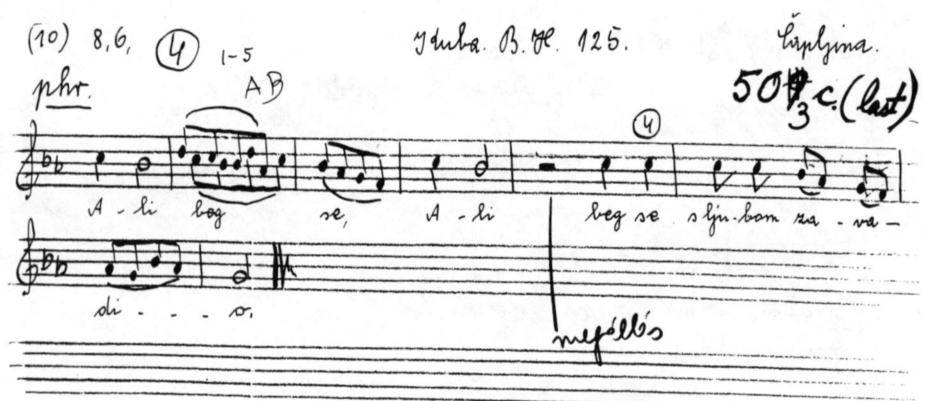
(10) 8, 6, ④ 1–5
phr.
AB
Kuba. B. H. 125.
Čapljina.
50 c. (last)
A - li beg se, A - li beg se s ljubom za - va -
di - - - o.
megállás

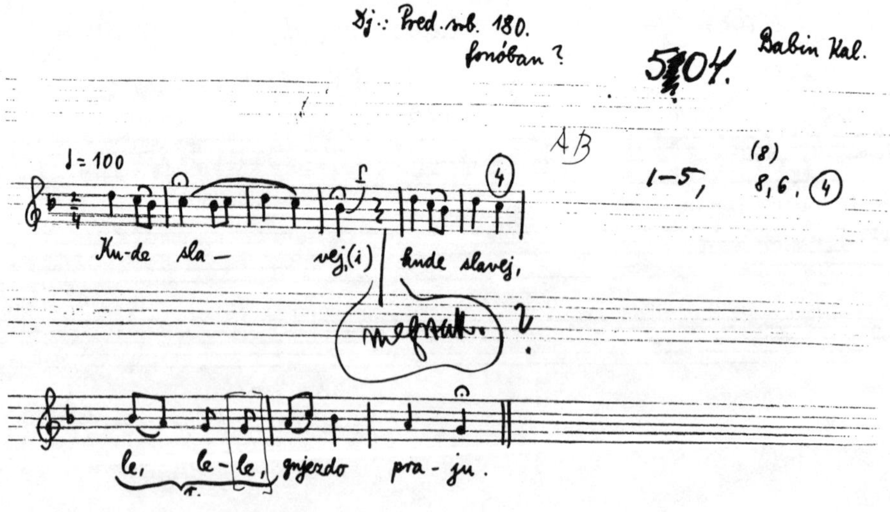
Babin Kal.
fonóban?
AB
♩= 100
(8)
1–5, 8, 6. ④
Ku-de sla - vej(i) kude slavej,
le, le - le, gnjezdo pra - ju.

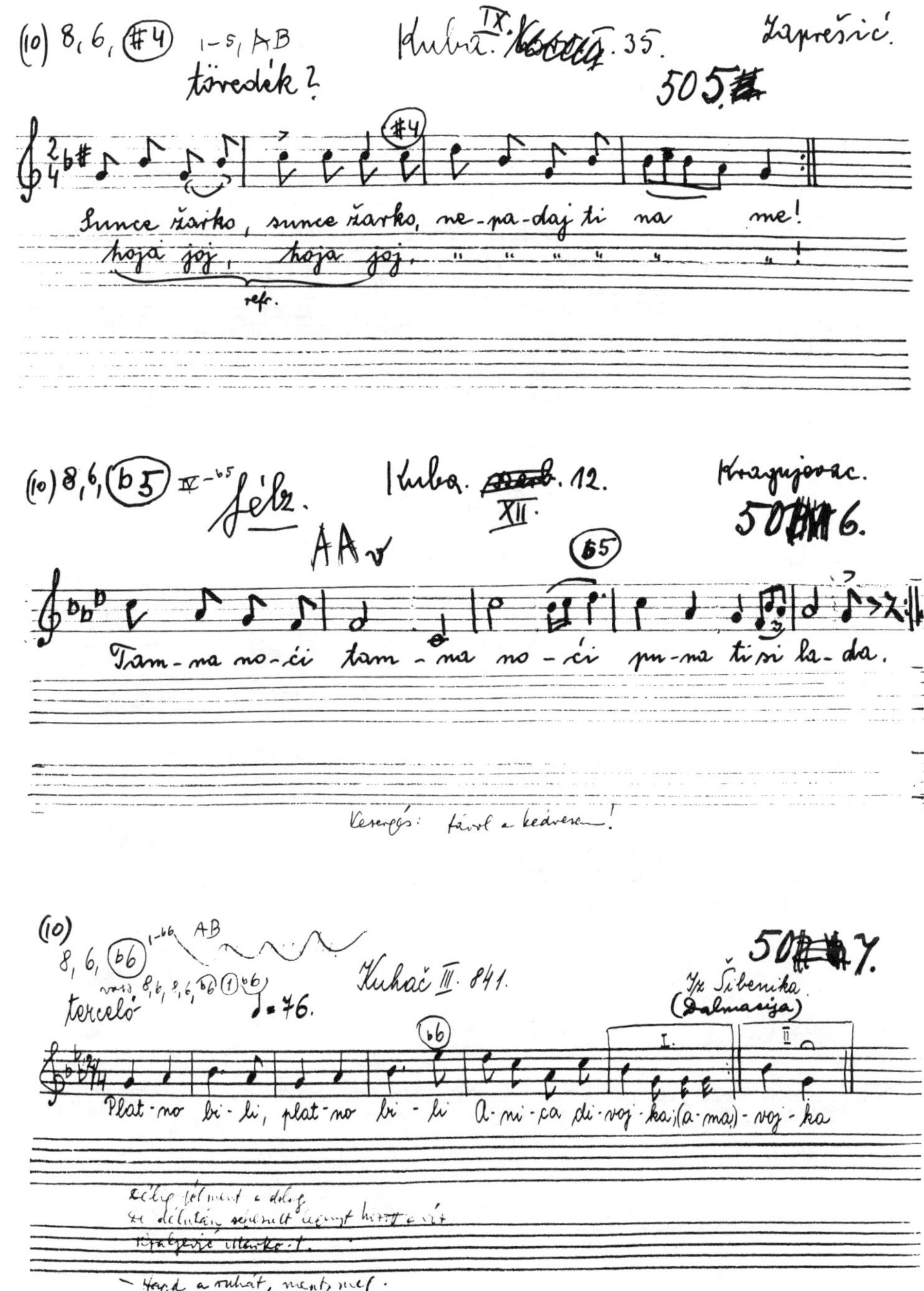

Zaprešić
505.
Sunce žarko, sunce žarko, ne-pa-daj ti na me!
Kragujevac.
Tam-na no-ći tam-na no-ći pu-na ti si la-da.
Kuhač III. 841.
Iz Šibenika (Dalmacija)
♩=76.
Plat-no bi-li, plat-no bi-li A-ni-ca di-voj-ka;(a-ma)-voj-ka

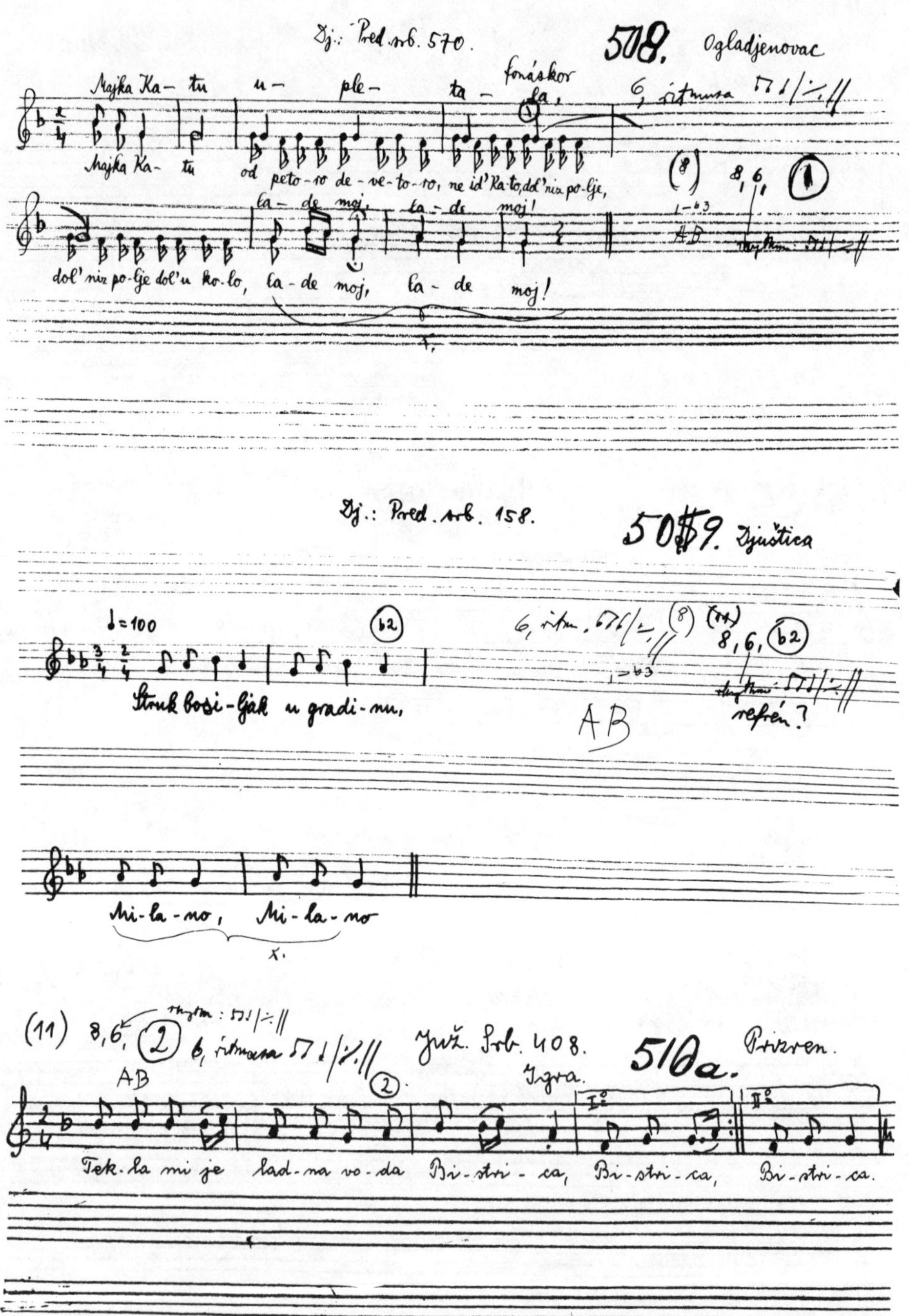
Dj.: Pred. srb. 570.
508.
Ogladjenovac
fonáskor
6, ritmusa
Majka Ka- tu u- ple- ta- la,
Majka Ka- tu od peto-ro de-ve-to-ro, ne id' Ka-to, dol' niz po-lje,
la- de moj, la- de moj!
dol' niz po-lje dol' u ko-lo, la-de moj, la- de moj!
AB
Dj.: Pred. srb. 158.
Djuštica
♩=100
Struk bosi-ljak u gradi-nu,
refrén?
AB
Mi-la-no, Mi-la-no
Juž. Srb. 408.
510a.
Prizren.
Igra.
AB
Tek-la mi je lad-na vo-da Bi-stri-ca, Bi-stri-ca, Bi-stri-ca.

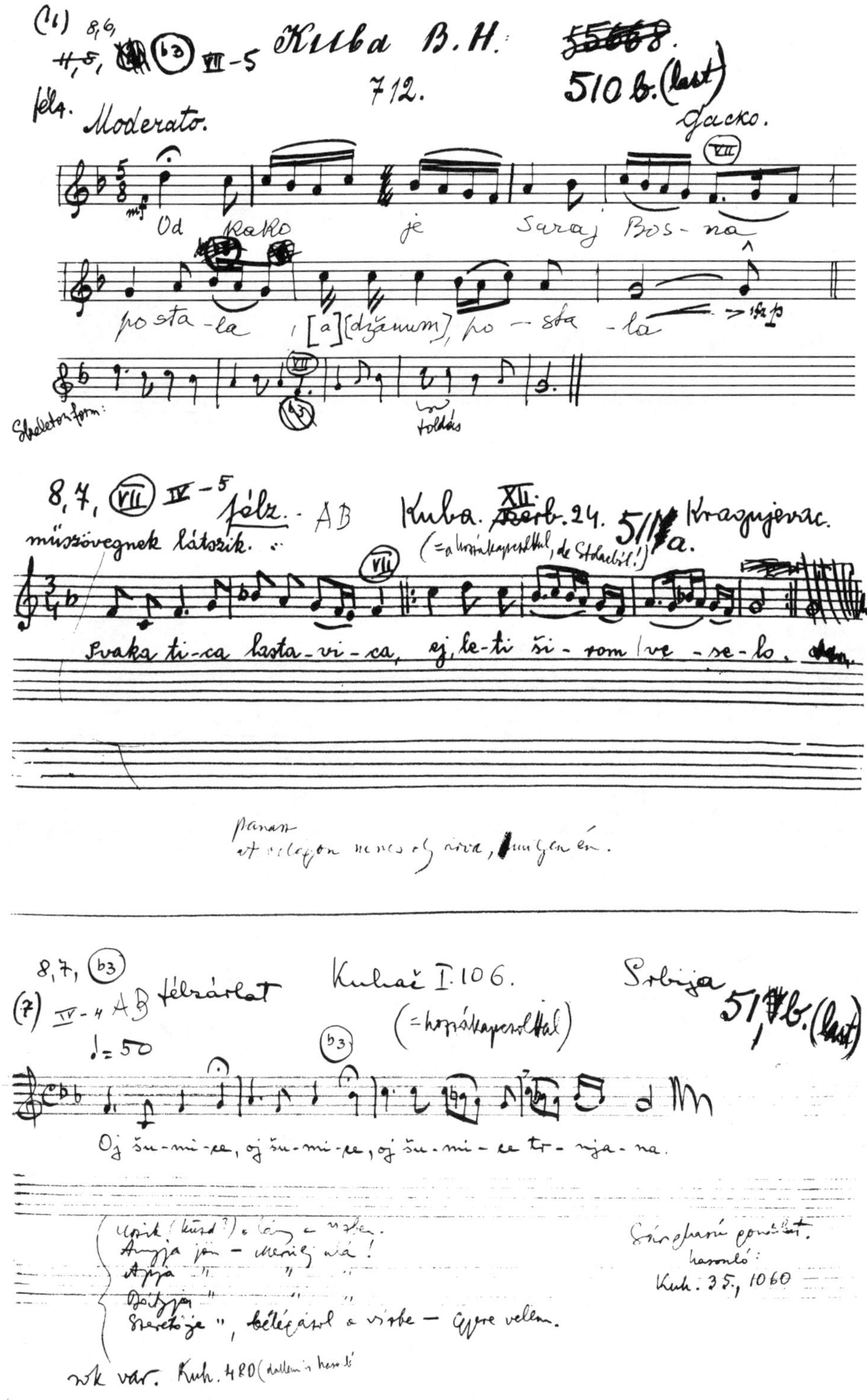
Kuba B.H.
712.
510 b.(last)
Moderato.
Gacko.
Od kako je Saraj Bos-na
po-sta-la
po-sta-la
Skeleton form:
toldás
8, 7,
félz.
AB
Kuba. XII. 24.
511 a.
Krapujevac.
műszövegnek látszik.
Svaka ti-ca lasta-vi-ca, ej, le-ti ši-rom ve-se-lo.
8, 7,
félzárlat
Kuhač I. 106.
Srbija
(=hopsákapcsolttal)
♩= 50
Oj šu-mi-ce, oj šu-mi-ce, oj šu-mi-ce tr-nja-na.
Kuh. 35., 1060

(8) 8,7, VII
Kuba B.H.
51/2.
AB
713.
Allegro moderato
Čapljina.
Šta se ču-je iz za grada, dži-do, dži-do; mo-re, dži-di-jo.
(11)
Kuhač I. 233.
Iz bivše hrv. Krajine
513a.
AB
Vi-ja-la se bie-la lo-za, bie-la lo-za vi-no-va, vi-no-va.
Kuh. 68.
(10) 8,6, VII
AB
Kuhač II. 486.
Iz Zente u Bačkoj.
♩= 52.
Mi-sliš di-ko, la-ne mo je, da mo-ram u-mre-ti ej!

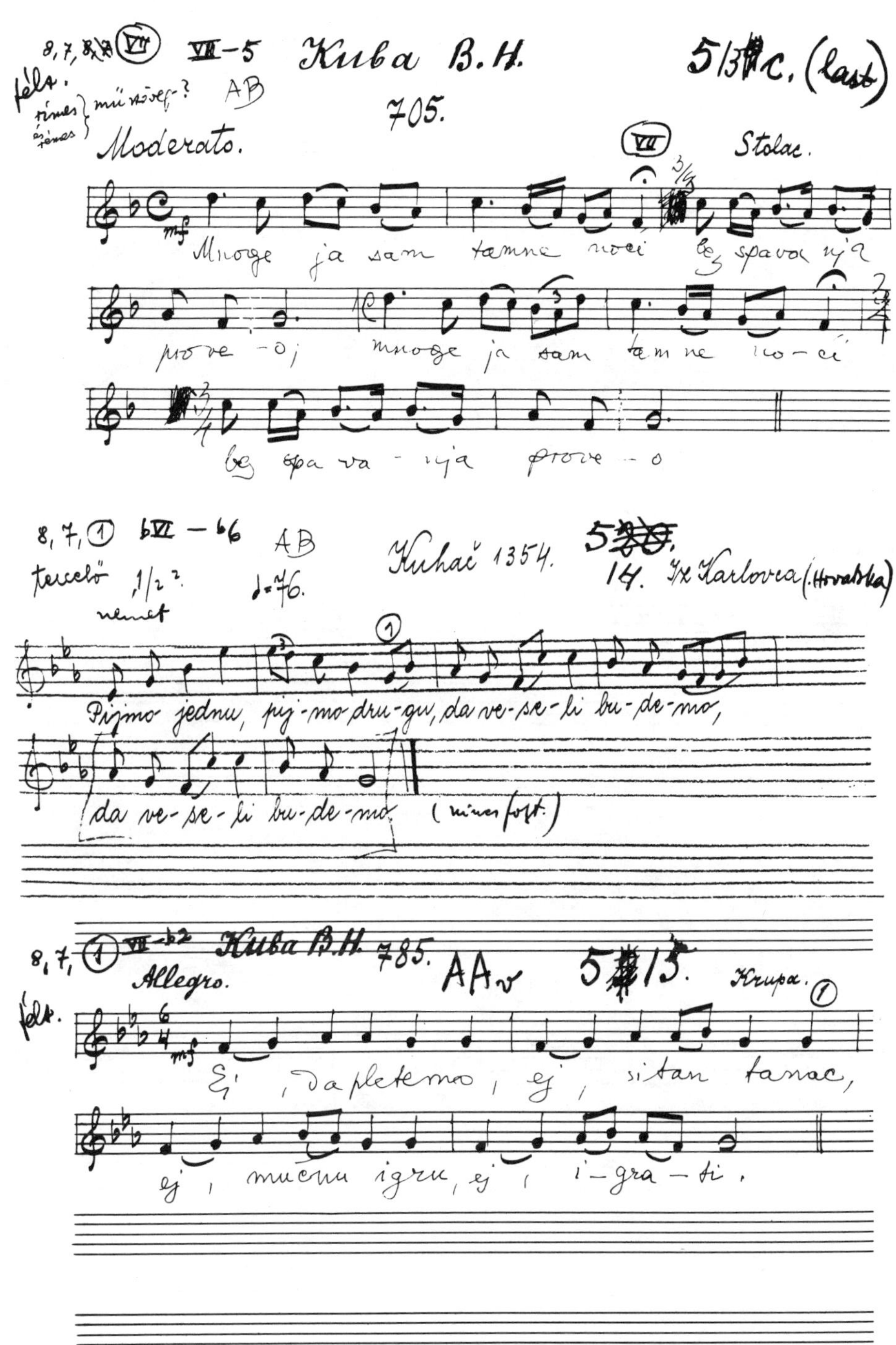
Kuba B. H.
705.
AB
Moderato.
Stolac.
Mnoge ja sam tamne noći bez spavanja
prove-o; mnoge ja sam tamne no-ći
bez spa-va-nja prove-o
AB
Kuhač 1354.
14. Iz Karlovca (Hrvatska)
♩=76.
Pijmo jednu, pij-mo dru-gu, da ve-se-li bu-de-mo,
da ve-se-li bu-de-mo
Kuba B. H. 785.
AA
Allegro.
Krupa.
Ej, da pletemo, ej, sitan tanac,
ej, mučnu igru, ej, i-gra-ti.

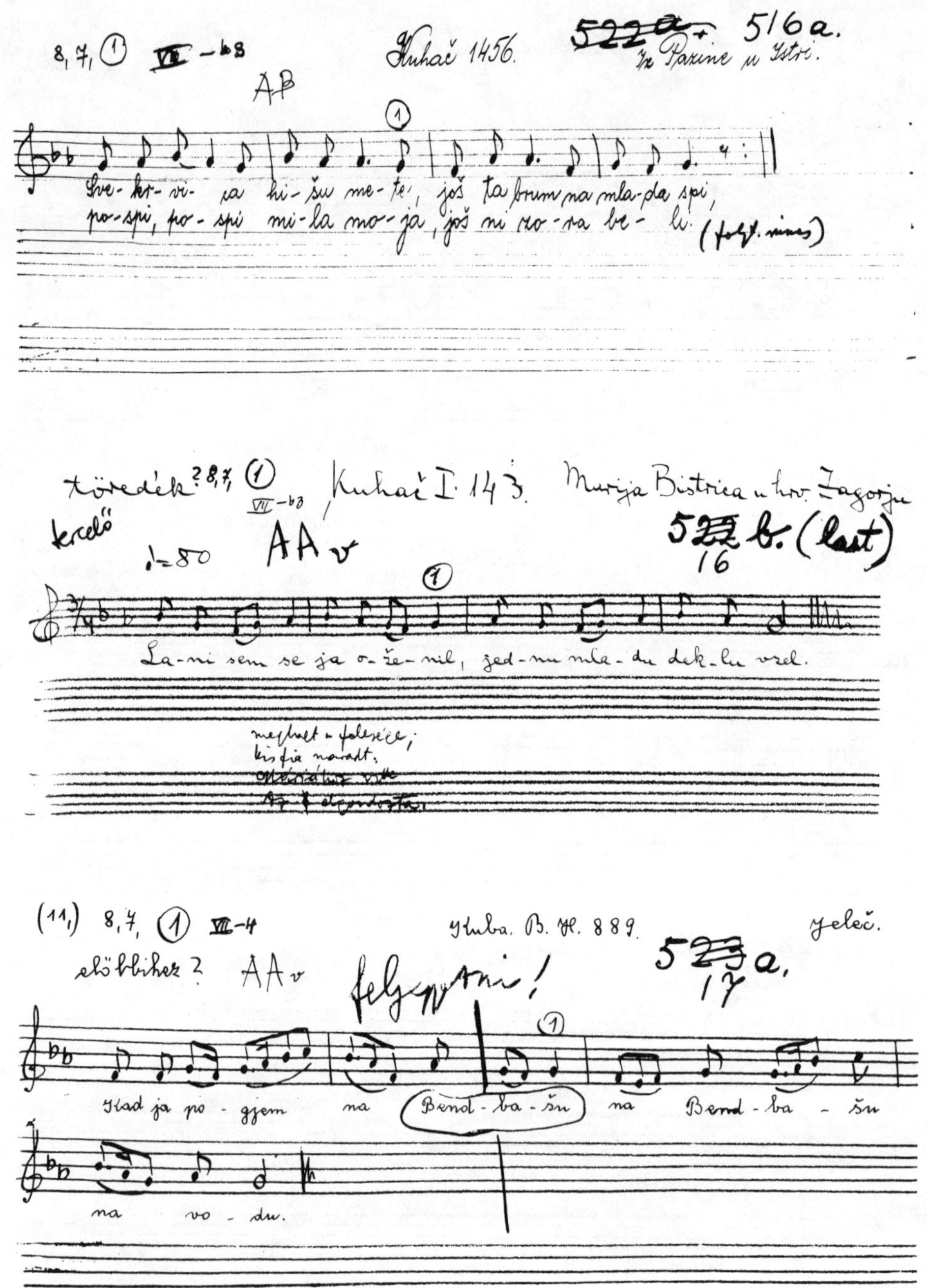
8,7, (1) VII—b3
Kuhač 1456.
522a
516a.
Iz Pazine u Istri.
AB
Sve-kr-vi-ca hi-šu me-te, još ta brum na mla-da spi,
po-spi, po-spi mi-la mo-ja, još ni zo-ra be-li.
(folyt. nincs)
töredék? 8,7, (1) VII—b3
Kuhač I. 143.
Marija Bistrica u hrv. Zagorju
kezdő
♩=80
AA v
522 b. (last)
16
La-ni sem se ja o-že-nil, jed-nu mla-du dek-lu vzel.
(11,) 8,7, (1) VII—4
Kuhač B. H. 889.
Jeleč.
előbbihez? AA v
523 a.
17
Kad ja po-gjem na Bend-ba-šu na Bend-ba-šu
na vo-du.

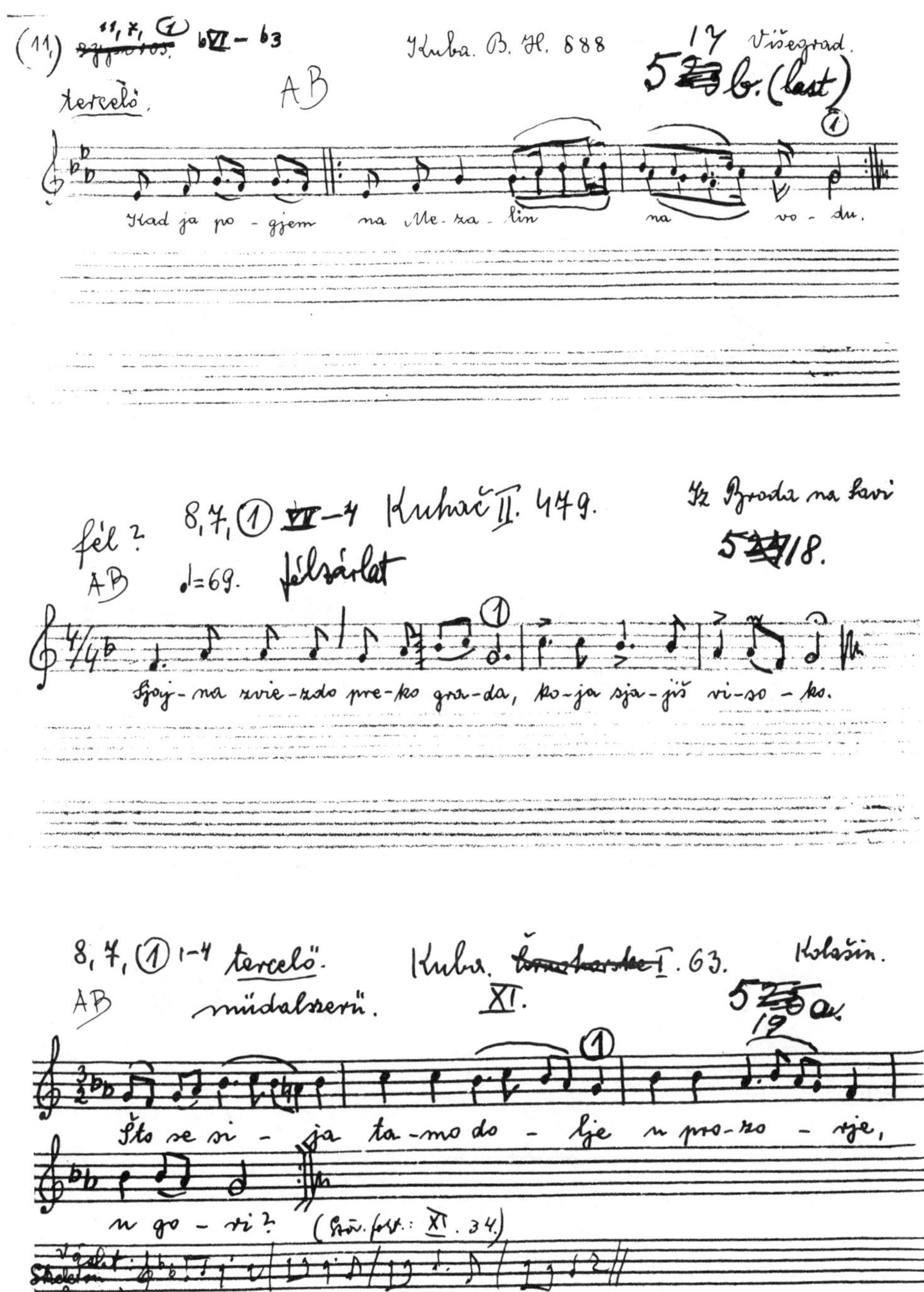
(11) 11, 7, ① bVI – b3
Kuba. B. H. 888
17 Višegrad.
5 b. (last)
tercelő.
AB
Kad ja po - gjem na Me - za - lin na vo - du.
fél?
8, 7, ① VI – 4
Kuhač II. 479.
½ Broda na Savi
5/18.
AB
♩=69.
félzárlat
Sjaj - na zvie - zdo pre - ko gra - da, ko - ja sja - jiš vi - so - ko.
8, 7, ① 1–4
tercelő.
Kuba. I. 63.
Kolašin.
AB
műdalszerű.
XI.
5 a.
19
Što se si - ja ta - mo do - lje u pro - zo - rje,
u go - ri? (Szöv. folyt.: XI. 34.)
Skeleton form:

8, 7, 7, ① 1–4
Kuba. B. H. 871.
Trebinje.
félz.
AB
519 b. (last)
Aj sva-ka ti - - ca la-sta-vi - ca aj le-ti ši - - rom
ve - se - lo.
(11) 8, 7, ① 1–4,
Kuba. B. H. 172.
526.
Višegrad.
AB
u-mje-la bi u-mje-la bi kaj-no bul-bul pje-va-ti,
(7) 8, 7, ① 1–5,
Kuba. B. H. 426.
Visoko.
vagy: 10, 9,
félz.
AA
tánc?
521.
Ej! aa ple-še-mo ej i na noć!
Ej! sit-ni ta-nac
Ej! muš-ku i-gru

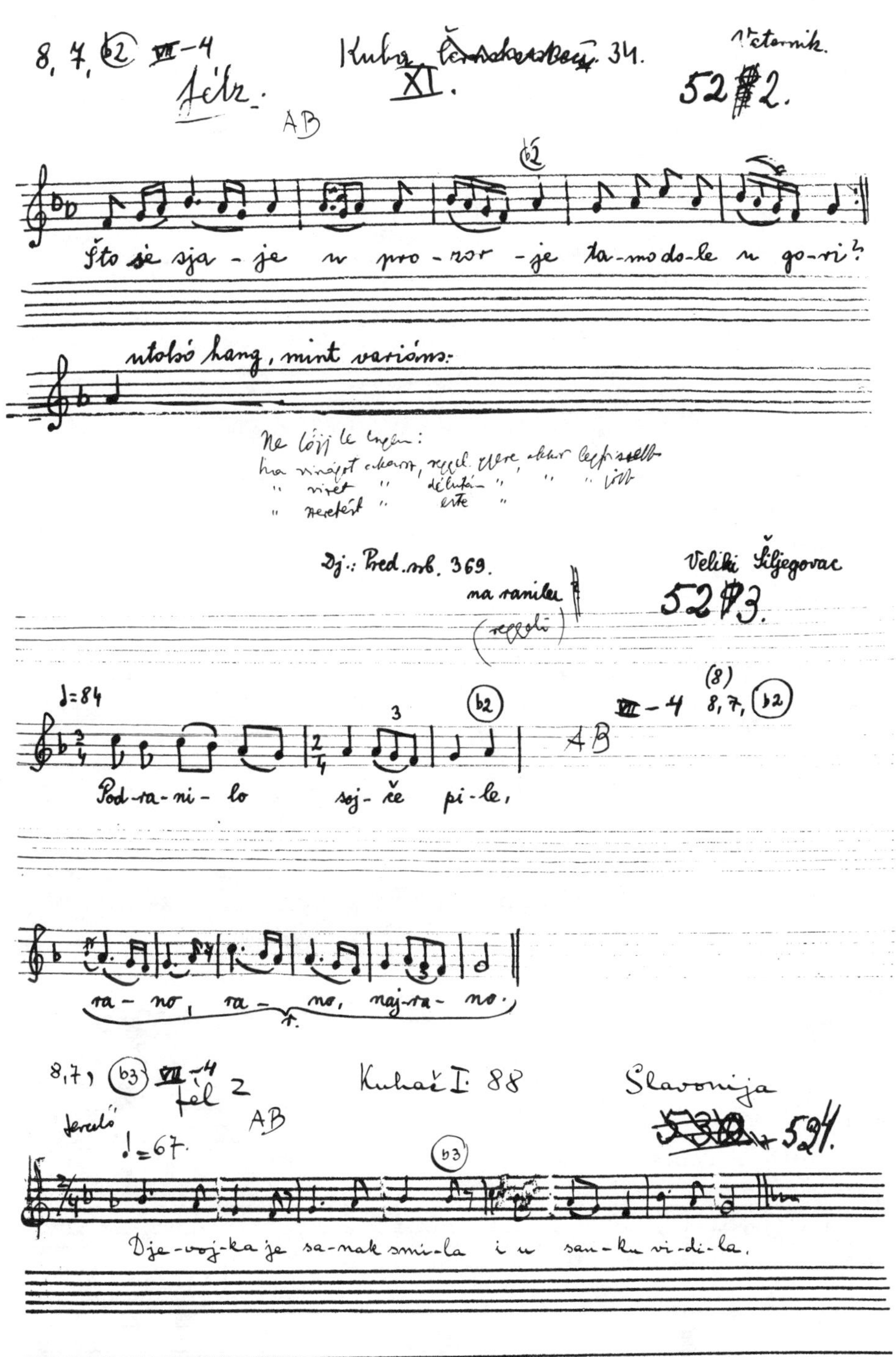

Što se sja - je u pro - zor - je ta-mo do-le u go-ri?
utolsó hang, mint variáns:
Dj.: Pred. sb. 369.
Veliki Šiljegovac
Pod-ra-ni-lo soj-če pi-le,
ra - no, ra - no, naj-ra- no.
Kuhač I. 88
Slavonija
Dje-voj-ka je sa-nak sni-la i u san-ku vi-di-la.

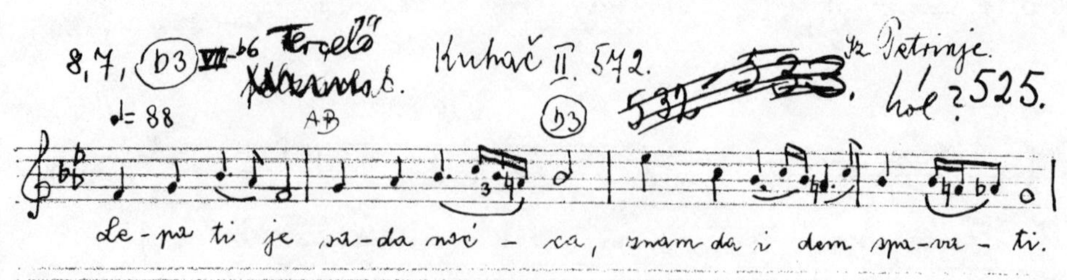
8,7, D3 VII-b6 Ercelő
Kuhač II. 572.
Iz Petrinje.
525.
♩= 88
AB
D3
Le-pa ti je za-da-rać-ca, znam da i dem spa-va-ti.

Kuba, B-H. 946.
1-7 AB
Jajce.
526a.
Adagio
4
Kako mo-reš, moja dra-ga, jedan da-nak bez mene?
Ja ne mo-gu, moja draga, ni pô sa-ta bez tebe!

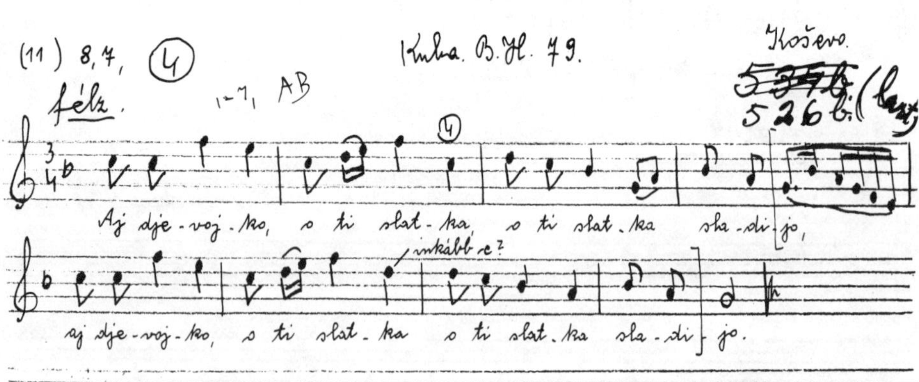
(11) 8,7, 4
Kuba. B.H. 79.
Koševo.
526b.
félz.
1-7, AB
4
Aj dje-voj-ko, o ti slat-ka, o ti slat-ka sla-di-jo,
inkább c?
aj dje-voj-ko, o ti slat-ka o ti slat-ka sla-di-jo.

Iz Novigrada kod Koprivnice.
Kuhač II. 665.
527.
Svadbarska
Pesme iz Levča, 11.
Jed-nu pe-smu pe-smo is-pe-va-mo,
Pe-smo is-pe-va-mo,
Sedeljka
Pesme iz Levča, 40.
Do-le-te-še la-ni go-lu-ba-ni,
La-ni go-lu-ba-ni

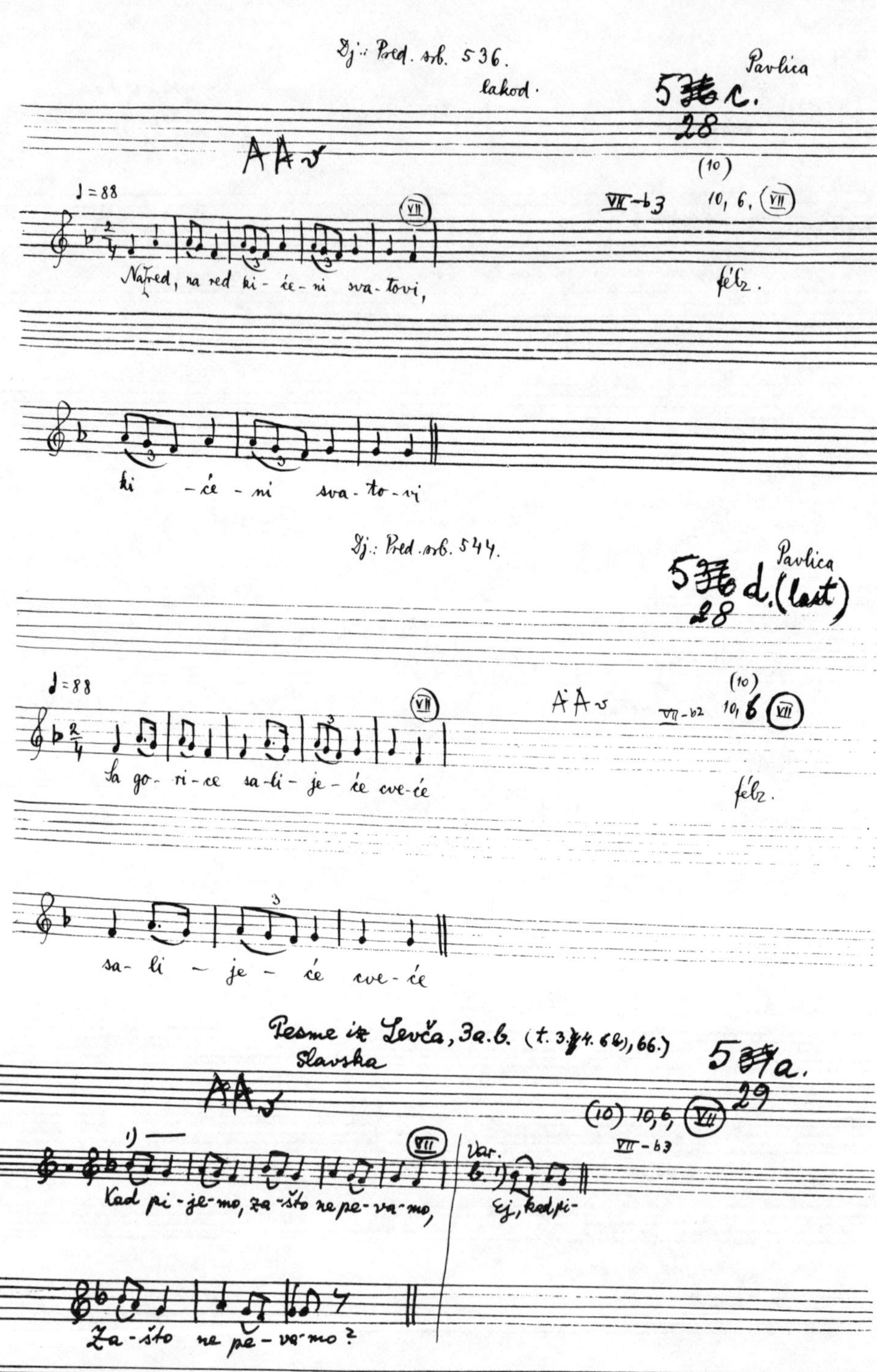

Dj.: Pred. srb. 536.
Pavlica
Lakod.
AA
♩= 88
Na red, na red ki-će-ni sva-tovi,
ki-će-ni sva-to-vi
Dj.: Pred. srb. 544.
Pavlica
♩= 88
Sa go-ri-ce sa-li-je-će cve-će
sa-li-je-će cve-će
Pesme iz Levča, 3a.b.
Slavska
Kad pi-je-mo, za-što ne pe-va-mo,
Var.
Ej, kad pi-
Za-što ne pe-va-mo?

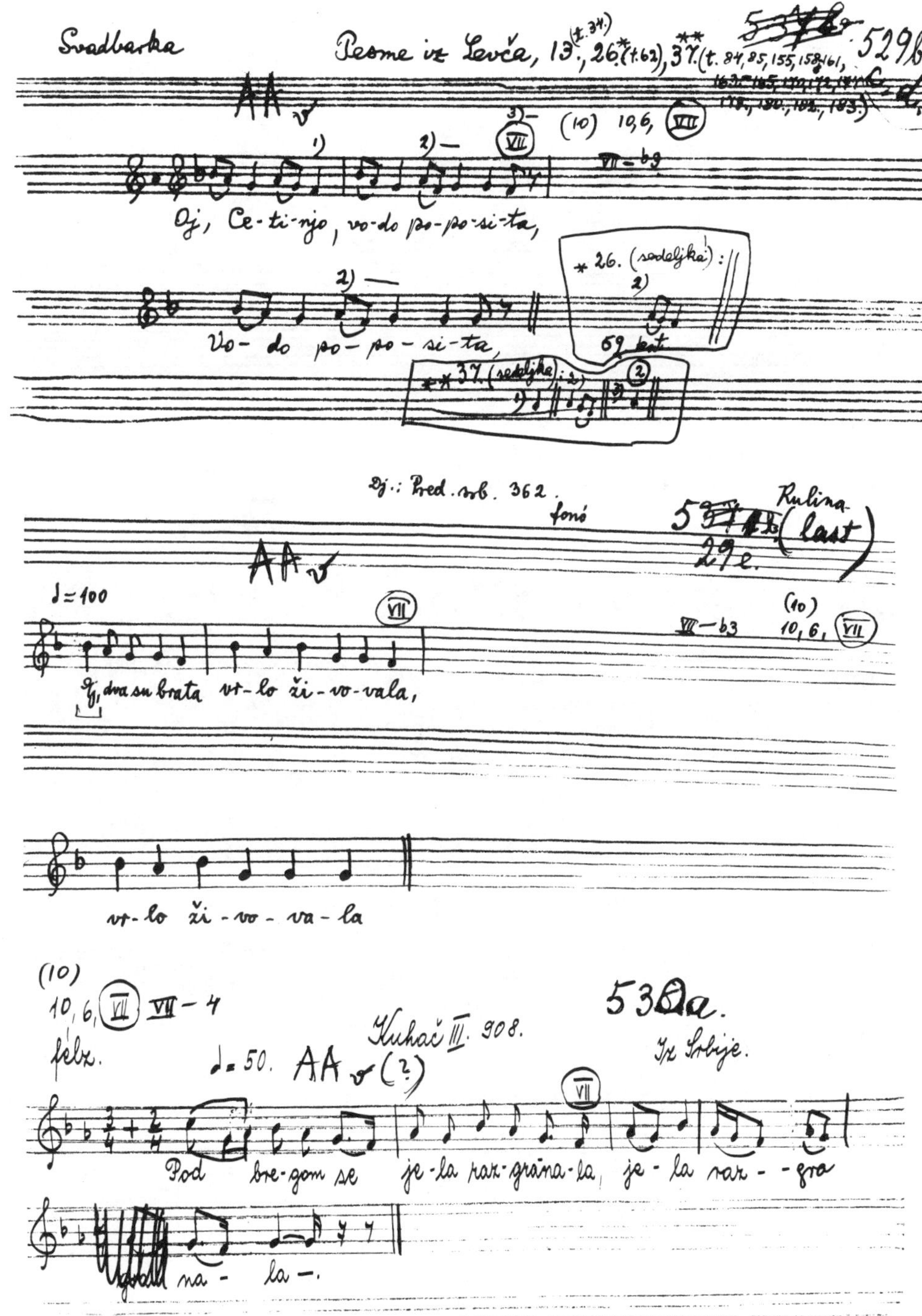

Svadbarka
Pesme iz Levča, 13, 26, 37
529b.
Oj, Ce-ti-njo, vo-do po-po-si-ta,
Vo- do po- po - si - ta,
26. (sedeljka)
37. (sedeljka)
Rulina (last)
529e.
Oj, dva su brata vr-lo ži-vo-vala,
vr-lo ži - vo - va - la
Kuhač III. 908.
Iz Srbije.
Pod bre-gom se je-la raz-grana-la, je - la raz - - gra
na - la -.

(10)
530 b.
Kuhač III. 831.
Iz okolice Zagreba.
Maj-ka na-- ju iz-van gra-da zva-la iz-van gra-da zva-la.
terceló
Kuhač II. 666.
Iz Srijema.
31.
2X
♩=120. AB
Što ću ji - nak, u-stre-li me stre-la, u stre-li me stre-la [oj!]
Ustaj di - ko, u-staj la-ne go-re, nespa-vaj do zo-re, [oj —!]
Svadbarska
Pesme iz Levča, Y. (t,9.10. 12.13. 14b), 15.÷18. 25. 29. 30a), 31. 33.)
AA
(10) 10,6, ① 532a.
U-staj, ka-me, u-staj, sta-ri sva-te,
U-staj sta-ri sva-te! ih!

Pesme iz Levča, 5. (t. 7)
Svadbarska
532b.
10,
VII – b2
O-bu-kuj se, pa-šo, o-de-baj se!
Svadbarska
Pesme iz Levča, 12. (t. 32.)
532c. (last)
7,
VII – b2
Skin' se škola de-voj-ko! ih!
(10)
10, 6, (1) VII – b3
Kuba B. H. 496.
533a.
Moderato
Višegrad.
Dva go-lu-ba svu noć pre-
pje-va-la, svu noć
pre-pje-va-la
Skeleton form:

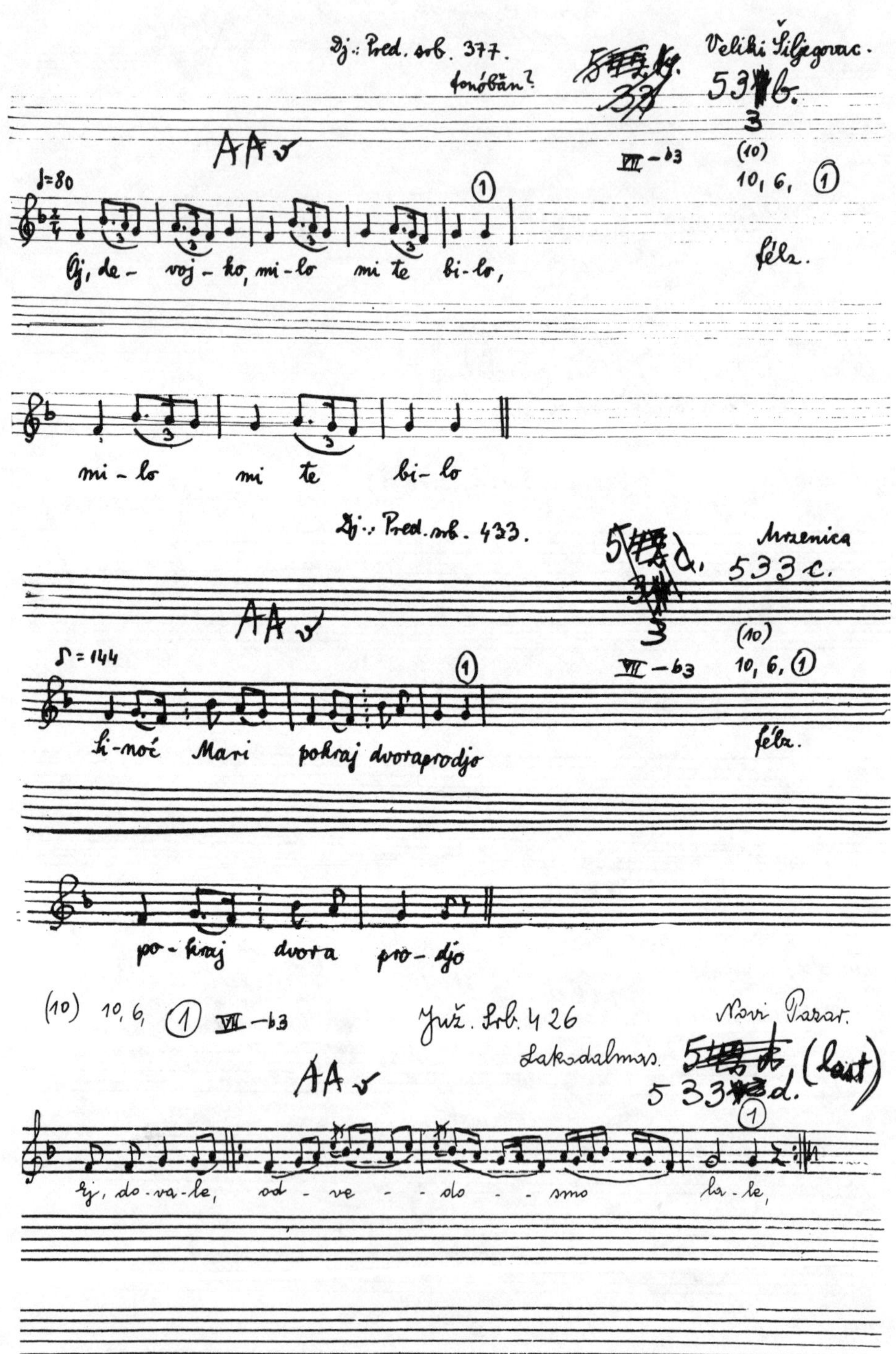

Dj.: Pred. srb. 377.
fonóbān?
Veliki Šiljegovac.
AA
Oj, de- voj- ko, mi-lo mi te bi-lo,
félz.
mi-lo mi te bi-lo
Dj.: Pred. srb. 433.
533 c.
AA
Si-noć Mari pokraj dvoraprodjo
félz.
po-kraj dvora pro-djo
Juž. Srb. 426
Novi Pazar.
Lakodalmas.
AA
Ej, do-va-le, od-ve-do-smo la-le,

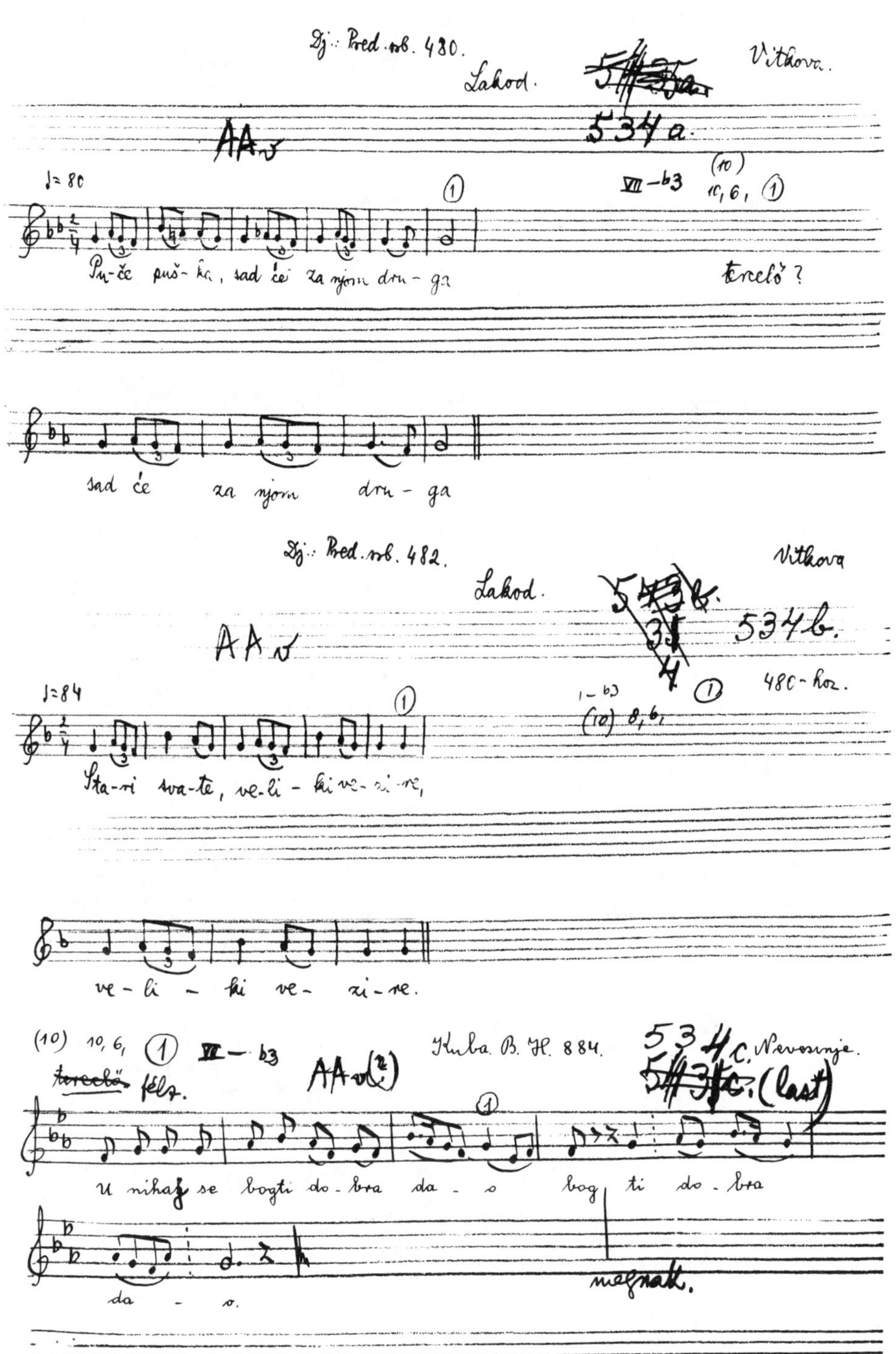
Dj.: Pred. sb. 480.
Lakod.
Vithova.
534a.
AAv
♩= 80
VII – b3
(10) 10, 6, ①
Pu-če puš-ka, sad će za njom dru-ga
tercló?
sad će za njom dru-ga
Dj.: Pred. sb. 482.
Vithova
Lakod.
534b.
AAv
♩= 84
480-hoz.
(10) 8, 6,
Sta-ri sva-te, ve-li-ki ve-zi-re,
ve-li-ki ve-zi-re.
(10) 10, 6, ① VII – b3
félz.
AAv
Kuba. B. H. 884.
534c. Nevesinje.
(last)
u nihaj se bog ti do-bra da-o bog ti do-bra
da-o.

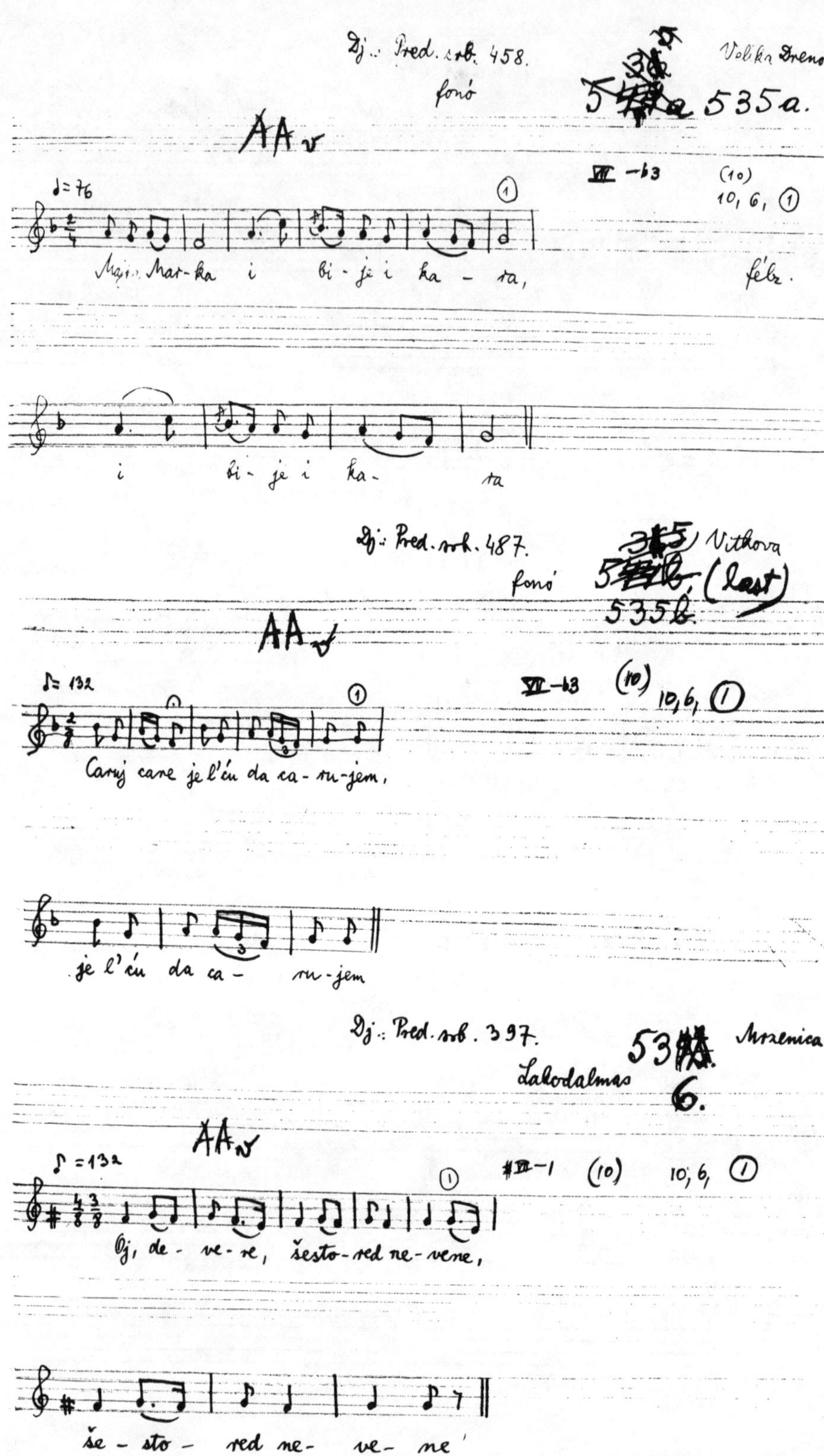

Dj.: Pred. sob. 458.
fonó
Velika Drenova
535a.
AA v
♩= 76
VII –♭3
(10)
10, 6, ①
Maj... Mar-ka i bi-je i ka – ra,
félz.
i bi- je i ka- ra
Dj.: Pred. sob. 487.
fonó
Vithova
(last)
535b.
AA v
♪= 132
VII –♭3
(10)
10, 6, ①
Carуj care je l'ću da ca-ru-jem,
je l'ću da ca- ru-jem
Dj.: Pred. sob. 397.
Lakodalmas
Mrzenica
536.
AA v
♪= 132
#VII –1
(10)
10, 6, ①
Oj, de- ve-re, šesto-red ne-vene,
še – sto – red ne- ve- ne'

Dj.: Pred. srb. 316.
lakodalmas
537.
Varoš
AA5
1–2
(10)
10, 6, ①
♩= 84
①
q! Vino piju dva - na - jec delija,
dva - na - jec deli - ja
(10)
10, 6, ①
1–63
Kuba B. H. 760.
538a.
AA5
Moderato
Ljeska kod Višegrada.
Bolna Jul - ko, zar si još dje -
voj - ka? zar si još dje -
voj - ka?
Skeleton form:
Kuba B. H. 762.
538b. (last)
Allegro moderato
Ljeska kod Višegrada.
Je - li ra - no, jel sun - ce vi - so - ko?

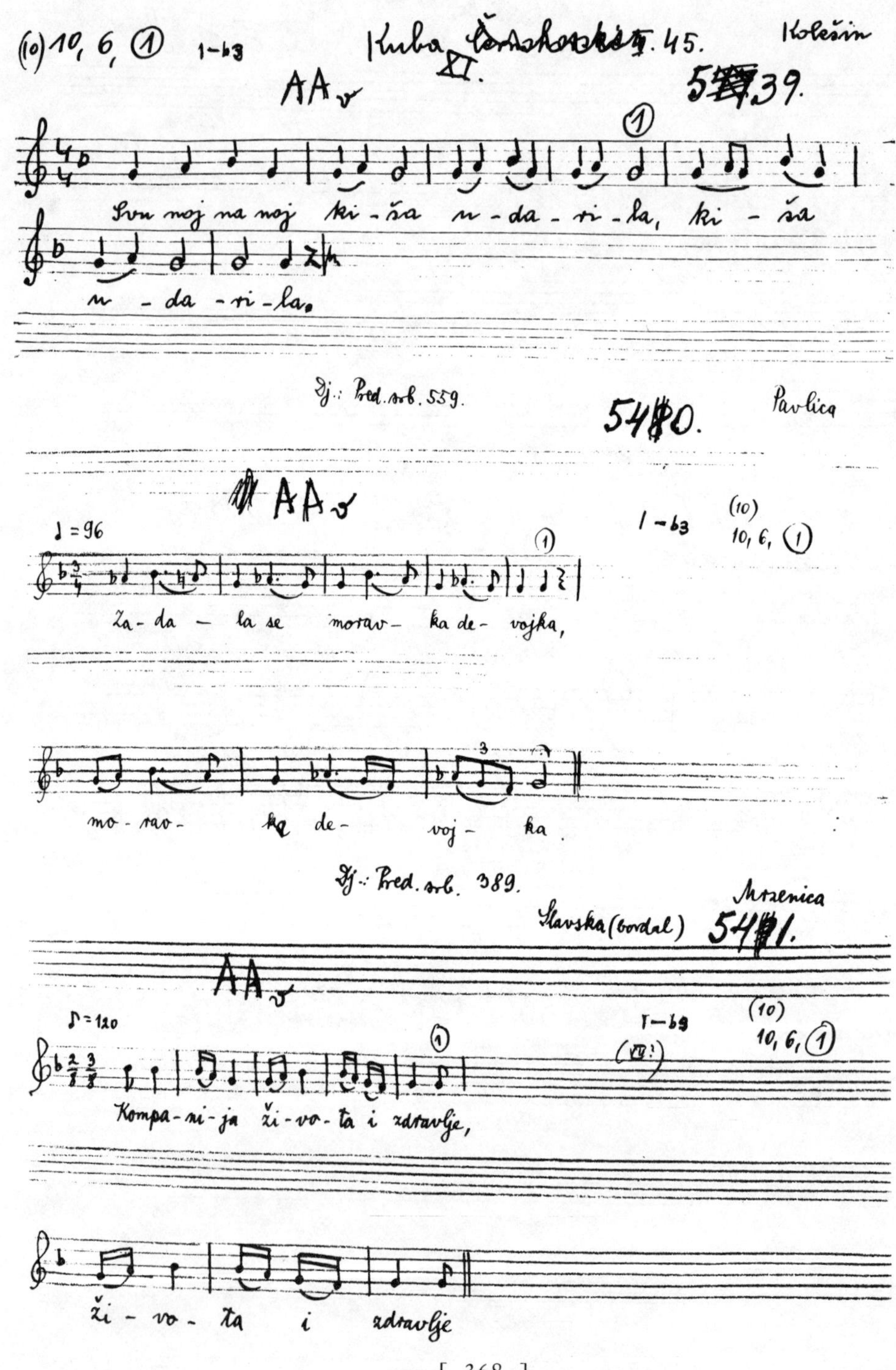

(10) 10, 6, ① 1-b3
Kolešin
AA
ki - ša u - da - ri - la, ki - ša
u - da - ri - la.
Dj.: Pred. sb. 559.
Pavlica
AA
♩= 96
1 - b3
(10)
10, 6, ①
Za - da - la se morav - ka de - vojka,
mo - rav - ka de - voj - ka.
Dj.: Pred. sb. 389.
Mrzenica
Slavska (bordal)
AA
♪= 120
(10)
10, 6, ①
Kompa - ni - ja ži - vo - ta i zdravlje,
ži - vo - ta i zdravlje

Dj.: Pred. zb. 205.
542. Striževac.
AA_v (?)
♩= 152
1–4
(10)
10, 6, ①
O-gre-ja-la sjajna mese-či-na,
félz.
sjaj- na me-se- či- na.
Dj.: Pred. zb. 476.
Vithova
arató 5 a.
43
AA_v
♩=66
1–4
(10)
10, 6, ①
Je- čam že- le Je-lač-ke de-voj-ke,
félz
Je- lač- ke de- voj- ke
Dj.: Pred. zb. 238.
Crvena Jabuka
5 b. (last)
43
AB
♩=84
1–4
(10)
10, 6, ①
Ka- raj, Doj- će, da ka- ra- mo
Na kraj, ka- ču, ze- le- nu liva-du,
félz.
da ka- ra- mo
ze- le- nu li-va- du.

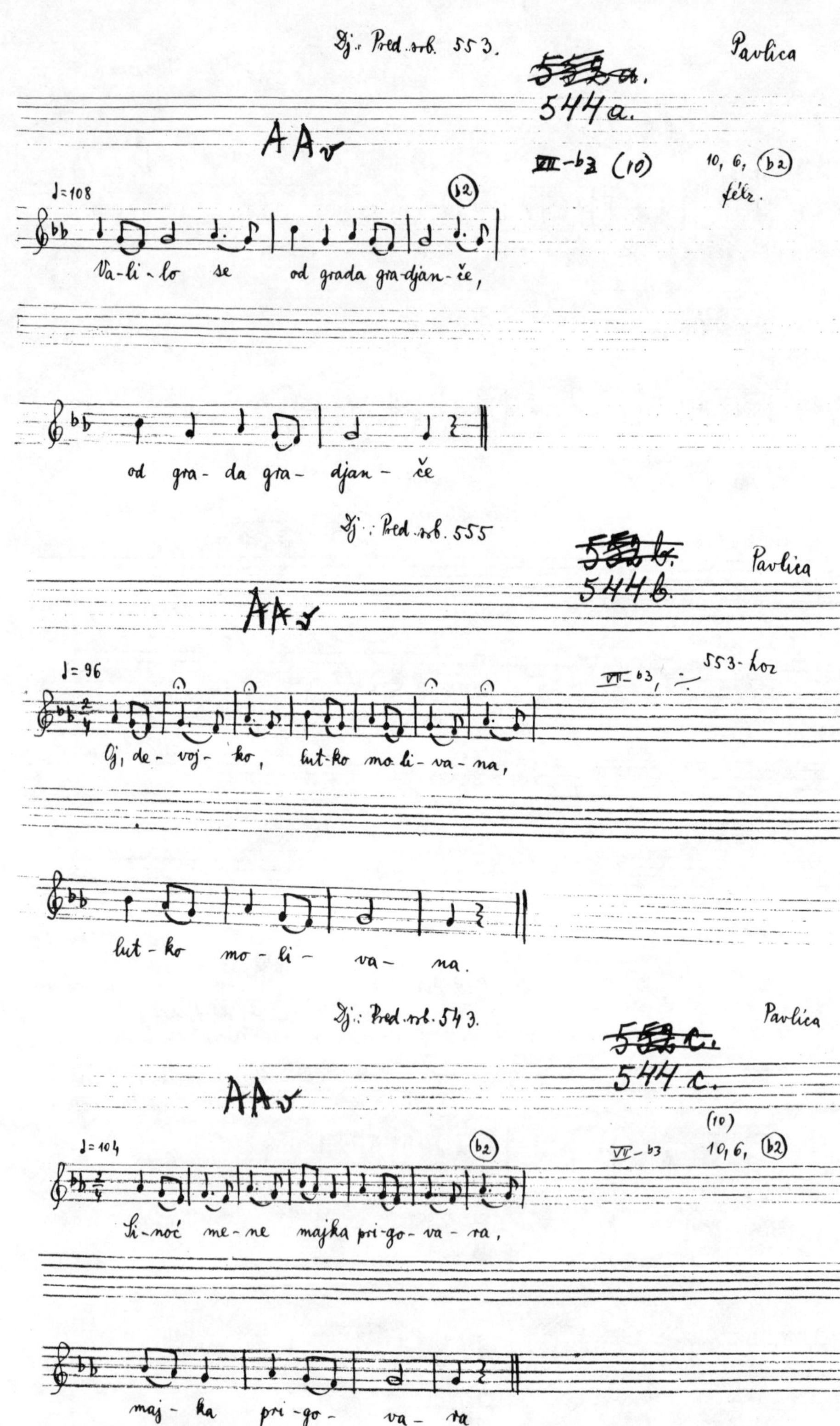
Dj.: Pred. srb. 553.
Pavlica
544a.
AAv
♩=108
VII-b3 (10)
10, 6, (b2)
félz.
(b2)
Va-li-lo se od grada gra-djan-če,
od gra-da gra-djan-če
Dj.: Pred. srb. 555
544b.
Pavlica
AAv
♩=96
VII-b3,
553-hoz
Oj, de-voj-ko, lut-ko mo-li-va-na,
lut-ko mo-li-va-na.
Dj.: Pred. srb. 543.
Pavlica
544c.
AAv
♩=104
(b2)
(10)
VII-b3
10, 6, (b2)
Si-noć me-ne majka pri-go-va-ra,
maj-ka pri-go-va-ra

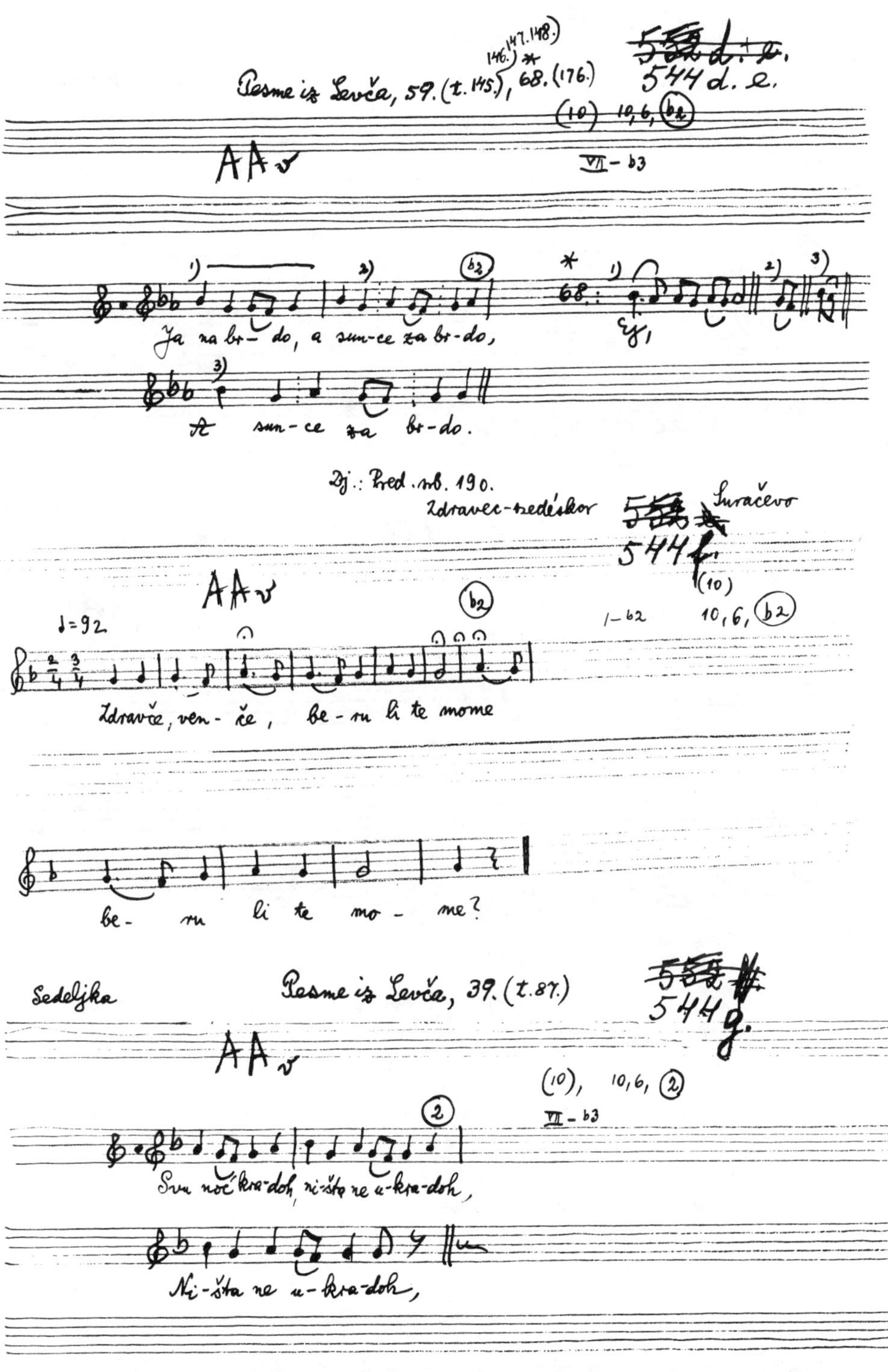
Pesme iz Levča, 59. (t. 145.), 68. (176.)
544 d. e.
(10) 10, 6, b2
AA
VII - b3
Ja na br- do, a sun-ce za br-do,
68.
A sun-ce za br-do.
Dj.: Pred. zb. 190.
Zdravec-sedéskor
Suračevo
544 f.
(10)
AA
♩=92
1 - b2
10, 6, b2
Zdravče, ven- če, be - ru li te mome
be- ru li te mo - me?
Sedeljka
Pesme iz Levča, 39. (t. 87.)
544 g.
AA
(10), 10, 6, 2
VII - b3
Svu noć kra-doh, ni-što ne u-kra-doh,
Ni-šta ne u-kra-doh,

Dj.: Pred. zb. 499.
Gordal
544 k.
Latkovac
AA5
♪=108
10, 6, ②
Kaa pi-je-mo zašto ne pe-vamo,
zašto ne pe- vamo?
Dj.: Pred. zb. 253.
544 k.
Mačkovac
AA5
♩=100
1-63
10, 6, ②
O, Cve-ti-njo, vodo pono- si-ta,
vo- do po-no- si- ta
Dj.: Pred. zb. 160.
545 a.
Djuštica
AB
♩=92
1-4
10, 6, ♭2
Sestra brata od de-la okala,
od de-la o- ka-la

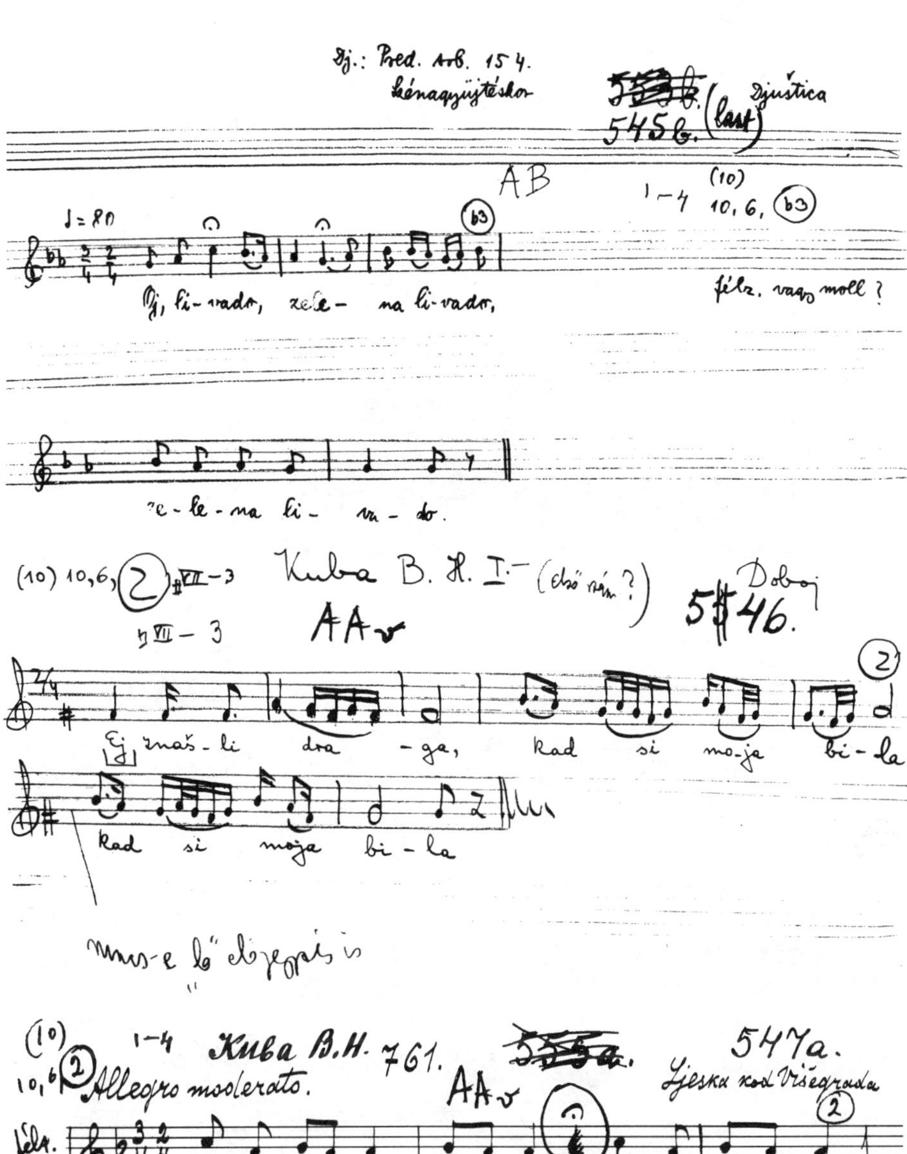

(10) 1–4 Kuba B.H. 761. 547a.

10,6 (2) Allegro moderato. AAv Ljeska kod Višegrada

félz.

Djevojka je bo-sjak posi-ja-la,

bo- sjak posi-ja-la.

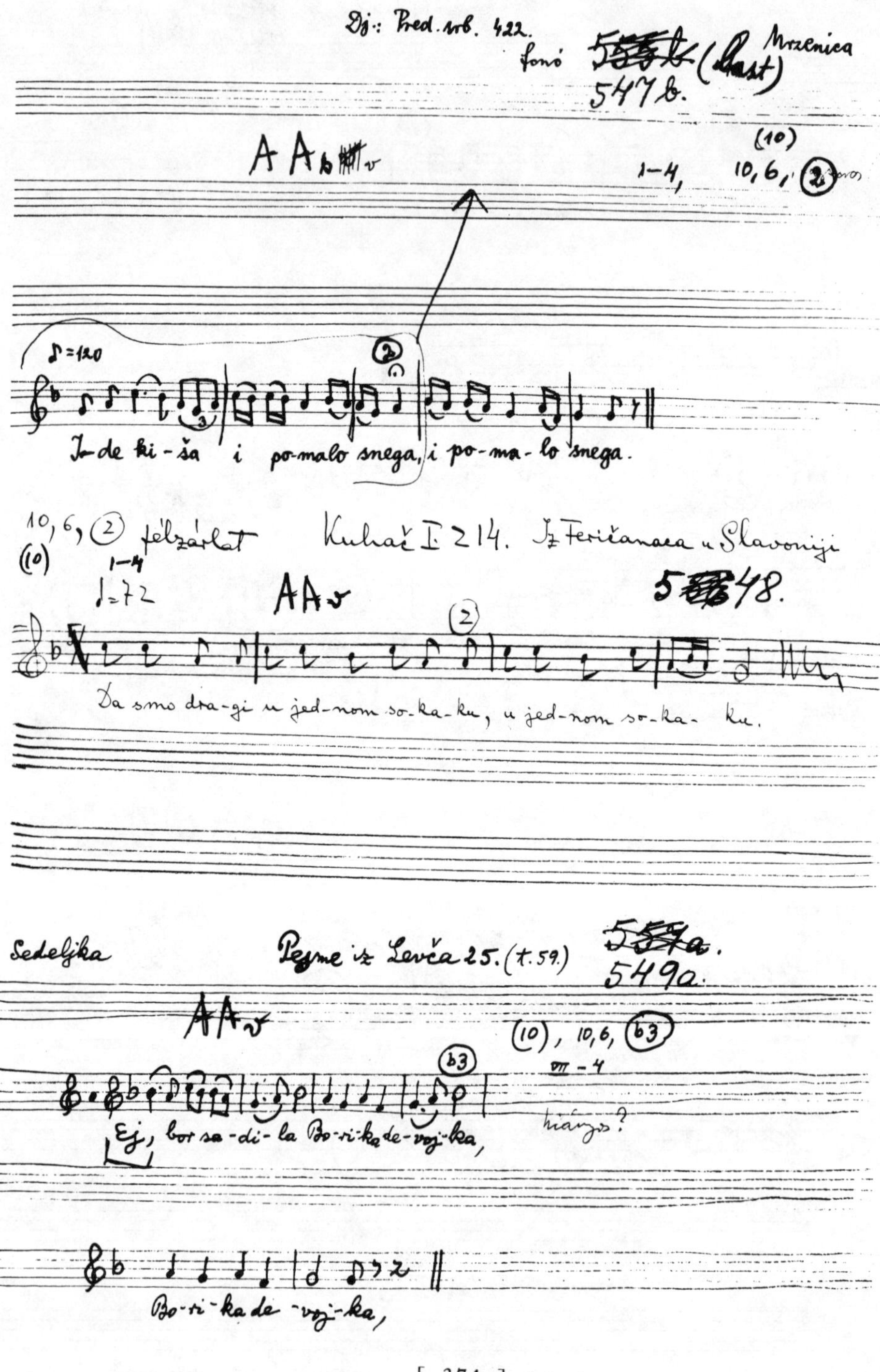
Dj.: Pred. srb. 422.
fonó 5478. (Mrzenica)
AA
1–4, 10, 6, (2) (10)
♪=120
I-de ki-ša i po-malo snega, i po-ma-lo snega.
10, 6, (2) félzárlat (10) 1–4
Kuhač I 214. Iz Feričanaca u Slavoniji
5548.
♩=72
AA
(2)
Da smo dra-gi u jed-nom so-ka-ku, u jed-nom so-ka-ku.
Sedeljka
Pesme iz Levča 25. (t. 59.)
549a.
AA
(10), 10, 6, (b3)
(b3)
VII – 4
hiányos?
Ej, bor sa-di-la Bo-ri-ka de-voj-ka,
Bo-ri-ka de-voj-ka,

Dj.: Pred. sb. 456.
Fonó
Velika Drenova
557 b. (last)
549 b. (last)
AA v
♩=76
(10)
1–4 10, 6, (b3)
Aj, šta-to zve-či niz to polje zvonce,
félz.
niz to po-lji zvon-ci.
(10) 10, 6, (4) 1–4
Kuba. XIII. 6.
(= B.H. 420*)
550a.
Bihać.
(Bosnia)
AA v
Toš-ko gra-du, ko-jim pa-ša pro-dje ko-jim pa-ša
pro-dje
* Doboj-ból; ezzel a szöveggel:
Sinoć sam si/š dragim zavadila:/
(10) 10, 6, (4) VII–4
Kuba. B. H. 582.
St. Majdan.
félz.
AA v
550b. (last)
Oj, Oj La-za-re na mo-ru vo-za-re na mo-ru vo-za'
elmyelés

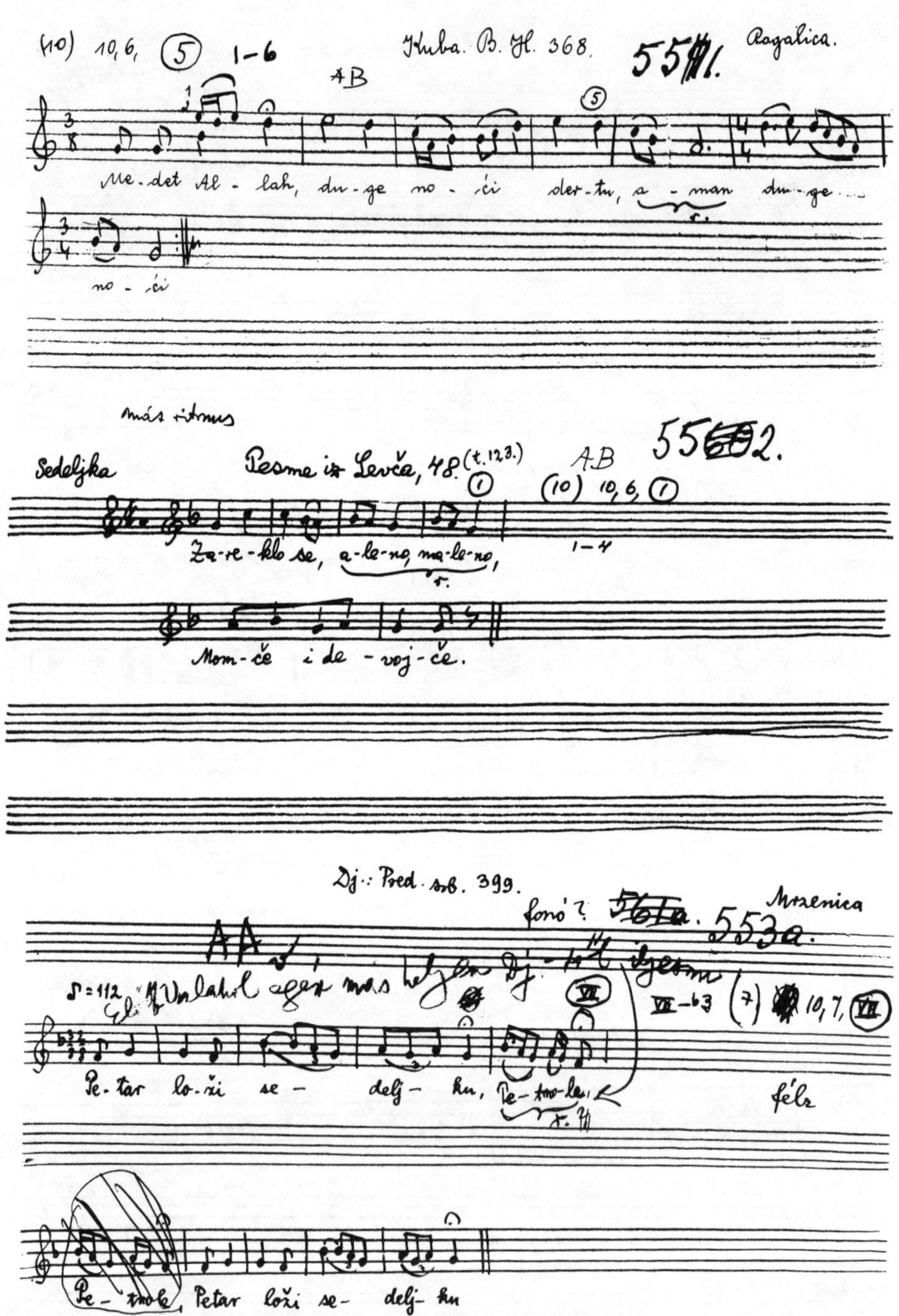
(10) 10,6, 5 1–6
AB
55
Rogalica.
Me-det Al-lah, du-ge no-ći der-tu, a-man du-ge-
no-ći
Sedeljka
Pesme iz Levča, 48. (t. 123.)
AB
55
(10) 10,6, 1
1–4
Za-re-klo se, a-le-no, ma-le-no,
Mom-če i de-voj-če.
Dj.: Pred. sb. 399.
Mrzenica
553a.
AA
♪=112
Pe-tar lo-ži se-delj-ku, Pe-tro-le,
félz
Pe-trole, Petar loži se-delj-ku

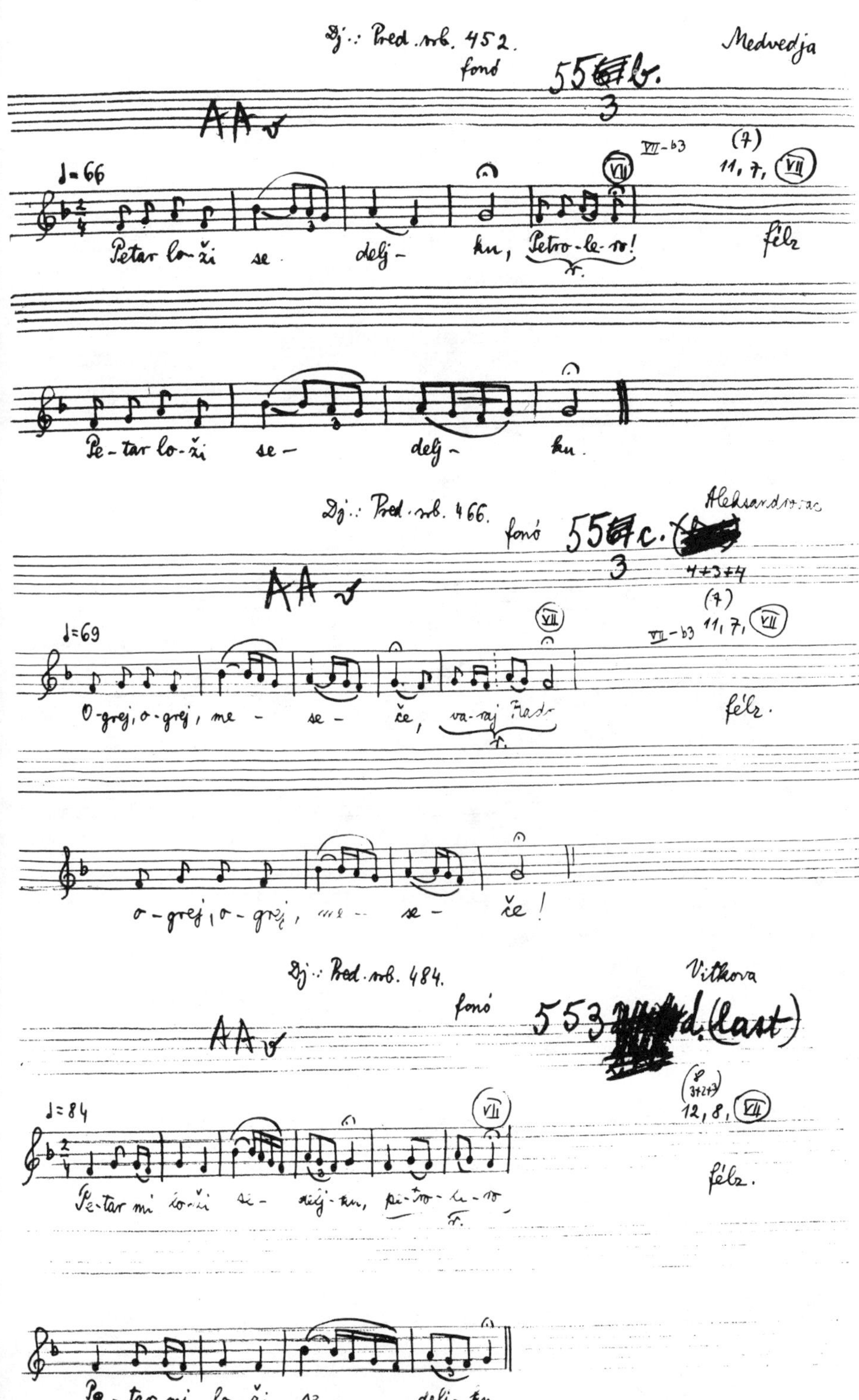

Dj.: Pred. srb. 452.
Medvedja
fonó
55b.
3
AA
♩= 66
VII–b3
(7)
11, 7, VII
Petar loži se delj- ku, Petro-le-ro!
félz
Pe-tar lo-ži se – delj – ku.
Dj.: Pred. srb. 466.
Aleksandrovac
fonó
55c.
3
4+3+4
AA
♩= 69
(7)
11, 7, VII
O-grej, o-grej, me – se – če, va-raj Rado
félz.
o – grej, o – grej, me – se – če!
Dj.: Pred. srb. 484.
Vitkova
fonó
553d. (last)
AA
♩= 84
12, 8, VII
Pe-tar mi lo-ži si- delj-ku, pi-tro-le-ro,
félz.
Pe-tar mi lo-ži se – delj-ku

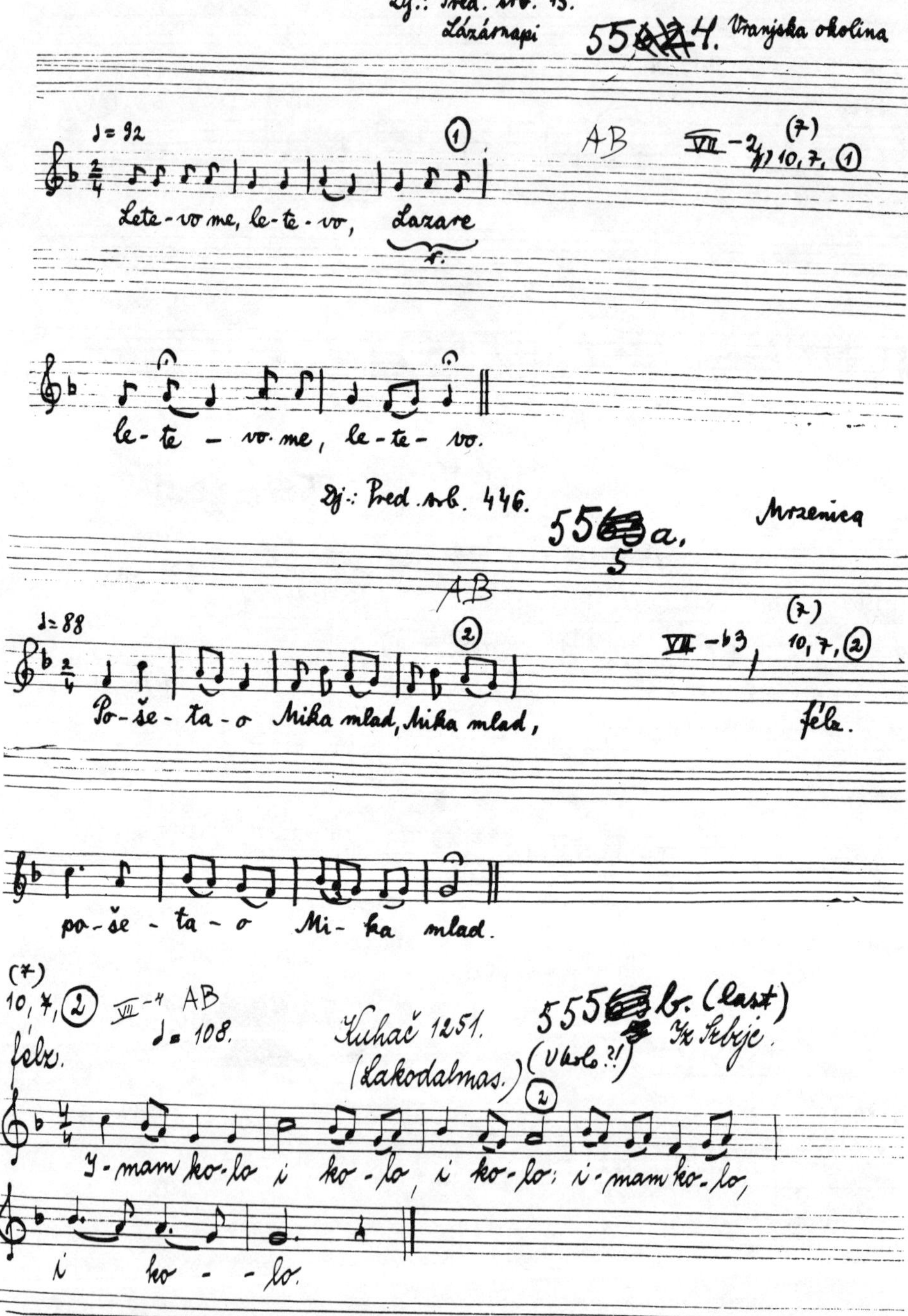
Dj.: Pred. srb. 15.
Lázárnapi
554. Vranjska okolina
♩= 92
AB
Lete-vo me, le-te-vo, Lazare
le-te - vo-me, le-te-vo.
Dj.: Pred. srb. 446.
555a.
Mrzenica
AB
♩= 88
Po-še-ta-o Mika mlad, Mika mlad,
félz.
po-še-ta-o Mi-ka mlad.
10,7, AB
félz.
♩= 108.
Kuhač 1251.
(Lakodalmas.)
555b. (last)
Iz Srbije.
(U kolo ?!)
I-mam ko-lo i ko-lo, i ko-lo; i-mam ko-lo,
i ko - - lo.

10, 8, ① VII – 11
Kuba. B. H. 943.
556.
Čajniče.
félbe.
AB
I - čin - di - ja ja za dr'je - - ma - la, za ve - če -
- dni - je -
- ru ništa ne - - mam
(10) 10, 8, ④
Kuba. XIII. 36.
557.
Kalinovik.
Zrinyi Miklósról és Szigetvárról.
Raz-bo-lje se ca-re Su-lej-ma-ne, a - man, aman, Su-lej-man.
Dj.: Pred. sb. 439.
558–559.
♩= 92
AB
VII – 4
(10) 11, 6, VII
Žalud maj-ci duši-ce dušo moja
što Ja - go - du i - ma

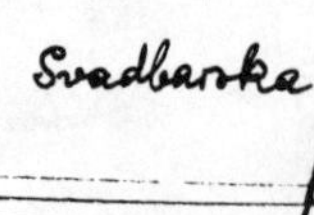

Pesme iz Levča, 10. (t.27.)

560.

(11) 11, 7, ①

VII–b2

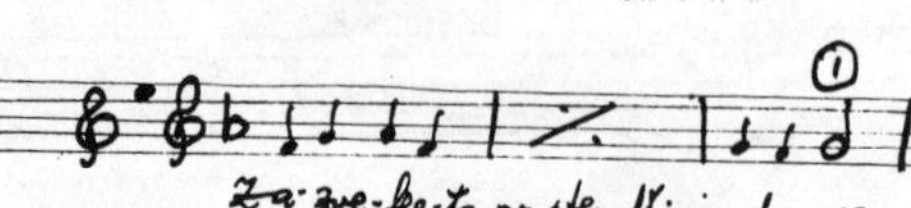

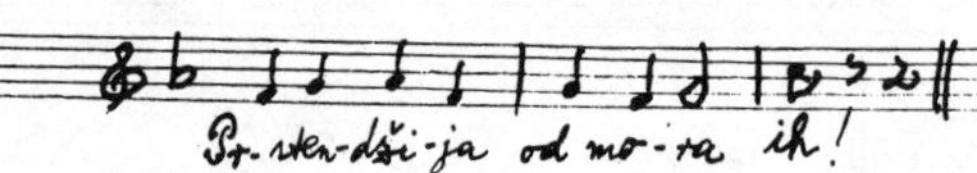

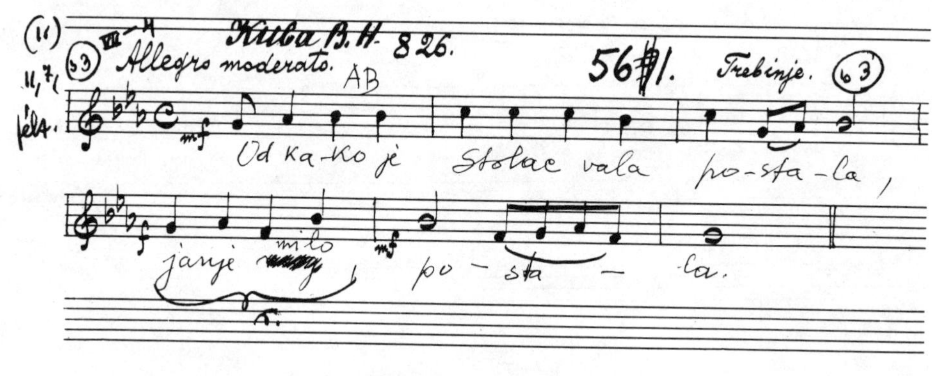

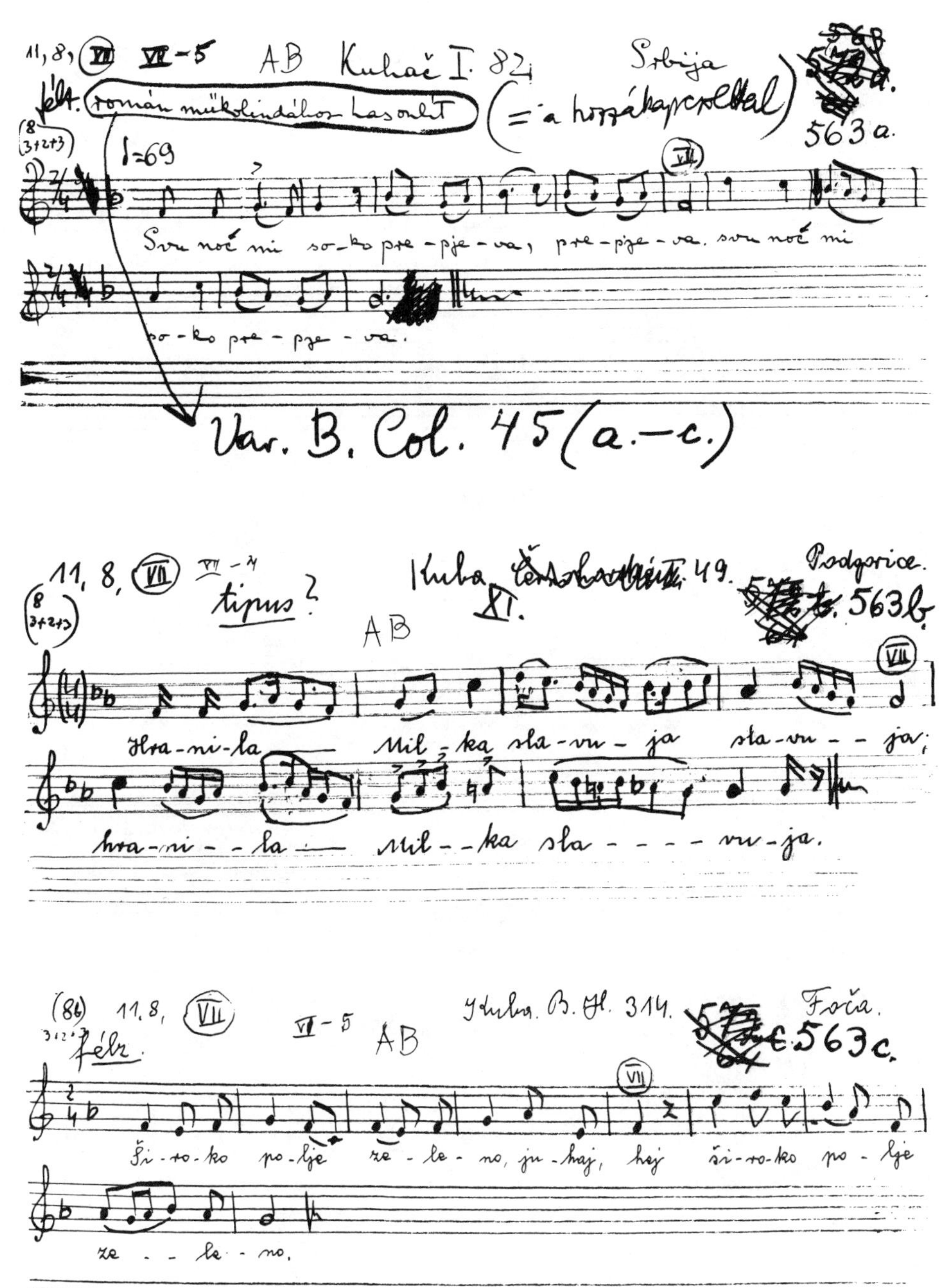
11, 8, VII
AB
Srbija
563a.
♩=69
Svu noć mi so-ko pre-pje-va, pre-pje-va. svu noć mi
so-ko pre-pje-va.
Var. B. Col. 45 (a.–c.)
11, 8, VII
tipus?
AB
XI.
Podgorice.
563b.
Hra-ni-la Mil-ka sla-vu-ja sla-vu-ja;
hra-ni-la Mil-ka sla-vu-ja.
11. 8, VII
AB
Foča.
563c.
Ši-ro-ko po-lje ze-le-no, ju-haj, hej ši-ro-ko po-lje
ze-le-no.

Bosiljevac 6 a) Kuhač 82.
Djordjević, Nar. Pev. 46 l/2
VII – 5 AB
Svu noć mi bul-bul pro-pje-va Um na-šeg I-va-na vra-tim
U-sta-ni I-vo, I-va-ne, Tvo-ja se lju-ba u-da-je
Dj.: Pred. srb. 117.
♩= 104
Pirot 564.
AA
VII – 4 11, 8, ①
So-kol mi le-ti vi-so-ko, mori dje-voj-ko*
* Ova je pesma doneta iz drugoga kraja, jer se u Pirotu ne kaže „djevojka". Vidi moje: Južna Srbija, strana 109.
so-kol mi le-ti vi-so-ko.
11, 8, ① VII – 5 tercelő. Kuhač 31. Imotsky. 565.
AA
Bu-di-la ma-jka I-va-na, I-va-na, bu-di-la ma-jka I-va-na.

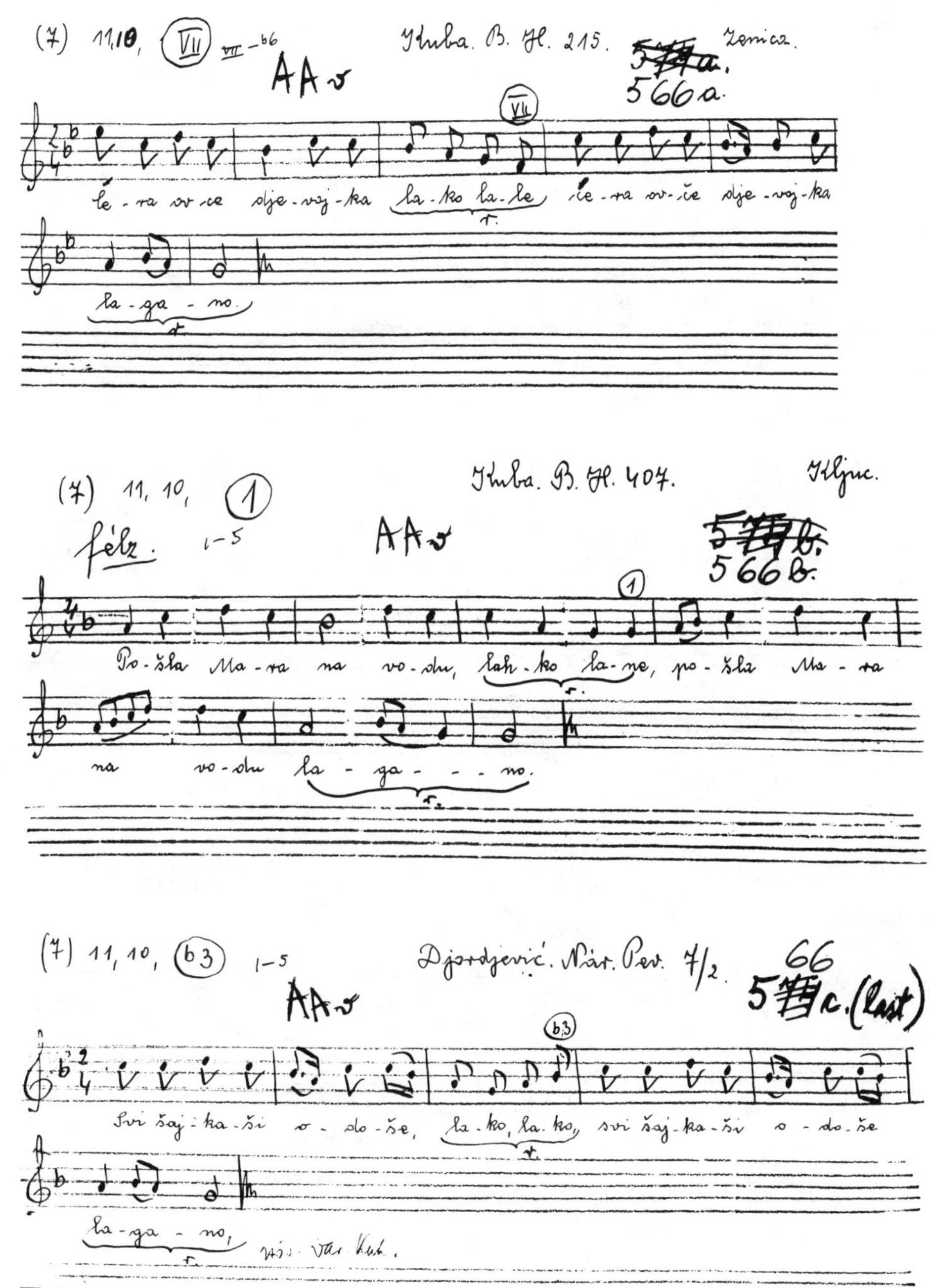
(7) 11,10, (VII) VII–b6
Kuba. B. H. 215.
Zenica.
566a.
AA
le-ra ov-ce dje-voj-ka la-ko la-le le-ra ov-če dje-voj-ka
la-ga-no.
(7) 11, 10, (1)
Kuba. B. H. 407.
félz. 1–5
AA
566 b.
Po-šla Ma-ra na vo-du, lah-ko la-ne, po-šla Ma-ra
na vo-du la-ga-no.
(7) 11, 10, (b3) 1–5
Djordjević. Nár. Pev. 7/2.
66
AA
Svi šaj-ka-ši o-do-še, la-ko, la-ko, svi šaj-ka-ši o-do-še
la-ga-no,

11, 10, ② VII – 5 AB
félz.
♩= 69.
Kuhač 1460.
557.a.
Iz Srijema.
Svi Šaj-ka-ši o - do-še (la-ko, la-ko); svi Šaj-ka-ši
o - do-še la- - ga - - - no.
félz
11, 10, ④
Kuba. B. H. 536.
AAv
557.b. (last)
Stolac.
Mo-mak ma-mi dje - voj - ku, La - ko la - ne Mo mak ma-mi,
dje - voj - ku la - ga - no.
568.
Obredno
Pesme iz Levča, 73.
AAv
11, 10, ①
1 – 5
Sla-va mi tvo-ja, Go-spo-de po-mi-luj,
Po-mi-luj nas Go-spo - - de, po-mi-luj!

Kuhač I. 344.
Iz Foče u Bosni
5769.
Ho-ćeš Lu-co, hoćeš Lu-co, že-ljo mo-ja, hej, po-šta-ni-ja
bi-ti?
Andantino.
Kuba B. H. 814.
570.
Maglaj.
Po-le-ti-la, do-šo, zla-
zla-to mo-je, dva bi-je-la
go-lu-ba.
félzárlat.
Kuhač II. 769.
571.
Iz Biograda.
Sla-vulj pi-le (mo-ri), sla-vulj pi-le (mo-ri) ne poj ra-no.
Ej, ne-de-ljo (mo-ri) dil-be-ro.

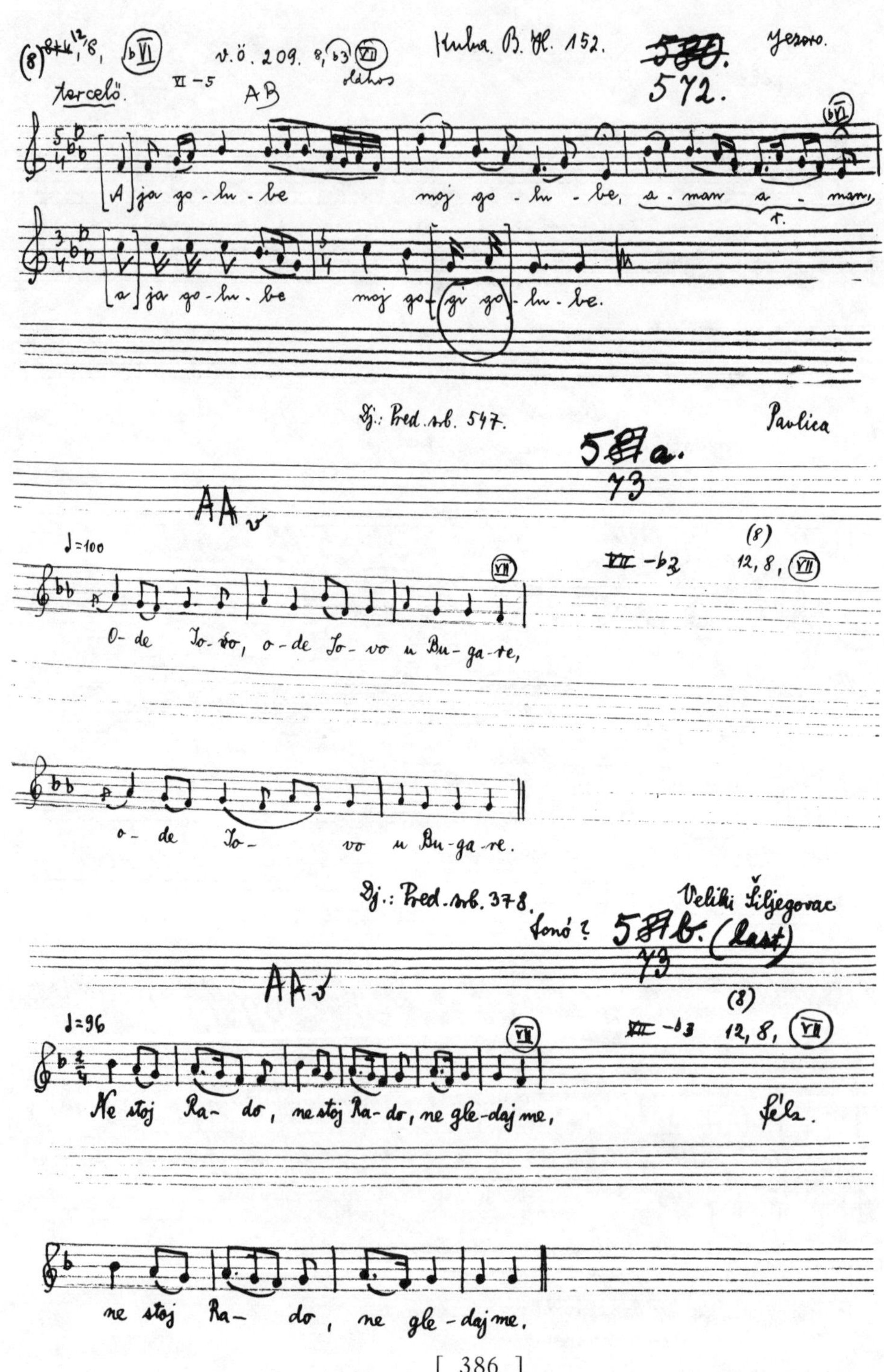
Kuba. B. H. 152.
Jezero.
572.
tercelö.
AB
Aja go-lu-be moj go-lu-be, a-man a-man,
aja go-lu-be moj go-gi go-lu-be.
Dj.: Pred. sb. 547.
Pavlica
573a.
AA
♩=100
O-de Jo-vo, o-de Jo-vo u Bu-ga-re,
o-de Jo- vo u Bu-ga-re.
Dj.: Pred. sb. 378.
Veliki Šiljegovac
573b.
AA
♩=96
Ne stoj Ra-do, ne stoj Ra-do, ne gle-daj me,
ne stoj Ra- do, ne gle-daj me.

Kuba B.H. 483.
Allegretto
Livno.
Oj, Mostaru, oj, Mostaru, si – rok
ti si, đumru – kano be – li ti si.
gümrük hanı
vám – háza
Kuba. B.-H. 974
Allegretto
Zenica.
Što s' Mo – ra – va za – mu – ti – la a – man a – man?
Što s' Mo – ra – va za – mu – ti – la?

Kuba B. H. 272.
Gacko.
Po-le-ti-o du-šo vran ga-vran čir-haj ha, po-le-ti-o du-šo
vran ga-vran!
Kuba B. H. 81.
ši-ro-ko je po-lje ze-le-no čir-haj-haj ši-ro-ko je
po-lje ze-le-no.
Kuba B. H. 72.
Livno.
Kolo.
Ko-lo vo-di a vaj, vaj, a oj vaj, vaj vaj, ko-lo
vo-di Jel-ka ma-te-ri-na vaj.

(10) 14, 12, (VII) VII – 4 AA v Kuhač II. 405.
Iz Kraljevice u hrv. Primorju.
tercelő.
579–580.
♩= 56.
Oj Je-le-na, vo-da ti le-de-na, (ni-na ne-na);
Oj Je-le-na, vo-da ti le-de-na (ne-na.)
Kidanoló növeg: Pokraj vode pero posajeno
A uz pero rumena rožica.
Ča je pero, to je mladi Ive,
Ča j' rožica, to j' mlada Marica.
stb.
(11) 15, 11, (1) VII-4 AB
Kuba B. H. 629
581.
Visoka
Andante
Po-le-će-la dva bi-je-la
go-lu-ba, a-man, a-man, ter pa-
du-še na dva bo-ra ze-le-na.
Skeleton form:
5, 7, (VII) bVII – b3 AB
Kuba. B. H. 882.
582.
Žepče.
tercelő.
Soj-če dje-voj-če, ku-pi-ću ti pa-pu-če.

5,7, (♭2) VII – 4, AB
Kuba, B-H. 991.
583. Mostar.
Allegro
Cu – nu malenu ne uzimaj za ženu.
Skeleton form:
Dj.: Pred. sb. 492.
fonó
5 84 a.
Vithova
AA
♩= 66
VII – ♭3
5, 8, (VII)
Za – spa-la Bo – ja,
félz
za – spala Boja, le-le, kraj mo – ra.
Dj.: Pred. sb. 464.
fonó.
5 84 b.
Aleksandrova.
AA
♩= 80
VII – ♭3
5, 8, (VII)
Pe – tri-ja plat – no
terelő
Pe-tri-ja platno be- li- la

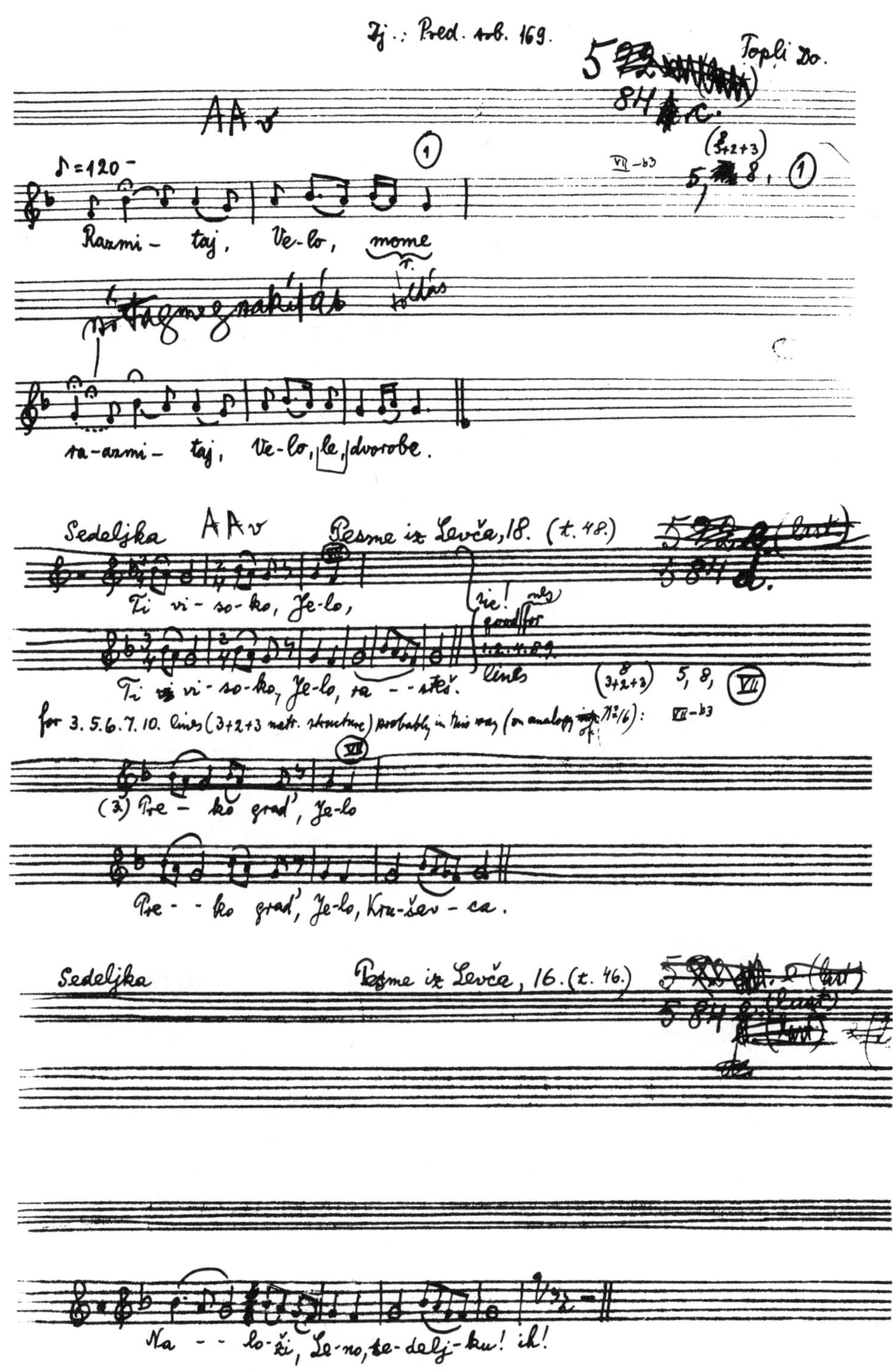

Topli Do.
♪=120
Razmi- taj, Ve-lo, mome
ra-azmi- taj, Ve-lo, le, dvorobe.
Sedeljka
Pesme iz Levča, 18. (t. 48.)
Ti vi-so-ko, Je-lo,
Ti vi-so-ko, Je-lo, ra- -stě.
lines
for 3. 5. 6. 7. 10. lines (3+2+3 metr. structure) probably in this way
(3) Pre- ko grad', Je-lo
Pre- -ko grad', Je-lo, Kru-šev-ca.
Sedeljka
Pesme iz Levča, 16. (t. 46.)
Na- -lo-ži, Le-no, se-delj-ku! ih!

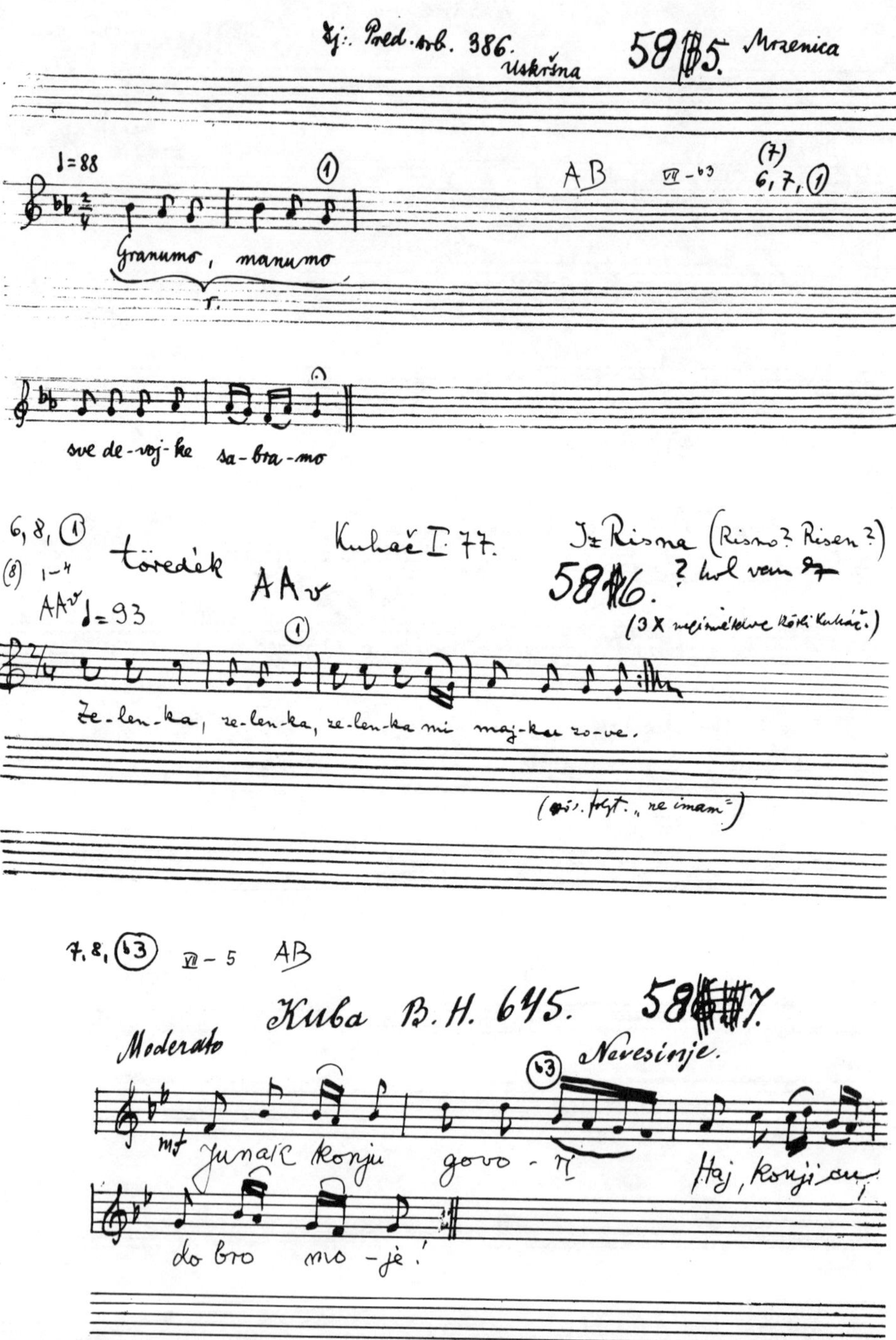
Iz: Pred. zb. 386.
uskršna
58 5. Mrzenica
♩=88
AB
6, 7, ①
Granumo, manumo
sve de-voj-ke sa-bra-mo
6, 8, ①
töredék
Kuhač I. 77.
Iz Risna (Risno? Risen?)
AAv
♩=93
58 6.
Ze-len-ka, ze-len-ka, ze-len-ka mi maj-ka zo-ve.
7, 8, ♭3
AB
Kuba B. H. 645.
58 7.
Moderato
Nevesinje.
mf
Junaić konju govo-ri
Haj, konjiću,
do bro mo-jè!

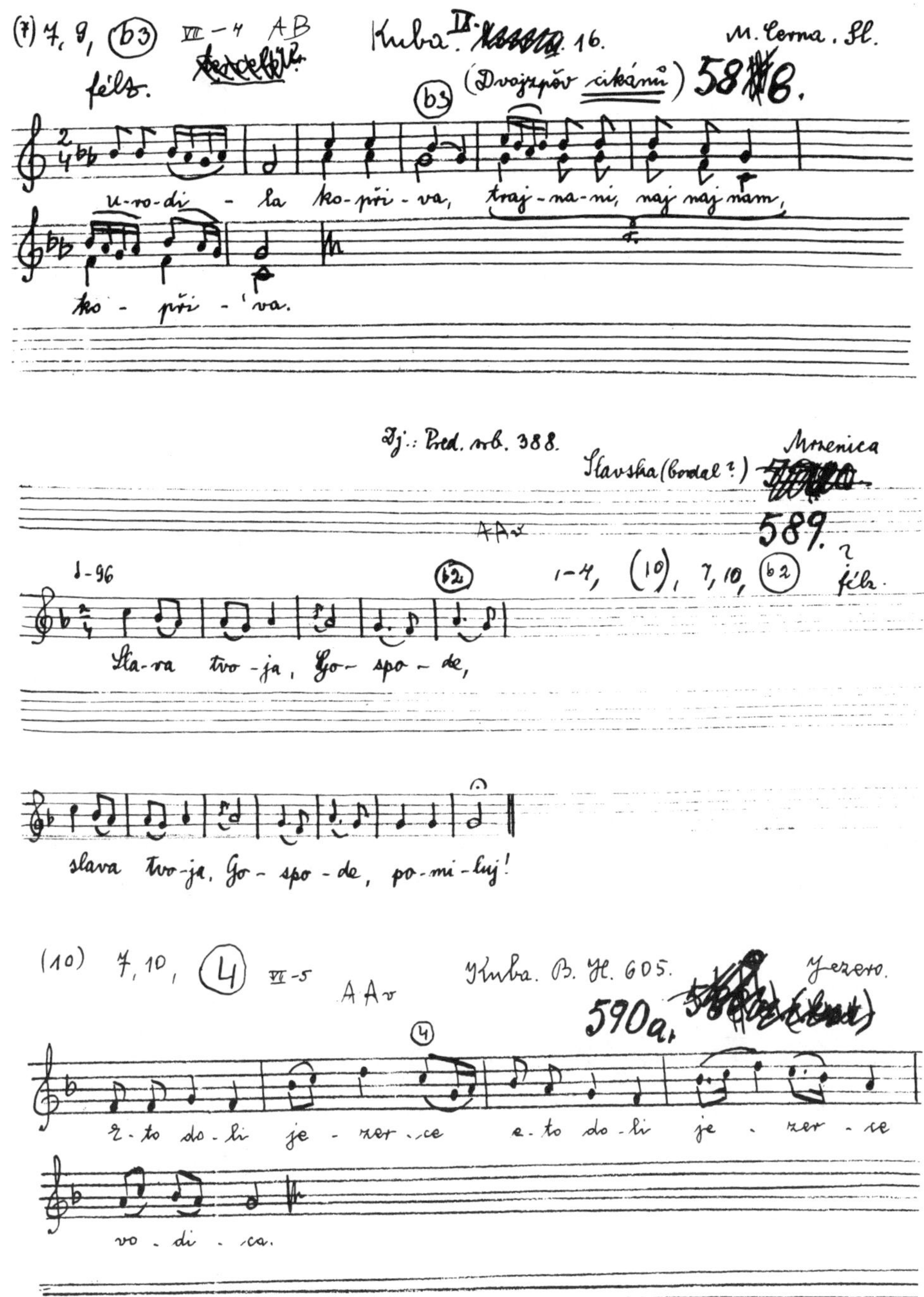

(7) 7, 8, (b3) VII – 4 AB
Kuba. II. 16.
félz.
(b3) (Dvojzpěv cikánů) 588.
u-ro-di - la ko-při - va, traj - na - ni, naj naj nám,
ko - při - 'va.
Slavska (bodal ?)
589.
AAv
1–4, (10), 7, 10, (b2) félz.
Sla-va tvo - ja, Go - spo - de,
slava tvo-ja, Go - spo - de, po-mi-luj!
(10) 7, 10, (4) VI-5 AAv
Kuba. B. H. 605.
Jezero.
590a.
z-to do-li je - zer - ce z-to do-li je - zer - ce
vo - di - ca.

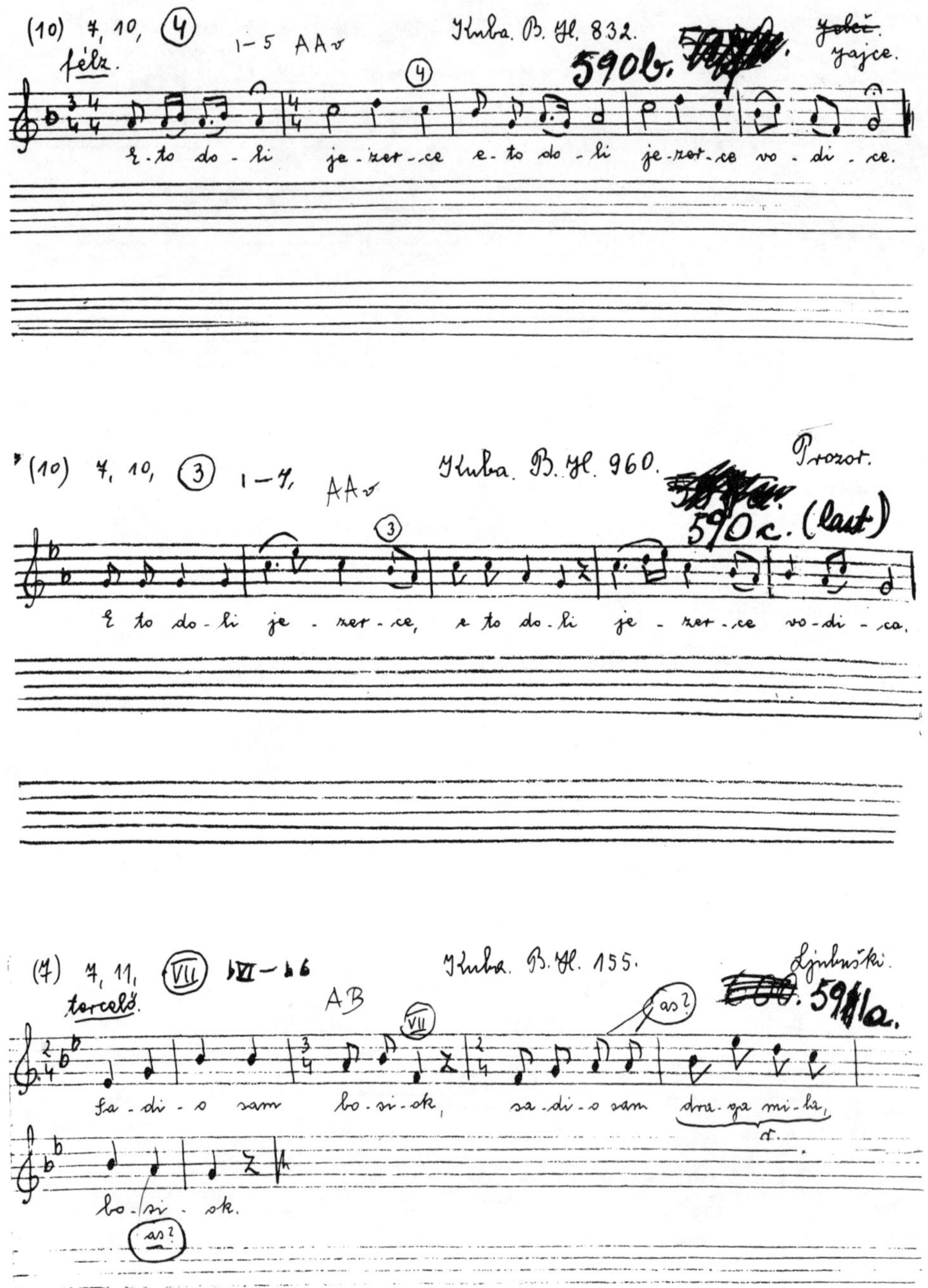

(10) 7, 10, (4) 1–5 AAv
Kuba. B. H. 832.
590b.
Jajce.
félz.
E-to do-li je-zer-ce e-to do-li je-zer-ce vo-di-ce.
(10) 7, 10, (3) 1–4, AAv
Kuba. B. H. 960.
Prozor.
590c. (last)
E to do-li je-zer-ce, e to do-li je-zer-ce vo-di-ca.
(7) 7, 11, (VII)
AB
Kuba. B. H. 155.
Ljubuški.
591a.
tercelő.
Sa-di-o sam bo-si-ok, sa-di-o sam dra-ga mi-la,
bo-si-ok.
as?
as?

AB
♩=56.
Kuhač III. 942.
Iz Senja.
(Hrv. Primorje)
Po-si-jal sam ba-se-lak, po-si-jal sam dra-ga ba-se-lak.
Kuba B. H. 805.
Allegro moderato.
AB
Doboj (Kolo)
592a.
Jad ja-do-vah, ja-do-vah, jad ja-do-vah, jad ja-do-vah, ja-do-vah
Skeleton form:
Kuba B. H. 799.
Kolo
592b.
Allegro moderato
Ženica (Kolo)
Ja pre-sa-dih ze-len bor, ja pre sa dih, ja pre-sa-dih ze-len bor.

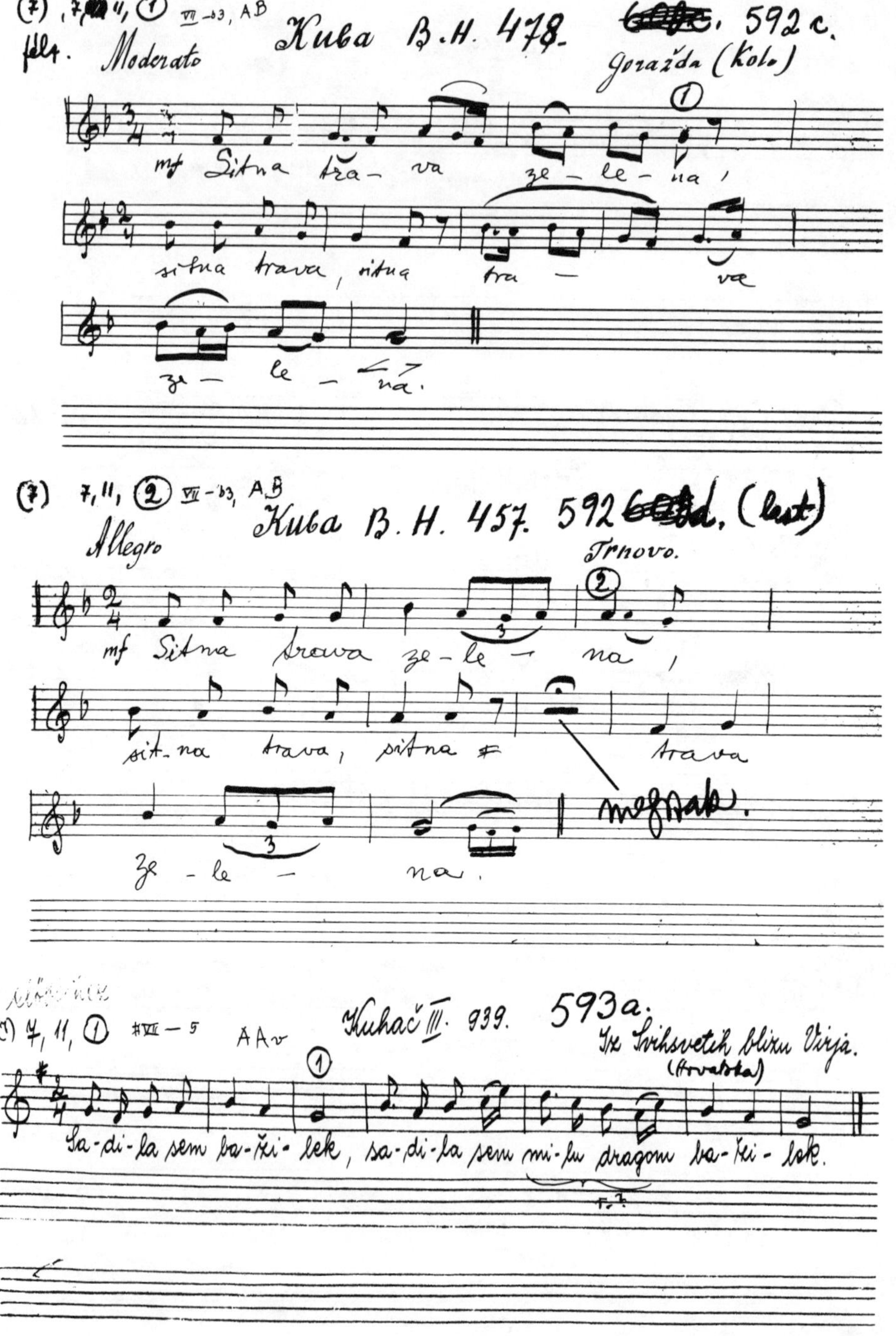
Kuba B.H. 478. 592c.
Moderato
Goražda (Kolo)
Sitna tra- va ze- le- na,
sitna trava, sitna tra- va
ze- le- na.
Kuba B.H. 457. 592
Allegro
Trnovo.
Sitna trava ze- le- na,
sit-na trava, sitna trava
ze- le- na.
Kuhač III. 939. 593a.
Iz Svihsvetih blizu Virja.
(Hrvatska)
Sa-di-la sem ba-ži-lek, sa-di-la sem mi-lu dragom ba-ži-lek.

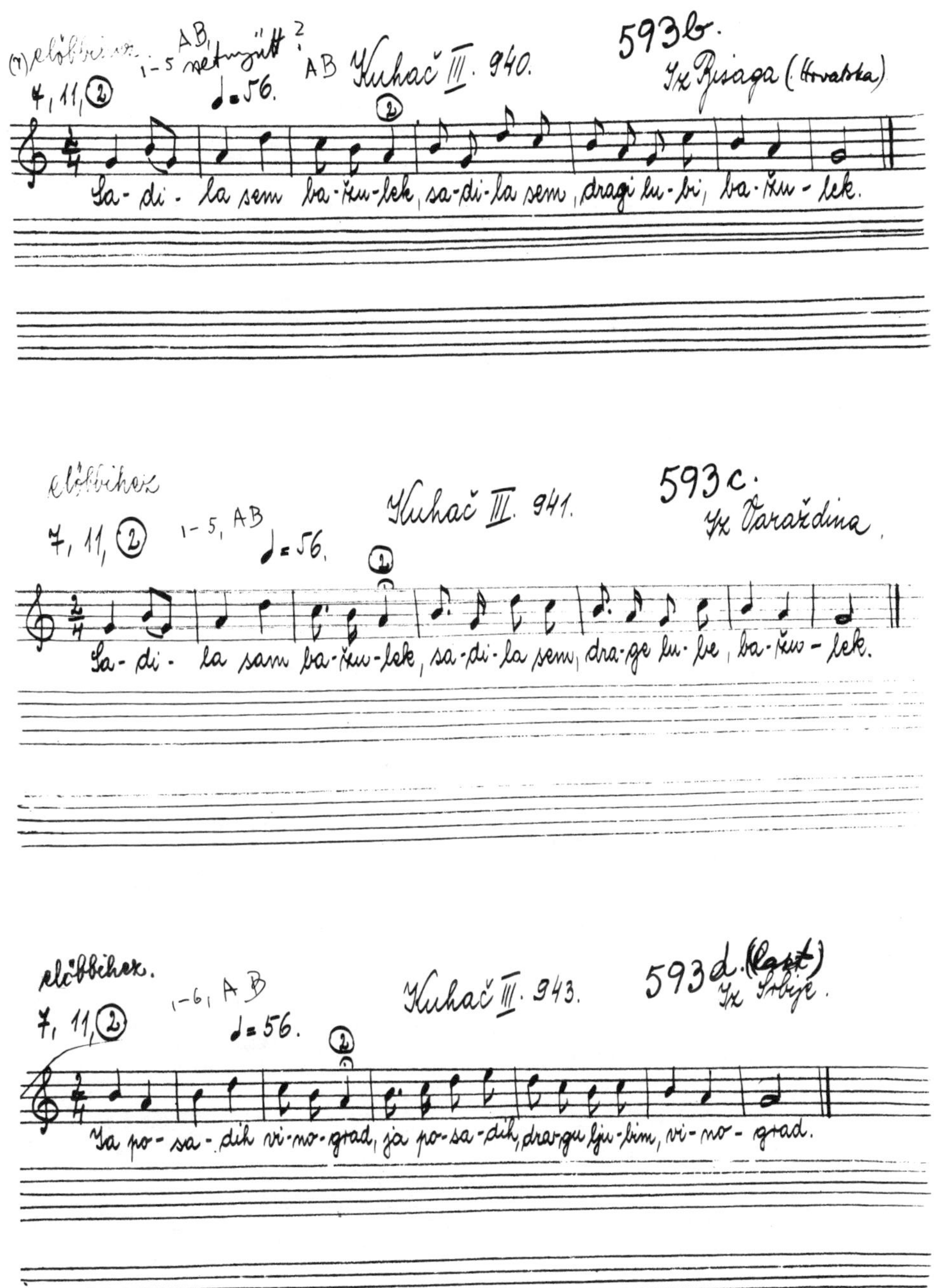

593b.
Kuhač III. 940.
Iz Bisaga (Hrvatska)
AB
♩=56.
Sa-di-la sem ba-žu-lek, sa-di-la sem, dragi lu-bi, ba-žu-lek.
előbbihez
7, 11, ②
1-5, AB
593c.
Kuhač III. 941.
Iz Varaždina.
♩=56.
Sa-di-la sam ba-žu-lek, sa-di-la sem, dra-ge lu-be, ba-žu-lek.
előbbihez.
7, 11, ②
1-6, AB
593d.
Kuhač III. 943.
Iz Srbije.
♩=56.
Ja po-sa-dih vi-no-grad, ja po-sa-dih, dra-gu lju-bim, vi-no-grad.

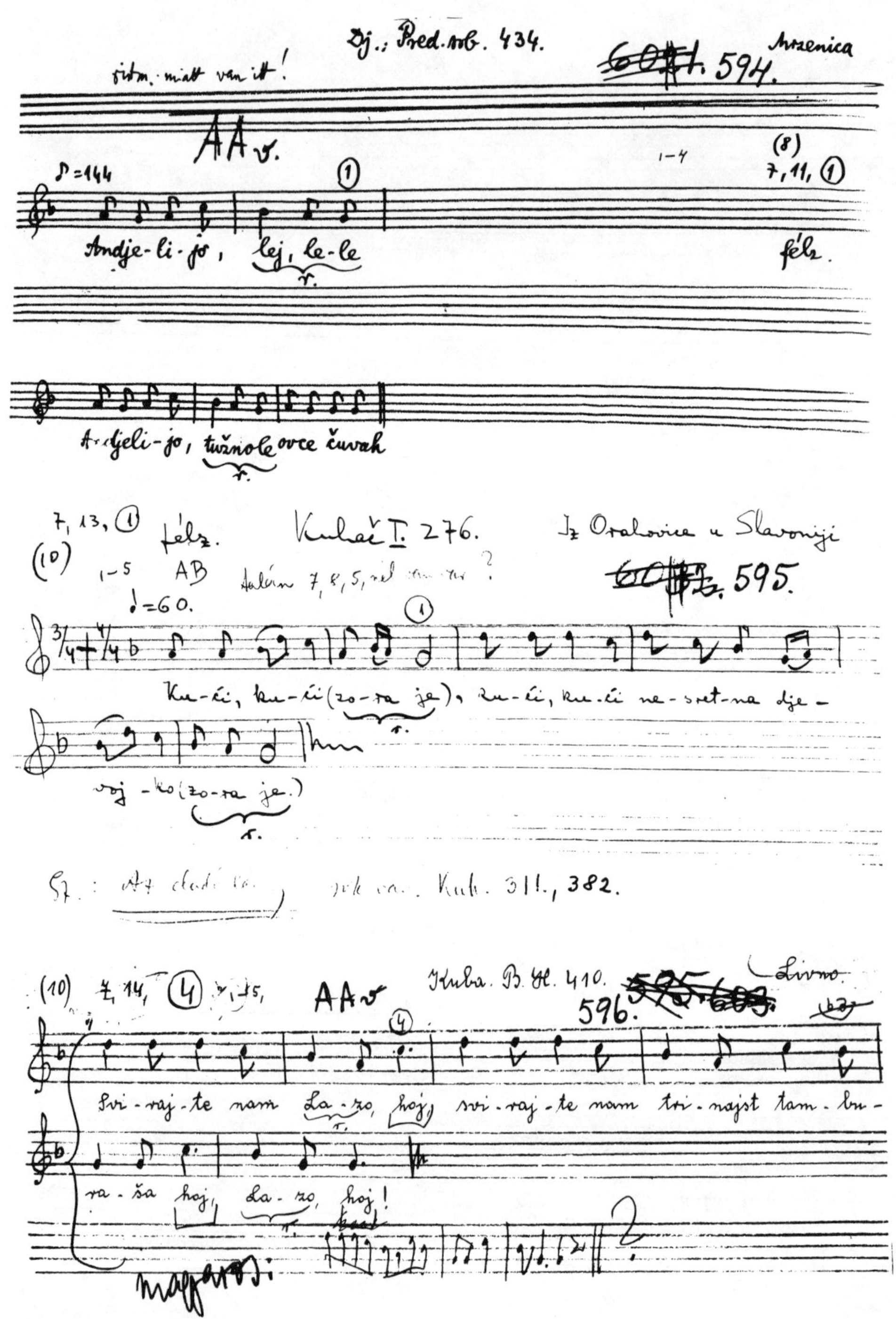

Dj.: Pred. zb. 434.
ritm. miatt van itt!
594.
AA v.
♪=144
Andje-li-jo, lej, le-le
félz.
Andjeli-jo, tužnole ovce čuvah
félz.
Kuhač I. 276.
595.
Ku-či, ku-či (zo-ra je), ku-či, ku-či ne-sret-na dje-
voj-ko (zo-ra je.)
Kuhač 311., 382.
Kuba. B. H. 410.
596.
Livno.
AA v
Svi-raj-te nam La-zo, hoj, svi-raj-te nam tri-najst tam-bu-
ra-ša hoj, La-zo, hoj!

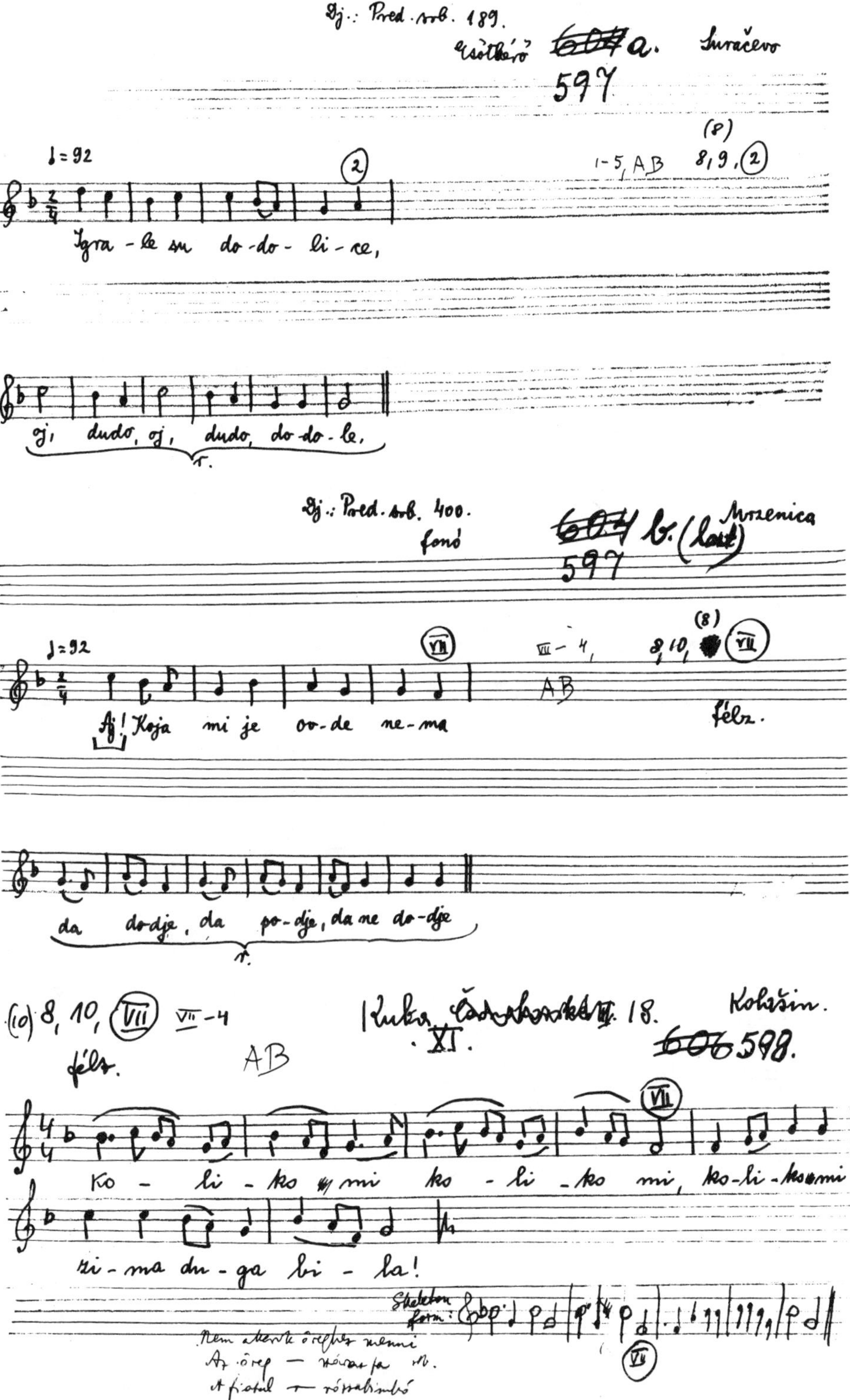
Dj.: Pred. sob. 189.
a. Suračevo
597
(8)
♩= 92
1-5, AB 8, 9, (2)
(2)
Igra - le su do - do - li - ce,
oj, dudo, oj, dudo, do - do - le,
Dj.: Pred. sob. 400.
fonó
b. Mozenica
597
(8)
♩= 92
VII
VII - 4, 8, 10, VII
AB
Aj! Koja mi je ov - de ne - ma
félz.
da dodje, da podje, da ne do - dje
(10) 8, 10, VII VII - 4
félz.
AB
18.
XI.
Kolašin.
598.
VII
Ko - li - ko mi ko - li - ko mi, ko - li - ko mi
zi - ma du - ga bi - la!
Skeleton form:
VII

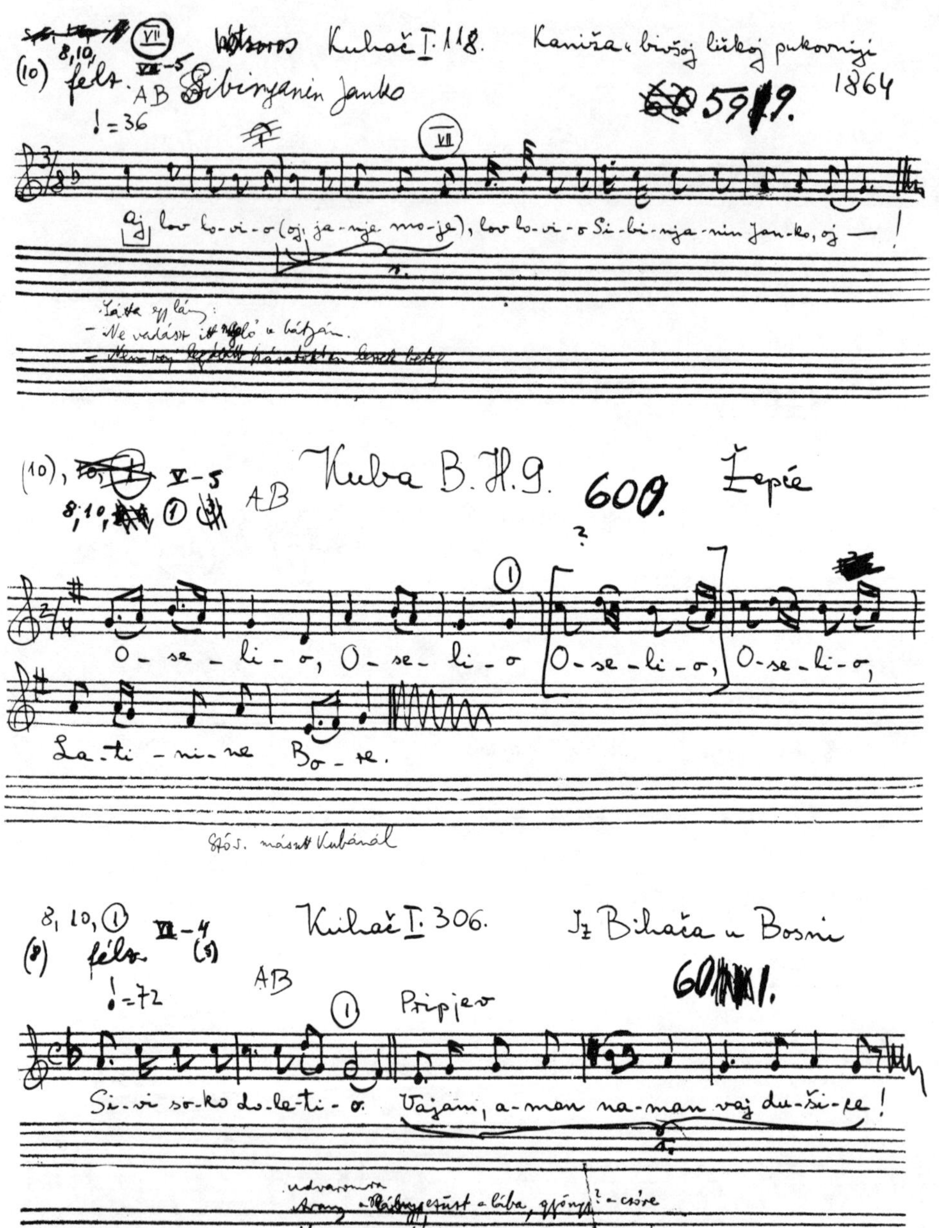

Kuhač I. 118.
Kaniža u bivšoj ličkoj pukovniji
1864
AB Sibinjanin Janko
♩=36
Oj lov lo-vi-o (oj, ja-nje mo-je), lov lo-vi-o Si-bi-nja-nin Jan-ko, oj —!
AB
Kuba B. H. 9.
600.
O-se-li-o, O-se-li-o O-se-li-o, O-se-li-o,
La-ti-ni-ne Bo-re.
Kuhač I. 306.
Iz Bihaća u Bosni
AB
♩=72
Pripjev
Si-vi so-ko do-le-ti-o. Vajam, a-man na-man vaj du-ši-ce!
Arany kalitkába zárnám

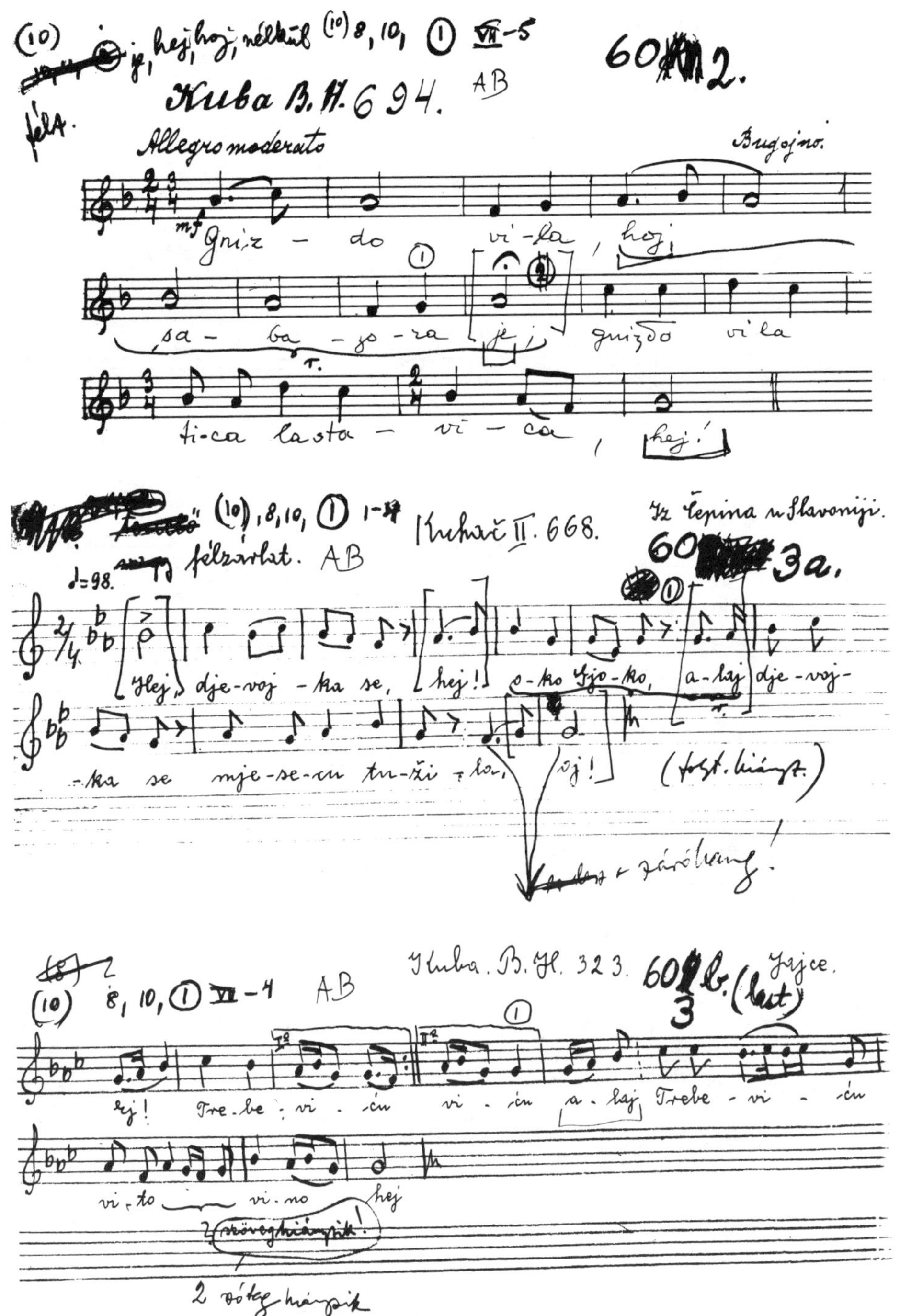

Kuba B. H. 694.
AB
Allegro moderato
Bugojno.
Gniz - do vi - la, hoj,
sa - ba - go - ra je, gnizdo vila
ti-ca lasta - vi - ca, hej!
(10), 8, 10, ①
Kuhač II. 668.
Iz Čepina u Slavoniji.
félzárlat. AB
♩=98.
Hej, dje-voj - ka se, hej! o-ko Gjo-ko, a-laj dje-voj-
-ka se mje-se-cu tu-ži - la, oj!
záróhang!
(10) 8, 10, ①
AB
Kuba. B. H. 323.
Jajce.
ej! Tre-be - vi - ću vi - ću a - laj Trebe - vi - ću
vi - to vi - no hej

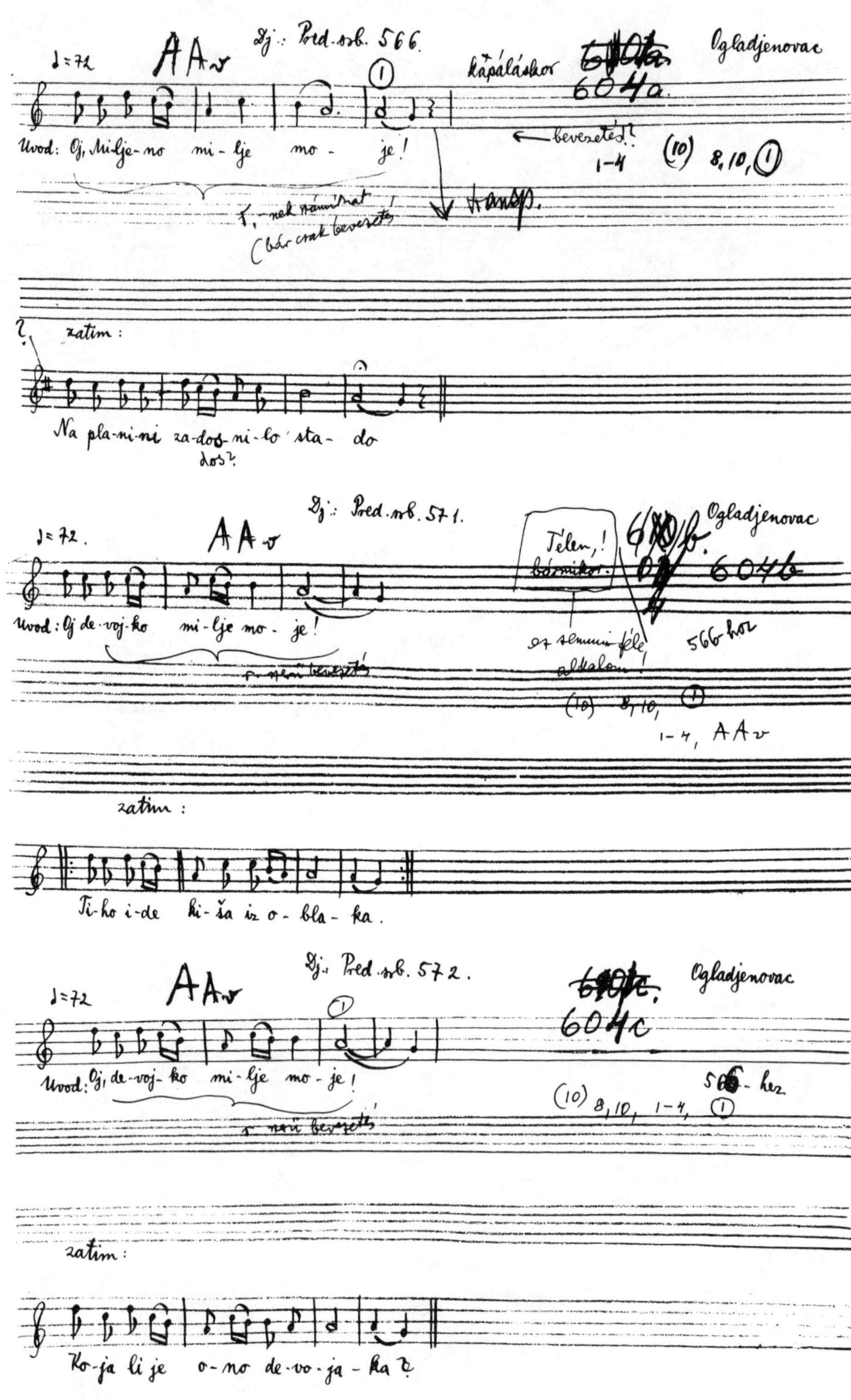
Dj.: Pred. srb. 566.
♩=72
AAv
kapáláskor
604a.
Ogladjenovac
Uvod: Oj, Milje-no mi-lje mo- je!
bevezetés!?
1-4
(10) 8,10,
zatim:
Na pla-ni-ni za-dos-ni-lo sta- do
dos?
Dj.: Pred. srb. 571.
♩=72.
AAv
Ogladjenovac
604b
Uvod: Oj de-voj-ko mi-lje mo- je!
566-hoz
(10) 8,10,
1-4, AAv
zatim:
Ti-ho i-de ki-ša iz o-bla- ka.
Dj.: Pred. srb. 572.
♩=72
AAv
Ogladjenovac
604c
Uvod: Oj, de-voj-ko mi-lje mo- je!
566-hoz
(10) 8,10, 1-4,
zatim:
Ko-ja li je o-no de-vo-ja-ka?

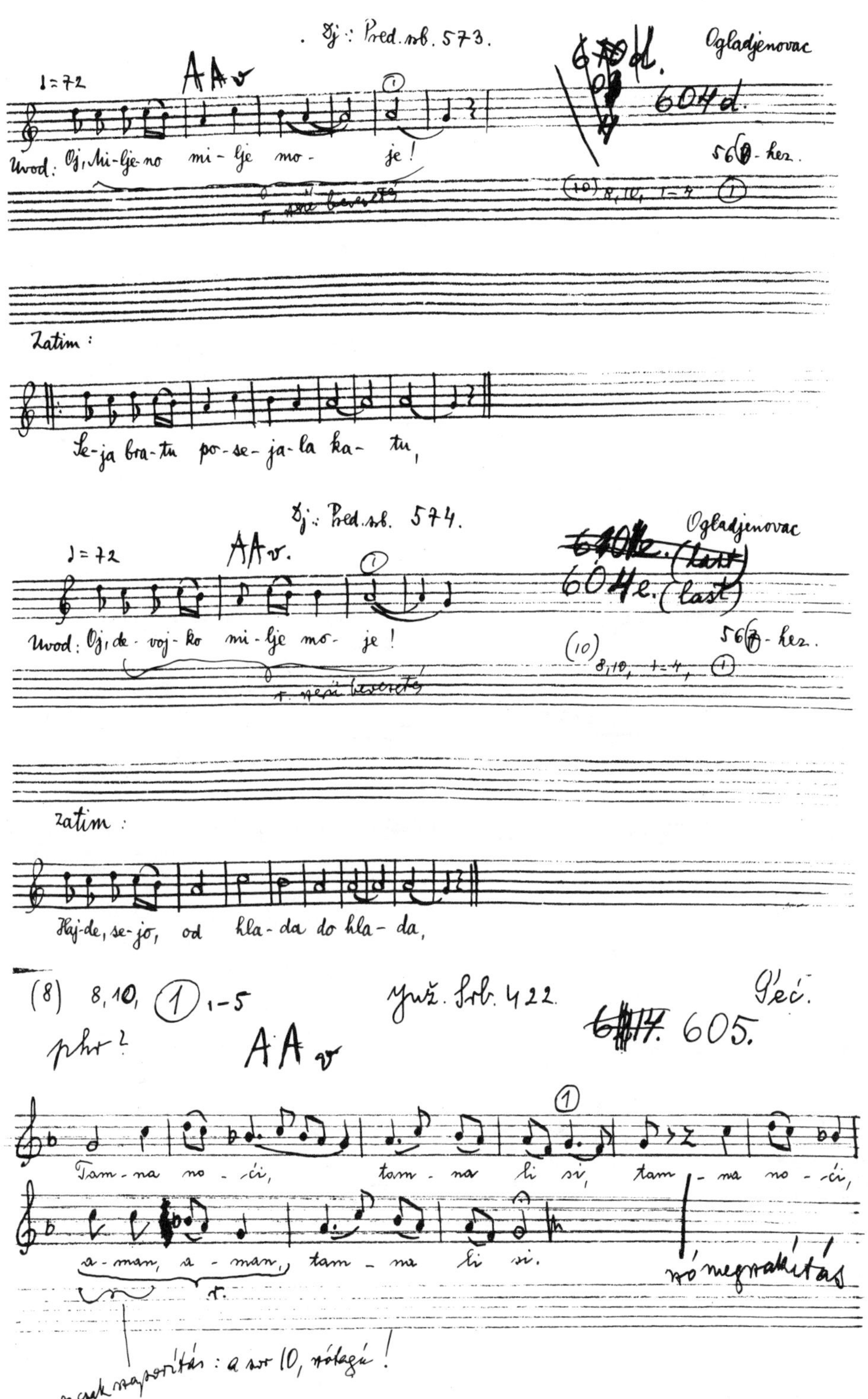

Đj.: Pred. zb. 573.
Ogladjenovac
604d.
56- hez.
AAv
♩=72
Uvod: Oj, mi-lje-no mi-lje mo- je!
(10) 8,10, 1–4 ①
Zatim:
Se-ja bra-tu po-se-ja-la ka- tu,
Đj.: Pred. zb. 574.
Ogladjenovac
604e. (last)
56- hez.
AAv.
♩=72
Uvod: Oj, de-voj-ko mi-lje mo- je!
(10) 8,10, 1–4, ①
zatim:
Haj-de, se-jo, od hla-da do hla-da,
(8) 8,10, ① 1–5
Juž. Srb. 422.
Peć.
605.
AAv
Tam-na no-ći, tam-na li si, tam-na no-ći,
a-man, a-man, tam-na li si.
szó megszakítás
ez csak szaporítás: a sor 10 szótagú!

Dj.: Pred. sb. 135.

Velika Lukanja

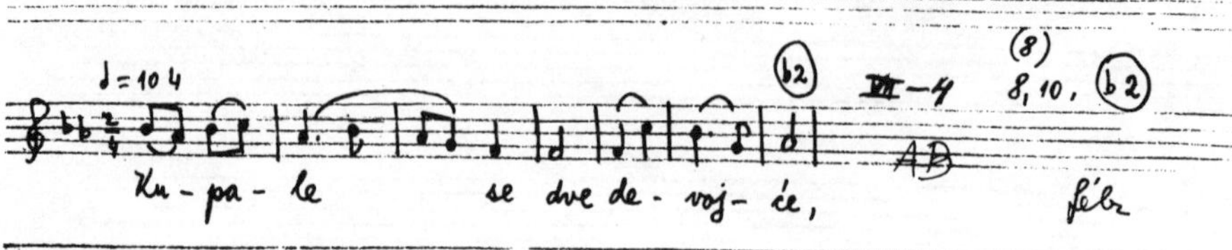

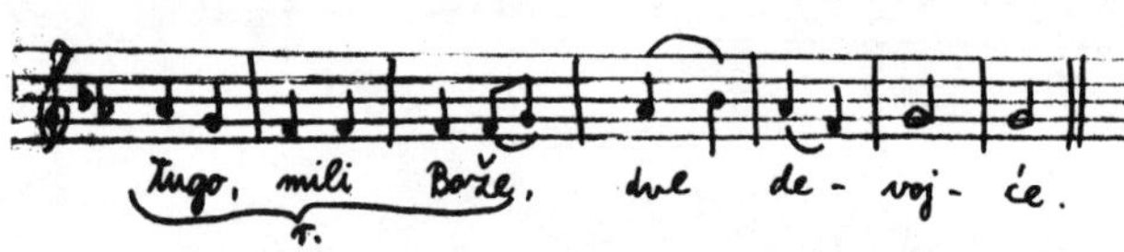

Dj.: Pred. sb. 315. arató Pirkovac

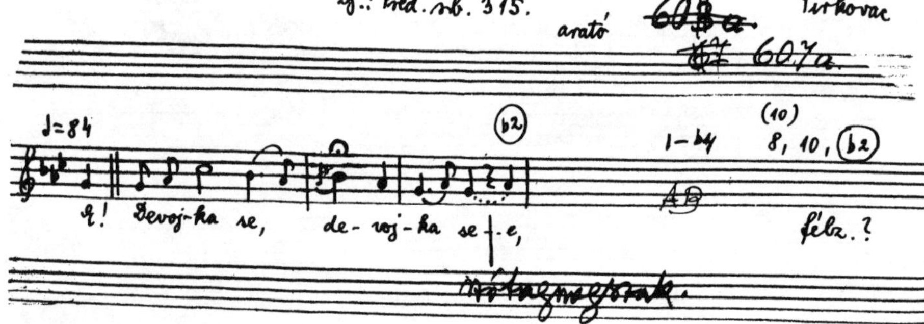

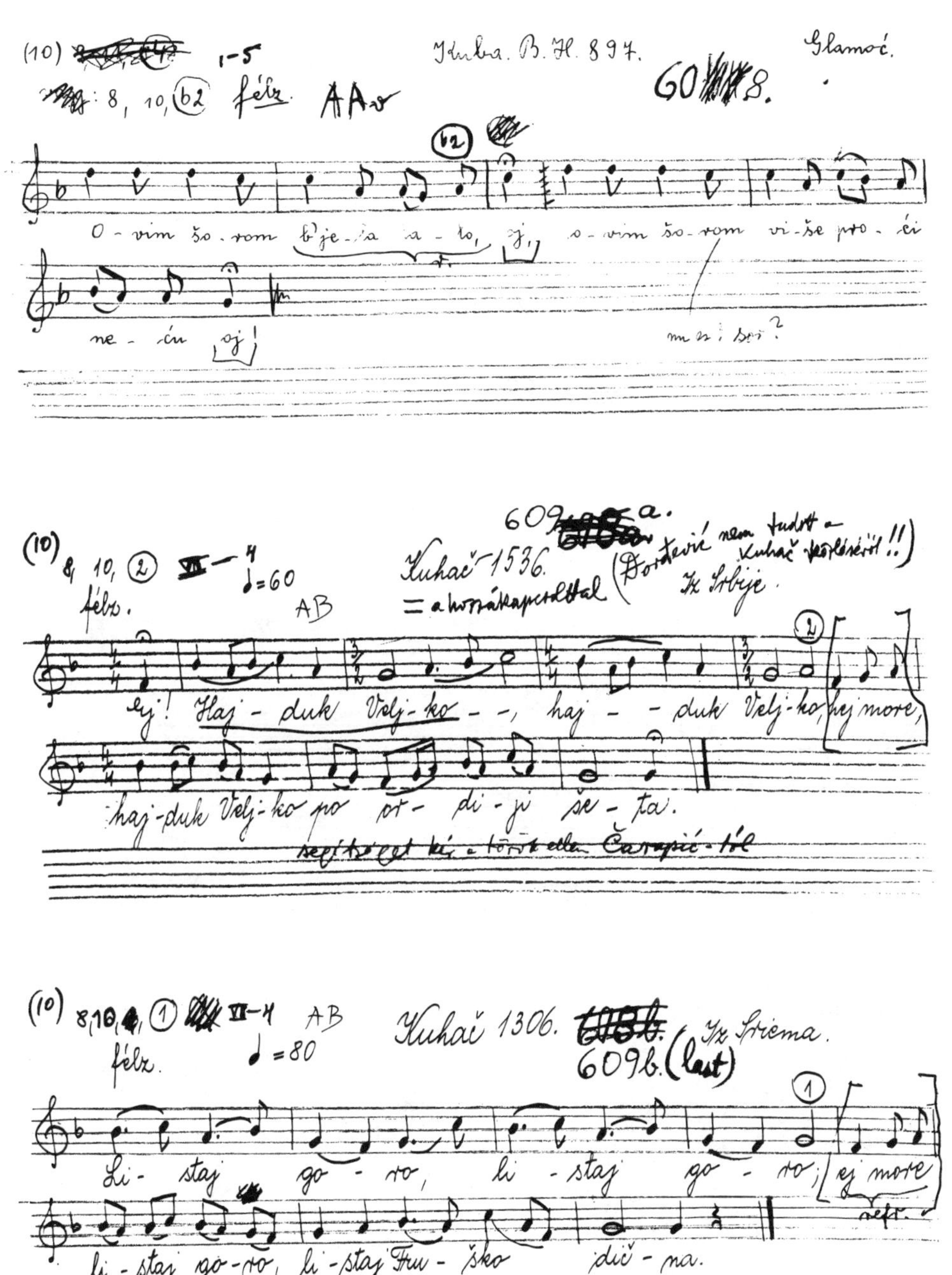
(10)
Glamoč.
O - vim šo - rom
ne - ću oj!
(10)
Kuhač 1536.
Iz Srbije.
ej! Haj - duk Velj - ko - -, haj - - duk Velj - ko, hej more,
haj - duk Velj - ko po or - di - ji še - ta.
(10)
Kuhač 1306.
Iz Srijema.
Li - staj go - ro, li - staj go - ro, ej more
li - staj go - ro, li - staj Fru - ško dič - na.

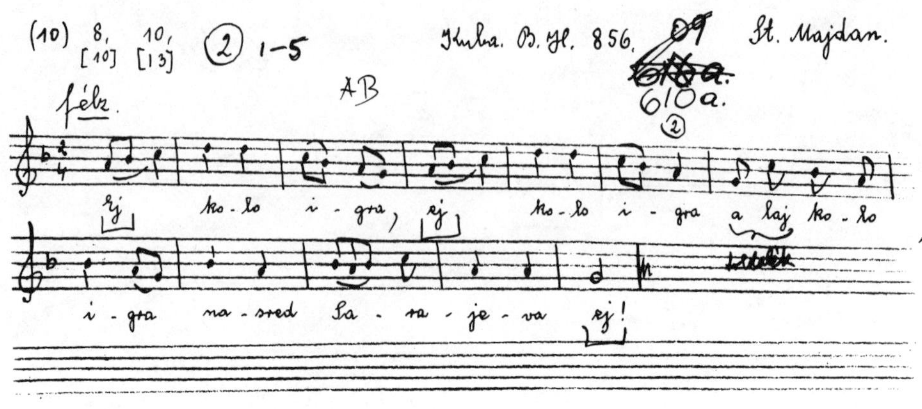
(10) 8, 10, [10] [13] ② 1–5
St. Majdan.
610a.
félz.
AB
ej ko-lo i-gra, ej ko-lo i-gra a laj ko-lo
i-gra na-sred Sa-ra-je-va ej!

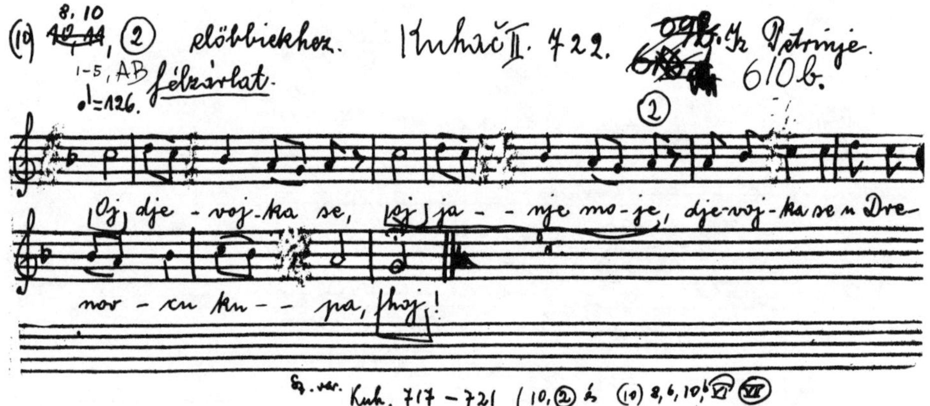
Kuhač II. 722.
Iz Petrinje.
610b.
1-5, AB félzárlat.
♩=126.
Oj dje-voj-ka se, ej ja-nje mo-je, dje-voj-ka se u Dre-
nov-cu ku-pa, hoj!
Kuh. 717 – 721

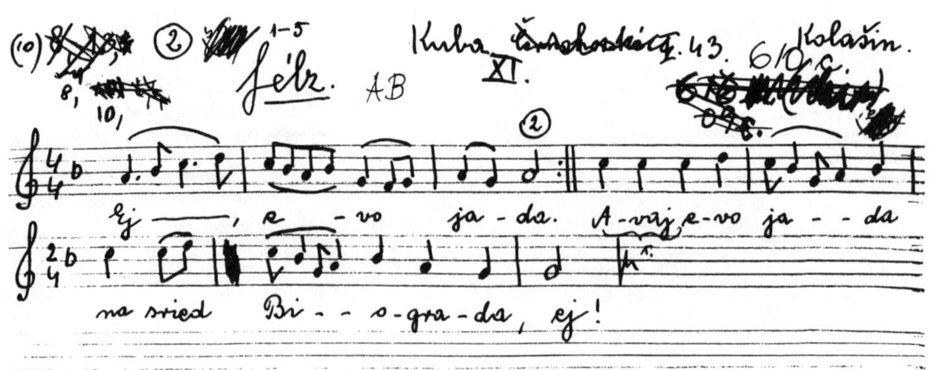
1–5
félz.
AB
Kolašin.
Ej e-vo ja-da. A-vaj e-vo ja-da
na sried Bi-s-gra-da, ej!

(10) 8, 10, (1)
félz.
1–5, AB
Kuhač II. 488.
Iz Otočca.
610 d.
Hej! aj moj Mi-je, hej, ja-nje moje! aj moj Mi-je, gaje si si-noć
bi-o? (hej!)
ref.
(10) 9, 10, (1) VII–4, AB
tipus. félz
Kuba IX. 46
Plaški
(Dvojzpěv hajných.)
610 e.
Oj, si-noć ka-sno, ej —, janješce mo-je. Si-noć ka-
sno ki-ša ro-mi-nja-la.
Dj.: Pred. sob. 391.
Slavska (bodal)
Mrzenica
♩=76
1–4
(10) 8, 10, (b3)
Ko u zdravlje, Ja-no, ra-no
ko u zdravlje pi-je ladno vi-no, hej!

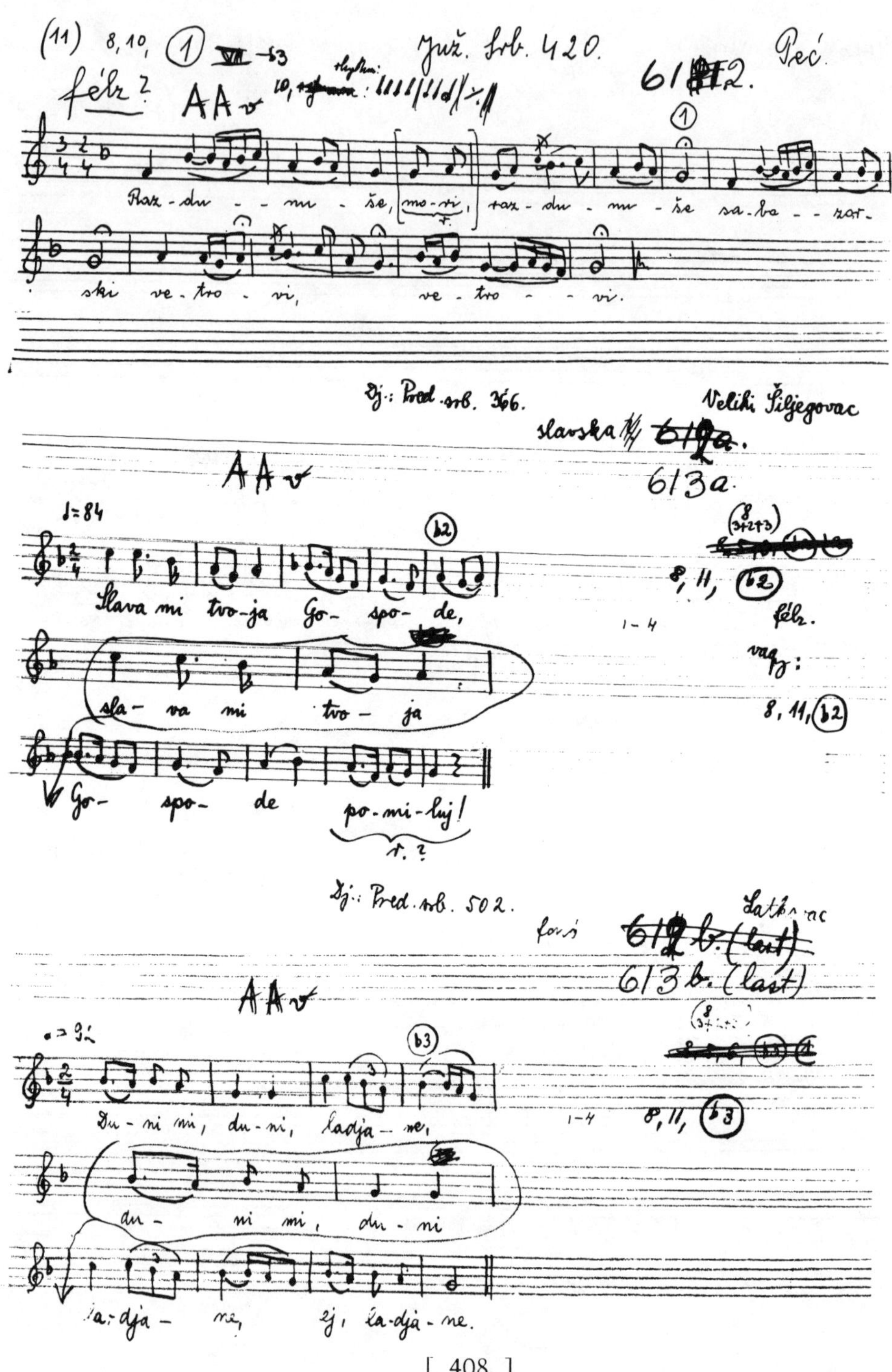
(11) 8, 10, ① VII – b3
Juž. Srb. 420.
Peć
félz ?
AA
Raz - du - - mu - še, mo - ri, raz - du - mu - še sa - ba - - zor -
ski ve - tro - vi, ve - tro - - - vi.
Dj.: Pred. srb. 366.
Veliki Šiljegovac
slavska
AA
613a.
♩= 84
Slava mi tvo-ja Go- spo- de,
8, 11, b2
1 – 4
félz.
sla- va mi tvo- ja
vagy:
8, 11, b2
Go- spo- de po-mi-luj!
Dj.: Pred. srb. 502.
613 b. (last)
AA
Du - ni mi, du - ni, ladja - ne,
1 – 4
8, 11, b3
du - ni mi, du - ni
la - dja - ne, ej, la - dja - ne.

(8) 8, 12, ① —4
Juž. Srb. 406.
Prizren.
félz.
AB
Igra.
614.
Go-ra-ni-ne, la-fa ni-ne, Go-ra-ni-ne, Go-ra-ni-ne
la-fa-ni-ne.
(8) 8, 12, (b2) 1–5, AB
Kuba. B. H. 320.
15 Trnovo.
Kolo.
Star se de-do po-ma-mi-o star se de-do po-ma-mi-o, po-ma-mi-o,
(8) 8, 12, ② 1–5, AB
Kuba. B. H. 353.
15
Trnovo.
Po-gji ko-lo po-gji bo-lje, po-gji ko-lo po-gji bo-lje po-gji bo-lje

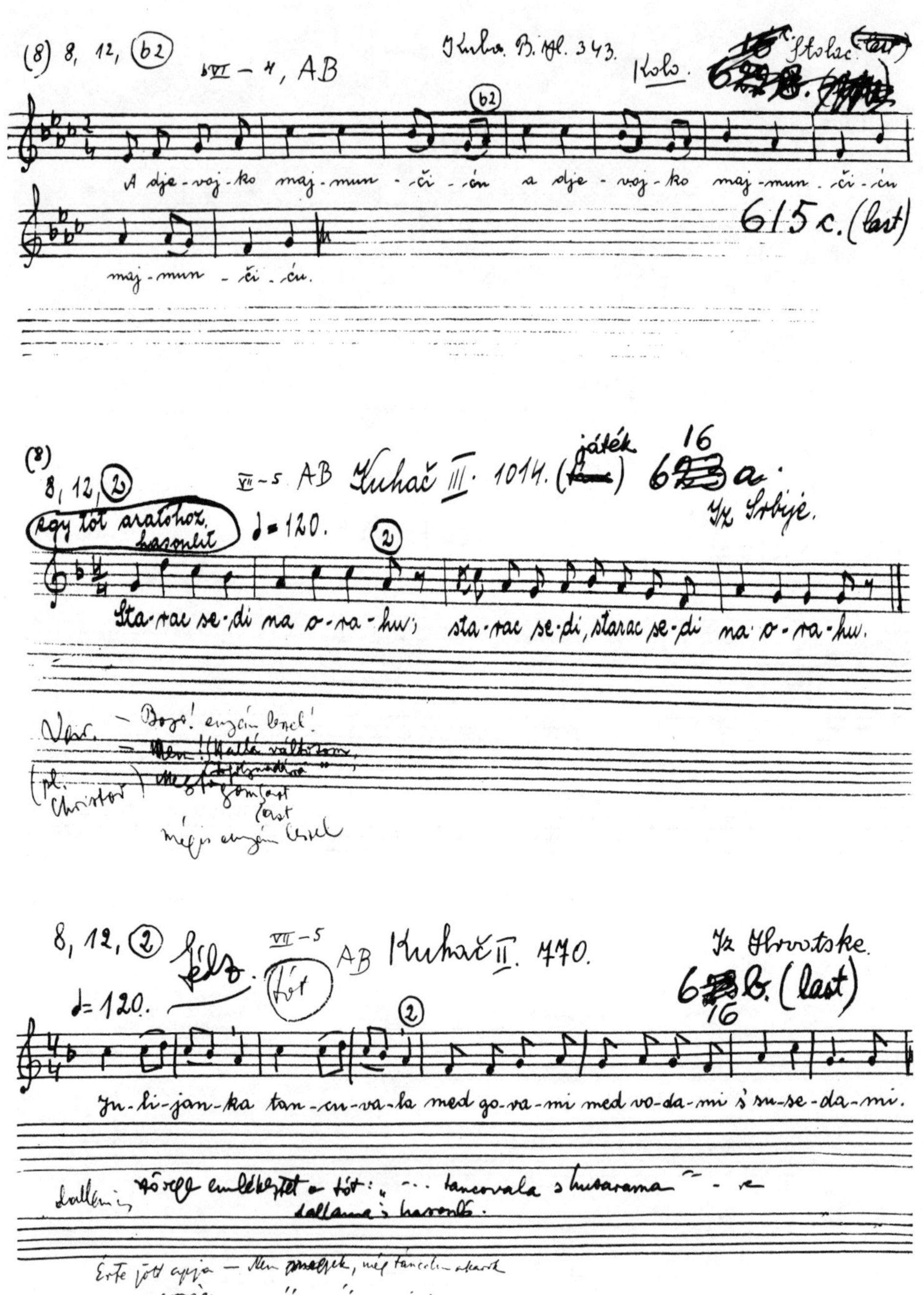
(8) 8, 12, (b2) bVI – 4, AB
Kolo.
A dje-voj-ko maj-mun-či-ću a dje-voj-ko maj-mun-či-ću maj-mun-či-ću.
615 c. (last)
8, 12, (2) VII – 5 AB Kuhač III. 1014.
Iz Srbije.
♩= 120.
Sta-rac se-di na o-ra-hu; sta-rac se-di, starac se-di na o-ra-hu.
8, 12, (2) VII – 5 AB Kuhač II. 470.
Iz Hrvatske.
♩= 120.
Ju-li-jan-ka tan-cu-va-la med go-ra-mi med vo-da-mi s' su-se-da-mi.

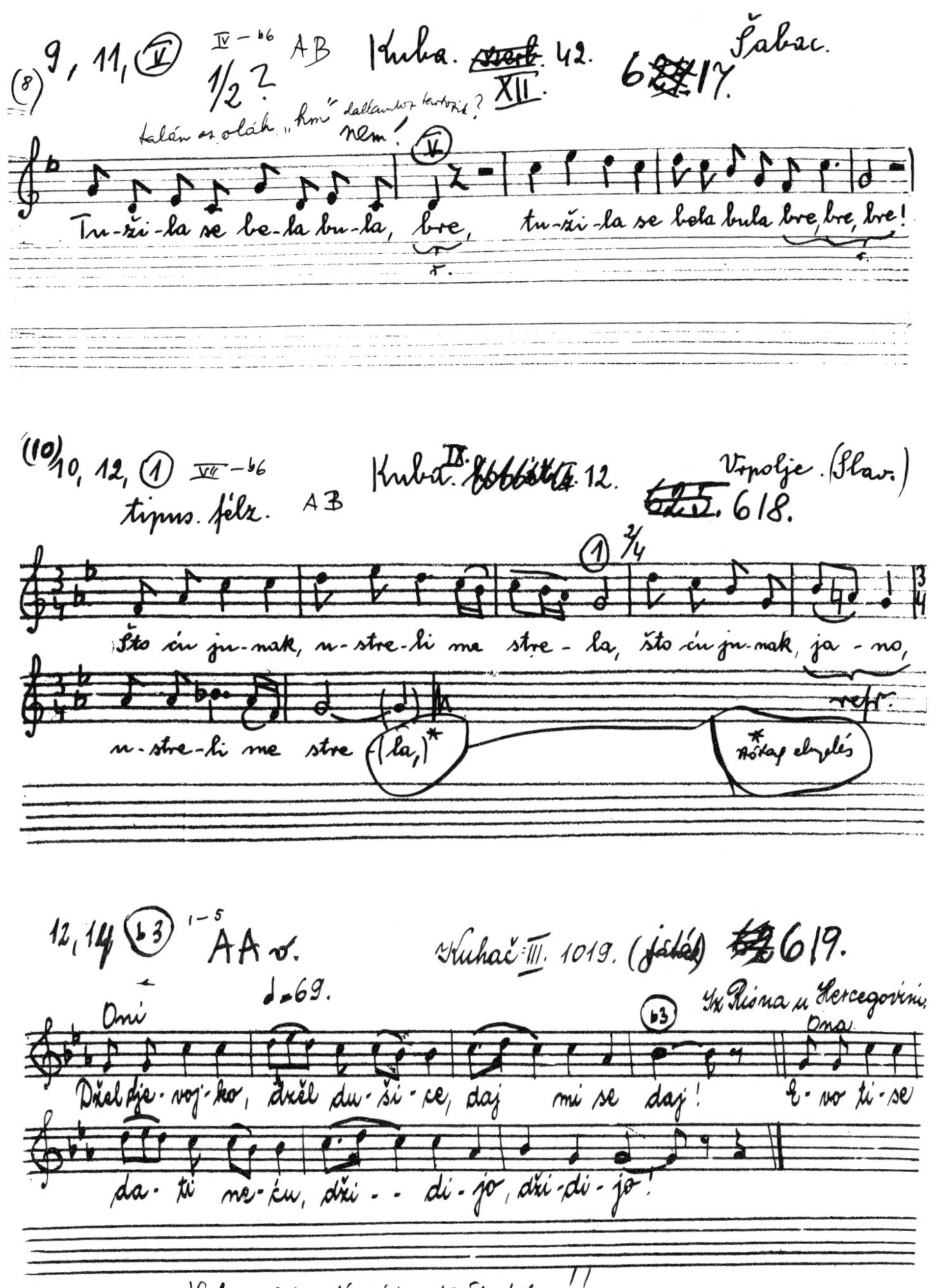
9, 11, (V) IV – b6 AB Kuba. XII. 42. Šabac.
Tu-ži-la se be-la bu-la, bre, tu-ži-la se bela bula bre, bre, bre!
10, 12, (1) VII – b6 Kuba. IX. 12. Vrpolje. (Slav.) 618.
tipus. félz. AB
Što ću ju-nak, u-stre-li me stre-la, što ću ju-nak, ja-no,
u-stre-li me stre (la,)*
12, 14 (b3) 1–5 AA v. Kuhač III. 1019. 619.
Iz Risna u Hercegovini.
Dželdje-voj-ko, dželdu-ši-ce, daj mi se daj! E-vo ti-se
da-ti ne-ću, dži-- di-jo, dži-di-jo!

General Index

GENERAL INDEX

General Index

AUSTRIA
GRAZ
Villach
Klagenfurt
R. DRAVA
Dravograd
POHORJE Mts.
Maribor
Murska Sobota
Lendava
BUDAPEST
R. SAVA
Jesenice
Bled
Radovljica
KAMNIK Alps.
Mt. Triglav
Kamnik
Kranj
Ptuj
R. DRAVA
Rogaška Slatina
Celje
Varaždin
ITALY
Tolmin
Ljubljana
R. SAVA
Gorizia
SLOVENIA
MILAN
Ajdovščina
Kalce
Klanjec
Durdevac
Postojna
Mt. Sljeme
Bjelovar
Trieste
Novo Mesto
Zagreb
Dugo Selo
Vitrovitica
VENICE
Piran
Koper
Portorož
Metlika
Umag
Buje
Novigrad
Crnomelj
CROATIA
Daruvar
Karlovac
Kutina
Opatija
Rijeka
Istria
Sisak
R. SAVA
Pakrac
Poreč
Pazin
Crikvenica
Glina
Vršac
Ogulin
Vojnić
Novska
Sl. Požega
Rovinj
Novi Vinodolski
Labin
KRK
Krk
Novi Gradiška
Cres
R. UNA
Bos. Dubica
Bos. Gradiška
VENICE
Pula
Senj
Bos. Novi
Prijedor
KVARNER
CRES
RAB
Rab
Otočec
Plitvice Lakes
R. UNA
Bihać
Bos Krupa
Osor
Sanski Most
LOŠINJ
Mali Lošinj
PAG
Banja Luka
Karlobag
Gospić
Bos. Petrovac
ADRIATIC SEA
SUSAK
Ključ
Udbina
R. UNA
Drvar
Gračac
ANCONA
Jajce
BO
Zadar
Bos. Grahovo
DALMATIA
Benkovac
Travnik
DUGI OTOK
Knin
Donji Vakuf
Biograd
Livno
Drniš
Šibenik
HERZ
Sinj
Trogir
Ugljane
Jablanica
Split
Omis
Posušje
Imoski
ŠOLTA
BRAČ
Brela
PESCARA
Makarska
Ljubuški
HVAR
Ploče
VIS
Orebić
Metković
BISEVO
Blato
Korčula
KORČULA
Slano
LASTOVO
MLJET
ADRIATIC SEA
0 kms
40
80
0 miles
25
50
N

YUGOSLAVIA

NGARY

KEY
Motorways
Main roads
Other roads
Railways
Car ferries
Cities
Large towns
Other towns
Airports

BUDAPEST
Szeged
Palić
Subotica
Senta
Kikinda
Ada
Sombor
R. DANUBE
VOJVODINA
Timisoara
Osijek
Srbobran
R. TISA
RUMANIA
Bačka
Vukovar
Zrenjanin
Bački Petrovac
Vinkovici
Novi Sad
Banat
R. DANUBE
Plandište
Srem
Alibunar
Vršac
Ruma
Sremska Mitrovica
R. SAVA
Brčko
Pančevo
Bijeljina
Šabac
R. SAVA
BELGRADE
Kovin
Vel Gradište
R. DANUBE
Tuzla
R. DRINA
Smederevo
Iron Gate (Dam)
Loznica
Požarevac
Kladevo
Zvornik
Mladenovac
Smed. Palanka
R. MORAVA
R. MLAVA
Petrovac
Vlasenica
Kladanj
Valjevo
Topola
Gornjak Gorge
Negotin
SERBIA
Žagubica
R. DANUBE
R. DRINA
Bor
rajevo
Rogatica
Kragujevac
Titovo Uzice
Požega
Čačak
Ćuprija
Paraćin
Zaječar
INA
Goražde
R. DRINA
Kraljevo
Ćićevac
Priboj
W. MORAVA R.
Foča
Maglić
Vranjačka Banja
W. MORAVA R.
Knjaževac
S. MORAVA R.
Nova Varoš
Ušće
Kruševac
Pljevlja
Prijepolje
Brus
Blace
Niš
Bela Palenka
Sacko
Raška
Prokuplje
Pirot
Žabljak
Novi Pazar
Kuršumlija
Babušnica
DURMITOR Mts.
Šavnik
Lescovac
S. MORAVA R.
SOFIA
MONTENEGRO
Kos. Mitrovica
cko L.
Nikšić
Kolašin
Ivangrad
Surdulica
Risan
Priština
Peč
Kotor
KOSOVO
BULGARIA
Tivat
Cetinje
Titograd
Lipljan
S. MORAVA R.
Dakovica
SOFIA
Uroševac
ALBANIA
Kjustendil
L. Skadar
Prizren
Stracin
Vratnica
Kumanovo
Bar
SAR PLANINA Mts.
R. VARDAR
Skopje
Ulcinj
Tetovo
BRINDISI
TIRANE
Mt. Popova Sapca
Kočani
Dulčevo
MACEDONIA
Gostivar
Titov Veles
Pehčevo
Mavrovo
Mt. Solunska Glava
Štip
Grasko
Radoviš
Stobi
Negotino
R. VARDAR
Kičevo
Brod
Debar
Izvor
Kavadarci
Kruševo
Strumica
Prilep
Velešta
Struga
L. Dojran
TIRANE
Ohrid
Resen
SALONICA
Otesevo
Mt. Pelister
Bitola
L. Ohrid
Heraclea
L. Prespa
ALBANIA
GREECE